Constitutionalism

Constitutionalism

Old Dilemmas, New Insights

'Proceedings from the XIII Academic Conference of the Colombian Constitutional Court'

Edited by
ALEJANDRO LINARES-CANTILLO
Associate Justice of the Colombian Constitutional Court

Assistant Editors
CAMILO VALDIVIESO-LEÓN
Law Clerk at the Colombian Constitutional Court
SANTIAGO GARCÍA-JARAMILLO
Constitutional Law Professor, Pontificia Universidad Javeriana (Bogotá, Colombia)

OXFORD
UNIVERSITY PRESS

OXFORD
UNIVERSITY PRESS

Great Clarendon Street, Oxford, OX2 6DP,
United Kingdom

Oxford University Press is a department of the University of Oxford.
It furthers the University's objective of excellence in research, scholarship,
and education by publishing worldwide. Oxford is a registered trade mark of
Oxford University Press in the UK and in certain other countries

First Edition published in 2021
Impression: 3

Published in the United States of America by Oxford University Press
198 Madison Avenue, New York, NY 10016, United States of America

British Library Cataloguing in Publication Data
Data available

Library of Congress Control Number: 2020948158

ISBN 978–0–19–289675–9

DOI: 10.1093/oso/9780192896759.001.0001

Printed and bound in the UK by
TJ Books Limited

To María Alejandra Gutiérrez,

Contents

IV. THE ROLE OF INTERNATIONAL, COMPARATIVE AND FOREIGN LAW IN DOMESTIC CONSTITUTIONAL LAW: DIALOGUE AMONG THE GLOBAL SOUTH

A) The Use of Foreign Precedents, A 'Global South' Monologue or a Conversation among Equals?

List of Abbreviations

ACHR	American Convention on Human Rights
ADR	alternative dispute resolution
NCA	National Constituent Assembly
ANC	African National Congress
AU	The African Union
BIT	bilateral investment treaty
BLS	Basic legal syllogism
CA	Constitutional Amendment
CEDAW	Convention for the Elimination of all Forms of Discrimination against Women
CEPAL	United Nations Economic Commission for Latin America and the Caribbean
CJEU	Court of Justice of the European Union
CCM	Community's constitutional morality
ECHR	European Convention on Human Rights
ECJ	European Court of Justice
ECtHR	European Court of Human Rights
ECOWAS	Economic Community of West African States
EHRS	European Human Rights System
FARC	Revolutionary Armed Forces of Colombia
FN	Frente Nacional (National Front)
FSLN	Sandinista National Liberation Front
GFA	Good Friday Agreement/Belfast Agreement
IAHRS	Inter-American Human Rights System
IACmHR	Inter-American Commission of Human Rights
IACtHR	Inter-American Court of Human Rights
ICC	International Criminal Court
ICCPR	International Covenant on Civil and Political Rights
ICESCR	International Covenant on Economic, Social and Cultural Rights
ICTY	International Criminal Tribunal for the former Yugoslavia
ICCR	International Criminal Court for Rwanda
IDP	Internally displaced persons
IHL	international humanitarian law
ILO	International Labour Organization
INSS	National Institute of Social Security
IRA	Irish Republican Army
JEP	Special Jurisdiction for Peace
MAS	Movement for Socialism
NAC	National Constituent Assembly
NCOP	National Council of Provinces
NGOs	Non-governmental organizations

NIAC	non-international armed conflict
OAS	Organization of American States
OAU	Organization of African Unity
OTP	Office of the Prosecutor of the ICC
PAU	Public Action of Unconstitutionality
PSC	Peace and Security Council
SJP	Special Jurisdiction for Peace
SALG	Southern African Litigation Center
TEU	Treaty of the European Union
TJ	Transitional Justice
TGC	Tribunal of Constitutional Guarantees
TPA	Treaty Passing Act
TRC	Truth and Reconciliation Commission
UHRS	Universal Human Rights System
UVF	Ulster Volunteer Force
VCLT	Vienna Convention on the Law of Treaties

List of Contributors

Juana I. Acosta-López (juanaacosta20@gmail.com) is a lawyer from the Universidad Javeriana. She holds a Master's degree in human rights and democratization from the Universidad Externado de Colombia and an LLM in human rights and democratization from New York University. She is currently undertaking doctoral studies at the Universidad Autónoma de México and is the head of the research department at the Universidad de La Sabana in Bogotá, Colombia. Professor Acosta was subdirector of the thematic area of the Office of the High Commissioner for Peace in the Peace Dialogues at La Havana, Cuba, and has served as external adviser to public and private entities as well as to international organizations on international and human rights law matters.

Diana Acosta-Navas (diana_acosta_navas@hks.harvard.edu) is a doctoral candidate in philosophy at Harvard, where she worked as adjunct lecturer on ethics and public policy at the Harvard Kennedy School of Government. She studied philosophy at the Universidad de Los Andes and obtained a Master's degree from the Universidad Nacional de Colombia. Professor Acosta's research centres on the analysis of the merits and risks of transitional justice institutions that seek to defend the rights and dignity of victims of human rights violations, particularly in the case of Colombia. She also works on other issues in political philosophy and the ethics of emerging technologies, especially issues related to freedom of speech.

Carlos Arévalo (carlos.arevalo1@unisabana.edu.co) holds an LLB from the Universidad de La Sabana in Colombia and an LLM in international legal studies from New York University. He is the former assistant justice (Magistrado Auxiliar) of the Colombian Constitutional Court. For two consecutive periods, he was president of the Colombian Academy of International Law. He was also fellow of the New York University Institute for International Law and Justice before the UN International Law Commission; human rights consultant for the Colombian Government, International Organizations and Corporations; and has been requested to act as an expert witness before the Inter-American Court of Human Rights, on issues related to state responsibility. Currently he is the head of the international law department at the Universidad de La Sabana.

David Bilchitz (davidb@saifac.org.za) is a Professor of Fundamental Rights and Constitutional Law at the University of Johannesburg and Director of the South African Institute for Advanced Constitutional, Public, Human Rights and International Law. He is also a Professor of Law at the University of Reading. He is a Member of the Academy of Science of South Africa and Vice-President of the International Association of Constitutional Law after serving as its Secretary-General for 7 years. He holds a BA (Hons) LLB from the University of the Witwatersrand and an MPhil in Philosophy (MPhil) and PhD in law from the University of Cambridge. He also worked as law clerk to Deputy Judge-President (then) Langa of the South African Constitutional Court in 2000.

Mario Alberto Cajas-Sarria (mcajas@icesi.edu.co) is a lawyer from the Universidad del Cauca with specialization in Public Law from the Universidad Externado of Colombia. He holds a Master's Degree from the Universidad Nacional of Colombia and a PhD in Law from the Universidad de Los Andes. Currently, he is the head of the legal studies department at the Universidad Icesi in Cali, Colombia. His academic interests vary from constitutional law to legal history.

Yenny Andrea Celemín (ya.celemin24@uniandes.edu.co) is a lawyer and MA in law from the Universidad Nacional de Colombia, and holds a PhD in Law from Universidad de Los Andes. She has been a professor of law at the Universidad Nacional de Colombia and the Universidad Jorge Tadeo Lozano, and is currently Assistant Law Professor at the Universidad de Los Andes. Her research interest is in the area of constitutional law.

Alma Diamond (alma.diamond@law.nyu.edu) is currently completing her doctoral studies at NYU Law under the supervision of Jeremy Waldron, where her research focuses on the relationship between law and state. She holds honours degrees in law and economics as well as an LLM from the University of Stellenbosch, South Africa. In 2019, she completed an LLM. in legal theory at NYU Law, where she was the recipient of the David H. Moses Memorial Prize. In South Africa, she lectured in contract law and microeconomics. She has written on contract theory and contract law, vagueness in legal reasoning, and constitutional legitimacy.

David Dyzenhaus (david.dyzenhaus@utoronto.ca) is a South African lawyer (LLB) from the University of the Witwatersrand, from which he also holds a BA. Following his doctoral degree in Philosophy of Law from Oxford University, he has been the law foundation visiting fellow at the University of Auckland, the Herbert Smith visiting professor in the Cambridge law faculty, the Arthur Goodhart visiting professor in legal science in Cambridge, and a senior scholar of Pembroke College, Cambridge. Currently he holds the Albert Abel Chair at the University of Toronto where he is University Professor of Law and Philosophy, and is a fellow of the Royal Society of Canada.

Cindy Vanessa Espitia-Murcia has a Bachelor of Law and Social Communication from the Universidad de La Sabana). Professor and researcher. Member of the Research Group on International Law, Universidad de la Sabana (Bogotá, Colombia).

Marie-Christine Fuchs (MarieChFuchs@gmail.com; marie-christine.fuchs@kas.de) is currently directing the Rule of Law Programme for Latin America of Konrad Adenauer Foundation, Bogotá, Colombia; she is a German lawyer and holds a BA, a LL.M and a doctorate degree in public international law, European Union law, and human rights law from Saarbrücken University, Germany; she has practiced law in law firms in Berlin, Hamburg and New York and worked as a researcher at Max Planck Institute for Comparative and International Privat Law. **Santiago García-Jaramillo (Assistant Editor)** (garciajaramillosantiago@gmail.com, santiagogj@corteconstitucional.gov.co) is a law clerk at the Chamber of Justice Alejandro Linares-Cantillo (Colombian Constitutional Court); Professor of Constitutional Law at Pontificia Universidad Javeriana (Bogotá, Colombia); visiting research scholar at Cornell University (Spring, 2018 and 2019). He has a LLB from Pontificia Universidad Javeriana (Colombia, 2013); and a specialization degree in public law from the Universidad Externado de Colombia (2016).

Roberto Gargarella (roberto.gargarella@gmail.com) is a lawyer and sociologist from the University of Buenos Aires. He holds various degrees including an LLM and a JSD from the

University of Chicago. Currently teaching at Torcuato Di Tella University, he has also taught at the University of Buenos Aires and has been a visiting professor at universities such as Columbia University, Chicago University, Pompeu Fabra Univeristy, New York University, and University of Bergen.

Tom Ginsburg (tginsburg@uchicago.edu) holds a BA, JD, and PhD Jurisprudence and Social Policy from the University of California at Berkeley. He was legal adviser at the Iran–US Claims Tribunal at The Hague, Netherlands, and has worked with foreign governments and international agencies on constitutional and legal reform. His research interests are in the areas of comparative and international law. Currently, he is the Leo Spitz Professor of International Law, Ludwig and Hilde Wolf Research Scholar at The University of Chicago.

Julián Huertas (julian.huertas@mail.utoronto.ca) is a doctoral student (SJD) at the University of Toronto Faculty of Law, under the supervision of Professor Karen Knop. He holds an LLM from Columbia Law School, where he was a Harlan Fiske Stone Scholar; a Master's degree in international law from Universidad de La Sabana (Colombia); and an LLB from Universidad del Rosario (Colombia). He has served as Executive Rapporteur of the Venezuela Accountability Project, a collaboration between the Global Accountability Network and the University of Toronto's International Human Rights Program. He is assistant professor of international law at Universidad de La Sabana School of Law and Political Sciences (on leave).

Samuel Issacharoff (Issacharoff@mercury.law.nyu.edu) is a lawyer from Yale University (JD). Having taught at the University of Texas, where he held the Joseph D. Jamail Centennial Chair in Law, he moved to Columbia University as the Harold R. Medina Professor of Procedural Jurisprudence. Professor Issacharoff's research has dealt with issues in civil procedure, law, and economics; constitutional law with particular focus on voting rights and electoral systems; and employment law. Currently he is the Reiss Professor of Constitutional Law at New York University and is a fellow of the American Academy of Arts and Sciences.

David Landau (dlandau@law.fsu.edu) holds an AB, a JD, and a PhD (political science) from Harvard University. Professor Landau has focused his writing primarily on the field of comparative constitutional law, concentrating on Latin America. Having served, in 2011, as a consultant on constitutional concerns for the Truth and Reconciliation Commission of Honduras, he has also been a founding editor of IConnect, the blog of the International Journal of Constitutional Law. Currently he is Mason Ladd professor and Associate Dean for International Programs at Florida State University College of Law.

Mitchel Lasser (ml355@cornell.edu) is a lawyer from Harvard Law School (JD). He later received a PhD in comparative literature from Yale University. His research interests are in the areas of comparative law, law of the European Union, and judicial process in the national and supranational contexts. He has been a visiting professor at the University of Paris-I (Panthéon-Sorbonne), the NYU School of Law, Yale Law School, the University of Geneva, the University of Lausanne, the Institut d'Etudes Politiques de Paris (Sciences Po), the University of Paris-5 (Descartes), and the Católica Global School of Law (Lisbon). Currently, he is the Jack G. Clarke Professor of Law and Director of Graduate Studies at Cornell Law School.

Alejandro Linares-Cantillo—Editor (a.linares.cantillo@gmail.com, alejandrolc@corteconstitucional.gov.co) is an associate justice of the Colombian Constitutional Court.

Justice Linares obtained his LL.B from the Universidad de Los Andes in Bogotá. He also obtained an LLM degree from Harvard University and has a PhD in Law from the Universidad Externado of Colombia. Justice Linares has practised law for more than thirty years in both the public and private sectors. He has taught in different universities in Colombia, including the Universidad de Los Andes, the Universidad del Rosario, and the Universidad del Norte. In the public sector, prior to becoming a justice at the Constitutional Court, he held different positions in the executive branch. Finally, in the private sector, he was partner of one of the most prestigious law firms in the country for more than twenty years, where his practice primarily focused on matters of transnational litigation and international business.

Andrei Marmor (am2773@cornell.edu) is a lawyer and a philosopher. He has been a professor at the University of Tel Aviv, where he obtained his first law and philosophy degrees, and at UCLA. He holds a PhD in philosophy from Oxford University. His research interests include philosophy of law and moral, social, and political philosophy. Professor Marmor is the founding editor of the Journal of Ethics and Social Philosophy and currently is the Jacob Gould Schurman Professor of Philosophy and Law at Cornell University.

Octávio Luiz Motta Ferraz (octavio.ferraz@kcl.ac.uk) is a Reader in Transitional Law at King's College London, where he co-directs the Transnational Law Institute. Following his LLB and MPhil degrees from the from the University of São Paulo, he obtained an MA in medical ethics & law from King's College London and a PhD in Law from University College London. , Professor Ferraz worked as a senior research officer to the UN special rapporteur for the right to health at the University of Essex and was also an associate professor at Warwick Law School.**Colleen Murphy** (colleenm@illinois.edu) holds an MA and a PhD in philosophy from the University of North Carolina at Chapel Hill and a BA from the University of Notre Dame. Having been an associate professor of Philosophy at Texas A&M University, she was a Laurence S. Rockefeller visiting faculty fellow at the University Center for Human Values at Princeton University. Currently she is a professor in the College of Law and the Departments of Philosophy and Political Science at the University of Illinois at Urbana-Champaign; director of the Women and Gender in Global Perspectives Program in International Programs and Studies. Professor Murphy is also an associate editor of the Journal of Moral Philosophy and a member of the American Philosophical Association's Committee on Philosophy and Law.

Professor Muna Ndulo (mbn5@cornell.edu), following his LLB from the University of Zambia, obtained an LLM from Harvard Law School and a DPhil from Trinity College, Oxford University. Professor Ndulo has acted as a legal officer in the International Trade Law Branch of the United Nations Commissions on International Trade, as well as an arbitrator under the International Chamber of Commerce. He has also been a political and legal adviser with the United Nations Mission Observer Mission in South Africa and to the Special Representative of the United Nations Secretary General to South Africa. In addition to his role as legal adviser to the United Nations Mission to Kosovo and to the United Nations Mission to Afghanistan, Professor Ndulo has also acted as a consultant to multilateral organizations including the World Bank, the African Development Bank, and the United Nations Development Program. Having been the founder of the Southern African Institute for Public Policy and Research, he is a member of its Board of Directors, a position which he also holds, amongst others, in the Board of the African Association of International Law and the Advisory Committee of Human Rights

Watch Africa. He is currently a professor of law at Cornell Law School and serves as the Director of the Cornell University Institute for African Development.

Yaniv Roznai (yaniv.roznai@idc.ac.il) is a lawyer from the Harry Radzyner Law School, Interdisciplinary Center Herzliya in Israel from which he holds a BA and LLB. Having obtained an LLM. and a Ph.D from the London School of Economics, he was a Post-Doc Fellow at the Minerva Center for the Rule of Law under Extreme Conditions, University of Haifa and the Hauser Global Law School, New York University. Currently, he is an Associate Professor at the Radzyner School of Law, Interdisciplinary Center Herzliya and a Co-Chair of the Israeli Section of the International Society of Public Law (ICON-S).

Axel Tschentscher (axel.tschentscher@oefre.unibe.ch) is a Swiss professor for law and philosophy. Having obtained an LLM. from Cornell University (U.S.A.), an MA in philosophy from Würzburg University (Germany), and a PhD in legal philosophy from Kiel University (Germany), he currently holds the Chair for Constitutional Law, Legal Philosophy, and Constitutional History at the Law Faculty of the University of Bern (Switzerland).

Camilo Valdivieso-León—Assistant Editor (valdiviesocamilo@gmail.com, camilovl@corteconstitucional.gov.co) is a law clerk at the Chamber of Justice Alejandro Linares-Cantillo (Colombian Constitutional Court). He was assistant professor of international investment law (Spring, 2017) and private international law (Fall, 2019) at the Universidad de Los Andes (Colombia). He holds an LLB from the Universidad de Los Andes (Colombia, 2015); and specialization degree in public management and administrative institutions from the Universidad de Los Andes (Colombia, 2018).

W. J. Waluchow (walucho@mcmaster.ca) is a Canadian philosopher. Having obtained his BA and MA in philosophy from the University of Western Ontario, and a DPhil in Philosophy from Oxford University where he studied under the direction of H. L. A. Hart, he is currently Emeritus Professor in McMaster University's Department of Philosophy, the Senator William McMaster Chair in Constitutional Studies, and an Adjunct Member of the Graduate Faculty of Osgoode Hall Law School, Toronto.

I
INTRODUCTION

Introduction

Alejandro Linares-Cantillo

This book is a compilation of the twenty essays prepared for the occasion of the XIII conference of the Constitutional Court of the Republic of Colombia held in Bogotá in January 2019. Following the accustomed annual tradition, during my year as Chief Justice of the Colombian Constitutional Court (2018–2019) it was among my responsibilities to organize and host an academic conference to discuss constitutional law issues which are of great interest to the academia and the Court itself. For the XIII conference, I decided to invite professors and scholars from Colombia and abroad to exchange views on and debate current trends in constitutionalism. By current trends, I mean mostly the classical debates, but with the novel approaches arising from the Colombian historical and political context in particular. Although constitutional judges are sometimes portrayed as not being open to criticism, I chose to focus the agenda on a critical approach towards the role of the Colombian Constitutional Court. Therefore, the idea was to have, as a source of inspiration, a critical reflection on our role from the academia. When I embarked on this project, I believed it was going to be an easy task. After all, the Colombian Constitutional Court is a bulwark of constitutionalism, even considered '*one of the most powerful courts in the world*'. [1] Therefore, inviting diverse professors and scholars to appraise the Colombian experience did not seem a complex enterprise.

As I started to reach out to leading international scholars and professors from around the world, I learned a lesson of judicial humility. I understood that our court, even as admired and important as it might be, has not been broadly studied by foreign academics. Moreover, there are very few publications on our court in the English language available for an Anglophone audience.[2] In addition, I found out that gathering this 'dream team' of national and international scholars demanded an impressive amount of work, since they all had previous and compelling commitments. Finally, it was hard to think of a dialogue between philosophers, who usually take a more a 'normative' approach towards discussions in constitutional law, and professors with

[1] Stephen Gardbaum, 'What Makes for More or Less Powerful Constitutional Courts?' (2018) 29 Duke Journal of Comparative & International Law 1–40; David Landau, 'Political Institutions and Judicial Role in Comparative Constitutional Law' (2010) 51 Harvard Law Journal 319.

[2] The most important one being Manuel José Cepeda-Espinosa & David Landau, *Colombian Constitutional Law: Leading Cases* (Oxford: Oxford University Press, 2017). See also Manuel José Cepeda-Espinosa, 'Judicial Activism in a Violent Context: The Origin, Role, and Impact of the Colombian Constitutional Court' (2004) 3 Washington University Global Studies Law Review 529; Santiago Garcia-Jaramillo, 'Colombian Constitutionalism: Challenging Judicial Supremacy through Pluralism' (2019) 2 International Comparative, Policy and Ethics Law Review 317; Samuel Issacharoff, *Fragile Democracies. Contested Power in the Era of Constitutional Courts* (Cambridge: Cambridge University Press, 2015); David Landau, 'A Dynamic Theory of Judicial Role' (2014) 55 Boston College Law Review 1501, among others.

Alejandro Linares-Cantillo, *Introduction* In: *Constitutionalism.* Edited by: Alejandro Linares-Cantillo, Camilo Valdivieso-León, Santiago García-Jaramillo, Oxford University Press (2021). © The various contributors.
DOI: 10.1093/oso/9780192896759.003.0001

an 'empirical' stance towards constitutional law. Fortunately, after months of planning and hard work, the conference was an academic success, and this collective work, as a collection of essays, reflects the numerous ideas and opinions written by scholars and international professors on the role of a constitutional court. At the end of the day, it was rewarding to see leading scholars from around the world making an effort to engage and establish a conversation not only with the Court, but also with local academics.

The lessons of the book are worth reviewing for comparative scholars, as well as by constitutional and regional courts. The reader will find that this book tries to bridge normative with empirical discussions, domestic with regional and foreign issues, 'Global South' approaches with 'Global North' stances on human rights, use of precedents, and transitional justice. This openness to hearing different points of view taught me a second lesson of judicial humility: our court, in its almost thirty years of existence, has developed creative and innovative precedents, but our history, the difficulties we have confronted, and even our jurisprudence, are not unique in the world of constitutionalism. Therefore, this book is also an invitation to be aware that constitutional law is context-dependent, as it aims at making sense in a particular society and time. In addition, the book proposes that conceiving the possibility of levelling and reaching a universal constitutionalism is not only utopic but counterfactual. However, it also offers an interesting perspective to abandon constitutional parochialism and dogmatism, to the extent that experiences from other regions, as well as critical normative positions on constitutionalism, can nourish and enlighten our national debates.

This collection of twenty chapters is divided into three thematic parts which illustrate five subjects at the spotlight of comparative constitutional law in light of the growing circulation and intensification of the idea of constitutionalism. Part I examines the evolving and leading role of constitutional courts in constitutional democracies. Part II allows constitutional experiences to speak for themselves and discusses tensions and debates in three topics: (1) the growing trend to judicially enforce 'constitutional unamendability'[3] under the doctrine of 'unconstitutional constitutional amendments'; (2) the idea of 'transformative constitutionalism' in the area of social rights enforcement; and (3) the models of transitional justice and their implementation in the Colombian case. Finally, Part III analyses vertical and horizontal movements of constitutional law doctrines and decisions.

* * *

Part I: The Role of Constitutional Courts in a Modern Democracy

A. Hercules at the Crossroads

Constitutional courts are today in the spotlight of legal, political, and social battles. Judges around the world try to imitate the '*Herculean Judge*' described

[3] The term is taken from Yaniv Roznai, *Unconstitutional Constitutional Amendments* (Oxford: Oxford University Press, 2018).

by Dworkin,[4] by deciding more and more cases in their forum of principles,[5] relying on opened-texture and highly moralized clauses included in many constitutions. It is hard to think that Justice Marshall in 1803[6] or Hans Kelsen[7] at the beginning of the twentieth century would anticipate what judicial review would become, and the centrality it would take, in solving moral-political disputes. While many theorists see judicial review as a necessary consequence of the supremacy of the constitution, considering its legally binding nature, the essays included in Part I of this book will cast some doubt on the necessary link between constitutionalism and strong judicial review, while also inviting the reader to analyse the rise of constitutional courts from a moral-political and historical point of view.

Part I will revert to the classical debates on the role of constitutional judges. From a normative stance, and by relying on legal and political philosophy, it will raise objections to the prominent role that judges have gained around the world. However, they will not be grounded solely on the classical counter-majoritarian objection. This first part will also engage in interpretative questions, it will focus on the existence or not of 'correct answers' in constitutional hard cases, as well as in the institutional designs needed to instantiate the quest for at least, a 'good answer'. In fact, Part I aims to examine the evolving roles of constitutional courts. This section bridges a moral political discussion on the legitimacy of powers conferred to constitutional courts to interpret the constitution, with an institutional design study, and a factual analysis of a concrete constitutional jurisdiction.

Two philosophers with a long-time struggle with constitutionalism open this chapter, Andrei Marmor and Wil Waluchow. First, Marmor in his chapter, entitled 'Constitutionalism, Liberalism and Democracy', sets the tone of the discussion by exposing his scepticism towards constitutional courts. He describes the tension between our commitment to democratic decision-making procedures and constitutional judicial review, showing that the liberal values that justify a democratic self-government may also vindicate some limits on majoritarian decision-making procedures, but not necessarily in the form of the constitutional regimes that we have. In his point of view constitutional courts are not a necessary feature of a liberal regime. And it is at this point that the reader will find a challenge to our faith in constitutional courts: Marmor acknowledges that democratic decision making has many defects (the fate of persistent vulnerable minorities, the tendency towards shortsightedness, a similar tendency to downplay people's rights and liberties for the sake of greater economic gains or in the force of external threats, and finally the dangers of populism and antiliberal politics gaining ground within a democratic system), but at the same time he doubts that courts will be able to deliver satisfactory results in these areas. In fact—by relying in the US experience—Marmor depicts courts as essentially conservative institutions which are not, and cannot be, as counter-majoritarian as depicted by legal scholars, mainly because their legitimacy and the acceptance of their decisions depends on

[4] Ronald Dworkin, *Law's Empire* (Cambridge, MA: Harvard University Press, 1986).
[5] Ronald Dworkin, 'The Forum of Principle' (1981) 56 New York University Law Review 469.
[6] See *Madison v Marbury*, 5 US 137 (1803).
[7] See Lars Vinx, *The Guardian of the Constitution: Hans Kelsen and Carl Schmitt on the Limits of Constitutional Law* (Cambridge: Cambridge University Press, 2015).

the people. Marmor, as a prominent legal positivist, believes that the acceptance and efficacy of judicial review is context-dependent, but that some fights still need to be fought in the political, not the legal arena.

To counteract this attack on constitutionalism, his old-time opponent, Wil Waluchow, in his chapter, entitled 'The Misconceived Quest for the Elusive Right Answer or Dedication to a Process, Not a Result', considers that constitutional courts must commit to a process rather than a result. He acknowledges that judges making political decisions have a considerable margin of discretion, and their cases fall into the 'hard cases' arena, as famously called by H. L. A. Hart.[8] As such, Waluchow believes that the answer to the interpretative concerns over constitutional judges should not be overcome by relying on the idea of a unique correct answer, as proposed by Dworkin, but rather by a dedication to the decision-making process, which presupposes the display of judicial virtues that Hart famously enumerated.[9] For Waluchow it is clear that, even if constitutional judges confront several 'hard cases' where discretion is at hand, judicial discretion does not consist of unbridled choice on the part of the one who exercises it. Waluchow revisits his idea of the 'Community Constitutional Morality', under which each legal system instantiates a set of moral values embedded in its constitution from which judges should not depart; it is the constitution and the local social practice that determines such 'constitutional morality', and not an ideal set of external objective morality. This idea mitigates the 'counter-majoritarian' objection, as judicial review would reflect the commitments deeply held by the society where it is being exercised. This proposal could be fertile soil for further research. It would be necessary to consider how this proposal works in those 'wicked legal systems'[10] where the 'Community Constitutional Morality' seems to be at odds with basic rights, or the objection that courts, instead of being an antidote to those shortcomings of democratic decision making—like the fate of persistent minorities—is simply becoming another institution aligned with the majoritarian views.[11]

In line with this discussion on constitutional interpretation and institutional design, Roberto Gargarella, in his chapter, entitled 'Dialogic Constitutionalism in Defective Democracies', initiates a conversation between the 'Global South' practice of judicial review, and the institutional framework set forth by the US founding fathers in the Federalist Papers. Gargarella's aim is to demonstrate how progressive constitutions of the Global South are 'trapped' by the Madisonian separation of powers. To overcome this situation, Gargarella believes that the institutional framework needs to be reshaped in order to accommodate the particular necessities of Latin American societies. In this sense, he agrees with Marmor that institutional design is context-dependent and needs to be fixed in line with particular moral-political considerations. To confront the objections raised by Marmor, Gargarella proposes rethinking the whole system of checks and balances towards a more participatory 'dialogic model', where constitutional courts are not entrusted with the final word on constitutional

[8] See generally H. L. A. Hart, *The Concept of Law* (Oxford: Clarendon Law Series, 1961).

[9] Ibid., at 205.

[10] See David Dyzenhaus, *Hard Cases in Wicked Legal Systems* (Oxford: Oxford University Press, 2010).

[11] See Andrei Marmor, *Interpretation and Legal Theory* (2nd edn, Oregon: Hart Publishing, 2005), 160–2; Andrei Marmor, 'What is Law and What Counts as Law? The Separation Thesis in Context' (2017) *Cornell Legal Studies Research Paper* No. 17-34.

interpretation—they would certainly have a word, but not the last one. This model has certain similarities with the 'departmentalist' approach that has been suggested by some prominent US scholars;[12] however, it departs from this idea by focusing on matters like social and economic rights, whose judicial enforcement has been mainly the domain of 'Global South' constitutionalism.

Part I concludes with an empirical chapter, departing from the philosophical, normative discussions to give the reader a valuable lesson in Colombian constitutional history and judicial politics. Mario Cajas, a Colombian professor, in his chapter, entitled 'From the Public Action of Unconstitutionality of 1910 to the Constitutional Court of 1991: The Political and Legal Struggles for Constitutional Justice in Colombia', provides an interesting historical account of the Colombian constitutional jurisdiction since 1910, when the public unconstitutionality action was first introduced into our legal system. Cajas' historical research evidences how the creation of a constitutional court is highly influenced by local history—as argued by Marmor—and the prominent role that local elites, in the political domain and legal academia, play within the consolidation of this process. Cajas demonstrates the idea that the institutional design to channel constitutionalism is context-dependent, but at the same time it is influenced by debates from other jurisdictions. For instance, he evidenced in his paper that the centralized Kelsenian model of judicial review[13] profoundly influenced the creation of the Colombian Constitutional Court. Hence, this chapter draws the readers' attention to another persistent discussion in 'Global South' countries: the influence and use of legal transplants and how they are 'translated'[14] into the concrete political context and society. Alongside Gargarella, Cajas instantiates a dialogue between 'Global North' and 'Global South' regarding institutional design. Cajas is careful not to assume that constitutionalism is a 'one-size-fits-all' idea, but his historical account invites the reader to consider how judicial review migrated from Europe into the Latin-American context.

One final topic, discussed by both Gargarella and Marmor refers to the current issue of 'populism', as a rising phenomenon in many countries around the world. It is interesting how both authors are sceptical about the role that courts can play to stop or mitigate this phenomenon. While the 'standard' depiction of constitutional courts as counter-majoritarian institutions makes us believe that apex courts are best situated to stop or at least limit populist impulses, Marmor maintains that courts need to rely on the people's acceptance and therefore are not truly in the best position to face populism. On the other side, Gargarella believes that instead of curtailing democracy, the best way to fight populism is by empowering democratic decision making and to confront the persistent basic inequalities (political exclusion, democratic dissonance, concentration of powers, hyper-presidentialism, among others). Even if the reader does not share this point of view, it leads to an essential question in the faith one may or may not have in judicial review, as both professors' critiques depict an imperfect

[12] See, among others, Kramer's proposal in Larry Kramer, *The People Themselves* (Oxford: Oxford University Press, 2005), and the reply by Post and Siegel in Robert Post & Reval Siegel, 'Popular Constitutionalism, Departmentalism, and Judicial Supremacy' (2004) 92(4) California Law Review 1027.

[13] Vinx (n. 7).

[14] See Esteban Restrepo-Saldarriaga, 'Inevitable Translations' (2017) 4 Revista del Centro de Estudios Constitucionales 111–68.

solution, rather than an ultimate one, and call attention to the need to defend constitutionalism and liberal values from the political arena.

It is now evident for the reader why in my mind, Part I is entitled 'Hercules at the Crossroads'. All the above-mentioned authors, despite their many theoretical approaches and differences, converge in the idea that there is more than mere textual analysis deployed by constitutional courts, and more than just the 'positive' or formal enactment of a constitution for Constitutional Courts to consolidate their powers. In the realm of institutional design, constitutional courts emerge in the midst of political circumstances, which determine the extent and scope of their powers. In their current role, judges intervene in highly contested moral-political and historical issues, with the uncertainty on whether they are or are not in the best position to do so. The question of whether they should intervene in such complex moral-political issues, to what extent they should, and the interpretative tools they should employ remains a contested domain, that not even the all-mighty Hercules judge could solve once and for all.

* * *

Part II: New Insights

While the topics discussed in this section are not new, the approach that the contributors to this volume take towards those topics are aimed at introducing new insights, perspectives, ideas, dilemmas, and proposals in the areas of constitutional amendments, the judicial enforcement of social and economic rights, and transitional justice. In Part II, the reader will engage in normative and empirical discussions, and in an ongoing dialogue between the so called 'Global South' and 'Global North' constitutional doctrines. In these examples from different jurisdictions, this section offers three similar constitutional issues which do not necessarily lead to similar solutions.

A. We the People or We the Judges—The Judicial Enforcement of Unconstitutional Constitutional Amendments' Theory

The discussion on unamendability in law, and vis-à-vis fundamental laws, is hardly a fresh topic.[15] Melissa Schwartzberg, for example, has carried out an exhaustive study on how it was a recurrent topic in classical Greece, how it was discussed in the fundamental laws of the Middle Ages, and also in the US Constitution—which includes the unamendable clause of equal representation in Senate, and the sunset clause regarding the slave trade.[16] However, as Schwartzberg and Roznai acknowledge, two

[15] Tierney traces it back to the discussions on the constitution of the Catholic Church and the extent of papal authority for the 'edification' and not for the 'destruction' of the Church Constitution. See Brian Tierney, *Religion Law and the Growth of Constitutional Thought, 1150-1650* (Cambridge: Cambridge University Press, 1982), 64.

[16] See Melissa Schwartzberg, *Democracy and Legal Change* (Cambridge: Cambridge University Press, 2007).

landmark events have boosted the development of constitutional unamendability. In the *explicit* form, the German Basic Law of 1949, with its unamendability clause comprising human dignity and other fundamental values; and in its *implicit* approach, the *basic structure doctrine* set forth by the Indian Supreme Court in *Kesavananda Bharati v State of Kerala* of 1973, by reaffirming and extending the idea proposed in 1967 in *Golaknath v State of Punjab*. As Yaniv Roznai illustrates in his seminal work 'Unconstitutional Constitutional Amendments', there is a worldwide trend towards constitutional unamendability. Not only have more constitutions included explicit unamendable clauses, but apex courts around the world are enabling themselves to be the guardians of the implicit 'basic structure of the constitution'.[17]

As Cajas has illustrated in his chapter, it is quite interesting that in Colombia the doctrine of implicit unamendability was enforced by our Supreme Court as early as 1978, perhaps inspired silently by the Indian *Kesavananda* decision in 1973. In 1977, the Colombian Congress approved summoning a limited 'constitutional assembly', with the specific purpose of amending the judicial branch and the territorial entities, and among others, creating a constitutional court, in spite of the fact that the 1886 Colombian constitution only allowed amendments by Congress. The Supreme Court of the time, in a highly divided decision, stated that the amendment power is inherently limited, as it cannot be delegated by Congress to a constitutional assembly. Thus, as the power to amend the constitution had to be considered a limited competence, only entrusted to Congress, it was the Supreme Court's role, as the guardian of the integrity of the constitution, to exercise an *ultra vires* judicial review to amendments duly approved by the legislature.[18] This precedent is not well known among comparative legal scholars, or in local academia, since we prefer discussing Decision C-551 of 2003 of the Constitutional Court. In this 2003 decision, by relying on the Indian Basic Structure doctrine, the Schmittean conception of constituent powers and his doctrine of the 'material' constitution, the Colombian Court enumerated the 'Constitutional Replacement Theory' while upholding most of the referendum.[19] The Court thus limited the power of constitutional amendment on substantial grounds, precisely by those implicit salient features that make the basic structure of the constitution, and consolidated the power of the Court to undertake such review, under the cloack of an *ultra vires*[20] doctrine. It should be noted, however, that the explicit text of the 1991 Colombian constitution limits the Court's competence to review amendments only on procedural grounds.

[17] Roznai (n. 3).

[18] In a Decision of 5 May 1978 the Chamber of Constitutional Affairs of the Colombian Supreme Court of Justice (Justice José Maria Velasco-Guerrero with Justice Guillermo González-Charry dissenting) declared as unconstitutional the Legislative Act 2 of 19 December 1977. The purpose of this act was to summon a Constitutional Assembly, following art. 213 of the 1886 Constitution, 2397 *Gaceta Judicial*, 91–125.

[19] Thus applying what Dixon and Issacharoff term a second-order deferral or 'Marbury Strategy'. See Rosalind Dixon & Samuel Issacharoff, 'Living to Fight Another Day: Judicial Deferral in Defense of Democracy'(2016) Wisconsin Law Review 683.

[20] For a comprehensive description on the use of this doctrine by the Colombian Constitutional Court, see, *inter-alia*, Jorge Roa-Roa, *Control de Constitucionalidad Deliberativo* (Bogotá: CEPC and Externado University Press, 2019); Vincente F. Benítez-Rojas, *Constitución Popular, No Judicial. Una teoría democrática del control de constitucionalidad de las reformas en Colombia* (Bogotá: University of La Sabana Press & Temis, 2014); Carlos Bernal-Pulido, 'Unconstitutional Constitutional Amendments in the

The Colombian Constitutional Court has become a landmark example of the judicial enforcement of implicit unamendability, as Issacharoff, Roznai, Celemin, and Ginsburg will show in their contributions to this volume. Perhaps the main reason for this reputation is that in 2010 the Court declared as unconstitutional a law summoning a referendum that, if approved by the people, would have allowed the president in office to run for a third term.[21] The Constitutional Court, in Decision C-1040 of 2005, upheld a constitutional amendment allowing one presidential re-election and made it quite clear that only another term would pass its constitutional test.[22] In this sense this precedent, as paradoxical as may sound, paved the way for halting the 2010 proposed amendment. This case has gained worldwide recognition because, as shown recently by Versteeg, it is the only successful case in the world of an apex court—or a successful *rara avis*[23]—to have put a halt to the consolidation of a powerful executive, by means of altering the presidential terms in office.[24]

The approach of this first section is rather more empirical. In fact, most of the contributors are devoted to comparative constitutional law, and to the study of the intersection of law and politics. Again, a chapter focusing on the Colombian discussions around the use of the unconstitutional constitutional amendment doctrine is included, to promote more comparative research based on the Colombian experience. This first section of Part II begins with a chapter by Samuel Issacharoff entitled 'Courts as Guarantors of Democracy'. Issacharoff has dedicated most of his academic life to the study of the rise of constitutionalism in new democracies; his ties to the 'Global South' have compelled him to direct his research efforts at countries such as Colombia, India, and South Africa, which are studied in depth in this section. By focusing on these countries, Issacharoff states that in these times, courts have been forced into the role of guarantors of the integrity of democratic institutions. He points out that legislatures are often dysfunctional, political parties are weak, and the critical faith of common initiative among political rules has faded. By undertaking a deep analysis of Indian political and constitutional reasons for the 'basic structure doctrine', the

Case Study of Colombia: An Analysis of the Justification and Meaning of the Constitutional Replacement Doctrine' (2013) 11 International Journal of Constitutional Law 339; Mario Cajas-Sarria, 'Judicial Review of Constitutional Amendments in Colombia: A Political and Historical Perspective, 1955–2016' (2017) 5 Theory and Practice of Legislation 245; Mario Cajas-Sarria, *El control judicial a la reforma constitucional. Colombia, 1910–2007* (Colombia: ICESI University Press, 2008); Cepeda-Espinosa (n. 2); Santiago García-Jaramillo & Francisco Gnecco-Estrada, 'La teoría de la sustitución: de la protección de la supremacía e integridad de la constitución, a la aniquilación de la titularidad del poder de reforma constitucional en el órgano legislativo' (2016) 65 Universitas Javeriana 59; Gonzalo Ramírez-Cleves, 'El control material de las reformas constitucionales mediante acto legislativo a partir de la jurisprudencia establecida en la Sentencia C-551 de 2003' (2006) 18 Revista Derecho del Estado 3; Esteban Restrepo-Saldarriaga, 'Reforma Constitucional y Progreso Social: La "Constitucionalización de la Vida Cotidiana" en Colombia' (2002) *SELA (Seminario en Latinoamérica de Teoría Constitucional y Política) Papers* 14.

[21] Decision C141 of 26 February 2010 invalidating Law no. 1354 of 2009

[22] Samuel Issacharoff, Santiago García-Jaramillo, & Vicente F. Benítez-Rojas, 'Judicial Review of Presidential Re-Election Amendments in Colombia' in Frauke Lachenmann and Rüdiger Wolfrum (eds), *Max Planck Encyclopaedia of Comparative Constitutional Law* (Oxford: Oxford University Press, 2017), https://oxcon.ouplaw.com/view/10.1093/law-mpeccol/law-mpeccol-e820, accessed 10 June 2020. .

[23] Ibid.

[24] Mila Versteeg et al., 'The Law and Politics of Presidential Term Limit Evasion' (2020) 120 Columbia Law Review 173.

South African Constitutional Court's decision rejecting the draft constitution to replace apartheid, and the decision of the Constitutional Court of Colombia to disallow a president from running for a third consecutive term, Issacharoff concludes that apex courts can play an 'emergency role' in the destiny of the democratic order, one that if limited to extreme situations and exercised with caution, sound reasoning, and judicial stewardship, can position judges in a good place to act as the guardians of deliberative democracy, and even to put a halt to populism.

The second contribution in this first section of Part II is a chapter by Tom Ginsburg. Ginsburg has studied the constitutions of several countries, especially those arising from what is called the 'third wave' of democratization. In his chapter, entitled 'The Machinery of International Law and Democratic Backsliding: The Problem of Term Limits', Ginsburg uses comparative constitutional law to cast some doubts on the necessarily good results that arise from apex courts enforcing the doctrine of unconstitutional constitutional amendments, and in this sense he invites us, in contrast to Issacharoff, to pause the faith in what courts can achieve as guardians of democracies, although he does not refute that they should play an important role. To cast these doubts, Ginsburg studies the abuse of the doctrine of unconstitutional constitutional amendments in Honduras, Bolivia, Sierra Leona, and Burkina Faso, and how in such contexts constitutional courts have become elements for legitimating autocratic regimes rather than guardians of deliberative democracy. Ginsburg's chapter reaffirms some of the normative questions raised in Part I of this book, especially the idea that the efficacy and good results of judicial review must be viewed and evaluated in a context-dependent analysis.

Yaniv Roznai, in his chapter, entitled 'The Straw that Broke the Constitution's Back? Qualitative Quantity in Judicial Review of Constitutional Amendments', also contributes to this comparative *tour d'horizon* on the judicial enforcement of the doctrine of unconstitutional constitutional amendments. As stated, his comparative research has become the milestone for any scholar or judge interested in the theoretical grounds of this doctrine, as well as its migration to different jurisdictions. In his chapter, Roznai examines the doctrines of constitutional unamendability, and how they can counteract revolutionary changes. He focuses mainly on developing the theory of quantity transforming into quality in the realm of constitutional amendments: under certain conditions, even small things can cause big changes. Roznai makes a deep theoretical analysis based on philosophical and natural sciences theories, and then proceeds to a more empirical approach. In fact, he takes the Colombian presidential re-election amendment as an example, departing from the question of why a second consecutive term is a valid constitutional amendment, while a third consecutive term is an unconstitutional replacement, and thus an unconstitutional constitutional amendment. He demonstrates how this 'new' re-election, seemingly a small change, subverted the democratic structure of the Colombian 1991 constitution. Roznai faces the recurrent criticism of the strong discretion that judges deploy when undertaking the judicial review of constitutional amendments by relying on implicit principles. He proposes that courts should consider the cumulative impact of a series of amendments affecting a certain constitutional rule or set of principles, since most of the time the dismemberment of a constitutional democracy occurs via a series of small changes, rather than by a single revolutionary change. By this approach, Roznai believes that constitutional courts will not disproportionately curtail democratic decision making, and might act, as Issacharoff depicts them, as the guardians of constitutional democracies in the face of populism and democratic decay.

In the final chapter, entitled 'Between the Explicit and Implicit Limits? An Analysis of Judicial Review of the Constitutional Amendment Doctrine in Colombia', Andrea Celemín illustrates the Colombian Constitutional Court's explicit and implicit powers to undertake the judicial review of constitutional amendments. She first describes and analyses the 'explicit' procedural limits of the Colombian 1991 constitution and the doctrine of implicit unamendability. Through a quantitative analysis of both types of judicial review, her chapter illustrates how the two approaches have developed in Colombia, and how in that context, there is an inverse relationship between the claims based on implicit limits (increasing behaviour) and those of explicit limits (decreasing behaviour). In fact, from 2010 to 2017, more amendment bills were challenged as unconstitutional on the grounds of the constitutional replacement doctrine (unconstitutional constitutional amendments) than on the grounds of violation of procedural terms. However, in the same vein as Roznai, Celemín sheds some insights on the discretion that judges deploy when enforcing these implicit limits. In fact, she raises some criticism over the fact that the Colombian Court does not have a clear interpretation of its own competence and scope to review constitutional amendments. In addition, Celemín claims that the excessive use of the doctrine of implicit unamendability has the undesired effect of focusing only on these 'substantive' principles thus 'relaxing' procedural judicial review. This can give the wrong idea of a less strict examination of the compliance with the rules governing the constitutional amendment process and therefore decreasing the quality in deliberation (at least with regards to the amendments duly approved by the legislature).

Overall, this section illustrates a recurring discussion between popular or 'political' constitutionalism and judicial supremacy. Should apex courts have the last word when interpreting the constitution? Or should the people and their representatives in Congress have the final say? Judicial supremacists used to reply to popular constitutionalists that they had the ultimate resort to a constitutional amendment when they disagreed with an interpretation set forth by constitutional courts. However, with the empowerment of judges to undertake the judicial review of duly passed constitutional amendments, this debate seems to take a different stance: should the last word on the process of constitutional amendments be shifted to the courts?[25] Indeed, it is a question of the ultimate source of sovereignty, of whether 'we the people' or 'we the court' have the final word on how to shape the constitution. This is certainly a challenging question, as Issacharoff, Roznai, Celemín, and Ginsburg have demonstrated.

In jurisdictions like Colombia, where those limits are implicit, and the competence to exercise a substantive review of constitutional amendments is not explicitly granted

[25] Schwartzberg advances an idea according to which constitutional unamendability enforced by courts, does not impede constitutional change, only shifts the final word on whether it is possible to make it or not to apex courts: Melissa Schwartzberg, *Democracy and Legal Change* (Cambridge: Cambridge University Press, 2007).

to the court by the constitution, judges should act with caution.[26] In this sense, all the authors in this section give us ideas on when to intervene. First, Issacharoff shows how courts can play an 'emergency role' for saving constitutional democracies. Even if it sounds like a modest role, one can think on a legal theory objection that apex courts are becoming 'the sovereign', under the famous Schmittean definition that 'sovereign is he who decides on the exception',[27] and that the sovereign precisely shows its existence during times when the survival or stability of the state is endangered. Indeed, in another chapter of this volume, Dyzenhaus criticizes the Colombian doctrine of implicit unamendability for relying on a 'Schmittean doctrine' of constituent power, which allows the Constitutional Court to exercise a muted constituent power, thus, relying on power and not on authority. Roznai's proposal of intervening when there is an accumulative impact of a series of amendments affecting a certain constitutional rule or set of principles presents us with a difficult dilemma: if courts intervene too soon, they might block amendments that are more aimed towards innovative pragmatism[28] than to subverting a constitutional democracy, but if they intervene too late, their decision might come at a time when democracy has been lost.[29] Finally, the doubts that Ginsburg depicts by studying the abuses of the use of the constitutional unamendability in order to legitimate autocrats,[30] reinvigorates the invitation that Gargarella and Marmor make in Part I to not only look at courts, but also address the recurring problems of our democracies. Perhaps this is the same invitation that Celemín makes when she warns against abandoning the focus on deliberation during the amending process to look only at substance.[31]

In short, this first section of Part II opens up countless opportunities for further research in the realm of the use of the doctrine of unconstitutional constitutional amendments. All of the authors set off a debate that is in the spotlight of today's constitutional discussions: to what extent can constitutional unamendability curtail the decay of constitutional democracies. This debate takes us back to the everlasting tension between democracy and constitutionalism, and invites us to think of pragmatic approaches for contributing to protect the fate of our constitutional democracies, and

[26] I myself have filed several concurring and dissenting opinions, calling to a self-restraint use of the doctrine of unconstitutional constitutional amendments in the Colombian context. For instance, I set out my doubts in the dissenting opinion to Decision C-285 of 2016. I have reaffirmed this view in concurring opinions to decisions C-084-2016; C-261 of 2016; C-699 of 2016, and the dissenting opinion to decision C-332 of 2017.

[27] Carl Schmitt, *Political Theology: Four Chapters in the Concept of Sovereignty* (Chicago: University of Chicago Press, 2006).

[28] The term is taken from Schwartzberg (n. 25).

[29] See Catalina Torres-Artunduaga & Santiago García-Jaramillo, 'Democratizing the Doctrine of Unconstitutional Constitutional Amendments: The Puzzle of Amending the Judiciary Branch' (2020) 14 Vienna Journal on International Constitutional Law 40.

[30] See David Landau, 'Presidential Term Limits in Latin America: A Critical Analysis of the Migration of the Unconstitutional Constitutional Amendment Doctrine' (2018) 12 Law and Ethics of Human Rights 225; David Landau & Rosalind Dixon, 'Abusive Judicial Review: Courts against Democracy' (2020) 53 UC Davis Law Review 1313; David Landau, Yaniv Roznai, and Rosalind Dixon, 'Term Limits and the Unconstitutional Constitutional Amendment Doctrine. Lessons from Latin America' in A. Baturo & R. Elgie (eds), *The Politics of Presidential Term Limits* (Oxford: Oxford University Press, 2019), 53.

[31] For instance, Dyzenhaus has shed doubts on this substance–process distinction. But see David Dyzenhaus, 'Process and Substance as Aspects of the Public Law Forum' (2015) 74 Cambridge Law Journal 284–306.

to call on more comparative and theoretical analyses on why cases like the second presidential re-election in Colombia are successful, not only with a 'positive law' approach, but by analysing political, historical, and social factors together.[32] This might give us an idea on how to achieve effective and assertive judicial interventions in favour of constitutional democracies.[33]

B. A Struggle for Equality or Judges as Policy Makers—The Judicial Enforcement of Socio-Economic Rights

The judicial enforcement of socio-economic rights, although more popular around the world, continues to be a contentious issue for constitutional law. In his book, *The Strange Alchemy of Law and Life*, Albie Sachs recalls his confusion when Ronald Dworkin advised him against including a socio-economic rights catalogue, and rather to rely on an equal protection clause. For Dworkin, an equality clause was enough for the transformation ahead. South Africa's constitutional framers did not follow Dworkin's advice.[34] Not only does the constitution include a catalogue of rights, but its Constitutional Court has a landmark set of decisions regarding the judicial enforcement of socio-economic rights. Decisions such as *Grootboom* are studied in comparative constitutional law as examples of how and when an apex court should intervene to secure such rights. Recently, Bruce Ackerman showed how socio-economic rights were at the centre-stage of the discussions between reformists and conservationists in revolutionary contexts, for example in the 'recent' constitutional history of France and Israel.[35]

The inclusion of catalogues of social and economic rights and their judicial enforcement has been considered a trademark of 'Global South' constitutionalism. The Mexican revolutionary constitution of 1917[36] included clauses aimed at securing the rights of workers and low-income citizens and, as such, can be considered the vantage point of today's so-called 'transformative constitutionalism'.[37] In basic terms, transformative constitutionalism is the product of constitutions that include a wide

[32] See Vincente F. Benîtez-Rojas, 'We the People, They the Media: Judicial Review of Constitutional Amendments and Public Opinion in Colombia', in Richard Albert, Carlos Bernal-Pulido, and Juliano Zaiden Benvindo (eds), *Constitutional Change and Transformation in Latin America* (Oxford: Hart Publishing, 2019) 143.

[33] Kim Lane Scheppele raises a proposal of unconstitutional constituent power worth considering: Kim Lane Scheppele, 'Unconstitutional Constituent Power' (2013). Paper prepared for the Penn Program on Democracy, Citizenship, and Constitutionalism 2012-1013, 22. Similarly, Dyzenhaus raises a normative attack towards the concept of constituent power: David Dyzenhaus, 'Constitutionalism in an Old Key: Legality and Constituent Power' (2012) 1(2) Global Constitutionalism 229–60.

[34] Albie Sachs, *The Strange Alchemy of Life and Law* (Oxford: Oxford University Press, 2011) 168–9.

[35] Bruce Ackerman, *Revolutionary Constitutions: Charismatic Leadership and the Rule of Law* (Harvard: Belknap Press, 2019).

[36] Böckenförde traces these clauses back to the III French Constitution. See Ernst Wolfgang Böckenförde, *Escritos sobre derechos fundamentales*, (1st edn, Baden-Baden: Nomos Verlagsgesellschaft, 1993).

[37] See, e.g., Armin Von Bogdandy et al. (eds), *Transformative Constitutionalism in Latin America: The Emergence of a New Ius Commune* (Oxford: Oxford University Press, 2017); Almut Schilling-Vacaflor et al. (eds), *New Constitutionalism in Latin America: Promises and Practices* (London and New York: Routledge, 2016).

catalogue of rights, which were drafted with the main aim of promoting change and social welfare in highly unequal societies. This approach towards constitutionalism usually demands a prominent role for constitutional courts, as the institutions committed to such transformation. However, as Hailbronner has suggested, this is not only a trademark of the 'Global South', and she illustrates in her study how those transformative ideas are also present and used in 'Global North' constitutionalism.[38]

In part I, this book opened with a discussion on the evolving role of constitutional judges. Both Gargarella and Marmor cast doubts over a strong intervention by courts, especially in the realm of public policies. This is precisely the main discussion of this second section of Part II. Given this approach, this section gathers two prominent scholars from the 'Global South', Octavio Luis Motta-Ferraz and David Bilchitz, who will engage in a dialogue with two renowned scholars from the 'Global North', David Landau and Axel Tschentscher. In his chapter, Motta-Ferraz will invite the reader to put aside the classical poles of activism or restraint, to think that the intervention of judges, in this realm, is really a matter of spectrum with extreme judicial deference (*abdication*) on one side, and extreme judicial assertiveness (*usurpation*) on the other extreme. But as with any spectrum, there is a wide range of possibilities in the middle.

Following Gargarella and Marmor, Tschentscher, in his chapter, entitled 'Constitutional Rights without the Notion of Optimization: Limiting Judicial Activism in the Realm of Social and Economic Rights', sets the discussion by affirming that apex courts should not take the place of the legislative or the executive branch. His departure point is theoretical as he takes a critical stance towards the notion of *optimization* that, according to Robert Alexy, legal principles—and as such rights—entail.[39] According to Tschentscher, optimization results in judicial activism that, in turn, shifts the power from politics to courts. Once the theoretical scenario is set, Tschentscher examines some decisions by the German Federal Constitutional Court considered 'activist decisions' in the realm of socio-economic rights, and compares their follow-up with the Colombian experience. As with all the authors in this second section, Tschentscher does not question the judicial enforcement of judicial rights, leaving aside an old debate and recognizing that it is a current trend, particularly when the constitutional text mentions explicitly socio-economic rights. He, however, thinks that judges must play a rather modest role, and limit themselves to a case-by-case rationale even if social rights are systematically under-enforced. Tschentscher also calls the courts' attention to the need to be aware of the financial restrictions of their countries, something that Justice Albie Sachs famously wrote in his concurring opinion in the *Sobramooney* case, stating: 'If resources were co-extensive with compassion, I have no doubt as to what my decision would have been. Unfortunately, the resources are limited, and I can find no reason to interfere with the allocation undertaken by those better equipped than I to deal with the agonizing choices that had to be made.'[40] Finally, Tschentscher asks courts to create incentives for legislatures and executive branches to commit to

[38] Michaela Hailbronner, 'Transformative Constitutionalism: Not Only in the Global South' (2017) 65(3) American Journal of Comparative Law 527–65.

[39] Robert Alexy, *A Theory of Constitutional Rights* (Oxford: Oxford University Press, 2010).

[40] Constitutional Court of South Africa, *Thiagraj Soobramoney v Minister of Health (Kwazulu-Natal)*, Albie Sachs, Concurring Opinion, 1997.

social and economic rights, and insists that follow-up measures should not be taken by apex courts, but rather by political branches.

Motta-Ferraz, in his chapter, entitled 'To Interfere or Not to Interfere? The Court's Dilemma in Social Rights' Enforcement', follows a similar line to Tschentscher. In fact, he doesn't call for abdication, but he invites the reader to take institutional constraints that courts face, as well as financial constraints, more seriously. Motta-Ferraz takes a critical approach towards the role that many courts are assuming in the protection of socio-economical rights in the Latin American context. He argues that the proper role of courts must necessarily vary according to the formulation of the social right in question. As a general rule, the more absolute and specifically formulated the right—or its corresponding obligation—the higher the institutional competence (legitimacy and competency) of courts will tend to be, and *vice versa*. When obligations are stated in vague fashion, such as the right to housing, health, and education in Colombia, Brazil, and South Africa, the room left for interpreting contending definitions is not only ample, but it often involves the intractable question of social policy design that must be studied by the executive and legislative branches. Further, Motta-Ferraz argues that courts should play, at most, a complementary role. In fact, Motta-Ferraz invites courts to take more creative approaches in the enforcement of socio-economic rights. For instance, he invites courts to look at the procedural method of judicial review, by focusing on evaluating the fairness of the decision-making process based on criteria such as transparency, non-discrimination, participation, and rationality, while leaving substantive review—which tends to be the trend in Latin American courts—as an exceptional method only.

Afterwards, taking a stance towards judicial assertiveness, and by reflecting on the South African experience, Bilchitzs' chapter, entitled 'How can Rights be Individuated?', focuses on how courts should individuate social and economic rights. Bilchitz argues that although all rights can be judicially enforced—something not denied by any of the contributors to this section—judges must have a different approach to each right, and that there are substantial differences even among social and economic rights themselves. In fact, Bilchitz revisits his approach towards socio-economic rights, and by doing so he opens a fertile terrain for further exploration on how to determine the so-called minimum *core* of these rights. He once argued in favour of the 'minimum core' being defined rather discretely in relation to a survival-based standard accommodation, but when analysing the recent *Dladdla* case of the South African Court, he concludes that it is not possible to confine human interests regarding housing to bare survival, as other dimensions of the right come into play. In this sense, Bilchitz seems to rely on the 'interest theory' of rights, set forth by Joseph Raz, according to which, despite their canonical formulations, rights have a dynamic character due to ever-evolving interests and duties that rights are there to protect and impose, and this dynamism is even more clear in pluralist societies where disagreement on those interests and duties flourishes.[41] In his chapter, Bilchitz calls attention to how courts should do their jobs with regards to the interpretation and enforcement of socio-economic rights. He suggests taking an 'integrated' approach, as proposed

[41] See generally Joseph Raz, *The Morality of Freedom* (Oxford: Oxford University Press, 1988); Andrei Marmor 'On the Limits of Rights', in *Law in the Age of Pluralism* (Oxford: Oxford University Press, 2007).

by Justice Edwin Cameron, which acknowledges the interconnection of the various rights and sought to use the Constitutional Court's reasonableness standard as a basis for his dissenting opinion.

To close this section, Landau, in his chapter, entitled 'The Colombian Model of Structural Socioeconomic Rights Remedies: Lessons from and for Comparative Experience', proposes an empirical analysis of the Colombian constitutional court's experience. He argues that the Colombian Constitutional Court's experience with structural injunctions is one of its greatest and most distinctive achievements, and thus believes that the approach towards socio-economic rights adjudication should be assertive, while avoiding the complete encroachment on the legislative and executive branches.[42] The influence of political context and cost also highlights a key point: the Colombian model should best be viewed as an invitation for further development and guided experimentation, rather than as a fixed formula for success. Landau argues that the Colombian court should seek ways to develop different types of monitoring mechanisms that are less expensive and that respond to variations in political context. In fact, constitutional experimentalism is the key in Landau's approach. This approach was first proposed by Dorf and Sabel, who stated that: 'courts can serve democracy better not only because they presume to provide fewer definite answers to legal, social and ultimately political questions, but also they can inquire into more of the political actor's own deliberate capacities'.[43] Even if the Colombian experience is successful, he doesn't think that it is a fixed model, but rather part of an ongoing experiment, not only for other jurisdictions but within Colombia itself. In fact, Landau, as Tschentscher and Motta-Ferraz, believes that economic and institutional constraints should be considered when deciding how courts should intervene to secure socio-economic rights. However, he departs from Tschentscher's insistence on the case-by-case approach, since he considers that individual remedies alone will not always ameliorate the underlining causes of constitutional violations, and in some situations may actually worsen them. As for Bilchitz, the author of this chapter believes that securing social and economic rights is a defining feature of the role of constitutional judges as guardians of the constitution.

It is undeniable that the 'Global South' constitutional texts include a diverse list of socio-economic rights and a commitment to transforming their historical inequalities. But this promise is common to many constitutional projects in the 'Global North' as well. In fact, the reader can recall the political and judicial struggles for the 'New Deal' measures, or the 'Obamacare' in the United States. As such, this chapter aims at promoting a dialogue between scholars and courts on how to intervene when social and economic rights are at stake. The dialogue between Motta-Ferraz, Bilchitz, Landau, and Tschentscher shows that it is possible to do, and there are many common points of view among truly different jurisdictions. I believe this debate underscores the fact that the project of 'transformative constitutionalism' should not rely solely on judges committed with its content, but it also needs to commit the executive and the legislative branches with its moral-political contents. In fact, social groups and

[42] Cepeda-Espinosa (n. 2).

[43] Michael C. Dorf & Charles F. Sabel, 'A Constitution of Democratic Experimentalism' (1998) 98 Columbia Law Review 267, 389.

common citizens should be at the centre stage of this project demanding action from all authorities, not only from those sitting on the judicial bench.[44]

The other point that calls my attention in this section, and I found it fertile terrain for further research, is how to create incentives to commit the executive and legislative branch with the enforcement of socio-economic rights. In fact, in his classical critique of judicial review, James Bradley Thayer affirmed that a strong and recurrent intervention by courts will negatively impact legislatures, since they would assume that there is always an authority to fix their mistakes or remedy their omissions.[45] On the other hand, the persistent inequalities of Global South countries have demanded from judges not to remain passive when political branches do not take their jobs seriously. I think the four chapters of this section invite the reader to move away from these poles, and to think of 'experimental' and creative ways in which socio-economic rights can be secured. In fact, it was not long ago that Fuller proposed an analysis of polycentric disputes and the limits of adjudication,[46] a discussion that, as this section illustrates, is not only far from over, but is not circumscribed to academic speculation any longer.

Finally, it is worth noting that Motta-Ferraz's point on considering judicial intervention as a spectrum, rather than classifying them as 'activist' or 'passive', gives us a better opportunity to rightfully assess the role that judges should play in the protection of socio-economic rights. While judicial activism is usually a term used to describe judges 'committed' to the transformative endeavour, it is true that judges can also array that 'activism' to deploy a conservative agenda—the Lochner era of the US Supreme Court is a great example—[47] while in some circumstance's restraint can allow the advance of a progressive political agenda—recall the US Supreme Court's late role after President's Roosevelt struggle for the New Deal,[48] or Chief Justice Roberts' closing statement when upholding Obamacare.[49] In fact, this whole section invites us to set aside all these confusing and sharp categories and to think about innovative ways that courts can contribute to achieve social and economic equality, while not renouncing our commitments to self-government and to have political-accountable policy makers. Perhaps legal problem-solving cannot replace policy making.

[44] In fact, there are many studies which cast some doubts on what constitutional courts can truly achieve in the enforcement of social and economic rights. See Ran Hirschl, *Toward Juristocracy* (Cambridge, MA: Harvard University Press, 2007); Mark Tushnet, *Weak Courts, Strong Rights* (Princeton: Princeton University Press, 2009); Michael Mandel, 'A Brief History of the New Constitutionalism, or "How We Changed Everything So That Everything Would Remain the Same"' (1998) 32 Israel Law Review; Michael Mandel, *The Charter of Rights and the Legalization of Politics in Canada* (Toronto, Ontario: Thompson Educational Publishers, 1994); see also Camilo Valdivieso-León and Santiago Garcia-Jaramillo, 'Transforming the Legislative: A Pending Task of Brazilian and Colombian Constitutionalism' (2018) 5 Journal of Constitutional Research 43–58.

[45] James Bradley Thayer, 'The Origin and Scope of the American Doctrine of Constitutional Law' (1893) 7 Harvard Law Review 129–56; see also Elizabeth Garrett & Adrian Vermeule, 'Institutional Design of a Thayerian Congress' (2001) 50 Duke Law Journal 1277.

[46] Lon L. Fuller, 'The Forms and Limits of Adjudication' (1978) 92 Harvard Law Review 353.

[47] Marmor, *Interpretation and Legal Theory* (n. 11), 166.

[48] Ackerman (n. 35).

[49] 'The Framers created a Federal Government of limited powers, and assigned to this Court the duty of enforcing those limits. The Court does so today. But the Court does not express any opinion on the wisdom of the Affordable Care Act. Under the Constitution, that judgement is reserved to the people': *National Federation of Independent Business v. Sebelius*, 567 US 519 (2012).

C. Courts as Mediators or Courts Setting the Ultimate Standards of Fairness: Transitional Justice

Transitional justice, understood as the set of processes designed to respond to past human rights violations,[50] has traditionally focused on transitions from authoritarian regimes to democracy.[51] More recently, it has shifted from its primary use and turned to address acts of violence committed during civil wars. In this context, the Colombian case has become an interesting example of the application of transitional justice models to socio-political agreements that seek to put an end to long-lasting conflicts. It has shown that justice is an essential feature in peace talks, and one aspect that demands careful attention in its design and subsequent implementation.

In 2016, as the peace process between the Colombian Government and the former FARC guerillas came to an end, the Colombian Constitutional Court was called upon to determine the constitutionality of the amendments and legislation adopted for the implementation of the peace agreement.[52] Here, one of the most critical aspects was the design and implementation of constitutional instruments of transitional justice, especially considering that this was the first peace process conducted under the Rome Statute,[53] which created the International Criminal Court. When exercising the judicial review of the constitutional instruments adopted for guaranteeing the victims' rights to truth, justice, reparation, and non-repetition, as well as the state's obligation to investigate and prosecute international crimes, it became clear that the Colombian peace process contained certain particularities that demanded a unique Colombian solution.

In the first place, the peace process had developed within the limits of a legitimate, stable, and enduring constitution, unlike previous transitional experiences in other parts of the world, like the one in South Africa, which concluded with the enactment of a new constitution. In this sense, despite the fact the transitional process aimed at developing peace as one of the main goals of the 1991 Colombian constitution, it was clear that the transitional rules could not replace the existing constitutional order, and that the Colombian Constitutional Court had to protect the defining set of principles incorporated in the constitution, applying the unconstitutional constitutional amendments discussed in Part II, Section I of this book.

On the other hand, the Colombian peace process with the FARC guerrillas portrayed multiple social and ethical questions regarding the decision to adopt a restorative model of justice. The Constitutional Court had to address political questions in legal terms, solving cases through traditional legalism,[54] and acting in the midst of a

[50] Andrew G. Reiter, Tricia D. Olsen, & Leigh A. Payne, 'Transitional Justice and Civil War: Exploring New Pathways, Challenging Old Guideposts' (2013) 1 Transitional Justice Review 1, Article 12.

[51] Ruti Teitel, 'Transitional Justice Genealogy' (2003)16 Harvard Human Rights Journal 69–94.

[52] See Corte Constitucional de la República de Colombia '*Resumen de las Decisiones de la Corte Constitucional en la Implementación del Acuerdo Final de Paz*' (Colombia: Imprenta Nacional de Colombia, 2019).

[53] Ratified by Colombia in 2002.

[54] In a broader sense, the participation of the Constitutional Court clearly shows that the peace process was built on a legalist perspective. This is, perhaps, due to the strong legalist tradition in Colombia; and/or because it is the first peace process under the Rome Statute; and/or because both parties wanted legal stability.

complex and polarized context. To do so, the Court acted as a '*third chamber*',[55] guaranteeing the constitution's principles of participation and deliberation. Additionally, as a palliative measure to the political divisions challenging the Colombian people, the Court sought to adopt balances in the midst of *knife-edge decisions*,[56] where the Court had to review a peace process formally rejected by popular vote, or what I have called 'the dance along the precipice', in order to avoid five to four decisions[57] in an already divided and convulsed political context.

This third section of Part II will provide new insights on the establishment, design, and implementation of constitutional instruments of transitional justice. Unlike previous sections, this one is focused mainly on the Colombian transitional justice integrated system, with certain specific references to the South African case. Ultimately, through the vision of both international and Colombian scholars, this section presents an analysis not only on the transitional justice model adopted by Colombia, but on the approach taken by the Constitutional Court. In the long run, it seeks to demonstrate that, as Professor Murphy points out, 'justice in transitional circumstances is not aimed at giving perpetrators what they deserve [but rather] at transforming a society, and doing so in a just manner by treating victims and perpetrators fairly'.[58]

This section begins with 'The Resilient Constitution', a chapter by David Dyzenhaus and Alma Diamond. In their chapter, the authors propose that transitions be thought of as 'bridges', not complete breaks, between the past and the present, and as such, the bridge of transitional justice represents quintessentially existential political problems. Therefore, they consider that if the problem and its solutions are political, the proper role of the courts and the law in these processes is not clear.

To better address this issue, the authors turn to examine the so called 'transitional constitution' of South Africa and the 'permanent constitution' of Colombia. Through a comparative approach, they conclude that constitutions are better understood in terms of their *resilience* rather than either being transitional or permanent, and that a 'resilient constitution' is one capable of springing back even after being subjected to extreme pressure, as long as leaders maintain their commitment to governing within the limits of the law. In this sense, they suggest that the differences between Colombian transitional justice and the South African case do not stem primarily from the 'permanence' of its constitution, but rather from the difficulties and tensions inherent to any transitional justice process, because it derives from some of the very rights it is designed to promote. By understanding this idea, Dyzenhaus and Diamond conclude

55 In Michael C. Dorf, 'Majoritarian Difficulty and Theories of Constitutional Decision Making' (2010) Cornell Law Faculty Publications, Paper 441, the author explains this concept by stating that: 'Just as the Senate and the House of Lords provide the opportunity for reconsideration of proposed legislation by a body of legislators with a somewhat different perspective and constituency from the Houses of Representatives and Commons, respectively, the Supreme Court provides yet a third look at the laws, or so the argument goes. The third legislative-chamber notion is only a metaphor, of course'.

56 In Jeremy Waldron, 'Judicial Review and Political Legitimacy' (2018) 27(1) Dikaion 7–28, the author stated that: 'The point would be to avoid knife edge disputes—where a knife edge in legislature is matched by knife edge in court'.

57 Jeremy Waldron, 'Five to Four: Why Do Bare Majorities Rule on Courts?' (2014) 123 Yale Law Journal 1694–730.

58 Colleen Murphy, *Judging the Justice of the Colombian Final Agreement* (Illinois: University of Illinois at Urbana-Champaign, 2018).

that the jurisprudence of the Colombian Constitutional Court on transitional matters can be understood as having moved from an understanding of the constitution as permanent to one of resilience that, they suggest, does not represent a new power seized by the Court. Rather, it signals an understanding of the role of the Court in maintaining a constitutional order even in the face of existential threats to it. Therefore, the authors concluded that the task of judges who manage a transitional justice process is then to educate their audience through the measures they take in times of normality. The only difference is that during transitional justice processes, judges should be primarily guided by the aim of achieving a condition of legality which will make it possible for the state to get on with a different task: remedying the circumstance of 'pervasive structural inequality'.

Dyzenhaus and Diamond also propose a challenging analysis to transitional justice. They avoid the classical debates on the fairness of alternative punishment or compliance with international standards. Instead, they provide an insightful and provocative analysis from the vantage point of legal theory.[59] The authors confront Carl Schmitt's legal theory with the work of the Colombian Constitutional Court in this transitional justice process. They find that the Colombian Court faced a dilemma: a failed plebiscite, which gave the sense that amendments were formally invalid, and a substantive view of the constitution, which posed a stringent test for amending the constitution.[60] On this point, Dyzenhaus and Diamond show what they consider a contradiction or at least a puzzle in Colombian constitutionalism in the realm of transitional justice, that is, the recourse to a Schmittean doctrine of unconstitutional constitutional amendments, rests on the idea of a substantive permanent constitution—which under Schmitt's constitutional theory also requires a homogeneous nation—while the transitional justice amendments require flexibility, and openness to accommodate plural groups. To overcome this situation, the authors suggest that the Colombian Constitutional Court should put the 'resilient' feature of its constitution at centre stage, and not its reliance on a substantive unchangeable core, as proposed by Schmitt.

The second contribution to this third section of Part II is presented by Colleen Murphy. Rather than studying the role of the constitutional courts in the transitional process like Dyzenhaus and Diamond, Murphy, in her chapter, entitled 'Judging the Justice of the Colombian Final Agreement', shifts her attention to examining the text of the Colombian peace agreement (also known as the Final Agreement), arguing that the justice component of this agreement depends on the extent to which the envisioned transitional process contributes to social transformation.

In her chapter, Murphy considers that despite the fact that societies emerging from periods of conflict or repression characteristically try to address past wrongs using processes that are not criminal punishment, there is deep disagreement as to whether true justice is achieved with alternative measures such as amnesty or a truth

[59] In fact, Dyzenhaus' research focuses on the legal theory of the Weimar Republic. See David Dyzenhaus, *Legality and Legitimacy: Carl Schmitt, Hans Kelsen, and Hermann Heller in Weimar* (Oxford: Oxford University Press, 1999).

[60] See, Daniel Currea-Moncada & Santiago García Jaramillo, 'The Colombian Tale of Two Legal Revolutions' (2020) 53 Cornell International Law Journal Online 1–25

commission.[61] To that extent, she argues that justice, in transitional circumstances, is not aimed at giving perpetrators what they deserve, but rather in transforming the political relationships among citizens and between citizens and officials, and in doing so in a just manner by treating victims and perpetrators fairly.

When examining the Colombian case under this lens, Murphy concludes that the justice process outlined in the Final Agreement is comprehensive, which is important in ensuring that victims and perpetrators are treated appropriately. She also notes that it deals with one critical aspect for transformation, already addressed by Dyzenhaus and Diamond: structural inequality. In that sense, she considers that the justice component contained in the Final Agreement effectively envisions a transitional process that contributes to a transformation in Colombian society and treats victims and perpetrators fairly. However, she warns that ongoing political will is required in order to achieve the envisioned standard of justice. To that extent, by drawing on the cases of Northern Ireland and South Africa, Murphy discusses the temporal dimension of transitional justice, and the constitutional changes that occur in the pursuit of it. In a way, one could consider that this temporal dimension envisions transitional justice in a similar way as the 'bridges' metaphor previously used by Dyzenhaus and Diamond.

The third chapter of this section focuses on the international consequences of the transitional justice model in Colombia. Rather than examining the role of the constitutional court or the components of the Final Agreement, Juana Acosta-López and Cindy Vanessa Espitia-Murcia, in their chapter, entitled 'The Transitional Justice Model in Colombia vis-à-vis the Inter-American Human Rights System: Amidst the Conventionality Control and the National Margin of Appreciation', seek to demonstrate that the Colombian transitional justice model, and particularly the integrated system for truth, justice, reparation, and non-repetition, are likely to successfully withstand the 'conventionality control' by the Inter-American Court of Human Rights.[62] For this purpose, the authors propose and delimit a model to be used by the Inter-American organs when analysing the Colombian transitional justice model. In seeking to accommodate the needs of the transitional process with the demands for justice, the model proposes a harmonizing technique between the notions of 'conventionality control', developed by the Inter-American Court since 2006, and the 'national margin of appreciation' doctrine, developed by the European Court of Human Rights. Acosta-López and Espitia-Murcia argue that this harmonizing approach would allow states to implement the most adequate mechanisms for the consolidation of a lasting peace scenario. Like Murphy, the bottom line for these authors is that the justice instruments of the Colombian system are compatible with Colombia's international human rights obligations.

[61] In Miriam J. Aukerman, 'Extraordinary Evil, Ordinary Crime: A Framework for Understanding Transitional Justice' (2002) 39 Harvard Human Rights Journal 15,the author questions whether prosecutions constitute the best method of redressing criminal actions in the context of transitional justice, as the rationale behind the preference for prosecution is the assumption that atrocious human rights violations are in fact crimes, and the Western conceptual framework for dealing with ordinary crime revolves around prosecutors, judges, and trials. In this context, the author asks whether ordinary crime really is an appropriate analogy for massive human rights atrocities or an extraordinary evil.

[62] Laurence Burgorgue-Larsen, *Conventionality Control: Inter-American Court of Human Rights (IACtHR)* (Oxford: Oxford Public International Law, 2018).

Finally, this third section of Part II closes with an interesting chapter that illustrates that interdisciplinary problems must be considered when examining transitional justice models. The contribution by Acosta-Navas is essential in shedding some light on one of the classical and most disputed debates in transitional literature: the ethical justification of the transitional justice measures, as opposed to its legal dimensions. By employing a conceptual analysis to spell out the 'retributive' and 'holistic' conceptions of justice, the author argues that both views fail to fully tailor their normative framework to the empirical conditions in which such institutions are implemented (e.g. large-scale wrongdoings and institutional weakness). In this sense, she draws out a proposal that synthesizes the motivating concerns behind both positions, and attempts to overcome the diagnosed flaws by drawing a conceptual bridge between the two opposing views. Acosta-Navas, rather than advocating for one position or the other, tries to articulate the crucial insights of both views in light of victims' right to justice, suggesting that transitional justice measures should be oriented towards creating appropriate conditions to enable and legitimize the future exercise of standardized procedures for redress.

As a final remark on this section, the authors have unquestionably illustrated and clearly depicted the social, political, and legal dimensions that revolve around the transitional justice debates. Contributors to this interesting topic bring new insights on the fact that there is no tailor-made transitional justice model which can be applied all around the world, but rather that each case poses its own particularities which must be considered when designing and implementing a transitional justice model. The Colombian model, as shown by Murphy and Acosta-López and Espitia-Murcia, combined no blanket amnesties, and some judicial and extra-judicial forms of accountability in order to comply with international human rights obligations. In addition to this, the Colombian Constitutional Court was given the power to examine the constitutionality of the model and, following its legalist tradition, it determined that transitional justice should be incorporated into the constitution in order to provide legal stability to political issues.[63] Constitutional courts, as shown by Dyzenhaus and Diamond, must adopt a new understanding of the constitution as a 'resilient' one, rather than a 'substantive' and closed document, as the Colombian Constitutional Court has argued, by relying on Carl Schmitt's constitutional theory. Constitutional courts in transitional contexts, should take the place of conciliators or mediators and an insurance for legal stability. As Acosta-Navas points out, whether the integrated system is able to bring about the social and structural transformations needed for enforcing victims' rights, will depend on whether or not its various components are sufficiently articulated. In that sense, all of the authors give us a clearer picture of the complexity that surrounds the Colombian transitional justice model. And in doing so, they invite us to carefully monitor its implementation to ensure that victims, perpetrators, and institutional actors such as our Constitutional Court, play an active role in guaranteeing its success.

* * *

[63] See Christine Bell, *On the Law of Peace. Peace Agreements and the Lex Pacificatoria* (Oxford: Oxford University Press, 2008).

Part III: The Role of International, Comparative, and Foreign Law in Domestic Constitutional Law: Dialogue among the Global South

A. The Use of Foreign Precedents: a 'Global South' Monologue or a Conversation among Equals

The classical debate regarding the relationship between international law and domestic law has been part of academic discussion since at least the early twentieth century. Traditionally, the interaction between domestic law and international law has been analysed through the prism of the theories of *monism* and *dualism*.[64] In Colombia, the Constitutional Court seems to have adopted moderate monism since 1998[65] in order to explain how the domestic legal order relates to international law. However, perhaps more importantly, it has developed a theory which illustrates the extent to which human rights law has penetrated domestic constitutional law.[66]

In these regards, Article 93 of the 1991 Colombian constitution grants international human rights law a higher status within the domestic legal order. This clause establishes that international treaties and agreements ratified by Congress that recognize human rights and that prohibit their limitation in states of exception will '*prevail*' in the domestic legal order. In interpreting this provision, the Colombian Constitutional Court has transplanted from France and developed the theory of the 'constitutionality block' (*bloque de constitutionalidad*), which has been understood as a tool for integrating international human rights law into the Colombian constitutional order, establishing itself as a mechanism for expanding constitutional provisions, a parameter of control of hierarchically inferior regulations, and a guarantee for the protection of human rights in the country. This theory, transplanted from the French doctrine of the *bloc de constitutionalité* has had a major impact on the precedents of the Colombian Court since its first inclusion in Decision C-225 of 1995. It shows that despite the importance of the classical distinction between monism and dualism in explaining the interactions between domestic law and international law, this debate should be approached in present times through the migration of constitutional ideas.[67] Those movements have been described as transnational

[64] See Ian Brownlie, *Principles of Public International Law* (Oxford: Oxford University Press, 2003); Antonio Cassese, *International Law* (Oxford, Oxford University Press, 2005).

[65] Constitutional Court, Decision C-400 of 1998.

[66] This step was not taken solely by Colombia, as shown by András Sajó & Renáta Uitz, *The Constitution of Freedom: An Introduction to Legal Constitutionalism* (Oxford: Oxford University Press, 2019). In the spirit of new constitutionalism, several Latin American constitutions opened up their legal systems before international human rights norms in the 1980s and 1990s.

[67] Sujit Choundhry (ed.), *The Migration of Constitutional Ideas* (Oxford: Oxford University Press, 2007).

constitutionalism,[68] strategic judicial borrowings,[69] global law,[70] or cosmopolitan constitutionalism.[71]

The third part of this book examines the growing informal trend of transnational conversation between courts. From a comparative perspective, it seeks to shed some light on both the migration of constitutional ideas from international law into domestic constitutional law and *vice versa*, and the lateral borrowings that constitutional courts undertake, sometimes silently. In that sense, Part III deals with both the vertical and horizontal movements of constitutional doctrines and experiences across the globe. The role of constitutional judges, the doctrine of 'unconstitutional constitutional amendments', the justiciability of socio-economic rights, and the transitional justice constitutionalism, all of which are topics that have been discussed in other sections of this book, are ideas that have penetrated and shaped different constitutional jurisdictions around the world. For that reason, this last part not only makes sense in terms of encompassing the different questions discussed in the book, but also has a special meaning, as it addresses a debate which has been a personal obsession of mine for years.[72]

This last and third part begins with a chapter by Muna Ndulo. In his contribution, entitled 'International and Foreign Law in Domestic Constitutional Law: A Comparative Examination of the Practice in United States and Post Conflict Countries', Ndulo attempts to illustrate the role of international and foreign law in domestic constitutional law. Through the case analysis of South Africa (a post-conflict state) and the United States (often seen as a country that is not too friendly to international and foreign legal systems), the author discusses the role of international and foreign law in reconciling the regional development of the rule of law in a country, by working closely together with domestic constitutional law.

In his chapter, Ndulo demonstrates the extent to which domestic courts both in the United States and South Africa resort to international and foreign law when interpreting different aspects of their constitutions. He shows that these courts, whenever they deem it appropriate, do consider them in the resolution of disputes before

[68] Jiunn-Rong Yeh and Wen Chen Chang, 'The Emergence of Transnational Constitutionalism. Its Features, Challenges and Solutions' (2008) 27 Penn State International Law Review 89; Vicky Jackson, *Constitutional Engagement in a Transnational Era* (Oxford: Oxford University Press, 2013); Rosalind Dixon & David Landau, *Transnational Constitutionalism and a Limited Doctrine of Unconstitutional Constitutional Amendments*, 13 International Journal of Constitutional Law (2015) 606.

[69] Vlad Perju, 'Constitutional Transplants, Borrowing and Migrations', in Michel Rosenfeld and András Sajó (eds), *The Oxford Handbook of Comparative Constitutional Law* (Oxford University Press, 2012), 1304.

[70] Willian Twining, 'Diffusion of Law. A Global Perspective' (2004) 36 Journal of Legal Pluralism and Unofficial Law 1; Neil Walker, *Intimations of Global Law* (Cambridge: Cambridge University Press, 2015).

[71] Matthias Kumm, 'The Cosmopolitan Turn in Constitutionalism. An Integrated Conception of Public Law' (2013) 20 Indiana Journal of Global Legal Studies 605.

[72] In fact, this topic was addressed in my doctoral dissertation regarding the applicable law in international investment arbitration. See, Alejandro Linares-Cantillo, *El Derecho Aplicable en el Arbitraje de Inversión: la tensión con el derecho interno* (Bogotá: Universidad Externado de Colombia, 2019).

them. The conditions under which each jurisdiction may resort to foreign or international law, as well as the criteria used for taking them into consideration, do vary. However, most importantly, he concludes that this practice should be encouraged as it promotes the uniform interpretation of international law and the progressive advancement of norms worldwide, which are aspects that are especially important in the field of human rights. In doing so, Ndulo shows himself as an advocate of the growing transnational conversation between courts, by considering it as a tool of empowerment and knowledge for both judges and lawyers. Through his chapter, we are able to see the emerging insistence of the protection of human rights with a shared language, an issue that is later addressed by Lasser and Fuchs.

After this general presentation on the interactions between international and domestic law, the second chapter by Mitchell Lasser, entitled 'The Inter-Institutional Dimension of the Fundamental Rights Revolution: The Colombian–American Implications of the Franco-European Experience', presents an interesting comparative study between the judiciaries of France/Europe and Colombia/Latin America, in the context of what he calls the 'fundamental rights revolution'. Lasser, an expert in comparative constitutional law, discusses how the fundamental rights revolution in Europe, and particularly in France, was fuelled, in part, by powerful international dynamics. He illustrates how fundamental rights operate as a common legal denominator across jurisdictions throughout Europe, describing the dynamic circulation of fundamental rights ideas among the numerous high courts in play, at the intersection of the domestic and supranational European judiciaries.

After explaining the Franco-European system of interaction, Lasser seeks to question what this analysis may suggest regarding the elaboration of human rights jurisprudence in Colombia and other Latin American countries that operate under the Inter-American Human Rights System. He finds that whereas Colombia has distinct 'judicial hierarchies' (Constitutional Court, Supreme Court, State Council), there is only one court at the international level: the Inter-American Court of Human Rights. This, as he shows, is one of the key differentiators with the European system, where there is institutional competition on the fundamental rights front between the European Court of Human Rights and the European Court of Justice. Therefore, he concludes that the differences among the systems affect the circulation and intensification of fundamental rights in the Latin American context. One might suggest that, as there is more inter-institutional competition at the local level than at the international level, courts tend to focus more on fighting for internal power in a 'battle of courts'[73] than on determining the value of supranational jurisprudence and its use.

In short, Lasser seeks to highlight the existence of inter-institutional dynamics that might contribute significantly to the spread of the fundamental rights idiom within judicial institutions operating at the intersections of the national and supranational domains. In doing so, he tries to draw some comparative insights for Latin American countries, especially ones like Colombia that have a legal culture based on the Napoleon Civil Code and, at the same time, are party to the Inter-American Human Rights System. To that end, through his chapter we see that despite the fact

[73] Sajó and Uitz (n. 66), 338.

that the European inter-institutional features appear to exist in the Inter-American context, they do not seem to trigger competitive interinstitutional features, with foreign human rights jurisprudence, as seen in Europe.

This conclusion leads almost directly to the third chapter of this section by Marie-Christine Fuchs entitled 'The Changing Role and Reception of International Law in Domestic Constitutional Law: Some Thoughts about Latin America and Europe'. From a comparative perspective, the author discusses the changing role and reception of international law into domestic constitutional jurisdictions in Latin America and Europe. In the same sense as Lasser, Fuchs begins by presenting a descriptive analysis of the differences between Europe and Latin America. As such, she shows that despite the existence of the 'conventionality control' doctrine developed in Latin America by the Inter-American Court of Human Rights, the European context seems more complex and diverse due to the 'three spheres of human rights protection': the European Court of Human Rights, the European Court of Justice, and the national constitutional courts.

Fuchs believes that, despite the fact that the multilevel architecture of protection provides states with a large range of opportunities for improving the effective protection of human rights both in Europe and Latin America, in practice the most relevant level of guaranteeing such protection still seems to be at the domestic constitutional level. After exploring the 'conventionality control' and the application of the 'constitutionality block' doctrine developed by the Colombian Constitutional Court, as well as the 'self-imposed' duty to interpret human rights 'in light of' the jurisprudence of the European Court of Human Rights by the German Federal Constitutional Court, she turns to examine the 'margin of appreciation doctrine'. Paradoxically, this doctrine, introduced by the European Court of Human Rights, has recently regained power both in Europe and Latin America as a bedrock of the 're-birth' of nationalistic movements. As proposals to bolster and reinstate the 'margin of appreciation doctrine' become more popular on both sides of the hemisphere, the author fears that the regional systems of human rights protection will suffer a serious backlash. In that sense, she presents a conflict between the return to national sovereignty and the use of international law as a benchmark to review and improve local legal systems.[74]

To confront these movements, Fuchs points out the need for analysis of legal problems in a more comprehensive and joint manner. Faced with these threats, she proposes that instead of combatting the multilevel system of human rights protection, there is a need for pragmatic compromise solutions that enhance the protection of human rights in a shared language. Just like Ndulo, Fuchs presents herself as a fierce advocate of multilevel interaction, especially in the human rights spectrum, by proposing a dialogue which includes vertical exchanges between regional bodies and constitutional tribunals, as well as horizontal relationships both among local constitutional courts and among regional courts.

[74] Recently, the German Federal Constitutional Court stated that the European Court of Justice's ruling on the European Central Bank's quantitative easing program had been 'objectively arbitrary', challenging the supremacy of the European Union system. Despite not being a decision on human rights, this shows the conflict between national sovereignty movements and the use of international law by relying on supranational judiciaries.

The final chapter of this section is presented by two Colombian scholars, Carlos Arévalo and Julián Huertas entitled 'Not so Moderate: The Relationship between the Colombian Legal System and International Law'. These authors focus specifically on the Colombian case. Through the examination of the Colombian Constitutional Court's jurisprudence, they show how this institution has shaped the relationship between municipal and international law by decisively defining the role of international law in Colombia.

Arévalo and Huertas, unlike the other authors of this section, resort to the classical distinction between monism and dualism as analytical tools to study the Colombian Constitutional Court's decisions. They show that our Court's position regarding the interaction between international and domestic law does not fit the 'moderate monism' model it has claimed to have followed since 1998, precisely because it has misrepresented Alfred Verdross' views. On the contrary, the authors consider that the answer to the question about the status of general international law in the Colombian constitutional order is at some point between constitutional monism and dualism. To that extent, after a thorough analysis of the Court's decisions, they suggest that with the exceptions of *jus cogens*, international human rights law, international humanitarian law, and border delimitation, the Colombian Constitutional Court follows what they call a 'sovereigntist or statist' position, in which there is a general prevalence of domestic legislation over international law. However, they do recognize that the Court has found a useful tool in international law to advance in significant social, political, and economic changes.

In sum, Arévalo and Huertas offer us an alternative view to the position that the Colombian Constitutional Court has assumed regarding the role of international law within the Colombian legal system. They defy the long tradition of Colombian academic literature that has considered that the Court has adopted a 'moderate monism' approach which is most visible in the application of the 'constitutionality block' doctrine. They suggest that by focusing solely on this doctrine, scholars have studied this issue from a narrow misconception. Therefore, they invite us to address the subject from a broader perspective in order to avoid a classification which is unsuccessful in showing the true role of international law as a whole in the Colombian constitutional order.

As shown by all the authors, studying the migration of constitutional ideas can help us to understand the interaction between international and domestic law. Vertically, ideas travel *top-down* from regional courts to national courts and influence domestic constitutional systems by strengthening the hierarchy of the rule of law, orienting the interpretation of the national constitutions, and filling the gaps in the interpretation of the domestic bills of rights. In Europe, ordinary courts point to decisions of the European Court of Justice, bypassing apex courts, as highlighted by Lasser in his chapter. In Latin America, the Inter-American Court of Human Rights has developed the monist doctrine of 'conventionality control', described not only in the chapters of Lasser, Fuchs, and Arévalo and Huertas, but also mentioned by Gingsburg and Acosta-López et al. in other parts of this book. The difficult question of whether national constitutional courts are bound by the case law of the Inter-American Court of Human Rights in a similar case of another member state remains open.[75] In the

[75] Sajó and Uitz, (n. 66), 461.

human rights arena, soft law is used as persuasive rather than as an authoritative or binding tool. Additionally, ideas also move *bottom-up*, particularly with the common denominator of multilevel protection, citizen oriented, human rights enforcement.

Horizontally, regional courts may borrow from their counterparts. In another section of this book, Acosta-López and Espitia-Murcia give us an example of this trend, by suggesting that the 'margin of appreciation doctrine', which was developed in 1956 by the European Court of Human Rights, could be used by the Inter-American Court of Human Rights when examining enduring transitional justice initiatives in the region. Additionally, national constitutional courts, sometimes without considering democratic legitimacy, adopt international and foreign legal decisions from other jurisdictions when addressing similar issues, or use them as persuasive arguments in their reasoning.

In the boosted use of comparative constitutional law[76] this chapter has shown, domestic courts sometimes transplant institutions mechanically '*lock, stock and barrel*', disconnected from local circumstances. Therefore, despite advantages of the growing transnational conversation between international, foreign, and domestic law, this last part invites us to examine these movements carefully in order to determine the distinctions between each region and each country. In the end, more than reviewing the interactions between international and domestic law through the traditional doctrines of monism and dualism, this section invites us to think of them as two interdependent legal orders that mutually inform and complement each other in multiple ways.[77]

* * *

This entire book is an unfinished experiment and simultaneously contains contributions from various ideas, decisions, and experiences concerning constitutional law. The dialogue between philosophers and empirical researchers, the bridges it tries to tend between 'Global North' and 'Global South' approaches to constitutionalism, the faith or scepticism that some authors deploy towards what constitutionalism can achieve ... all of the above, is not aimed at giving definite answers on what courts or legal scholars should do, but rather it is an invitation to reopen the classical debates on constitutionalism, and provide new insights that can enrich the current discussions in comparative constitutional law. I hope the reader will enjoy this collection of essays, and—as I did—will find it a provocative call to question our deeply held convictions on constitutional interpretation, institutional design, and moral-political

[76] See Roger Masterman & Robert Shutze (eds), *The Cambridge Companion to Comparative Constitutional Law* (Cambridge: Cambridge University Press, 2019); Daniel Peat, *Comparative Reasoning in International Courts and Tribunals* (Cambridge: Cambridge University Press, 2019); Andrea Buratti, *Western Constitutionalism: History, Institutions, Comparative Law* (2nd edn, Cham: Springer, 2019); Tom Ginsburg & Rosalind Dixon (eds.). *Comparative Constitutional Law* (Cheltenham: Edward Elgar, 2017); Vicki C. Jackson & Mark Tushnet, *Comparative Constitutional Law* (3rd edn, Cambridge: Foundation Press, 2014); Mark Tushnet, *Advanced Introduction to Comparative Constitutional Law* (Cheltenham: Edward Elgar, 2014); Rosenfeld & Sajó (n. 69); Vikram D. Amar & Mark V. Tushnet (eds), *Global Perspectives on Constitutional Law* (1st edn, Oxford: Oxford University Press, 2008).

[77] Together with my assistant editors we want to thank Vicente Benítez-Rojas, Catalina Torres-Artunduaga, and Daniel Currea-Moncanda for the concrete suggestions and proofreading which enriched and improved this introduction.

goals. Ultimately, it is in itself a source of inspiration and obviously, a call for further academic research.

I want to thank all the leading international and Colombian scholars who submitted the papers published in this collection. I am grateful to them for their patience during the publishing and editing process, and for their willingness to edit and review their papers several times. Unfortunately, some great Colombian and foreign scholars who participated in the Constitutional Court's conference could not submit their papers for this collection. However, I am also thankful to all of them, since their thoughtful lectures at the conference allowed me to write this introduction, and to re-evaluate and revisit some of my stances on constitutional law. This event, and as such these memoirs, were possible due the generosity of many Colombian institutions, as well as many universities in Colombia and the United States. To all of them I extend my most sincere gratitude. Putting together this 'dream team' of legal scholars was one of the most overwhelming and rewarding tasks I have had in my judicial career. But I could not have done this alone. I want to thank the team that made this event possible. First of all, my Deputy Justice Catalina Torres-Artunduaga, who worked tirelessly as the leading coordinator of this event. She was helped by a group of brilliant young lawyers, Antonio Laborde-Baena, Natalia Negret-Garrido and Nicolás Parra-González, who along with my wife, María Alejandra Gutiérrez-Camacho, made sure that the academic content, as well as every detail of the event was a success. Many Colombian scholars helped me shape the ideas and gave me some necessary criticism on how to conduct an event of this magnitude. In this sense, I want to especially thank Manuel José Cepeda-Espinosa, Vicente Benítez-Rojas, Esteban Restrepo-Saldarriaga, Helena Alviar-García, and Carlos Bernal-Pulido. I would also want to thank two law clerks from my chamber, Camilo Valdivieso-León and Santiago García-Jaramillo, who dedicated invaluable time to elaborating the academic programme of the event, inviting the scholars, working on the logistical aspects, and assisting me in editing this volume, as well as helping me draft and review several versions of this introduction. Finally, I am grateful to the OUP team, led by Jamie Berezin and John Smallman, for their willingness to help us in publishing this book. I must thank the anonymous peer-reviewers, whose thoughtful comments and sharp criticism helped to better shape this volume and this introduction. Any persistent are mine alone.

II
THE ROLE OF CONSTITUTIONAL COURTS IN MODERN DEMOCRACIES

A)

Hercules at the Crossroads

1
Constitutionalism, Liberalism, and Democracy

Andrei Marmor

The tension between our commitment to democratic decision-making procedures and constitutional judicial review is widely recognized in the literature. Most liberal jurists and political theorists take this tension to be somewhat regrettable but unavoidable. A constitutional democracy, they think, is the best liberalism can offer. I will not necessarily dispute this conclusion. Perhaps some form of a constitutional democracy is what liberalism justifies. My purpose in this essay, however, is to show that these tensions are deep, their underlying conflicts are serious and intricate, and the solutions we have, manifest in strong constitutional courts with extensive powers of judicial review, are far from the best. I will, here and there, try to offer some ways in which we might be able to do better. But my main purpose in this essay is to unpack the connections between liberalism's commitment to democracy and constitutionalism, showing that the liberal values that justify a democratic regime may also justify some limits on majoritarian decision making procedures, but not necessarily in the form of the constitutional regimes we have.

I will begin with some elaboration on the ways in which I understand the tensions between constitutionalism and democracy. I will then outline a framework argument that might be thought to resolve this tension, focusing on a line of thought that purports to show how the same liberal values that justify democracy are also the ones that justify the constitutional constraints on it. I will try to show that these arguments are very limited in what they actually entail, falling short of justifying the constitutional regimes we have. In some respects, at least, we should be able to do better.

I. The Tensions between Constitutionalism and Democracy

A constitution is a legal instrument and its legal-political status is determined by certain features, not by its title or formulations. In previous work I identified five or six constitutive features of constitutions which make the constitution the kind of legal instrument that it is.[1] First and foremost, the constitution is deemed to be the supreme law of the land, claiming normative superiority over any other type of law, including,

[1] See Andrei Marmor, *Interpretation and Legal Theory* (rev. 2nd edn, Hart Publishing, 2005), ch. 9; and Andrei Marmor, *Law in the Age of Pluralism* (Oxford: Oxford University Press, 2007), ch. 4.

Andrei Marmor, *Constitutionalism, Liberalism, and Democracy* In: *Constitutionalism*. Edited by: Alejandro Linares-Cantillo, Camilo Valdivieso-León, Santiago García-Jaramillo, Oxford University Press (2021). © The various contributors.
DOI: 10.1093/oso/9780192896759.003.0002

crucially, enactments of ordinary democratic institutions like congress or parliament. Secondly, constitutions tend to establish the courts' power of judicial review.[2] In order to implement the constitution's claim to supremacy, legal systems invariably entrust the interpretation of the constitution into the hands of the courts, giving the constitutional court the final say in determining its content.[3] Most importantly, constitutional judicial review is normally implemented by the power of the constitutional court to strike down legislation as constitutionally invalid, overriding ordinary democratic processes. Constitutions are also the kind of legal instruments that purport to be in force for a long time, typically for generations, and they achieve this longevity by making constitutional amendments more difficult, sometimes much more difficult, than ordinary changes by way of democratic legislation. There is also a remarkable similarity, though historical and contingent, in the kind of content constitutions tend to have. Most constitutions are divided between establishing and regulating the main organs and institutions of the regime, setting up various structural features of the legal system and its democratic institutions, and having a bill of rights, that is, listing some fundamental principles and basic rights that are meant to be secure from encroachment by governmental authorities and ordinary legislation. Finally, though this is the least uniform aspect of constitutions, their respective bill of rights and fundamental principles tend to be formulated in rather general, abstract, and high-minded ways, leaving countless details to be filled out by legislatures and the courts. This is so, partly because constitutions aim to have a very wide scope of application, purporting to regulate all aspects of the legal system, and partly because they aim to be in force for a very long time, entrenching rights and principles to be respected for generations to come.

All this comes to show that constitutionalism is, essentially, a *pre-commitment* device.[4] By having a constitutional regime with the courts' powers of judicial review, we essentially pre-commit to the entrenchment of certain individual rights and principles of governance, removing them from the ordinary democratic decision making processes. The enactment of a constitution purports to bind current and future generations to certain principles, by making changes to those principles subject to some form of a super-majority rule (i.e. constitutional amendments). In short, the very essence of constitutionalism is to remove certain issues from the ordinary democratic decision-making processes, entrusting their interpretation and implementation in the hands of the courts. But then, quite obviously, by removing certain issues from the realm of democratic processes, we would seem to violate the principle of majority rule, whereby one person gets one vote in the distribution of power to make public decisions. Essentially, constitutionalism is a counter-majoritarian device. But is it also counter-democratic? Are the tensions here deeper? I think they are, and I would like to elaborate on that.

Constitutional democracies entrust the courts with tremendous legal and political powers. Three of those stand out: the power of judicial review, the power of shaping

[2] Or, as in some countries, later came to be recognized as having so established. This happened in the United States of course, and much more recently in Israel.

[3] A note on usage: I will use the term 'constitutional court' to designate any higher-level court that has jurisdiction over constitutional matters, whether it's a separate constitutional court or, as in the United States for example, the Supreme Court.

[4] See, e.g., Jon Elster, *Ulysses Unbound* (Cambridge: Cambridge University Press, 2009).

the content of the constitution, and agenda-setting powers. All these are familiar, so let me rehash briefly. The legal power of judicial review is the power to override decisions of the executive and legislative branches of the government, invalidating, limiting, or modifying, in some cases even instructing, decisions reached by ordinary democratic processes. Evidently, given our commitment to democratic decision making processes, and the massive resources invested in maintaining an electoral system and a democratic regime, the power granted to a constitutional court to strike down or modify results of these democratic processes is very significant indeed. Secondly, constitutional courts have very considerable legal power in shaping the content of constitutional principles, rights, and obligations; tacit constitutional conventions; and generally, the ways in which the content of the constitution is understood and implemented. Over time, and especially in systems with a strong tradition of *stare decisis*, constitutional courts get to shape what the constitution means and what it entails. Finally, but not least importantly, constitutional courts have great agenda setting powers. Given the very large number of petitions that tend to reach constitutional courts, access to constitutional litigation at the highest level must be constrained by certiorari. The legal power of granting or withholding cert amounts to a very considerable influence on the moral-political agenda that is publicly debated. Constitutional courts get to choose what issues to elevate to public debate and what issues to bracket, set aside for another day, or even sometimes to silence.

Constitutional courts' powers *de jure*, just listed, are not necessarily reflective of their actual powers. The actual, *de facto*, power of constitutional courts is a much more complicated matter of course, largely depending on how much independence the court has relative to other political forces in the country. If judges can be replaced at will by politicians, or if they can be bribed, politically or otherwise, to take extreme examples, then the courts will be subservient to politicians and all this tremendous *de jure* power will not amount to much, not for the court, anyway. Bearing this in mind, I will bracket such issues from now on, and assume that we are talking about robust, independent courts, who can exercise their legal and political powers at will, unencumbered by other political branches of the government. But now, to see how much these constitutional powers are at odds with democratic principles, we need to dwell for a moment on the essentially non-democratic character of the courts themselves. I do not mean to refer here, or to be overly concerned about, ways in which judges are appointed to the court.[5] My concern is with the lack of democratic accountability that is essential to constitutional courts.

Lack of democratic accountability is twofold. First, the judges on the constitutional court are not legally or politically accountable to the public, or to the legislatures elected by the public. Judges' decisions and their record on the court is not subject to re-evaluation and response by others. In an orderly constitutional democracy, even if judges are somehow elected to their position on the court, they would not be subject to re-election over time. Which means, quite simply, that judges are

[5] Justice Brennan, who has been a staunch liberal on the US Supreme Court, used to tell the story of President Eisenhower who, when asked by a journalist at the end of his term what his biggest mistake was during his presidency replied: 'I made two mistakes and both of them are still on the supreme court.' Justice Brennan was one of them.

not subject to any process of democratic accountability. Secondly and additionally, the court's constitutional decisions are also subject to very limited democratic accountability. Constitutional decisions can only be changed by constitutional amendments. The more rigid the constitution, that is, the more difficult it is to amend it, practically speaking, the less democratic accountability applies to the courts' decisions. In other words, constitutional decisions amount to the imposition of a super-majority requirement: they can be changed, democratically, but only by following the super-majority requirements embodied in the amendment processes, and those are sometimes very difficult to accomplish.[6]

This lack of democratic accountability is no accident of course; constitutional courts are meant to be independent of the ordinary democratic process, it's what constitutional judicial review is meant to achieve. As I mentioned earlier, the whole point of a constitutional regime is to remove certain decisions from the ordinary democratic decision-making processes, aiming to secure certain rights and principles, and certain structural aspects of the legal system, from the vagaries of majority rule. Making judges and their decisions on a constitutional court democratically accountable would clearly undermine this basic rationale of constitutionalism. However, we should bear in mind that majority rule is precisely the core idea of a democratic decision-making procedure. When we subject a certain public decision to majority vote, we aim to implement the principle that all voters get to have an equal say in the decision to be reached. Normally, deviations from majority rule would entail a deviation from the principle of one person one vote, that is, a principle of an equal distribution of political power. Which is simply to say that the tension between constitutionalism and the underlying principle of a democratic decision-making process is direct and obvious. Constitutionalism can only be understood as a deviation from, or as a constraint on, the principle of equal distribution of political power. Perhaps it is a justified constraint, and this is the question I will address below.

II. Justifications

Understanding the basic idea of constitutionalism in terms of a pre-commitment device may help us to see how it operates as a precaution against shortsighted or otherwise distorted decisions that democratic procedures may lapse into. Following the analogy to the famous myth of Ulysses, who had good reason to suspect that his judgement would be seriously curtailed in the face of the sirens, and thus had himself tied to the mast, ordering his subordinates to ignore his pleadings to be untied when the time came, constitutionalism also ties us to the mast, making untying relatively difficult, in order to guard against corrupting temptations. In other words, the basic idea here is that constitutionalism is a safeguard, a kind of preemptive precaution against likely lapses of majority rule. Ordinary democratic procedures, it must be assumed, work

[6] The Colombian system is particularly challenging in this respect since it is one of the only legal systems I'm aware of where the Constitutional Court gets to have fairly substantive review powers over constitutional amendments, occasionally striking them down as unconstitutional. See Part III., *A) We the People or We the Judges: The Judicial Enforcement of Unconstitutional Constitutional Amendments* later in this volume.

well enough generally. But sometimes they are prone to corruption or grave moral errors, and therefore certain issues need to be removed from the ordinary process and handed to the courts, assuming that the courts' constitutional decisions are likely to be better, at least in the long run.

Obviously, this line of thought has a great deal of instrumentalism built into it. The argument requires substantiating a number of premises. First, it is based on the assumption that ordinary democratic procedures work well enough, generally. If we dispute this assumption, then constitutionalism is not the remedy, and we would need an alternative to democracy. Secondly, we must be able to identify, in advance, the kind of cases in which ordinary democratic procedures are likely to lead us astray; we need to know, *ex ante*, who are the sirens and where they lurk. Finally, we must assume that in those same cases where sirens are present, where democracy is likely to fail as it were, courts are likely to do better. Again, at least generally and in the long run. But of course these last two assumptions, particularly the third, are very questionable at best.[7]

I am not suggesting that we cannot identify some of the sirens lurking along the way. We know, for example, that majority rule, by itself, is not going to guarantee adequate protection for persistent vulnerable minorities. We know that ordinary democratic procedures tend to perform miserably in times of national emergency and similar widely perceived threats to security and stability. We know that in various contexts ordinary democratic procedures tend towards shortsightedness, discounting future gains or losses for more immediate benefits. I will elaborate on these concerns in greater detail below. First, however, I would like to spell out the moral argument for constitutionalism, in order to see more clearly how far a moral argument can take us and where exactly practical and instrumental concerns come into the picture.

Democracy, as a system of governance and decision-making process, is in need of moral-political justification. The best moral justification of democracy comes from liberal political morality. But then, so the argument would go, those same liberal values which justify democracy would also justify certain limits on democratic decision procedures, and those are the kind of limits that are imposed by a constitutional regime. Let's call this the argument from liberalism.[8] Needless to say, if the argument from liberalism can be filled in properly and made to work, it would be a good one. I think it can be filled in, and it can be made to work, but only up to a point.

Liberal justifications of democracy are varied and complex, and I cannot dwell here on all or any one at great length. But for our purposes, a broad-brush picture should be enough. So let's begin with a consequentialist approach. According to this line of thought, democratic procedures are not inherently valuable; they don't necessarily instantiate anything of intrinsic value. The reasons to prefer a democratic system to its alternatives are essentially instrumental.[9] Democracies tend to yield the right results in terms of the values and objectives that a liberal-political morality would care for. Outcomes of democratic procedures, assuming a representative democracy is well structured, tend to do a decent job of aggregating the preferences of people to maximize their overall satisfaction. Therefore, if you are a consequentialist, holding that

[7] See, e.g., Jeremy Waldron, *Law and Disagreement* (Oxford University Press: Oxford, 1999), chs 10–13.
[8] See, e.g., Thomas Christiano, *The Constitution of Equality* (Oxford University Press: Oxford, 2008) ch. 7.
[9] See, e.g., Joseph Raz, 'Liberalism, Skepticism and Democracy' (1988–1989) 74 Iowa Law Review 761.

maximizing overall preferences (or some other variant of a similar conception of the good) is the ultimate moral objective, you would find democratic procedures justified so long as they achieve this objective better than any feasible alternative. To what extent this argument is tied to liberalism would obviously depend on the question of how close the ties are, generally speaking, between consequentialism and liberalism. But this is not going to be my concern here.

I would not deny that there is a great deal of plausibility to a consequentialist justification of democracy. Representative democracy is well structured to yield results, in the long run, that approximate a decent level of welfare maximization, probably more so than any feasible alternative. Furthermore, it would not be very difficult to see how certain constraints on majority rule could be thought to improve the welfare maximization mechanisms of the legal system. But then, of course, empirical questions loom large: do we have good evidence to support the assumption that precisely in those areas in which democratic procedures are likely to fail, constitutional courts are likely to do better? As I will argue in more detail below, we have good reason to be doubtful.

More pertinently, however, liberal critics of the consequentialist approach to the justification of democracy tend to point out the fact that on any strong instrumentalist approach the intrinsic moral values we find in democratic decision-procedures are lost.[10] And, they claim, rightly so in my mind, that democracy, at least in certain contexts, does manifest things we care about intrinsically, regardless of consequences. We care about political equality, for example; we care about fairness, and things like that. But again, if your justification of democracy is purely instrumental, you have no way of explaining aspects of it that are non-instrumentally valuable. On the other hand, since consequentialism does not regard democratic procedures as intrinsically valuable to begin with, the tension between constitutionalism and democracy would not be all that deep either. And this, above anything else, renders the consequentialist approach somewhat tangential to the debate. If you don't think that things like fairness, equality, and a right to political participation, capture aspects of human interaction that we hold intrinsically valuable, then the whole debate about constitutionalism loses its moral edge; it becomes a debate in political science. Since I am not a political scientist, and my interest here is purely moral, I will bracket the consequentialist approach from here on, and discuss the kind of liberal justifications of democracy that do take certain underlying moral principles to be independently and intrinsically valuable.

There is hardly a consensus on the constitutive elements of a liberal-political morality. But some fundamental ideas loom large. Those are the moral-political ideals of freedom and equality. Liberalism is a deep commitment to the idea that people's freedom to do and to think whatever they want is the baseline or point of departure for any legal order, whereby constraints and limits on those freedoms are the ones that need to be justified. People should be free, unless there are very good reasons, mostly harm prevention reasons, to limit some freedoms. And then, liberalism is also a commitment to the idea that people should be treated as equals, at least in some fundamental respects. The very idea of a democratic regime is justified by an ideal of equality, that is, the idea that people's ability to influence political decisions should be

[10] See, e.g., Christiano (n. 8).

divided equally, one person one vote. At least in principle, democracy aspires to attain some form of an equal distribution of political power. Needless to say, equality is a very complex and controversial ideal. The main divisions between liberal left and right on the ideological spectrum stem from different understandings of what it is that people should be equal in, and to what extent. Roughly and crudely put, the right maintains that an equality of rights, opportunities, and legal status is all that is needed, whereby the left aspires to a more egalitarian distribution of welfare or at least a much more egalitarian distribution of socio-economic resources.

Either way, the point I want to make here is that liberalism, understood as commitment to freedom and equality, plays a dual role in a justifying democracy: liberalism is what justifies the need for a democratic decision-making process, and also what justifies the constitutional limitations on it. Taken together, the idea is that a proper construal of the fundamental values of freedom and equality justify, by and large, a majoritarian decision-making process, essentially a 'one person one vote system', but only up to a point and with certain constraints, constraints that are derived from those same fundamental values that justify democracy to begin with.

So this is the line of thought that I want to focus on. There are two similar versions of the argument from liberalism I want to explore. Both arguments lead to the conclusion that people have a right to political participation and the right needs to be allocated to all equally. But they reach this conclusion somewhat differently. According to one line of thought, heavily influenced by Rawls's *A Theory of Justice*,[11] one's ability to have an impact on public decisions is a *primary good*, the kind of good that every rational person would want to have more of rather than less, regardless of one's conception of the good. And this makes a lot of sense. Regardless of your conception of the good, of what makes your life worth living and the kind of things you generally value, you would have an interest in shaping your social, economic, cultural, and natural environment. Even a hermit needs an environment where he can be left to be alone. And of course, most of us are not hermits; our ability to materialize our conception of the good and other things we value is hugely dependent on the environment we live in. So, quite obviously, we all have an interest in our ability to shape that environment and make it more conducive to our way of life and our ethical and practical concerns.

There is a lot going for the idea that political participation, the power to have some impact on public decisions, is a primary good. And then, like any primary good, it should be subject to fair distribution. According to Rawls, and many other liberals, the starting point for any fair distribution, the baseline as it were, is always equality. Things ought to be distributed equally, unless there are compelling reasons to deviate from equality. So now I hope you can see how we get a two-stage argument for constitutional democracy: the baseline is an equal distribution of political power, that is, the principle of 'one person one vote', which practically entails majority rule. But we don't necessarily have to end there. If political power is a primary good, subject to distributional fairness, there might be compelling reasons to deviate from equal distribution in some cases or under certain conditions. So at least

[11] John Rawls, *A Theory of Justice* (Harvard University Press: Cambridge MA., 1971).

the door is open to consider various constraints on equal distribution of political power that might be justified. In particular, it would seem to be plausible to assume that some constraints on majority rule are needed to safeguard the fair distribution of other primary goods, such as socio-economic status, self-esteem, and freedoms of various kinds.

Before we move on, let me mention a slightly different argument that leads to very similar conclusions. According to this line of thought, we do not need to think about political power as a primary good. We care about political power only because we care about our freedoms. We care about our freedoms to shape our lives in the way we want, which is to say, we value our personal autonomy, we care about our freedoms to go wherever we please, to think and feel whatever we want, to be able to express ourselves freely, and so on and so forth. Now, obviously, if you care about these freedoms and consider them essential for human flourishing and wellbeing, you would care about *securing the conditions* that make it possible to have the freedoms and the ability to exercise them. Needless to say, the relevant conditions are multifarious. They include conditions of economic prosperity; social and cultural support of one's life projects and self-esteem; legal rights; environmental conditions; and so forth. In short, all the things that are subject to public-political decisions. Thus the first step here is to realize that we all have an interest in having a say in shaping the kind of environment that would be conducive to our freedoms. That would be something like a right to political participation. The equal distribution of this right would follow from the same Rawlsian idea, namely, the idea that an equal distribution is the baseline of a fair distribution, unless compelling reasons justify deviation from equality.[12] So we get the same two-step argument here, whereby the principle of one person one vote is the default principle, but the door is left open for restrictions and modifications in light of other values which might be even more compelling from a liberal point of view. For example, there would be no point in securing an equal right to political participation if the exercise of that right is likely to undermine other fundamental freedoms, such as freedom of speech or freedom of religion.

Both arguments, then, and similar arguments for democracy based on the fundamental values of freedom and equality, lead to the same kind of conclusion, namely, that a principle of majority rule, instantiating the ideal of an equal distribution of political power, is what liberalism requires, but that those same values may also justify deviations from majority rule and various constraints on it.[13]

Let me acknowledge before we proceed, however, that the move from an ideal of equal distribution of political power to the principle of majority rule, especially when that principle is instantiated by a complex representative model of democracy, is not all that straightforward, and certainly not simple. If you have ten people

[12] I have tried to develop an argument for democracy along these lines in Marmor, *Law in the Age of Pluralism* (n. 1), ch 1.

[13] There is a long tradition in liberal political philosophy that purports to justify democracy by way of deriving its values from some forms of consent, from the idea of the consent to be governed. See, e.g., D. Estlund *Democratic Authority* (Princeton University Press: Princeton, 2009). I am largely ignoring this tradition here, partly because I am very doubtful of any attempt to base the legitimacy of political authority on consent, and partly because consent-based arguments, even if successful, would not change the general picture I try to depict here.

in a room and a decision has to be made, you would distribute the power to make that decision equally by granting each person one vote, and making the decision favoured by a simple majority. But even in this hugely simplified model, there is more you might need to secure for the power to make the decision to be really equal. You have to make sure, for example, that nobody in the room is subject to the possibility of undue pressure from, or extortion by, somebody else. If there is room for debate before the decision, you would need to make sure that everybody would have equal opportunity to speak up and make their case to the others. And so on and so forth. Now of course, political reality is vastly more complex, and the problems of equal access to political power, and equal opportunity to influence political decisions, is correspondingly vastly more complicated and often very difficult to implement. Nevertheless, I will bracket these complications here, and assume that we can work out a system of representative democracy that instantiates, as well as possible, the ideal of an equal distribution of political power. It is now time to consider whether this ideal can be overridden by other liberal values that can justify constitutionalism.

In principle, the answer has to be affirmative. No single principle that instantiates an important liberal value can be secure from conflicts with other liberal, moral, ethical values, and when conflict arises, one may need to give way to the other. In other words, even if we regard the principle of equal distribution of political power as essential to a liberal democracy, we cannot maintain that it should always be secure from the challenge by conflicting values and principles liberalism cherishes as well. So the idea that under certain conditions majority rule may need to be constrained, and sometimes overridden, by other concerns is surely correct. Somewhat differently put, it would make no sense to suggest that the principle of equal distribution of political power is so fundamental that no other principles can ever outweigh it. Even if you think that some values are truly foundational, admitting of no justified exceptions, like the value of human dignity, or perhaps the value of life itself, the principle under consideration here merits no such foundational status. Its value is derived from other things we care about, things like freedom, autonomy, and fundamental equality. Which comes to show that the difficult questions about the justification of a constitutional democracy with powers of judicial review and the like, cannot be answered in a very abstract and high-minded way; the debate is bound to be more mundane, delving in to a myriad of practical concerns.

Let us assume then, that a liberal justification of democracy may well require some constraints and limits on majority rule, limits on the power of democratic institutions to have the final say on public decisions. Some balance between conflicting values needs to be drawn. But the need to balance different fundamental concerns does not yet tell us how to constitute the mechanisms for attaining an acceptable balance. It does not yet show us that a relatively rigid written constitution, accompanied by a constitutional court with the power of judicial review, is the best option. There are many other options on the table. For example, we could have a written constitution, and perhaps even a fairly rigid one at that, but without granting the constitutional court the power to strike down legislation that violates the constitution. Courts may be allowed only the power to issue declarative judgments, proclaiming, if they so deem, that the law violates the constitution, leaving the legal outcome to depend on legislatures, eventually accountable to the public.[14] Or, we could have, of course, a regular constitutional democracy with a non-rigid constitution, making amendment procedures relatively easy to carry out. Alternatively, we could have a non-constitutional democracy, as it were, where some types of public decisions, determined in advance, would require a super-majority vote in parliament or perhaps by referenda. Article 33 of the Canadian Charter provides another interesting model. It grants the democratic legislatures the power to override constitutional decisions of the Supreme Court, while imposing certain costs in doing so, requiring the override to be made very explicit and imposing a sunset provision. Other similar models can be conceived.

The difficult question here is how to proceed in thinking about these issues, inevitably combining, as they do, questions about institutional design and moral considerations. I will proceed in three stages: starting with the moral considerations, I will outline, albeit briefly and incompletely, the main moral concerns that would justify the need to impose limits on majority rule. I will then proceed to the institutional issues, outlining some of the characteristic features of constitutional courts, aiming to show that there are some inherent limits, serious limits, to how well courts can be expected to address the moral concerns about majority rule. Finally, I will suggest some ways in which institutions can be re-designed to address at least some of those concerns better.

III. Moral Concerns and Institutional Design

Let us begin by identifying the main sirens that lurk in the background of democratic decision-making procedures. As I mentioned earlier, the most obvious moral concern about majoritarian decision procedures relates to the fate of vulnerable minorities. Take a simple model: suppose we have a country with two main ethnic groups, the Reds, forming about 70 per cent of the population, and the Greens, forming about 30 per cent of the population. Now suppose that this ethnic identity, of being a member of the Reds or the Greens, is of considerable and wide-ranging significance to these people. Their ways of life are different, their conceptions of the good are partly defined by their ethnic identities, and so forth. In other words, let us assume that the kind of things Reds care about and wish to accomplish are very different from, and often at odds with, the concerns and desires of the Greens. Needless to say, if you just leave public decisions to the fate of simple majority rule, the Greens are going to be on the losing end all the time. Even if we assume that there are some public decisions that should be, as a matter of the right moral result, sensitive to numbers, so that if more people prefer X to Y, going for X is morally the correct way to go, we would still not think that this applies to all matters of public concern. Some fundamental needs and important interests of people should be met regardless of numbers, regardless of how many people might prefer otherwise. Therefore, a situation in which the Greens are going to lose pretty much 100 per cent of the time would be totally unacceptable. This much, I think, we can all agree on. But let us be a bit more precise about what is, morally speaking, at stake here.

[14] This is roughly the case, though without a written constitution, in the United Kingdom.

To say that minorities need to be protected from the tyranny of the majority, without further elaboration, is ridiculous. Most minorities in any given population do not require any particular protection; billionaires, legal philosophers, brain surgeons, and so forth, are all tiny minorities, but none is particularly vulnerable or in need of any protection from majority rule. More importantly, even if we think about the hypothesis of the Reds and the Greens, we cannot tell how much protection the Greens need without further context and historical background. Suppose it is the case that the Greens have been the colonial power in the country for centuries, with a long history of exploiting and subjugating the Reds to their selfish interests. Consequently, the reality is that the Greens are much more powerful than the Reds, economically, socially, and otherwise. Now it is no longer so clear how much protection from majority rule the Greens are morally entitled to have, not so? In other words, and this is the main lesson I'm hoping we learn here, the moral concern we have with the need to protect minorities is a concern with certain types of minorities. The kind of minorities that do merit our special concern would have to be persistent and vulnerable minorities, weak and unpopular. The kind of minorities whose members' interests and wellbeing tend to be ignored or, worse, deliberately undermined by the majority, and who systematically lack the economic and political power to gain their protection by majoritarian decision procedures. So yes, the protection of the interests of persistent and vulnerable minorities is, no doubt, one of the main moral concerns we should have with ordinary democratic decision procedures. Bearing in mind that these kinds of minorities tend to be very unpopular, often regarded with disdain, suspicion, or worse, by the dominant majority, this makes the means for protection often challenging and difficult.

I have already mentioned that a familiar problem with democratic procedures consists in a tendency towards shortsightedness. We see this very clearly in cases of national emergencies and perceived threats to security and stability, when ordinary democratic procedures tend to perform miserably, running roughshod over people's rights. But the problem of shortsightedness is more prevalent. Politicians need to showcase accomplishments to their constituents in order to be re-elected, which means that they would typically need to show what they had already gained for their potential voters, not what they will have ascertained for the distant future. Furthermore, given the relatively short time span of election cycles it is easy for politicians to downplay costs that will materialize in the distant future; they may not be in power when those costs need to be addressed. So there is, no doubt, a certain pressure in democratic procedures to prefer visible gains in the present, even if future costs are too high, to costly long-term investments. Although these dangers of shortsightedness tend to affect mostly economic and environmental issues, there is a similar concern with greater moral impact. The temptation to set aside certain individuals' rights and moral interests in favour of greater gains in overall prosperity is often very strong. We see it these days with the enormous economic boom of the Internet economy, where huge profits and prosperity seem to sideline important privacy protections and important safeguards against abuse and manipulation. We see it in the domain of tax law in the United States, for example, whereby in the name of economic growth taxes are reduced for the rich and increased for the lower middle classes. And we see it in many countries where people are required to forgo certain liberties in order to secure economic prosperity. Combined with the concern about inadequate protection of persistent vulnerable minorities, the dangers of shortsightedness loom large. It is not just tempting, but practically all too easy in a democratic system to sidestep the moral interests of the weak and vulnerable in order to gain greater economic prosperity. Rawls, for one, saw this danger clearly and was at some pains to justify a principle of *the priority of liberty*, suggesting that when nations reach beyond a certain minimal level of prosperity, it should be forbidden to sacrifice liberties in favour of any greater gains in prosperity.[15] Though Rawls was not directly concerned with mechanisms of democracy, the temptations he warned against are precisely those we have in mind here.

Finally, let me dwell on the danger of populist xenophobia. It is becoming all too evident these days that democracies can slip to frightening forms of xenophobic populism, without relinquishing any of the institutional structures and safeguards of an orderly democratic regime. What we see these days, at least so far, is a form of ballot-box populism, gaining a lot of traction in many liberal and not so liberal democracies.

Populism is much easier to recognize than to define. Without attempting a precise definition, let me say what I mean by it. Metaphorically, at least, populism is a kind of political Protestantism, striving to relinquish institutional mediation between leadership and ordinary people. Populist leaders present themselves as direct representatives of the people, a directness they purport to convey by bypassing anything they can label as the "establishment", be it legislatures, courts, political parties, the media, etc. Populism is a kind of anti-establishment democracy, aiming to represent the 'ordinary folks' directly and what it is that they really want. And of course, this is what makes populism so dangerous. Liberal democracy values procedures and institutions in full recognition that there is no such thing as 'what the people really want'. People want and value many conflicting things, and hard choices need to be made; they value different things to different degrees, and often in ways that are not entirely coherent even from an individual's perspective. The role of procedures and institutions in a representative democracy is precisely that of aggregating and balancing conflicting interests, preferences, and value judgements, in fair and equitable ways. Representative democratic institutions, a free and thriving press, well-organized political parties, and other 'establishment' institutions, serve important functions in enabling a process of bargaining and compromise. Populism, on the other hand, is based on the illusion that political leaders can simply know what most people want, as if there is something knowable and simple about it.

And yet, with all the anti-establishment rhetoric and disdain for compromise and subtlety, populism seems to thrive, no doubt in part aided by social media and new communication technologies, within the confines of orderly democratic regimes. This raises the serious concern that just as an ordinary democratic procedure is unlikely to provide sufficient protection against oppression of vulnerable minorities, it is also unlikely to safeguard against xenophobic populism. And we should bear in mind that xenophobic populism is dangerous both domestically and internationally; its negative effects are present both internally, within the domestic setting, and externally, in the international domain in relation to other countries and other populations.[16]

[15] Rawls (n. 11), section 11.

[16] There is an old myth, propagated extensively in the aftermath of World War I, that liberal democracies do not wage war against each other; it is inherently against their interests to do so. Perhaps there is some

It may be too early to say how much of this new trend of nationalist, xenophobic populism rising in democracies[17] these days exposes an inherent or structural weakness of liberal democracies, as such, or just thrives regardless of the underlying type of regime in question. Either way, I think we can safely say that there might not be anything in the structure of an orderly democratic regime to stop the emergence of xenophobic nationalism. Xenophobic populists seem to win in the ballot box and advance their agenda democratically, not so much despite but probably because of their vocal disdain for the 'establishment', the 'mainstream media', even for political parties and legislatures; for all we can tell now, it is partly what enables this populism, xenophobic, immoral, and anti-liberal as it is, to thrive in democratic regimes.

To sum up: we have identified four or five main types of serious moral concerns about the workings of an orderly democratic system. The fate of persistent vulnerable minorities, the tendency towards shortsightedness, a similar tendency to downplay people's rights and liberties for the sake of greater economic gains or in the face of external threats, and, finally, the dangers of populism and anti-liberal policies gaining ground within a democratic system. The next question we need to address is the institutional one: whether constitutional courts, with their extensive powers of judicial review, agenda setting, and the like, can be expected to mitigate these serious concerns, and how well they are likely to safeguard against them.

We have already mentioned the fact that constitutional courts are made to be non-democratic institutions, deliberately shielded from popular accountability. And this makes it tempting to think that precisely because the courts are not democratically accountable, they can operate as safeguards against the shortcomings of democratic procedures. I think that we have reason to be doubtful about this. If we take a closer look at the institutional features of constitutional courts we might be able to see why having too much faith in judicial review is faith misplaced. There are three main institutional features of constitutional courts I want to flag here: the courts' basis of political power, the elitist nature of the institution, and its inherently traditionalist leanings. Taken together, I will argue, these features might explain why courts are not going to do a tremendous job in protecting vulnerable minorities, in safeguarding fundamental rights, when those rights seem to hinder prosperity and perceptions of the collective good, and perhaps somewhat more speculatively, I doubt that courts can be relied on to curtail the emergence of xenophobic populism.

Let's start with the issue of power base. The *de facto* power of the court is largely a function of its respectability in the eyes of the public and the level of popular assent it enjoys. Political leaders have armed forces at their disposal, they can intimidate others

truth to this; at least in the last few decades, exceptions are rare. But there is not even a myth that liberal democracies are unlikely to be bellicose. Many wars have been waged and grave atrocities committed by liberal democracies in the last few decades. There is nothing, it seems, in the nature of a liberal democratic regime to make it less bellicose externally, often embarking on unjust wars and unjust international interventions. I am not suggesting that any other type of regime is likely to do better on this front. Probably not.

[17] Prominent examples these days include the United States, of course, but also countries such as Hungary, Poland, Turkey, Russia (though to call these democracies might be a bit of a stretch), and Brazil, and who knows what other countries might join the club soon. There is a great deal of speculation about the long-term effects of the Coronavirus pandemic, some suggesting that these populist and particularly nationalist-xenophobic trends might gain even greater momentum. That, of course, remains to be seen.

to comply with their wishes, so they can often cling on to power with very little popular support. But courts have none of that. Courts derive all their power from the assent or, at the very least, acquiescence, of other officials in the system and the general public. The courts' popularity, so to speak, is the courts' *de facto* power. In order to function as constitutional courts, they need to be respected. Interestingly, in many countries the popularity of the court, and its public esteem, tends to be inversely related to the popularity and respectability of the legislature. There is, in fact, a remarkably uniform pattern whereby countries in which the legislature is deemed by the general public as one of the least respected institutions, the supreme or constitutional court is deemed very highly. When the legislature is seen as dysfunctional, people tend to look at the court as the responsible adult in the family.[18] Either way, the main point to bear in mind here is the familiar one, that the courts' *de facto* legal-political power is greatly a function of perceptions. Courts gain their power from their respectability in the eyes of the general public.

A related institutional aspect of constitutional courts is the very public nature of their agenda and reasoning. As I mentioned earlier, courts have very considerable agenda-setting powers. But the flip side of this power is that the agenda they set, the decisions they make, and the reasons the court provides for those decisions, are all in the public domain, for anyone to observe. Constitutional courts operate in the limelight. You might think that the same goes for the legislative branches of government, even if less so for the executive. But that's not quite true. Legislatures have means of hiding their agenda and their ulterior motives much more effectively. That is so partly because the legislative process is often very complicated and cumbersome, subject to complex bargaining procedures behind closed doors, and partly because the resultant laws enacted can be hugely complex and not easily understood by the public. What we often see is a complex law enacted, and then a cacophony of incoherent explanations by different political parties of the reasons behind the legislation and its ulterior motives. Constitutional courts, on the other hand, make much fewer decisions over time, reasons for them need to be provided publicly and officially, and decisions tend to be single-issue decisions, not all that difficult to grasp by ordinary people. Generally speaking, then, the decisions of constitutional courts are out in the daylight, salient and easily observable. This makes constitutional courts particularly vulnerable to populist pressure and easy targets for populist propaganda.[19]

The third feature of constitutional courts I want to mention is their inherent elitism. Elitism is a function both of the sociology of the profession, and also, more importantly, a function of the very nature of the institution itself. Constitutional courts get to make rather high-minded decisions, typically in some adversarial process, based on arguments and the weighing of reasons, almost in an academic fashion. In other words, the decision-making process in constitutional courts, and the subject matters

[18] The truth is that there might be some causal connection here, at least in some places, whereby the strengths of the constitutional court actually diminishes, causally speaking, the general popularity and respectability of the legislature. I have no evidence for this, and I suspect that establishing such causal connections empirically would be very challenging.

[19] A good US example of this can be observed in the massive support Trump has received from the Evangelical community, almost entirely based on their desire to change the composition of the Supreme Court in order to repeal *Roe v Wade* (410 US 113 (1972)) and similar liberal holdings.

to be decided upon, inevitably require a form of reasoning and argumentation that can only be attained by skilled, highly educated and knowledgeable individuals. It is a very respectable and in many ways admirable form of institutional decision-making, and as such, it is by its very nature highbrow, civilized, and elevated from the yelling and shouting of ordinary politics. Higher courts, just like universities, are essentially elitist institutions. Their whole rationale, as it were, is to be elevated from unrefined passions and prejudices of ordinary politics. Elitism is built into the role of constitutional courts, and it is no accident that courts are run by a professional elite. It's what constitutional courts are meant to do.

Finally, but not least importantly, constitutional courts tend to exhibit, again, institutionally and inevitably, a high level of deference to tradition. By which I mean not just legal tradition, but social and cultural tradition generally. Why is that? First, remember that courts gain the power they have from general perceptions and public respectability. Thus their powerbase is socially conventional, relying on the prevailing social order. Respect for the prevailing order and its entrenched traditions is what gives courts the respectability and security they need. Secondly, there is something in the very nature of the legal profession and legal modes of reasoning that tie it to the past, to long standing traditions. For example, think about the fact that decisions courts need to make cannot be all governed by enacted regulation; regulation is bound to run out, and then judges need to make decisions on the basis of the past, past legal doctrines, past legal conventions and, generally, deference to legal tradition. Perhaps this is more evident and out on the surface in common law systems, but to some extent it must be true across the board, it's just the nature of law and legal reasoning that it is closely tied to past decisions and long-standing traditions.

Of course I'm aware of the fact that courts, including constitutional courts, sometimes render radical decisions, departing, sometimes sharply, from prevailing traditions. The example of *Obergefell v Hodges*[20] (legalizing gay marriages) in the United States is perhaps one such recent case. But there are two points to bear in mind here. First, radical departures from the past tend to be exceptional cases; exceptions are possible, here and there, without undermining the general trend. Secondly, and this you might think is a bit speculative, I think that courts embark on a radical shift from long-standing traditions only when they sense, clearly enough, that public opinion is behind them, even if politicians and legislatures are not quite there.[21] Sure enough, there are more or less activist courts, and sometimes courts ford the river ahead of the public, but very rarely so. The general background against which constitutional courts operate is always in deference to long standing traditions.

None of these general institutional features of constitutional courts, however, necessarily tilt the court's decisions towards any particular ideological direction. The same institutional constraints that apply to constitutional courts across the board leave great leeway for decisions along a very broad spectrum, from traditionally conservative or right-wing ideologies to liberal or left-wing ones. To the extent

[20] 576 US 644 (2015).

[21] *Obergefell* is a good example of this. The decision to legalize gay marriages in the United States had very wide support in the general public, much wider than in the states and federal legislatures and the political establishment.

that some ideologies are ruled out, as it were, those would tend to be only of the radical, revolutionary kind. Within the bounds of traditional moral-political ideologies, courts can lean either way. Nevertheless, I would argue that the institutional features of constitutional courts should make us doubt that they are all that well positioned to solve the problems we mentioned about the shortcomings of ordinary democratic procedures.

Start with the issue of protection of minorities. What tends to make certain salient social groups into a persistent vulnerable minority is a very complex and deep rooted set of ills of human nature and human social organization. Nobody wakes up one day to think that people with a certain identity or feature are to be discriminated against. Discrimination and ill treatment of minorities always has deep historical and social roots, entrenched in the traditions and belief systems of the dominant majority. Courts, of course, cannot be expected to rectify the ills of our nature, but the problem is that they are subject to the same forces that afflict society at large. Since the court's bases of support and power consist in public perceptions, those public perceptions, particularly deep rooted ones, are bound to influence the courts as well. The courts' relative immunity to democratic accountability does not make them immune to the forces that constitute social consensus. When the dominant majority in a society regard some smaller social group with disdain and moral contempt, people tend to think that they have reasons for it. Those reasons, bogus and questionable as they inevitably are, tend to draw on the long-standing traditions of the society in question, fed and reinforced by the myths and prejudices of the culture of the dominant majority. To expect that judges would be largely immune to these forces is naïve, at best. Now couple this with the fact that the courts' bases of power reside in public perceptions and overall popularity, and you can see that there is only so much courts can be expected to do in order to protect minorities subject to deep rooted social hostility.

But the courts, as we noted before, are also inherently elitist institutions, both emerging from educated classes and speaking to them, as it were. Would this elitism not tilt the courts towards greater concern for the plight of vulnerable minorities? Alas, elitism has never been a close associate of justice, fairness, and equality. Sometimes it is, but not typically and not necessarily. Social elites are typically more refined in their expression of hostility and moral indignation, but they are not less prone to prejudice and bias than anybody else. In fact, the elitism of the court often has an additional entrenching effect; prejudices and biases that gain the support of elites tend to become even more entrenched by gaining an air of respectability that makes the prejudices even harder to uproot.

You may be puzzled about why would we need to speculate about the courts' ability to protect vulnerable minorities when we have ample evidence out there in the history of judicial review in many countries. Some of this history, like that of the United States, spans centuries, others several decades, but there is a lot of it; countless cases of constitutional courts dealing with the protection of minorities, all over the world. No doubt, we have a lot of evidence out there, but the problem is that the evidence is far from conclusive. Alongside many admirable, sometimes even courageous, decisions there are countless failures and disappointments. We cannot just count the good ones and the bad ones, and compare the numbers, that would be too silly. There are too many variables at work, and comparisons are very difficult to draw. Think about some landmark cases from the United States.[22] Alongside the admirable and important decisions, such as *Brown v Board of Education*,[23] ending racial segregation in American schools, there are also striking failures. The US Supreme Court signed off on the incarceration of Japanese Americans during World War II,[24] much more recently reiterated similar results with incarceration camps at Guantánamo,[25] and allowed the Trump administration to blatantly discriminate against visitors and potential immigrants from Muslim countries.[26] The US Supreme Court, only a few years ago, struck down parts of the Voting Rights Act of 1965 which were designed to protect racial minorities from disenfranchisement in traditionally racist counties,[27] and these days the Court is consistently making it more and more difficult to litigate claims of wrongful discrimination in employment and service provision.[28] Finding a clear and steady trend in courts' decisions about protection of minorities is not easy. I think that the safest we can say is that the record is at best patchy. And , if my speculative arguments are correct, this record is going to remain patchy for structural reasons.

For different reasons, the role of the constitutional courts in safeguarding against the almost inevitable shortsightedness of democratic procedures is also very problematic. We have ample historical evidence to show that in times of national emergency courts tend not to perform better than legislatures and the executive.[29] In matters of economic and financial expenditures and investments, courts usually shy away from intervention, and for good reason. They lack the expertise, as well as the democratic mandate, to force legislatures or executives into making very costly investments for the distant future. Furthermore, there is very little in constitutional documents and constitutional doctrines to ground such decisions legalistically. The more pertinent question, however, is whether courts can do a better job in safeguarding something like Rawls's *priority of liberty* principle? Can they put the brakes on measures intended to increase economic prosperity when those measures jeopardize people's liberties and rights? I doubt that there is a clear answer to this question. Circumstances vary considerably. Generally speaking, I think that what we tend to see is limited success. Just as courts tend to find it very difficult to counter the government when the latter threatens that undermining their policy is going to endanger national security and international relations, courts are often wary of countering the government when huge

[22] The focus on the United States is not scholarly justified, it is due to the limits of my background. My Canadian colleagues tend to regard their Supreme Court's constitutional judicial review with greater esteem, and perhaps rightly so. The Canadian Charter is a much more recent document than the US Constitution, it is more liberal in content, and the Court itself tends to more liberal leanings than the US Court. Nevertheless, I am far from sure that realities on the ground, particularly with respect to protection of indigenous minorities, is all that different.

[23] 347 US 483 (1954).

[24] *Korematsu v United States*, 323 US 214 (1944).

[25] *Hamdi v Rumsfeld*, 542 US 507 (2004). Although *de jure*, the Court ruled that Guantánamo detainees have rights of *habeas corpus*, the Court actually legitimized the detentions and watered down the *habeas corpus* procedures to internal military tribunals.

[26] *Trump v Hawaii*, 585 US _ (2018).

[27] *Shelby County v Holder*, 570 US 529 (2013).

[28] The obstacles to anti-discrimination litigation come in two main forms: the Court makes it more difficult to file class action suits in this domain, and the courts routinely enforce mandatory arbitration clauses in employment contracts even when the arbitration clauses apply to employment discrimination or sexual harassment claims.

[29] As some of the cases mentioned earlier attest; see, e.g., *Korematsu* and *Hamdi*.

economic costs and benefits are at stake.[30] But sometimes they do, and it's very difficult to generalize.

Finally, thinking about the prospects of constitutional protections in the face of xenophobic nationalism is presently even more of a speculative game. Some of the pessimism I expressed about the courts' ability to protect persistent vulnerable minorities surely apply here is as well, perhaps even more forcefully. But the problems in this case are wider and deeper. The institutional features of constitutional courts make the institution particularly vulnerable to the kind of populist pressure that comes with this new trend of ballot-box populism. The demagogy and enlivening spirit of xenophobic populism, as we mentioned earlier, is hugely driven by disdain for 'mainstream' institutions, disdain for elitism and liberal values, and disdain for anything that can be associated with 'the establishment'. Obviously, this puts the courts in a very precarious position. Couple this with the fact that courts' *de facto* power resides mostly in popular perceptions, their inherently elitist character, the tendency to preserve traditions, and the fact that the courts operate in the public limelight, and you can see how powerless courts may become in the face of this xenophobic, nationalist, anti-liberal wave.

Now you might think that pessimism comes cheap. The real question is whether we can think of better alternatives. After all, we did acknowledge that ordinary democratic procedures are far from perfect and are in need of correction. There are sirens out there and we know, at least partly, where they lurk. Are there better ways to safeguard against these shortcomings of democratic procedure? I am not going to answer the question directly, partly because I am probably not competent to do so, and partly because there are too many variables in play, some of them jurisdiction specific, others not yet fully researched. Nevertheless, given the concerns we have raised so far, a few tentative conclusions may follow.

One problem we can generalize from the discussion is that constitutionalism seems flawed by offering one type of medicine for very different ailments. A strong constitutional court with extensive power of judicial review might be good to solve some problems, but not others. In particular, I doubt that it is the best solution for the need to protect persistent vulnerable minorities. What makes minorities particularly vulnerable is lack of political power. Finding ways of increasing the political bargaining power of minorities would seem to be much more effective, particularly when the minority group is relatively salient and persistent in time. Remember that poor people tend to get much more from their voting rights and the ballot box than they get from the courts. And that is so because voting in elections is almost the only political power they have, and sometimes that power is significant. Similarly, minorities that manage to gain some *de facto* veto rights on political decisions tend to do much better than those who have only a litigation avenue to pursue in the protection of their rights and interests. Goodwill takes you only so far; outcomes tend to be determined by political and social power.

[30] A nice example is the Obamacare decision of the US Supreme Court (*King v Burwell*, 576 US 988 (2015)) where despite the conservative majority on the court, it eventually refrained from striking down a key component of Obamacare, leaving the legislation in place, partly, no doubt, due to the huge cost-benefit impacts involved. However, the Obamacare litigation still continues and the end is not in sight.

All this would indicate that when we think about protection of persistent and vulnerable minorities, much more attention should be paid to the structuring of electoral systems than to constitutional rights. Some of the main parameters are well known. Minorities tend to do much better in electoral systems of proportional representation; regional, first-past-the-ballot systems (which exist in most countries), dilute the votes of minorities, rendering their ability to influence outcomes, and their ability to have serious bargaining powers, considerably less effective. But then we also know that the more proportional the representative system is, the less stable governments and parliamentary coalitions tend to be. So there is always a trade-off here and the right balance is not easy to achieve. Nevertheless, even if details are debatable, I would venture to guess that vulnerable minorities are better served by ways of increasing their relative political power in the electoral system, than by constitutional protections.

Another factor to bear in mind is that there is a great deal that can be achieved in the protection of minorities by way of ordinary legislation. In fact, judging by the experience of the United States, much more has been achieved at the statutory level than the constitutional one. Most of the important protections of vulnerable minorities in the United States, and by far the greater amount of progress in this area, has been accomplished by the Civil Rights Act 1964 and the Voting Rights Act 1965 (and some subsequent additions and amendments). If anything, constitutional intervention in these Acts tended to undermine, not to foster, the levels of protection of minorities. I am not claiming that US legal experience can be generalized across the board, or that it reflects some necessary state of affairs. But at the very least, it's a good cautionary tale.

As I mentioned earlier, there are many more options on the table. Some of those options would curtail, to some extent, the power of constitutional courts, shifting greater responsibility to the legislatures and to voters. In my mind, that would be a good thing. Too much power in the hands of the courts tends to undermine the responsibilities legislatures assume, and consequently tends to undermine institutional functioning and respectability of representative democracy. That cannot be a good thing. Admittedly, however, some of the shortcomings of democratic procedures are not easy to amend by any acceptable means. The inherent shortsightedness we discussed above is not the kind of problem that lends itself to constitutional solutions, but it may not lend itself to any other kind of solution that would be consistent with an acceptable form of democracy. And then, needless to say, the rise of xenophobic populism is even more vexing. It would be very difficult to think of any institutional design that can safeguard us against the evils of anti-liberal forces gaining the upper hand in democratic regimes. Some fights need to be fought in the political arena, not the legal one.

2

The Misconceived Quest for the Elusive Right Answer or Dedication to a Process, Not a Result

*W. J. Waluchow**

I. Introduction

Among the long-standing questions of legal theory is whether judges ever make new law when they decide legal cases. Many legal theorists believe that the exercise of this creative power is inevitable, perhaps even desirable. They think this is so even in modern constitutional democracies rooted in the common law, where deliberation and voting among elected legislators is now widely accepted as the principal forum for the creation of new law. Other legal theorists reject both the necessity and desirability of judge-made law. Ronald Dworkin was perhaps the foremost contemporary proponent of this view and set out to develop a complex theory that purports to eliminate the need for judges ever to create new law. According to Dworkin's famous *right answer thesis*, there is always, in a mature legal system, an antecedently existing right answer to any legal question on which a case might turn. And it is the duty of the judge to find and apply that answer in deciding a case.

One needn't dig too deeply to understand the reluctance of those, like Dworkin, who reject the necessity and desirability of judge-made law. The thought that judges create new law poses a threat to the archetypal image of the judge as an impartial, neutral arbiter whose role is to apply legal norms created elsewhere, by individuals who possess the democratic authority to do so. In this view, justice is, or ought to be, blind to extra-legal considerations—including all those reasons one might have to create the laws judges are supposed to apply in an impartial manner. In modern constitutional democracies those who properly engage in law creation are, of course, members of elected legislatures, who are viewed as representing and furthering, in their law-making activities, the values, interests, and preferences of the electorate they were legitimately chosen to serve. According to this archetypal image, a judge's reasoning should map onto what we might call a 'basic legal syllogism' ('BLS'). The law provides the major premise of the relevant BLS; a statement of the facts of the case provides its minor premise; and the conclusion states the legally right answer it is the duty of the judge to affirm in her judgment. On this picture, there both is and ought to be little

* The title of this paper is a take on Paul Brest's classic article 'The Misconceived Quest for the Original Understanding' (1980) 60 Boston University Law Review 204.

W. J. Waluchow, *The Misconceived Quest for the Elusive Right Answer or Dedication to a Process, Not a Result*
In: *Constitutionalism*. Edited by: Alejandro Linares-Cantillo, Camilo Valdivieso-León, Santiago García-Jaramillo, Oxford University Press (2021). DOI: 10.1093/oso/9780192896759.003.0003

room for judicial creativity. The law both does and ought to provide the antecedently existing right answer to the pivotal question raised in the case: Is this defendant liable for committing an actionable tort? Is this defendant guilty of a crime? Is this contract legally valid? Is this statute constitutionally valid? And so on.[1]

Despite this archetypal image, most deny that it, and the BLS it embraces, accurately reflects the judicial reasoning that actually goes on in most, if not all, legal cases. Legal realists are often characterized as denying the image entirely, suggesting instead that the law *never* fully determines the conclusions reached by judges. Rather, a host of non-legal factors significantly contribute to (or determine) the outcome of any case. These include the judge's own individual sense of fairness; his broader, possibly quite partisan, convictions of political morality; and political pressure from some other government body. This is so even in cases where there appears to be a singular legal rule which itself seems to supply the required right answer. In any such case, the realist will say, the rule requires interpretation. And as English Bishop, Benjamin Hoadly famously said: 'Whoever hath an absolute authority to interpret written or spoken laws; it is he who is truly the lawgiver to all intents and purposes and not the person who wrote or spoke them.'[2]

But one does not have to embrace an extreme form of legal realism in order to deny that the archetypal image fully captures the nature of all judicial decision making. Many less sceptical scholars and judges believe that judges are inevitably required in some cases to fill in 'gaps' or indeterminacies left by the law and its makers in the effort to supply judges with their major premises. And in so doing, they employ a mode of reasoning commonly referred to as *judicial discretion*. Theorists as vastly different as Aquinas, Austin, Kelsen, and Hart all accept that there are inevitably cases where the law runs out and the judge must, of necessity, exercise a kind of law-making discretion in supplying, supplementing, or specifying the missing or incomplete major premise of the relevant BLS.[3] But as I noted earlier, not all theorists think it inevitable, let alone desirable, that judges should sometimes be called on to create new law in this way. After distinguishing two innocuous forms of *weak discretion*, one having to do with the use of judgment, the other with finality of decision, Dworkin distinguishes a third form—what he calls *strong discretion*—and argues that its exercise is far from inevitable. Strong discretion is characterized by the judge's freedom to step beyond the confines of authoritatively binding legal norms for grounds on which to decide a case. In such instances the law fails to provide a uniquely right answer, and the judge is free to choose on grounds she sees fit to consult and in any way she deems desirable. It is this third, strong sense of discretion that Dworkin denies is necessary, let alone desirable, in constitutional democracies like the United States, Canada, and Colombia. If the coercive measures the law purports to license are to be justified in such systems, Dworkin reasons, the law must be a *seamless web* in which the antecedently existing, legally right answers can always be found by judges. Were such right answers not always available,

[1] Henceforth I will use the term *pivotal question* to mean the question the relevant BLS is meant to answer.

[2] As quoted by John Chipman Gray, 'A Realist Conception of Law', in Feinberg and Gross (eds), *The Philosophy of Law* (3rd edn, Belmont, CA: Wadsworth), 12.

[3] By *specification* I mean what Aquinas meant by this term. That is, I mean the process of choosing from among a number of readings or interpretations the norm itself leaves open. On some translations, specification is described as the *determination of common notions*, that is, *determinatio*.

and judges were instead permitted to exercise strong discretion, the costs would be too great. These include a loss of democratic legitimacy and a failure to respect basic fairness. Democratic legitimacy would be sacrificed because, as the archetypal image suggests, the role of the judge in a democracy that embraces a separation of powers is to be an impartial arbiter who renders decisions according to standards set by others with democratic authority to create them. Fairness is compromised because 'if a judge makes a new law and applies it retroactively in the case before him, then the losing party will be punished, not because he has violated some duty he had, but rather a new duty created after the event.'[4] Basic fairness demands that we be judged by a law that existed at the time we acted, and that this be used as the major premise in the BLS deciding our fate. So too does the rule of law.

My aim in this paper is to question the need for antecedently existing right answers to all pivotal legal questions. Put another way, my aim is to question whether the exercise of judicial discretion in answering pivotal questions is, as Dworkin and the archetypal image suggest, necessarily illegitimate in a constitutional democracy. I will argue that legitimacy does not necessitate existing right answers and a rejection of judicial discretion. My case will ultimately rest on two factors: first, the difficulty of determining, in any particular case, whether there is a right answer and what that might be; and second, the fact that judicial discretion does not consist in unbridled choice on the part of one who exercises it—a consequence that might seem inevitable if the law has indeed 'run out'. As Dworkin himself once remarked, 'discretion is not tantamount to license, and it does not exclude criticism. Almost any situation in which a person acts … makes relevant certain standards of rationality, fairness, and effectiveness.'[5] And as Hart observed in *The Concept of Law*, it certainly does not amount to 'blind, arbitrary choice'.[6] As we shall see, it requires, at least within the confines of a constitutional democracy, the observance of a range of limitations on the types of reasons to which the judge may appeal, and on the type of reasoning in which the judge may legitimately engage when exercising discretionary choice in creating new law. This makes a crucial difference. When the appropriate limitations are observed, democratic legitimacy need not be compromised by the exercise of judicial discretion. So long as a judge reasons in the right way, her decision can be legitimate, even when the law fails to provide a clearly right answer to her pivotal question. Indeed, even if there is no singularly right answer at all, clear or otherwise. In developing this argument, my focus will be on cases where judges review acts of legislation for conformity with constitutional rights.[7] Here the issue of judicial discretion takes on a particular poignancy because it is tempting to think that the law quite often fails to provide the clearly right answers seemingly required for democratic legitimacy. More specifically, it fails to provide pre-existing right answers to morally loaded questions concerning the meaning of constitutional provisions invoking concepts like equality, dignity, and the principles of fundamental justice. In the view of many, these are precisely the type

[4] Ronald Dworkin, *Taking Rights Seriously* (2nd edn, London: Duckworth, 1977), 84.

[5] Ibid., 33.

[6] H. L. A. Hart, *The Concept of Law* (3rd edn, Oxford: Clarendon Press, 2012), 204.

[7] Henceforth, when I use the term *constitutional review* this is what I should be taken to mean. And when I use the term *charter* I should be taken to mean a constitutional charter or bill of rights, or sections of a constitution that recognize constitutional rights such as the right to equality, free expression, or dignity.

of fundamentally contentious moral questions that admit of no determinate answers and that must be dealt with and settled by elected legislatures, not the supposedly neutral arbiters figuring in our archetypal image of judges.[8] Section 7 of the Canadian Charter of Rights and Freedoms specifies a right to 'life, liberty and security of the person'. But it fails to say anything more that might illuminate what precisely this constitutional right amounts to in concrete cases. Suppose that Parliament has introduced legislation that a court later strikes down because of a perceived conflict with this right. In ruling against Parliament, the court not only announces its disagreement with Parliament, it overrides the latter's understanding and substitutes its own view of the matter. But on what basis could such a substitution be justified? Had the law provided a clear, antecedently existing right answer to the pivotal question concerning the meaning and implication of the Section 7 right for the case, and if the court in ruling as it did simply applied that answer so as to generate the required BLS, then legitimacy might not be threatened. The court would have simply applied superior, pre-existing law set elsewhere. But if there is no such right answer, or if no one cannot say with any degree of confidence what it might be even on the assumption that it does exist, and if the court has the freedom to substitute its own moral views for that of the legislature, then it's far from clear that the requirements of democratic legitimacy can be met. Without a pre-existing legally right answer for the judges to find and apply, the worry is that constitutional review substitutes rule by appointed judges for rule by the people and their democratically elected representatives. And this worry is enough to convince many people that we should do away with constitutionally guaranteed rights of political morality, and the democratically dubious judicial practices they generate. My aim is to question this line of thinking by supporting the thesis that finding a uniquely right answer in constitutional rights cases is not required for democratic legitimacy. All it requires is that answers be arrived at *in the right way*.

II. Right Answers?

For purposes of argument, let's begin by observing that in many instances of constitutional review, there simply is no *clearly* right answer to the relevant pivotal question upon which all reasonable, well-informed individuals will agree. That is, whether in fact there is a right answer, it remains true that the law fails fully to determine *clearly* what it is. That is, it fails undeniably to determine whether an act of the legislature stands in conflict with a morally-based constitutional right. And so it fails to provide an uncontroversial major premise of a BLS on which a court might base its decision. Of course to say that this is true in *some* cases is not to say that it's true in *all* cases. This is crucial to stress. There is a noticeable tendency in arguments over the legitimacy of constitutional review to focus exclusively on the abstract moral terms in which many highly contentious constitutional rights provisions are couched. I have already noted Section 7 of the Canadian Charter. But consider as well Section 15, which specifies

[8] Among the most prominent defenders of this position is Jeremy Waldron. See, e.g., Jeremy Waldron, 'A Rights Based Critique of Constitutional Rights' (1993) 13 *Oxford Journal of Legal Studies* 19; Jeremy Waldron, *Law and Disagreement* (New York: Oxford University Press, 1999).

that 'every individual is equal before and under the law and has the right to the equal protection and equal benefit of the law ...'. Taken in and of itself, Section 15 is obviously as open as Article 13 of the Colombian constitution to a variety of different, quite plausible interpretations, each based on a different moral theory concerning the nature of equality.[9] Philosophy text books are filled with such theories. Even if there were a true moral theory, as well as uniquely correct answers flowing from it, the fact remains that there is widespread, deep-seated disagreement on what these might be. There is, in other words, a plethora of different understandings of equality, none of which is obviously correct, or uncontestably superior to all the others. And if the law provides no clear, authoritative instructions as to which of these plausible understandings is, for legal purposes, correct, judges will be forced to choose on some other basis, most likely their own personal understandings of the relevant moral issues. This not only threatens our archetypal image of judges as neutral arbiters, it threatens to undermine all efforts to justify constitutional review. Judges would be authorized to exercise a level of discretionary choice that would indeed be difficult to reconcile with democratic legitimacy.

But all this follows only if we focus on nothing but the constitution's abstract moral terms and ignore the long history of attempts, by both the legal and political systems of the relevant jurisdiction, to deal with questions of equality. Is Section 15's right to equality consistent with a failure to recognize same-sex marriage? Read independently of Canadian legal and political history, it is doubtful that there is a legally right answer to that question, let alone a *clear* or *indisputable* one. But read in the context of the string of Canadian laws and legal decisions that have recognized the rights of same-sex couples to share spousal pension entitlements, to adopt children together, to inherit from one another according to the same rules that apply to opposite-sex couples, and so on, Canadian law probably *did* provide a right answer, one that became clear to the Supreme Court in the deliberations underpinning its same-sex marriage reference.[10] I hazard to suggest that the same might be said of the state of Colombian law in the years preceding the Constitutional Court's historic 2016 ruling affirming the right of same-sex couples to the full benefits and protections of marriage. As one news source put it: 'the Constitutional Court has handed down one decision after another since it first extended the legal standing of Colombia's LGBT community in 2007. When the Court heard arguments in the gay marriage case in July, the writing was already on the

[9] Article 13 specifies that: 'All individuals are born free and equal before the law and are entitled to equal protection and treatment by the authorities ...'.

[10] *Reference Re Same-Sex Marriage* [2004] 3 SCR 698, 2004 SCC 79. Many Canadian courts had held earlier that an opposite-sex requirement for civil marriage violates the equality guarantee enshrined in s. 15(1) of the Charter. As a result, same-sex marriages generally came to be viewed as legal and were regularly taking place in British Columbia, Ontario, Quebec, Yukon, Manitoba, Nova Scotia, and Saskatchewan. See *EGALE Canada Inc. v Canada (Attorney General)* (2003) 225 DLR (4th) 472, 2003 BCCA 251; *Halpern v Canada (Attorney General)* (2003) 65 OR (3d) 161 (CA); *Hendricks v Quebec (Procureur General)* [2002] RJQ 2506 (SC); *Dunbar v Yukon* [2004] YJ No. 61 (QL), 2004 YKSC 54; *Vogel v Canada (Attorney General)* [2004] MJ No. 418 (QL) (QB); *Boutilier v Nova Scotia (Attorney General)* [2004] NSJ No. 357 (QL) (SC); *N.W. v Canada (Attorney General)*, [2004] SJ No. 669 (QL), 2004 SKQB 434. In each of those instances, the Attorney General of Canada conceded that the common law definition of marriage was inconsistent with s. 15(1) of the Charter and was not justifiable under s. 1, and publicly adopted the position that the opposite-sex requirement for marriage was unconstitutional.

wall.'[11] As the courts in both Canada and Colombia recognized, any legal system that accords same-sex couples virtually every right associated with opposite-sex marriage, short of the right to be legally recognized *as married*, violates the right of same-sex couples to the equal treatment and protection of the law. According to The Canadian Human Rights Commission, it amounts to endorsement of the notorious *separate but equal* doctrine.[12]

Many theorists who support constitutional review draw on legal history in the manner just described. Ronald Dworkin is perhaps the most famous example. Recall that Hercules must ensure that his interpretive theory *fits* legal history to some appreciable degree. He is not free to decide on the basis of what he, personally, thinks is morally best. This despite the fact that he is a judge of super-human capabilities and, let's assume, infallible moral insight. It's a consequence of Dworkin's theory that Hercules, and the judges who strive to emulate him, are sometimes constrained to render decisions they view as morally suboptimal. And this is because legal history shapes the understanding of the moral principles and values for which a legal system stands. It is these understandings that courts must respect in their decisions, not the personal moral views of judges.[13] Of course Dworkin also thought that Hercules would always discover, in his interpretive theory of law, a uniquely right understanding entailing a uniquely right answer to the relevant pivotal question. Only if he were able to do that, Dworkin surmised, could democratic legitimacy be maintained—even for Hercules. But one needn't share Dworkin's conviction that the law *always* succeeds in providing right understandings and answers in order to share his insight that it does so *often*, and that legal history serves as a significant constraint on judges in all cases, including those in which abstract constitutional rights are in play. Absent legal history, there might well be few if any right understandings and answers in such cases, and there might well be far too much discretion. But with legal history in the picture, this conclusion by no means follows.

Others who share this view that legal history serves to constrain discretion include common law constitutionalists such as David Strauss and myself. Both of us have developed theories according to which constitutional practice constrains but does not always eliminate discretionary choice on the part of judges. To be sure, our theories aim to show that the law does in fact sometimes provide the right answers the archetypal picture demands. And we are also at pains to stress that, even when this is not so, both legal practice and the particular words chosen by constitutional authors can significantly reduce the scope of a judge's discretion. As Strauss puts it: 'Even when the constitutional provisions are open-ended, as in the case of the [US] Religion Clauses, for example, having the text of the clauses as the shared starting point at least narrows the range of disagreement.'[14] Strauss is here pointing out that the particular words chosen for a constitutional right provision can narrow the range of possible disagreements

[11] See 'Colombia Says "I Do" to Gay Marriage', *the city paper*, 7 April 2017, https://thecitypaperbogota.com/news/colombia-says-yes-to-gay-marriage/10653 accessed 20 January 2019.

[12] Canadian Human Rights Commission, *Submission to the Standing Committee on Justice and Human Rights—Same Sex Marriages*, https://www.chrc-ccdp.gc.ca/eng/content/submission-standing-committee-justice-and-human-rights-same-sex-marriages accessed 20 January 2019.

[13] On the important role the dimension of fit plays in Dworkin's constitutional theory, see Wilfrid Waluchow, 'Constitutional Rights and the Possibility of Detached Constructive Interpretation' (2015) 9 *Problema: Anuario de Filosofía y Teoría del Derecho* 23–52.

[14] David Strauss, *The Living Constitution* (Oxford: Oxford University Press, 2010) 104.

over the associated moral value. For instance, in using the term *expression* instead of *speech,* the authors of the Colombian constitution ruled out many tricky questions with which US courts have had to grapple. They have not had to puzzle over whether expressive freedom encompasses more than the ability to express thoughts and feelings by articulate sounds. Burning a flag or a government document can be clearly expressive, even if no words are uttered.

So the words actually chosen can narrow the range of disagreement. But so too can precedent, and what I have elsewhere called a 'community's constitutional morality', or 'CCM'.[15] By this term I mean a morality attributable to the community and anchored in the moral commitments it makes by way of its constitutional practices. It is a morality developed largely in a case-by-case manner in constitutional review cases. Earlier cases decided under the relevant constitutional rights provision rule out certain understandings of the incorporated moral concept, ones that the words and the associated moral concepts might appear to have left open. As these cases are decided, specific, more detailed, understandings and doctrines emerge that provide further content to what would otherwise be significantly underdetermined provisions. Once same-sex couples were legally recognized as entitled to shared pension benefits, adoption of children, and so on, any questions there might have been regarding the constitutional recognition of same-sex marriages were answered. To deny the validity of same-sex marriage would almost certainly have violated the constitutional right of same-sex partners to equal protection and treatment in both Colombia and Canada.

So there are options other than *all* right answers, on the one hand, and *no* right answers, on the other. In at least some constitutional rights cases, the law rules out certain answers as incorrect but appears to leave us with a range of reasonable alternatives from which judges will have to choose. But this brings us back to our central question: can such discretionary choices, even from among a restricted range of options, be justified in a constitutional democracy? If so, how so? Are there special restrictions a judge must observe before her discretionary choice can be considered legitimate? It is to these questions that I would now like to turn.

III. The Epistemic Condition

As a matter of pure theory, constitutional charter cases can be divided into two categories. First there are those possibly rare cases where the law does in fact successfully determine a uniquely right answer. Let's call these *D* cases. Then there are those cases where this is not so. Here the law is *underdetermined,* that is, no constellation of law and fact entails one and only one answer to the relevant pivotal question. Call these *U* cases. The Canadian same-sex marriage reference case was arguably a *D* case, though there are no doubt some who would disagree. And there were almost certainly many *U* cases in the Canadian Charter's early days, when the constraining hand of

[15] See, e.g., Wilfrid Waluchow, *A Common Law Theory of Judicial Review: The Living Tree* (Cambridge: Cambridge University Press, 2007); Wilfrid Waluchow, 'Constitutional Morality and Bills of Rights', in Grant Huscroft (ed.), *Expounding the Constitution* (Cambridge: Cambridge University Press, 2008), 65–92.

precedent-setting case law was largely absent. It's important to observe that the existence of these two theoretical categories is of little, if any, genuine practical consequence when it comes to questions concerning the legitimacy of judicial discretion. This is because none of us, judges included, can normally say, with any degree of confidence, into which category any particular case falls. In almost all instances, a case does not come neatly labelled as either a *D* case or a *U* case. In practice, and leaving aside Dworkin's super judge Hercules, all we have is considerable uncertainty over which possibility actually obtains. More specifically, we usually have some mixture of the following five epistemic scenarios:

(1) Some people firmly believe that there *is* a uniquely right answer to the pivotal question of the case, and that it is X;
(2) Other people firmly believe that there *is* a uniquely right answer to the pivotal question of the case, but that it is Y;
(3) Some people firmly believe that there *must be* a uniquely right answer to the pivotal question of the case, but they're unsure whether it is X or Y, or some other, third answer, Z;
(4) Some people firmly believe that there is *no* uniquely right answer to the pivotal question of the case, only rival answers such as X, Y, or Z; and finally
(5) Some are just not sure which of the above four possibilities actually obtains—that is, they are unsure whether there is a right answer to the pivotal question of the case, or whether, if indeed there is such an answer, it is X or Y or Z.

I will refer to the fact that constitutional review cases typically combine some mixture of these five scenarios as the *epistemic condition*.

The epistemic condition is important to stress for a number of reasons, not least of which is the following. Setting aside those very rare cases in which the law provides an indisputably clear answer to the relevant pivotal question upon which all reasonable people can agree, constitutional review almost always takes place under conditions of significant uncertainty: there is insufficient reason to believe that what we have is a *U* case and insufficient reason to believe that what we have is a *D* case. In other words, we really don't know what kind of case we have—and whether, as a consequence, judges in deciding the case are creating new law, or instead applying pre-existing law. Given this important fact, it would be quite unreasonable to require that judges engage in different forms of reasoning in the two types of cases. That is, it would be unreasonable to require of them that they engage in one form of reasoning when they are faced with a *D* case and another, quite different form whenever they are called on to adjudicate a *U* case. Given significant uncertainty over the category into which any given case falls, judges can only reasonably be asked to employ one form of reasoning—a form that is appropriate in either scenario, and hence would be legitimate *regardless* of the category into which the case, theoretically, happens to fall. Put another way, judges should be required to employ the same type of reasoning in *all* controversial review cases, and independently of whether this reasoning results in law creation or successful law application. Given the epistemic condition under which they labour, judges must employ the same form of reasoning in all cases, regardless of the category into which, in a particular instance, their case could be seen to fall were we somehow able to rise above that condition and take the god's-eye point of view.

A second reason to stress the epistemic condition is that it arguably rules out what might otherwise seem to be a reasonable solution in contentious constitutional review cases: automatic deference to the legislature and its views about the meaning and import of the relevant constitutional principle or value. Suppose a citizen comes before a court arguing that his constitutional right to free expression has been violated by passage of a law banning hate speech. He firmly believes this to be so even though he acknowledges that other reasonable people—most notably the legislators who enacted the law—disagree with him. Now suppose that the court rejects this citizen's argument, not on its merits, but out of deference to the legislature. What could possibly warrant such a move? The only obvious answer is an argument that runs something like this:

> Since there is deep disagreement and uncertainty over the meaning of the rights provision and whether, as a consequence, the legislation in question violates it, democracy demands that we respect the legislature's choice from among the understandings of the right seemingly left open by the meaning of constitutional provision. Judges must therefore defer to the legislature's understanding and deny the citizen's claim.

How might a citizen respond to a dismissal of his claim based on such an argument? Would he not point out that the court has, in effect, simply ignored the epistemic condition and assumed that the controversial case is a *U* case in which the constitutional provision is, in fact, underdetermined? In other words, has the court not inferred from the fact that there is no *clear* answer to the pivotal question that there is no answer at all? In drawing this inference, the court would have effectively ruled out the possibility that the citizen's right to free expression has in fact been violated—that, disagreement and uncertainty notwithstanding, the citizen's case is in fact as the citizen firmly believes it to be: a *D* case in which the law is on his side. Yet uncertainty over whether a right has been violated does not entail that it hasn't because the case is a *U* case. On the contrary, it is quite possible that the case really is a *D* case in which a violation has actually occurred. And the court owes our citizen a full and fair hearing on whether or not this is so. A court, which routinely defers to the legislature in controversial cases, does a great injustice to citizens whose rights may in fact have been violated.

So given the epistemic condition, justice seems to require that citizens be given their day in court even when the violation of their constitutional rights is far from clear. In such cases, judges will have to weigh the citizen's arguments against those of the government, accepting the case for infringement only when the government's arguments are judged better, on the relevant standards of proof, than the citizen's. What the burden of proof is in such cases, and who is required to shoulder it, are questions that different jurisdictions can answer differently. Section 1 of the Canadian Charter, as interpreted in *Regina v Oakes*, incorporates a two-stage process of analysis.[16] What is widely known as the *Oakes* test, places the initial burden on a complainant to show,

[16] *R. v Oakes* [1986] 1 SCR 103.

on the balance of probabilities, that an infringement on her Charter right has occurred. In most cases this is easily demonstrated because the courts have in effect set the bar very low, owing to their very expansive understandings of Charter rights. In cases of free expression, for instance, any measure that in any way restricts one's ability to express oneself is likely to be viewed as an infringement on one's right to express oneself freely. The only question that remains is whether such an infringement can be justified. Most of the hard work is done at this second stage of the *Oakes* test where the government assumes the leading role. If the government wishes its rights-infringing measure to stand, it assumes the burden of showing, on the balance of probabilities, that the infringing law represents a 'reasonable limitation that can be demonstrably justified in a free and democratic society'.[17] There is no talk of certainties here, and no talk of a citizen's responsibility to demonstrate an unjustifiable infringement. For good reason, most notably the imposing power of the state leviathan, the decks are stacked against the government and in favour of the citizen. If anyone is given the benefit of the doubt, it's the citizen, a benefit that would be lost were deference automatically shown to the legislature in all controversial cases—cases that might in fact have right answers that favour the citizen's complainant.

So automatic deference in a controversial case is unwarranted, whether or not there is, in theory, a right answer to the relevant pivotal question concerning the violation of a constitutional right—that is, regardless of whether the case in question is a *U* case or a *D* case. If the government's claim is to be accepted, justification for doing so must be established. But now we come to the important question that must be faced: how is the judge to decide in such cases? In those exceedingly rare cases where constitutional law and practice provide indisputably right answers to the relevant pivotal questions, the judge's duty is obvious: apply the relevant major premise of the relevant BLS and decide accordingly. But none of the cases under consideration are, of course, of this nature. They are ones in which there are inevitably good, though not indisputable, reasons in favour of the citizen's case, and good, though not indisputable, reasons in favour of the government's. And the law fails to provide clear instructions on how they are to be balanced against one another.[18] So how is a judge to decide? Once again, it is of no use to continue to say, à la Dworkin, that the judge must find and apply the uniquely right answer. And once again, the reason is obvious. Given the nature of the case, it is far from clear that there *is* such an answer and what it might be assuming it does exist. There are good reasons to think it might be answer A (e.g. the government's case should win), good reasons to think it might be answer B (e.g. the citizen's case should win)—and perhaps good reason to think that neither answer is ruled out. So what is a judge to do under these circumstances? There appears to be but one possibility: she should use her best judgement and select an answer that can be reasonably defended, regardless of whether the case is a *U* case or a *D* case. What else could she

[17] Canadian Charter of Rights and Freedoms, Section 1.

[18] I am assuming, here, that this is so even after the legally prescribed steps for considering constitutional rights cases—such as those prescribed by the *Oakes* test—have been taken into consideration. There might, for example, be good, though not indisputable, reasons for thinking that the government's case for a justified limitation has been met—*and* good, though not indisputable, reasons for thinking that it has not.

do? But now the important question is this: how should that best judgement be exercised in such circumstances? It's to a brief consideration of that question that we now turn.

IV. Discretionary Judgement

Consider the following passage from *The Concept of Law*. In exercising discretionary judgment, Hart observed, judges are not:

> confined to the alternatives of blind, arbitrary choice, or 'mechanical' deduction from rules with predetermined meaning... Judicial decision, especially on matters of high constitutional import, often involves a choice between moral values, and not merely the application of some single outstanding moral principle; for it is folly to believe that where the meaning of the law is in doubt, morality always has a clear answer to offer. At this point judges may again make a choice which is neither arbitrary nor mechanical; and here often display characteristic judicial virtues, the special appropriateness of which to legal decision explains why some feel reluctant to call such judicial activity 'legislative'. These virtues are: impartiality and neutrality in surveying the alternatives; consideration for the interests of all who will be affected; and a concern to deploy some acceptable general principle as a reasoned basis for decision. No doubt because a plurality of such principles is always possible it cannot be *demonstrated* that a decision is uniquely correct: but it may be made acceptable as a reasoned product of informed, impartial choice. In all this we have the 'weighing' and 'balancing' characteristic of the effort to do justice between competing interests.[19]

Now consider the following statement, endorsed by well over 2,400 US law professors in their letter of 4 October 2018, urging the US Senate to reject the nomination of Brett Kavanaugh to the US Supreme Court:

> Judicial temperament is one of the most important qualities of a judge. As the Congressional Research Service explains, a judge requires 'a personality that is even-handed, unbiased, impartial, courteous yet firm, and dedicated to a process, not a result'.[20]

These two passages can serve as a useful starting point in our search for conditions under which the exercise of discretionary judgement in constitutional cases can be legitimate.

Such an exercise can be legitimate if it is:

(1) not arbitrary;
(2) impartial and neutral in surveying the alternatives;

[19] Hart (n. 6), 204–5.
[20] 'The Senate Should Not Confirm Kavanaugh', https://www.nytimes.com/interactive/2018/10/03/opinion/kavanaugh-law-professors-letter.html accessed 20 January 2019.

(3) one that gives equal consideration to the interests of all affected parties; and
(4) based on a general principle (or set of principles) that extends by its terms to cases beyond the one being decided.

To these we might add that it must be:

(5) based on sound reasoning (empirical and logical);
(6) offered from the point of view of the community's legal system and its CCM; and
(7) respectful of what Rawls calls the *duty of civility*.

And last, but by no means least, it must be:

(8) dedicated to process not result.

I can offer only a few, preliminary comments on these eight conditions, some of which are fairly uncontroversial and in little need of explanation. Condition 5 is more or less self-explanatory. In exercising judgement under conditions of uncertainty, judges should attempt to ensure (as all practical reasoners should) that their arguments are sound according to ordinary, accepted standards of reasoning applicable to the natural and social sciences, and to discourse and argumentation more broadly construed.

To say that a discretionary decision must not be arbitrary (condition 1) is essentially to say that it must be based on reasons. As Simon Blackburn notes in relation to the reasoned basis of morality: 'Perhaps there cannot be laws without a lawgiver. But Plato tells us that the ethical laws cannot be the arbitrary whims of personalized gods.'[21] In short, even the gods must have reasons for the norms they prescribe. The same is true of discretionary decisions by judges in constitutional review cases. If a choice is to be made between one understanding of a constitutional right and another, some reason must be found for that choice. It cannot be based on pure whim. But not any old reason will do, of course. Rendering a decision based on a coin flip is ruled out, arguably by conditions 2 and 4. But so too is a decision based on pure personal preference. The simple fact that the judge prefers understanding A over understanding B, or that A is to the advantage of the judge or others with whom she identifies, perhaps politically, is not an acceptable reason. Steven Burton sums up this point nicely when he writes:

> Ad hominem reasons ... are always excluded. Clear instances of opportunism occur, accordingly, when a judge acts for reasons of advantage to self, friends, or groups with which he or she identifies ...The reasons warranted by law as grounds for judicial decision are a subset of all otherwise relevant reasons consisting of those on which judges are authorized to act. They are justificatory reasons, not the ad hominem reasons that animate ordinary and transformative political contexts.[22]

[21] Simon Blackburn, *Ethics: A Very Short Introduction* (Oxford: Oxford University Press, 2009), 17.
[22] Steven J. Burton, *Judging in Good Faith* (Cambridge: Cambridge University Press, 1992), 156.

Burton's point extends to cases where the reason given is that the decision accords with the judge's own personal moral beliefs. Judges play a public role in which their decisions must be publicly justifiable. That is, they must be *justifiable* to those affected by those decisions.[23] And the sheer fact that one decision as opposed to another, accords with her own personal moral beliefs, or those of some group of persons, such as the members of a particular political party with whom the judge shares his political leanings, offers no such justification.

But of course the exclusions just listed are quite minimal and tell us very little about the range of acceptable reasons for judgement. This is largely because the realm of all possible reasons extends well beyond the range of reasons excluded by the considerations just mentioned. But fortunately, our list of conditions offers considerably more guidance.

Condition 4, that reasons be based on a general principle, demands that the factors considered in rendering the decision extend beyond the case in question. Faithful observance of this condition is one way to minimize the chances that *ad hominem* or purely partisan reasons are at play. If reason R is a good reason for a decision in circumstances C, then it is an equally good reason for that very same decision in any other similar case, real or hypothetical, in which circumstances C obtain.[24] Importantly, this includes cases in which I or those I personally care about are on the losing end of the deal. In other words, as Kant and Hare famously argued, a decision maker may accept a reason for decision only if she is willing to accept its implications for her own situation should she or anyone else she cares about be in a position to be adversely affected by that decision. As Kant put it, I must be prepared to will, as universal law that applies equally to me as well as all others, the maxim on which I act. This feature of reasoned judgement is one that Rawls seeks to capture when he introduces his famous *original position*, where each rational contractor is denied personal information upon the basis of which she might choose principles that work to her own personal advantage, or to the advantage of those with whom she shares a special bond of some kind. In thinking about how judges should decide hard, controversial constitutional rights cases, we might view judges as occupying a role analogous to Rawls' contractors. There would be differences, of course. Among the most important of these—the focus of condition 6—is that the facts to which judges have access include relevant facts of constitutional practice and history with which they must reconcile their decisions.

Complying with condition 4 also inclines one towards observance of conditions 2 and 3, that the decision maker be impartial and neutral in surveying the alternatives, and that she give equal consideration to the interests of all affected parties. Basing a decision on reasons that extend beyond the case at hand, and that apply to real or hypothetical situations where the judge is adversely affected, will help ensure

[23] In my view it is appropriate for judges to base their decisions on the moral beliefs and commitments of the community they serve, as revealed in that community's CCM. Of course in difficult cases judges will have to rely on contentious personal beliefs about what those moral beliefs and commitments happen to be. But such beliefs are different from the judge's own personal moral beliefs.

[24] The feature to which I am alluding is often called *universalizability.* The universalizability of moral reasons and judgements is a hallmark of several moral theories including those of Immanuel Kant and R. M. Hare. See, e.g., Immanuel Kant, *Groundwork of the Metaphysics of Morals* (multiple editions); R. H. Hare, *Freedom and Reason* (Oxford: Oxford University Press, 1963).

impartiality—more specifically, that her decision is even-handed, unbiased, and impartial.

Condition 6, that a discretionary decision be offered from the point of view of the community's legal system and its CCM, is one I touched on earlier and on which I elaborate at much greater length elsewhere.[25] Though made by individual judges, legal decisions, discretionary or otherwise, are undertaken in fulfilment of a public role, a role the archetypal image mentioned at the outset was, in part, meant to represent. Though faulty in several ways, the archetypal image does capture one important truth: judges are required to decide cases, not in terms of their own personal norms and commitments, but of those ascribable to the community they serve. It would be seriously wrong for a judge to ignore the latter in deciding a case, and to rely instead on his own personal moral beliefs. If his community, via its settled legal norms, fails to provide a clear major premise to a relevant BLS, it is nonetheless incumbent upon the judge to draw on other norms and commitments attributable to the community in providing one. Among the most fundamental of these commitments and norms are those established in that community's constitutional practices and the moral and legal commitments that practice establishes. This, I suggested above, helped justify the recognition of same-sex marriage in Canada and, I am led to believe, Colombia. A judge who, for moral or political reasons he personally thinks best, ignores his community's CCM steps beyond the limits of legitimacy. His discretionary decision, even if morally justified in the abstract and independently of the context in which it is made, fails the test of legitimacy for one whose role is to serve his community by enforcing its norms. Echoing Section 1 of Canada's Charter of Rights, it fails to be justifiable in a free and democratic society.

Condition 7, that the judge respect the duty of civility, in effect follows from the considerations just canvassed. As mentioned earlier in relation to the epistemic condition, and as Rawls repeatedly stressed in his later writings, reasonable people of good faith and integrity disagree deeply on many moral issues, including those around which constitutional rights cases revolve. And yet they realize that much of their life in common requires common standards for the governance of their conduct. Legislative choices create many of these common standards, and judicial decisions set out to implement and sometimes supplement them. But constitutional review cases are often ones in which some of these legislative choices are rejected. As noted earlier, in those exceptionally rare cases where everyone agrees that a constitutional rights provision has clearly and undeniably been violated by the legislature's choice, most of us would be comfortable with a court's decision to strike it down. It would simply be enforcing superior law. Questions of legitimacy arise only in those much more typical cases where the epistemic condition prevails and where judges are called on to exercise discretionary judgment in choosing among rival understandings of the relevant constitutional right. Condition 7 reminds judges that their decisions set common standards for our common life together. It reminds them that, in the face of reasonable pluralism

[25] See Waluchow, *The Living Tree* (n. 16); Waluchow, 'Constitutional Morality and Bills of Rights' (n. 16); Wilfred Waluchow, 'Normative Reasoning From a Point of View', in Ken Himma, Miodrag Jovanovich, & Bojan Spaıç (eds), *Unpacking Normativity: Conceptual, Normative and Descriptive Issues* (Oxford: Hart Publishing, 2018), 119–34.

and the epistemic condition, it is important that they base their decisions on reasons each of us can at least recognize as an acceptable, if not always fully embraced, basis for establishing a common standard. Though these will not always be reasons each of us will particularly like or think ideally best, they should nevertheless be reasons we can all at least recognize as acceptable under the conditions. In alluding to this fact, condition 7 invokes Rawls' notion of public reason and the ideal of reciprocity or civility it embodies. As Rawls puts it:

> Th[is] ideal ... expresses a willingness to listen to what others have to say and being ready to accept reasonable accommodations or alterations in one's own view. Public reason further asks of us that the balance of those values we hold to be reasonable in a particular case is a balance we sincerely think can be seen to be reasonable by others. Or failing this, we think the balance can be seen as at least not unreasonable in this sense: that those who oppose it can nevertheless understand how reasonable persons can affirm it. This preserves the ties of civic friendship and is consistent with the duty of civility. On some questions this may be the best we can do.[26]

To summarize, condition 7 demands that judges base their decisions on reasons that all others could accept as a reasonable basis for decision. As a result, it excludes reasons deeply tied to comprehensive ideologies and doctrines not all of us share, and that would be labelled by some as unreasonable. In Rawls' view, it excludes reliance on religious reasons and reasons stemming from controversial moral and political ideologies. To be sure, the surviving reasons are not necessarily ones everyone would prefer, even under ideal conditions of deliberation and choice. Nor are they reasons which every reasonable person in such circumstances would consider particularly strong, or ideally worthy of support but for the fact of reasonable pluralism and the need to come to some sort of mutually acceptable compromise. But they are reasons, as Rawls would have it, that such persons would all judge to be at the very least 'not unreasonable', in the sense that those who oppose them can at least understand how reasonable persons could affirm them in justifying an exercise of public power in the circumstances of reasonable pluralism and the epistemic condition.

This brings us to the eighth and final condition on our list. The requirement that judges be dedicated to process not result, returns us once again to the archetypal image of judging with which we began. Let's assume, for the moment, that the archetypal image accurately captures reality. That is, let's assume that the law somehow always provides judges with a clear major premise from which they could deduce a legally right answer to the relevant pivotal question in a constitutional rights case. Under these conditions, it would be fair to characterize judging as little more than the neutral, impartial derivation of the legally right result flowing from the relevant BLS. In this scenario, a judge's concern would be—or at least should be—to achieve the right result. Process might be important too, but her primary responsibility would be to ensure that she gets the right result for the case. But of course the archetypal image fails badly to capture the true nature of judging in virtually all constitutional rights cases.

[26] John Rawls, *Political Liberalism* (New York: Columbia University Press, 1993), 253.

In light of the uncertainty and deep disagreement surrounding such cases, we cannot reasonably ask our judges to get the right result. And this is because none of us can be sure, in any particular case, whether there actually is a right answer, or whether instead we are faced with a *U* case where the law is underdetermined. What we *can* ask of judges, however, is that they observe the right process of reasoning, a process meant to be captured, at least partially, by the eight conditions of legitimacy outlined and discussed in this paper. We can also ask that those chosen to judge our conduct and our laws display the judicial virtues embodied in those conditions, virtues so obviously lacking in (now) Supreme Court Justice, Brett Kavanaugh.[27] At his confirmation hearings, in which allegations of sexual assault were brought forward, Kavanaugh had this to say:

> This whole two-week effort has been a calculated and orchestrated political hit, fueled with apparent pent-up anger about President Trump and the 2016 election. Fear that has been unfairly stoked about my judicial record, revenge on behalf of the Clintons, and millions of dollars in money from outside left-wing opposition groups.
>
> This is a circus. The consequences will extend long past my nomination... And as we all know, in the United States political system of the early 2000s, what goes around comes around.[28]

Hardly the stuff of dispassionate, even-handed, and impartial deliberation. In describing his former acquaintance, Robert Post, former Dean of the Yale Law School, put the point this way:

> His performance is indelibly etched in the public mind. For as long as Kavanaugh sits on the court, he will remain a symbol of partisan anger, a haunting reminder that behind the smiling face of judicial benevolence lies the force of an urgent will to power. No one who felt the force of that anger could possibly believe that Kavanaugh might actually be a detached and impartial judge ... Kavanaugh will thus join the court as the black-robed embodiment of raw partisan power inconsistent with any ideal of an impartial judiciary. As the court moves to the right to accommodate Trump's appointments, Kavanaugh will inevitably become the focus of distrust and mobilization. His very presence will undermine the court's claim to legitimacy; it will damage the nation's commitment to the rule of law. It will be an American tragedy.[29]

That a person so obviously lacking in the judicial virtues embodied in our eight conditions could make it to the US Supreme Court is troubling. It only serves to strengthen

[27] Larry Solum has done much to highlight the importance of judicial virtues, both for the process of judging cases and for the process of choosing individuals who will engage that process i.e. judges. See, e.g., Larry Solum, The Virtues and Vices of a Judge: An Aristotelian Guide to Judicial Selection' (1987–1988) 61 South California Law Rev*iew* 1735.

[28] Brett Kavanaugh, 27 September 2007 (Senate Hearing transcript, courtesy of Bloomberg Government), https://www.washingtonpost.com/news/national/wp/2018/09/27/kavanaugh-hearing-transcript/?utm_term=.7bae3ab982cb accessed 20 January 2019.

[29] Robert Post, 'Brett Kavanaugh Cannot Have It Both Ways', *Politico Magazine*, 6 October 2018, https://www.politico.com/magazine/story/2018/10/06/kavanaugh-confirmation-temperament-yale-dean-221086 accessed 20 January 2019.

concerns about the American political system, and the rampant partisanship and tribalism that threatens to undermine its legitimacy, including the legitimacy of its Court and its decisions. One can only hope that such incidents will spark a renewed interest, among all those embrace the ideals of constitutional democracy, in ensuring that the men and women selected to sit in judgement of our conduct and our laws are not ones for whom securing the right partisan result counts more than honouring the right process.

3
Dialogic Constitutionalism in Defective Democracies

Roberto Gargarella

In what follows, I shall study the theory and practice of constitutional dialogue, in the context of defective democracies. I want to explore the meaning, scope, and limits of this practice, although—for the purposes of this paper—I shall basically limit my study to the working of the judicial branch.

In this paper, I shall first present the dialogic view that I take as a starting point; then I shall present some of the problems that seem to be affecting our constitutional democracies; and after this I shall reflect on the tasks that a committed judiciary could assume, in order to confront the existing social and institutional difficulties. Finally, I shall illustrate the previous analysis through different cases related to actions and omissions by the Colombian Constitutional Court.

I define 'constitutional dialogue' as an ongoing conversation that is developed by the different branches of government and the people, aimed at interpreting the constitution. Similarly, Bradley Bakker stated: 'constitutional dialogue encompasses the idea that different governmental branches and people interact in ways that shape the dominant views of constitutional interpretation over time'.[1]

By 'defective democracies' I mean certain political organizations that are usually affected by at least two significant difficulties, both related to a centennial history of inequality. The first difficulty concerns an institutional system that concentrates power (particularly, but not only, in the hands of the executive), expressing and reproducing, in that way, *political inequalities*.[2] This first difficulty, as we shall see, has generated democratic instability and the gradual erosion of the system of 'checks and balances'. The second difficulty concerns *socio-economic inequalities* that generate situations of domination, subordination, political violence, and social protests. The notion of defective democracies should be distinguished from the notion of 'wicked democracies' ('legal orders in which law is used as the instrument of an immoral political ideology')

[1] Bradley Bakker, 'Blogs as Constitutional Dialogue: Rethinking the Dialogic Promise' (2008) 63 New York University Annual Survey of American Law 215, 216; Gal Dor, 'Constitutional Dialogues in Action: Canadian and Israeli Experiences in Comparative Perspective' (2000) 11 Indiana International & Comparative Law Review 1, 17–18.

[2] Juan José Linz & Alfred Stepan, *The Breakdown of Democratic Regimes* (Baltimore: The John Hopkins University Press, 1978); Juan José Linz & Arturo Valenzuela, *The Failure of Presidential Democracy* (Baltimore: The John Hopkins University Press, 1994); Carlos Nino, 'Hyperpresidentialism and Constitutional Reform in Argentina', in Arendt Liphart and Carlos Waisman (eds), *Institutional Design in New Democracies* (New York: Westview Press, (1996).

Roberto Gargarella, *Dialogic Constitutionalism in Defective Democracies* In: *Constitutionalism*. Edited by: Alejandro Linares-Cantillo, Camilo Valdivieso-León, Santiago García-Jaramillo, Oxford University Press (2021).
DOI: 10.1093/oso/9780192896759.003.0004

which has been examined by David Dyzenhaus.[3] I believe that numerous modern democracies can be characterized as 'defective democracies,' but I shall still take most of my examples from the Latin American region. Also, I think that democracies may be deemed 'defective' for different reasons, although in this paper I shall mainly concentrate on the referred problems.

I. Constitutional Dialogue: Why and What?

Why does dialogue matter? Dialogue does not matter with regards to independent questions about the way in which it is developed (how is this dialogue carried out? between whom? why? etc.). Those of us who conceive of democracy as an ongoing dialogue between all those potentially affected,[4] value this practice because we see it as an expression of a decision-making process that takes our equal moral dignity seriously.[5]

There are other reasons that come in support of this approach. We value that this dialogic practice assumes that: none of us is in a privileged position (as a consequence of her knowledge, intelligence, social status, racial origin, etc.) for deciding in the name of the collective; that each person is the 'best judge' of his or her own interests; that we are all fallible and that a conversation with others may illuminate us regarding viewpoints we have not recognized or properly balanced; that a conversation with others may help us recognize errors we had not seen in our own positions; and that in such a way we may begin to empathize with the views and interests of others.

In my approach to constitutional dialogue I shall have in mind the ideal of a *deliberative conception of democracy*. Although there are different versions of what a deliberative democracy is, in this work I will define deliberative democracy in agreement with the basic features that I mentioned in previous paragraphs. Therefore, I will here assume that deliberative democracy is directly linked to the (Habermasian) ideal of an ongoing discussion about issues of public interest (or public morality) among all those potentially affected.[6] According to this definition, a proper deliberative democracy, that is to say one that is capable of creating impartial public decisions, is characterized by the presence of two fundamental features, namely (1) *social inclusion*; and (2) *public debate*. To state it differently, public decisions tend to lose impartiality or become unduly biased when certain individuals or groups of people become unjustifiably excluded from the debate (i.e. because of poverty or social marginalization); and also when those decisions are not preceded by a robust, wide-open process of collective discussion (i.e. because of the influence of money in politics and the public life in general). The same reasons that support dialogic democracy—as asummed in this paper—(iii) prevent democracy from interfering with issues of *private or self-regarding*

[3] David Dyzenhaus, *Hard Cases in Wicked Legal Systems* (Oxford: Oxford University Press, 2010), vii.

[4] Jurgen Habermas [1992] (1996), *Between Facts and Norms* (Original Faktizität und Geltung) (trans. W. Rehg, Cambridge, MA: MIT Press).

[5] Jeremy Waldron, *Law and Disagreement* (Oxford: Oxford University Press, 1999).

[6] Jurgen Habermas. *The Inclusion of the Other: Studies in Political Theory* (Cambridge, MA: The MIT Press, 1998); Jon Elster, 'The Market and the Forum: Three Varieties of Political Theory', in Jon Elster & Aanund Hylland (eds), *Foundations of Social Choice Theory* (Cambridge: Cambridge University Press, 1986), 104–32; Nino (n. 2).

morality, that is to say issues where no one else is affected.[7] When third parties are not affected, the matter is about individual autonomy, rather than collective self-government. And democracy has to be reserved to issues of public morality (as Carlos Nino would put it: it lacks epistemic capacities to intervene in matters of self-regarding morality). It is in this context, for those reasons, and with those limits, that I value dialogic justice. In other words, constitutional dialogue shall not be valued here, whatever its content, the reasons behind it, its scope, its motivations, or the actors that are involved in the conversation.

Within the framework of a deliberative democracy, I will advocate for a dialogic approach to constitutionalism where, as stated, the different branches of government and the people at large engage in a conversation with the aim of interpreting the actual implications of the fundamental constitutional values. This approach already says something regarding what a constitutional dialogue is, and what is not. In the end, not everything qualifies as a constitutional dialogue.

In my view, such conversation about the constitution includes basic considerations about who discusses it, about what they discuss, how they do it, and why they do it. I have explored these issues in other works, where I made reference to the importance of issues such as transparency, information, openness and the like. For that reason, I shall here limit myself to underline the following two points, which I find particularly relevant. First, constitutional dialogue should not be limited to a mere exchange amongst the branches, where 'We the People' are mere spectators of what public agents decide about issues of public interest. In addition, the idea of a constitutional dialogue is based on fundamental egalitarian considerations, which are incompatible with an institutional schema where one of the branches has, in fact, the 'last say'. This is the same in a dialogue within the family: the conversation does not qualify as an egalitarian, valuable dialogue, if the father can begin or end the conversation at will, with a blow on the table.

II. Defective Democracies and the Corrosion of Constitutional Dialogue

Herein, I want to highlight some problems that I consider distinctive of non-ideal, defective constitutional systems, which severely affect the functioning of a dialogic democracy. Although they all seem a result of basic inequalities, some of them are more related to the imperfect working of the institutional system, and some of them are more directly related to the injustices generated by the existing economic inequalities.

A. Political Exclusion, Economic Oppression, and Social Subordination

Latin America gained its independence after four centuries of a brutal colonization process that created extreme inequalities. Those extreme inequalities became reflected

[7] Carlos Nino, *The Ethics of Human Rights* (Oxford: Oxford University Press, 1991).

in all the different spheres of society—social, economic, political, and constitutional—and since then remained fundamentally in place: Latin America became and remained as the most unequal region in the world. Inequality (is the product of, and) has generated numerous social injustices, which are perceived as such.[8]

The presence of unjust inequalities—and their permanence—obviously affects the legitimacy of the democratic system, eroding its foundations. In most cases, the existing inequalities are not limited to a minority group, but rather extended to the majority of the population. Social injustices and social exclusion of the kind create a major problem for the law. When the law is created within a context characterized by social exclusion, it tends to bend in favour of the 'socially included' or the politically more powerful.

The consequences of inequality are multiple, and among them I would mention the *political exclusion* that it generates; the situations of *economic oppression* that it favours; and the states of *social subordination* that it promotes. In Latin America, during the colonial period extreme situations of inequality included, for example, the presence of slaves; the domination of aboriginal groups; the dominion of men over women; the deprivation of all political rights to the poor; etc. After independence, most countries in the region introduced some changes in the law and in their social organization, so as to address the worst aspect of those situations of oppression. The region moved from a situation of state oppression to one of *formal equality*.

By the mid-1850s most Latin American countries had effectively abolished slavery and titles of nobility. However, the struggle to establish legal equality was still not consolidated (i.e. women were still deprived of all their political rights; and indigenous minorities remained in the margins of society, usually living in extreme poverty). The 'social question' that was mostly unattended during the nineteenth century gained presence in the twentieth century, particularly after the world economic and political crisis that erupted in the first decades of the new century. Initially, Latin American countries took note of the demands of the urban workers. Only later did a majority of countries begin to take into consideration the demands of other marginalized groups, and women in particular.[9]

Undoubtedly, many of the reforms that were then adopted represented a significant improvement in the situation for women in Latin America. However, none of them managed to overcome the situation of social subordination created and enforced by the law over centuries, much less solve situations of brute social inequality that still

[8] Terry Karl, 'The Vicious Cycle of Inequality in Latin America', Working Paper 2002/177, http://citeseerx.ist.psu.edu/viewdoc/download?doi=10.1.1.565.1033&rep=rep1&type=pdf accessed on 20 June 2019 For Karl, Latin America is the most unequal region in the world. This acute inequality affects virtually all aspects of economic, social and political life; it is fundamental for explaining why the results of the past two decades of development have been so disappointing in this area of the world. Economic growth has been surprisingly low despite having embraced neoliberal economic models, which succeeded almost everywhere in cutting inflation to single digits, reducing budget deficits, and generally lowering public external debt during the 1990s ... As the region enters the 21st Century, more than a third of its citizens live in poverty, and nearly 80 million people suffer from extreme poverty, with incomes less than $1 a day ... Not surprisingly, in a region characterized by the most unequal distribution of income and assets in the world, most believe that their societies are fundamentally unjust.

[9] For instance, with regards to gender rights, a majority of countries in the region began to recognize equal voting rights for women by the mid twentieth century. Argentina did so in 1947; Brazil in 1934; Colombia

affects the vast majority of Latin American women (i.e. those concerning reproductive rights, unequal salaries, unequal access to work, etc.[10]

Only by the end of the twentieth century, through legal reforms, constitutional changes, and the signing of new international treaties, did Latin America begin to take note of the demands and rights of aboriginal groups, which had remained fundamentally ignored until then—they were the marginalized among the marginalized.[11] In spite of these legal advances, many serious difficulties remain. The United Nations Economic Commission for Latin America and the Caribbean ('CEPAL') stated that:

> after centuries of exclusion and denial, the 10% of the region's population that is of Indigenous origin, and another 30% of African origin, including black and mixed race people, continue to be treated like minorities, even when they are actually majorities in their own countries. Furthermore, throughout Latin America and the Caribbean, ethnicity tends to be synonymous with poverty.[12]

B. 'Democratic Dissonance'

The first institutional problem that I want to mention refers to tensions that exist between the extremely high democratic expectations and demands of the citizenry, which have continuously grown in recent decades ('overloading democracy'), and the limited democratic opportunities offered by our institutional system (which thus appears as a 'narrow jacket' that constrains, rather than channels the citizens' claims).

The 'high democratic expectations and demands' of the citizenry refer to what we could call *the fact of democracy*, this is to say the presently shared conviction that our voice must be considered for deciding those matters that significantly affect our

in 1954; Costa Rica in 1949; Ecuador in 1929; El Salvador in 1961; Nicaragua in 1955; Paraguay in 1961; Uruguay in 1932; and Venezuela in 1946: Paola Bergallo, *El género en el constitucionalismo latinoamericano contemporáneo. Tendencias y desafíos desde una perspectiva feminista* (Buenos Aires: *ILADD*, mimeo, 2013). Later on, some legal and constitutional reforms began to make explicit references to affirmative action programmes favouring substantive gender equality.

[10] See Paola Bergallo, Isabel Jaramillo Sierra, & Juan Marco Vaggione (eds), *El aborto en América Latina*, (Buenos Aires: Siglo XXI, 2018).

[11] Raquel Z. Yrigoyen Fajardo, 'El horizonte del constitucionalismo pluralista: del multiculturalismo a la descolonización', in César Rodríguez Garavito (ed.), *El derecho en América Latina. Un mapa para el pensamiento jurídico del siglo xxi* (Buenos Aires: Siglo xxi , 2011), 132. An important step favouring a more respectful legal approach to the matter was the enactment *Convenio 169*, which was enacted in 1989 by the International Labour Organization ('ILO'). The agreement included clauses guaranteeing respect for the culture, way of life, and institutions of the indigenous peoples. It also made reference to the right to effect consultation to these peoples, in the case of public legislation that directly affected those groups. Most of the constitutions that emerged after the enactment of the *Convenio 169* included complete lists of indigenous rights in their texts, and adopted views favourable to legal pluralism. Among these new constitutions, it is worth mentioning those of Colombia, 1991; Bolivia, 1994; Ecuador 1996 (and 1998), and Venezuela, 1999.

[12] https://www.cepal.org/cgi-bin/getProd.asp?xml=/prensa/noticias/comunicados/2/132/P132.xml accessed on 20 June 2019. ECLAC, 'Current Situation of Indigenous and Afro-American People in Laitn-America and the Caribbean'. Similarly, according to a recent report by the World Bank, indigenous peoples continue to be confronted with 'glass ceilings and structural barriers that limit their full social and economic inclusion': http://www.worldbank.org/en/region/lac/brief/indigenous-latin-america-in-the-twenty-first-century-brief-report-page accessed on 20 June 2019.

lives.[13] I think that the fact of democracy represents a distinctive feature of contemporary democracies, which explains the so-called 'democratic crises' or 'disenchantment' that seems typical of our time.[14] In the case of Latin American—one could claim—the tensions between citizens' expectations/demands and what the institutional system actually delivers, are higher than in other contexts, due to the significant and historical level of social mobilization and popular participation that has characterized the public life of the continent.[15]

The 'limited democratic opportunities' offered by the institutional system refer to the fact that the prevailing constitutional systems were designed at a time distinguished by a certain 'discomfort with democracy'—elitist assumptions that Roberto Unger characterized as the 'dirty little secret' of constitutionalism.[16] As a result of those assumptions, the institutional system that was then created organized a representative system that assumed representation as a first desired option, rather than as a 'necessary evil' or a 'second best'; showed a clear preference for internal or endogenous controls, rather than external or popular ones; and also established a 'hypertrophy of

[13] This claim about the 'fact of disagreement' is different from, although consistent with, what John Rawls named 'the fact of pluralism,' which would be distinctive of our time (John Rawls, *Political Liberalism* (New York: Columbia University Press, 1993)), or what Jeremy Waldron referred to, in a similar fashion, as 'the fact of disagreement' (Waldron (n. 5). Herein, I shall only presume the existence of this 'fact', but—I believe—its origins can be located far back in the past. One significant moment in that story appeared during the so-called 1848 democratic revolutions. Those revolutions symbolized the strong participatory demands and the widespread level of discontent that prevailed at the time concerning a situation of systematic political exclusion for the vast majority of the population. In Latin America, as some historians have put it, the 'old colonial order' became virtually disintegrated at the beginning of the twentieth century (Tulio Halperín Donghi, *Historia Contemporánea de América Latina* (Alianza: Buenos Aires, 2007). The breakdown of the old (political, economic, social) order was followed by the emergence of growing demands for political democracy—as had happened in Europe after 1848. From then to the present, in America as in Europe, the breakdown of the old order was followed by growing democratizing demands, which today are at a climax.

[14] The existing tensions between the 'overload of democratic demands' and an institutional system that is unable to satisfy most of those demands, have been the object of recurrent theoretical studies. Robert Dahl and Joseph Schumpeter examined those tensions during the early twentieth century: Robert Dahl, *A Preface to Democratic Theory* (Chicago: University of Chicago Press, 1956); Joseph Schumpeter, *Capitalism, Socialism and Democracy* (London: Harper Classics, 2008). At that time, the restriction of the participatory claims of the citizenry seemed the only possible solution to the existing democratic crisis. In the mid twentieth century, the well-known *Trilateral Report* produced by Michael Crozier, Samuel Huntington et al., returned to those early democratic concerns, and insisted on similar anti-democratic solutions: Michael Crozier, Samuel Huntington, & J. Watanuki, *The Crisis of Democracy: Report on the Governability of Democracies to the Trilateral Commission Paperback* (New York: New York University Press, 1975).

[15] Just to mention one indication of this state of dissatisfaction, I could quote the *Latinobarómetro Report*. According to the 2017 report, 'the decline of democracy is accentuated in 2017, with a systematic decline in the support and satisfaction of democracy, as well as the perception that governments rule only in favor of a few'. The report [also shows that regional] governments suffer the same fate: each year, Latin Americans approve them less': http://www.latinobarometro.org/latNewsShow.jsp accessed 20 June 2019. In a similar direction, see the numbers offered for Europe by Van Reybrouck, and his reference to what he called a 'syndrome of democratic fatigue': David Van Reybrouck, *Against Elections. The Case for Democracy* (London: Bodley Head, 2016).

[16] Roberto Unger, *What Should Legal Analysis Become?* (New York: Verso, 1996), 72.
For Unger, the 'secret' consists of a 'discomfort with democracy' that 'shows up in every area of contemporary legal culture: in the ceaseless identification of restraints upon majority rule, rather than of restraints upon the power of dominant minorities, as the overriding responsibility of judges of and jurists; in the consequent hypertrophy of countermajoritarian practices and arrangements; in the opposition to all institutional reforms, particularly those designed to heighten the level of popular political engagement, as threats

counter-majoritarian practices and arrangements'.[17] For our purposes, I should also highlight that the first goal of such system appeared to be that of 'preventing mutual oppressions', rather than favouring democratic deliberation of any kind.[18]

The goal of preventing 'mutual oppression' undoubtedly represents an important social good, but clearly not one that advocates of deliberative democracy would demand and celebrate. It is true that the prevention of mutual oppression may be deemed a pre-condition of dialogue, but the distance that exists between *preventing civil war and promoting dialogue* is too big to be ignored.[19]

C. Concentration of Powers and Hyper-Presidentialism: Violation of Rights, Political Instability, and an 'Unbalanced System of Checks and Balances'

Inequalities of all kind have favoured the concentration of (economic and political) powers in Latin America. Hyper-presidentialist systems have become, in such contexts, the main expression of political inequalities within the institutional system. According to Carlos Nino—who coined the concept—the idea of 'hyper-presidentialism' can be understood comparatively, particularly when we examine the faculties assigned to (and achieved by) the president in the constitutions of Latin America, vis-à-vis those that they were reserved for the position in the Constitution of the United States, which served as a model.[20] Nino alludes to, then, the (additional) powers granted to Latin American Presidents in matters such as the state of siege; federal intervention in the provinces (outside the American constitutional right); and the appointment and discretionary removal of ministers; or the legislative powers.[21]

To begin with, it seems clear that the concentration of powers can imply, and has actually implied, the suspension, suppression, or violation of rights. These violations of rights can derive from different circumstances, but in Latin America they have been frequently related—as we have already mentioned—to the strengthening of the

to a regime of rights ... in the single-minded focus upon the higher judges and their selection as the most important part of democratic politics.'

[17] Ibid., 72, 198;

[18] In fact, the 'logic' of the system of 'checks and balances' seems to still be that which James Madison defined in *Federalist Papers* n. 51, namely to prevent mutual oppressions by providing the members of the different branches of powers the 'constitutional means and personal motives to *resist* encroachments of the others'. The rationale behind the whole idea of 'checks and balances' was that 'the provision for *defense* must ... be made commensurate to the danger of *attack*' (James Madison, Federalist Paper 51. https://avalon.law.yale.edu/18th_century/fed51.asp accessed on 19 June 2019).

[19] Of course, I understand that many authors do not share this view and actually assume the opposite position to be right. For instance, in a recent article that is the consistent continuation of a long series of writings, Cass Sunstein has insisted on the deliberative structure of the system. The connection that he establishes between the original system of 'checks and balances' and public deliberation, is direct. He describes it as a 'complex system of checks' which includes 'national representation, bicameralism, indirect election, distribution of powers, and the federal-state relationship': Cass Sunstein, 'Lessons from the American Founding', in Cass Sunstein (ed.), *Can it Happen Here? Authoritarianism in America* (New York: Harper Collins, 2018), 72.

[20] Nino (n. 7), 524ff.

[21] Nino refers, in particular, to the partial enactment of laws, and to the extensive regulatory functions reserved for the President. These powers are added to the special powers reserved for the President in

executive's authority. States of siege; states of internal commotion; states of emergency; states of exception; and federal intervention represent only some of the many ways in which political power has been accumulated in a few hands and rights have been consequently put under serious threat.[22]

In addition, the combination of a system of 'checks and balances' and a very strong executive power is problematic. In fact, the entire point of having a system of 'checks and balances' is ensuring the internal equilibrium between the branches, thus preventing mutual encroachments.[23] However, when we design a system of mutual controls between the branches, and at the same time make one of the branches more powerful than the others, we put into question—if not directly undermine—what we have done in the first place. The adoption of such a peculiar (unbalanced) system of 'checks and balances' has created numerous problems in the life of Latin American countries. Probably the most important one relates to the level of *political instability* that it helped to generate, and which has characterized Latin America's political life since the early twentieth century when the first military coups took place.[24]

Worse still, the 'unbalanced system of checks and balances' generated another crucial difficulty—the *gradual erosion of the division of powers*. The weakness of the system of 'internal controls' allowed the President to gain gradual control over Congress, and put the entire administrative bureaucracy under its discretional authority. In

jurisprudential developments (i.e. in favour of delegated legislative faculties), and doctrines such as those of 'nonjudiciable political issues'.

[22] The creation of these 'hyper-presidentialist' systems resulted from the compact between liberals and conservatives that had taken place in most countries in the region, by the mid nineteenth century, that is to say when Latin Americans defined the basic structure of their constitutional organizations. In what concerns the organization of powers, liberals advocated for the adoption of (something like) the US model, which was based on the idea of 'equilibriums'. Liberals pushed for the adoption of a system of 'checks and balances', like the one that characterized the US Constitution, which promised a political life with 'neither anarchy nor tyranny'. Conservatives distrusted that model. They instead favoured the model of concentrated political authority and centralized territorial organization, which they had come to know through the European monarchies. In order to overcome their differences, most countries finally adopted a 'system of checks and balances', where one of the branches—obviously the executive, according to the conservatives' demands—had the powers necessary to prevail over the rest. They shaped, in the end, what we could call an 'unbalanced system of checks and balances'.

[23] As James Madison put it in *Federalist Papers* n. 51: 'the great security against a gradual concentration of the several powers in the same department, consists in giving to those who administer each department the necessary constitutional means and personal motives to resist encroachments of the others. The provision for defense must in this, as in all other cases, be made commensurate to the danger of attack. Ambition must be made to counteract ambition. The interest of the man must be connected with the constitutional rights of the place.'

[24] In effect, during the early 1980s, most academics seemed to agree on the existence of a strong connection between so-called hyper-presidentialism and democratic breakdown. Some years later, however, numerous academics began to challenge what had seemed to be 'revealed truths' of the anti-presidentialist movement. In particular, many of them challenged the alleged link between hyper-presidentialism and democratic instability. Some of these new studies maintained that the then common assertions that presidentialism tended to suffer cyclical crisis that provoked the breakdown of democracy were not empirically sound (i.e. Matthew Shugart & John M. Carey, *Presidents and Assemblies, Constitutional Design and Electoral Dynamics* (Cambridge: Cambridge University Press, 1992)); or that the real causes of the instability of presidentialism resided in some other place (see Matthew Shugart & Scott Mainwaring, 'Presidentialism and Democracy in Latin America: Rethinking the Tems of the Debate', in Matthew Shugart & Scott Mainwaring (eds), *Presidentialism and Democracy in Latin America* (Cambridge: Cambridge University Press, 1997)); discussing some of this literature see, e.g., M. Alegre, 'Democracy without Presidents', 2009, http://www.law.yale.edu/documents/pdf/Democracy_without_Presidents.pdf accessed 20 June 2019.

addition—something of particular importance for the purposes of this text—in contexts marked by the concentration of economic and political powers, we must be prepared to have judges who work under the persistent pressures of powerful economic and political actors (typically, the executive), and become gradually deferent to those demands.

D. Social Rights and the Problem of the 'Engine Room of the Constitution'

There are at least two elements that are worth considering in what concerns the status of social rights in Latin American constitutionalism. On the one hand, Latin America continues to be the most unequal region in the world, and not surprisingly, in it, elemental social rights are systematically and massively violated every day. On the other hand, Latin American constitutions are filled with social, economic, human, cultural, and multicultural rights, like no other constitutions in the world. Regional constitutions have been the first in the world to adopt a long list of social and economic rights, and are also the ones that continue being the most generous in this respect.[25] The fact is, unfortunately, that social rights are systematically unenforced, and institutional systems show severe difficulty in ensuring the implementation of those rights. These situations of systematic breach of the law create additional problems for constitutionalism: they affect the legitimacy of the system and favour a loss of collective faith in it.

In previous writings, I maintained that those problems originate, at least in part, on an erroneous understanding of constitutionalism. The fact is that, since the beginning of the twentieth century, Latin Americans introduced drastic changes in their organization of rights (they began to introduce more and more social rights in their constitutional texts), but they did not change their organization of powers accordingly. As a result, Latin American constitutions exhibit very 'progressive' declarations of rights, and at the same time very old-fashioned (eighteenth century-style) organizations of powers, which are still characterized by an accentuated concentration of powers. In several works I have dealt with this problem, which I call the problem of the *engine room* of the new constitutions, which consists in the introduction of radical changes in the area of rights, while preserving, basically untouched, the old structure of powers. As I have tried to demonstrate in other work, this institutional framework tends to be fatal for the enforcement or actual life of the 'new rights': those progressive rights thus appear entirely dependent on the discretionary will of the few (and particularly the will of the President) that are (is) in control of political power.[26]

[25] As we know, since the enactment of the Mexican 1917 constitutions, which was the first in the world to include social, economic, and cultural rights in its constitution, most Latin American countries began to incorporate long lists of social, economic, and cultural rights into their constitutions—which allows us to refer to Latin America's 'obsession with constitutional rights'.

[26] Roberto Gargarella, *Latin American Constitutionalism* (Oxford, Oxford University Press, 2013)

E. Moral Perfectionism

Political conservatism has frequently combined with moral perfectionism. By moral perfectionism I understand the view that maintains (1) that there are certain objective or correct moral values; and (2) that state authorities have to use the coercive powers at their disposal in order to enforce those objectively defensible moral values. In the case of Latin America, political conservatism and moral perfectionism have frequently combined in the context of conservative governments, democratic governments, and more frequently authoritarian regimes. This kind of authoritarianism was particularly common during the nineteenth century, and could be described as the legacy of the colonial period—the time of 'the cross and the sword', which actually expressed the enduring alliance between the Army and the Church. Usually, this type of political conservatism also found expression in the constitution. In fact, in the initial decades after independence, most conservative regimes created new constitutions or modified the existing ones, so as to enact a new kind of constitution that defined the organization of powers according to politically elitist assumptions, and organized the declaration of rights according to the morally perfectionist demands of the Church. By the end of the nineteenth century, and the beginning of the twentieth century, most of those constitutions had disappeared, but the legacies of conservatism remained. At the present moment, Latin America's political life continues to oscillate between liberal and conservative initiatives, which implies that, once again, public authorities (political or judicial) try to enforce or implement morally perfectionist policies, including the criminalization of purely private behaviour; the ban or prosecution of homosexuality; and extremely conservative policies in matters of reproductive health.

F. Political and Social Violence

The existence of unjust inequalities (and their byproducts, namely situations of political domination; social oppression; economic discrimination; etc.) has been one main (but not exclusive) reason behind frequents outbreaks of political and social violence. Political violence was a common phenomenon after independence, when opposing political forces disagreed about how to reorganize the new societies in the face of existing social injustices. The first half of the nineteenth century was the scene of numerous civil wars, and recurrent confrontations between opposing factions. By the mid nineteenth-century, and following the wave of the 'democratic revolutions' in Europe, new explosions of civil discontent appeared in Chile, Peru, and Colombia. At the beginning of the new century, with the world's economic crisis (that implied, in Latin America, the definite crises of the authoritarian model of 'order and progress' that had prevailed since the 1880s) a new wave of socio-political violence emerged in most of the region's countries, beginning with the Mexican 1910 revolution.[27] Undoubtedly, however, the most significant and influential outburst of political

[27] Eric Hobsbawm (1995) *Age of Extremes* (London. Little, Brown and Co.); Eric Hobsbawm (1998) La *era del Imperio, 1875*-1914 (Buenos Aires: Grijalbo Mondadori); Allan Angell (1994) 'The left in Latin America since c. 1920', en L. Bethell (ed.), *The Cambridge History of Latin America*, vol. 6, part 2, 163–233.

violence in the region appeared in the mid-1960s, with the Cuban Revolution and the numerous politically violent outbreaks that followed suit, including the revolution led by the Sandinista National Liberation Front ('FSLN'), which put an end to Antonio Somoza's dictatorship in 1979.

On a different note, I should make reference to the history of social protests that also distinguished the political life of Latin America. During the twentieth century, many of those protests were led by powerful trade unions, which had grown enormously during the middle of the century, following the period of import-substitution that took place during the years of World War II, particularly in countries like Argentina and Mexico. Notably, however, social protests were not extinguished after the period of economic adjustments, privatization, and de-industrialization that became common in the entire region during the 1990s, and which ended with unprecedented levels of unemployment. Trained in the defence of their rights during the trade-unions period, numerous workers, now unemployed, still organized themselves and protested against the prevalence of *neoliberal* economic programs. The protests included those that exploded in 2001 in Argentina promoted by the *piqueteros* (usually unemployed people who blocked the national roads to call public attention to their demands); the consistent and powerful protests in defence of their right to land, promoted by the movement of the *Sim Terra* ('MST') in Brazil; the 'wars' for 'water and gas in Bolivia during 2000 and 2005; the 'invasions' produced in Peru; the taking of both private and public land that was carried out in Chile; the protests of the young students—*pingüinos*—in Chile; the fights lead by the *mapuches* in the Patagonia of Argentina and in the south of Chile in defence of indigenous rights; the numerous environmental disputes, particularly against mining companies, which appeared in the entire region in the last decades; etc.[28]

In the end, social violence would need a different remedy, even though both political and social violence seemed to be related to massive poverty and unjustified inequalities. Poverty tends to generate social unrest, favouring on many occasions crime and the emergence of criminal organizations. Meanwhile, high inequality tends to favour violent crime. According to a recent (2018) report, Latin America is the world's most violent region: it includes only 8 per cent of the world's population, but accounts for 33 per cent of its homicides (which tend to be concentrated in just four countries, namely Brazil, Colombia, Mexico, and Venezuela. Latin America is also home of 17 out of 20 countries (and 43 of the 50 cities) in the world with the highest murder rates. The main causes behind these impressive numbers, according to this report, are inequality, unemployed young men, dislocated families, poor government services, and easily available firearms.[29] Through the many faces of social violence (criminal organizations, drug-traffickers, gangs, police forces that get involved in crime, etc.) Latin

[28] A recent study confirms the remarkable and surprising social support gained by most of these popular expressions, which included the occupation of land and blockading of roads (Germán Lodola (2011) Cultura política de la democracia en Argentina, 2010. Consolidación democrática en las Américas en tiempos difíciles,' LAPOP, Vanderbilt University).

[29] Amanda Erickson, Latin America is the world's most violent region. A new report investigates why, 25 April 2018, https://www.washingtonpost.com/news/worldviews/wp/2018/04/25/latin-america-is-the-worlds-most-violent-region-a-new-report-investigates-why/?utm_term=.d60be774170d, accessed 23 January 2019.

America remains not only the most unequal, but also the most insecure region in the world. Social violence provokes the corrosion of civic life and seems to be a critical factor in explaining an extended loss of faith in contemporary democracies.

III. Judicial Dialogue

In the following pages I shall examine the judiciary's potential contribution to the reparation or strengthening of our defective democracies, in agreement with the values of dialogic constitutionalism. But I shall do it with an initial warning: I do not think that the judicial system is well-prepared to favor that possible contribution. More precisely, I shall maintain that judges are not prevented to make that important contribution, but at the same time lack the proper incentives for assuming the desired role. In that respect—I will conclude—we should encourage judges to work in line with the goals of a deliberative democracy, even though we do not have reasons for believing that they will tend to do so.

A. Required, Possible, but Unlikely

The point is that judges not only lack incentives for engaging in a dialogic exercise, but also find more limits than opportunities to act in such a conversational way. They could opt for deciding according to what a dialogic theory requires, or not, but nothing in the institutional system induces them to make their decisions according to the principles and methods that a deliberative theory would demand. To begin with, the function of judges is not well-defined and the scope and limits of their mission remains unclear. When we say that judges have to 'guard the constitution' we say, on the one hand, *too little*, because judges need much more specific instructions, but also *too much*, because the constitution potentially compromises all relevant public issues. Things become much more complicated when we realize that we do not have (and will not have) widely shared interpretative formulas. By contrast, there are interpretative responses and interpretative theories of all kinds, which may allow judges to decide one way or the other, and always do so by invoking the support of the law. The question is, then: why would judges tie their own hands; intervene only in a limited range of cases; and decide in a 'narrow and shallow' way (say, according to the requirements of a dialogic theory)?[30] Why, if they could do just the opposite (decide about everything in a 'broad and deep' way) would they adopt the path of self-restriction if, by adopting the opposite path, they could expand their own powers, or increase their capacities to 'threaten' political authorities?

Maybe, at a time when many of their colleagues—in other tribunals, local and international—decide to explore dialogic (or other kind of) strategies, judges will find the motivation to imitate and follow the actions of their peers so as to share the prestige that may become attached to this or that other behaviour. At a certain point of time,

[30] Cass Sunstein *One Case at a Time* (Cambridge: Harvard University Press, 2001).

it may be fashionable to behave in one way or another. Also, at a moment when political and judicial institutions are seen as part of a distant elite, public officers may find it attractive to look for alternatives that allow them to regain some of the lost public respect. In certain contexts, dialogic alternatives became popular, among judges, as a strategy for recovering the popular legitimacy and consideration that they had lost on the way. Moreover, it may well happen, for example, that judges engage in a dialogic relationship with the political branches (i.e. by requiring Congress to assume or re-assume certain duties), but mostly as a way of eluding certain responsibilities, or avoiding the adoption of certain costly political decisions.

Judges do not want to incur reputational costs; they also do not want to pay political costs (lose the legitimacy they need to stabilize the decisions they produce); and—more significantly—they tend to fear formal and informal sanctions coming from the political branches. All these motivational elements are important for understanding their behaviour or predicting their reactions, but, again, none of them suggest that they will consistently engage in the desired conversational exercise. In the context of weak institutional systems judges may tend to act more prudently towards the current government (and more aggressively towards the coalition that left power) but that does not say much about their motivation to engage in a cooperative conversation with the political branches.[31]

In sum, it seems unreasonable to think that judges will limit themselves to act in the ways required by, say, a dialogic theory; or renounce to act in more expansive and non-conversational ways, whenever they wanted or found it necessary: they are not irrational. In the end, and taking into account the institutional powers typically assigned to high judicial positions, we could predict that judges will not stick to a dialogic or similar approach, even though they will be open to adopt it occasionally, probably out of convenience or as a result of a self-interested calculation (i.e. as a way to regain legitimacy).

B. What Could (Should) Judges do, in Favour of a Constitutional Dialogue?

In principle, by engaging in dialogue with the public or with the other branches, the judiciary may not only help to strengthen the collective dialogue in ways otherwise difficult to achieve, but also help to avoid the common and reasonable criticisms directed against its limited legitimacy.

Before going on with the study of judicial dialogue, let me try to say something more about what judicial dialogue is—particularly in the face of the disagreements we have in this respect.[32] Some authors, for example, began to use the language of judicial

[31] Gretchen Helmke, *Courts under Constraints* (Cambridge: Cambridge University Press, 2004).

[32] Actually, one of the main problems we face in the study of this topic is that authors seem to be using different definitions of what judicial dialogue is. For Canadians Peter Hogg and Allison Bushell—two authors who played a crucial role in the development of these studies—dialogue 'consists of those cases in which a judicial decision striking down a law on Charter grounds is followed by some action by the competent legislative body' (Peter W. Hogg & Allison A. Bushell, 'The Charter Dialogue Between Courts and Legislatures' (1997) 35 Osgoode Hall Law Journal 75). According to Rosalind Dixon 'dialogue theory … assumes that courts are entitled to intervene either coercively or communicatively (or, potentially, in both ways), where

dialogue and conversation to (re)describe exactly the type of judicial review that came to characterize US legal practice.[33] Others—including myself—want to use the idea of dialogue to refer to certain novelties or changes that have gradually appeared in our democracies in relation to the practice of judicial review. These novelties range from subtle changes in the attitude of our judges (more openness or sensitivity towards the opinions of the political branches) to the unprecedented organization of public hearings with representatives of social movements, non-governmental organizations ('NGOs'), and the government. In my view, we find a situation of dialogue when judges abandon their traditional approach to judicial review and—rather than simply upholding or invalidating legislation—openly engage with the political branches and/or the people at large in the task of constitutional interpretation.

The judiciary's possible contribution to the collective, democratic dialogue mainly derives from its peculiar institutional position. The judiciary's fundamental institutional mission is that of receiving complaints from all those who consider themselves improperly treated by the majoritarian decision-making process.[34] Judges are obliged to listen and take note of those complaints and give them a justified answer based on public reason.[35] In this sense, judges are situated in an exceptional position for integrating the views of the wronged—for giving due weight to the interests of those unduly displaced from the democratic arena.[36]

From their particularly relevant institutional place, judges may help improve the democratic system precisely in those aspects where our defective democratic system is more in need of help. Fortunately, and in spite of the lack of incentives they have for behaving in the desired way, judges have numerous means at their disposal, which may help us work in the direction of a dialogic democracy. Some of those means are constitutionally established and formally regulated. Many others are not institutionally established but may still be considered within the scope of their attributions—at least, within the scope of the attributions that a reasonable conception of the judicial

there are arguable failures of foresight, perspective, accommodation, or responsiveness. From a dialogic perspective, in particular, such intervention will be aimed at introducing new ideas, perspectives, or even equilibriums into the political process, all with a view to encouraging the legislature and the broader constitutional culture to reconsider its allegiance to the previous status quo' Rosalind Dixon, Creating dialogue about socioeconomic rights: Strong-form versus weak-form judicial review revisited I•CON, Volume 5, Number 3, 2007, 407.

[33] The most interesting case, in this respect, is that of Barry Friedman. See, e.g., Barry Friedman, 'Dialogue and Judicial Review' (1993) 91 Michigan Law Review 577..

[34] For Daniel Thompson, 'deliberative democracy does not exclude judicial review as a possible institutional arrangement, but it insists that there will often be reasonable disagreement about what liberties should be inviolable, and that even when there is agreement there will be reasonable dispute about their interpretation and how they should be weighed against other liberties': Daniel Thompson, 'Democratic Theory and Global Society' (1999) 7 Journal of Political Philosophy 112.

[35] This is to say reasons that everyone is reasonably capable of understanding and accepting (Rawls 1991).

[36] Sandra Liebenberg presented a similar, although not identical, approach. For her, 'Within a deliberative model of democracy, courts potentially play a valuable role in protecting the vital interests and values which human rights norms seek to protect. In addition, they seek to preserve the conditions for fair and equitable participation in decision-making processes through which human rights are given concrete effect': Sandra Liebenberg, 'Engaging the Paradoxes of the Universal and Particular in Human Rights Adjudication. The Possibilities and Pitfalls of 'meaningful Engagement' (2012) 12 African Human Rights Law Journal 11.

function and deliberative democracy may accept.[37] All the means and remedies that we will be considering are instruments that would allow judges to make an important contribution to constitutional dialogue, *without unduly intruding in areas that are of exclusive competence of the political branches* (i.e. the design of particular public policies).

Let me, in what follows, list some of the things judges could do, in order to favour the values of dialogic constitutionalism. I shall here assume that we need to rethink the constitutional duties of judges, in agreement with the teachings of history. I maintain, as Cass Sunstein put it, that constitutions should be understood as pre-commitment strategies, used to 'protect (society) against the most common problems in their usual political processes. Constitutions should therefore work against a nation's most threatening tendencies'.[38] The same goes—I submit—for judges: judges need to rethink their mission in agreement with the nation's most threatening tendencies.

Herein, I shall list a series of possible responses to the evils of a defective democracy that we have already revised. The list is not-exhaustive, and refers to actions that may be finally required of the different branches of powers, *according to their institutional position and democratic legitimacy*. I shall only focus on the possible intervention of the judicial branch, and, whenever possible, I illustrate my claims with judicial decisions and doctrinal opinions.

1. Democracy: democratic reconstruction

The first possibility that I want to explore refers to judicial actions directed at repairing situations of democratic failure that are eroding the legitimacy of our constitutional democracy. So far, we know about judges who work as guardians of the democratic procedure— for instance, in John Ely's process-oriented, representation-reinforcing approach to interpreting the constitution (more about this below). In addition, we know about proposals suggesting that judges use the powers at their disposal in order to confront situations of structural injustice, for example, in Owen Fiss' view about structural injunctions[39] (more about this below). Procedural approaches to judicial review ask judges to safeguard, rather than reconstruct, the democratic system. Meanwhile, structural injunctions are mainly directed at repairing the damages derived from the violation of rights. However, we have not yet properly studied proposals favouring *democratic reconstruction*. In this case, judges would use the means and remedies under their control in order to 'repair' or restore sections of our democratic organization that are no longer working in the required way. The idea would be to recuperate the damaged character of our constitutional democracies—in other words, make possible that the people at large recover their republican capacity to *directly decide and control what their agents do*—as Thomas Jefferson once proposed. Judges could, in this sense, and for example, require affected groups to be consulted directly

[37] Katie Young has explored and described different possible dialogic judicial responses, which she attributes to the South African Constitutional Court (Katharine G. Young, *Constituting Economic and Social Rights* (Oxford: Oxford University Press, 2012)).

[38] Cass Sunstein 'The Anticaste Principle' (1993) Chicago Unbound. University of Chicago Law School, https://chicagounbound.uchicago.edu/cgi/viewcontent.cgi?referer=https://www.google.com/&httpsredir=1&article=12206&context=journal_articles, 36, accessed 19 June 2019.

[39] Owen Fiss, *The Civil Rights Injunction* (Bloomington: Indiana University Press, 1978).

when their interests are seriously affected by relevant public decisions; or organize public hearings so as to ensure that affected groups participate in the elaboration of those programs addressing their fundamental interests. The remarkable series of public hearings summoned by Argentina's Supreme Court in the *Matanza-Riachuelo River Basin* case are, in principle, attractive in this respect. Initiated in 2004, the case involved damages stemming from the contamination of the Matanza-Riachuelo River, which affected millions of people. A typical example of structural reform, the case involved a massive violation of rights, and also numerous actors, with different levels of responsibility, including the national government; the province of Buenos Aires; the city of Buenos Aires, and 44 private companies that dumped hazardous waste into the river. The initial audiences organized by the Court seemed to be oriented in the right direction: the tribunal called for the participation of those directly affected and forced political authorities to present a suitable plan for addressing the contamination of the river. From the very beginning, however, the process showed its significant limits: private companies and disadvantaged groups were situated at an equal level in those audiences; and the most affected gradually lost control of the decision-making and decision-controlling process.

2. Deliberation: safeguarding the procedures of a deliberative democracy

Courts may make an important contribution to constitutional dialogue not only by actively promoting a conversation between political actors, as we shall see below, but also through more 'defensive' measures, oriented to safeguard the procedural (pre) conditions of democratic dialogue. John Ely popularized a similar view, arguing that the Supreme Court should interpret the constitution so as to reinforce democratic processes and popular self-government. In order to comply with this mission, judges would be first required, he claimed, to 'clear the channels of political change'.[40] Now, what could this notion of 'clearing the channels of political change' actually imply?

According to Ely, his 'participation-oriented' or 'representation-reinforcing' approach implied, first, a special protection for the rights of speech, press, assembly, petition, and political association, which are central to the functioning of a representative democracy. In other words, judges should examine all restrictions in the area (i.e. limitations imposed on political discourse) with the highest scrutiny, and presume that the political decision of the case is contrary to the constitution. The same goes for voting rights and cases of political 'gerrymandering' (which basically occurs when voting districts are redrawn to benefit one party over another during elections).

The problem that I see with this view is that it is based on a still narrow (pluralist) conception of democracy.[41] I would agree with it, but having in mind, instead, a deliberative understanding of democracy. As a consequence, the judges' mission would be that of safeguarding the procedural conditions of democracy, in ways where 'democracy' is read in agreement with a deliberative view. For instance, courts may require

[40] For Ely, the political process is 'malfunctioning'—in other words, 'the process is undeserving of trust', first, when 'the ins are choking off the channels of political change to ensure that they will stay in and the outs will stay out' (John Hart Ely, *Democracy and Distrust* (Cambridge: Harvard University Press, , 1980), p. 103).

[41] See also Sunstein (n. 38).

legislators to open the decision-making process to the public, in order to avoid or reduce the influence of interest groups; or require political authorities to call public hearings to supervise crucial aspects of the application of the law. More radically, the Court may scrutinize the legislative process, so as to ensure that the legislative debate is not merely a facade of a decision actually made by interest groups.

In recent years, some 'activist' courts seemed to have adopted an approach of this kind. For instance, scholars Scott and Macklem have studied and described the jurisprudence of the Indian Court, with particular focus on the 'continuing interplay' or conversation amongst the branches, stimulated by the Highest Court. For them, 'the Indian experience suggests that it may be appropriate to allow the judiciary to advocate certain solutions in order to prod the other branches into general debates and concrete responses that in the long run are more democratically legitimate and effective'.[42] I believe that, in certain occasions, the Indian Court went beyond the demands and limits suggested by a deliberative scheme, and assumed responsibilities that it should have left to the political branches. However, I still think that this Court is capable of offering us unique examples of how a tribunal that is committed to a deliberative view could decide.

3. Inclusion: expanding the political dialogue

Judges may contribute to collective dialogue by different means and in different ways. One crucial contribution would be that of expanding the political conversation, so as to ensure that the decision-making process does not remain encapsulated or under the exclusive control of the dominant political elites. For instance, the South African Court explored an interesting route of dialogic intervention, through what came to be called a process of 'meaningful engagement'. The Court first explored this alternative in the *Olivia Road* case, where the applicants challenged the municipality of Johannesburg's practice of evicting residents of so-called 'bad buildings' for health and safety reasons.[43] In a crucial passage of its decision, the Court stated:

> The City of Johannesburg and the applicants are required to engage with each other meaningfully and as soon as it is possible for them to do so, in an effort to resolve the differences and difficulties aired in this application in the light of the values of the Constitution, the constitutional and statutory duties of the municipality and the rights and duties of the citizens concerned.[44]

Through this decision, the Court showed that it could facilitate the resolution of situations of massive violations of rights, through means that honoured the dialogic

[42] Craig Scott & Patrick Macklem, 'Constitutional Ropes of Sand or Justiciable Guarantees? Social Rights in a New South African Constitution' (1992) 1 University of Pennsylvania Law Review 130.

[43] Lilian Chenwi, 'Democratizing the Socio-Economic Rights Enforcement Process', in Helena Alviar García, Karl Klare, & Lucy A. Williams, *Social and Economic Rights in Theory and Practice* (London: Routledge, 2015), 1851; Liebenberg (n. 36), 14; Sandra Liebenberg, 'Toward an Equality-Promoting Interpretation of Socio-Economic Rights in South Africa. Insights from the Egalitarian Liberal Tradition' (2015) 132 South African Law Journal, part 2, 411–37.

[44] Occupiers of 51 Olivia Road, Berea Township and 197 *Main Street Johannesburg v City of Johannesburg and Others* (24/07) [2008] ZACC 1; 2008 (3) SA 208 (CC) ; 2008 (5) BCLR 475 (CC) (19 February 2008), accessed on June 19, 2019 www.saflii.org/za/cases/ZACC/2008/1.html.

ideal. The alternative of the 'meaningful engagement' ensured that the affected community had a decisive voice in the decision-making process, which could not then be limited—as it usually was—to the wishes or interests of the ruling elite.[45]

In addition, judges could ensure that the process does not unjustly exclude the *voices* of disadvantaged minorities or affected groups, that is to say the voices of those who are usually unheard as a result of their situation of marginalization or social exclusion. More particularly, the judiciary could guarantee that the decision-making process does not ignore the viewpoints of potentially affected individual or groups occupying a socially disadvantaged position; and also that it does not exclude *arguments* that are worth considering for the sake of impartiality; or that it does not include arguments that are constitutionally impermissible. A good example of these possibilities appears in *Doctors for Life*, a case that was decided by the active and always creative South African Constitutional Court.[46]

In *Doctors for Life*, a doctors' organization brought a complaint to the Court, claiming that the National Council of Provinces ('NCOP'), 'in passing certain health bills, failed to invite written submissions and conduct public hearings on these Bills as required by its duty to facilitate public involvement in its legislative processes and those of its committees'. The Court was asked to reflect upon the constitutional obligation of legislators to facilitate public involvement in its legislative processes, and it said:

> In the overall scheme of our Constitution, the representative and participatory elements of our democracy should not be seen as being in tension with each other. They must be seen as mutually supportive. General elections, the foundation of representative democracy, would be meaningless without massive participation by the voters. The participation by the public on a continuous basis provides vitality to the functioning of representative democracy. It encourages citizens of the country to be actively involved in public affairs, identify themselves with the institutions of government and become familiar with the laws as they are made. It enhances the civic dignity of those who participate by enabling their voices to be heard and taken account of. It promotes a spirit of democratic and pluralistic accommodation calculated to produce laws that are likely to be widely accepted and effective in practice. It strengthens the legitimacy of legislation in the eyes of the people. Finally, because of its open and public character it acts as a counterweight to secret lobbying and influence peddling. Participatory democracy is of special importance to those who are relatively disempowered in a country like ours where great disparities of wealth and influence exist.

[45] Against this creative remedy, however, one should note that this initiative was undermined by the same Court the following year in the case *Joe Slovo*. (Surprisingly, in this case, namely *Joe Slovo*, the Court not only supported the eviction of the community's residents, but also did so in ways that undermined its previous statements in *Olivia Road* concerning 'meaningful engagement': the Court ordered the parties to engage in a process of 'meaningful engagement', but just with regard to the different aspects of the eviction and relocation process, which it took for granted.) This unexpected reversal of its own criteria reaffirmed what we have already suggested: courts have ample room for manoeuvre, which allows them to opt, basically at will, for creative and attractive alternatives, or do just the contrary.

[46] *Doctors for Life International v The Speaker of the National Assembly and Others* (CCT12/05) [2006] ZACC 11; 2006 (12) BCLR 1399 (CC); 2006 (6) SA 416 (CC) (17 August 2006).

This decision was interesting for different reasons, but particularly because of the centrality that some members of the tribunal attributed to the elements of *voice and discussion* in the decision-making process and, more specifically, for the importance that some of those judges attributed to the voices of the 'disempowered'.[47]

4. Authoritarianism: restoring the system of checks and balances

I have already made reference to the way in which Latin American constitutional systems, since the early nineteenth-century, have allowed the concentration of political authority to be held in the hands of a few, and erected controversial hyper-presidential systems. Hyper-presidentialism—I suggested—was in part responsible for some of the worst institutional evils affecting the region. To mention the two most important: the system of concentrated authority favoured political instability (and military coups), which generated the most serious violations of human rights of the twentieth century, and provoked the gradual erosion of the entire system of 'checks and balances'. As I mentioned above, the system of 'checks and balances', which seeks to balance the power of the different branches of government, seems logically inconsistent with having one of those branches assigned much more power than the rest. In such conditions, the entire schema of controls comes under threat: predictably, the most powerful branch will begin to use its threatening powers to thwart the will of the rest and impose its own authority. This is why judges need to work, not so much, or not only, towards *preserving* the system of 'checks and balances' or preventing its deterioration, but also for the *restoration* of the system.

History has taught us about the tremendous risks posed by the concentration of powers over democracy, and constitutionalism needs to be configured and reconfigured while acknowledging history. Therefore, in countries deeply damaged by the evils of hyper-presidentialism, they should definitely work against its worst consequences and, more generally, work for preventing the expected, recurrent emergence of such risks.

Fortunately, we may find numerous examples of courts properly fulfilling their accountability function in the context of new democracies.[48] Not surprisingly, however, and given the potential importance of their accountability function, courts tend to be the first institutional victims in systems defined by the presence of hyper-powerful presidents.

[47] As Justice Sachs put it: 'A vibrant democracy has a qualitative and not just a quantitative dimension ... Dialogue and deliberation goes hand in hand. This is part of the tolerance and civility that characterize the respect for diversity the Constitution demands ... Indeed, public involvement may be of special importance for those whose strongly-held views have to cede to majority opinion in the legislature. Minority groups should feel that even if their concerns are not strongly represented, they continue to be part of the body politic with the full civic dignity that goes with citizenship in a constitutional democracy. Public involvement will also be of particular significance for members of groups that have been the victims of processes of historical silencing. It is constitutive of their dignity as citizens today that they not only have a chance to speak, but also enjoy the assurance they will be listened to. This would be of special relevance for those who may feel politically disadvantaged at present because they lack higher education, access to resources and strong political connections. Public involvement accordingly strengthens rather than undermines formal democracy, by responding to and negating some of its functional deficits.'

[48] Siri Gloppen et al. (eds), *Democratization and the Judiciary. The Accountability Function of Courts in New Democracies* (London: Frank Cass, 2003).

5. Social rights: the material preconditions of democracy

Usually, in contexts of profound social injustice, we find situations of massive—rather than isolated or occasional—violations of rights. In Latin America, these massive violations of rights dramatically contrast with constitutional documents that are extremely generous in what concerns the—economic, social, cultural, or multicultural—rights that they explicitly recognize as fundamental interests.

Surprisingly or not, and until quite recently, judges did not tend to see most of those rights—social and economic rights in particular—as enforceable rights. Judges insisted on this restrictive approach, in spite of the massive number of fundamental rights that were affected; the long list of rights incorporated in most Latin American constitutions; or the consistency of this Latin American commitment towards social and economic rights (in every new reform, Latin American constitutions always expanded, rather than reduced, the list of recognized rights). The reasons they offered in their support were different, but usually very poor. Judges usually alleged that socio-economic rights (in contrast with individual rights) were too costly; that their satisfaction required active actions, rather than mere inactions or omissions from state authorities; that they had no democratic legitimacy for enforcing those rights; or that they had no control over the budget; etc.

Contrary to these views, judges could and should adopt a different approach to fundamental rights so as to avoid new violations of rights and allow vast sectors of the population to gain democratic agency. More precisely, they should understand that the mission of safeguarding the conditions of democracy also includes the protection of the *material preconditions* of democracy.

In recent years, different courts around the world offered examples about how judges could fulfil this important, delicate, and difficult task. For instance, in the case of *Mariela Viceconte v Ministry of Health and Social Welfare*, an Argentinean court held that the government had to produce and provide a particular vaccine—'Candid 1'—that had been shown to be effective against the hemorrhagic fever. This was an illness that threatened the lives of more than three million people who lacked access to preventive medical services. More interestingly still, in South Africa the Constitutional Court decided the *Treatment Action Campaign* (TAC) case[49] in the midst of an HIV/AIDS epidemic with more than six million people infected. The Court ordered the South African government to make an anti-retroviral drug, Nevirapine—which offered the potential of preventing the infection of thousands of children per year—available to infected mothers giving birth in state institutions. In addition, the Court ordered the government to present a plan explaining how it would extend provision of the medication to its birthing facilities countrywide.

6. Moral perfectionism

According to the dialogic view that I have here defended, each person is and should be considered sovereign in what concerns his or her own personal life; neither legislators nor judges should interfere with those basic, personal choices. An occasional majority, or the dominant political coalition, should not transform perfectionist principles into

[49] *Minister of Health and Others v Treatment Action Campaign and Others (No. 2)* (CCT8/02) [2002] ZACC 15; 2002 (5) SA 721; 2002 (10) BCLR 1033 (5 July 2002).

legal norms, and judges should not decide their cases in ways that implied the imposition of a comprehensive view upon individuals. For similar reasons, the political branches should prevent the judiciary from enforcing a particular morality. In the end, in a pluralist democracy nobody should deprive individuals of the right they have to live their personal lives in the way they want.

We find an example of political perfectionism, for instance, in an initiative adopted in the state of Colorado in 1992, when the community decided to prevent the adoption of legislative, executive, or judicial action that recognized homosexuals or bisexuals as a protected class. The case is particularly interesting given that it was not the legislature that pushed for the adoption of this perfectionist legislation. Rather, the legislative change was the product of a majority decision: voters promoted the amendment of the state's constitution through a popular initiative. The judicial response in the face of that political decision was appropriate: in *Romer v Evans*,[50] the majority of the Supreme Court stated that the amendment lacked 'a rational relationship to legitimate state interests'. Delivering the opinion of the majority of the Court, Justice Anthony Kennedy affirmed a principle of legal *neutrality* (see below). He stated: 'One century ago, the first Justice Harlan admonished this Court that the Constitution "neither knows nor tolerates classes among citizens." Unheeded then, those words now are understood to state a commitment to the law's neutrality where the rights of persons are at stake. The Equal Protection Clause enforces this principle and today requires us to hold invalid [Amendment 2].' From the perspective that is here defended, the Court's view was right in recognizing that 'the people' had no right to impose its own views about how to live a good life on any other person or group—not even through a plebiscite (as anticipated, the fact that the majority's decision was based on a plebiscite gives this decision even more significance.

Of course, the line that divides issues of self-regarding morality and issues of public morality is thin, and on some occasions obscure. Given the importance that this distinction has in order to define the division of labour between courts and legislatures, the lack of 'clear frontiers' between the two realms is worrying. This situation creates a problem for our view (one that puts a special emphasis on the distinction between the 'private' and the 'public' spheres). However,—it should be admitted—it also creates a problem for all alternative views. We would neewd to know whether 'the people at large' or the legislature are authorized to enforce their own moral views or not; when and for what reasons; or how to prevent decisions such as that of *Bowers*. The dialogical model, in addition, takes part of its force from those ambiguities: its basic claim is that the different branches and the people have to work together in defining the precise demands of the constitution through an endless, ongoing, open, and collective conversation.

7. Oppression/exclusion: the anticaste principle and structural reparations

Contexts of economic oppression and social subordination may end up creating 'castes' or groups of people living under the dominion of others. In such contexts,

[50] 517 US 620 (1996).

judges may take as one of their main missions that of preventing oppression and terminating with those grave injustices. Cass Sunstein aptly defined this potential mission through what he named an *anticaste principle*. In his words:

> The anticaste principle forbids social and legal practices from translating highly visible and morally irrelevant differences into systemic social disadvantage, unless there is a very good reason for society to do so. On this view, a special problem of inequality arises when members of a group suffer from a range of disadvantages because of a group-based characteristic that is both visible for all to see and irrelevant from a moral point of view.[51]

In the same way that courts should work for the elimination of oppressive situations, they should do their best to eliminate the structural causes and consequences of social exclusion and marginalization. As already suggested, courts could issue orders to manage, and even reform, institutions such as prisons or hospitals in ways that allowed them to work according to the mandates of the law. Owen Fiss studied these particular remedies, which he called 'structural injuctions', and explained how they could help to address and eventually challenge or overcome historical situations of unjust inequality. The rationale behind his structural proposal can be seen in an example like this: different police officers may be sanctioned at different times for their racist behaviour, but none of those sanctions would be sufficient or efficient to address the structural problem that is present—the structural problem that finally explains why, again and again, police officers engage in racist behaviour. Such situations of pervasive and long-standing injustice call for the adoption of more structural measures.[52] One possible illustration of this approach is a series of orders issued by the Indian Court on 28 November 2001, through which the tribunal directed all state governments to provide cooled midday meals for all children in government financed schools, even defining the minimum quantities of calories and protein that should be in the diet provided.[53] In that way, the Indian Court tried to address a structural situation of injustice, which implied the marginalization of vast sectors of the population.

[51] Sunstein (n. 38), 2411–12. In terms of the reasoning that judges could develop in these situations, we find an interesting illustration in *People's Union for Democratic Rights v India* [1983] 1 SCR 456, which the Court of India resolved according to the norms banning forced labour. The Court interpreted the existing norms as including a positive duty to avoid and also to alleviate 'the compulsion of economic circumstances,' and extended that duty to both state and private actors. For the Court, there was no reason that justified reading the word 'forced' in a 'narrow and restricted manner so as to be confined only to physical or legal force'. By contrast—it claimed—'[a]ny factor which deprives a person of a choice of alternative and compels him to adopt one particular course of action may properly be regarded as "force"... Where a person is suffering from hunger or starvation ... he would have no choice but to accept any work that comes his way, even if the remuneration offered to him is less than the minimum wage.'

[52] Fiss (n. 39); Owen Fiss, *The Law as It Could Be* (New York: New York University Press, 2003).

[53] R. Sudarshan, 'Courts and Social Transformation in India', in Roberto Gargarella, Pilar Domingo, & Theunis Roux (eds), *Courts and Social Transformation in New Democracies* (Aldershot: Ashgate, 2006), 159. See also, e.g., *People's Union for Civil Liberties v Union of India*.

8. Protests: the expressive component of social protests

For the truly disadvantaged in Latin America, social protests have become the main means for demanding the end of grave violations of fundamental rights.[54] This situation says something troublesome about the state of our constitutional democracies: on the one hand, it reveals the presence of serious and extended situations of violation of constitutional rights, and on the other hand it suggests the lack of adequate institutional channels. In other words, the victims of grave violations of constitutional rights are confronted with significant difficulties in democratically expressing their demands and complaints.

In the face of such situations, judges should start taking social protests more seriously, rather than simply treating them as unlawful or even non-democratic political responses. In contexts characterized by the lack of adequate institutional channels, people may go to the streets, unduly occupy public spaces (i.e. squares, public avenues) so as to make their demands audible. Rather than dismiss the protests as mere 'actions' that in one way or another defy the law, they should make an effort to preserve the *expressive component* of these actions, if that were possible.[55] The 'flag burning' cases, among others, have forced legal scholars to think along those lines.[56] These efforts to preserve the expressive component of the acts in question are consistent with recent proposals advanced by theorists of democracy who have opened up space for the consideration of the *illocutionary aspects* of non-verbal acts within a theory that emphasizes democratic deliberation.[57]

As the dissenting minority maintained in the case *Adderley v Florida*:[58]

> The right to petition for the redress of grievances has an ancient history and is not limited to writing a letter or sending a telegram to a congressman; it is not confined to appearing before the local city council, or writing letters to the President or Governor or Mayor. [Conventional] methods of petitioning may be, and often have been, shut off to large groups of our citizens. [Those] who do not circulate elaborate pamphlets may have only a more limited type of access to public officials. Their methods should not be condemned as tactics of obstruction and harassment as long as the assembly and petition are peaceable, as these were.[59]

[54] Roberto Gargarella y Ramiro Álvarez Ugarte, 'Freedom of expression and social protest' en J. González Bertomeu y R. Gargarella (eds), *Latin American Casebook: Courts, Rights and the Constitution* (Rutledge, 2016).

[55] In *NLRB v Fruit Packers*, 377 US 58, (1964), and examining the issue of picketing, Justice Black maintained that when the action of patrolling and that of speech were so intertwined, the court should 'weigh the circumstances' and 'appraise the substantiality of the reasons advanced' for the regulation of the activity of picketing (*NLRB v. Fruit Packers* (377 U.S. 58, 1964)., at 77–78). As M. Scott summarized his position, Black stated that: 'If information conveyed by the picketers is lawful, picketing to convey that information cannot be deemed unlawful.' See M. Scott, 'Picketing under the First Amendment' (1974) 26 Hastings Law Journal 167, 175.

[56] *Texas v Johnson*, 491 US 397 (1989); *Tinker v Des Moines Sch. Distr.*, 393 US 503 (1969).

[57] See Iris Marion Young, *Inclusion and Democracy* (New York: Oxford University Press, 2000), 45. See also J. Mansbridge, 'Deliberation Everywhere', 2005, unpublished manuscript presented for *IVR Conference*, Granada, Spain, 1–2.

[58] 385 US 39, (1966)).

[59] In *Brown v Louisiana*, 383 US 131 (1966), a similar case (although without Justice Brennan's vote), the minority group maintained the same position as in *Adderley*. In *Tinker v Des Moines*, 393 US 503, 1969, the

IV. Dialogic Constitutionalism in the Context of Defective Democracies. The Case of Colombia and its Constitutional Court

Having the dialogic ideal in mind, and also considering the problems that allow referring to many contemporary democracies as defective democracies, we can now begin to critically examine the workings of the Colombian Constitutional Court in its short history. Of course, my opinions should be taken as merely tentative and provisional.

I can anticipate that, in general, the balance seems pretty good from the particular standpoint that I have here adopted: the Colombian Constitutional Court has been exemplary in many of the initiatives that it has adopted, and in many of the decisions that it has produced. Since its creation, and with good reason, the Court has attracted the attention of the legal community, both at national and international levels. However, it is not clear that the tendencies that we can now see as prevalent within the Court are the most promising, according to our defined standards. Since 1991, the Court has (regularly) used certain opportunities to change its composition, and after so many years of work, some of the most attractive features of its jurisprudence seem to have weakened a little. In addition, as we shall see, the Court's many courageous, intelligent, and creative decisions are usually contrasted with other much less attractive and polemic decisions, in the same area. This situation calls our attention to some of the problems that were examined above. First, the constitution does not offer courts good incentives for developing their work in agreement with, say, dialogical principles. I understand that we may have different interpretations concerning how to define the precise content of those principles but, in the end, the problem transcends our adhesion or not to a certain specific understanding of democracy and constitutionalism: the problem seems different and more serious when courts are allowed to make decisions at their discretion without restraints, while certain interest groups or power structures, including a powerful executive and a traditional elite, exercise pressure in favour of specific decisions, and disadvantaged groups living in conditions of extreme inequality are not equipped with like means of influence. Having said this, let me now offer a very succinct picture of the Court's work.

The trajectory of the Court in its relationship with the executive seems quite revealing of the way in which the tribunal operates. In this area, and concerning very similar problems, we find both courageous and unduly deferent decisions on the part of the Court. Since its creation, in fact, the Court upheld the constitutionality of many norms that unduly expanded the executive's power, while it also managed to curtail the authority of the President at many different and significant

majority of the Court accepted part of the arguments of the minority (at least regarding a more expansive theory of the public forum), and claimed that the First Amendment permitted 'reasonable regulation of speech-connected activities in carefully restricted circumstances'. But, it added: 'we do not confine the permissible exercise of First Amendment rights to a telephone booth or the four corners of a pamphlet, or to supervised and ordained discussion in a school classroom' (at 513).

opportunities.[60] In particular, I should mention that the Court issued many decisions limiting the President's capacity to declare 'states of siege' or '*states of exceptions*'. Decision C-004 of 1992 was the first decision to control a declaration of a state of emergency. In 1994, the Court went a few steps further and invalidated President Gaviria's decree establishing a state of internal commotion. This was the first time in Colombia's history that a Colombian court had disallowed a President to use its emergency powers. The Court made a similar decision one year later.[61] Also, in Decision C-327 of 2003, the tribunal limited the President's chances of renewing an existing state of internal commotion, and later it invalidated legislation that enabled the President to grant general amnesties or individual pardons during a state of exception and regulated the cases in which the President could declare an emergency. Decisions of these kinds generated repeated tension between the Court and political power.[62] More significantly, in 2005 the Court approved a constitutional amendment that authorized President Alvaro Uribe's *re-election*, which was not allowed under the 1991 constitution. However, in 2010, the Court blocked President Uribe's bid for a third term by rejecting as unconstitutional a proposed referendum that would have asked voters whether to allow him to seek a new re-election. From the perspective that has been defended here, this courageous decision represents an important step forward in the defence of democracy. However, I understand that a proper approach to that case required, from the Court, a different theoretical approach: not its 'theory of the substitution' (which came to prevent the enactment of 'unconstitutional constitutional reforms'), but rather a theory favourable to the *dispersion of power*, to be applied in the face of recurrent attempts from those in power to self-expand its institutional capacities.

Among the novelties introduced by the Court, there is one that merits particular attention, and which the tribunal has repeatedly used in order to confront structural situations of violations of fundamental rights: the *unconstitutional state of affairs* or 'estado de cosas inconstitucional'. The unconstitutional state of affairs is somehow related to the structural injunction that was examined above. The Court may declare such a state in the face of grave and massive violations of rights, which are not attributable to a single authority, but rather the product of long-standing structural problems.

[60] For example, in Decision C-283 of 1995, the Court contributed to delimit the powers of Congress and the President regarding the preservation of public order, trying to preserve the autonomy and authority of the latter. Also, in Decision T-683 of 1999, the Court argued for the superior authority of the executive in issues concerning public order. In this way, it allowed the President to freely decide how to deal with an extremely difficult situation that involved a mass kidnapping in Cali (while the plaintiff wanted the Court to seek alternative solutions that the President was not willing to explore). And, in Decision C-048 of 2001, the Court validated a law that allowed the President to withdraw national armed forces from certain areas of the country, in order to facilitate the President's strategy regarded as the promotion of peace.

[61] See Decision C-300 of 1994; Decision C-466 of 1995.

[62] For instance, President Samper threatened to promote a constitutional reform in order to limit the Court's controlling powers, but reviewed his initiative after the Court moderated some of its initial criteria. See, for instance, Decision C-027 of 1996, which came after the assassination of a presidential candidate, Alvaro Gómez, and Samper's declaration of a state of 'internal commotion'. Taking into account the social impact of this dramatic event, the Court recognized, at least in part, the validity of the President's decision (Rodrigo Uprimny Yepes, 'The Constitutional Court and Control of Presidential Extraordinary Powers in Colombia', in Siri Gloppen, Roberto Gargarella, & Elin Skaar (eds) *Democratization and the Judiciary* (London, Frank Cass, 2003), 59).

In those cases, the Court may adopt 'structural' remedies, which do not only benefit the plaintiffs in an individual *tutela,* but also other persons who share the same situation. This doctrine was first advanced by the Court in its Decision T-153 of 28 April 1998, where the tribunal had the chance to examine the living conditions of inmates within national prisons.[63] More significantly, the Court declared an unconstitutional state of affairs in the case of the situation faced by the forcibly displaced population. Its responses in the case were not limited to the plaintiff, but instead referred to the entire displaced population in Colombia. In the words of Manuel Cepeda, former president of the Court, on that opportunity the Court 'issued orders for remedying the budgetary and administrative capacity shortfalls and established minimum mandatory levels of protection of [internally displaced population's] rights that were to be secured in an effective and timely fashion'.[64] From this perspective, initiatives such as those seem well-directed in order to begin confronting problems that are so entrenched that they require the cooperative effort of different sections of the government in order to deal with them. It should be noted, however, that these remarkable initiatives promoted by the Court were fundamentally directed at confronting grave situations of massive violations of rights, but not to help restore or radically strengthen the basic foundations of the democratic system. In fact in Colombia, more than in other countries, democratic politics has historically been affected by numerous factors, from severe political violence to radical inequality, narco-criminal activities, and the pressure of powerful elites. In the face of such extreme circumstances, the Court could have made a much more significant contribution to democracy. However, it did not. As we shall see, it did a decent job of fulfilling its *representation-reinforcing* function, but did not work in the same way in its *democratic-reconstructing* function.

The decisions that allowed the Court to gain increasing international attention were perhaps those produced in the area of social rights. The substance of many of these decisions, as well as the means employed by the Court, and the remedies that it used—which in many cases were carefully designed so as to respect dialogic principles—had extremely attractive results.[65] Among numerous significant decisions, the Court forced the government to develop a vaccination plan in order to grant children's health rights;[66] it ordered the provision of medicines to AIDs patients;[67] and forced a public institution to provide particular individuals expensive medical treatment.[68]

[63] On that opportunity, the Court decided to set in motion a collective process in which representatives coming from all the different affected parties were required to participate. The Court also established a period of four years for these actors to define and implement a solution to the problem. Libardo Ariza , 'La prisión ideal: intervención judicial y reforma del sistema penitenciario en Colombia', in Daniel Bonilla & Manuel A. Iturralde (eds), *Hacia un nuevo derecho constitucional* (Bogotá: Universidad de Los Andes, 2005). See also Manuel José Cepeda-Espinosa, 'How far may Colombia's Constitutional Court go to protect IDP rights?' (2005), https://www.fmreview.org/sites/fmr/files/FMRdownloads/en/brookings/cepedaespinosa.pdf. See further Decision T-590, related to the protection of human rights defenders.

[64] Cepeda-Espinosa (n. 63).

[65] For instance, through the *principle of connection* or 'principio de conexidad' the Court established that social and economic rights virtually acquire the character of fundamental rights and thus can be the object of judicial protection through *tutelas* when the violation or non-satisfaction of those rights puts fundamental rights under risk.

[66] See Decision SU-225 of 1998.

[67] See Decision T-484 of 1992.

[68] See, e.g., Decision T-516 of 2000 or Decision T-590 of 1999.

Moreover, in 2000 the Court declared that part of the national budget was unconstitutional because it did not contemplate an appropriate increase in public official's wages (a decision that was partially reviewed one year later).[69] More recently, through Decision T 760/8, the tribunal cooperated in the restructuring of the entire health system in Colombia. The decision, which appeared after intense judicialization in that area (more than 320,000 cases came to the judiciary between 1999 and 2005), succeeded in organizing and clarifying the profuse and sometimes contradictory regulation existing in the area, after so many legal reforms and judicial decisions. Through its ruling, the Court required the reorganization of the existing plans through transparent and participatory mechanisms, and demanded the reconstructive process to be supervised by public audiences.[70]

Even though there is much to say in favour of what the Court achieved in this particular area of the law, one should also note that, not unusually, the Court went beyond the limits of the judicial sphere and assumed a quasi-legislative role. For instance, in the so-called 'UPAC' decision, the Court had the chance to scrutinize the national system of loans, created under President Pastrana's administration, which had come under severe crisis.[71] Through numerous and subsequent decisions, the Court had the chance to carefully evaluate the constitutional validity of the state's plan. The Court's rulings amounted to the virtual elimination of the UPAC and the creation of a new system, whose interest rates would be governed not by the market but by the Central Bank.[72] To sum up: the dialogic view challenges, instead of accepting, traditional approaches to judicial review and the division of powers. However, the innovative character of this doctrine does not amount to an authorization for the judiciary to assume tasks corresponding to the political sphere. For a dialogical approach, the Court could and should do numerous things in order to 'activate' politics, but not replace it altogether.[73]

The Court also made enormous efforts in order to ensure proper protection of the rights of disadvantaged groups, including members of indigenous communities.[74] With respect to the latter, the Court tried at the same time to articulate a proper defence of individual rights, and also develop an adequate understanding of cultural differences. However, it seems clear that its decisions in the area did not follow a consistent doctrine or set of principles. On some occasions, for instance in Decision T-254/94, which referred to the sanctions imposed by the community on one of its

[69] See Decision C-1433 of 2000.

[70] A. Yamin & O. Parra, 'The Role of Courts in Refining Health Policy: The Case of the Colombian Court' (2009), manuscript.

[71] Through this system, the government wanted to promote the construction of houses in a country where it was extremely difficult to obtain long-term credits from the banks. Due to unfortunate circumstances, and after a period of macro-economic instability, the system became inefficient, and its credits enormously expensive—it is said that 200,000 families were on the verge of losing their homes because they could not afford their mortgages.

[72] Mauricio Pérez Salazar, 'Razones y sinrazones de un debate: la crítica económica de la jurisprudencia constitucional colombiana, 1999-2002' (2003) (14) Revista Derecho del Estado. There were three rulings concerning the UPAC system, the first of which was issued in May 1999—Decision C-383.

[73] Jeremy Waldron, 'Judicial Review and Political Legitimacy (2017), manuscript on file with the author.

[74] In 2006, the Court determined the constitutionality of abortion in some limited circumstances. In 2016, the Court recognized that gay marriage was not against the constitution and that, consequently, heterosexual and same-sex couples had the same fundamental rights. The following year, the Court also accepted that gay couples had the right to adopt children.

members, including sanctions on the family of the offender and his properties, the Court ruled against the community's decision, and grounded its ruling on the primacy of liberal values. In other cases, for instance in Decision T-349/96, the Court seemed to vary its philosophical perspective. This decision referred to an indigenous community that condemned one of its members for different crimes, and—after the condemnation, and without the presence of the offender—the indigenous authorities augmented the punishment that had been previously determined. On this occasion, the Court assumed a renewed position, which was more open to cultural diversity than the previous one, and which affirmed that indigenous communities had to enjoy the highest possible degree of autonomy. Contrary to what it had affirmed in Decision T-254/94, liberal values now did not seem prevalent. In another case, namely Decision T-349/96, the Court partially changed its previous approach. On this occasion, the Court had to decide on a case where members of an indigenous community had imposed restrictions on the religious freedom of some of its members. Here, the Court maintained that indigenous authorities had to respect, in principle, the individual rights of its members, and that the only exception to this principle appeared when the restriction represented the only available means capable of avoiding the erosion of the community's cultural traditions.[75]

As anticipated, the Colombian Court also made clear that it was prepared to safeguard the procedural conditions of a deliberative democracy, and was therefore ready to invalidate norms that appeared to be the product of mere 'naked interests'. Thus, on numerous opportunities, it challenged legislative decisions that had not been the object of a careful deliberative process. For instance, in an important 2004 decision, it objected to the so-called Anti-terrorist statute, which represented a crucial part of (then recently re-elected and extremely powerful) President Uribe's political agenda. In spite of the complexity of the case, the Court rejected the legislative's initiative after recognizing that more than a dozen of the representatives who voted for the polemic statute had changed their views on the topic from one day to the next, without giving any public explanation about their change of views. The Colombian Court offered many other examples of its commitment to open deliberation. For instance, in Decision SC-668 of 2004 the Court declared that Article 16 of law no. 1, 2003 was unconstitutional, as a consequence of the lack of debate in the Plenary of the House of Representatives.[76]

In spite of these significant efforts in defence of the deliberative character of the democratic procedures, the Court failed to ensure due respect to those deliberative procedures in other relevant cases. For instance, in different cases related to the implementation of the right to free, prior, and informed consultation, the Court seemed unable to ensure due respect to the principles of public deliberation. For instance, in its recent Decision SU-095 of 2018, the Court decided in favour of a *tutela* interposed by the oil company Mansarovar Energy Ltd, trying to prevent the development of a popular consultation in the city of Cumaral, Meta. The Court's ruling appeared in tension with other decisions by the same Court in similar circumstances, and the existing

[75] This analysis is based on Daniel Bonilla, 'Los derechos fundamentales y la diferencia cultural' (2003) *SELA*, manuscript on file with the author.

[76] Leonardo García Jaramillo, *Constitucionalismo* deliberativo (México: UNAM, 2015).

legal framework (such as Article 33 of law no. 136, 1994). On this occasion, the Court maintained that municipalities lacked the competence for organizing popular consultations in these circumstances.[77]

The Court also had the opportunity to intervene in other crucial cases involving popular consultations, such as those originated after the failed consult in the case of the historic 'Acuerdos de Paz' or *Havana Peace Agreements*. The agreement was signed in Colombia between official authorities and representatives of the Revolutionary Armed Forces of Colombia ('FARC'), and put an end to more than 52 years of internal armed conflict, which had caused the death of more than 260,000 people (215,000 civilians), and forced the displacement of millions of others. The Peace Agreements were then subject to a popular consultation, where the majority of the people expressed opposition to the Treaty.[78] Consequently, and following the failed consultation process, an intense process of negotiations took place between the Agreement's political opponents in the plebiscite and the Colombian government in order to review the general Agreement and conclusively try to achieve a great national pact. After around 10 meetings over 4 weeks, government negotiators received 455 reform proposals that were later discussed with FARC representatives in Cuba. Afterwards, a new version of the general Agreement emerged. In addition, the Colombian Congress issued many decisions trying to give life and stability to the new version of the Agreement, and the Court has had the opportunity to delve into many of the complex intricacies of those norms. In what follows, I will only make a few observations about two of the Court's main decisions in the area, one that I consider to be fundamentally well decided, and the other that I consider, in principle, to be wrong.

First, let me say something about the Court's decision of May 2017, when the tribunal examined the norm allowing the government to fast track laws related to the Agreement (Constitutional Amendment 1, 2016). The government had promoted these procedural reforms in order to accelerate the implementation of the Agreement (and particularly the amnesty law that the members of the guerrilla organization demanded). However, in its May decision, the Tribunal considered (Decision C-332/17) that two basic parts of the 'fast-track' mechanism created by Congress were unconstitutional.[79] For the Court, implementing those two clauses would have involved replacing the constitution by altering the deliberative and decision-making powers of Congress—powers that would have been transferred to the then President Juan

[77] See, e.g., the opinion of the legal NGO DeJusticia, in https://www.dejusticia.org/solicitamos-la-anulacion-de-la-sentencia-que-le-pone-limites-a-las-consultas-populares/?utm_source=Observatorio+de+Discriminaci%C3%B3n+Racial&utm_campaign=a66f01399c-EMAIL_CAMPAIGN_2018_12_10_01_33&utm_medium=email&utm_term=0_f10e561b57-a66f01399c-85561809 accessed on 19 June 2019.

[78] The Colombian Constitutional Court has had the opportunity to deal with different aspects of the Treaty, which the National Congress tried to constitutionalize and implement, in troublesome political circumstances: unfortunately, a slight majority of the Colombian voters (50,2 %) voted against ratifying the Agreement. The consultation that was carried out in October 2016, and the the 49, 76 per cent of the electoral roll voted in favour of the Peace Agreement. The electoral abstention was over 62 per cent, the greatest in 22 years.

[79] According to one of the objected clauses, all changes to each of the laws developing different aspects of the Agreement had to be approved by the government before coming to a congressional vote. According to the second objected clause, Congress could only vote to approve or deny the law, implementing the peace process without the possibility of debating and voting each of the articles individually.

Manuel Santos.[80] In the words of the President of the Constitutional Court at that time, Luis Guillermo Guerrero, the ruling was not aimed at undermining the force of the Peace Agreement, but rather to 'open up spaces for democratic deliberation'. From the dialogic perspective that was defended here, the Court's decision looked, in principle, right: the concerns exposed by the Court were appropriate. They expressed reasonable worries about the democratic-reinforcing character of the law, and the procedures that it established. The Court's strict scrutiny of the 'fast-track' law seemed totally justifiable: the government needed to show that it was doing its very best to 'build democratic legitimacy', but it instead demonstrated that it was willing and ready to circumvent the constitutional/procedural requirements of democratic deliberation. The Colombian Constitutional Court reasonably said 'no' to the government's ill-fated initiative, and in that way reaffirmed its commitment to deliberative democracy.

Secondly, let me now refer to a different example, related to the Court's ruling of 11 October 2017 (Decision C-630/17). On that occasion, the Court upheld Congress-approved legislation, which established that the Peace Agreement between the government and the FARC could not be amended for the next 12 years (Constitutional Amendment 2, 2017). This is to say, that the following three governments would be unable to modify approved parts of the accord.[81] The short-term purpose of the political initiative was obvious: to shield the Agreement from potential changes that may be introduced by the coming government—a coalition led by right-wing candidate Iván Duque who, unsurprisingly, became the President of the country. In my view, the same principles that justified the Court's decision in the 'fast-track' case required a different approach on this occasion—particularly so in the face of a historical Peace Agreement of extraordinary complexity and importance, which had received a negative response by the majority of the Colombian citizenry in a recent plebiscite. If—in spite of that popular decision—the incumbent government still wanted to adopt, develop, and implement the historical Agreement, then it was obliged to carefully craft a new consensus, rather than shield the Agreement from politics. Contrary to this goal, the government showed (again) that it had no confidence in the Colombian people, and tried to use the law to guard an agreement that required, instead, full and open democratic support. And that the Court finally supported those initiatives, in the name of an uncertain and imprecise 'principle of stability and security' adds nothing relevant to its decision.

V. Final Words

Having reached this point, one crucial question to answer is the following: How we—advocates of dialogic constitutionalism—should act, in the face of the kind of

[80] https://lasillavacia.com/historia/las-dos-caras-del-golpe-al-fast-track-60989 accessed on 19 June 2019.

[81] Gonzalo Ramírez-Cleves, 'The Colombian Constitutional Court Rules that the Peace Agreement is Mandatory for Three Presidential Terms', 2017, http://www.iconnectblog.com/2017/10/the-colombian-constitutional-court-rules-that-the-peace-agreement-is-mandatory-for-three-presidential-terms/ accessed 29 June 2019. According to the norm that was upheld by the Court, 'institutions and authorities of the state have the obligation to comply with what is established in the final accord in good faith ... until the end of three complete presidential periods following the signing'. For the Court, that article incorporated a 'principle of stability and security that is deferential to the purposes of the Agreement'.

defective democracies in which we live. In these conditions, I would suggest, if we get—by chance or other unexpected reasons—judges, or other public officers, with good dialogical dispositions, or find public decisions oriented in the 'right' dialogic way, we should, at least in principle, applaud and celebrate them. This, as long as those actions and decisions accord with the principles described here. It is, in the end, always a good thing to have more public hearings; or more public debates about issues of fundamental importance (e.g. about how to solve an environmental catastrophe). The problem is that we need to rely on good institutions, rather than on good public officers or good luck. As James Madison put it, in the Federalist Papers no. 51, 'if men were angels, no government would be necessary'. Given that men are not angels, and also given that the prevailing institutional structure is not prepared to foster democratic deliberation, we proponents of dialogic constitutionalism should work for the adoption of a different institutional system, more capable of advancing our collective conversations.

4

From the Public Action of Unconstitutionality of 1910 to the Constitutional Court of 1991

The Political and Legal Struggles for Constitutional Justice in Colombia*

Mario Alberto Cajas-Sarria

I. Introduction

The Constitutional Court of Colombia established by the onstitution of 1991 is widely recognized for its activism when it comes to rights,[1] and it is considered as one of the courts representing the *Neo-constitutionalism* of the Global South.[2] Nevertheless, the constitutional control prior to the Constitutional Court is far less known: Indeed, the trajectory of Colombian judicial review is still relatively ignored, both by comparative law and constitutional law, since both fields tend to focus on the so-called 'American standards' of judicial review or the 'European' (centralized model); or the variants and mixtures of both 'models'.[3] Perhaps, in part, this narrative remains almost denied due to the 'geopolitics of knowledge' that usually operates on the institutional trajectories of a large part of Latin-America.[4]

Colombia had rich judicial review experiences throughout the nineteenth and twentieth centuries: some of them were more local, and others had to do with the possibility of

* This chapter is based on my paper: 'La construcción de la justicia constitucional colombiana: una perspectiva histórica y política, 1910–1991', published in Spanish in Revista Precedente, Vol. 7, 2015, 109–152, and also on my book chapter: 'Trayectoria de la creación de un tribunal constitucional en Colombia', published in Spanish in: *Historia Constitucional de Colombia*, Vol. IV, 2019, edited by Augusto Trujillo et al, Academia Colombiana de Jurisprudencia, Bogotá, Colombia, 2019.

[1] For an overview of the leading cases and the activist role of the Colombian Constitutional Court, see Manuel Cepeda & David Landau, *Colombian Constitutional Law: Leading Cases* (New York: Oxford University Press, 2017).

[2] On the constitutional change in the Americas, see Collin Crawford & Daniel Bonilla Maldonado, *Constitutionalism in the* Americas (Cheltenham: Elgar, 2018).

[3] There are numerous examples of this in the legal scholarship, for instance see Jean Louis Halpérin, 'The Triumph of Judicial Review: The Evolution of Post-Revolutionary Legal Thought', in Olivier Moréteau et al. (eds), *Comparative Legal History* (Cheltenham: Edward Elgar, 2019); Morton J. Horwitz, 'Constitutional Transplants' (2009) Theoretical Inquiries in Law 10–535; Nuno Garoupa & Tom Ginsburg, 'Judicial Audiences and Reputation: Perspectives from Comparative Law' (2009) 47 Columbia Journal of Transnational Law 451.

[4] In general, on the need to change the approaches to the 'Euro—Latin American legal spaces' in the politics of comparative law, see Diego Medina-López, 'The Latin-American and Caribbean Tradition', in Mauro Bussani & Ugo Mattei (eds), *The Cambridge Companion to Comparative Law* (Cambridge: Cambridge University Press, 2012).

Mario Alberto Cajas-Sarria, *From the Public Action of Unconstitutionality of 1910 to the Constitutional Court of 1991*
In: *Constitutionalism*. Edited by: Alejandro Linares-Cantillo, Camilo Valdivieso-León, Santiago García-Jaramillo,
Oxford University Press (2021). © The various contributors. DOI: 10.1093/oso/9780192896759.003.0005

reviewing state acts against federal laws or constitutions. But the most important moment of that trajectory was the enactment of the Public Action of Unconstitutionality ('PAU') by the Constitutional Assembly of 1910, which for the first time allowed any citizen to challenge the constitutionality of laws and decrees before the Supreme Court.[5] The same constitutional amendment (Legislative Act 3 of 1910) also entrusted the Supreme Court, which was a court of cassation until then, the judicial review of legislation.[6]

Over the decades of the twentieth century, both legal scholars and political actors began to criticize the role of the Supreme Court as a constitutional judge. Some considered that the Court lacked specialized knowledge to perform such a role, others felt that the PAU congested the judicial corporation and delayed the decisions too much.

And for the second half of the twentieth century, the expansion of the Austrian or European 'concentrated model' of the constitutional court provoked legal scholars and political actors to give rise to a need to transform Colombian constitutional justice, and to implement a constitutional court:[7] perhaps the prestige and the origin of the aforementioned model helped to influence the attempts at 'legal borrowing'.[8] By the end of the 1980s, in part because of Supreme Court decisions unfavourable to governments, initiatives to create a constitutional court were increased, and it was finally established by the National Constituent Assembly in 1991.

This chapter tells the history of the transformations and the attempts to change Colombian constitutional justice since the establishment of the PAU in 1910 to the creation of the Constitutional Court in 1991. This trajectory highlights how political actors and legal scholars with different purposes and strategies in certain political contexts and under particular legal doctrines, shaped the national judicial review. The narrative will also show how a local institutional development was transformed under the influences of foreign legal institutions that local jurists as well as politicians invoked, adapted, and 'used' for different purposes and at different times: in this way, it will account for the legal and political struggles to establish a constitutional court, which seemed in part to transplant the model expanded from Europe to the world in the second half of the twentieth century.[9]

[5] Mario Cajas, 'Lessons from the History of Courts on the Review of Constitutional Amendments in Colombia', in Joshua C. Tate, Jose Reinaldo de Lima, & Andres Botero-Bernal (eds), *Global Legal History: A Comparative Law Perspective* (Abingdon: Routledge, 2019), 90.

[6] 'The popular action *in rem* is more novel. It was developed too early for Colombia to be indebted to Hans Kelsen and his Austrian experiment. If there was any borrowing, it was in the opposite direction . . . ': J. A. C. Grant, 'Judicial Control of the Constitutionality of Statutes and Administrative Legislation in Colombia: Nature and Evolution of the Present System' (1950) 23 South California Law Review 489.

[7] For an overview of the *models* of constitutional justice and its expansion in Latin America, including Colombia, see Phanor Eder, 'Judicial Review in Latin America' (1960) 21 Ohio State Law Journal 570; Grant (n. 7); Héctor Fix-Zamudio, 'La justicia constitucional en América Latina' (1989) IV *El Constitucionalismo en las postrimerías del Siglo XX colaboraciones extranjeras y nacionales* 451–532; Francisco Fernández Segado, 'El control de la constitucionalidad en Iberoamérica: sus rasgos generales y su génesis en el siglo pasado (1996) *Pensamiento Constitucional* 2–3 (Lima: Pontificia Universidad Católica del Perú).

[8] On the 'prestige' as a factor to explain legal transplants, see Jonathan M. Miller, 'A Typology of Legal Transplants: Using Sociology, Legal History and Argentine Examples to Explain the Transplant Process' (2003) 51 American Journal of Comparative Law 839; Mathhias Siems, *Comparative Law* (Cambridge: Cambridge University Press, 2014).

[9] For a political history of the Colombian judicial review before 1991, see my work in two volumes: Mario Cajas, *La Historia de la Corte Suprema de Justicia de Colombia, 1886-1991* (vols I–II, Bogotá: Universidad de los Andes, 2015).

The path of constitutional justice proposed here is described in five phases. The first phase starts when the Legislative Act 3 of 1910 established the PAU. The second phase is set in the mid-twentieth century with the military rule of General Gustavo Rojas Pinilla, who first tried to establish a 'Tribunal of Constitutional Guarantees' to replace the Supreme Court as a constitutional judge in 1953, and then created the 'Chamber of Constitutional Affaires' within the Supreme Court itself in 1956; thus replacing the constitutional control exercised by the plenary chamber of the same court.

The third phase is related to the attempt to create a constitutional court in 1968, which ended in a constitutional amendment that established the constitutional chamber of the Supreme Court. The fourth phase deals with the failed constitutional amendment of 1979, which modified the functions of the constitutional judge of the plenary chamber of the Court and its constitutional chamber that was declared unconstitutional by the Supreme Court itself in 1981. Finally, it deals, in a comprehensive way, with the creation of the constitutional court by the National Constituent Assembly ('ANC'), which brought an end to the function of the constitutional judge of the Supreme Court in the constitution of 1991.

II. The Public Action of Unconstitutionality of 1910 as a 'Path-breaker' in Colombian Constitutional Justice

The political projects that converged in the so-called 'Regeneration' led by President Rafael Nuñez materialized in the constitution of 1886. Thus, it embodied the conservative, centralist, confessional, and authoritarian reaction against the liberal and federal regime that dominated much of the second half of the nineteenth century. It also established the Supreme Court as the head of the national judiciary, and a legal reform then decided that the same institution would be a 'court de cassation'. One of the measures that sought to ensure the dominance of the President of the Republic over the Court established that the justices would be appointed by the former and confirmed by the Senate. Indeed, the 'first national Court' was composed of a majority of justices of conservative origin, faithful to the 'regenerative' ideal, and for lifetime tenure.[10]

But the authoritarian *Regeneration* paved the way for the bloody Thousand Days War, a civil armed conflict that pitted the liberals against the conservative government between 1899 and 1902, and from which the latter emerged victorious. The conservative President, Rafael Reyes (1904–1909), then tried to govern without the politicians and rebuild the country after the war. With the opposition of Congress to his ambitious reforms, he decided to close it in 1905. The same year, a constituent assembly, which replaced Congress, approved several constitutional amendments that strengthened the executive power.

An alliance between conservative and liberal factions created opposition to the Republican Union Party, which forced the elections to Congress in 1909, and then the convocation of a new Constituent Assembly in 1910, in which the opposition won a majority of seats. With the end of the Reyes dictatorship, path-breaking amendments were enacted by the Constituent Assembly, all aimed at guaranteeing a true system of

[10] Mario Cajas, 'La Corte Suprema de Justicia de Colombia, 1886-1910: de juez de la Regeneración a juez constitucional' (2013) 14 Historia Constitucional 430–4.

checks and balances and limiting presidential power. For instance, it established that the justices of the Supreme Court would be elected by Congress from a short list of three candidates whom the executive would nominate.

As previously stated, the Constituent Assembly approved the Legislative Act 3 of 31 October 1910, which established the PAU and entrusted the Court with the jurisdiction to decide the constitutionality of the law before a lawsuit filed by any citizen.[11] In this way, Colombia was among the first countries to establish in the constitution an *actio popularis* of judicial review of legislation.

These factors, together, help to explain the institutional change. By 1910, an important legal discussion on constitutional supremacy had been developed, and it gradually permeated the political and intellectual circles in the context of a growing opposition to the regeneration and and its project that subordinated the constitution to the legislation ; a regime that also excluded the liberal dissent and a conservative-opposed faction. Thus, the 'culture' of constitutional supremacy was gradually 'recovering' political power to the point that it captured the interest of those mentioned factions in different political moments from 1886 to 1910. However, it was when Reyes released the power, that the need to rebuild the constitutional order and to achieve the inter-partisan peace in the critical juncture of the political regime between 1909 and 1910 arose, and the conditions for the PAU were created.[12] Therefore, both, the Supreme Court and the judicial review of legislation were seen as legal guarantees for the political parties fearful of the political hegemonies[13] nor the Court easily adjusted to the new institutional design. For example, with the argument that the PAU made the Court inconveniently prevail over the other branches, Congress tried to eliminate that constitutional complaint by 1912.[14]

The Supreme Court itself did not seem comfortable with its new role as constitutional judge; at times expressing that it 'blurred' its role as a court of cassation. The Court even showed signs of resisting the change:[15] in 1916 and 1919 it proposed to Congress to divest it of that responsibility, as it considered that judging the constitutionality of laws implied an interference in the responsibilities of the other branches: that is to say, it had been assigned a role oblivious to it.

It is also important to mention that, at times, the Court did not seem to facilitate citizens' access to the constitutional complaint of the PAU: since 1910 the case law set strict procedural parameters that were more similar to the cassation than to an *actio popularis*. Law 96 of 1936, promoted by sectors of the Court itself, which with 'anti-formalistic' spirit specified the requirements of the PAU, undoubtedly contributed to expand popular access.

[11] Legislative Act 3 of 1910, Article 41. Carlos Restrepo Piedrahita, *Constituciones Políticas Nacionales de Colombia* (Bogotá: Universidad Externado de Colombia, 2004), 259.

[12] On the period between the constitution of 1886 and the amendment of 1910, see Fernando Correa Uribe, *Republicanismo y reforma constitucional* (Medellín: Universidad de Antioquia, 1996).

[13] Cajas (n. 10).

[14] Mario Cajas, *La Historia de la Corte Suprema de Justicia de Colombia, 1886-1991* (vols I–II, Bogotá: Universidad de los Andes, 2015).

[15] The historiographic and political reconstruction of judicial review appears in ibid.

Finally, it is also very important to clarify that, by the middle of the twentieth-century the Colombian judicial review of constitutionality, the so-called 'mixed' system, was in effect, which combined elements of the 'diffuse' American standard with the 'concentrated' European type. That is, it did not align itself with the two canonical models of constitutional control.[16] Indeed, although the Supreme Court was the only one empowered to review the constitutionality of laws, other institutions also exercised judicial constitutional control: Legislative Act 3 of 1910 established that the governors of the departments would challenge the 'acts of the municipalities for reasons of unconstitutionality or illegality' before the corresponding 'judicial authority'. A little later on, Legislative Act 1 of 1945 entrusted the Council of State to judge the constitutionality of the decrees issued by the government.

III. A Military Rule Looking for Judicial Review in Europe?

Laureano Gómez, a strong opponent of the liberal party was elected President in 1950, after an election campaign marked by bipartisan violence in which the liberals withdrew their candidate in the absence of electoral guarantees and in the midst of accusations by the sectarian repression of the conservative government of Mariano Ospina Perez (1946–1950). Gómez's mandate advanced in an uneven way: due to health problems, the position was held by Roberto Urdaneta, appointed to the Presidency from the end of 1951.

With Urdaneta, Congress, exclusively integrated by conservatives, convened a National Constituent Assembly ('ANC'), which was to dismantle the liberal constitutional amendment of 1936. The ANAC was formed, but could not carry out its mission to ammend the constitution because in 13 June 1953, the general commander of the armed forces, General Gustavo Rojas Pinilla, assumed the executive power after a *coup d'état* of President Gómez. Rojas was widely supported by the conservative faction opposed to Gomez and led by the former President Mariano Ospina Perez (1946–1950), for the liberal party, and other important sectors of opinion.

An overwhelming population celebrated General Rojas due to the crude bipartisan violence that had increased with Gómez's government. But this 'national happiness' was soon interrupted by the tensions between the executive and the Supreme Court, whose justices had been in office since 1950. One of the first factors that weakend the atmosphere was the proposal for judicial reform that Antonio Escobar Camargo, Minister of Justice, announced on 4 November 1953, in a radio conference. The bill proposed modifying the system of election of the justices, as the government considered that the design established in 1910 politicized the Supreme Court. The solution he proposed was to give the President the 'historical and moral responsibility of selecting a staff of honest and brilliant Justices' for constitutional periods that would not coincide with that of the government.[17]

[16] Cajas, Mario, 'La construcción de la justicia constitucional colombiana: una aproximación histórica y política, 1910-1991' (2015) 7 Revista Precedente. Ibid. See Legislative Act 1 of 1945, Article 41. Restrepo (n. 11, 492).

[17] Antonio Escobar Camargo, *La reforma judicial: Conferencia del señor Ministro de Justicia, doctor, Antonio Escobar Camargo, dictada el 5 de noviembre de 1953* (Bogotá: Imprenta Nacional, 1953).

Rojas also seemed to look at the still incipient 'European constitutional justice', as he proposed creating a Tribunal of Constitutional Guarantees ('TGC') to replace the Supreme Court as a constitutional judge. The TGC would be assigned the study of 'the enforceability of laws and decrees with the force of law'. According to Minister Escobar, it was a 'necessary reform' to 'technify' constitutional justice. However, it seemed more like a strategy to deprive the Court of its jurisdiction as constitutional judge, and also to give the government interference in appointment of justices to the new Tribunal.Indeed, the TGC would be integrated by the presidents of the Supreme Court chambers, the Council of State, and by three representatives of the President of the Republic. That is to say, all its justices would be appointed by the executive, because the same amendment proposed that he would appoint the Supreme Court and the Council of State justices. For the Minister, there were no 'technical' arguments to justify the jurisdiction of the Supreme Court to 'decide on the validity of Congress and Government acts', which made it the arbiter of the branches of power and placed the other two branches in a position of inferiority in relation to the judiciary. In the same way, it considered that it was necessary to assign this task to specialists in public law and not to experts in the cassation technique.[18]

The 'Colombian TGC' arose after World War II, when the 'concentrated constitutional justice' model proposed by Hans Kelsen began to expand in Europe,[19] according to which a specialized and independent court was entrusted with the review of the constitutionality of laws, as well as the defence of the constitution.[20] The Kelsenian model was inaugurated with the Constitutional Court of Austria of 1920, and this body would have inspired the Tribunal of Constitutional Guarantees in the Spanish constitution of 1931.[21] Then, in the postwar period, the Constitutional Court of Italy was created in the constitution of 1947; and finally, the Constitutional Court of Germany of the Fundamental Law of Bonn of 1949 was created, which began operating in 1951.[22]

It is very likely that Rojas's TGC picked up elements from the above-mentioned Spanish TGC, although the proposal differed from this model and the 'Kelsenian model':[23]

[18] Mario Cajas, 'La Justicia constitucional del general Gustavo Rojas Pinilla: entre el Tribunal de Garantías Constitucionales y la Sala de Negocios Constitucionales. Colombia, 1953-1957' (2016) 7 Revista de Historia Constitucional 286.

[19] See Sara Lagi, 'Hans Kelsen and the Austrian Constitutional Court' (2012) Revista Coherencia 9–16.

[20] 1 Luís Cervantes, Los tribunales constitucionales en el derecho comparado: Un estudio introductivo sobre sus antecedentes y situación jurídica actual, Estudios básicos de Derechos Humanos, VI. (San José: IDH, 1996, 358)..

[21] The bibliography on the influence of the Kelsenian model in the Court of Constitutional Guarantees of 1931 is extensive. Among others, see Niceto Alcalá- *Significado y funciones del Tribunal de Garantías Constitucionales* (Madrid: Editorial Reus, 1933); José Luís Cascajo Castro, 'Kelsen y la Constitución española de 1931' (1978) 1 Revista de Estudios Políticos; Francisco Rubio Llorente, 'Del Tribunal de Garantías al Tribunal Constitucional' (1985) 16 Revista de Derecho Político 3; Héctor Fix-Zamudio, *Los Tribunales Constitucionales y los Derechos Humanos* (México, DF: UNAM, 1980); José F. Palomino Manchego, 'Los orígenes de los Tribunales Constitucionales en América Latina', in Professor Allan R. Brewer Carías, A. Arismendi,. & J. Caballero (eds), *El derecho público a comienzos del siglo XXI: Estudios en homenaje al* (vol. 1, Madrid: Civitas, 2003). See also John Bell and Marie Lucie Paris (eds), *Rights-Based Constitutional Review: Constitutional Courts in a Changing Landscape* (Cheltenham: Edward Elgar, 2016); Halpérin (n. 4).

[22] Mauro Cappelletti, 'La justicia constitucional en Italia' (1960) 41 Boletín del Instituto de Derecho Comparado de México 41.

[23] The Colombian legal scholar Eustorgio Sarria had proposed a TGC 'similar' to the Spanish model of 1931, but with a different composition of justices (Eustorgio Sarria: Tratado de Derecho Administrativo, 2nd edition (Bogotá:Crítica Jurídica, 1952, 46).

the Spanish TGC did not belong to the judiciary and was composed of twenty-six members, including the presidents of the Council of State and the Court of Audit,[24] while its other members were elective and some of them were not required to be lawyers.[25]

The proposal for judicial amendment was added to the speech given by General Rojas, in which he reacted to the decision of a criminal judge to release a notorious citizen accused of alleged conspiracy at a time when he commanded the Army. Rojas accused the Judiciary Branch of being politicized and said that:

> The Minister of Justice . . . talked about the amendments that, in his concept, are necessary so that the application of the laws and the imposition of sanctions are in charge of carefully selected professionals . . . who guarantee their independence from political pressures and bribes. While the judiciary cannot isolate itself from the flag camp and there are no fast and effective procedures to punish judges and magistrates who fail to comply with their duties, the administration of justice is potentially the most shameful deception . . . and a permanent disrepute of one of the main branches of public power.[26]

The Supreme Court justices reacted to Rojas by resigning from their positions. Rojas issued a decree replacing the full court, which was formed with an equal number of justices from both the liberal and conservative parties in January 1954. The resignations and the arrival of the new court seemed to postpone the proposal of reform to constitutional justice.

By 1956, General Rojas Pinilla had already lost the support of the two traditional political parties and was organizing his own political party: 'the third force'. He also gradually showed its ambition to govern with the less possible limit. In that context, he, perhaps partly reprising his project to create a TGC, wanted to further limit the independence of the Supreme Court and established a constitutional affairs chamber within the same Court. The chamber would be composed of eight justices from other chambers of the Court, and would have the jurisdiction to:

> definitively decide on the enforceability of the legislative acts that have been refuted as unconstitutional by the Government or on the laws or decrees that in compliance with the Constitution, may be denounced as unconstitutional by any citizen before it after holding a hearing with the National Attorney General.

Rojas stated that the creation of the new chamber was necessary because 'the practice has demonstrated the need to create a specialized Chamber in Public Law within the Supreme Court'. But, while this change could be interpreted as a reform aimed towards the *specialization* of the Colombian Judicial Review, with it, the military rule was able to ensure that a small group of justices, chosen by Rojas, were in charge of the judicial review instead of the plenary chamber of the Supreme Court. Several justices resigned their positions as a reaction to this institutional change.

[24] Rubio (n. 21), 31.

[25] Héctor Álvarez García, "La naturaleza política del Tribunal de Garantías Constitucionales de la segunda república española", Revista de Derecho Político (Madrid: UNED, 2011- 80, 194) .

[26] Paz, Justicia, Libertad, Postulados Invariables del Actual Gobierno: trascendental discurso del Presidente en Cartagena". El Tiempo, Bogota: November 12, 1953, 12. .

The new chamber also received criticism from different sectors of jurists, to which General Rojas replied:

> The Constitutional Affairs Chamber would consecrate in this way, significantly, the correct and modern tendency to end the promiscuous knowledge in the administration of justice of the most developed countries and the permanent aspiration of our reformers.[27]

The constitutional affairs chamber, a kind of 'small constitutional court', would review the constitutionality of the Decrees of State of Siege issued by the military rule, given that Congress had been closed since 1953. The chamber was running until 18 July 1957, when the Government Military Board that replaced Roja's terminated its functions and the plenary chamber of the Court regained its former duties.

In sum, the constitutional justice of General Rojas Pinilla claimed to respond to the argument of 'modernization' following the European trend of specialized or 'concentrated courts'. Although, with the reform, the military rule obtained greater influence in the Supreme Court.[28]

IV. The Attempt to Create a Constitutional Court in 1968

The liberal and conservative parties agreed on the return to the civilian government, and the start of the new political regime began to materialize in the plebiscite that amended the constitution in 1957. The Frente Nacional (National Front) ('FN') agreements established the alternation in the power and the parity distribution of the public offices between the two parties. The same reform established that the Supreme Court would be integrated by the two parties on an equal basis, that its justices would have life tenure, and that the vacancies would be filled by the justices themselves (the cooptation system).

Within the FN, President Carlos Lleras Restrepo (1966–1970) proposed to make a profound change in the design of the institutions, which would be based on the 1968 constitutional amendment. The amendments package discussed by Congress included the creation of a constitutional court that would be responsible for exercising the judicial review instead of the Supreme Court.[29]

The idea of a constitutional court had been driven by constitutionalists, such as Carlos Restrepo Piedrahita, and supported by former President Dario Echandía, both members of the First Committee of the Senate of the Republic. Their purpose was to strengthen and *modernize* constitutional justice.[30] Indeed, as Restrepo Piedrahita

[27] Gustavo Rojas Pinilla, 'Respuesta del Presidente' (1956) Gaceta Judicial 2171–73.

[28] Cajas (n. 19).

[29] Secretaría Jurídica de la Presidencia de la República, *Historia de la Reforma Constitucional de 1968* (Bogotá: Imprenta Nacional, 1969), 4.

[30] 'In 1966, then-Senator of the Republic, *Carlos Restrepo Piedrahita*, supported by former President *Dario Echandía* and other Senators, managed to achieve that, in the draft of the constitutional amendment which was being processed, were accepted the creation of a Constitutional Court. The project radically restructured the constitutional control system' (Bold in original text). Carlos Restrepo Piedrahita, *Tres Ideas Constitucionales: supremacía constitucional, Corte Constitucional, el Ombudsman* (Bogotá: Universidad Externado de Colombia, 1978), 99.

stated, with such an initiative, they wanted a specialized Court similar to the model of a 'concentrated' constitutional court installed a few decades ago in countries like Germany and Italy:

> The creation of the Constitutional Court is one of the best contributions of the Commission to the project. With this new institution, the national Public Law will reach the highest degree of rationalization of our State Judicial Law ...The Colombian State will thus be aligned in the front row with the other modern States, which have improved and streamlined the role of the jurisdictional review of the constitutionality of the Government laws and acts ... Henceforth, just one authority, the Constitutional Court, located on the highest peak of the State, will be the one that will express the content of the Constitution being legally binding for everybody, ruling people and organs.[31]

According to Restrepo, the creation of the Constitutional Court and the renewal of judicial review, was a contribution to the 'rationalization of the State', which was consistent with the purposes of the Lleras government: strengthening judicial review meant limiting the branches of power and allowed the country to move towards a constitutional state, which coincided with the idea for the development of the State announced by Lleras in his presidential campaign.

Restrepo also noted that prestigious legal scholars such as the Italian, Mauro Cappelletti, and the American, J. A. C. Grant, had already expressed the dangers of not having a well-defined scheme of 'diffuse' or 'concentrated' judicial review; such a situation represented legal uncertainty: on one hand, there were various 'constitutional judges' (Council of State, contentious administrative courts), and on the other hand, it led to the application of the 'exception of unconstitutionality' by all judges and even by administrative staff, a form that already had a long-running history in the Colombian legal tradition. The creation of the Constitutional Court tried to change once and for all 'the variegated system of judicial review in Colombia', which, according to Restrepo, was 'the most anti-technical of the ones that simultaneously exist in the States, [and] the most hypertrophic and sophisticated form of the so called mixed control'.

Restrepo did not hesitate to state that: 'the Constitutional Court is my pretty girl, the apple of my eyes'[32] Likewise, he again raised the 'technical' argument, formulated in previous attempts to deprive the Supreme Court of its function as constitutional judge: '... The Court, being essentially a Cassation Court ... is not organically adequate to fulfill one of the most difficult functions ... which is the jurisdictional control of the laws and acts of government ... With the creation of the Constitutional Court we have achieved a concentrated control'.[33]

Under the bill discussed in the Senate, the Constitutional Court would be composed of six justices appointed by Congress from joint lists made up of candidates

[31] Ibid.
[32] El Tiempo, Bogotá: 26 de marzo de 1967, 18.
[33] Ibid.

nominated by the Council of State, the President of the Republic, and the Court of Cassation (the new name proposed for the Supreme Court). The justices would hold office for six-year terms and could be re-elected indefinitely.

The approval of the project in the first round in Congress suggested that the Constitutional Court was becoming a reality, and that the proposal seemed important in the equipment needed for the reorganization of the state that Lleras was looking for. For example, in March 1967, the Minister of Government, Misael Pastrana, described it as one of the six 'fundamental bases' of the constitutional amendments.[34]

By mid-1967, although approval of constitutional amendment projects was stalling in Congress amid severe political tensions between factions of political parties, the government seemed to keep alive the hope that the constitutional court would be created. On 20 July 1967, for example, when installing the session of Congress, President Lleras insisted on the package of amendments and referred to the Constitutional Court as the body that would henceforth replace the 'diffuse or multiple control system of constitutionality of laws' with that of 'concentrated and uniform control'.[35]

By the end of 1967 the situation regarding the creation of the new court would change dramatically. A report of the First Committee of the Senate states that it was concluded that the Colombian judicial review system was a 'legal instrument well known by the country, and that it offers originality that has made it noticeable to strangers, and that in general has been successful, while the new proposal has not been matured enough neither in the political circles nor in the academic circles'. In addition, besides these circumstances, 'in full setting of the current formula and none for the replacement one, which bowed the revising commission of the constitutional projects to return to the existing system, showing with this their agreement with the authoritative voices of the Supreme Court and with the legal scholars'.[36]

The proposal of the constitutional court was subject to much criticism. For example, several congressmen asked for the project to be shelved, such as the very influential Senator and lawyer Hernan Toro Agudelo, who said that the amendment was a setback for the broad judicial review of the Supreme Court:[37]

> Although it was not clearly stated, the intention of the amendment ... is that in the future there may not be any claims of unconstitutionality of the resolutions and other Government acts, different to the decrees, nor from the decrees, nor from the acts of other national, departmental and municipal authorities or establishments, whether they are decrees, resolutions, ordinances or agreements, because the suppression of public action of unconstitutionality regarding all of them is implicit ... In short, a fundamental change occurs ... And that change looks as if it does not have any practical or doctrinaire utility, we already have a great tradition in the diffuse constitutional control, which in the end ... is unified throughout the Court.

[34] Ibid.

[35] (El Tiempo, 21, 07, 1967) 31.

[36] Secretaría Jurídica de la Presidencia de la República. 1969. Historia de la Reforma Constitucional de 1968, Bogotá: Imprenta Nacional..

[37] Restrepo (n. 30), 107.

Congress stated: 'The important initiative of Professor Carlos Restrepo Piedrahita has consecration in some countries, mainly European, and it represents a more sophisticated system, but it is contrary to the Colombian legal tradition, and it has not been studied further not even in the Colombian legal scholarship'.[38] Besides this, there was the argument that the integration model of the Constitutional Court was contrary to the political independence of the High Courts, that had pursued the plebiscite of 1957, with the cooptation system, so it would be a change from 'judicial constitutional control' to 'political constitutional control', given that the amendment bill left the election of justices of the Constitutional Court in the hands of Congress.

The Congress also stated that the proposed amendment had technical defects as it accumulated many functions in the Constitutional Court that would eventually overload it, as its jurisdiction would be to review the constitutionality of the 'Ordenanzas' of the Departmental Assemblies and of the agreements of the Municipal Councils.[39]

Undoubtedly, it was not only the 'technical' opposition to the creation of the constitutional court that ruined the initiative: the rarefied political environment contributed to the burial of the project too. Presidente Lleras lacked majority in Congress, because it was fragmented in factions of the liberal and conservative parties, as well as the ANAPO Party. For example, in July 1967, after nine months of debate, the House of Representatives rejected the bill approved by the Senate; subsequently, in March 1968, the House approved it, but then the Senate denied it in June of the same year. It was at this last moment that Lleras resigned from the Presidency as a mechanism to put pressure on the negotiation between the factions of Congress. The Senate did not accept the resignation, but it did not commit to approve the amendment either. After intense negotiations the Senate approved the project, although later in another debate it was rejected: this time Lleras reacted by requesting the resignation of his entire cabinet. After complex negotiation, which included several concessions made by the executive to Congress, the amendment was finally approved in December 1968.[40]

Thus, with the described scenario, all the executive's energy was focused on passing the amendments that he considered of greater political urgency: for example the measures in electoral matters, the departmental and municipal regime, the gradual dismantling of the political parity agreed by the FN, and of course the amendment of the two-thirds majority rule that required the approval of any law in Congress.

Despite the failure of the initiative to create a constitutional court, Legislative Act 1 of 1968 established the constitutional chamber in the Supreme Court. The chamber was a specialized body made up of *iuspublicists* (public law lawyers) who would conduct the processes and would write the draft of decisions to be considered and finally decided by the plenary chamber of the Supreme Court. In this way, the new chamber would share the full court that was also integrated by the civil, criminal. and labour cassation chambers.[41] The amendment also authorized President Lleras to issue a decree posting the first four justices of the constitutional chamber.

[38] Secretaría Jurídica de la Presidencia de la República. 1969. Historia de la Reforma Constitucional de 1968, Bogotá: Imprenta Nacional, 38.

[39] Ibid., 466.

[40] El Tiempo, Bogotá: 13 de diciembre de 1968, 1.

[41] 'ARTICLE 71 … : The Supreme Court is entrusted of safeguarding the integrity of the Constitution … The Supreme Court will fulfill these functions in the Plenary Chamber, after examining the Constitutional Chamber composed by Justices specialized in Public Law … ', *Diario Oficial*, 1968).

V. The Supreme Court puts an end to the 'Small Constitutional Court' of 1979

President Julio Cesar Turbay Ayala (1978–1982) had majority in Congress that facilitated the endorsement of the Legislative Act 1 of 1979, which took up the topics proposed to be debated by the so-called 'small constituent of 1977', when at the time of Alfonso Lopez Michelsen's government Congress approved an amendment whereby a body of deputies in charge of reforming the constitution would be elected. The amendment of 1977 was declared unconstitutional by the Supreme Court in the Decision of 5 May 1978, before the assembly was elected.[42]

Legislative Act 1 of 1979 sought a profound transformation of the judiciary. It established the Superior Judicial Council, responsible for managing judicial careers and also for sending lists of candidates to fill the vacancies of justices in the Council of State and the Supreme Court.. Then, the Court and the Council of State will appoint the justices only based on those lists. The same Superior Council would also send lists to the high courts for them to nominate the magistrates of district courts. They would respectively nominate the judges, and it would also be in charge of the disciplinary control of the Supreme Court justices, the Council of State, as well as the lawyers, magistrates, and judges.[43] The amendment also abolished the life tenure of the judiciary in the higher courts and fixed eight-year terms without a re-election possibility.

As for constitutional justice, the 1979 amendment attributed new competences to the constitutional chamber of the Supreme Court, which were withdrawn from those who were at the head of the plenary chamber. The full court would only decide on claims against Legislative Acts and Decrees of State of Siege, while all other functions of judicial review passed to the constitutional chamber; this then became a *small constitutional court* within the Supreme Court.

In such a context, the Legislative Act 1 of 1979 significantly affected the Supreme Court. It forced the Court to give up a large part of judicial review in favour of its constitutional chamber, that is, that which used to be called the 'Cinderella' of the Court, because it was stated that the four justices specialized in public law conducted verdicts that were eventually decided by 20 lawyers who cultivated other areas of law in the civil, criminal, and labour cassation chambers. Under the amendment, the constitutional Chamber not only increased its justices to eight, but would now also have important decision-making roles.

The Supreme Court would also lose the guarantee of life tenure for justices. Furthermore, the Court would have to fill its vacancies of justices according to the mentioned lists. And if that was not enough, the Court would no longer freely appoint the magistrates of the district courts, nor would they ever appoint the judges within their respective jurisdictions. Henceforth, the Superior Council would be the body in charge of presenting the respective lists of eligible judges to the Court and the district courts.

[42] In that Decision, the Court, for the first time, assumed its jurisdiction to review the constitutionality of the Legislative Act, even though the constitution of 1886 did not explicitly state that the Court had such an attribution. One of the purposes of the call for the 'small constituent' was to establish a constitutional court. Cajas (n. 10).

[43] Legislative Act 1 of 1979, Article 6.

In Decision 57 of 3 November 1981, with the Opinion of Justice Fernando Uribe Restrepo, the Court declared unconstitutional the Legislative Act 1 of 1979, two years after it came into force. The Court stated that Congress had committed serious procedural irregularities in the issuance of the amendment.[44] The decision caused such tension between the executive and the Court, that when it was about to decide, the first tried to change the quorum of the Court with a decree.

After the unconstitutionality of Legislative Act 1 of 1979, the full chamber of the Supreme Court recovered its full jurisdiction on judicial review from the constitutional chamber. The decision was also a heavy political and legal setback for President Turbay. Finally, it gave cause to many to perceive that Colombia had fallen into a *government of judges*.

VI. The Last Years of the Judicial Review by the Supreme Court and the Creation of the Constitutional Court in 1991

During the 1980s there was broad debate on the advisability of creating a constitutional court to replace the Supreme Court, after the decisions of unconstitutionality of the Legislative Act of 1979 as well as the Decrees of Economic Emergency declared by the government of President Belisario Betancur (1982–1986). Thus, in 1984, in an academic forum held at the Externado de Colombia University, in Bogotá, prominent legal scholars, justices of the Supreme Court, and members of the government spoke for or against creating a constitutional court, as the Betancur government had proposed to Congress.[45]

Jaime Castro, Minister of Government, defended the idea of the constitutional court. In his opinion, the 'model of concentrated' judicial review was much more adequate than the 'diffuse' one, and that required a constitutional judge who acted according to law, but who knew the 'politics' of the constitution. He also stated that judicial review by the Supreme Court 'does not barely reflect the political will of the Nation. It can go, therefore, against such political will'. Similarly, he noted that there were decisions that seemed to place Colombia in a 'government of Judges', because the Supreme Court had invaded Congress grounds. For Castro, the solution to the problems was 'simply to synchronize the political will of the Nation with the exercise of the so-called constitutional jurisdiction, through the formula that has been adopted in all parts of the world'. That is, to create a constitutional court composed by justices chosen by Congress from short lists of three candidates that would be sent to it by the Council of State, the Supreme Court, and the President of the Republic.[46]

On the other hand, justices of the Supreme Court invited to the forum spoke in favour of judicial review by the same Court. For example, Manuel Gaona Cruz, said that the project to create a Constitutional Court sought to replace judicial control 'by a political control held by a Constitutional Court', and that it was a proposal that had come

[44] Corte Suprema de Justicia. 1981, Decision 57, November 3, 1981, Gaceta Judicial 2405, CLXIV, 408

[45] Carlos Restrepo Piedrahita, *Aspectos del Control Constitucional en Colombia* (Bogotá: Universidad Externado de Colombia, 1984).

[46] Ibid., 122.

'after an orchestrated publicity of renowned chroniclers and columnists', because the campaign on this amendment was 'mounted on attractive but erroneous and despicable arguments.' 'If the system is going to be changed, it is good to know why'.[47]

For Justice Gaona the 'right to the Constitution' was what justified constitutional judicial review, and that control was only guaranteed if the judges were granted an 'independence or autarky of origin, of organization and of action against the political decision-making powers, governmental, legislative and administrative powers, which are precisely those which issue such acts', because in the absence of such autonomy 'the control would be reduced to an institutional strategy of simulation of the Constitution keeper, or of ineffective and conciliatory political control ... If this is what they are looking for, any form of political control is better than the current one. But I hope this is not about that, at least in the constituent intention'.[48] He also highlighted the objectivity and independence of the Supreme Court: 'The judgments have never had a partisan character not even by dissents circumstantial numerical coincidence ... no one can predict, not even its own members, what its pronouncements will be about. That is the best guarantee of safekeeping the constitutional integrity of any Country.'[49]

As possible adjustments to the current system, but without changing the Supreme Court, Justice Gaona Cruz said that it was possible to find a way for the Court to have jurisdiction to review Legislative Acts due to proceeding vices, and also international treeties. In those cases, the Plenary Chamber would decide by to two thirds of its members , and also in the review of the Decrees of Emergency; or in any change of its precedent..

Former promoters of the creation of the constitutional court were also heard in the forum of 1984. Carlos Restrepo Piedrahita recalled the attempts to create that court and did not miss the moment to criticize the two decisions of the Supreme Court that invalidated the amendments of 1977 and 1979, accusing the Court of having invaded the 'field of action and power' of Congress as a constituent power. He stated that the need to create a constitutional court was so solid from the perspective of the doctrine, that, unanimously 'seventeen specialists law professors from Europe and the American Continent, who ... participated in the symposium of 1977 ... ' without exception, had declared that 'as a culmination of this progressive evolution (the jurists refer ... to the process of rationalization of the defense methods of the Constitution that is being carried out in Iberoamérica and in other States) it is convenient to create specific Constitutional Courts or Tribunals, whose competence—because of the complexity of the political life of the Modern State—should be extended to all those aspects that may determine attacks or violations of the constitutional order'.

Of course, Restrepo not only referred to this global trend, but also alluded to the criticisms that he had regarding judicial review by the Supreme Court, which in his view required an immediate amendment, and which were basically the same topics suggested during the failed attempt to create a constitutional court in 1968.

[47] Carlos Restrepo Piedrahita, *Aspectos del Control Constitucional en Colombia* (Bogotá: Universidad Externado de Colombia, 1984) 73.

[48] Ibid.

[49] Carlos Restrepo Piedrahita, *Aspectos del Control Constitucional en Colombia* (Bogotá: Universidad Externado de Colombia, 1984) 73.

To sum up, the 1984 forum shows that although in 1968 similar arguments had been heard to promote the creation of a constitutional court, other factors were now added to justify the need for change, related to the Supreme Court decisions that caused discomfort to the executive. After the 1984 proposal to create a constitional court, during the administration of President Virgilio Barco Vargas (1986–1990), there was a new attempt to establish it in 1988.

A couple of years later, a National Constituent Assembly—ANC—achieved what had failed to materialize for nearly three decades: to replace the judicial review of the Supreme Court with that of a constitutional court. The constitutional court was included in the constitutional amendment that President César Gaviria presented to the ANC in 1991. However, as one of its promoters, Manuel José Cepeda expresses it, the idea of the constitutional court in the project was not peaceful:

> [There were] serious disagreements within the government of President Gaviria whether ... the proposal to establish a Constitutional Court should be [included], or whether it was preferable to keep the judicial review powers in the hands of the Supreme Court. This divergence—that in fact became the most intense internal discrepancy of the government—was finally resolved by President Gaviria in favor of the creation of a CC, against the position supported, among others, by the Minister of Justice, a former magistrate of the Supreme Court.[50]

According to Cepeda, President Gaviria 'actively supported the creation' of the constitutional court for the following reasons: the material inability of the Supreme Court to fulfil its increased tasks now that it would have to review all judicial decisions under the *tutela*; the need for 'entrusting a new Court the mission to preserve the innovative spirit that inspired the new Constitution'; and because a constitutional court could 'make legitimate and definitive decisions to resolve disputes of high political significance on the content and the scope of the new Constitution'.[51]

Within the debates of the ANC, on 7 March 1991, Pablo Caceres, President of the Supreme Court insisted on the serious risks that posed stripping the Court of its role as constitutional judge to transfer it to the 'political-type control' that the constitutional court would exert. He stated that the creation of the constitutional court was announced 'referring again to the comparative law', arguing that 'a Constitutional Court resolves the issue of the guarantee needed by those who exert the public power for their situational policies because such Court shall be composed of representatives, or rather spokespersons of the political chambers, the Government, and to respect a little bit the modesty of the independence, by members suggested by the Courts of justice'.[52] He also highlighted the judicial review exercised by the Supreme Court, which he described as the best, and according to the needs of the country, although he acknowledged that some minor adjustments could be made. Some of the tweaks to be made to

[50] Manuel José Cepeda Espinosa, *Polémicas Constitucionales* (Bogotá: Legis, 2007), 35.
[51] Ibid.
[52] Asamblea Nacional Constituyente, *Gaceta Constitucional* No. 57, martes 23 de abril de 1991. Bogotá, DE, 96.

the Supreme Court—proposed or accepted by him—were to redistribute the caseload between the constitutional chamber and the plenary chamber of the Court.

Returning to the testimony of Manuel José Cepeda, he stated that President Gaviria exercised his political leadership to convince the members to establish a constitutional court: 'Let's think about the future. The new Constitution requires for its full implementation, a new system of judicial review.' After intense negotiation, a secret ballot of 44 against 27 constituents approved the establishment of the constitutional court.

As can be seen, at the end of the 1991 constituent process, the Supreme Court did not succeed in its campaign to avoid their replacement as constitutional judge. This time, it could not stop the convergence of factors and varied interests. On the one hand, the interest of the Gaviria administration, driven by constitutionalists, in an era of global expansion and growth of the constitutional courts. Likewise, the interest of the constituents, who consented to the insistence of the government towards the necessity of creating a new court to uphold a new constitution, which would not be bound to the criteria of traditional jurists from the Supreme Court who would not understand the deep political change. Also, the interest of the political sectors, which had been insisting for a long time that the executive and legislative branches should participate in shaping constitutional justice: in particular in the election of the justices. Finally, the echoes of the rising human rights movement, which following the influence of the global context, stressed the need to defend the broad bill of rights that had been incorporated into the new constitution..

Finally, the 1991 constitution maintained the 'mixed' system of constitutionality control: it adapted the specialized constitutional court model with the constitutional court, but it was still accompanied by the Council of State and the contentious-administrative jurisdiction; and in addition, all of the country's judges became part of constitutional justice as judges of guardianship actions.

VI. Conclusion

This chapter has shown how different political actors, including the Supreme Court—with its interests and strategies, as well as legal scholars, under certain political contexts and legal doctrines—shaped Colombian constitutional justice in five different moments of national history. Thus, it was proposed to recall the complex paths to the creation of the constitutional court in the constitution of 1991, from the establishment of the PAU in 1910.

For this narrative to be made possible, it is important to appreciate that, although local constitutional justice had interesting developments, once the concentrated constitutional justice model inspired by the 'concentrated model' spread throughout Europe, Colombian legal scholars began to judge the local design and to demand its reform.

The trajectory also shows how different academic voices defended the Supreme Court, as a constitutional judge, with convincing arguments at different times when the substitution of a constitutional court was announced before 1991. Likewise, the active participation of other legal scholars in support of the creation of that court should be appreciated.

This chapter has shown how, during a great part of the twentieth century, different technical arguments and political reasons were combined to amend Colombian judicial review, and that many of those debates arose because the local design was examined under the lens of models, such as the aforementioned concentrated constitutional court of Kelsenian origin.

Finally, this trajectory put in evidence the resistance to adopt foreign legal institutions, as well as the 'strategical' adaptation by different judicial and political actors, and at the same time, how the prestige operated as a factor for legal transplants. In this way, it could open new perspectives to explore legal transplants on judicial review in a comparative, political, and historical perspective.

III
NEW INSIGHTS

A)

We the People or we the Judges: The Judicial Enforcement of Unconstitutional Constitutional Amendments

5

Courts as Guarantors of Democracy

Samuel Issacharoff

I. Introduction

Each era carries forward the logic of its formation. Out of the experience of the totalitarian and military regimes of the mid- to late twentieth century came the demand for human rights and the rule of law. As against tanks in the street, political opponents in prison or worse, and the wanton use of repression as a primary instrument of political control came the simple and compelling demand for respect of the individual. Human dignity was the touchstone of the challenge to authoritarianism, and the protection of human rights defined the legal agenda the world over.

That era has largely come to a close, fortunately. Despite hold out regimes in places like North Korea, and despite provocative tributes to state repression of the past, as in Brazil, the main challenge to democratic rule comes from the subversion of the democratic process from within, rather than assault from without. Populist regimes around the world, armed with a generally legitimate electoral mandate, assert a form of popular will that bleeds all too easily into majoritarian tyranny. Under the sway of charismatic leaders, these populist governments seek to entrench themselves in office through centralized executive power, clientelist rewards to supporters, and threats to compromise the liberties that generally permitted their assumption of power.[1]

Too often the current moment of populist unrest is assessed as if a return to older-style authoritarianism were imminent.[2] However, the current iteration of populism challenges the underpinnings of democratic governance in a more subtle way.[3] These regimes need democratic legitimacy and so must stand for election and re-election,

[1] See Jan-Werner Müller, *What is Populism*? (2016), 41–49 (identifying these and other antidemocratic tendencies of populist governments); see also David Fontana, 'Unbundling Populism', (2018) 65 UCLA Law Review 1482, 1487–96 (differentiating authoritarian, anti-establishment, and xenophobic tendencies within populist movements).

[2] See, e.g., Daniel Boffey, 'Macron: Political Divisions in Europe Are Like a Civil War', *Guardian* (17 April 2018 10:50 AM), https://www.theguardian.com/world/2018/apr/17/emmanuel-macron-europe-civil-war-illiberalism-nationalism (quoting French President Emmanuel Macron describing '[t]he deadly tendency which might lead [Europe] to the abyss' and warning 'a generation that's forgotten its own past'); *'Decline in Democracy Spreads Across Globe as Authoritarian Leaders Rise'*, NPR (3 August 2017 4:35 PM), https://www.npr.org/2017/08/03/541432445/decline-in-democracy-spreads-across-the-globe-as-authoritarian-leaders-rise; Ruth Ben-Ghiat, 'An American Authoritarian', *Atlantic* (10 August 2016), https://www.theatlantic.com/politics/archive/2016/08/american-authoritarianism-under-donald-trump/495263/ (comparing Donald Trump to Benito Mussolini).

[3] See Steven Levitsky & Daniel Ziblatt, *How Democracies Die* (2018), 5 ('Blatant dictatorship ... has disappeared across much of the world. Military coups and other violent seizures of power are rare.... Democracies still die, but by different means.'); Martin Wolf, 'The Rise of the Populist Authoritarians', *Financial Times* (22 January 2019), https://www.ft.com/content/4faf6c4e-1d84-11e9-b2f7-97e4dbd3580d

Samuel Issacharoff, *Courts as Guarantors of Democracy* In: *Constitutionalism*. Edited by: Alejandro Linares-Cantillo, Camilo Valdivieso-León, Santiago García-Jaramillo, Oxford University Press (2021). © The various contributors.
DOI: 10.1093/oso/9780192896759.003.0006

and generally cannot move outright to abolish rule of law constraints.[4] Most notably, these regimes often face judicial resistance to outright executive command.

At the same time, the populist challenge responds centrally to democracy's own institutional failures.[5] The reality of democratic governance today is that legislatures are oftentimes dysfunctional, political parties are weak, and the critical faith of common initiative among political rivals has faded.[6] As Michael Ignatieff has observed, adversaries become enemies. In these times, courts are forced into the role of guarantors of the integrity of democratic institutions.[7] More directly, 'the role of the judge in a democracy is to protect the constitution and democracy itself'.[8]

Three cases indicate how courts act as guarantors of constitutional democracy, suggesting ways they could react to current populist challenges. First, from India, the basic structures decisions set forth the principle that certain constitutional changes, even if procedurally proper, can go too far in undermining the fundamental character of a democratic order. This series of decisions also claims for the judiciary the power and duty to judge when an amendment oversteps this line. Next, the South African Constitutional Court's decision rejecting the draft constitution to replace the apartheid system establishes that protections against untrammeled majority rule are among these basic features of constitutional democracy. Last, a decision of the Constitutional Court of Colombia to disallow a president from running for a third term goes to show how courts can protect competition in the political process. Rejecting a properly enacted constitutional amendment that would have permitted a president to run for a third term, the Court feared lack of rotation in office would chill political debate and contestation. Together, these decisions articulate a distinct challenge for apex courts confronting a challenge to the democratic process itself.

What follows is an unfolding story of judicial oversight of democracy, a play in three acts, if one wills. This chapter does not argue that these formal constitutional alterations at issue in the three cases are the chief threat to democracy. Indeed, serious abuses occur under established law today irrespective of any constitutional

('The autocracies we are seeing today have important differences from those of the fascist parties . . . They are manipulative more than incontinently brutal.').

[4] See Samuel Issacharoff, *Fragile Democracies. Contested Power in the Era of Constitutional Courts* (Cambridge: Cambridge University Press, 2015), 168 (2015) ('All of the democracies created in the late twentieth century necessarily internalized the rights commitments, at least formally. Even in states with horrific human rights records, there is generally a formal legal commitment to rights protections for the citizenry.'); Tom Ginsburg & Aziz Z. Huq, *How to Save a Constitutional Democracy* (2018), 38–48 (categorizing declines in democracy as either 'authoritarian collapse' or 'democratic erosion' and describing the tools used to fight the two forms of decline).

[5] See David Brady, John Ferejohn, & Aldo Paparo, *Political Economy and Immigration: A Seven Nation Study*, NYU School of Law Public Law Research Paper No. 19-03 (2017) (discussing how the effects of the Great Recession and economic liberalization led to a gap between major political parties and their bases in advanced democracies, creating a space for populist movements).

[6] See Samuel Issacharoff, 'Populism Versus Democratic Governance', in Mark A. Graber, Sanford Levinson, & Mark Tushnet (eds), *Constitutional Democracy in Crisis?* (2018), 447–58(discussing these features of healthy democracies and how populists weaken them).

[7] See Ginsburg & Huq (n. 4), 240–5.

[8] Aharon Barak, 'Foreword: A Judge on Judging: The Role of a Supreme Court in a Democracy' (2002) 116 Harvard Law Review 16, 36.

amendment.[9] It also leaves to the side the propriety of the amendment process that creates the provisions that are struck down. Instead, its animating concern is how courts have claimed a role for themselves as guarantors of the democratic process, and what this role might entail against today's challenges.

II. Basic Structures

Perhaps the leading international authority on the judicial role in democracy is found in the jurisprudence of the Indian Supreme Court.[10] Beginning with independence, the Supreme Court and the Congress Party government were locked in confrontation over government efforts at land redistribution. The Indian courts resisted in the familiar language of protecting fundamental rights, including the right to property.[11] Populist governments through the 1950s and 1960s repeatedly passed legislation to seize large land estates without compensation, and the Court repeatedly tried to frustrate these efforts.[12] Finally, in *Golak Nath*,[13] the Court construed a constitutional provision allowing for judicial review of any law infringing upon fundamental rights to include constitutional amendments as well as statutes, and having established its own jurisdiction, proceeded to invalidate the challenged amendments.

Undeterred, the dominant Congress Party under the leadership of Indira Gandhi pushed through a new amendment to insulate certain legislative acts from judicial scrutiny under the 'Ninth Schedule' that made certain legislative enactments unreviewable.[14] Indian constitutional amendment only required a majority vote in both chambers of parliament to amend, giving a legislative majority unchecked power.[15] Finally, the declaration of national emergencies,[16] allowed Gandhi to create a one-party system with severe constrictions of basic civil liberties.[17]

In *Kesavananda Bharati*,[18] the Court pushed back, articulating what would become the basic structures doctrine for the first time. That doctrine established the right of judicial review of any legislative enactments deemed violative of the core functioning of democracy.[19] Although the Court permitted the limitations on property rights at issue, it reserved a sphere of 'basic structures' of constitutional rule that the judiciary

[9] See, e.g., Human Rights Watch, *Eroding Checks and Balances: Rule of Law and Human Rights under Attack in Poland* (2017) (documenting the legislative and policy measures that threaten the rule of law in Poland).

[10] See Issacharoff (n. 4), 159.

[11] See Raju Ramachandran, 'The Supreme Court and the Basic Structure Doctrine', in B. N. Kirpal et al. (eds), *Supreme but Not Infallible* (2000), 107.

[12] Ibid., 159–60; Manoj Mate, 'Two Paths to Judicial Power: The Basic Structure Doctrine and Public Interest Litigation in Comparative Perspective' (2010) 12 San Diego International Law Journal 175, 179–81.

[13] *Golak Nath v State of Punjab*, AIR 1967 SC 1645 (India).

[14] See Constitution Act (Twenty-Fourth Amendment), Sections 2–3 (1971) (India).

[15] See ibid.

[16] See P. N. Dhar, *Indira Gandhi, The 'Emergency,' and Indian Democracy* (2000) (memoir from advisor to Gandhi detailing the use of emergencies throughout the 1970s in India to deal with mounting unrest).

[17] See Issacharoff (n. 4), 161.

[18] *Kesavananda Bharati v State of Kerala*, AI.R 1973 SC 1461.

[19] See ibid.

could act to preserve.[20] In a move reminiscent of *Marbury v Madison*,[21] the Court allowed the legislature to win the battle over the immediate enactment, because by reserving this sphere of authority for the judiciary, it was fighting a larger war.

The Court left the scope of the basic structure doctrine undefined, and in part due to its length and fractured nature, the decision did not provide guidance on how to determine whether something was considered a basic structure.[22] In the years following, the Court began to flesh out the doctrine by finding certain emergency decrees unconstitutional.[23] The confrontation between the two branches finally came to a head when the Court applied the basic structures doctrine to provisions that limited the power of judicial review. In *Minerva Mills*,[24] the Court struck down a constitutional amendment that, among other things, demoted the right to property from being fundamental, thus insulating ongoing nationalizations of industry from judicial review, and essentially stripped all review jurisdiction over constitutional amendments from the Supreme Court.[25] In what emerged as the most important decision in this area of law, Justice P. N. Bhagwati's concurring opinion identified two basic structures that had been violated by these acts: the inherent limits on the power of the parliament to amend the constitution and the power of judicial review to enforce the provisions of the constitution.[26] The concurrence grounded the Court's assertion of power in the idea that the structural limits on governmental power inherent in a democracy are necessarily enforced by the court system.[27]

The basic structures doctrine allows courts to thwart attempts to compromise key features of the democratic nature of the political system. Although scholarship has focused on the ostensibly paradoxical idea of unconstitutional constitutional amendments,[28] more relevant here is how the series of decisions setting out the doctrine begins to claim a role for courts as guardians of the integrity of a larger democratic structure. No doubt, as in *Marbury* itself, the Court's intervention can be discounted as an attempt to safeguard its own power from attack. Yet, the doctrine developed in the context of ongoing centralization of power within a parliamentary majority and other authoritarian trends, does not simply attack the judiciary.[29]

[20] See ibid., para. 316 ('[E]very provision of the Constitution can be amended provided in the result the basic foundation and structure of the Constitution remains the same.').

[21] 5 US (1 Cranch) 137 (1803).

[22] See Vivek Krishnamurthy, 'Note, *Colonial Cousins: Explaining India and Canada's Unwritten Constitutional Principles*' (2009) 34 Yale Journal of International Law 207, 227–8 (summarizing the various justices' opinions in *Kesavananda* on what was included within the basic structures of democracy).

[23] See Mate (n. 12), 185.

[24] *Minerva Mills Ltd v India*, AIR 1980 SC 1789.

[25] See ibid., _. The Amendment was couched, as authoritarian measures frequently are, in the language of democracy and preservation of the constitutional order. See Statement of Objects and Reasons, The Constitution (Forty-Second Amendment) Act, 1976 (India) ('A Constitution to be living must be growing. If the impediments to the growth of the Constitution are not removed, the Constitution will suffer a virtual atrophy.').

[26] *Minerva Mills* (n. 24), paras 91–5 ('It will therefore be seen that the limited amending power of Parliament is itself an essential feature of the Constitution, a part of its basic structure . . .').

[27] Ibid. ('It is for the judiciary to uphold the constitutional values and to enforce the constitutional limitations.').

[28] See David Landau, 'Abusive Constitutionalism' (2013) 47 UC Davis Law Review 189, 232, n. 165 (collecting scholarship criticizing the idea).

[29] See Issacharoff (n. 4), 164; Ramachandran (n. 11), 115–17.

Courts around the world cite the Indian Court for the proposition that the judiciary is uniquely situated to safeguard democracy.[30] However, as the Indian Supreme Court itself struggled with it after it had sketched the key features of the doctrine, it can be difficult to determine what exactly the basic structures of democracy are.[31] It is also noteworthy that in *Kesavananda Bharati*, the Court grounded the doctrine specifically in the structures of the existing Indian constitution, as opposed to deeper principles of democracy or other external sources.[32] Much as the basic structures doctrine introduced the concept of safeguarding democracy, it left unanswered what features of democracy were actually the basic structures demanding judicial vigilance.

III. Limits on Majorities

India asks the question of what forms the basic structure of democracy; South Africa begins to answer it. As part of the transition out of apartheid, the newly formed Constitutional Court was tasked with reviewing a draft constitution written by a Constitutional Assembly (both houses of the legislature) to govern the new state. By itself, this reflected an extraordinary innovation in the pacted transition from apartheid. The negotiations between the white rulers and the African National Congress ('ANC') yielded a set of 34 principles that would frame any new governmental structure. In particular, these principles granted important protections for civil liberties and fundamental rights, including property rights. The transitional process did not create a fully elaborated constitutional structure and instead left that to the post-apartheid political process.

To recast the history very briefly, South Africa's apartheid regime was slowly collapsing as international condemnation and internal dissent grew.[33] It also became clear that the ANC, the largest organization fighting for liberation, and its leader Nelson Mandela, who had become an international hero while imprisoned, would take power when apartheid fell.[34] However, negotiating a peaceful transition posed its own problems. The white minority owned the vast majority of land in the country, and feared uncompensated seizures of its property.[35] Although the apartheid system had

[30] See Richard Albert, 'How a Court Becomes Supreme: Defending the Constitution from Unconstitutional Amendments' (2017) 77 Maryland Law Review 181, 183–4 (collecting examples); Ramachandran (n. 11), 108 ('The "basic structure" doctrine alters the emphasis of democratic constitutionalism and had an immediate effect on the thinking of many Constitution makers and judiciaries throughout the world.').

[31] See, e.g., *Supreme Court Advocates on Record Ass'n v India* (1993) 4 SCC 441 (finding an independent judiciary to be a basic structure); *S. R. Bommai v India*, AIR 1994 SC 1918 (finding secularism to be a basic structure); *L. Chandra Kumar v Union of India* (1997) 1 SCJ 552 (finding judicial, rather than administrative, process to be a basic structure).

[32] While the opinion fractured, the summary endorsed by nine of the thirteen justices found that the amendment process 'does not enable Parliament to alter the basic structure or framework of the Constitution'. See Ramachandran (n. 11), 114.

[33] See Issacharoff (n. 4), 166–7.

[34] Ibid., 171.

[35] See *In re Certification of the Constitution of the Republic of South Africa*, 1996 (4) SALR 744 (CC) (S. Afr.), para. 12 (describing 'the fear in some quarters that the constitution ... might not sufficiently address the anxieties and the insecurities of such constituencies'); Issacharoff (n. 4), 172–3 (discussing the resistance to including a bill of rights within the interim constitution, because it 'was seen as inevitably entrenching the privileged position of the white minority').

been largely majoritarian for the few who were allowed to participate in politics, the prospect of the black majority taking power led the white government to call for the codification of property rights and structural protections against majorities.[36] For its part, the black majority demanded changes to the unequal distribution of wealth, and any agreement that ceded too much ground to the ancien regime would lack popular support, diminishing the chances for a peaceful transition.[37]

From 1991 to 1993, the government and the ANC (as well as other organizations) negotiated over an interim constitution and the eventual form of the government in Kempton Park, Johannesburg.[38] These negotiations produced an interim constitution, to be in place for a five-year transition, and a set of thirty-four principles that would be the basis of the new constitution.[39] Among these principles were constitutional supremacy, multiparty democracy, and the separation of powers with an impartial judiciary.[40] A new legislature, chosen in elections with universal adult suffrage, would draft a permanent constitution during the transitional period, a process that would involve a public outreach campaign to build popular support and garner feedback.[41]

Eventually, the draft constitution would be submitted to a new constitutional court, which would then decide if it comported with the 34 principles.[42] In the *Certification Decision*, the Court found the proposed constitution lacked sufficient protection for minorities, both individuals and minority parties, and thus needed redrafting to satisfy the constitutional principles agreed upon during transition negotiations. In other words, the decision found the constitution to be in significant parts unconstitutional. While the framework of the *Certification Decision* was as a guarantor of the underlying negotiated principles, the Court nonetheless had to reach further into the questions left open in the Basic Structures doctrine as to what exactly were the prerequisites for democratic governance.

The Court found the draft constitution 'satisfied the basic structures and premises ... contemplated by the applicable [Constitutional Principles]' and 'complie[d] with the overwhelming majority of the requirements'. Yet the Court found certain principles violated, including a requirement for special majorities for constitutional amendments and the entrenchment of fundamental rights and freedoms.[43] Also problematic was how the Public Protector, a government watchdog position analogous to an Inspector General, was subject to removal by a simple legislative majority.[44]

[36] As Albie Sachs, an ANC leader who became a justice of the Constitutional Court, put it, '[n]ow that the majority is going to be black, South African whites suddenly believe majority rule is a terrible thing ... Now that the majority stands to change color, you no longer hear people talking about majority rule but "majoritarianism" ... '. Donald L. Horowitz, *A Democratic South Africa? Constitutional Engineering in a Divided Society* (1991), 98.

[37] See *Certification Decision* (n. 35), paras 12–13.

[38] See Issacharoff (n. 4), 172.

[39] See ibid.; *Certification Decision* (n. 35), paras 14–30 (giving procedural and historical background leading up to the certification process).

[40] See *Certification Decision* (n. 35), para. 45 (synthesizing various constitutional principles into a set of 'basic structures and premises').

[41] See ibid., para. 20.

[42] See ibid., para. 13 ('[A]n independent arbiter would have to ascertain and declare whether the new constitution indeed complied with the guidelines before it could come into force.').

[43] Ibid., paras 45, 483.

[44] See ibid., para. 163.

Unifying the defects the Court identified was a sense that majority power, against minority parties and individuals, needed stronger institutional checks.[45]

After the Court's remand, the Constitutional Assembly made the requested fixes, making the amendment process more difficult, formally entrenching fundamental rights and providing for their judicial enforcement, and requiring a two-thirds vote for removal of the Public Protector.[46] The revised constitution was then resubmitted for judicial approval, which the Constitutional Court granted in the *Second Certification Decision*,[47] and the new constitution went into effect in February 1997.[48]

The conventional reading of the *Certification Decision* is that the Court was giving force to the thirty-four constitutional principles agreed upon during the transition negotiations, and these principles provide the full basis for rejecting the draft.[49] Indeed, the Court connects each of the provisions in the draft constitution that it strikes down to a specific constitutional principle.[50] However, the decision also discusses how the principles 'must be applied purposively and teleologically to give expression to the commitment "to create a new order".'[51]

Because the principles were written broadly, the Court must pull from other sources to apply them to specific language. For example, one principle declared that minority political parties be allowed to participate 'in a manner consistent with democracy',[52] and to determine whether a voting scheme met this criterion, the Court looked to comparative law.[53] In another portion on individual rights to compensation for seized property, '[a]n examination of international conventions and foreign constitutions' guides the Court's reasoning.[54] In its preamble, the Court cites the 'aspirational ideal' of 'the Montesquieuan principle of a threefold separation of state power'.[55] Although the objections are fit within the framework of the 34 Principles, a common theme runs through them, about the need to protect individual rights and liberties, and thwart the ability of a simple legislative majority to wield power. In other words, these protections go to the basic structures of constitutional democracy.

[45] See Issacharoff (n. 4).

[46] See Issacharoff (n. 4), 186. In drafting the new version of the constitution, the Assembly made extensive changes, some related to the reasons for rejection, while 'others simply tightened up the text'. *Court of South Africa, The Certification Process*, https://www.concourt.org.za/index.php/constitution/the-certification-process, accessed 22 March 2019.

[47] *In re Certification of the Amended Text of the Constitution of the Republic of South Africa*, 1997 (2) SA 97 (CC) (S. Afr.).

[48] See Norman Dorsen, et al., *Comparative Constitutionalism* (2010), 129.

[49] For example, the website of the South African Constitutional Court describes the decision as 'identif[ying] the features that did not comply with the principles' and explaining how the draft 'failed in several respects to satisfy the conditions thrashed out in multiparty talks'. *Constitutional Court of South Africa, The Certification Process*, https://www.concourt.org.za/index.php/constitution/the-certification-process, accessed 22 March 2019).

[50] See *Certification Decision* (n. 35) para. 482.

[51] Ibid., paras 34–8.

[52] Ibid., para. 222.

[53] See, e.g., ibid., para. 227 ('In the German Bundesrat, on which the NCOP appears to have been modeled, [a similar voting scheme is in place], and there is nothing to suggest that the Germany system has proved unsatisfactory or undemocratic.').

[54] Ibid., para. 73.

[55] Ibid., para. 6.

In a key section, the Court finds that '[i]t is no coincidence that the drafters of the [constitutional principle]s, having in [constitutional principle] I established the principle that the state they contemplated would be a democracy, immediately proceeded to describe one of its key attributed in [constitutional principle] II'. Principle 2 guarantees that 'all universally accepted fundamental rights ... shall be provided for and protected by entrenched and justiciable provisions in the Constitution'. It defines these 'fundamental rights, freedoms and civil liberties' according to the norms 'established in human rights jurisprudence' as those 'recognised in open and democratic societies', and defines 'universal' as applying only to those rights 'that have gained a wide measure of international acceptance as fundamental'.[56] The Constitutional Court cites to various sources to determine these, including 'South African jurisprudence and academic writing', the law of 'Germany and similar European countries', 'a survey of international instruments', and the African Charter on Human and People's Rights. Thus, though the Court's task is nominally limited to giving force to the constitutional principles, the incorporation of the modifier 'universally accepted' into the text functionally delegates the question of what rights are included to the Constitutional Court. The Court then turns to outside sources and broader conceptions of democracy to realize the principles.

It is of course a tribute to the leadership of Nelson Mandela that the government readily accepted the Court's ruling. By the time the *Certification Decision* came down, Nelson Mandela commanded sizeable legislative majorities, served as the Head of State, and controlled the police and military.[57] The need to placate the white minority to assure peaceful transfer of power would have seemed less pressing because transition was a fait accompli.[58]

However, the Court's attention to minority rights makes sense for two reasons. First, underpinning the fight against apartheid was a belief in fundamental human dignity.[59] The memory was still fresh of a political system that did not protect individuals' civil rights against an unjust government. Secondly, the Court understood that circumstances had changed, and instead of guarding against a collapse into chaos, it had to protect against a different threat. The new government had been designed with the singular figure of Nelson Mandela in mind, and accordingly concentrated power in the office of the President.[60] Mandela and the ANC were synonymous with the anti-apartheid struggle and had, as expected, dominated the first round of free elections. When the Constitutional Court spoke of a dominant parliamentary majority, it feared the power of an entrenched ANC.

The concerns evident in the *Certification Decision* became all the more pressing as the ANC consolidated its power, and as that power passed from Mandela to less enlightened successors.

[56] Ibid., paras 48–52.

[57] See Issacharoff (n. 4), 189.

[58] See ibid.

[59] See ibid., 172 ('The campaign against apartheid had been largely waged in the name of human dignity and human equality. It was simply impossible not to enshrine these inspirational values in a political system based on fundamental treatment of all individuals as repositories of basic civil rights.').

[60] See ibid., 171 ('[T]here was no escaping the fact that the ANC would control the parliament and that as a result Nelson Mandela would serve as head of state.').

IV. Protection of Political Competition

Any discussion of the Colombian Constitutional Court's decision in the *Second Re-Election Case*[61] is necessarily inadequate in the circumstances of a discussion before the Court that delivered that important ruling. Among the many decisions that have articulated a principle of 'unconstitutional constitutional amendments', as framed by David Landau and Rosalind Dixon, no decision stands out so forcefully as the Court's confrontation with the prospect of a third presidential term for President Álvaro Uribe.

Uribe had taken took office in 2002, assuming leadership of a country riven by violence from drug cartels and guerrilla paramilitary groups.[62] His first term restored a measure of peace and security to the country, causing his popularity to soar.[63] Because the Colombian constitution, responding to the Latin American tradition of strongmen, limited presidents to only one term in office, the legislature had to pass an amendment to allow Uribe to run for a second term.[64] Though the amendment was procedurally proper, it was challenged as undermining the constitutional order.[65] The Constitutional Court disagreed, first finding the validity of the amendment justiciable and then upholding it.[66] The majority found the legislature could amend the constitution pursuant to the authorized procedure, but could not replace constitutional regimes entirely. Allowing Uribe to run for two terms in office was on the correct side of that line, because an eight-year presidency did not change defining features of the state.[67]

Uribe won and served a second term, stabilized the country, and remained a popular figure.[68] Perhaps unsurprisingly, he then attempted to run for a third term, and again, the legislature passed a constitutional amendment to allow him to do so.[69] The amendment went before the Constitutional Court, which struck it down in the *Second Re-Election Case*.[70] Although the Court cited procedural defects in the amendment process, none was serious enough to justify overturning an amendment that had just been endorsed by the people in a referendum vote.[71] Instead, the decision makes two important moves: it names 'alternation in office' as one of the core, inalienable

[61] See Corte Constitucional, 26 de febrero de 2010, Sentencia C-141/10, Gaceta de la Corte Constitucional, http://www.corteconstitucional.gov.co/relatoria/2010/c-141-10.htm (translation by author).

[62] See Issacharoff (n. 4), 146.

[63] See ibid.

[64] See ibid., 147; Ley de Garantias Electorales, L. 996, 24 de noviembre de 2005.

[65] See ibid.

[66] See Corte Constitucional, 19 de octubre de 2005, Sentencia C-1040/05, Gaceta de la Corte Constitucional.

[67] See ibid. See also Constitutional Claim Decision C-1040, 2005, http://english.corteconstitucional.gov.co/sentences/C-1040-2005.pdf (summarizing in English the *First Re-Election Case*). The Court describes how the 'substitution of the Constitution occurs when a defining element... instead of being amended is replaced with another element, opposed to it or completely different' (internal quotations omitted), and how '[t]wo terms is not a substitution.' Ibid.

[68] See Issacharoff (n. 4), 147.

[69] See ibid., 148; L. 1354/09, 8 de septiembre de 2009, D.O. No.47.466.

[70] Corte Constitucional, 26 de febrero de 2010, Sentencia C-141/10, Gaceta de la Corte Constitucional, http://www.corteconstitucional.gov.co/relatoria/2010/c-141-10.htm.

[71] See Issacharoff (n. 4), 150 ('None of these [procedural] defects alone was of sufficient magnitude to justify overturning what appeared a clear popular mandate.').

features of democracy and allows the judiciary a role in fostering meaningful electoral competition.

What changed? It is difficult to construct a categorical principle that two terms are permissible, but three are not. Instead, the Court's multiple opinion stressed that, under the circumstances of Colombia's nascent democracy, allowing a three-term President would violate 'the principle of separation of powers and the system of checks and balance, [and] the rule of alternation in office according to pre-established periods'.[72] Had Uribe been permitted to serve a third term, due to the length of fixed terms for various appointed positions, he would have been able to shape much of government, including consequential officeholders outside the executive branch.[73] This would concentrate power in one individual who would control the administrative state and judiciary into the future in a way not contemplated by the original constitution.[74]

The decision reflected shifts in the political framework that allowed the Court to intervene. First, Uribe's popularity, while still high, was not unimpeachable in the same way it had been before, so the Court could feel more comfortable in acting as a check against him.[75] Secondly, Colombian voters had taken advantage of the period of comparative stability to sort themselves into political parties, and voters were now sufficiently affiliated to permit meaningful competition.[76] In other words, the choice was no longer between anarchy and Uribe. The country had stabilized to allow for robust democratic contestation, and allowing Uribe to participate would prevent this, because he was so closely tied to this new stability and would dominate any election.

The Court, therefore, acted to preserve competition in the political sphere, finding 'the alternation of power constitutes an element or essential component of the democratic model established by the 1991 Constitution'.[77] The risk to democracy it perceived was that without alternation among candidates, power inevitably concentrates. In time, disputes over many questions—including economic affairs, public sector employment, and how private industry operates—would be channeled through the same small group of people. The Court feared this would lead to the development of the pathologies of corruption, clientelism, and cronyism, common to functionally single party states.[78] If the success of any petition for government action turns

[72] Corte Constitucional (n. 70); Rosalind Dixon & Samuel Issacharoff, 'Living to Fight Another Day: Judicial Deferral in Defense of Democracy' (2016) Wisconsin Law Review 683, 692 (giving the quoted translation).

[73] See Corte Constitucional (n. 70), §6.3.6 (analysing 'the possibility of a second reelection and its institutional impact').

[74] Ibid.

[75] See Dixon & Issacharoff (n. 72), 718 ('While Uribe's personal popularity never fell below sixty-five percent during his time in office, by 2009 Colombia had seen a marked decrease in its rate of economic growth, and thus the strength of the underlying factors sustaining Uribe's popularity.').

[76] See ibid. at 718–19.

[77] Corte Constitucional (n. 70), §6.3.6.1.3.

[78] See Issacharoff (n. 4), 135 ('Where dependence of connections to the incumbent regime becomes the basis for employment or government contracts or social welfare benefits, no opposition can ensure its supporters that disloyalty to the incumbent does not mean isolation and penury. Even where elections are reasonably free and fair, and even where the opposition does not face direct oppression, the suffocating consequences of perpetual rule will be manifest.').

on one's connections to who is in power, then dissent becomes too risky. This in turn chills political challenge: why run against someone who controls all levers of power in the state?

For the Court, the need to 'assur[e] checks and balances on presidential power' would be undermined if 'a president with popular power could have a decisive influence on the configuration of legislative power in such a way that the political parties supporting him would have a clear majority in Congress . . .'.[79] Anticipating the problem of executive unilateralism under populist regimes, the Court went on: 'the advantage of having served as president for eight years' allows 'the progressive increment in presidential periods [that] can allow a leader to perpetuate himself in power and potentially create a vicious cycle permitting the consolidating of only one person in power.'[80]

Two additional factors can compound this risk: first, in much of the democratic world, administrative and executive powers have tended to merge over time, meaning more government functions are handled through the executive.[81] The Colombian Court well anticipated the risk that consolidated executive authority would take a democratic system and 'convert it into the deformed version known as *presidencialismo*, which is characterized precisely by that exaggerated predominance and by the tendency to exceed the maximum time allowed for the exercise of presidential power in order to maintain the *caudillo* and his political project in power . . .'.[82]

Secondly, in states that do transition to democracy, the party formed of the liberation movement tends to entrench itself as a supermajority, following in the historic tradition of the Mexican Partido Revolucionario Institucional. For example, in Namibia, the anti-apartheid group SWAPO now acts as essentially the country's sole political party, leading to the problems described above.[83] This also describes the current status of the ANC in South Africa, lending credence to the concerns of the Constitutional Court in the *Certification Decision*.[84] The Colombian Court feared that Uribe would quash political opposition, not necessarily through overt means but instead by simply continuing to hold office and appoint officials over an extended period of time.

Thus, the Court stepped in to protect and indeed, foster competition in the political arena. Because civil society and political institutions were weak in light of the decades-long conflict, the Court intervened in the *Second Re-Election Case* to support their fledgling efforts. Uribe accepted the Court's decision, and allowed for the peaceful transition of power to his successor.[85]

[79] Manuel José Cepeda Espinosa & David Landau, *Colombian Constitutional Law: Leading Cases* 355 (Oxford: Oxford University Press, 2017) 355).

[80] Ibid., 356.

[81] See Francesca Bignami, 'From Expert Administration to Accountability Network: A New Paradigm for Comparative Administrative Law' (2011) 59 American Journal of Comparative Law 859, 879–84 (surveying developments in administrative law in presidential and parliamentary systems).

[82] Cepeda Espinosa & Landau (n. 79), 357.

[83] See Henning Melber, 'From Controlled Change to Changed Control: The Case of Namibia' (2003) 21 Journal of Contemporary African Studies 267, 277–9.

[84] See Issacharoff (n. 4), 264 ('Already there are ominous signs in South Africa of political attacks on the constitutional court as an institution . . . But the court remains the only significant institution not under direct ANC control . . .').

[85] See ibid, 151.

V. Conclusion

There is no escaping the difficult task that apex courts have assumed the world over. Core issues of democratic governance that would have been deemed political questions decades ago are now standard fare before courts empowered with constitutional judicial review. And, perhaps inevitably, this power has now extended to the structures of the constitutions themselves.

Once stripped of the pretense of narrow textual exposition, such constitutional tribunals must begin to articulate a theory of democratic governance that justifies their intervention into the domain of the proper allocation of political power and electoral accountability. The three acts presented thus build on each other. First, the Indian Supreme Court carves out the category of basic structures of democracy, claiming for itself the power to identify and act to protect them. The South African Constitutional Court names one of the structures: constitutional democracies necessarily protect minorities, both individuals and political parties, against a legislative majority. It then applied this principle by refusing to approve a formal constitutional structure until these protections were added. This active role for the judiciary continues in the Colombian Constitutional Court's disapproval of a constitutional amendment to permit a three-term president. The Court acts to foster a dynamic and contested political sphere, fearing the consequences of power accruing over time.

When taken together, the decisions demonstrate an emerging institutional role for courts. Although the Indian basic structures decisions and the *Certification Decision* concern in part individual rights, these liberty interests are not the focus, and instead, the courts act as safeguards of a larger constitutional order. This includes actively policing the separation of powers to preserve their own role as an independent check on power and creating the conditions for civil society organizations to grow. Rather than liberty or simple majority rule, they act on behalf of constitutional democracy. This guardian role suggests how courts can react to novel issues of this phase of resurgent populism globally.

First, they must be vigilant against changes in law that penalize opposition parties or protect against challenges to incumbents. The Taiwanese constitutional court provides an example. After enjoying decades as the dominant party, the Kuomintang ('KMT') began to lose its hold on power due to political challenge.[86] It reacted by postponing parliamentary elections and insulating the allocation of seats for parties in the National Assembly from the direct results of elections.[87] After a non-KMT candidate won the Presidency, the Constitutional Court struck down the changes the KMT had made as 'alter[ing] the existing constitutional provisions concerning the fundamental nature of governing norms and order', demonstrating the long reach of the ideas set forth in the Indian basic structures decisions.[88]

[86] See Samuel Issacharoff, *Judicial Review in Troubled Times: Stabilizing Democracy in a Second Best World* (2019) 98 North Carolina Law Review 1, 14.

[87] See ibid., 14–15.

[88] Interpretation No. 499 (Taiwan Constitutional Court Interpretation, 24 March 2000), available at https://www.judicial.gov.tw/constitutionalcourt/EN/p03_01.asp?expno=499.

Another example comes from the United States. After North Carolina Republicans lost a gubernatorial election, the Republican-controlled state legislature promptly stripped powers from the office, with the Republican incumbent signing the legislation before his Democratic successor took office.[89] This was struck down by the North Carolina Supreme Court as violating state constitutional provisions creating a separation of powers and interfering with the governor's ability to ensure that the laws are faithfully executed.[90] As in the *Second Re-Election Case*, the courts intervened to prevent incumbents from entrenching their own power.

Next, courts can also channel disputes into the formal mechanisms of democracy to foster deliberation. When Theresa May's government asserted the right to implement Brexit directly, as a command decreed by the people, the United Kingdom Supreme Court stepped in to force the executive to go through the proper procedural channels of parliamentary authorization.[91] The Court recognized that the action came out of the inability of the major political parties to resolve their intra-coalitional differences, an attempt to escape the duty of deliberation.[92] However, as a major constitutional change, Brexit 'must be effected ... by Parliamentary legislation'.[93] As opposed to exit by essentially decree, going through the regular legislative process will (at least theoretically) confer the benefits of democratic legitimacy and improved outcomes it is intended to provide.

If courts perform these functions, they will do so in their capacity as guarantors of the basic structures of democracy. Just as they have acted to protect political competition and the rights of minorities, they may also identify and protect other features of constitutional democracy. Whether vibrant opposition parties, the soft power of democratic deliberation, or an independent judiciary, more can no doubt be included under the umbrella of basic structures of democracy. No doubt more such challenges will force courts to further elaborate the structural preconditions for democracy as much of the democratic world currently grapples with a wave of populist movements. This is fraught terrain for judiciaries the world over. Given the current weaknesses of many democratic institutions, it is difficult to escape this critical new judicial undertaking.

[89] See Issacharoff (n. 87), 25.

[90] See *Cooper v Berger*, 809 SE 2d 98, 112–13 (NC 2018).

[91] *See R (on the application of Miller and another) v Secretary of State for Exiting the European Union* [2017] UKSC 5 (appeal taken from Northern Ireland, England, and Wales).

[92] See Issacharoff (n. 86), 23.

[93] *Miller* (n. 91), [82].

6

The Machinery of International Law and Democratic Backsliding

The Problem of Term Limits

Tom Ginsburg

Our era is one of democratic backsliding, in which there is great anxiety about the future. As the number of democracies decline, and formerly 'consolidated' democracies leave the ranks entirely, we are prone to wonder whether the future is even darker. This mood coincides with a general scepticism about human rights. Both from the academic right and the academic left, we are confronted with the claim that human rights law is hypocritical, lacks efficacy, or sets the wrong goals.[1] *Mutatis mutandis*, it is unlikely to serve as a force for the protection of democracy.

In this chapter I address a phenomenon at the intersection of these trends that is occurring with increasing frequency. In some cases, the idea of rights is abused to facilitate democratic erosion and incumbent takeover. The cases I focus on are the abuse of international rights to political participation so as to facilitate a leader remaining in office beyond the constitutionally mandated term. This involves not only the abuse of the interpretation of rights, but also the abuse of the doctrine of unconstitutional constitutional amendments, which has spread around the world in recent years. How does this happen and what, if anything, can international law do about it?

After introducing a motivating case, the famous decision of the Colombian Constitutional Court in the second re-election decision, in which courts stood for the protection of democracy, I examine recent 'bad' cases in which rights and constitutional amendments are abused to extend leaders' terms. I survey recent developments in the law of term limits, and briefly propose a normative interpretation of the right to political participation which ought to be consistent with the emerging doctrine. My suggestion is that there is an emerging consensus, at least in some regions of the world, that there are limits in states' abilities to modify term limits unconditionally.

This point is part of a broader argument I am making, that courts, international institutions, and international human rights adjudicators all ought to be engaged in the promotion, support, and disciplining of democracy. Even if there is no 'right' to democracy in international law, it remains the case that human rights are best protected by structure of democratic governance that rest on the consent of the governed. This is true notwithstanding ample evidence that democracies are certainly capable of

[1] Samuel Moyn, *Not Enough: Human Rights in an Unequal World* (Cambridge: Harvard University Press, 2018); Eric Posner, *The Twilight of Human Rights Law* (New York: Oxford University Press, 2014); Stephen Hopgood, *The Endtimes of Human Rights* (Ithaca: Cornell University Press, 2013).

Tom Ginsburg, *The Machinery of International Law and Democratic Backsliding* In: *Constitutionalism*. Edited by: Alejandro Linares-Cantillo, Camilo Valdivieso-León, Santiago García-Jaramillo, Oxford University Press (2021). © The various contributors.
DOI: 10.1093/oso/9780192896759.003.0007

human rights abuses against minorities at home and populations abroad. But it is still the case that the worst atrocities are committed by non-democratic governments, and the electoral constraint on democratic leaders means that they are unlikely to be able to sustain the same kind of massive human rights abuses. To the sceptic on this point, I ask that you suspend disbelief for the duration of the essay.

It is appropriate to put these ideas on paper for a conference celebrating the jurisprudence of the Constitutional Court of Colombia. The Court's two decisions on re-election are justly famous in the universe of comparative constitutional law, building on a longer history in which the Court had pioneered doctrines of review of amendments for constitutionality.[2] They remain, as I will describe below, the paradigm for clear reasoning and substantive protection of democracy by constitutional adjudicators. But Colombia's lead has not always been followed, as we shall see.

I. Some Preliminaries: Democracy

My working definition of democracy is a drawn from my recent book with Aziz Z. Huq, in which democracy consists of three linked elements: government characterized by competitive elections, in which the modal adult can vote and the losers concede;[3] the enforcement of a minimal set of rights to speech, association, and the ability to run for office; and what we call the bureaucratic rule of law, which governs administration.[4] As we argue, this is a relatively thin definition, not tied to any particular vision of political economy or thick version of policy. But it is also one that emphasizes the systemic quality of democracy. The three elements work together and are mutually reinforcing: elections will not matter much if alternative parties cannot organize, campaign, and run for office, and rights will be of little use without bureaucracy to enforce them.

Recognizing the systemic quality is critical to the defence of democracy. If enough slight deviations occur on multiple dimensions, it is possible that a country's democracy can erode far enough so as not to be worthy of the term. Kim Lane Scheppele has identified the problem of what she calls the 'Frankenstate' in which each formal element of liberal democracy is present, but the operations of the elements interact to produce a regime of entrenched power. This could be because of amendments to particular aspects of the system, each one acceptable on its own. A court or other international actor confronted with this kind of institutional structure may have trouble identifying what single reform constitutes a potentially fatal threat to democracy, or which single institution it is that crosses the line to merit illegality. Identifying this involves some sense of the 'basic structure' of democracy. But it is not a formulaic set of principles or rules so much as a recognition of the forces that threaten democracy

[2] Mario Alberto Cajas-Sarria, 'Judicial Review of Constitutional Amendments in Colombia: A Political and Historical Perspective' (2017) 5(3) Theory and Practice of Legislation 245–75.

[3] Adam Przeworski, *Democracy and the Market* (New York: Cambridge University Press, 1991), 10 ('Democracy is a system in which parties lose elections').

[4] Tom Ginsburg & Aziz Z. Huq *How to Save a Constitutional Democracy* (Chicago: University of Chicago Press, 2018), 10

from within, and that must be checked. Only with this kind of vision can law effectively respond to the threat of the day.

The threat of the day, as I have already implied, is one of democratic erosion—the slow death of democracy by a thousand cuts, rather than the quick collapse of democracy through a coup d'etat or revolution. Increasingly, democracy dies slowly. And so one underlying question is what can be done to stop that process. The last part of my chapter considers the role of international law in this regard. To be clear, I usually take a sovereigntist vision of international law, in which there is no universal 'right to democracy', and a variety of ways of achieving a good society, compatible with basic human rights. However, we are observing recent developments of a normative framework, at the regional level, to address problems of democratic erosion.

With these working definitions in mind, let us proceed with the analysis.

II. All Good Things Go Together: Colombia

Colombian readers will recognize the threat of erosion and the role of the Court in identifying it. By 2004, when President Alvaro Uribe's allies in the Congress sought to allow his immediate re-election by passing a constitutional amendment to allow a second term, the Court had already declared several constitutional amendments to violate the constitution under the constitutional replacement doctrine. In response to a challenge, the Court issued Decision C-1040/2005, authored by Justice Manuel J. Cepeda, holding that that the essential features of the constitution would not be replaced, in part because the system of checks and balances would remain in place. Uribe subsequently won re-election in a landslide.

In 2009, with his second term soon to come to a close, Uribe's allies again sought a referendum to allow him a chance at a third term. Uribe remained, and remains, popular. But in 2010, the second re-election decision constrained him from running for a third term. The decision, which is the subject of widespread commentary, took just the kind of broad, systemic approach that is in my view needed for courts to address problems of democratic backsliding. It not only identified some procedural irregularities in the proposal, a standard task of courts, but it also noted that the power that Uribe would accumulate as a result of three terms, particularly in regard to appointments or key government officials, would amount to an unconstitutional 'replacement'. The logic of the original constitution had been based on a single term for the presidency. With multiple terms, a president could potentially dominate other branches of government, undermining the separation of powers in the constitutional order.

As President Uribe complied with the decision, his chosen successor Juan Manuel Santos won office in 2010. This led to significant policy reversals and adjustments, particularly with regard to the peace negotiations with rebel groups, that need not detain us here.

The whole incident amounted to what Professor Huq and I have called a 'near miss'.[5] By this we mean situations in which democracy is under some threat of backsliding,

[5] Tom Ginsburg and Aziz Z. Huq, 'Democracy's Near Misses', (2018) 29 Journal of Democracy 16–30.

but, at a critical juncture, the backsliding is arrested and democracy survives. One of our findings in that research is that, in many countries, it is actors that do not themselves have democratic electoral legitimacy whose intervention is key to preserving democracy. In the case of Colombia it was an unelected constitutional court. In other cases, it might be a military, a bureaucracy, or an electoral commission that plays the crucial role.

This point is an important one to consider when thinking about what international institutions can and cannot do. Obviously international courts and bureaucracies are not democratically legitimate. But they can, under some circumstances, play a critical role in arresting democratic backsliding by holding leaders to account, or slowing down processes of erosion. We shall return to this point at the end of this essay.

III. Abuses of Human Rights Law for Incumbent Takeover

The major threat to democracy in our era is that of incumbent takeover, in which a leader seeks to remain in office past his or her constitutionally mandated term, and to erode democracy as well. Term limits are thus critical for the protection of democracy.

Honduras has been a major battleground for novel institutional design and conceptions of executive term limits. In light of a regional history of term limit abuses, the constitution of Honduras, originally adopted in 1982, allowed only a single term presidency. Not only was the term limit unamendable, but there was a kind of 'poisoned pill' provision whereby anyone who even *proposed* changing the term limit would be punished with immediate removal from office.[6]

In 2009, incumbent president Manuel Zelaya called for a non-binding referendum on changing the limit, provoking a claim that he had violated the constitutional provision.[7] The Attorney General and Congress resisted, and Congress passed a law forbidding the poll, yet Zelaya pushed on. After the country's Supreme Court ruled that Zelaya was in violation of the constitution and enjoined the plebiscite, the military implemented an order to arrest Zelaya, and he was forcibly spirited out of the country.

The Organization of American States quickly turned the issue into an international one, labelling it a coup d'etat, and calling for Zelaya's reinstatement. Every country in the hemisphere condemned Honduras, as did many European governments, including Russia. Honduras was suspended from the Organization of American States

[6] Constitution of Honduras, Article 239 ('A citizen who has previously served as President cannot be President or Vice President of the Republic. Whoever breaks this provision or proposes its reform, as well as those who support him directly or indirectly, will immediately cease in the performance of their respective offices and will be barred for ten years from the exercise of any public function.' This provision was retained from Honduras' constitution of 1957, and similar provisions were found in the constitutions of Peru 1933 and Guatemala 1945. As Rosalind Dixon, David Landau, and Yaniv Roznai note, this was accompanied by two others that made sure proposing term limit extensions was to be treated as a most serious infraction: Article 42(5) threatens that those who support re-election of the president could lose their citizenship, and Article 4 calls any infringement of alternation in the presidency to be 'treason. See David Landau, Rosalind Dixon, & Yaniv Roznai, 'From an Unconstitutional Constitutional Amendment to an Unconstitutional Constitution? Lessons from Honduras' (2019) 8 Global Constitutionalism 40.

[7] See Noah Feldman et al., Report to the Commission on Truth and Reconciliation of Honduras: Constitutional Issues 10–11 (March 2011), https://papers.ssrn.com/sol3/papers.cfm?abstract_id=1915214[accessed 20 January 2020].

('OAS'), and was not re-admitted until 2011, when Zelaya and his successor announced a deal under which he could return. Zelaya eventually resumed a minor role in politics, though he was never reinstated to the presidency.

OAS has always had a concern with external intervention and unconstitutional changes in government. Article 9 of its Charter allows suspension, by a 2/3 vote of member states, of any country whose 'democratically constituted government has been overthrown by force'. In 2001, the member states adopted the Inter-American Democratic Charter, designed to strengthen and protect the democratic order. It refers expressly to a 'right to democracy' enjoyed by peoples of the region.[8] Article 7 asserts boldly, that '[d]emocracy is indispensable for the effective exercise of fundamental freedoms and human rights in their universality, indivisibility and interdependence, embodied in the respective constitutions of states and in inter-American and international human rights instruments'. Constitutions, it seems, are indeed a central part of the domestic order for human rights and such. Article 20 goes on to lay out the mechanisms for responding to 'unconstitutional alteration of the constitutional regime that impairs the democratic order'.

In its reactions to Zelaya's ouster, in my view, the OAS was overly concerned with one kind of threat to democracy—the coup d'etat—and paid too little attention to the problem of incumbent takeover. The organization was extremely quick to enforce its anti-coup norm, but was not sensitive to the risk of erosion if Zelaya had been allowed to run for office in the face of explicit constitutional language that prohibited him from doing so.[9]

The region has traditionally suffered from coups and so this reaction is perhaps understandable. But the OAS was, in many ways, focused on yesterday's problem rather than today's. The number of coups and attempted coups has fallen dramatically since the early 1990s. After a series of failed attempts in the early 1990s, the number of coups has declined precipitously. Only two brief coups in Ecuador and a failed attempt in Venezuela have occurred since then. But the fact is that, in Article 20 of the Democracy Charter, the OAS had the normative resources to criticize Zelaya as well.

Against this background, term limits again emerged on the scene a few years later. With Zelaya's opponents in the National Party having consolidated power, the constitutional chamber of the Supreme Court had been packed. In a 2015 decision, the Supreme Court found the constitutional provisions limiting the discussion of presidential term limits to be a violation of fundamental rights of freedom of expression.[10] Importantly, it sourced these rights not only in the domestic constitution it was reviewing, but in international human rights instruments. This was rhetorically critical, for how else could the Court hold provisions that had been a part of the original constitutional design to be unconstitutional? The Court set aside the term limit as well as the 'poison pill' provisions and those forbidding advocacy of reform. This allowed

[8] Article 1.

[9] Micha Wiebusch, 'The Role of Regional Organizations in the Protection of Constitutionalism', International IDEA Discussion Paper 17/2016, 39.

[10] Supreme Court of Justice, Constitutional Chamber, Decision of 22 April 2015, available at http://www.poderjudicial.gob.hn/Documents/FalloSCONS23042015.pdf accessed 20 January 2020.

the incumbent, Juan Orlando Hernandez., to run for a second term in 2017, which he won.[11]

This remarkable decision is one which shows how international law can be utilized for regressive purposes. As Landau and his co-authors note, the 'theory of the unconstitutional constitution appears to rest primarily on international law and a resultant hierarchy of norms'.[12] The Supreme Court noted that since the Inter-American Convention preceded the Honduran Constitution, the country was bound to observe the Convention in its formulation of all national law. This view, as Landau and his colleagues note, takes a very broad view of the role of international law, displacing in many respects the ideas of a sovereign people exercising constituent power.

To be sure, I am not saying that moving from a one-term to a two-term limit in a constitution equates with democratic backsliding. Democratic practices differ in this regard. Most presidential systems have some form of term limit, but some others do not. Using Cheibub et al.'s coding of different types of systems of government, which distinguishes presidential, parliamentary, and semi-presidential democracies from various kinds of dictatorships, we find that thirty out of thirty-five presidential democracies have some form of term limit for the Head of State, as do twenty-four out of twenty-five semi-presidential democracies.[13] In short, the weight of democratic practice is towards some form of term limit. But of course even if *all* presidential democracies had term limits, this would not mean that they were *required* as a matter of international law or democratic theory. The background condition of international law is noninterference with the domestic choices of states, and uniformity in democratic practice does not turn a domestic norm into an international obligation.

In assessing the Honduras situation, context is important. It seems that the National Party of Honduras played significant hardball in pushing through the reform, including packing the Supreme Court's constitutional chamber. Thus this seems to be a case, at a minimum, of the abuse of international law in service of a local political faction, and potentially worse. Only time will tell if Hernandez stays around and erodes democracy.

A similar decision striking constitutional term limits on the basis of the regional human rights treaty has been adopted in Bolivia.[14] Perhaps even more bizarrely, in Bolivia, the Plurinational Constitutional Tribunal went to the original draft of the constitution, and rejected term limits on the grounds that they had only been agreed to as a political compromise.[15] The political context here was even more troubling than in Honduras. First elected in 2006 as the country's first indigenous president, Evo Morales headed a leftist party, the Movement for Socialism ('MAS') which sought transformative social and political change. In 2009, the movement succeeded in its project of promulgating an innovative constitution, including several novel institutional structures and an extensive set of rights. The constitution had a limit of two

[11] 'The President of Honduras Starts his Second Term under a Cloud', *Economist* (27 June 2018).

[12] Ibid., 10.

[13] Data on file with author. Jose Cheibub, Jennifer Gandhi, & James Raymond Vreeland, 'Democracy and Dictatorship Revisited' (2010) 143 Public Choice 67–101.

[14] Tribunal Constitucional Plurinational, Sentencia Constitutional Plurinacional No. 0084/2017, 28 November 2017, 5 (Bol.).

[15] Ibid.

terms for the presidency, and this led to a challenge to Morales' attempt to stand for re-election in 2014. The country's Supreme Court ruled that, since he had been initially elected under a prior constitution, his first term would not count against his total number of terms. In 2016, with his second term under the new constitution coming to a close, Morales' supporters sought a constitutional amendment that would allow him to run for a third term. However, to their surprise, the proposal failed in a public referendum. Not to be deterred, Morales turned to his Constitutional Tribunal, reliably filled with his appointees. In 2017, the Tribunal issued a decision finding that the term limit provision was itself unconstitutional.

The Tribunal again relied heavily on international law and the fact that the constitution integrated these principles in Article 256.I.[16] It invoked Article 23 of the American Convention. Article 23(1) grants every citizen the rights:

> [T]o take part in the conduct of public affairs, directly or through freely chosen representatives; to vote and to be elected in genuine periodic elections, which shall be by universal and equal suffrage and by secret ballot that guarantees the free expression of the will of the voters; and to have access, under general conditions of equality, to the public service of his country.[17]

The Court noted that under the Pact of San Jose, the only limitations on these rights were for age, nationality, residence, language, capacity, or criminal activity; since prior service was not on this list, it could not be used to exclude a candidate from exercising their political rights to run again.[18] Under this view, term limits would seem to be a *per se* violation of international human rights law.[19]

These decisions, while sounding in the preservation of democracy, in fact pose a threat to it, as they are being used to facilitate executive entrenchment by particular individuals.

IV. What Can International Law Do About All of This?

Part of the problem is that international law, and specifically the Inter-American human rights system, had not yet crystallized a view of term limits, which is an issue of institutional design on which democratic practice differs. Term limit violations embody the threat of democratic erosion rather than collapse. As we shall see below, international law has done a good deal to develop rules against unconstitutional changes of government. But it is only recently becoming equipped to deal with instances of democratic erosion. In this section, we discuss what different regional organizations

[16] Constitution of the Republic of Honduras, Article 256.I (18 January 1982) ('The international treaties and instruments in matters of human rights that have been signed and/or ratified, or those that have been joined by the State, which declare rights more favorable than those contained in the Constitution, shall have preferential application over those in this Constitution.').

[17] American Convention on Human Rights (1969) OASTS No. 36 (in force 18 July 1978).

[18] Tribunal Constitucional Plurinational (n. 14), 74

[19] Cf. Venice Commission, Report on Term-Limits: Part I-Presidents, adopted at 114th Plenary Session 17–18 March 2018, para. 84.

can do about the problems of democratic erosion, focusing especially on the term limit issue.

It is perhaps not surprising that regional organizations have taken the lead in this regard. At the global level, the so-called right to democratic governance is hardly the topic of consensus, but norms have been easier to articulate at the regional level, where countries share common concerns. One powerful motivator has been the fear of external intervention. Indeed, it seems that the regions most effective in developing frameworks for protecting democratic governance have been Africa and Latin America, in part because of both continents' long histories of colonialism and external manipulation from the United States and Europe. These histories spurred actors to come up with regional solutions.

To be sure, as documented by Murray, Alston, and Weibusch, there has been increasing attention by United Nations actors to the phenomenon of term limits. Kofi Annan referred to term limits positively in 2003, and more recently Secretary General Antonio Gutteres noted, in a 2017 report on elections and democratization, that term limits were important safeguards against 'winner-take-all' politics, and that attempts to change or remove them were inadvisable.[20] But the primary actors have been regional.

One interesting phenomenon has been the development of *networks* of regional institutions, which can articulate norms and standards even if they are not formally binding. A good example of an external actor making some difference without any formal legal authority to do so is the European Commission on Democracy through Law, popularly known as the Venice Commission, which is a body under the Council of Europe. The body issues reports on national constitution-making and constitutional amendment processes as well as other institutional reforms that impact democracy and the rule of law.[21]

In 2018, beset by the confusion in its region about term limits, the Organization of American States requested an advisory opinion from the Venice Commission on four questions: (1) whether or not re-election was a human right, and if so, whether term limits constrain the rights of either (2) voters or (3) the candidate themselves? Finally, they asked (4) about the best way to modify term limit provisions if they needed it.

In a nuanced opinion, the Commission expressed its scepticism towards presidential or semi-presidential constitutions that allowed the president more than two terms.[22] It found that the international standards guaranteeing rights to political participation were not inconsistent with some restrictions on the number of terms a president could stand for, and indeed noted that democratic quality is often enhanced by restriction on terms. The risks of personal aggrandizement and subsequent restrictions on participation suggest a positive relationship between term limits and democracy, not an inherent tension. Even if the term limits prevented the people from making a choice to retain a popular president, this could in a necessary case be circumvented by properly

[20] U.N. Secretary-General, *Strengthening the Role of the United Nations in Enhancing the Effectiveness of the Principle of Periodic and Genuine Elections and the Promotion of Democratization*, UN Doc A/72/260 (1 August 2017).

[21] Paul Craig, 'Transnational Constitution-Making: The Contribution of the Venice Commission on Law and Democracy', in Gregory Shaffer et al. (eds), *Transnational Legal Orders* (New York: Cambridge University Press, 2019), 156.

[22] Venice Commission (n. 19), para. 63.

adopted constitutional amendments. It found that restrictions on re-election are not unreasonable restrictions on voters' rights of choice. Further, the role of constitutional courts should, in the Commission's view, be focused on *ex post* review of constitutional amendments, 'after the amending text has been adopted by the constitutional legislator pursuant to the relevant, special constitutional requirements'.[23] This statement seems to implicitly reject the decisions of the Bolivian and Honduran courts that struck down term limits on the basis of international human rights. In reacting to this decision, the OAS asserted that the report had 'full legal validity'.[24]

As a normative matter of international law, it seems particularly odd to assert that term limits violate the personal rights of the leader to run for repeated re-election. When a person assumes the office of president, they will typically, by law, enter into a position of special status. In many systems they cannot be sued, and have immunities for professional actions. They may also, by law, lose the right to manage their own financial affairs, as well as to speak in a personal capacity. It is no surprise, then, that the special status means that one's political rights are limited as well.

V. A Note on Africa

The African Union ('AU') has been playing a major role in the articulation of norms focused on unconstitutional changes of government, as well as on term limits. The approach began with regional reactions to contrary incidents, such as the 1997 coup d'etat in Sierra Leone. A major first step was the Constitutive Act of the Union, adopted in 2000 at Lomé, Togo, which in Article 30 prohibits unconstitutional changes in government.[25] It was accompanied by a Declaration on OAU responses to unconstitutional changes of government, and expressed concern over the 'resurgence' of coups in the region.[26] The categories of unconstitutional changes included coups, intervention by mercenaries, replacement of government by rebels, and the refusal of an incumbent to step down after free and fair elections. The timing of this set of interventions reflected the concerns of African leaders about rebels and outside intervention. Since the wave of constitutional reforms in the early 1990s had typically allowed for two presidential terms, there had not yet been a wave of amendments seeking to extend the terms of those leaders.[27] Other leaders had just secured amendments to allow them to remain in office.[28]

[23] Ibid., para. 114.

[24] OAS 2018. Mansaje de Secrtario General de OEA sobre opinion de la Comision de Venexia sobre releccion presidential, discussed in Christina Murray, Eric Alston, & Micha Wiebusch, 'Presidential Term Limits and the International Community' Institute of Development Policy, Working Paper, 2018.9: 5–29 (2018), at 16.

[25] Organization of African Unity (OAU), Constitutive Act of the African Union, 1 July 2000, Article 4(p).

[26] AHG/Decl.5 (XXXVI).

[27] The amendments followed in Guinea (2001), allowing Lansana Conte another term. Angola's Jose Eduardo Dos Santos' constitutionally mandated third term still went to 2007. Mozambique's Joaquim Chissano's second term went to 2004, and he ended up declining to run for a third. Uganda's Yoweni Museveni's term went to 2005, when he amended the constitution to allow continued rule. Chad's Idriss Deby amended the constitution in 2005 to allow a third term. Zambia's Frederick Chiluba had a term that was to run out in 2002. Tom Ginsburg, Zachary Elkins, & James Melton, 'On the Evasion of Executive Term Limits' (2011) 52 William and Mary Law Review 1807.

[28] Namibia's Sam Nujoma had secured a constitutional amendment in 1999 allowing a third term. He successfully ran, but stepped down after that term in accordance with the constitution.

Further developing these norms, the African Charter on Democracy, Elections and Governance (Governance Charter) of 2007 further clarifies what such an unconstitutional change is: the category includes coups; intervention by mercenaries or rebels to replace a democratically elected government; a refusal of an incumbent to yield office after losing an election; and 'any amendment or revision of the constitution or legal instruments, which is an infringement on the principles of democratic change of government'.[29] We thus see in the first decade of the century a new attention to term limit extensions as a potential risk for democratic governance.

The norms of the AU are to be enforced by the Peace and Security Council, which can impose sanctions for failure to abide by the policies.[30] The decisions require consensus, which might not seem forthcoming in a body whose members include non-democratic members like Egypt; but there is the possibility of a 2/3 vote if consensus is unattainable.[31] The AU adopted a protocol to allow the African Court of Human and People's Rights to include criminal jurisdiction for violations.[32]

In 2009, at a meeting in Swaziland, the Peace and Security Council ('PSC') established the Ezulwini Framework for the Enhancement of the Implementation of Measures of the African Union in Situations of Unconstitutional Changes of Government. This set up a sanctioning committee and a framework for the PSC to reserve the constitutional order, develop sanctions, and make decisions about when a country has returned to constitutional governance. And a whole series of other instruments address other aspects of the democratic process.[33]

How has this normative framework played out in practice? These and other AU norms are enforced by the Commission and the African Peer Review Mechanism, which is a continent wide mechanism looking at rule of law, and explicitly include fixed terms.[34] They have in their reports criticized Zambia and Uganda for removing term limits. Then, in 2009, Mamadou Tandja sought to amend the constitution to remove term limits in Niger, only to be prevented by his own constitutional court. The subsequent turmoil, when Tandja was removed by a military coup, led the AU to suspend the country from AU activities. This sequence highlighted that the norm of condemning coups was stronger than the norm of condemning incumbent takeovers, even though the latter is now a much more common way of ending democracy. Following this, the AU's PSC adopted a principle that the constitution 'should not be manipulated in order to hold on to power against the will of the people'.[35] It further

[29] African Union, African Charter on Democracy, Elections and Governance, Art. 23, 30 January 2007.

[30] Ibid., Article 25.

[31] Protocol Relating to the Establishment of the Peace and Security Council of the African Union, Article 13, (2003).

[32] Protocol on Amendments to the Protocol on the Statute Establishing the African Court of Justice and Human Rights, Article 4, (2014). At the time of writing the protocol had 15 signatures but no ratifications.

[33] Wiebusch lists several from the African Commission on Human and People's Rights, including the Resolution on Electoral Process and Participatory Governance (1996); the Dakar Declaration on the Right to a Fair Trial (1999); the Declaration on Principles of Freedom of Expression (2002); the Resolution on Elections in Africa (2008): Wiebusch, note 9, above.

[34] Murray et al. (n. 24), 10, n. 4.

[35] AU 2009, Ezulwini Framework for the Enhancement of the Implementation of Measures of the African Union in Situations of Unconstitutional Changes of Government in Africa; see Murray et al. (n. 24), 11

noted the next year that failure to respect provisions of the constitution 'could trigger political crisis'.[36]

The framework was tested in Burkina Faso in 2014, when President Blaise Compaore introduced constitutional amendments to extend his rule, which had begun in 1987. The constitution of 2000 had limited the president to two new five-year terms, which were due to end in 2015. The opposition called protests, which led to a military intervention and Compaore fleeing the country. The PSC called for a transition to civilian rule within two weeks. The Economic Community of West African States ('ECOWAS') then sent a delegation of heads of state to mediate a solution, which involved a transitional government. A failed coup attempt the next year was followed by a democratic election.

The AU has used targeted sanctions several times, including in Mauritania (2008), Guinea (2009), Madagascar (2010), and the Central African Republic (2013).[37] It played a critical role in inducing the military in Sudan to allow a majority civilian government. It did not, however, have much effect in the case of the Egyptian coup in 2013. And in a later crisis in Burundi, the head of the AU Commission called on Pierre Nkurunziza to avoid running for a third term, while heads of state were a bit more reticent. This call, however, went unheeded.

VI. Conclusion

This chapter has surveyed the interaction of international law with a major channel of democratic erosion: the extension of executive terms. While much of our constitutional imagination and our international legal norms focus on military coups and other mechanisms of democratic collapse, the fact is that incumbent takeover is the greater risk in our era. Term limit extensions are an essential element of incumbent takeovers.

We are beginning to observe two contradictory and related trends: the abuse of human rights law to facilitate incumbent bypass of term limits, and the hints of a thicker normative framework in international law, still incompletely enforced, to make this more difficult. It is at the level of the region where this will play out, and Africa and Latin America have taken the lead. But the consequences for the global future of democracy may be great.

[36] AU 2010, Decision on the Prevention of Unconstitutional Changes of Government and Strengthening the Capacity of the African Union (Assembly/AHG/Dec. 269 XIV). Addis Ababa

[37] Wiebusch (n. 9), 23.

7

The Straw that Broke the Constitution's Back?

Qualitative Quantity in Judicial Review of Constitutional Amendments

*Yaniv Roznai**

I. Introduction

According to the doctrine of constitutional unamendability, certain constitutional principles that provide the constitution its identity are deemed as unamendable. They are beyond the power of the formal amendment process. And such unamendability may also be enforced through substantive judicial review even of constitutional amendments.

Perhaps one of the most famous jurisdictions in which constitutional unamendability is applied is Colombia. The Colombian Constitutional Court has proven to be a central player in constitutional change, often blocking major constitutional amendments. Famously, the Constitutional Court held that President Alvaro Uribe could amend the constitution to seek a second consecutive term in office, but not a third consecutive term.[1] The question is raised as to why a second consecutive term is a valid constitutional amendment while a third consecutive term is an unconstitutional replacement?

Throughout history, philosophers and scientists have postulated the contradiction that individual small changes, which are powerless to effect a qualitative change, at a certain point do exactly that: quantity changes into quality. The idea that, under certain conditions, even small things can cause big changes finds its expression in all kinds of modern sayings and proverbs: 'the straw that broke the camel's back', 'many hands make light work', 'constant dripping wears away the stone'; 'a death in thousand cuts', and so on.

This concept was first brought forward by the Megarian Greek philosophers in the fourth century BC. The paradox attracted little subsequent interest until the late nineteenth century when it was conceptualized first by Hegel as an abstract concept and then by Marxist philosophers in the neo-Hegelian tradition, especially Engels, who developed materialistic and scientific applications of the theory.

In this chapter I wish to propose that this theory of quantity transforming into quality was at play in the Colombian term limits case, and this notion may be a model for future aggregated review of constitutional amendments. This chapter

* I would like to thank my research assistant, Achinoam Harel for her excellent work.

[1] Colombian Constitutional Court, Decision C-141 of 2010.

Yaniv Roznai, *The Straw that Broke the Constitution's Back?* In: *Constitutionalism.* Edited by: Alejandro Linares-Cantillo, Camilo Valdivieso-León, Santiago García-Jaramillo, Oxford University Press (2021). © The various contributors.
DOI: 10.1093/oso/9780192896759.003.0008

proceeds as follows: Section II provides an overview of the doctrine of constitutional unamendability and its protection against revolutionary changes thereby its limited utility against minor constitutional changes. In Section III an overview of the notion of transition from quantity into quality in philosophy and science is provided. Section IV then moves to law in order to demonstrate how quantitative aggregation may be considered during legal analysis. Section V then focuses on two major constitutional decisions—from Colombia and Israel—to demonstrate how qualitative quantity can rationalize the application of constitutional unamendability even against constitutional amendments that do not revolutionize the constitutional order. Section VI concludes.

II. Constitutional Unamendability and the Protection against Revolutionary Amendments

There is a global trend towards imposing substantive limitations (explicit or implicit) on constitutional amendment powers.[2] In recent decades, including explicit limits ('eternity clauses') in constitutions has become a central feature of modern global constitutional design.[3]

Moreover, even in countries where the constitution does not include any 'eternity clause', courts around the world have recognized a core of basic principles which is implicitly protected from amendments. The doctrine of 'implied limitations' on the constitutional amendment power was most famously applied by the Indian courts. In *Kesavananda Bharati v State of Kerala* of 1973, the Indian Supreme Court held that the power of the parliament 'to amend the constitution does not include the power to alter the basic structure, or framework of the constitution so as to change its identity'.[4] This has come to be known as the 'basic structure doctrine'.[5]

Since its adoption in India, the basic structure doctrine has migrated to various other states, and was adopted and applied in numerous variations, as courts in Bangladesh, Pakistan, Uganda, Kenya, Taiwan, Peru, Belize, Malaysia, and Slovakia, declared that some basic features or principles of the constitution are so imperative to the constitutional order and its identity that they are beyond the amendment power even without

[2] For elaboration, see Yaniv Roznai, *Unconstitutional Constitutional Amendments: The Limits of Amendment Powers* (Oxford: Oxford University Press, 2017).

[3] Ibid., at 20–2 (showing that between 1789 and 1944, only 17 per cent of world constitutions enacted in this period included unamendable provisions; between 1945 and 1988, already 27 per cent of world constitutions enacted in those years included such provisions, and out of the constitutions which were enacted between 1989 and 2015, already more than half (54 per cent) included unamendable provisions). See also Richard Albert 'Constitutional Handcuffs' (2010) 42(3) Arizona State Law Journal 663; Yaniv Roznai, 'Unamendability and The Genetic Code of The Constitution' (2015) 27(2) European Review of Public Law 775; Michael Hein, 'Impeding Constitutional Amendments: Why are Entrenchment Clauses Codified in Contemporary Constitutions?' (2019) 54(2) Acta Politica 196.

[4] *Kesavananda Bharati v State of Kerala*, AIR 1973 SC 1461.

[5] Much has been written about this doctrine. See, e.g., Sudhir Krishnaswamy, *Democracy and Constitutionalism in India: A Study of the Basic Structure Doctrine* (New Delhi: Oxford University Press, 2010).

any explicit limitations.[6] Constitutional amendments, according to this notion, are distinguished from revolutionary changes to the constitution. Amendments can indeed change the constitution but must operate within the boundaries of the existing constitutional order and its foundational principles; they must not comprise a change so radical that it has to be regarded as a new constitution.[7]

A central variation of this doctrine is the one developed in Colombia. The Colombian constitution of 1991 creates a distinction between amendment (which can be carried out by Congress alone or by referendum) and replacement carried out by the Constituent Assembly. However, it does not include any unamendable provisions and does not establish any principles determining when each route must be used. It also expressly limits judicial control over constitutional amendments to 'procedural errors' only. Nonetheless, the Constitutional Court gave a wide definition of the concept of 'procedural error', noting, in a line of judicial decisions, that the amendment power does not extend to the replacement of the constitution with a different one. It is only the constituent power, acting through extraordinary mechanisms such as a Constituent Assembly that can constitute a new constitution:

> Congress derives its power to reform the Constitution from the constitution itself. It has a derivative or secondary status as a constituent force. Therefore, it can reform or amend the Constitution, but it cannot replace it or substitute it for another constitution. If Congress crosses the line between amending the Constitution, and replacing it, it violates its constitutional powers and competence. If that happens, the Court can overturn Congress' decision, not on the grounds of content review, but based on the fact that a branch of government has ignored its constitutional competence, and therefore, violated constitutional procedural rules.[8]

Accordingly, there is a difference between amending the constitution and replacing it. An amendment can indeed reform the constitution but may not be so radical so as

[6] See, e.g., Yaniv Roznai, 'The Migration of the Indian Basic Structure Doctrine', in Malik Lokendra (ed.), *Judicial Activism in India—A Festschrift in Honour of Justice V. R. Krishna Iyer* (New Delhi: Universal Law Publishing Co. Pvt Ltd, 2012), 240.

[7] The basic theory behind this doctrine is that the constitutional amendment power is a delegated legal competence which acts in trust and therefore limited both explicitly and implicitly. First, it must obey those explicit conditions stipulated in the constitution. Secondly, the body which holds the constitutional amendment power in trust cannot use it in order to destroy the constitution, from which its authority derives. The amendment power is the internal method that the constitution provides for its self-preservation. By destroying the constitution, the delegated amending power undermines its own raison d'être. To amend the constitution so as to destroy it and create a new constitution would be an action *ultra vires*. In addition, since every constitution consists of a set of basic principles and features, which determine the totality of the constitutional order and make up the 'spirit of the constitution' and its identity, the constitutional amendment power cannot be used in order to destroy the basic principles of the constitution. The alteration of the constitution's core results in the collapse of the entire constitution and its replacement by another—but this is for the people's primary constituent power, not the delegated organs, to decide via a proper channel of higher-level democratic participation and deliberations. See Yaniv Roznai, 'Towards A Theory of Constitutional Unamendability: On the Nature and Scope of the Constitutional Amendment Powers' (2017) 18 *Jus Politicum* 5.

[8] Opinion C-1040/ 05, taken from the English summary of the decision which is available at the website of the Constitutional Court of Colombia, https://www.corteconstitucional.gov.co/english/Decision.php?IdPublicacion=9203 accessed on 14 December 2020.

to replace it with something completely different. This has become to be known as the 'substitution' or 'replacement' doctrine.[9]

But how do we know whether a constitutional amendment 'replaces' the constitution with a new one? Of course, a constitutional amendment can blatantly destroy the basic elements of the constitutional order replacing them with new ones. This was the case, for example, with the transition in Hungary from communism to democracy, a transformation brought about through formal constitutional amendments.[10] But what if the amendment only slightly deviates or infringes the basic constitutional principles? According to the doctrine, such an amendment—that does not replace the constitution with a new one—is surely allowed to stand.

Indeed, according to the established standards of review, only an extraordinary infringement of unamendable principles, or a constitutional change that 'fundamentally abandons' them, would allow judicial annulment of constitutional amendments. As the German Constitutional Court explained regarding the German 'eternity clause' (Article 79.3 of the Basic Law):[11]

> The purpose of [the unamendable provision] ... is to prevent both abolition of the substance or basis of the existing constitutional order, by the formal legal means of amendment ... and abuse of the Constitution to legalize a totalitarian regime. This provision thus prohibits a fundamental abandonment of the principles mentioned therein. Principles are from the very beginning not 'affected' as 'principles' if they are in general taken into consideration and are only modified for evidently pertinent reasons for a special case according to its peculiar character ... Restriction on the legislator's amending the Constitution ... must not, however, prevent the legislator from modifying by constitutional amendment even basic constitutional principles in a system—immanent manner.[12]

[9] See, e.g., Carlos Bernal, 'Unconstitutional Constitutional Amendments in the Case Study of Colombia: An Analysis of the Justification and Meaning of the Constitutional Replacement Doctrine' (2013) 11(2) International Journal of Constitutional Law 339; Gonzalo Andres Ramirez-Cleves, 'The Unconstitutionality of Constitutional Amendments in Colombia: The Tension between Majoritarian Democracy and Constitutional Democracy', in Thomas Bustamante & Bernardo Gonçalves Fernandes (eds), *Democratizing Constitutional Law* (Switzerland: Springer, 2016), 213; Mario Alberto Cajas-Sarria, 'Judicial Review of Constitutional Amendments in Colombia: A Political and Historical Perspective, 1955-2016' (2017) 5(3) Theory and Practice of Legislation 245; Juan Gonzalez Bertomeu, 'The Colombian Constitutional Court's Doctrine on the Substitution of the Constitution', in Richard Albert, Carlos Bernal, & Juliano Zaiden Benvindo (eds), *Constitutional Change and Transformation in Latin America* (Oxford: Hart Publishing, 2019), 119.

[10] Yaniv Roznai, 'Constitutional Transformations: The Case of Hungary', in David Law (ed.), *Constitutionalism in Context* (Cambridge University Press, forthcoming 2021).

[11] The German eternity clause prohibits amendments to the Basic Law that affect the division of the Federation into Länder; human dignity; the constitutional order; or basic institutional principles describing Germany as a democratic and social federal state. On the German eternity clause, see Helmut Goerlich, 'Concept of Special Protection for Certain Elements and Principles of the Constitution against Amendments and Article 79(3), Basic Law of Germany' (2008) 1 NUJS Law Review 397; Ulrich K. Preuss, 'The Implications of "Eternity Clauses": The German Experience' (2011) 44(3) Israel Law Review 429.

[12] 30 BVerfGE 1, 24 (1970); see the English translation in Walter F. Murphy & Joseph Tanenhaus (eds), *Comparative Constitutional Law— Cases and Commentaries* (New York: St. Martin's. Press 1977) 659, 661–2.

This notion seems to be applicable also to the Colombian Constitutional Replacement Doctrine. As Carlo Bernal wrote, concerning that doctrine, an amendment would count as a 'replacement of the constitution if, and only if, the infringement is of such magnitude that the political system can no longer be considered as an institutionalization of deliberative democracy'.[13] In other words, an amendment has to fundamentally abandon the principle of deliberative democracy in order to be deemed unconstitutional. Thus, the theory of unamendability allows, at least in theory, 'for a gradual deconstruction of the constitutional system, brought about piece by piece via constitutional amendments'.[14]

What if the constitution is being replaced with a new one not through a one-time revolutionary amendment à la Hungary 1989, but through an incremental series of amendments that each—on its own—may not amount to a replacement, but when examined accumulatively in the context of an ongoing gradual process, such a series of amendments may prove to be part of an incremental constitutional replacement in which the whole is greater than the sum of its parts?

In this chapter, I wish to claim that a possible solution for relaxing this difficulty may be by adopting the law of 'quantity turns into quality' when considering the accumulative impact of a series of amendments affecting a certain constitutional rule or principles. I will demonstrate this by two constitutional decisions from Colombia and Israel. But before showing how, perhaps it is better to delve into first explaining what the law of 'quantity turns into quality' is.

III. The Transition from Quantity into Quality in Philosophy and Science

The Megarian philosopher Eubulides is usually credited with the first formulation of the 'sorites paradox'.[15] The paradox asks: Is one grain of sand a heap of sand? The answer is invariably—no. Then are two grains of sand a heap? Again, the answer is no. If we continue adding individual grains of sand—at what point will they transform into a heap? In a similar fashion, the 'Bald Man paradox' presents a man with a full head of hair who is obviously not bald. The removal of a single hair will not turn a non-bald man into a bald one. And yet it is obvious that a continuation of that process must eventually result in baldness.

A modern rendition of these puzzles was coined by Dorothy Edgington as 'the mañana paradox': 'the unwelcome task which needs to be done, but it's always a matter of indifference whether it's done today or tomorrow; [or] the dieter's paradox: I don't care at all about the difference to my weight one chocolate will make'.[16]

[13] Bernal (n. 9), 357.

[14] Roznai (n. 1), 226.

[15] The name 'sorites' is derived from the Greek word soros, meaning 'heap'. Dominic Hyde, 'The Sorites Paradox', in Giuseppina Ronzitti (ed.), *Vagueness: A Guide* (Switzerland: Springer, 2011), 1.

[16] Dorothy Edgington, 'Vagueness by Degrees', in Rosanna Keefe & Peter Smith (eds), *Vagueness: A Reader* (Cambridge, MA: MIT Press, 1996), 296. Many theorists of the Ideal Language doctrine took the paradox to the direction of the vagueness of the term 'heap', concentrating on its semantic vagueness (see the Stanford Encyclopaedia of Philosophy article on the Sorties Paradox, https://plato.stanford.edu/entries/sorites-paradox/#SoriHist accessed on 14 December 2020. However, it was also specifically used by later

From these examples, it is clear that the numerical accumulation of minor changes may bring a major paradigmatic shift. Georg Wilhelm Friedrich Hegel was perhaps the first one to point to the significance of the transition from quantity to quality in social evolution. Hegelian dialectic is usually presented in a threefold manner, comprising three dialectical stages of development: a thesis, giving rise to its reaction; an antithesis, which contradicts or negates the thesis; and the tension between the two being resolved by means of a synthesis.[17] In more simplistic terms, one can consider it thus: problem → reaction → solution.

Another important dialectical principle for Hegel is the transition from quantity to quality, which he terms 'measure'.[18] Hegel describes a dialectic of existence: first, existence must be posited as pure Being (*sein*); but pure Being, upon examination, is found to be indistinguishable from Nothing (*nichts*). When it is realized that what is coming into being is, at the same time, also returning to nothing (in life, for example, one's living is also a dying), both Being and Nothing are united as Becoming.[19] As he elaborated in his *Encyclopaedia of the Philosophical Sciences*:

> Each of the three spheres of the logical idea proves to be a systematic whole of thought-terms, and a phase of the Absolute. This is the case with Being, containing the three grades of quality, quantity and measure.
>
> Quality is, in the first place, the character identical with being: so identical that a thing ceases to be what it is, if it loses its quality. Quantity, on the contrary, is the character external to being, and does not affect the being at all. Thus, e.g. a house remains what it is, whether it be greater or smaller; and red remains red, whether it be brighter or darker.
>
> Measure, the third grade of being, which is the unity of the first two, is a qualitative quantity. All things have their measure: i.e. the quantitative terms of their existence, their being so or so great, does not matter within certain limits; but when these limits are exceeded by an additional more or less, the things cease to be what they were. From measure follows the advance to the second subdivision of the idea, Essence.[20]

Hegel further explains in later passages of the book:

> The identity between quantity and quality, which is found in Measure, is at first only implicit, and not yet explicitly realised. In other words, these two categories, which unite in Measure, each claim an independent authority. On the one hand, the quantitative features of existence may be altered, without affecting its quality. On the

theorists such as Hegel and Engels in the context relevant to our discussion of incremental changes accumulating into significant ones.

[17] See e.g. G. E. Mueller, 'The Hegel Legend of "Thesis-Antithesis-Synthesis' (1958) 19(3) Journal of the History of Ideas 411–14, http://hegel.net/articles/Mueller1958-TheHegelLegendOfThesisAntithesisSynthesis.pdf accessed on 14 December 2020

[18] G. W. F. Hegel *The Logic of Hegel. The Encyclopaedia of the Philosophical Sciences* (Oxford: The Clarendon Press, 1874), §§107–11.

[19] Ibid., at §§86–88.

[20] Hegel (n. 18), §85.

other hand, this increase and diminution, immaterial though it be, has its limit, by exceeding which the quality suffers change. Thus the temperature of water is, in the first place, a point of no consequence in respect of its liquidity: still with the increase of diminution of the temperature of the liquid water, there comes a point where this state of cohesion suffers a qualitative change, and the water is converted into steam or ice. A quantitative change takes place, apparently without any further significance: but there is something lurking behind, and a seemingly innocent change of quantity acts as a kind of snare, to catch hold of the quality. The antinomy of Measure which this implies was exemplified under more than one garb among the Greeks. It was asked, for example, whether a single grain makes a heap of wheat, or whether it makes a bald-tail to tear out a single hair from the horse's tail. At first, no doubt, looking at the nature of quantity as an indifferent and external character of being, we are disposed to answer these questions in the negative. And yet, as we must admit, this indifferent increase and diminution has its limit: a point is finally reached, where a single additional grain makes a heap of wheat; and the bald-tail is produced, if we continue plucking out single hairs. These examples find a parallel in the story of the peasant who, as his ass trudged cheerfully along, went on adding ounce after ounce to its load, till at length it sunk under the unendurable burden. It would be a mistake to treat these examples as pedantic futility; they really turn on thoughts, an acquaintance with which is of great importance in practical life, especially in ethics. Thus in the matter of expenditure, there is a certain latitude within which a more or less does not matter; but when the Measure, imposed by the individual circumstances of the special case, is exceeded on the one side or the other, the qualitative nature of Measure (as in the above examples of the different temperature of water) makes itself felt, and a course, which a moment before was held good economy, turns into avarice or prodigality.[21]

Interestingly, this idea is not only relevant to physical science but also to political science, and may be important also for the study of constitutions:

The same principles may be applied in politics, when the constitution of a state has to be looked at as independent of, no less than as dependent on, the extent of its territory, the number of its inhabitants, and other quantitative points of the same kind. If we look, e.g. at a state with a territory of ten thousand square miles and a population of four millions we should, without hesitation, admit that a few square miles of land or a few thousand inhabitants more or less could exercise no essential influence on the character of its constitution. But on the other hand, we must not forget that by the continual increase or diminishing of a state, we finally get to a point where, apart from all other circumstances, this quantitative alteration alone necessarily draws with it an alteration in the quality of the constitution. The constitution of a little Swiss canton does not suit a great kingdom; and, similarly, the constitution of the Roman republic was unsuitable when transferred to the small imperial towns of Germany.[22]

[21] Hegel (n. 18), §§108.
[22] Ibid.

Trotsky, a self-proclaimed Marxist, and dialectician,[23] expanded on Hegels' dialectics in his *Defense of Marxism*:

> Every individual is a dialectician to some extent or other, in most cases, unconsciously. A housewife knows that a certain amount of salt flavours soup agreeably, but that added salt makes the soup unpalatable. Consequently, an illiterate peasant woman guides herself in cooking soup by the Hegelian law of the transformation of quantity into quality. Similar examples from daily life could be cited without end. Even animals arrive at their practical conclusions not only on the basis of the Aristotelian syllogism but also on the basis of the Hegelian dialectic. Thus a fox is aware that quadrupeds and birds are nutritious and tasty. On sighting a hare, a rabbit, or a hen, a fox concludes: this particular creature belongs to the tasty and nutritive type, and—chases after the prey. We have here a complete syllogism, although the fox, we may suppose, never read Aristotle. When the same fox, however, encounters the first animal which exceeds it in size, for example, a wolf, it quickly concludes that quantity passes into quality, and turns to flee. Clearly, the legs of a fox are equipped with Hegelian tendencies, even if not fully conscious ones.[24]

In the writings of Hegel there are many examples of the law of dialectics drawn from history and nature. But Hegel's idealism necessarily gave his dialectics a highly abstract, and arbitrary character. Marx and Engels created a scientific, materialist basis to dialectics in their Dialectical Materialism theory which emphasizes the importance of real-world conditions—Marx mainly in terms of class, labour, and socio-economic interactions,[25] and Engels through the natural sciences.

Engels postulated three laws of dialectics from his reading of Hegel's *Science of Logic*, which he elucidated in his work *Dialectics of Nature*:

a. The law of the unity and conflict of opposites.
b. The law of the passage of quantitative changes into qualitative changes.
c. The law of the negation of the negation.

Thus, he writes, on the law of the transformation of quantity into quality and vice versa:

> All qualitative differences in nature rest on differences of chemical composition or on different quantities or forms of motion (energy) or, as is almost always the case, on both. Hence it is impossible to alter the quality of a body without addition or subtraction of matter or motion, i.e. without quantitative alteration of the body concerned.

[23] L. Trotsky, 'Testament of Leon Trotsky' (February 27, 1940), https://www.marxist.com/testament-of-leon-trotsky.htm accessed on 14 December 2020.

[24] L. Trotsky, 'In Defense of Marxism, An Open Letter to Comrade Burnham, (1940)' (London, 1966), 91–119, https://www.marxists.org/archive/trotsky/idom/dm/14-burnham.htm accessed on 14 December 2020.

[25] Marx did not expound greatly on the principle of quantity turning into quality, enlarging mainly on other parts of Hegelian dialectics, and therefore there are no subsequent explanations of his philosophy.

> In this form, therefore, Hegel's mysterious principle appears not only quite rational but even rather obvious.[26]

Finally, the law of the transformation of quantity into quality also applies to natural sciences. The phrase 'phase transition' is used in science to denote what is essentially a qualitative leap. Similar processes can be seen in phenomena as varied as the weather, DNA molecules, and the mind itself. Thus, the dialectic principle of transitions between quantity and quality can be found in various scientific fields through phase transitions, in chemistry, for example. The existence of atomic weight was discovered in 1862 by Cannizzaro. In 1869, Russian scientist Dimitri Ivanovich Mendeleyev, in collaboration with the German chemist Julius Meyer, worked out the periodic table of the elements, so-called because it showed the periodic recurrence of similar chemical properties. Mendeleyev's innovation lay in the fact that he did not approach the elements from a purely quantitative standpoint in that he did not see the relation between the different atoms merely in terms of weight. The whole of Mendeleyev's periodic table is based on the law of quantity and quality, deducing qualitative differences in the elements from quantitative differences in atomic weights.

Chemistry also involves changes of both a quantitative and qualitative character, both changes of degree and of state. This can clearly be seen in the change of state from gas to liquid or solid, which is usually related to variations of temperature and pressure. In 'Dialectics of Nature', Engels gives a series of examples of how, in chemistry, the simple quantitative addition of elements creates qualitatively different bodies:

> The sphere, however, in which the law of nature discovered by Hegel celebrates its most important triumphs is that of chemistry. Chemistry can be termed the science of the qualitative changes of bodies as a result of changed quantitative composition. That was already known to Hegel himself (*Logic*, Collected Works, III, p. 488). As in the case of oxygen: if three atoms unite into a molecule, instead of the usual two, we get ozone, a body which is very considerably different from ordinary oxygen in its odour and reactions. Again, one can take the various proportions in which oxygen combines with nitrogen or sulphur, each of which produces a substance qualitatively different from any of the others! How different laughing gas (nitrogen monoxide N_2O) is from nitric anhydride (nitrogen pentoxide, N_2O_5)! The first is a gas, the second at ordinary temperatures a solid crystalline substance. And yet the whole difference in composition is that the second contains five times as much oxygen as the first, and between the two of them are three more oxides of nitrogen (NO, N_2O_3, NO_2), each of which is qualitatively different from the first two and from each other ... the Hegelian law is valid not only for compound substances but also for the chemical elements themselves. We now know that 'the chemical properties of the elements are a periodic function of their atomic weights' (Roscoe-Schorlemmer, *Complete Text-Book of Chemistry*, II, p. 823), and that, therefore, their quality is determined by the quantity of their atomic weight. And the test of this has been brilliantly carried out. Mendeleyev proved that various gaps occur in the series of related elements arranged according to atomic weights

[26] F. Engels, C. P Dutt, & J. B. S Haldane, 'Dialectics of Nature' (1940), https://www.marxists.org/archive/marx/works/1883/don/ch02.htm accessed on 14 December 2020.

> indicating that here new elements remain to be discovered. He described in advance the general chemical properties of one of these unknown elements, which he termed eka-aluminium, because it follows after aluminium in the series beginning with the latter, and he predicted its approximate specific and atomic weight as well as its atomic volume. A few years later, Lecoq de Boisbaudran actually discovered this element, and Mendeleyev's predictions fitted with only very slight discrepancies. Eka-aluminium was realised in gallium (ibid., p. 828). By means of the—unconscious— application of Hegel's law of the transformation of quantity into quality, Mendeleyev achieved a scientific feat which it is not too bold to put on a par with that of Leverrier in calculating the orbit of the still unknown planet Neptune.[27]

The law of quantity and quality also applies in physics. For example, it serves to shed light on the controversial contradiction called the 'uncertainty principle'. Whereas it is impossible to know the exact position and velocity of an individual subatomic particle, it is possible to predict with great accuracy the behaviour of large numbers of particles. A further example: radioactive atoms decay in a way that makes a detailed prediction impossible. Yet large numbers of atoms decay at a rate so statistically reliable that they are used by scientists as natural 'clocks' with which they calculate the age of the earth, the sun, and the stars.[28] The fact that the laws governing the behaviour of subatomic particles are different to those that function at the 'normal' level is an example of the transformation of quantity into quality. Thus, Engels writes:

> In physics, bodies are treated as chemically unalterable or indifferent; we have to do with changes of their molecular states and with the change of form of the motion which in all cases, at least on one of the two sides, brings the molecule into play. Here every change is a transformation of quantity into quality, a consequence of the quantitative change of the quantity of motion of one form or another that is inherent in the body or communicated to it. 'Thus, for instance, the temperature of water is first of all indifferent in relation to its state as a liquid; but by increasing or decreasing the temperature of liquid water a point is reached at which this state of cohesion alters and the water becomes transformed on the one side into steam and on the other into ice.' (Hegel, *Encyclopedia*, Collected Works, VI, p. 217.) Similarly, a definite minimum current strength is required to cause the platinum wire of an electric incandescent lamp to glow; and every metal has its temperature of incandescence and fusion, every liquid its definite freezing and boiling point at a given pressure—in so far as our means allow us to produce the temperature required; finally also every gas has its critical point at which it can be liquefied by pressure and cooling. In short, the so-called physical constants are for the most part nothing but designations of the nodal points at which quantitative addition or subtraction of motion produces qualitative alteration in the state of the body concerned, at which, therefore, quantity is transformed into quality.[29]

[27] Ibid.

[28] Alan Woods & Ted Grant 'Reason in Revolt; Marxist Philosophy and Modern Science' (2015), https://www.marxist.com/reason-in-revolt-marxist-philosophy-and-modern-science/2.-philosophy-and-religion.htm accessed on 14 December 2020.

[29] Ibid.

In biology, we can see the law of the transformation of quantity into quality at work when we consider evolutionary processes of species. In biological terms a specific 'breed' or 'race' of an animal is defined by its capacity to inter-breed. But as evolutionary modifications take one group further away from another a point is reached where they can no longer inter-breed. At this point a new species has been formed. Paleontologists Stephen Jay Gould and Niles Eldredge have demonstrated that these processes are sometimes slow and protracted and at other times extremely rapid.[30] They show how a gradual accumulation of small changes at a certain point provokes a qualitative change. The term used to describe long periods of stability, interrupted by sudden bursts of change, is 'punctuated equilibria'. When this idea was proposed by Gould and Eldredge of the American Museum to Natural History in 1972, it provoked a hostile debate among biologists, for whom, until then, Darwinian evolution was synonymous with gradualism.

For a long time, it was thought that evolution precluded such drastic changes. It was pictured as a slow, gradual change. However, fossil records, although incomplete, present a very different picture, with long periods of gradual evolution punctuated by violent upheavals, accompanied by the mass extinction of some species and the rapid rise of others. Whether or not the dinosaurs became extinct as a consequence of a meteorite colliding with the earth, it seems highly improbable that most of the great extinctions were caused in this way. While external phenomena, including meteorite or comet impacts, can play a role as 'accidents' in the evolutionary process, it is necessary to seek an explanation of evolution as a result of its internal laws. The theory of 'punctuated equilibria', which is now supported by most paleontologists, represents a decisive break with the old gradualist interpretation of Darwinism, and presents a truly dialectical picture of evolution, in which long periods of stasis are interrupted by sudden leaps and catastrophic changes of all kinds. Gould wrote that:

> ... when presented as guidelines for a philosophy of change, not as dogmatic precepts true by fiat, the three classical laws of dialectics embody a holistic vision that views change as interaction among components of complete systems and sees the components themselves not as a priori entities, but as both products and inputs to the system. Thus, the law of 'interpenetrating opposites' records the inextricable interdependence of components: the 'transformation of quantity to quality' defends a systems-based view of change that translates incremental inputs into alterations of state, and the 'negation of negation' describes the direction given to history because complex systems cannot revert exactly to previous states.[31]

It is precisely this idea of incremental imputes that translate to alterations of state—or in other words the transformation of quantity to quality—that I wish to apply in constitutional law, and more precisely in constitutional change.

[30] Stephen Jay Gould & Niles Eldredge, 'Punctuated Equilibria: An Alternative to Phyletic Gradualism', in Thomas J.M. Schopf (ed.), *Models in Paleobiology*, (San Francisco: Freeman, Cooper and Company, 1972), 82–115.

[31] Stephen Jay Gould, 'Nurturing Nature', in *An Urchin in the Storm: Essays about Books and Ideas*, (London: Penguin Books, 1990), 194.

IV. Quantity Turns into Quality in Law

Considerations of quantity in qualitative legal analysis are not new. One can consider this as a subset of aggregation in legal analysis.[32] For example, Ariel Porat and Eric A. Posner have examined examples of how aggregation might take place in torts, contracts, criminal law, and public law.[33] International law, for example, is one field where aggregation, and more specifically the transformation of quantity into quality, can take significance.

William Thomas Worster examined the situation where 'the quantitative growth and dispersion of a certain norm or other legal fact at some point results in a qualitative shift in the state of the law'.[34] This, to Worster, may be relevant for the creation of customary international law: 'the formation of customary international law could be described as a phase transition from one equilibrium state (e.g. rule of permissiveness) to another (e.g. rule of prohibition) that is characterized as a build-up of quantitative practice eventually sufficient to reach a critical mass that forces a qualitative shift in the norm.'[35]

Another example from international law is the 'accumulation of events' or 'needle prick' doctrine. According to this doctrine, a specific act of terrorism, or needle prick, though may not individually qualify as an armed attack that allows the victim state to respond with armed force in self defence, could amount to an armed attack entitling response when the totality of incidents are taken into consideration.[36] Put differently, the quantity of small events transform to a different legal state—that of an armed attack that allows action in self defence.

Such accumulation can also be relevant in judicial review. Consider, for example, these two cases from Israel. The first concerned the legality of the long-standing arrangement whereby 'Yeshiva students' (students of Jewish educational institutions that focus on the study of traditional religious texts) were granted postponement of their military service for so long as they continued their full-time studies. This has been confirmed by successive Ministers of Defence since 1948. Writing for the majority, Justice Aharon Barak wrote that the petitioners have not discharged the burden placed on them of showing that the Minister acted in an unreasonable manner. However, he also added that 'there is ultimate significance to the number of Yeshivah students whose service is deferred. There is a limit which no reasonable Minister of Defence may cross. Quantity makes a qualitative difference.'[37]

[32] See, e.g., Alon Harel & Ariel Porat, 'Aggregating Probabilities Across Cases: Criminal Responsibility for Unspecified Offenses' (2009) 94 Minnesota Law Review 261; Brandon L. Garrett, 'Aggregation and Constitutional Rights' (2012) 88 Notre Dame Law Review 593, 641–8; Zemer Blondheim & Nadiv Mordechay, 'Towards a Cumulative Effect Doctrine: Aggregation in Constitutional Judicial Review' (2014) 44(2) Mishpatim 596 (Hebrew).

[33] Ariel Porat & Eric A. Posner, 'Aggregation and Law' (2012) 122 Yale Law Journal 2.

[34] William Thomas Worster, 'The Transformation of Quantity into Quality: Critical Mass in The Formation of Customary International Law' (2013) 31(1) Boston University International Law Journal 4.

[35] Ibid., 20.

[36] Norman Menachem Feder, 'Reading the U.N. Charter Connotatively: Toward a New Definition of Armed Attack' (1987) 19 New York University Journal of International Law and Politics 395, 415

[37] H.C. 910/86, *Yehuda Ressler and Others v Minister of Defense*, 32(2) PD 441 (1988) para. 69 of Barak's judgment (Isr.)

In the second case, an extended panel of nine justices of the Supreme Court decided the question of the constitutionality of the arrangement enacted by the Knesset (Israeli Parliament) in 2012, in amendment no. 3 of the Prevention of Infiltration Law (Offenses and Adjudication), 5714-1954, which allows holding infiltrators in custody for a period of three years. All nine justices of the panel held, unanimously, that the arrangement was unconstitutional because it disproportionately limited the constitutional right to liberty determined in Basic Law: Human Dignity and Liberty. In his judgment, Justice Amit emphasized that the content of his opinion relates to the situation today, in which the number of infiltrators stands at approximately 1 per cent of the population of Israel, as a fait accompli. At the same time, Justice Amit commented that one wonders about the numerical 'red line' of what the state can bear without concern for a real limitation of its sovereignty, its character, its national identity, its cultural-societal character, the makeup of its population, and the entirety of its unique characteristics, and without concern for its stability and of 'breaking its neck' in terms of crowding, welfare and economy, internal security, and public order. Against that backdrop, Justice Amit noted that when balancing between various basic rights or between basic rights and the vital interests of the state, we must be aware of the data, the assessments and the forecasts, as there are situations in which 'quantity makes quality'.[38]

So, the idea that the accumulation of minor changes can bring about a major change may also be relevant to legal analysis, and in our case, in the judicial review of constitutional amendments. But before turning to exemplify this, allow me to explain the problem first. Nowadays, democratic breakdowns occur not by an immediate break in the legal order but by subtle and gradual legal means that ultimately dismantle the constitutional system.[39] As Tom Ginsburg and Aziz Huq demonstrate in their book, *How to Save a Constitutional Democracy*, one of prime elements of the current wave of democratic erosion is its incrementalism: 'democratic erosion is typically aggregative process made up of many smaller increments. But those measures are rarely frontal assaults on one of the three institutional predicates of liberal constitutional democracy, of the kind that might be associated with an overly totalitarian or fascist regime.'[40] However, when such measures are taken accumulatively, the affect is momentous. As they state: 'a sufficient quantity of even incremental derogation from a democratic baseline ... can precipitate a qualitative change that merits a shift in classification'.[41] Likewise, Wojciech Sadurski writes that the 'a broad assault upon liberaldemocratic constitutionalism produces a cumulative effect, and the whole is greater than the sum of its parts'.[42] And this is the crucial point. Often, each constitutional change on its own may not transform the constitutional order or be considered as a constitutional

[38] HCJ 7146/12, *Adam v the Knesset*, 64(2) P.D. 717 (2013) (Isr.), para. 2 of Amit's judgment.

[39] See Kim Lane Scheppele, 'Autocratic Legalism' (2018) 85 University of Chicago Law Review 545; Steven Levitsky & Daniel Ziblatt, *How Democracies Die* (New York: Crown, 2018).

[40] Tom Ginsburg & Aziz Z. Huq, *How to Save a Constitutional Democracy* (Chicago: University of Chicago Press, 2018), 90–1.

[41] Ibid., 45.

[42] Wojciech Sadurski, *Poland's Constitutional Breakdown* (Oxford: Oxford University Press, 2019), 58.

replacement, but the incremental aggregation of the changes may lead to a constitutional revolutionary change.[43]

The problem, as mentioned earlier in the chapter, is that constitutional unamendability is not aimed to prevent minor constitutional changes that deviate from or contradict unamendable principles, and which preserve the state's constitutional identity but aimed to preserve the constitutional order and guard it against revolutionary changes. Constitutional unamendability, as currently applied, allows for an incremental, gradual crumbling of the constitutional order brought about bit by bit by constitutional amendments. It is here, I claim, that the idea of 'Quantity transforms into Quality' may be of use in judicial review of constitutional amendments.

V. When Quantity Transforms into Quality in Judicial Review of Constitutional Amendments: Two Examples

A. Colombia

Probably the best known of the recent term limits cases are those issued by the Colombian Constitutional Court after President Alvaro Uribe, who held power from 2002 until 2010, first amended the constitution to allow a single consecutive re-election, and then attempted to amend it again to allow a possible third term. Both amendments were challenged as possible substitutions of the constitution. The Court allowed the first amendment, permitting Uribe to run for (and win) a second term in 2006.[44] However, the Court blocked the second attempt, to run for a third term, holding *inter alia* that allowance of a third consecutive term would constitute a substitution of the constitution and thus an unconstitutional constitutional amendment.[45] Uribe complied with the decision and was replaced with Juan Manuel Santos at the end of his second term in 2010.[46]

The reasoning of these two decisions mixed consideration of the domestic political context with comparative examination.[47] For example, in the first re-election decision, the Court noted that allowance of two consecutive terms in office did raise some risks that the president would abuse his power but held essentially that those risks were far from certain and fell within a tolerable range. It further strengthened its decision with a comparative analysis showing that permitting two consecutive presidential terms was fairly normal and common in other liberal democracies with pure presidential systems, and that there is no 'consensus' within Latin America as to the proper scope of presidential re-election. Thus, according to the Court, 'a constitutional amendment

[43] See Gary J. Jacobsohn & Yaniv Roznai, *Constitutional Revolution* (New Heaven: Yale University Press, 2020).

[44] Colombian Constitutional Court, Decision C-1040 of 2005.

[45] Colombian Constitutional Court, Decision C-141 of 2010.

[46] See, e.g., Samuel Issacharoff, *Fragile Democracies: Contested Power in the Era of Constitutional Courts* (Cambridge University Press, 2015); Rosalind Dixon & David Landau, 'Transnational Constitutionalism and a Limited Doctrine of Unconstitutional Constitutional Amendment' (2015) 13(3) International Journal of Constitutional Law 606.

[47] This is based upon M. J. Cepeda & D. Landau, *Colombian Constitutional Law: Leading Cases* (Oxford: Oxford University Press, 2017), 342–60.

that suppresses the ban on presidential re-election, allowing it for one time only, does not constitute, in and of itself, a substitution of the Constitution.'[48]

In sharp contrast, in the second re-election decision, the Court held that allowing three consecutive presidential terms would constitute a replacement of the existing principle of the separation of powers by creating an unduly strong and unchecked president. The Court carefully described the procedures for selecting all of the various bodies charged with checking presidential power, including courts, ombudspersons, procurators, and comptrollers. It noted that many of these institutions had long terms in office or terms staggered from that of the president, in order to preserve institutional independence. Yet it emphasized that with twelve consecutive years in office, the president would be able to select essentially all of these officials (or the institutions charged with selecting them), in many cases more than once. The Court also explained that it was likely that a president with twelve consecutive years in office would be able to exercise a dominant influence on the composition of Congress, and—even after eight years in office—hold dominating advantages over any potential opponents. Thus, the electoral playing field would inevitably be very tilted, regardless of any legal guarantees given to opposition candidates.

These conclusions from domestic constitutional design and constitutional theory were again bolstered by comparative analysis. Based on regional experience from both inside and outside of Latin America, the Court concluded that the current Colombian design allowing two consecutive four-year terms was already at the 'outer limit' of common practice, and that going beyond that limit raised 'serious risks of perversion of the regime'. The Court emphasized that allowing presidents to serve more than eight years in office also seemed to be associated with executive dominance, in other words with the distorted form of government called *presidencialismo* rather than a merely presidential form of government, and with problematic democratic outcomes. The Court thus prevented Uribe's attempt to amend the constitution in order to run for a third term: 'since the presidential system adopted in the Constitution of 1991 works from the presidency, a second re-election would rupture and substitute the Constitution in all cases ... a second presidential re-election substitutes structural axes of the Political Constitution, and thus [the law] ... violates the Constitution and must be declared unconstitutional.'[49]

I want to suggest an explanatory reasoning for this decision, based upon the logic of qualitative quantity. If one analyses the case in a 'purely scientific', mathematician way, one can wonder why running for a second term is allowed—as a matter of constitutional change—but changing the constitution in order to run for a third term is tantamount to a constitutional replacement? To put it differently, if +4 (years of term) is a constitutional amendment and not a replacement, why is another amendment that brings about +4 (years of term) considered a constitutional replacement? Precisely because the constitutional change was examined in a cumulative manner (4+4+4). The aggregated result (12) was so sever in its effect on the constitutional order to declare the amendment seeking for a third term as a prohibited replacement, notwithstanding the fact that the amendment itself brought about only a minor change (4). Here, the

[48] Colombian Constitutional Court, Decision C-1040 of 2005; cited in Cepeda & Landau (n. 47), 353.

[49] Colombian Constitutional Court, Decision C-141 of 2010; cited in Cepeda & Landau (n. 47), 359.

quantity (3 terms x 4 years) turned into quality—fundamentally abandoning the principle of term limits and thus an unconstitutional constitutional replacement.

B. Israel

In 2017, the Israeli Supreme Court delivered a dramatic decision in which, for the first time in its history, it issued a nullification notice to a temporary Basic Law (a law carrying a constitutional status) that changed the annual budget rule to a biennial one, for the fifth time in a row, by applying a doctrine of 'misuse of constituent power'.[50]

This historical background is important. According to the established constitutional principle, the government must ordinarily submit an annual budget for the approval of the Knesset. This is a central mechanism for the Knesset to supervise the government. The importance of this constitutional rule is evident in light of the constitutional consequences of the budget proposal being rejected: dissolvency of the Knesset.

Notwithstanding his rule, in 2009, considering the global economic crisis, the Ministry of Finance proposed a biennial budget for the years 2009–2010. Accordingly, due to special circumstances, the government decided that the biennial budget would be enacted as a temporary amendment to Basic Law: The State Economy. The Minister of Finance made it clear that this was a one-time amendment, stemming from a true case of urgency. This meant that government expenditures for the two-year period would be determined in advance, with the entire budget voted and approved by the Knesset only once. After this one-time temporary amendment, the government amended the Basic Law again, in another temporary amendment, proposing that the new temporary amendment is meant to be an experimental legislation, a 'pilot' to examine whether the mechanism of a biennial budget should be permanent.

This amendment was challenged before the Supreme Court in *MK Roni Bar-On v The Knesset*,[51] but was rejected by a seven-judge panel. Writing the main opinion of the Court, the President of the Supreme Court at that time, Dorit Beinisch, held that the use of temporary ordinances to establish the biennial budget is problematic and there may be certain cases in which a temporary amendment to a basic law will be considered a misuse of the title 'basic law'. However, at this time, the Supreme Court would not intervene, because the government was justified in temporarily experimenting with the unconventional biennial budget before deciding whether to adopt it as a permanent arrangement. While the Court reasoned that biennial budgets do not constitute a serious danger to democracy, it did harshly criticize the use of temporary Basic Laws, declaring that such instruments contradict the fundamental concept which states that constitutional provisions are enduring and detract from the status of the Basic Laws. Accordingly, temporary constitutional amendments, President Beinisch urged the legislature, should be used sparingly and in extreme circumstances.

[50] HCJ 8260/16 *Academic Center of Law and Business v Knesset*, (6 September 2017). This section is built upon Yaniv Roznai, 'Constitutional Paternalism: The Israeli Supreme Court as Guardian of the Knesset' (2018–2019) 51(4) *Verfassung und Recht in Übersee* 415.

[51] HCJ 4908/10 *Bar-on, MK v Knesset*, 64(3) PD 275 (2011).

This advice, as we shall see, was ignored. At the end of the experimental period, it became clear that the budget deficit had only increased. As a result, the Minister of Finance and the Chairman of the Finance Committee announced that there would be no further amendments to the Basic Law and that future budgets will be approved year by year, according to the established constitutional rule. Even so, biennial budgets were approved for 2013–2014 and 2015–2016, against professional opinions from within the Finance Ministry and the Knesset legal advisor's office.

In 2017, the government decided, for the fifth time, to approve a biennial budget by way of another temporary order, which was challenged before an expanded panel of seven judges of the Supreme Court in the case of *Ramat Gan Academic Center of Law and Business v. Knesset* delivered on 6 September 2017.[52]

Justice Elyakim Rubinstein, writing the majority opinion, opened the judgment with the following statement: '[T]he case before us raises two worrying trends within Israeli parliamentary democracy, which are intertwined: one, the decreasing importance of the Knesset as a body responsible for supervising the government actions. The second, the undermining of the basic laws status, constitutional texts ...'[53] The Supreme Court reiterated the presuppositions that the Knesset is the Israeli legislature, according to Article 1 of Basic Law: The Knesset, and that the government, on the other hand, is 'The Executive Authority of the State', according to Article 1 of Basic Law: The Government. One of the Knesset's main supervisory roles of the government's activities is approving the state budget. Although the government shapes the budget, it is the Knesset that approves it. Without this approval, the Knesset will be dissolved, and new elections will be held.

The state budget is largely based on taxes collected from the public, and from this stem the fundamental principle of democracy by which the parliament decides on taxing policy and expenditure priorities, which the government then implements. More than just technical issues, the state budget and its approval are essential and lie at the root of democracy. When the Knesset lost its ability to frequently monitor the budget—it has lost its power. Approving a biennial budget does just that, by denying the Knesset one of its most essential tools of government supervision.

Beside the decline in the status of the Knesset, the Supreme Court notes also a decline in the status of the Basic Laws. The increasing use of temporary orders to amend Basic Laws is an example of the intolerable triviality with which the legislature and the executive authorities consider the constitutional documents of the state. The use of temporary orders is prevalent in the Israeli landscape regarding ordinary laws and other legislation, yet the Court fails to understand how amendments with a wide impact on the constitutional framework of the country are done time after time, without public deliberation, through temporary orders amending Basic Laws. The result of these actions is a continuous decline in the status of the Basic Law. As the concept of temporary orders itself contradicts the basic principle of a constitutional democracy, the use of temporary orders in cases such as these should be done very cautiously.

In his ruling, Justice Rubinstein used the doctrine of misuse of constituent power. This doctrine, which was already discussed in the case of *Bar-On*, centres on whether

[52] *Academic Center of Law and Business* (n. 50)

[53] Ibid.

the use of temporary orders to amend Basic Laws, is, in itself, a 'wrongful use of constituent power, in a way which withholds the validity of the Basic Law via Temporary Orders as a basic law'.[54] In the case of *Bar-On*, as mentioned, it was ruled that under certain and extreme circumstances, the use of a temporary order to amend Basic Laws could justify judicial intervention. Justice Rubinstein stated that the amendment of the Basic Law by temporary orders, time after time and under the current circumstances, constitutes a misuse: 'the repeated use of a temporary order to amend the Basic Law not only overrides the public debate, but also undermines the status of the Basic Laws in a way that justifies a judicial action.'[55]

As for judicial remedy, Justice Rubinstein adopts the Knesset's position and instead of striking down the amendment he declares a 'nullification notice'. The practical meaning was that the Court allowed the current amendment yet forbade another future amendment of the Basic Law by a temporary order. If in the future such a temporary amendment would be passed, it will be struck down. The reasons for choosing this relief are twofold: first, the Court has yet to invalidate Basic Laws and therefore would rather practice extreme caution when doing so; second, the state budget had been enacted long before this verdict. Striking the budget now would have far-reaching implications on the government and the economy.[56]

This judgment raises an important question; why in the first challenge, the *Bar-On* case, was the temporary amendment establishing a biennial budget allowed but in the second challenge, in the *Academic Center of Law and Business* case, it was declared as an unconstitutional constitutional change? Why was the second regarded as a prohibited abuse of constituent power, while the first was not such an abuse?

The first and obvious answer is that the circumstances that allowed a temporary biennial budget had changed. In the first case, it was based on an experiment. But that experimental period that heavily justified the previous temporary amendment ended and was no longer relevant. With these circumstances, it is hard to justify the existence of a temporary order that serves only a specific government at a specific point of time, without an external objective anchoring. It was only governmental convenience that lead to the continuation of the temporary amendments and the removal of the constitutional rule imposing upon it a political burden.

But it is more than that, I wish to suggest. It was the accumulation of the temporary amendments that was conclusive. As Justice Hanan Melcer explained in his opinion, a one-time temporary change of the annual budget rule to a biennial one is an infringement of the constitutional rule without essentially modifying the basic rule (annual budget). However, the recurring use of the temporary amendment turned the 'infringement' of the constitutional rule into its 'modification'. In other words, the Court has taken an aggregated review, considering not only the 'qualitative' effect of the fifth amendment on its own but also the 'quantity'—all the previous amendments that, when considering all the amendments together, have led the country not to have an annual budget for a decade. This was explained by Justice Hanan Melcer in his

[54] *Bar-on, MK* (n. 50), para. 17 of Justice Beinisch Judgment.

[55] *Academic Center of Law and Business* (n. 51), para. 33 of Justice Rubinstein's judgment.

[56] Ibid., para. 34.

support of the majority's decision in the biennial budget case: 'The quantity turned into quality'.[57]

VI. Conclusion

In a recent article,[58] Tamar Hostovsky Brandes and I argue that the time has come to consider an aggregated form of judicial review of constitutional amendments in order to face populist constitutionalism and democratic erosion. Assume the following scenario; a state is undergoing a process of democratic erosion. In an attempt to capture the court, the executive enact distinct changes to the legal structure, undermining separation of powers and judicial independence. Each of these in itself is not a constitutional replacement. None of them fundamentally abandon the constitutional order's fundamental principles and replaces them with new ones. However, taken accumulatively, these changes bring about a constitutional replacement. Accordingly, one may ask themselves why the court should not take into its consideration all prior constitutional changes in addition to a single constitutional change it is currently reviewing.

An aggregated review may relax—even if not solve—the challenge posed by the incremental use of subtle constitutional amendments undermining basic constitutional principles. One method to be applied in such scenarios is to consider the quantitative changes to basic constitutional principles in order to examine the qualitative effect on them. In other words, although the currently reviewed amendment is in itself of a minor extent, taken together with its preceding amendments, it may be regarded as 'the Straw that broke the Constitution's back'.

As I have attempted to demonstrate in this chapter, in many areas 'a gradual accumulation of quantity at some point results in a change in the quality of the situation'.[59] Another such area may be constitutional change. Surely it is difficult to tell when a constitutional change becomes a constitutional replacement just as it is difficult to draw a bright-line to tell high from low. Hegel's dialectical principle provided a philosophical foundation for the transition from quantity change to quality change. One scholar suggested that from Hegelian philosophy one can infer the following proposition: 'constitutional courts must keep an open and reliable channel for the observation of "quantity change" because factual understanding via effective measurement ... is required to judge whether the transition happens'.[60]

As I have tried to demonstrate in this chapter, such logic was precisely what stood at the basis of two dramatic judicial decisions in Colombia and Israel, where courts reviewed constitutional amendments declaring them to be prohibited modifications and thus unconstitutional: in these two cases the quantity transformed into quality.

57 Ibid., para. 7 of Justice Melcer's judgment.

58 Yaniv Roznai & Tamar Hostovsky Brandes, 'Democratic Erosion, Populist Constitutionalism, and the Unconstitutional Constitutional Amendments Doctrine', (2020) 14(1) Law & Ethics of Human Rights, 19.

59 Worster (n. 34), 13.

60 Wen-Yu Chia, 'Utilizing External-Knowledge in Means-Ends Analysis: A Comparative Study on Taiwanese and U. S. Cases Regarding Interdisciplinary Approaches to Constitutional Reasoning' (2018) 13(1) National Taiwan University Law Review 1, 23.

8

Between the Explicit and Implicit Limits? An Analysis of Judicial Review of the Constitutional Amendment Doctrine in Colombia

Yenny Andrea Celemín

I. Introduction

A common feature in the literature about constitutional design consists of the identification of different mechanisms for entrenching constitutional provisions in order to avoid recurrent constitutional changes. These mechanisms have been labelled as the principle of constitutional rigidity,[1] and they are conceptualized as 'an aggravated difficulty with respect to ordinary legislation to modify or derogate the Constitution'.[2]

Constitutional entrenchment devices are diverse in form and nature. Some of them have a procedural essence, mainly intended to distinguish regular legislation from the constitutional amendment process. An overlap of the competence to create regular legislation and constitutional rules in the same body—parliaments—serves as an explanation for this distinction. On the contrary, other constitutional rigidity mechanisms have a material or substantive nature. In this way, some constitutions contain specific clauses declared as immune to changes in the same text of the constitution. These devices are quite common in modern constitutions: 'Many constitutions have some provisions that are unamendable. Roznai (2013) reports that 40% of constitutions have some provisions that are unamendable. Some 11% entrench certain basic rights.'[3] Thus, the incorporation of these types of clauses implies that no organ with authority to modify a constitution has the competence to change these specific provisions under any circumstances.

These manifestations of the principle of constitutional entrenchment constitute one type of limits to carry out constitutional changes: explicit limits on constitutional amendments. They are explicit because the literal text of the constitution is the

[1] Richard Albert 'The Structure of Constitutional Amendment Rules' (2014) Wake Forest Law Review 912.

[2] Alfonso Ruiz, 'Constitucionalismo y Democracia' (2005) 21 Isonomia No 52

[3] James Melton and Tom Ginsburg, 'Does the Constitutional Amendment Rule Matter?' (2014) Coase-Sandor Institute for Law & Economics Working Paper No. 682 (May), 1.

Yenny Andrea Celemín, *Between the Explicit and Implicit Limits? An Analysis of Judicial Review of the Constitutional Amendment Doctrine in Colombia* In: *Constitutionalism*. Edited by: Alejandro Linares-Cantillo, Camilo Valdivieso-León, Santiago García-Jaramillo, Oxford University Press (2021). © The various contributors. DOI: 10.1093/oso/9780192896759.003.0009

parameter that determines them. Nonetheless, the explicit limits are not the only ones that organs authorized to modify constitutions must abide by when they intend to pass a constitutional amendment. Contemporary constitutionalism is discussing, with more frequency nowadays, the necessity for derivative powers to follow implicit limits in the constitutional amendment process. The intervention of constitutional courts through judicial review in the determination of these implicit limits is crucial: courts decide what these restraints are.[4]

In the Colombian context, the Constitutional Court carries out both types of judicial review of constitutional amendments based on examining explicit and implicit limits on the constitutional amendment process. On the one hand, the Colombian Constitution does not have any unamendable clauses that work as explicit limits. Explicit limits, in this paper, refers just to 'strategies [aimed] at enforcing the constitutionally mandated procedures for formal amendment'.[5] On the other hand, the judicial review of implicit limits is a strategy with the purpose of 'evaluating the content of the amendment and its conformity with the existing constitution'.[6]

Due to the intensity with which the Constitutional Court exercises judicial review of constitutional amendments, the number of papers that analyse the two types of decisions made by the Court are significant in the Colombian juridicial field. However, although there are a robust number of works explaining the doctrines about judicial review of constitutional amendments based upon explicit[7] and implicit limits,[8] there is not enough information about the types of relationships that exist between them in Colombian constitutionalism.

The purpose of this paper is to contribute to filling this gap by means of revision and a contrasting of the Colombian Constitutional Court's doctrine on judicial review of constitutional amendments based on both explicit and implicit limits. This analysis shows that, in Colombian constitutionalism, there is an inverse relationship between the two types of doctrines. Although there is no constitutional authority to exercise judicial review based on implicit limits, the emergence of this doctrine has influenced judicial review based on explicit limits as established in the literal text of the Colombian constitution.

[4] Yaniv Roznai, *Unconstitutional Constitutional Amendments: A Study of the Nature and Limits of Constitutional Amendment Power* (London: London School of Economics, 2014).

[5] Richard Albert, 'How a Court Becomes Supreme: Defending the Constitution from Unconstitutional Amendment' (2017) 77 Maryland Law Review 181, 180.

[6] Ibid.

[7] See, e.g., Alfonso Palacio, Concepto y Control del Procedimiento Legislativo (Bogotá: Universidad Externado de Colombia, 2005); Guillermo Otálora, 'El Deber de Deliberación Mínima en el Debate Parlamentario' (2013) 38 Revista Pensamiento Jurídico 65; Yenny Celemín, 'La Influencia de la Jurisprudencia de la Corte Constitucional en el Proceso Legislativo en Colombia' (2017) 11 Revista Precedente 53.

[8] See, e.g., Carlos Bernal, 'Unconstitutional Constitutional Amendments in the Case Study of Colombia: An Analysis of the Justification and Meaning of the Constitutional Replacement Doctrine' (2013) 11(2) International Journal of Law Review 339; Eloy García, 'La Sustitución de la Constitución en el Derecho Constitucional Colombiano' (2016) 95 Revista de Derecho Político 229; Santiago García & Francisco Gnecco,. La teoría de la sustitución de la Constitución: de la protección de la supremacía e integridad de la Constitución, a la aniquilación de la titularidad del poder de reforma en el órgano legislativo (2016) 133 Vniversitas 59.

II. The Explicit Limits to Pass Constitutional Amendments and its Control within the Colombian Constitutional Court's Doctrine

The identification of the requirements that determine explicit limits on the constitutional amendment process is not an easy task in any constitutional context. The complexity of this labour rests in the existence of a set of diverse legal sources for the amending process, which surpass the text of the constitution.[9] As in other countries, in the Colombian constitution, the explicit limits on constitutional amendments are not found in the same part. They are placed throughout the entire constitutional text and in other statutory laws too. Among the constitutional rules governing the constitutional amendment process comprised in the 1991 Colombian constitution are: Title XIII, which regulates the constitutional amendment process; Title VI, which regulates ordinary legislation procedures; and Title VIII, which determines judicial review.

In order to clarify the meaning of explicit limits on the constitutional amendment process, due to the open texture of the constitutional material, these rules are subject to permanent interpretation by the Colombian Constitutional Court. The Court safeguards the constitution based on the terms of Article 241 of Paragraph 1 of the Colombian Constitution, which establishes that the exercise of judicial review must be based just on the control of explicit limits due to errors of the procedure in the formation of constitutional amendments as established in Title XIII of the Colombian Constitution.

However, in the Colombian context, several problems on the way to understand the meaning of these explicit limits have emerged. One of these problems dealt with the way to solve conflicts of interest before debates. In Decision C-1040 of 2005, a lawsuit of unconstitutionality was brought to the Court regarding this scenario of constitutional litigation. According to the plaintiff, in process of Legislative Act 2 of 2004, which approved a constitutional amendment to allow presidential re-election, there was a discussion about a conflict of interests. The press at that time called it 'the carousel of impediments'.[10] In this specific case, the conflict of interests was about having relatives holding public positions in the governmental body who wanted to be immediately re-elected through the constitutional amendment. This situation made these congressmen have a direct interest in the approval of the amendment. However, by means of the carousel, each congressman refrained from voting against his own impediment but voted for revoking the impediment of their colleagues, who also had relatives holding public offices. This allowed them to participate in the debates and vote for the approval of the amendment. This practice was pleaded before the Court by several citizens (C-1047/2005, C-1049/2005), including members of the House of Representatives (C-1041/2005). However, the aforementioned judicial decision considered this form of voting and handling conflicts of interest to be in line with the constitution. To explain the ruling, the Court said:

[9] Elizabeth Garret, 'Framework Legislation and Federalism' (2008) 83 Notre Dame Law Review 1495.

[10] https://www.elespectador.com/noticias/politica/el-carrusel-de-los-impedidos/ (https://www.elespectador.com/impreso/politica/articuloimpreso-el-carrusel-de-los-impedidos). Consulted in January 10, 2018.

> If good faith governs the legislative impediments, it must be presumed that both the congressmen's statement and their conduct prior to the acceptance are carried out with honesty, neatness and loyalty, which allows us to conclude that not only the communication addressed to the Chairman is transparent, but also their participation in the decision of the impediments of their colleagues.[11]

Other interpretation problems of these rules are related with the majority vote requirements to manage reports of debates,[12] and the existence of voting cycles inside debates to reduce the majority's will. In Decision C-277 of 2007 the Court examined Constitutional Amendment 5 of 2001. The lawsuit that initiated the Court ruling alleged that there was a procedural defect in the amendment. The amendment sought to eliminate a payment from the social security system that had been denied by 45 votes to 33 in the eighth debate held in the plenary Senate. Once the voting happened, the Secretary of the plenary said that the proposal to eliminate the payment had been denied in plenary session. However, the Minister of Social Security requested a recess to reflect on the impact of the article that had just been denied for the purposes of the constitutional amendment, which was aimed at giving economic stability to the social security system. The President of the Senate said that the Minister's proposal would be studied, and, because of this, he created a special commission to introduce a new proposal to vote on in plenary session. The new proposal eliminated the payment for those who received higher pensions, but it maintained it for those who received lower pensions. The Speaker indicated that the Chamber Secretary should make a clarification stating that: 'When the voting on section eight was read, I said that it had been denied. It was not. What happened was that it was not approved, there was a decision of no approval, not denial.' After this statement, the special commission's new proposal was put to a vote. It then reached 79 votes in favour and 9 against. Sectors representing labouring unions contested the amendment. Finally, the Court declared that the amendment had been adjusted to the Constitution. According to its consideration:

> In the reconstruction of the approval process under study, it was determined that, after the unfavorable vote, interventions continued in this regard, which had as a corollary the invitation of the Minister of Social Security to a recess. This undoubtedly indicates that the discussion had not ended; in addition, among other things, because if this had not been the case, progress would have been made in the debate and voting on the other sections and the paragraph of the aforementioned section eight of the legislative act object of analysis, a situation that did not occur.[13]

Nevertheless, inside these scenarios of constitutional dispute on the meaning of explicit limits, a particular limit has a leading role in Colombia due to the frequency of its presence.[14] One of the rules of the constitutional amendment process in Colombia

[11] Decision C-1040 of 2005 also ratified in Decision C-337 of 2006.

[12] See, e.g., Decision C-816 of 2004.

[13] Decision C-277 of 2007

[14] The quantitative analysis presented in the last part of this paper (especially the data in Figure 8.1) shows that, in Colombia, most unconstitutionality lawsuits claim the violation of this specific explicit limit on the constitutional amendment process.

says that during the second reading stage, the Congress can only discuss initiatives presented in the first reading stage.

According to cases solved by the Court, constitutional committees, plenary sessions, and even harmonization committees have violated it on several opportunities. Nonetheless, the Court has not declared the unconstitutionality of constitutional amendments in all of these cases. The reason for this absence of constancy in the Colombian Court's doctrine relates to different forms in which judges interpret the rules. Some judge's decisions are based more on an anti-formalist point of view than others, in the process of controlling the fulfillment of procedures.

At the beginning of the doctrine on judicial review of constitutional amendments based on explicit limits, the Colombian Constitutional Court was a strict guardian of the constitution. Through a formalist interpretation of Article 375, the Court demanded that the text of a constitutional amendment approved in the first reading was the same as that approved in the second reading (Decision C-277 of 1997). In later judgments, such as Decision C-40 of 2010,[15] and Decision C-141of 2010, the Court acted in the same way.

Nevertheless, this doctrine was not stable enough. Thus, in decisions such as C-543 of 1998 and C-1052 of 2012, the Court changed its interpretation, and introduced a new approach, which turned its doctrine into a more anti-formalist interpretation of rules. In the former of the rulings the Court undertook judicial review of Constitutional Amendment 1 of 1997. This amendment modified Article 35, which, in 1991, established as a fundamental assumption an absolute prohibition on the extradition of Colombian citizens. The amendment removed this prohibition; however, in the enactment, the moment from which it would begin to have effect was different. Several actors, including the Legal Secretary for the Presidency of the Republic, alleged this amendment. One of the charges on which the request for declaration of unconstitutionality of the amendment is based refers to the inclusion of the modification on the effective term to revoke the prohibition of extradition of Colombian citizens that the amendment pretended to include. While in the first period of approval the text indicated that such prohibition would be established when dealing with crimes committed prior to the validity of the respective extradition treaty, in the second reading, the validity of the amendment was modified. Based on this modification, the effective term of extradition of Colombian citizens would be: 'Extradition will not proceed in the case of criminal acts committed prior to the promulgation of this norm.' The Court proved the charge. However, in its decision, it considered that the constitutional amendment had been processed in accordance with the explicit limits of the constitution. In its interpretation, the Court used the following decision rule:

[15] In the process of Constitutional Amendment 1 of 2009, Congress intended to make several reforms to the Colombian political system structured in the constitution. One of these reforms sought the creation of an ineligibility clause for those who were elected in more than one corporation, in those cases in which there was a coincidence of the periods. Faced with this specific issue, there was no deliberation in the debates of the plenary senate (fourth debate (first round) and eighth debate (second round)). After finishing the debates, plenary sessions created a conciliation committee to look at the legislative chamber's - topics of disagreement. Finally, this commission included, in the second round, a transitory paragraph to the rule that created a temporary exception to ineligibility that the Senate never discussed or voted on in the plenaries. The Court declared the amendment unconstitutional on the basis that Congress included the transitory exception of ineligibility that was never discussed in the fourth and eighth debates.

> Having said that, what is the main issue that is regulated in the accused subparagraph? Unquestionably, the non-retroactivity of extradition. So, if this is the substantive issue—that is, that the will of the Congress was to establish the prohibition of extraditing Colombians by birth because of criminal acts committed before the treaty, or the constitutional norm—the date from which it would have effect becomes an accessory matter, which could be modified in the second round.[16]

As noted, from this flexibility of the interpretation of the rules on the amendment process, the Constitutional Court considered that the discussion on the entry into force of extradition and the determination on who was going to be affected or who benefited from the measure could not be considered as an essential issue that should be discussed in the second reading stage necessary to process a constitutional amendment.

In this new approach, the Court does not revise word by word the items discussed in the first reading and contrast them with the ones discussed in the second reading; the judicial review is less strict. The Court does not consider a violation of the rule, a scenario in which some issues do not appear explicitly discussed in the first reading but do so in the second reading, if it can determine some connection between discussions. In this scenario, the tribunal considers the requirement as satisfied. In other words, the control of these limits needs to find the existence of some kind of connection between the issues discussed in the first stage with issues discussed in the second stage.

According to this flexible criterion of interpretation, not every item of a constitutional amendment bill must appear integrally or identically in each one of the eight debates required by the 1991 Colombian constitution in order to be approved. The Constitutional Court named this contrasting a *relative identity principle.*

The *relative identity principle* in the constitutional amendment process is flexible enough to allow items never discussed in the first stage to be included in the second stage without declaring them unconstitutional.

Another example of the use of this principle is related to Constitutional Amendment 3 of 2011. This bill had the purpose of adding a new article to the constitution, which enshrined the right of fiscal sustainability or stability. Many political parties with representation in Congress were opposed to this bill; in their view, the purpose of the amendment was to subordinate the guarantee of socio-economic and cultural rights to the availability of resources.

In the first stage, which included four debates in committees and plenaries of both chambers, the amendment's draft was seriously modified in order to reach an agreement about the scope of the concept of fiscal sustainability. This accord consisted of a change to the legal status of the concept. Thus, fiscal sustainability turns in a standard more than a constitutional right. In this sense, the principle of fiscal sustainability changed its appearance; it began to look like a guideline for the materialization of socio-economic rights, but did not have the competence to limit them.[17] These changes cleared the political parties' doubts about the convenience of the constitutional amendment. Finally, it passed in the fourth debate of the first reading.

[16] Decision 543 of 1998.
[17] Gaceta del Congreso, Issue 758/2010.

However, something happened during the second stage of Constitutional Amendment 3 of 2011. In the seventh debate, some members of the First Constitutional Committee of the Senate proposed to include a measure that had never been discussed previously. This proposal was the introduction of an incident of fiscal impact in the *Acción de Tutela* and other constitutional actions, upon which the Constitutional Court and other high courts adjudicate socio-economic rights. According to this incident, the government (represented by d Secretaries of State) could start a particular procedure in order to explain to the courts the economic effects of this specific decision and its impact on the national budget. After hearing these explanations, the Court could modify its decision, clarify it, and even differ its decision during the time of compliance, when the Court found the government's arguments on the incident of fiscal impact reasonable.[18] This proposal was never published either in the Gaceta del Congreso or in the government's magazine, as required in Article 375 to approve constitutional amendments. It was also not discussed in any of the four debates in the first reading or the fifth and sixth debates of the second reading.

Once Constitutional Amendment 3 of 2011 was approved, some citizens contested the unconstitutionality of it before the Colombian Constitutional Court. However, despite the transgression of the explicit limit in Article 375, the Colombian Constitutional Court considered that the constitutional amendment was constitutional. To decide on this, the Court based its decision on the *relative identity principle* discussed previously, The Court said that it was possible to find a connection between the fiscal impact incident and the concept of fiscal sustainability discussed in the first stage of the constitutional amendment process: 'The inclusion of the incident of fiscal impact is framed within the parameters required by this Corporation for the additions that are introduced during the second round of a bill, as it was the product of the legislative deliberations that intended to make the criterion of sustainability compatible with the clause of the social rule of law.'[19]

Nevertheless, this interpretation has some problems. It can stimulate legislators to avoid facing thorny discussions related to a specific amendment transparently. Therefore, when parts of a bill are likely to be ruled out in the first committees, discussion of them are postponed until the very end, so they are more likely to be passed.

In some scenarios, legislators plan such manoeuvres to try to include controversial items in the last discussions in order to obtain the result they want. Strategies, such as the use of records (declarations about specific issues that are not introduced as proposals to vote on at the beginning of the process, but finally appear stuffed in an amendment bill), were observed in the amendment or legislative process in some cases in Colombian constitutionalism.[20] Nevertheless, there are not enough studies about the effects of these maneuvers yet.

Additionally, this sort of interpretation definitively makes the process of constitutional amendment easier, due to the possibility of deferring discussions or reducing

[18] Gaceta del Congreso, Issue 490/2011.

[19] Decision C-1052 of 2012.

[20] The following press note relates these kinds of strategies in to the discussion of a statutory bill in Colombia: https://www.eltiempo.com/politica/congreso/de-donde-salio-mico-para-reactivar-ordenes-de-captura-a-exfarc-304496. Consulted in 10 January 2018.

the quantity of debates. It blurs the original constitutional rigidity principle from the original design of the Colombian constitution.

In sum, the control of explicit limits in the Colombian Constitutional Court's doctrine does not have a stable parameter when it exercises procedural judicial review.

III. Implicit Limits to Write and Control Constitutional Amendments: Judicial Review Based on the Constitutional Replacement Doctrine in Colombia

At the beginning of its role as the guardian of the 1991 Colombian constitution, the Colombian Constitutional Court acted literally as established under Articles 241 and 379 of the constitution. Some scholars have assessed this role as a minimalist one in the exercise of judicial review of constitutional amendments.[21] In this way, the Court acted as a self-restrained body, which founded the rationale of judicial review of constitutional amendments only on its function of checking the regularity of the procedure followed by Congress when amending constitutional provisions.

However, this way of reviewing amendments changed in 2003 (Decision C-551 of 2003), when the Colombian Constitutional Court took over the competence of the Colombian Congress to amend materially any constitutional provision. From this moment, the Court divided its doctrine about judicial review of constitutional amendments into two parts: one doctrine based on implicit limits (to revise content), and another based on explicit limits (to revise procedures). In this Decision, the Colombian Constitutional Court argued that its new way of exercising judicial review was founded on the interpretation of the word *amend*, which in the Latin *emendere*, means to correct or improve. Therefore, it does not imply either 'deconstitute' or 'reconstitute'. According to Gozler:

> Parting from this meaning of word 'amend', some scholars, and even a Supreme Court, asserted that the power to amend cannot replace one constitutional system with another or alter the basic structure or essential features of the constitution. Likewise, some authors argued that the constitution has an 'inner unity', 'identity' or 'spirit' and the amending power cannot ruin this 'inner unity', 'identity' or 'spirit' of the constitution.[22]

Deciding to act this way, the Colombian Court started its path as a maximalist body exercising judicial review of constitutional amendments beyond the procedural limits set by the constitution. According to this new perspective, the constitution gives the parliament, as derivative power, the power to amend, but not to replace, the constitution. In this interpretation, the distinction between original and derived constituent powers is crucial, as Bernal has pointed out, because each agent of the constitutional change has a different scope to alter a constitution.[23]

[21] Mario Cajas, 'La reforma constitucional: límites de la Corte al Congreso' (2004) Revista Precedente 13

[22] Kemal Gozler, *Judicial Review of Constitutional Amendments* (Turkey: Ekin Press, 2008).

[23] Bernal (n. 8).

The theoretical construct of the constitutional replacement doctrine elaborated by the Colombian Constitutional Court to carry on judicial review based on implicit limits can be considered as a kind of substantive judicial review of constitutional amendments.[24] Nonetheless, the absence of textual authorization granted by the constitution to exercise judicial review of constitutional amendments based on substantive grounds has made the Court insist on the procedural nature of the doctrine.

In the Court's view, the constitutional replacement doctrine is not a form of substantive judicial review, but a sort of judicial review by which the tribunal only checks a procedural issue: the competence of the derived constituent power to amend the constitution. In several decisions that follow Decision C-551 of 2003, the Court focused on supporting its thesis of the procedural nature of the constitutional replacement doctrine with different strategies.

The first strategy consists of a regular reiteration of this idea in all the rules in which it uses the doctrine from 2003 until today.[25] This sort of reiteration of an old doctrine is quite infrequent in the Court's activity due to the widening of its rulings.

The second strategy, more sophisticated than the first one, aimed at denying some association between the doctrine and a sort of substantive judicial review of constitutional amendments, consists of the creation of a methodology to use the constitutional replacement doctrine. The methodology is, for instance, recorded in decisions such as C-1040 of 2005. According to it, the methodology of the constitutional replacement doctrine is composed of three steps constituted in the form of a syllogism with a major premise, a minor premise, and a conclusion.[26]

The study of cases of judicial review based on this doctrine shows some consistency on the grounds of certain specific constitutional clauses; clauses that serve as major premise in this doctrine:

> The identity, for *foundational structuralism theory* is 'the normative identity of the Constitution, supported by a coherent interpretation of its core constitutional principles of basic features.' Changing this identity would result in the formation of a new constitution. The constitutional identity is the constitution's 'genetic code'.[27]

Therefore, the *genetic code* of the Colombian Constitution has eight link clauses according with the constitutional replacement doctrine of the Colombian Court. The first clause relates to the provision of fundamental rights, especially: equality, privacy, due process, and political participation. The second clause is the ongoing materialization of socio-economic and cultural rights as constitutional rights. The third is the separation of powers, that is, the autonomy and independency of the branches,

[24] Juan Esteban Jaramillo, 'La problemática de los límites al poder de reforma de la Constitución Política de 1991' (2013) Revista Facultad de Derecho y Ciencias políticas, Facultad de Derecho 43; Eloy García, 'La Sustitución de la Constitución en el Derecho Constitucional Colombiano' (2016) Revista de Derecho Político 95; Santiago García y Francisco Gnecco, 'La teoría de la sustitución de la Constitución: de la protección de la supremacía e integridad de la Constitución, a la aniquilación de la titularidad del poder de reforma en el órgano legislativo' (2016) Revista Universitas 133.

[25] See, e.g., Decision 674 of 2017.

[26] Bernal (n. 8).

[27] Roznai (n. 4).

mainly, the judicial branch. Also, the idea of the identity of the constitution is regularly connected to the principles of representative and participatory democracy. Finally, elaborating the major premise of the constitutional replacement doctrine rests in arguments related to political decentralization, constitutional roots and traditions, constitutional rigidity, and constitutional rationality.

While the Court has exerted itself in elaborating a solid doctrine to exercise judicial review based on implicit limits in the Colombia context, the declaration of unconstitutionality of constitutional amendments on the grounds of constitutional replacement is unusual. One of the scarce cases[28] in which the Court declared a constitutional amendment as unconstitutional relates to the enactment of Constitutional Amendment 2 of 2015, decided by the Court in Decision C-373 of 2016.

In July 2015, the Colombian Congress enacted a constitutional amendment introducing several changes in the organic structure of the Colombian constitution. First, the amendment eliminated presidential re-election approved in Constitutional Amendment 2 of 2004). Secondly and foremost, the original design of the 1991 constitution was modified in order to re-organize the judicial branch and to perform a kind of horizontal control on it.

The purpose of Constitutional Amendment 2 of 2015 was to create a special body called the *Comisión de Aforados*,[29] a new organ in charge of controlling the public conduct of the members of the judicial branch. In this sense, the amendment aimed at correcting faults in the naïve design of the constitution regarding the judicial branch. This original design established Congress oversees the functions of the judicial branch, but did not set clear procedures or proper technical and bureaucratic resources to do so.

The Constitutional Amendment 2 of 2015 established a two-stage procedure. The first stage would be led by the *Comisión de Aforados*, an autonomous body elected by the members of the Chamber of Representatives but outside it. Its function consisted of investigating and bringing charges against members of high bodies of the judicial branch when they did not exercise their functions properly. The second stage put the Chamber of Representatives and the Senate in charge of judging those incriminated by the *Comisión de Aforados*.

In 2016, Amendment 2 of 2015 was the object of a lawsuit for unconstitutionality because it allegedly replaced the constitution. According to the plaintiff,[30] the creation of this commission substituted some axial principles of the Colombian Constitution—the autonomy of the judicial branch, the rule of law clause, and the due process clause.

The plaintiff argued that the nature of the new body was not explicitly specified. Such vagueness was against the rule of law clause because it was not clear where in the state structure the new organ would be placed. Moreover, the new design would cause confusion for the reasons why a body, which does not belong to any of the political branches nor has democratic legitimacy, would have the power to charge or accuse the members of the judicial branch.

[28] See Decisions C-373 of 2016, C-285 of 2016, C-588 of 2009, and C-1200 of 2003.

[29] A special commission created to investigate those granted immunity, that is, those who are not investigated by means of ordinary procedures; in this case, the Attorney General and the magistrates of the high courts.

[30] In this specific case, the plaintiff of the lawsuit was one of the possible subjects of investigation by the new body created in the constitutional amendment.

In Decision C-373 of 2016, the Colombian Constitutional Court stated the unconstitutionality of the constitutional amendment contained in Amendment 2 of 15. In its ruling, the Court declared that the necessity of establishing a body with political responsiveness as the organ in charge of controlling the high authorities of the judicial branch was an essential part of the Colombian constitution. The Court argued that such body must have the capability to balance imposing sanctions on high authorities with considerations such as 'the pursuit of the common good', 'the institutional stability', as well as the 'exceptional nature' of these kinds of trials, exceptionality that rests in maintaining the autonomy of the judicial branch.

According to this ruling, the autonomy of the judicial branch is the element of the constitution being replaced by the constitutional amendment challenged. This substitution is the major premise; in the Court's view, the body with competence to oversee the members of the judicial branch must have democratic legitimacy in order to balance sanctions that could affect institutional stability, being that this is the only way to guarantee judicial independency. Since Legislative Act 2 of 2015 lacks this feature, the Court finally declared it unconstitutional on the grounds of a transgression of the implicit limit explained above.

The previous sections of this paper dealt with describing explicit and implicit limits on the constitutional amendment process in Colombia. It also outlined the judicial review doctrines based on the two sorts of limits. The next part will analyse how these types of judicial review function in the Colombian context.

IV. Judicial Review on Constitutional Amendments: A Revision from a Quantitative Analysis

A. Methodology

In order to analyse relations between the judicial review of explicit and implicit limits in the Colombian Constitutional Court's doctrine, the paper undertakes a quantitative revision of 110 rules of judicial review on constitutional amendments enacted from 1995 (the year of the first unconstitutionality lawsuit) to 2017: see Figure 8.1.

It is important to clarify that from 1993 (when the first constitutional amendment was enacted) until 2017, the 1991 Colombian constitution had been amended on 41 occasions. Nevertheless, not all the amendments had been objects of judicial review; despite in Colombia any citizen can bring a lawsuit for a declaration of its unconstitutionality.[31]

From 2017 to 2018, the 1991 Colombian constitution was amended on seven other occasions: five in 2017 and two more in 2018. According to these data, the Colombian constitution suffered 48 constitutional amendments from 1993 to 2018.

[31] The list of constitutional amendments never charged as being unconstitutional are: (1) 01/1993 Constitutional Amendment ('CA'); (2) 02/1993 CA; (3) 03/1993 CA; (4) 01/1995 CA; (5) 01/1999 CA; (6) AL 02/2000 CA; (7) AL 02/2002 CA; (8) 02/2005 CA; (9) 02/2005 CA; (10) 03 /2005 CA; (11) AL 03/ 2007 CA; (12) AL 01/2013.

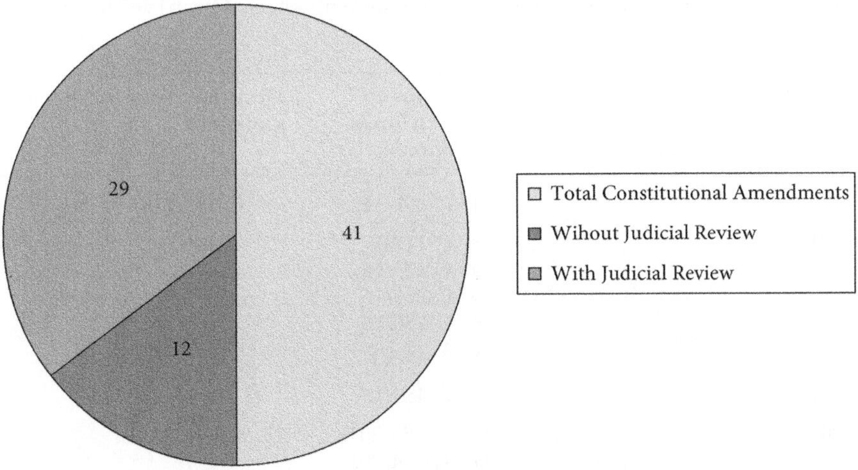

Fig. 8.1 Constitutional amendments checked through judicial review from 1995 to 2017

However, these last amendments are not part of this study for two reasons. The first is that the amendments suffered by the 1991 constitution in 2017 are not comparable to regular constitutional amendments. This is because the derivative power effected the amendments made to the 1991 constitution using a special procedure (the Special Legislative Peace Process), which had specific and transitory requirements to execute constitutional amendments in a compressed way (less debates and requirements), in order to allow the consolidation of the 2016 Peace Agreement, quickly. It is therefore not possible to make an adequate comparison between these amendments and the other amendment's set elaborated through constitutional rules established in the 1991 Colombian constitution. In addition, this paper does not analyse judicial review on constitutional amendments made during 2018, as data on them are currently unavailable. Table 8.1 shows all the rulings analysed in the period selected for the analysis.

To carry out the analysis, each one of the 110 decisions were analysed through a scheme. This helps capture the same information about all of the content. The data collected about it indicates the presence or absence of different information categories: (1) constitutional amendment reviewed in the decision; (2) decisions over explicit limits violations lawsuit; (3) type of charges due to explicit limits transgressions; (4) decisions over implicit limits violations lawsuit; (5) type of charges by implicit limit transgression; and (6) judicial review decisions.

3.2 Findings

Figure 8.2 shows the percentage and numerical sharing of the different lawsuits. Violation of explicit limits charges in the lawsuit and violation of implicit limits charges in the lawsuit are tied with 44 (40 per cent), and 44 (40 per cent) appearances, respectively. On the other side, violation of both types of limits in the same lawsuit have 22 appearances (20 per cent). These data are significant when

Table 8.1 Total judicial review decisions of amendments enacted from1997 to 2016 in Colombia

Constitutional Amendment	Decisions on explicit limits violations	Decisions on implicit limits violations	Decisions on both types of violations
01/2016		1. C-699/16	2. C-332/17
02/2015		3. C-112/17 4. C-373/16 5. C-285/16 6. C-230/16	7. C-94/17
01/2015		8. C-085/16	
06/2012		9. C-433/13	
02/2012		10. C-855/2013 11. C-754/2013 12. C-756/2013	13. C-754/2013
01/2012		14. C-577/14 15. C-579/13	
05/2011	16. C-538/13	17. C-470/13 18. C-121/13 19. C-10/13	20. C-317/13 21. C-106/2013
04/2011		22. C-305/2012 23. C-249/2012 24. C-243/2012	
03/2011	25. C-490/12 26. C-457/12 27. C-420/12 28. C-419/12 29. C-416/12 30. C-397/12 31. C-384/12 32. C-371/12 33. C-288/12 34. C-132/12 35. C-367/11 36. C-332/11		37. C-1052/12
02/2011	38. C-294/2012	39. C-170/2012	
01/2011		40. C-138/2013 41. C-1056/2012 42. C-846/2012	
1354/2009 Act for calling a referendum			43. C-141/2010
AL 02/2009			44. C-882/2011
01/2009	45. C-40/2010 46. C-294/2010	47. C-702/2010 48. C-599/2010 49. C-569/2010 50. C-541/2010 51. C-303/ 2010	

Table 8.1 Continued

Constitutional Amendment	Decisions on explicit limits violations	Decisions on implicit limits violations	Decisions on both types of violations
01/2008	52. C-461/2010	53. C-764/2009 54. C-588/2009 55. C-15/2010	
01/2007			56. C-757/2008
02/2007	57. C-33/2009		
04/2007	58. C-427/2008	59. C-058/2008 60. C-803/2008 61. C-737/2008	
01/2005	62. C- 317/2007 63. C-337/2006 64. C-277/2007 65. C-178/2007	66. C-530/2007 67. C-216/2007 68. C-180/2007 69. C-153/2007 70. C-740/2006 71. C-472/2006	72. C-293/2007 73. C-292/2007
01/2004	74. C-1121/2004 75. C-1173/2004 76. C-973/2004		
02/2004	77. C-1049/2005	78. C-174/2006 79. C-278/2006 80. C-34/2006	81. C- 1047/2005 82. C-1044/2005 83. C-1043/2005 84. C-1041/2005 85. C- 1040/2005
01/2003	86. C-332/2005 87. C-208/2005 88. C-971/2004 89. C-757/2004 90. C-753/2004 91. C-372/2004 92. C-313/2004		93. C-242/2005, 94. C-688/2004,
02/2003			95. C-818/2004 96. C-817/2004 97. C-816/2004
03/2002	98. C-786/2005 99. C-013/2004 100. C-966/2003 101. C-1092/2003	102. C-970/2004 103. C-888/2004	
796/2003 Act for calling a referendum			104. C-551/2003
01/2001	105. C- 692/2002 106. C-617/2002 107. C-14/20002		
01/1997	108. C-543/1998		
02/1995	109. C-387/1997 110. C-222/1997		

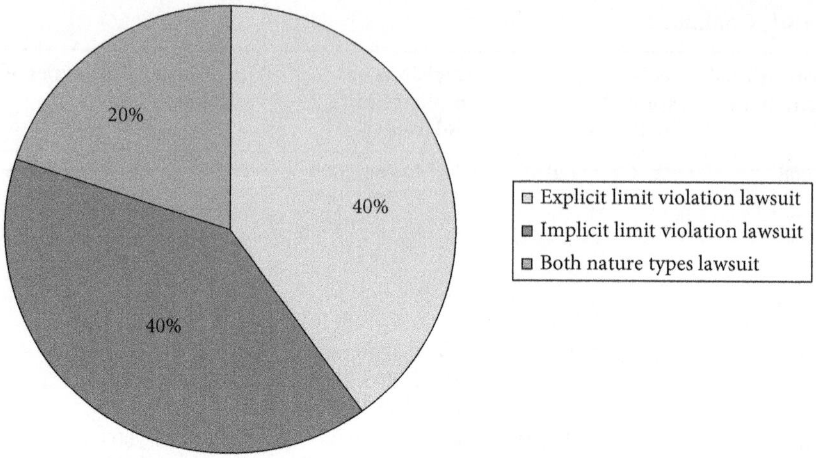

Fig. 8.2 Lawsuits' nature

taking into consideration that lawsuits by implicit limits appeared in Colombian Constitutionalism after Decision C-551 of 2003, seven years later than the first lawsuits on explicit limits transgressions.

Figure 8.3 shows the discrimination of results after judicial review by a number of occurrences. Sorted from higher to lower the judicial review results show the following data. Res Judicata, a type of decision by which the Court resend the decision to a previous decision, that had already decided the issue has 40 appearances. Constitutional or partially constitutional types of decisions have 34 appearances.

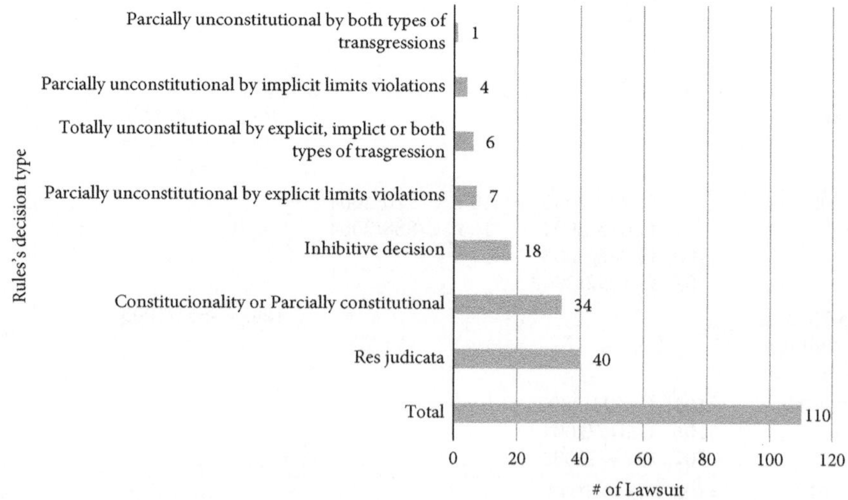

Fig. 8.3 Decision types

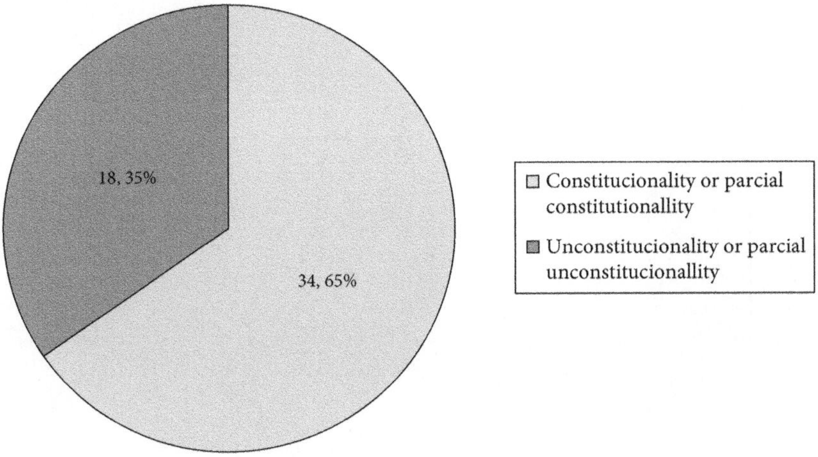

Fig. 8.4 Relation between constitutional or unconstitutional decisions

An inhibitive decision is a type of decision in which, due to the poor construction of charges, the Court omits to undertake a study of the case (this has appeared 18 times). Another type of judicial review decision is partially unconstitutional. This type of decision is splitting in explicit limits violations, with 7 appearances and implicit limit violations with 4 appearances. In addition, the figure shows another type of decision, a totally unconstitutional decision due to explicit, implicit, or both types of violations, with 6 appearances. Finally, the Court declares a partial unconstitutionality by both types of limits violations on just 1 occasion: Decision 551 of 2003. According to the data, the majority of decisions are decisions in which the lawsuit does not have a definitive answer of the Court because it has already decided the case, or due to flaws in the lawsuit. These data serve as an indicator of the complexities of judicial review of constitutional amendments.

In addition, it is important to highlight the contrast between constitutional or unconstitutional decisions. Figure 8.4 shows a court's preference for declaring constitutional amendments as constitutional (65 per cent) instead of declaring them unconstitutional (35 per cent).

A closer study of these last data in Figure 8.5 shows a slight success for charges of unconstitutionality by procedural or explicit limits than lawsuits by the use of the constitutional replacement doctrine. A relation of this finding contrasted with initial data about lawsuits' nature confirms this important outcome. In this sense, if there is a tie of lawsuits on the unconstitutionality of constitutional amendments presenting before the court by charges of constitutional replacement occurrences and lawsuits by procedural transgressions, the relations over data confirm the trend of favourability of unconstitutional decisions due to breakdowns of procedural limits.

Additionally, data displayed in Figures 8.6 and 8.7 provide an insight into types of breakdowns of explicit and implicit limits claimed by plaintiffs in the unconstitutionality of constitutional amendments process.

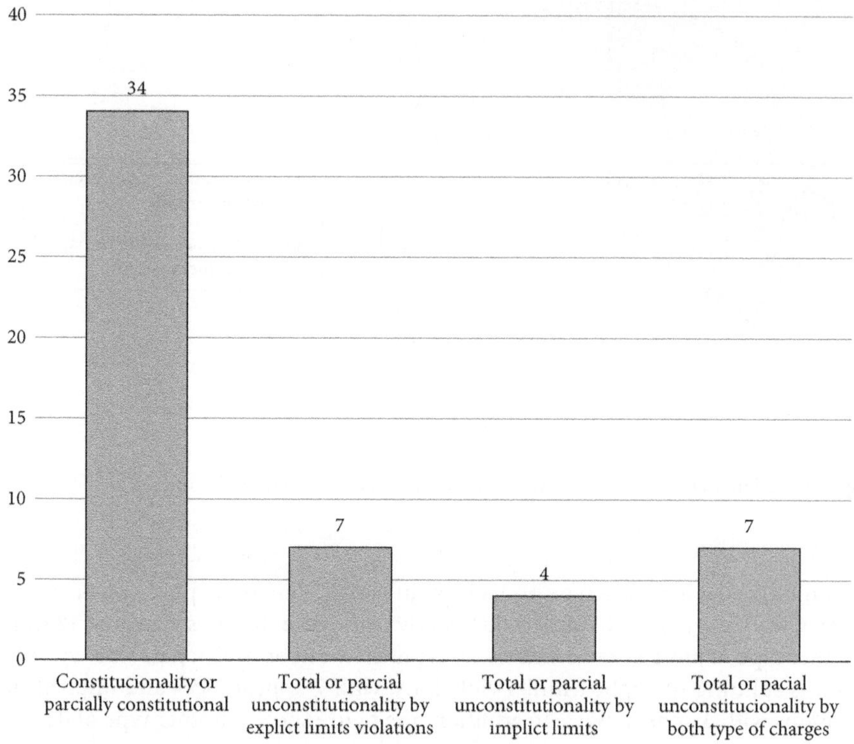

Fig. 8.5 Kinds of constitutional or unconstitutional decisions

In relation to procedural limits breakdowns, it is possible to identify the following charges in the lawsuit that originates court's rules:

Figure 8.6 shows the frequency of different arguments in the lawsuit charges due to explicit limits violations. Introduction of one part, article matter, or issue of the bill in the second reading stage at twenty-three is the most violated rule according to a plaintiff's view. The second, it appears, is a charge related to the absence of discussion of one part, article, matter, or issue of the bill or the committee, plenary, or harmonization to inform in some of the eight debates necessary to approve a constitutional amendment bill at eighteen appearances. Manoeuvres in the voting procedures in order to break the majority will and facilitate cycle voting has fifteen appearances. Finally, elaboration of the amendment without actual participation of the people in the process registered seven appearances. On the other side, the lowest three types of charges are: simultaneity in undertaking debates in committee and plenary sessions with two appearances. Likewise, breaching the terms stipulated in the constitution for undertaking the debates, absence of clarity about what exactly is being voted by the committee or the plenary, and other irregularities in the voting stage have the same presence with one appearance.

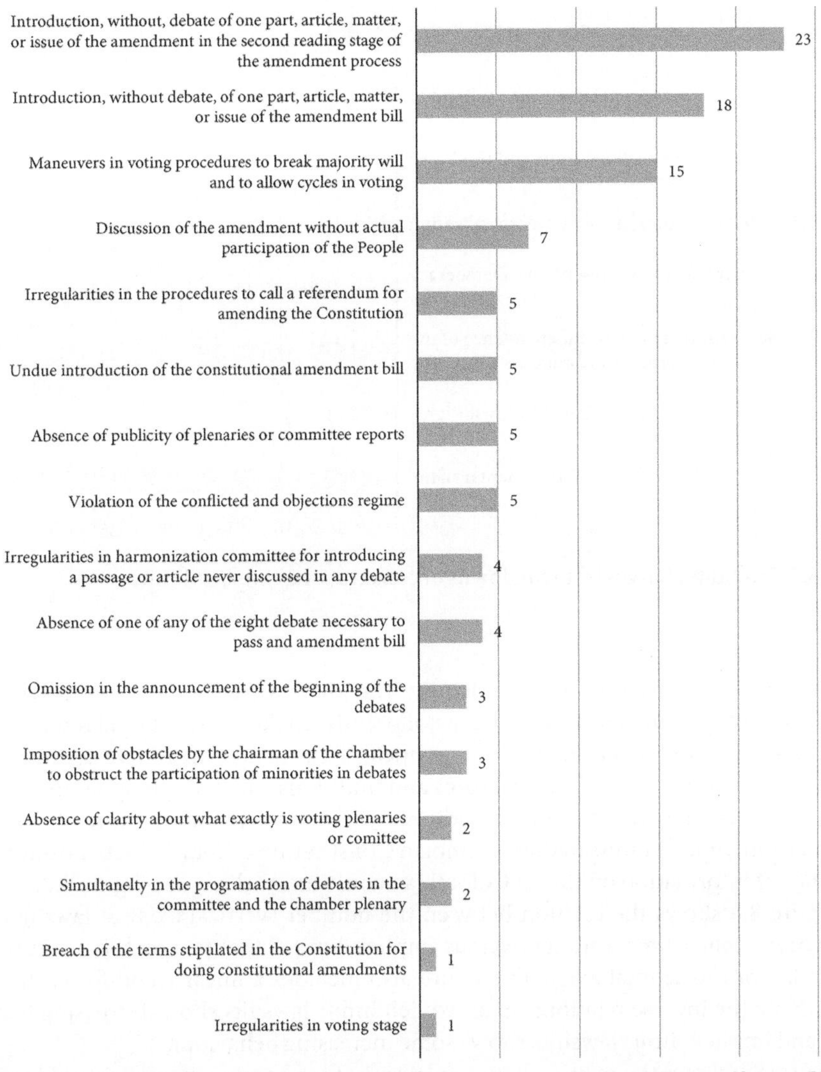

Fig. 8.6 Lawsuits charges by breakdowns of constitutional explicit limits

In the same way, Figure 8.7 shows the frequency of different arguments in the lawsuit charges due to implicit limits violations:

The top three causes were: fundamental rights, with thirty one appearance, separation of powers and independence or autonomy of the branches has twenty-three appearances. Democracy principles have eleven appearances, and constitutional rigidity seven appearances. These categories follow the former essential elements of the 1991

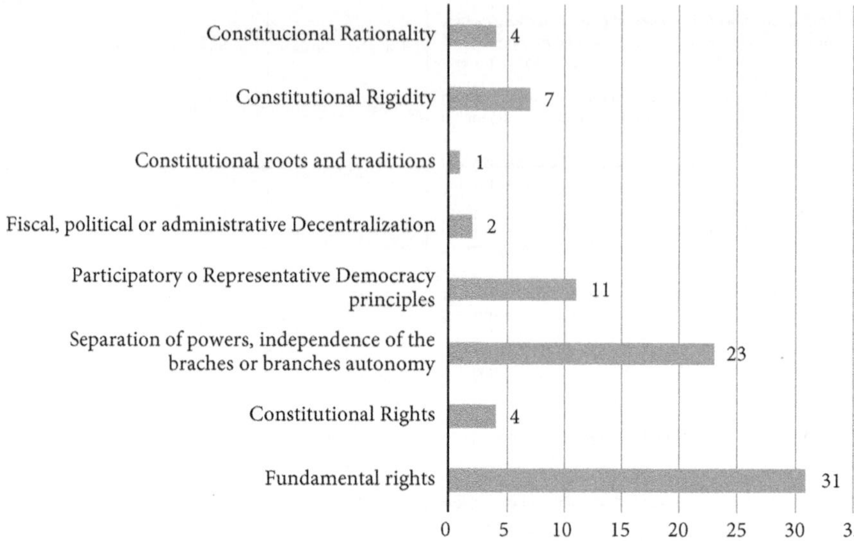

Fig. 8.7 Lawsuits charges by breakdowns of constitutional implicit limits

Colombian constitution's spirit or identity. The lowest three reasons argued were in implicit limits lawsuits as in a way the major premise in the constitutional replacement test are: constitutional rationality, four; political, fiscal, or administrative decentralization, two; and finally constitutional roots and traditions with a single apperance.

Finally, it is important to contrast judicial review on constitutional amendments by explicit and implicit limits in the Colombian Constitutional Court's doctrine due to an absence of information on this in Colombian constitutionalism: see Figure 8.8.

Figure 8.8 shows the relation between the number (vertical axis) of lawsuits per category: explicit limit (orange) versus implicit limit (blue) per each constitutional amendment (horizontal axis). This figure also includes a linear trend for each category. Note the inverse relationship as explicit limits lawsuits show decreasing behaviour and implicit limits lawsuits shows some increasing behaviour.

Figure 8.9 shows the relation between lawsuits filed because of explicit and implicit limits according to the Colombian Court's doctrine. The figure divides the Court's exercise of functions into three periods. The first one from 1995 to 2002, when the Court exercised just procedural judicial review of constitutional amendments, that is, according to the explicit limits established in the Colombian Constitution. The second period from 2003 to 2009, when the Court started reviewing constitutional amendments based on implicit limits. This period comprised the emergence and consolidation of the constitutional replacement doctrine. Finally, the last one from 2010 to 2017.

In Figure 8.9, the y-axis represents the number of lawsuits brought before the Court. The line shows the number of lawsuits filed in the three different periods—the blue line represents the lawsuits for the violation of implicit limits and the orange line for the violation of explicit limits. Note the inverse relationship between the two kinds of lawsuits, that is, the number of cases alleging the violation of implicit limits, in the last

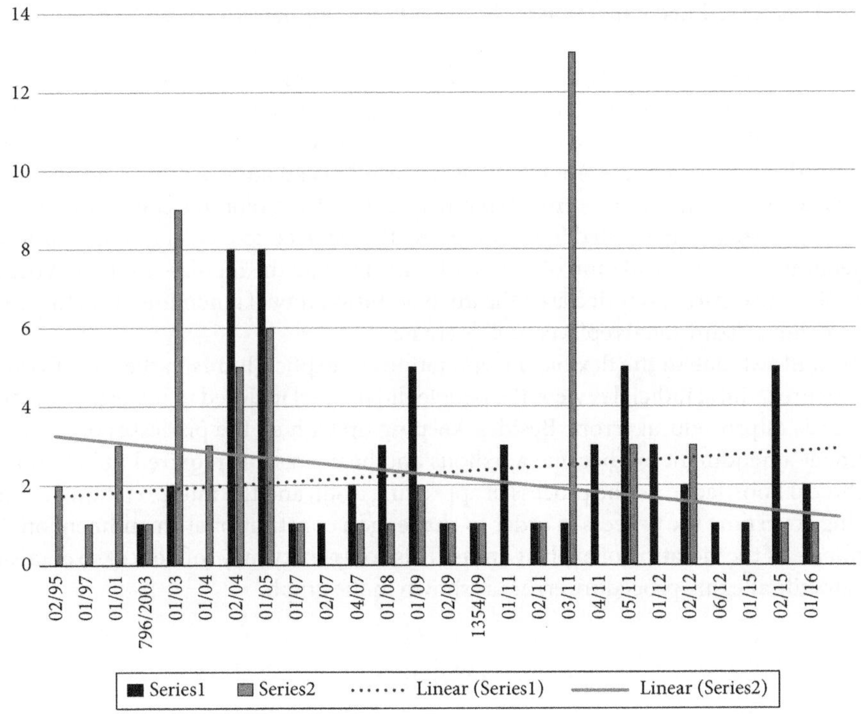

Fig. 8.8 Relation between implicit and explicit lawsuits

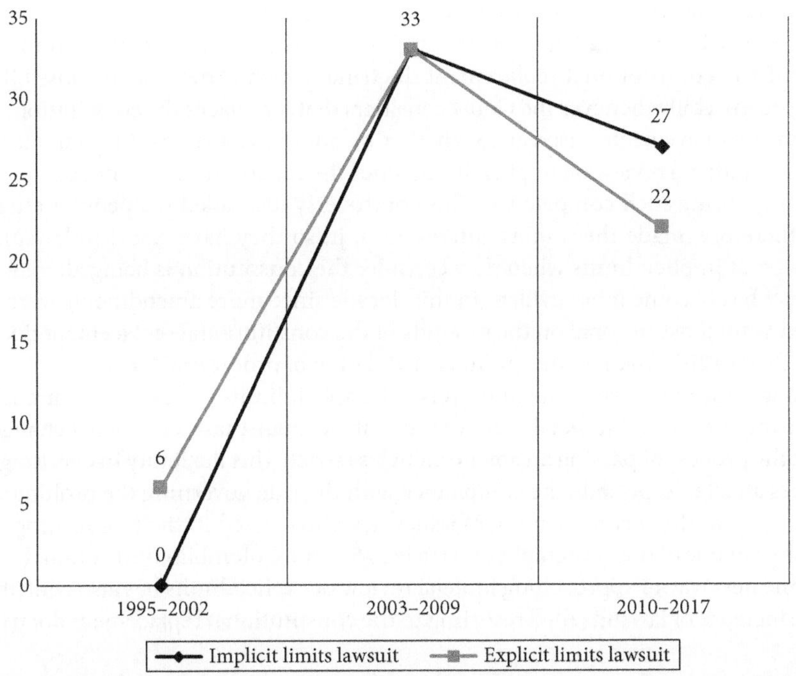

Fig. 8.9 Relation between implicit and explicit lawsuits

period, increased in comparison to the other type. This behaviour can be explained as follows.

In order to face the critiques raised on judicial review on explicit limits, the Colombian Constitutional Court had to construct a theoretical framework to justify the lack of a provision in the constitution allowing for the competence to carry out substantive judicial review. After the Court started to explain what this kind of review consisted of, as well as the control of implicit limits in the Colombia constitutionalism, the people became interested in it. Therefore, they started to challenge constitutional amendments for the violation of implicit limits. Despite the increase in these types of lawsuits, the Court barely declared the unconstitutionality of amendments in the exercise of the constitutional replacement doctrine.

In contrast, due to the flexible interpretations of explicit limits in the Court's exercise of procedural judicial review, the people did not feel inclined to make a lawsuit on the basis of procedural errors. Besides, keeping up with all the processes of a constitutional amendment bill became a tedious and heavy task. It required full attention, technical knowledge on the process of approving a bill, and the interpretation of every ruling governing the process in order to challenge a constitutional amendment on the rationale of the violation of explicit limits. This complexity may influence the decrease of lawsuits alleging procedure errors as shown in the graph.

V. Conclusion

Although the Colombian constitution only grants competence to review constitutional amendments on explicit limits, that is, to check for breaches in procedures, the Colombian Constitutional Court began to exercise judicial review on implicit limits more intensely. This tendency led the high court to create a theoretical framework to justify its constitutional replacement doctrine, which allows for the possibility to strike down a bill whenever the Court considers that it replaces the constitution.

Concerns have been raised as to whether or not the Court has the competence to carry out judicial review on implicit limits since the constitution does not contain provisions granting such competence. This controversy has called the people's attention and, therefore, made them more interested in it, so they have resort to lawsuits for violation of implicit limits when they consider the constitution is being altered. Such conduct has become more evident in this decade since more amendments were challenged as unconstitutional on the grounds of the constitutional replacement doctrine from 2010 to 2017 than on the grounds of violation of procedural terms.

Along with the more frequent exercise of implicit limits review, the Court started exercising procedural judicial review in an anti-formalist fashion. Such a change has made the process of passing an amendment less strict. This flexibility in checking procedures affected especially the compliance with the rule governing the prohibition of discussions in the second reading of issues never discussed in the first reading as established in one of the paragraphs of Article 375 of the Colombia constitution. In addition, the new way of approaching judicial review of explicit limits has also contributed to the increase of lawsuits filed resorting to the constitutional replacement doctrine.

Despite the two ways the People may challenge amendments, the Court does not tend to declare constitutional amendments unconstitutional very often either because of breaches in implicit limits or explicit limits. Nonetheless, it is still easier to strike down an amendment by means of challenging procedural errors than cases of constitutional replacement.

Finally, it is important to promote research of the actual impact of the two doctrines exercised by the Court, given the fact that the way in which the Court interprets the competence to review constitutional amendments is still unclear.

B)

A Struggle for Equality or Judges as Policy Makers: The Judicial Enforcement of Socio-Economic Rights

9

Constitutional Rights without the Notion of Optimization

Limiting Judicial Activism in the Realm of Social and Economic Rights

Axel Tschentscher

I. Introduction

In the realm of social and economic rights, when they are enforced like other fundamental rights, there has been near universal consensus that the role of constitutional courts everywhere is to improve the political reality by optimizing the result. The Colombian Constitutional Court is at the forefront of this fight for social justice. It has continued the tradition of judicial review with *erga omnes* effect under the 'public action' procedure. It has extended the *inter partes* effect of *tutela* actions by giving them precedential weight within the country's court system.[1] And it has adopted structural or even 'systemic'[2] remedies under the 'state of unconstitutional conditions' doctrine. For some, it has gained the stature of a 'super court'.[3]

I do not presume to know the Colombian legal system well enough to evaluate it on my own cognizance. Also, the innovative conceptual and methodological tools crafted by the Colombian Constitutional Court might be more appropriate for Latin America than any doctrines developed for Europe or North America.[4] Therefore, I have to rely on the judgement of others: From what I have read about the powers in Colombia, the Congress seems to be neither forceful nor consistent or reliable in its policy making. The Colombian Constitution Court, on the other hand, is known to be a major power in promoting social and economic rights.[5] This institutional setting seems to call for more judicial activism than is commonly accepted in comparative constitutional law. The rising number of *tutela* actions show an ongoing need for judicial remedies. The

[1] Manuel José Cepeda Espinosa & David Landau, *Colombian Constitutional Law, Leading Cases* (New York: Oxford University Press 2017), 13.

[2] *Manuel José Cepeda-Espinoza*, 'Social and Economic Rights and the Colombian Constitutional Court' (2011) 89 Texas Law Review , 1699ff., 1702.

[3] Cf. *Oscar Vilhena Vieira*, 'Ambitious Constitutions: Prominent Courts', in Rosalind Dixon & Tom Ginsburg (eds), *Comparative Constitutional Law in Latin America* (Cheltenham/Northampton: Edward Elgar, 2017), 253ff., 257.

[4] Carlos Bernal, 'The Constitutional Protection of Economic and Social Rights in Latin America', in Dixon & Ginsburg (n. 4), 325ff., 339.

[5] Cepeda Espinosa & Landau (n. 2), 17.

Axel Tschentscher. *Constitutional Rights without the Notion of Optimization* In: *Constitutionalism*. Edited by: Alejandro Linares-Cantillo, Camilo Valdivieso-León, Santiago García-Jaramillo, Oxford University Press (2021).
DOI: 10.1093/oso/9780192896759.003.0010

Court itself stated in 1992 that the lack of leadership in the legislature must be compensated by strengthening the judicial power.[6]

Nevertheless, while judicial activism might be beneficial or even necessary in the short run, the short-term gains might be offset by systemic risks in the long run. There have been objections to activist courts particularly as adjudicators in the realm of social and economic rights.[7] I also want to place a question mark behind judicial activism—or at least one particular aspect of this activism—the notion of optimization. This notion in our current constitutionalism is closely tied to the theory about legal principles.[8] When fundamental rights are viewed as principles rather than rules, their application becomes open ended and inevitably leads to a balancing procedure where their effect is matched with countervailing principles. The call for universal health care, for instance, is balanced against the financial restraints of the state. Balancing is, for the most part, implemented by the proportionality test. This proportionality test, in a kind of international judicial career,[9] has even encroached upon constitutional systems like the British that used to rely on a loose unreasonable test.[10] Once a court starts the balancing within the proportionality test, the theory of principles as developed by Ronald Dworkin, Robert Alexy, David Beatty, and others inevitably links the decision to an optimization task. For instance: the legislator is forced to implement universal health care as far as it is at all possible financially.

While some have argued that proportionality and balancing itself need to be curtailed,[11] I am not averse to the theory of legal principles in general, but critical towards the practical and institutional consequences an *optimization* by constitutional courts entails. Therefore, I have for some time tried to conceptualize legal principles without the notion of optimization. Basically, that approach starts with the theory of principles in adhering to the balancing approach, but leads to a less fine-tuned control of the constitutional court over the laws and their application. It tries to limit judicial activism and avoid a hyper-judicialization triggered by fundamental rights adjudication.

In order to address the issues raised in this chapter, I will start out with a brief analysis of two decisions by the German Federal Constitutional Court that are examples of judicial activism, followed by the monitoring decisions that are not. I will then contrast this with the Swiss experience where the Federal Court has only limited powers of constitutional review and therefore only nudges the national politicians in the right direction. Finally, I will return to legal theory in order to defend a concept of

[6] Decision T-406 of 1992, quoted in Cepeda Espinosa & Landau (n. 2), 17.

[7] See, e.g., Aoife Nolan, 'Ireland: The Separation of Powers vs. SocioEconomic Rights', in Malcolm Langford (ed.), *Social Rights Jurisprudence: Emerging Trends in International and Comparative Law* (Cambridge: Cambridge University Press, 2009), 295ff.; Katharine G. Young, *Constituting Economic and Social Rights* (Oxford: Oxford University Press, 2012), 133ff., 196ff.

[8] , 'Constitutional Rights, Balancing, and Rationality' (2003) 16 Ratio Juris 131–40, 135ff.; Robert Alexy, 'Proportionality and Rationality', in Vicki C. Jackson & Mark Tushnet (eds.), *Proportionality. New Frontiers, New Challenges* (Cambridge: Cambridge University Press, 2017), 13ff.

[9] Cf. Jackson & Tushnet (n. 9), 1ff.

[10] See Eva Julia Lohse, *Rechtsangleichungsprozesse in der Europäischen Union. Instrumente, Funktionsmechanismen und Wirkparameter effektiver Harmonisierung* (Tübingen: Mohr Siebeck, 2017), 218ff.—with further references.

[11] See, e.g., Francisco J. Urbina, *A Critique of Proportionality and Balancing* (Cambridge: Cambridge University Press, 2017), 125ff., 197ff.

constitutional rights without the notion of optimization. This will also serve as a basis for commenting on the four issues presented to this panel.

II. Cases of Activism and Restraint by the German Federal Constitutional Court

A. Cumulation of Income and Property Taxes

The first case of judicial activism concerns the economic rights of the German middle class.[12] Until this ruling of 1995, the Federal Constitutional Court had always stressed that the extent to which citizens are taxed by the state is subject to political discretion. The duty to pay taxes, even very high taxes, was not considered a violation of property.[13] Accordingly, there have been no fixed limits on taxation. With the exception of prohibitive taxation,[14] only relative limits were imposed by the Court, for example the rule that married couples may not be forced to pay higher taxes than similar couples that are not married.[15] Therefore, when the Court was faced with the decision regarding cumulated tax on income and property, the adequate result should have been that only unreasonable inequalities are prohibited, therefore adopting another relative limit without infringing on the legislator's power of taxation. However, a seven to one majority of the Court held that the legislator was duty bound to limit the property tax to an extent where the total tax does not exceed 50 per cent.[16] This new rule on 'sharing in half' between citizens and state ('Halbteilungsgrundsatz') came as a surprise to the legal community.

According to the published opinion of the one dissenting judge,[17] the new ruling lacked the self-restraint that is adequate for the Constitutional Court. The Court should have acknowledged the legislator's prerogative in developing criteria for who has to pay what as a tax. Even if a legislator is asking for guidance, this task should

[12] BVerfGE 93, 121—Einheitswerte II (standardized evaluation II); decision by the 2nd Senate of the German Federal Constitutional Court; 2 BvL 37/91 of 22 June 1995 https://www.servat.unibe.ch/dfr/bv093121.html accessed on 22 December 2020.

[13] BVerfGE 4, 7 (17)—Investitionshilfe, https://www.servat.unibe.ch/dfr/bv004007.html accessed on 22 December 2020; 78, 249 (277)—Fehlbelegungsabgabe https://www.servat.unibe.ch/dfr/bv078249.html accessed on 22 December 2020; 89, 48 (61)—Versorgungsausgleich.

[14] 'Erdrosselnde Steuer'; see BVerfGE 16, 147 (161)—Werkfernverkehr, https://www.servat.unibe.ch/dfr/bv016147.html accessed on 22 December 2020; 38, 61 (80 f.)—Leberpfennig, https://www.servat.unibe.ch/dfr/bv038061.html accessed on 22 December 2020; 78, 232 (243)—Landwirtschaftliche, Altershilfe, https://www.servat.unibe.ch/dfr/bv078232.html accessed on 22 December 2020; 82, 159 (190)—Absatzfonds, https://www.servat.unibe.ch/dfr/bv082159.html accessed on 22 December 2020; 95, 267 (300)—Altschulden, https:www.servat.unibe.ch/dfr/bv095267.html accessed on 22 December 2020.

[15] BVerfGE 6, 55 (76)—Steuersplitting, https:www.servat.unibe.ch/dfr/bv006055.html accessed on 22 December 2020; 69, 188 (205)—Betriebsaufspaltung.

[16] BVerfGE 93, 121—Einheitswerte II, at 138: 'Die Vermögensteuer darf deshalb zu den übrigen Steuern auf den Ertrag nur hinzutreten, soweit die steuerliche Gesamtbelastung des Sollertrages bei typisierender Betrachtung von Einnahmen, abziehbaren Aufwendungen und sonstigen Entlastungen in der Nähe einer hälftigen Teilung zwischen privater und öffentlicher Hand verbleibt ...', https:www.servat.unibe.ch/dfr/bv093121.html#138 accessed on 22 December 2020.

[17] BVerfGE 93, 121, 149 ff.—dissenting opinion by Judge Böckenförde; https://www.servat.unibe.ch/dfr/bv093121.html#149 accessed on 22 December 2020.

not be taken up by the Court because tying the decision to constitutional law would exempt it from political innovation and would render the political system powerless in face of future dynamics. With the new decision, the dissenting judge held, the property guarantee of the constitution would be used as a limiting factor on taxation—a task it was never designed for. The new 'sharing in half' rule was the Court's invention based on its own estimate of what could still be considered adequate taxation.[18] In effect, this rule would bind the hands of the legislator in the future. It would ignore the fact that the constitution does not want to pre-determine social politics, but leaves this to the legislator's discretion.

What happened to this activist decision of the Federal Constitutional Court in Germany? Nine years later, when all of the former justices had finished their tenure and the Court's Second Senate was composed of a renewed panel, that same Senate of the Court revoked its earlier decision.[19] The citizen who brought the case had been taxed with a cumulated rate of close to 60 per cent. He claimed the 'sharing in half' rule was violated by the tax laws. The Court with the renewed panel of justices now held that the former decision was only *obiter dictum* and not binding as a general rule. The binding part was exclusively based on equality, therefore establishing a relative limit rather than any kind of absolute restriction for the legislator. While the justices still used a proportionality test to check on the violation of the property right, the balancing no longer supported a 'sharing in half' outcome. Rather, it was deemed the legislator's domain to find an adequate balance for the property principle and the social state principle. By leaving this task to the politicians, the Court made sure that a proper result could be achieved under changing circumstances. The Court held that the principle of proportionality might warrant absolute limits on taxation, but that any restriction of that kind would run the risk of imposing restrictions on the legislator that were not explicitly intended by the constitution.[20] So, in the end, judicial restraint prevailed over judicial activism.

B. Eligibility for Medical Studies

A second, more recent case of judicial activism concerns the social right of participation in the subsidized German medical education system.[21] The much coveted university places can cost as much as 190,000 Euros per student per year with all of the cost carried by the state university system and only a minimal administrative fee required from the students. For decades, there have been many more applicants for medical school than there were places. Since education within the federal system is a matter for

[18] BVerfGE 93, 121 (157)—consideration no. 2 of the dissenting opinion https://ww.servat.unibe.ch/dfr/bv093121.html#157 accessed on 22 December 2020.

[19] BVerfGE 115, 97—Halbteilungsgrundsatz ('sharing in half' rule); https://www.servat.unibe.ch/dfr/bv115097.html accessed on 22 December 2020active justices were now Hassemer, Broß, Osterloh, DiFabio, Mellinghoff, Lübbe-Wolff, and Gerhardt Landau; formerly active justices were Limbach, Böckenförde, Klein, Graßhof, Kruis, Kirchhof, Winter, and Sommer.

[20] BVerfGE 115, 97—Halbteilungsgrundsatz ('sharing in half' rule), 115, https://www.servat.unibe.ch/dfr/bv115097.html#115 accessed on 22 December 2020.

[21] BVerfGE 147, 253—numerus clausus III; http:www.servat.unibe.ch/dfr/bv147253.html accessed on 22 December 2020.

the states, the German state governments have come up with an elaborate system to assign places to the applicants. Some get admitted right after finishing high school on the basis of their outstanding academic performance. Some are admitted on the discretion of the medical schools. And the rest can apply on the basis of a waitlist period in order to improve their chances in the future.

The Federal Constitutional Court had already decided about the general framework for the assignment of limited university places in the so-called *numerus clausus* jurisdiction.[22] This was far back in the 1970s. When the issue came up a year ago, the Court had a much closer look at the question. On the basis of an individual right to participation in medical education, the Court now held some of the distribution provisions unconstitutional and came up with very detailed guidelines for the rest. The waitlist, for instance, was limited to the 20 per cent of places it assigned under the current scheme. By setting a maximum threshold, the Court limited the states in re-designing the procedure. Furthermore, the Court forced the states to adopt a new limitation on the waitlist procedure. This incursion on a state sponsored scheme was based on an elaborate empirical analysis of student group access in the past. By curtailing the waitlist procedure, the Court restricted the states so much that the current political discussion leans to abolishing the waitlist altogether.

The medical studies case is an example of judicial activism. The Court's decision is part paternalism, part political regulation. It is paternalism towards the students who are no longer allowed to wait for the medical school place, as it tells them that their chances are worse than those of other groups, and therefore, they would be better off choosing a different course of studies. It is political regulation towards the states because it curtails the current distribution scheme and even sets guidelines for future designs without waiting for politicians to come up with their own ideas. All of this is based on the Court's own cost-benefit analysis that, in effect, prioritizes utilitarianism over the autonomy aspects of the right to choose one's course of studies. We will see that this result, as with the example of the 'sharing in half' rule before, is caused by a misguided notion of optimization in decision making.

C. Monitoring Decisions Regarding Social Security Payments

In the realm of social and economic rights, monitoring decisions have a firm place in the case law of the Federal Constitutional Court of Germany.[23] This form of decision is used during the preparation of new legislation. Generally, the Court acknowledges the politicians' prerogative of factual prognosis about what kind of regulation

[22] BVerfGE 33, 303—numerus clausus I; https://www.servat.unibe.ch/dfr/bv033303.html accessed on 22 December 2020; BVerfGE 43, 291—numerus clausus II; https:www.servat.unibe.ch/dfr/bv043291.html accessed on 22 December 2020.

[23] Cf. Karl-Jürgen Bieback, 'The Legislature's Duty to Evaluate its own Legislation According to the Case-Law of the German Federal Constitutional Court' (2018) 38 Zeitschrift für Rechtssoziologie 42–59, doi.org/10.1515/zfrs-2018-0003 accessed on 22 December 2020; Andrea Kießling, 'The Legislature's Duty to Evaluate its own Legislation According to the Case-law of the German Federal Constitutional Court. Comment on Karl-Jürgen Bieback (2018) 38 Zeitschrift für Rechtssoziologie 60–8, doi.org/10.1515/zfrs-2018-0004 accessed on 22 December 2020.

fits the demands of the future. However, if the fact finding by the legislator has been lacking or the context of the social right is subject to dynamic change, the Court uses the monitoring duty in order to ensure a *dynamic protection* of fundamental rights.[24] In the case of reduced social security payments, the so-called *Hartz IV* decision,[25] the Court found the legislative fact finding lacking in consistency and detail. Rather than just stating the error and requiring the politicians to fix it, the Court, by way of *obiter dictum*, stated that the legislator was duty-bound to 'continuously monitor social security payments and adapt them whenever any change in the economic context occurs'.[26]

If we compare this monitoring duty with the more robust system for monitoring the Colombian Constitutional Court's orders, two differences are quite tangible. First of all, the German Court is not itself an actor of the monitoring, but just triggers a duty that has to be fulfilled by the legislator in the future. Therefore, there is no additional burden on the Court in administering the consequences of its past decision. If the legislator violates its monitoring duty, a new case challenging this mistake can be brought before the Court to address the grievance. While establishing a monitoring duty is in itself an example of judicial activism, because it significantly reduces the discretion of parliament about how frequently it wants to update the law, the kind of triggered self-monitoring the German Court uses is less intrusive on the balance of power than the Colombian monitoring system seems to be.

III. Limited Judicial Review of the Swiss Federal Court

A. General Concept of Limited Review

Switzerland has a non-centralized system of constitutional review with the Federal Court as the final arbiter of fundamental rights protection. That Court often declares cantonal laws null and void because they violate constitutional rights. In that sense, the Federal Court works like a Constitutional Court. Its power of judicial review is, however, significantly reduced in all matters of federal law (Article 190 of the Swiss Constitution). Whenever a law has been adopted by the national parliament, it may be criticized by the Courts and can even be declared unconstitutional. Notwithstanding exceptions of public international law violations, the declaration of unconstitutionality does not lead to the law's demise because it does not in itself reduce the normative power of the law. In order to invalidate an unconstitutional provision, the federal legislator itself must act again to change the law. This is a judicial restraint not by choice of the Court, but by order of the constitution. Its main purpose is to clearly establish that the legislator's authority trumps that of all the Courts, even the highest one on the federal level.

[24] Bieback (n. 24), 45.

[25] BVerfGE 125, 175 (257)—Hartz IV, https:www.servat.unibe.ch/dfr/bv125175.html#257 accessed on 22 December 2020.

[26] BVerfGE 125, 175 (257)—Hartz IV: 'Pflicht zur fortwährenden Überprüfung und Weiterentwicklung der festgesetzten Leistungen bei sich ändernden wirtschaftlichen Rahmenbedingungen', https://www.servat.unibe.ch/dfr/bv125175.html#257 accessed on 22 December 2020.

B. Unconstitutional Tax Burden on Single Parents

How does the limited constitutional review work in practice? One of the recent examples in social rights adjudication is the Federal Court's finding of 2005 that the tax burden on single parent families was unconstitutional.[27] It violated the social right to taxation according to one's economic power (Article 127, Para 2 of the Swiss Constitution). There was no way for the Court to avoid the unconstitutionality by interpretation since the tax law explicitly treated single parent families the same as couple families and parliament had actually discussed the matter without differentiating the tax burden.

Under normal circumstances a Federal Court ruling on the unconstitutionality of a provision in federal law works as a strong appeal to the Federal Parliament to change the law. Accordingly, the Federal Parliament did amend its tax law in 2009 to abolish the unconstitutionality with legal effect starting 2010, that is, more than four years after the Court's decision. This, however, is not even the end of the story. Since the amendment only allowed for a differentiation that then had to be implemented both by the Federation and the Cantons, the injustice was not abolished for more than six years after the Court's decision. This delay in providing redress against violations of constitutional rights is the cost to be paid if a limited review power takes care of the judicial restraint problem.

IV. Conceptualizing Legal Principles without Optimization

A. Examples of Harm Done by Optimization

As we have seen in the first two cases of social and economic rights adjudication in Germany, optimization results in judicial activism that, in turn, shifts the power from politics to courts. The 'sharing in half' rule for combined taxation came as a surprise out of nowhere. It was invented by an activist Court that wanted to enforce absolute tax thresholds on the legislature in order to protect citizens' property. Without stating so, the Court resorted to economic rationales by doing this. There has long been an economic discussion about tax optimization that takes into account the limits on people's motivation when the tax rate exceeds the optimization point. According to the *Laffer* curve, the total government revenue of taxes first increases with the tax rate, but falls when the optimization point has been passed. Notwithstanding the practical problems of calculating this,[28] the picture of legitimate taxation drifting over into an illegitimate burden lies at the heart of the notion of optimization, both in economics and in law.

In the taxation case, the later panel of justices exposed the limits of this rationale. The Court declared the 'sharing in half' rule as non-binding *obiter dictum*, thereby in

[27] BGE 131 II 697—Alleinerziehende; https://www.servat.unibe.ch/dfr/bge/c2131697.html accessed on 22 December 2020.

[28] Walter E. Block & William Barnett, 'On the Use and Misuse of the Laffer Curve' (2005) 24(3) Journal of Public Finance and Public Choice, ssrn.com/abstract_id=1845164 accessed on 22 December 2020.

effect revoking the earlier judgment. However, the damage had already been done. In 1997, only two years after the first decision, the legislator changed the system of taxation by no longer raising any property taxes at all. Frequent attempts to re-establish property taxation in order to achieve a more just overall taxation of very wealthy citizens have since failed. Even the recent discussion about Picketty's theses in his book on wealth distribution[29] has not yet made a revision possible.

It is still too early to estimate the full effect of the Court ruling in the very recent case about medical school applications. Politics might very well do something similar to the combined taxation ruling and abolish the controversial waitlist altogether—much like raising property taxes was abolished altogether twenty years ago. Notwithstanding future changes in the law, there is one harmful effect evident in the Court's reasoning itself. With the decisive focus on efficient allocation of funds, the legal rationale has been switched from Kantian deontology to utilitarianism. While the Court used to picture fundamental rights as a means to further individual autonomy, it now calculates its usefulness for the state. It is no longer the individual desire to become a doctor that counts, but the investment of public funds in the most promising human instrument of health care.

B. How to Avoid the Optimization Trap

There are at least three ways to avoid the optimization trap that has been outlined by the German cases—two of them easy and one more complicated. The easiest and most effective way is the Swiss method of prohibiting judicial activism altogether. If constitutional review is limited to non-binding advice given to the federal legislator, the Court will never impose on politics. However, this easy way comes at a high price. Unconstitutional laws can stay in power for many years if the legislator does not pick up on the Court's appeal for change. The price, therefore, is a less effective implementation of fundamental rights.

The second easy way against optimization in Court rulings is to avoid legal principles and rely on legal rules as far as possible. I have tried to show elsewhere that this is an approach related to Anglo-American law.[30] To avoid legal principles means avoiding the proportionality test and balancing that come with those principles. In a framework of legal rules rather than principles simpler tests can be used that do not lean towards optimization by courts.

The third and more controversial way to avoid optimization by Courts is to re-conceptualize legal principles and the balancing procedure.[31] In my view, it is the most appealing way of dealing with the problem of undue judicial activism. We should abolish the notion of optimization while adhering to the balancing approach where

[29] Thomas Piketty, *Capital in the Twenty-First Century* (Cambridge: Harvard University Press, 2014).

[30] Axel Tschentscher, 'Privacy and Data Protection by Rules Rather Than Principles', dx.doi.org/10.2139/ssrn.3013830 accessed on 22 December 2020. Sometimes this is called the US 'exceptionalism' to proportionality: Jacco Bomhoff, 'Beyond Proportionality: Thinking Comparatively about Constitutional Review and Punitiveness', in: Jackson & Tushnet (n. 9), 148ff.

[31] See Axel Tschentscher, 'Interpreting Fundamental Rights—Freedom versus Optimization', in Hermann Pünder & Christian Waldhoff (eds), *Debates in German Public Law* (Oxford: Hart Publishing, 2014), 43–56,

unavoidable with respect to fundamental rights. That way, we will understand legal principles as open ended norms that still require balancing wherever they collide. But we will avoid the fine-tuned rulings commonly associated with the balancing procedure. The Court's decision would be restricted to an 'all or nothing' statement regarding the relative weight of the colliding principles under the specific circumstances of the case at hand. A good example for this is the rationale of the renewed panel of justices in the German tax case.[32] The Court restricted the former ruling to the combination of property and income tax to avoid its application to a cumulation of income and business tax. It also restricted the binding part to the combination of the property right with an inequality challenge, thereby avoiding any general limitation on the tax rate.

V. Conclusion

We have seen that actual harm can result from judicial activism in the field of social and economic rights. At least some of this harm can be traced back to the notion of optimization entailed with the concept of legal principles. Avoiding the notion of optimization seems to be the most promising remedy in these cases.

VI. Panel Questions

Along the lines of this approach, my statement regarding the four issues raised for this panel is as follows:

(1) No Constitutional Court should actually take the place of the legislative or executive branch. Even if social rights are systematically under-enforced, the Court should stick to case by case rationales in order to preserve regulative discretion for the future. At most, the Court can aggregate various cases into one common decision about remedies, as was done in Decision T-760 of 2008 on medical treatment prescribed by physicians, but denied by Health Promotion Entities (EPSs). If decisions avoid the generalizations of law making as much as possible, the short time benefits of judicial activism are not offset by systemic harm to the balance of powers.

The legislator deserves the final say regarding the normative framework even if the outcome is not optimized. When in the housing finance crisis of 1999 the Colombian Constitutional Court struck down the UPAC system (Units of Constant Acquisitive Power) in Decision C-700 of 1999, Congress adopted a new UVR system (Real Value Units) that was upheld as mostly constitutional in

53ff.; for an updated version see the SSRN Working Paper at dx.doi.org/10.2139/ssrn.1630393 accessed on 22 December 2020.

32 BVerfGE 115, 97—Halbteilungsgrundsatz, https:www.servat.unibe.ch/dfr/bv115097.html accessed on 22 December 2020.

Decision C-955 of 2000.[33] In the literature, this has been characterized as 'back-tracking' by a court disappointed in the effects of its earlier ruling.[34] But notwithstanding substantive disappointment the legislator *did* do its job and the judicial branch only took care of fine-tuning afterwards.

With the structural enforcement of health care in Decision T-760 of 2008, the Court added general orders to the model of individual remedies.[35] The Ministry of Social Protection was ordered to perform a list of obligations (e.g. develop a new health plan, sanction EPSs, improve regulation of treatment, submit periodic reports) within specific deadlines to be controlled by a court monitoring system—with special compliance personnel, with public hearings, and with follow-up orders (*autos*).[36] In addition, the Court struck down the health cost related state of social and economic emergency declared by the Uribe government in 2009 (Decision C-252 of 2010). At the same time it kept some of the taxes adopted to finance the health care system. Notwithstanding the popularity of the Court's decision and its secondary goal to 'empower civil society',[37] this selective intervention looks quite intrusive with regards to the balance of powers. To some extent this might in retrospect have been warranted when Congress eventually passed a statutory law governing health (upheld by the Court in Decision C-313 of 2014), but the dynamics of state powers have been tilted towards the Court to achieve this outcome.

In my opinion, Decision T-025 of 2004 is on a different level from the health care issues.[38] Enforcing the Guiding Principles of Internal Displacements adopted by the United Nations High Commissioner on Refugees goes towards the right to a dignified life that lies at the core of fundamental rights protection. With emergency humanitarian aid there is *no balancing at all* because it belongs to the minimal core of human rights (human dignity plus the essential nucleus of fundamental rights) that must be satisfied under all circumstances and at all costs. Within the three substantive testing levels commonly used for fundamental rights: the unreasonable test, the proportionality test, and the essential minimum test, this is the strongest safeguard of all. Therefore, when the Court adopted a robust monitoring in this case by installing a Monitoring Commission[39] and by generally developing a 'Dialogic Judicial

[33] Cepeda Espinosa & Landau (n. 2), 156ff.

[34] César Rodríguez-Garavito, 'Beyond the Courtroom: The Impact of Judicial Activism on Socioeconomic Rights in Latin America' (2011) 89 Texas Law Review 1669, 1690.

[35] For details, see Aquiles Ignacio Arrieta-Gómez, 'Realizing the Fundamental Right to Health through Litigation: The Colombian Case' (2018) 20 Health and Human Rights Journal 133, 137; Cepeda Espinosa & Landau (n. 2), 175ff.

[36] For a detailed description of the hearing regarding T-025 of 2004 see Rodríguez-Garavito (n. 35), 1669ff.

[37] Cepeda-Espinoza (n. 3), 1704.

[38] Cf. César Rodríguez Garavito & Diana Rodríguez-Franco, *Radical Deprivation on Trial: The Impact of Judicial Activism on Socioeconomic Rights* (Cambridge: Cambridge University Press, 2015), 3ff., 30ff., 144 ff.; for the case itself, see Cepeda Espinosa & Landau (n. 2), 179ff.

[39] See Cepeda Espinosa & Landau (n. 2), 179ff., 186.

Activism'[40] this might be warranted, not because it is innovative, but because it is a measure of last resort even though strongly infringing on the balance of powers.[41]

(2) Financial restraints of the state are a necessary part of the balancing of countervailing principles, and therefore should be taken into account with the enforcement of social and economic rights. In particular, to avoid unnecessary bailout funds or other expensive emergency measures, the Court should leave macroeconomic discretion to the legislative and executive branches of government. The Court has enabled such flexibility in the past, for example when it decided, in the budget decision, C-1064 of 2001, that it was not disproportionate to limit public servants with better salaries.[42]

(3) Strong remedies according to Tushnet's distinction,[43] that is, precise outcome-oriented orders with no legislative or administrative leeway as to their realization, are a legitimate instrument to enforce social rights. To preserve the balance of power, however, they should be narrow in design, that is, adopted by *individual* litigation and in the form of *specific* remedies or damages. In other words: the strength of remedies should be based on the degree of obligation, not on the scope of the order.

(4) The monitoring system established in the IDP decision, T-025 of 2004, and the health care decision, T-760 of 2008, is both innovative and disturbing from the perspective of comparative constitutional law. If a panel of the Court maintains jurisdiction over the case, devotes high-ranking personnel solely to monitoring, issues follow-up orders, requires periodic reports, holds public hearings and appeals to civil society to aid in the monitoring process, then the Court clearly steps into the role commonly associated with the legislative and executive branches.[44] Rather than implementing a monitoring system run by the Court, the follow-up, if necessary, should be required by monitoring instruments within the legislative and executive branches since this is less intrusive for the balance of power. As it is now, the Columbian Constitutional Court simply retains its jurisdiction indefinitely rather than issuing a final decision to pass back the ball to the other powers.[45]

[40] Characterization of the approach by Rodríguez Garavito & Rodríguez-Franco (n. 39), 171ff.; Rodríguez-Garavito (n. 35), 1669ff.

[41] Congress passed a statute in 2008 that implemented the Monitoring Commission's indicators for progress; see Cepeda Espinosa & Landau (n. 2), 187.

[42] Ibid., 161ff., 165.

[43] Mark Tushnet, *Weak Courts*, Strong Rights: Judicial Review and Social Welfare Rights in Comparative Constitutional Law (Princeton/Oxford: Princeton University Press, 2009), 227ff., 247ff..

[44] A total of twenty-one public follow-up hearings and nearly 100 follow-up decisions within seven years: see Rodríguez-Garavito (n. 35), 1694. Also, the stronger monitoring correlates with a higher impact in T-025 compared to T-760; see ibid. at 1695, 1697.

[45] For this unique aspect of the Colombian *tutela* situation see Cepeda-Espinoza (n. 3), 1700.

10
The Court's Dilemma in Social Rights' Enforcement*

Octávio Luiz Motta Ferraz

The democratic process is a gamble on the possibilities that a people, in acting autonomously, will learn how to act rightly.[1]

Can courts play a legitimate and competent role in the adjudication of social and economic rights such as health, education, and housing? How? This debate, which we may call here the question of social rights *justiciability*, is far from academic, as it once was. As more and more constitutions now expressly recognize these rights, courts around the world are increasingly called to adjudicate disputes arising under them, prominently in Latin America but also increasingly elsewhere. The difficulties this raises are thus becoming more evident and more urgent. This paper aims to contribute to this debate.

Express legal recognition of these rights, especially in the constitution as it has occurred in most Latin American countries and many others beyond, has weakened considerably the once widespread argument that social rights justiciability was an illegitimate practice.[2] Yet, what precisely the judiciary can and should do to protect these rights remains deeply problematic and open for debate. The difficulties stem mostly from the high complexity of the issues often involved in social rights disputes, in particular the intractable problem of how to allocate scarce resources among the myriad of competing needs salient in any modern complex society, and from important limitations on the institutional competence of courts to deal with those issues.

The paper will aim to expose these difficulties in order to enable a fruitful discussion of potential ways of addressing them. The animating questions will be *whether* and *how* it may be possible, given the intractable nature of the exposed difficulties, to come up with a proper role for the courts. I will argue that it may indeed be possible for courts to play a proper role in the protection of social rights, but that this

* Some sections of this chapter draw on my book, *Health as a Human Right. The Politics and Judicialisation of Health in Brazil* (Cambrige: Cambridge University Press, 2020). I am grateful to Jeff King for insightful comments and suggestions on an earlier version.

[1] Robert Dahl, *Democracy and Its Critics* (New Haven: Yale University Press, 1989), 192.

[2] Unless recognition is expressly made with the proviso that courts may not be invoked, such as under the 'directive principles of state policy' model, which has not been adopted in that many places beyond Ireland and India as far as I know.

Octávio Luiz Motta Ferraz, *The Court's Dilemma in Social Rights' Enforcement* In: *Constitutionalism*. Edited by: Alejandro Linares-Cantillo, Camilo Valdivieso-León, Santiago García-Jaramillo, Oxford University Press (2021). © The various contributors.
DOI: 10.1093/oso/9780192896759.003.0011

role should be different from the one envisaged by some commentators and currently being played by many courts, in particular in Latin America.

The paper proceeds as follows. I start with some methodological clarifications on how I believe the question should be approached. Too often the justiciability debate is carried out as if this issue were already settled or simply overlooking the question. I adopt a so-called 'institutional approach' and explain, in Section I, what this approach entails and how it differs from other, more familiar 'formalist' approaches. Section II is dedicated to a detailed exposition of the difficulties involved in social rights adjudication mentioned above, that is, complexity of the subject matter and limited judicial competence. Once these preliminary issues are discussed, I move on to address the main question of the paper in Section III. As the title of my paper gives away, I see it as a genuine quandary faced by democratic regimes, and courts in particular. I make no pretence, therefore, to offer a final and clear solution to the problem. I do think however that there are better and worse approaches to it, which I discuss in light of some real social rights cases that have reached the courts of different countries.

I. Some Methodological Clarifications

Before I embark on the substantive discussion, it is necessary to make some clarificatory methodological points. How does one assess the proper role of courts in the enforcement of social rights? A full treatment of the question would of course require a lengthy incursion in normative political theory to discuss complex and highly contested issues including conceptions of democracy, separation of powers and rights. I cannot carry out such a wide-ranging discussion here. What I will do, instead, is make explicit and briefly explain some of the assumptions that underlie my approach to the topic.

A. Institutional Approaches

I follow here an *institutional approach* rather than a *formalist approach*, to use Canadian scholar Jeff King's helpful distinction.[3] As he aptly describes them, formalist approaches 'are premised on a formalist separation of powers between legislatures, the executive and the courts'. Familiar conceptual distinctions used in such approaches are those between *law and politics*, *principle and policy*, and *justiciability*

[3] For a much more thorough treatment of the topic, see the monograph *Judging Social Rights* by Jeff King, on which I draw heavily below: Jeff King, *Judging Social Rights* (Cambridge: Cambridge University Press, 2012), in particular chapter 5 for a discussion of 'institutional approaches'. See also the longer piece, J. A. King, 'Institutional Approaches to Judicial Restraint' (2008) 28 Oxford Journal of Legal Studies 409–41. Other defenders of this approach are: Neil Komesar, *Imperfect Alternatives: Choosing Institutions in Law, Economics and Public Policy* (Chicago: University of Chicago Press, 1997); Neil Komesar, *Law's Limits: The Rule of Law and the Supply and Demand of Rights* (Cambridge: Cambridge University Press, 2001); C. R. Sunstein, *Legal Reasoning and Political Conflict* (New York: Oxford University Press, 1996); C. R. Sunstein, *One Case at a Time: Judicial Minimalism on the Supreme Court* (Cambridge, MA: Harvard University Press, 2001); C. R. Sunstein & A. Vermeule, 'Institutions and Interpretation' (2003) 101 Michigan Law Review 885–951.

and non-justiciability. 'Institutional approaches' reject the usefulness of such distinctions and focus, rather, on 'the comparative merits and drawbacks of the judicial process as an institutional mechanism for solving problems'.

It is not because an issue can be classified as 'political', or 'a matter of policy', or as a 'non-justiciable' issue, that courts ought not to adjudicate them. These *a priori*, formalistic, and bright-line divisions of competence among legislatures, executives, and courts are not really helpful; they are theoretically vague, giving just 'a veneer of objectivity to a number of inarticulate major premises'.[4] To cite King again, 'the appropriate question is which [institutional arrangement] is the best among the available alternatives for resolving a given problem'.[5] The idea of 'comparative institutional competence' is therefore the central one to institutional approaches.

Once this is acknowledged, it also becomes clear that the appropriate role of courts and other state institutions can be neither *static* nor *universal*, that is, determined once and forever and applicable everywhere. They rather vary and evolve depending on how the institutions perform in a particular time and place. This will certainly seem too undefined to the formalist mind, yet it is an inevitable corollary of acknowledging the shortcomings of the formalist approach and the superiority of institutional approaches. On reflection, moreover, it fits much better the actual history of the development of institutions and their roles in democracies. Think of the practice of judicial review of legislation for instance. Not even in the United States, where it seems to have emerged originally, has it always been an established feature of constitutional arrangements.[6] Moreover, despite its significant advancement globally, there are still some important democracies where it is not regarded as an adequate practice in the constitutional architecture. As American political scientist Robert Dahl persuasively argues:

> It is misleading to suggest that there is one universally best solution to the problem of how best to protect fundamental rights and interests in a polyarchy. Although American lawyers typically assume that the solution must include a supreme court with the authority to strike down national legislation that violates fundamental rights and interests, such a system of quasi guardianship is neither necessary nor, on American experience, sufficient. In the absence of a universally best solution, specific solutions need to be adapted to the historical conditions and experiences, political culture, and concrete political institutions of a particular country.[7]

Under a formalist approach, one is forced to conclude, implausibly, that a certain model is intrinsically correct, that is, universal, and all other models that deviate from

[4] King *Judging Social Rights* (n. 3), 132.

[5] The original reads simply 'institutions'. I prefer 'institutional arrangement', as we are not simply comparing institutions and deciding that one is best and therefore will be entrusted exclusively with social rights implementation, but rather looking at a combination of potential institutional arrangements, that is, legislation + administration + judicial review, or just legislation + administration, or just administration + ombudsman etc. Jeff King has agreed that this conveys better his own views in personal communication.

[6] According to the most accepted version it was in the famous case of *Marbury v Madison* that the Supreme Court asserted itself the role of judicial review at the turn of the nineteenth century. Although historians dispute the existence of earlier cases, the fact is that it is not there in the constitution itself nor was it practiced in its first decades.

[7] Dahl (n. 1), 192..

it are therefore intrinsically defective. Under an institutional approach, variations are actually expected and ought to be assessed in light not only of normative theory but also of the empirical data, which is necessarily contextually dependent on the performance of the institutions in the particular regime in question.

So, whether social rights should be justiciable or not cannot be decided in the abstract, as if there were a blueprint that prescribed one way or another to be adopted by every single country in the world.[8] Social rights justiciability, under the institutional approach I am defending here, is a piece in a democratic regime's puzzle (much like the electoral system, the government regime, the composition of the legislature, and many others) whose usefulness and precise design is to be decided by each country, according to their local political culture and institutional performance, in their ever elusive quest towards the ideal democratic system,[9] or, as Robert Dahl puts it 'to adapt political reality in some significant measure to [democracy's] demanding requirements'.[10]

It is perfectly acceptable and expected, thus, that democracy 'x' may decide to confer ample power for courts to adjudicate social rights whereas democracy 'y' may decide to forbid courts from ever entertaining these rights, through say the constitutional doctrine of directive principles of state policy. Both countries can of course be criticized for adopting an inadequate system. But not because they depart from some formalistic blueprint that determines in the abstract that social rights adjudication is appropriate or not. They can be criticized, under the institutional approach, if it can be shown that their systems produce worse results, from a democratic perspective, than they would if they operated differently.

But accepting an institutional approach does not mean, contrary to what might at first appear, that no interesting comparison and learning can occur among countries. As democratic regimes are grounded on similar generic values such as political equality, freedom, human rights, it is also expected that different countries, despite their different cultures and contexts, will follow similar practices and have institutions that function in broadly similar ways.[11] It would be hard to conceive, for instance, a modern democracy without a legislature, an executive, and a judicial branch. How these bodies are selected, organized, and operate are however all specific features that will likely vary among different democratic regimes, and they can certainly (and do) learn from observing (and sometimes experimenting with) the ways in which other

[8] See Octávio Luiz Motta Ferraz, 'Harming the Poor through Social Rights Litigation' (2011) 89 Texas Law Review 1643, 1643–68.

[9] I use democracy here in the thick, substantive sense of the term, that is, as encompassing the protection of human rights and going beyond mere majority rule . For a classic discussion of these different conceptions of democracy and a defence of a substantive conception, see, inter alia, Ronald Dworkin, *Taking Rights Seriously* (Cambridge, Mass.: Harvard University Press, 1977) *Law's Empire* (Cambridge, Mass.: Harvard University Press, 1986).

[10] Dahl (n. 1), 1.

[11] Another way of capturing this is through Robert Dahl's distinction between democracy as an ideal and as 'actual regimes that fall considerably short of the ideal'. As he explains, the challenge is to determine when a regime 'is sufficiently proximate to the ideal that we can properly regard it as a democracy ... It is a problem of deciding on a reasonable threshold'. The way forward, he suggests, and I agree, is to combine 'both the normative and the empirical aspects of democracy ... in a single theoretical perspective', warning, though, that 'the task is a wide-ranging one': ibid., 6.

countries do things. In a highly integrated world, moreover, it is expected that practices will be influenced from outside and become more convergent.

In my view, thus, it is perfectly possible to adopt an institutional approach to the analysis of the proper role of courts in the judicial enforcement of social rights, recognizing thus its strong dynamic and contextual nature, and still develop a generic discussion of the topic that can be useful in different contexts. Although a more final and detailed conclusion on the question will necessarily demand in-depth data and analysis that are specific to a certain country, some issues are likely to occur in all democratic regimes and thus allow a more generic and universal discussion.

B. Criteria of Assessment: Legitimacy and Capacity

Under the institutional approach adopted here the main question is therefore whether courts can play a role in the protection of social rights that is appropriate, from an institutional competence perspective, in light of other existing and potential institutional arrangements. But how do we gauge *institutional competence*? I will focus here on two broad criteria of institutional competence often found in the literature on social rights justiciability and cited in passing in the introduction above: *legitimacy* and *institutional capacity*.[12] Can courts perform a role that is legitimate and capable of protecting social rights compared to what can be achieved through other potential institutional arrangements that do not involve the courts? [13] This is of course still too generic and in need of explanation. What do legitimacy and capacity mean when the protection of social rights is in question? We can only fully apprehend and specify the meaning of these generic terms in light of a detailed discussion of what is actually involved in the protection of social rights. This will be the topic of the next section of this paper. It is however useful to anticipate, here, a couple of general points that will hopefully become clearer later.

Although the ideas of legitimacy and capacity are interrelated in important ways, they refer to two separate dimensions of the operation of decision-making institutions in democratic regimes.

Taking democracy to be a regime with a distinctive set of political institutions and practices with a unique process of making collective and binding decisions that ensures certain desirable results, we want to populate these institutions in a manner, that is, with the personnel most likely to reach those desirable results. Institutional capacity and legitimacy are to be understood precisely as the *qualities* (i.e. characteristics and abilities) of the decision-making institution that enable it to reach as well as possible those desirable results.[14] Whereas legitimacy has to do

[12] See King, *Judging Social Rights* (n. 3) and David Landau, 'The Reality of Social Rights Enforcement' (2012) 53(1) Harvard International Law Journal 189–247.

[13] Like most of the literature I will focus on the legislature and the executive as comparators to courts. For a thorough consideration of other relevant mechanisms such as administrative tribunals, ombuds, and alternative dispute resolution ('ADR') see King*Judging Social Rights* (n. 3), 85–95.

[14] This is my own formulation combining some of the classic conceptions of democracy put forward in the political science literature. See Dahl (n. 1), 5.

more with the pedigree of the decision maker (how they came to office) and the process of decision making (majority rule, secret or open ballots, reasoned decisions) capacity has to do more with the technical ability to reach the correct outcomes. Democratic regimes will normally combine legitimacy and capacity criteria when selecting the members and defining the competence of their governance institutions in varying measures. This is because of the vague, contested, and varied nature of the notion of 'desirable results' when it comes to political collective decision making. In more technical domains, where the results desired are clearer, we are happy to select decision makers solely on capacity grounds.[15] Think of medicine for instance. As the desired result sought by society is clearly to get the best possible medical care, we will aim at selection and regulation rules for health professionals that guarantee they are capable (i.e. have capacity) to exercise that particular task. Legitimacy does not arise as an issue. In the political domain, on the contrary, it arises with particular force. Even if we may agree that the desirable results of legislation and administrative action are good government, we are bound to fiercely disagree about what good government means in all the myriad areas where modern government gets involved. To cite just a couple of issues: What should the income tax rates be? Should abortion be permitted? In what circumstances? Should citizens have the right to bear arms?

It is because of this fact of pervasive disagreement in political issues (i.e. issues about how we ought to live together in society)[16] that the notion of legitimacy is so important in political institutions of democratic regimes. As John Rawls has concisely put it, a legitimate procedure is required 'when collective decisions must be made and agreement is normally lacking', that is, 'when the conflicts and disagreements in political life make unanimity impossible or rarely expected'.[17] Under such conditions of uncertainty about the desirable outcomes, it is important that decisions are taken through a fair process, that is, one that everyone can accept as legitimate. In a democracy, we normally relate fairness to the idea of political equality, that is, of equal consideration of everyone's interests and some measure of participation in the decision-making process.

A final general point about legitimacy and capacity is in order before we move on to discuss them in more concrete manner in the next section. These are not always perfectly complementary or substitutive qualities in political institutions. That is, it is not that legitimacy should prevail whenever the outcome is uncertain, and capacity should prevail whenever it is. They may also and will often conflict. We can have a situation for instance in which a legitimately selected institution is nonetheless not the best capable to reach the correct decision. When that happens, a trade-off needs to take place. As we shall see, this is precisely the difficult situation that arises in social rights adjudication.

[15] As Isaiah Berlin aptly wrote: 'Where ends are agreed, the only questions left are those of means, and these are not political but technical, that is to say, capable of being settled by experts or machines like arguments between engineers or doctors.': Isaiah Berlin, 'Two Concepts of Liberty', in *Four Essays on Liberty* (Oxford: Oxford University Press, 1969),166.

[16] John Rawls, *A Theory of Justice* (Cambridge, Mass.: Harvard University Press, 1971).

[17] J. Rawls, *Reply to Habermas, in Political Liberalism* (New York: Columbia University Press, 1991), 428.

II. Understanding the Complexity of Social Rights

If my arguments in the previous section are plausible, to determine the proper role of courts in the enforcement of social rights we need to assess whether and how, as institutions of a democratic regime, they are institutionally competent—that is, have legitimacy and capacity—to contribute to the enjoyment of these rights by the population, which is what democracies understood in a substantive sense are about. This analysis, I argued, is inherently comparative, that is, it has to be carried out in light of the institutional performance of other existing and potential institutional arrangements of the democratic regime in question.

In order to perform this analysis well, we need to flesh out in more detail, first, what precisely is involved in the enterprise of implementing social rights, that is, making them a reality for the population where they are constitutionally recognized. Legitimacy and capacity, as I argued, are strongly determined by the nature and complexity of the enterprise in question and significantly influenced by whether it is possible to identify clear and consensual desirable results of that enterprise and whether there are well established technical methods to achieve them. To recall the example from medicine, as the desirable result of the enterprise is clearly finding the best possible treatment to a certain condition, determining who ought to lead the task of selecting and implementing the adequate therapeutic strategy presents little difficulty: the health professionals with the appropriate qualifications. If the patient has cancer, an oncology team; if the patient has a heart condition, a cardiology team, and so on and so forth.[18]

Social rights cases are rarely, if ever, of that sort of simplicity, although many lawyers and judges seem to wrongly believe that they are, which often leads, as I will argue, to problematic models of judicial enforcement. It is therefore very important to dispel this popular misconception in order to properly understand and analyse whether there is a proper role for courts in social rights protection and, if so, what exactly it is or should be.

A. Two Types of Obligations: Absolute and Qualified

We should start by noting that social rights are not a 'homogenous species' that come in a single shape. They rather exist in significantly variable formulations in different jurisdictions and this has an important bearing on our question. Jeff King's work is again very useful here, in particular the important distinction he highlights between what he calls *absolute* and *qualified* obligations.[19] The difference has to do with potential justifications available for non-compliance. Whereas *absolute* obligations admit of no justification for non-compliance, qualified ones do. Another way of expressing this difference is this: absolute obligations are automatically violated whenever the conduct they specify is not observed by the duty-holder, whereas qualified obligations are

[18] I am of course simplifying it, as most health conditions demand multi-disciplinary teams, but the simplification does not in my view affect the strength of the argument.

[19] King, *Judging Social Rights* (n. 3), chapter 4.

not. If non-observance can be justified by one of the available potential justifications the duty-holder will not be found responsible for violating the corresponding right.[20]

Whether a social rights' obligation is formulated in an absolute or qualified manner in a constitution is extremely relevant for the issue of justiciability for reasons that are easy to understand. It will be in general much simpler to determine the violation of absolute obligations than of qualified ones, assuming that the specification of the content of the obligation is clear. Here is an example of an absolute social rights' obligation of that sort found in the Brazilian constitution.

Article 203: Social assistance will be provided for those who need it, independent of contribution to the social security system, and has as its aims:

> V—the guarantee of one minimum wage monthly to individuals with disabilities and to the elderly who prove not to be able to subsist on their own or with the support of their family, in the terms specified by law.[21]

The obligation seems to be absolute as there is no express mention in its formulation or anywhere else in the constitution of any possible justification for it not to be fulfilled. It is expressly not conditional on any behaviour of the right-holder, such as contribution to the social security system. The entitlement guaranteed to the right-holder is very precisely set as one minimum wage. The only aspects left slightly open for interpretation are the notions of 'disability', of incapacity to subsist, and the age threshold. But these are all notions that can be specified with relative ease and have actually been specified through complementary legislation, as mandated by the constitution itself at the end of the Article (the age threshold was set at 65, and the incapacity for subsistence at an income of less than one quarter of the minimum wage).[22]

Constitutional provisions of that nature present very little difficulty in the determination of what is required to be done. They invite the exercise of a mere logical intellectual operation. Whenever a disabled or elderly person above the age of 65 proves to be unable to subsist from her own resources the state ought to provide her with a monthly income of the value of one minimum wage. In terms of comparative institutional legitimacy and capacity there is also little to debate. As the legislature has already complemented the constitutional provision through the specification of the open notions of need and age, the executive must simply organize an

[20] Other ways of expressing the same distinction is through the use of the expressions prima facie and definitive obligations, or conditional and unconditional obligations. See David Bilchitz, *Poverty and Fundamental Rights: The Justification and Enforcement of Socio-Economic Rights* (Oxford: Oxford University Press, 2007) for another useful more detailed development of this point.

[21] My translation from the Portuguese. In the Colombian Constitution the equivalent provision seems less clear but also of an absolute nature: 'Article 46. The State, society, and the family shall all participate in protecting and assisting individuals in the third age bracket and shall promote their integration into active and community life. The State shall guarantee to them services of integral social security and food subsidies in cases of indigence.' (English version available at https://www.constituteproject.org/constitution/Colombia_2005.pdf, accessed 7 January 2021). There seems to be no qualification on the duty of the state to provide social security and food subsidies in cases of indigence. There is still a lot of scope for clarification of what 'integral social security', 'food subsidies', and 'indigence' mean though.

[22] Federal Law n. 8.742 (7 December 1993). For details, see the webpage of the Brazilian Government at https://www.inss.gov.br/beneficios/beneficio-assistencial-ao-idoso-e-a-pessoa-com-deficiencia-bpc accessed on 6 January 2021

administrative system to implement the programme. Should for any reason a citizen who is entitled to the benefit not receive it, courts are perfectly legitimate and capable of issuing an order to force the executive to fulfil its clear duty. The same absolute nature and a similar degree of content specificity is often found in rights to pensions.[23]

But not all constitutional provisions recognizing social rights are of that nature. Many are *qualified* obligations and often formulated in rather *vague* terms. Good examples of this kind can be found in many of the provisions of the Colombian, Brazilian, and South African constitutions, especially in the areas of health, education, and housing. The following provisions on housing in the constitution of these three countries illustrate the point well:

> *Colombia*: Article 51
>
> All Colombian citizens are entitled to live in dignity. The State shall determine the conditions necessary to give effect to this right and shall promote plans for public housing, appropriate systems of long-term financing, and community plans for the execution of these housing programs.
>
> *Brazil*: Article 6
>
> Education, health, food, work, housing, leisure, security, social security, protection of motherhood and childhood, and assistance to the destitute are social rights, as set forth by this Constitution.
>
> Article 21. The Union shall have the power to:
>
> XX—establish directives for urban development, including housing, basic sanitation and urban transportation;
>
> Article 23. The Union, the states, the Federal District and the municipalities, in common, have the power to:
>
> IX—promote housing construction programs and the improvement of housing and basic sanitation conditions;
>
> *South Africa*: Section 26. Housing

1. Everyone has the right to have access to adequate housing.
2. The state must take reasonable legislative and other measures, within its available resources, to achieve the progressive realisation of this right.

[23] See, for instance, Article 48 of the Colombian Constitution, which states, rather strongly, that 'All inhabitants are guaranteed the irrevocable right to Social Security', and goes on to specify it in no less than 21 further paragraphs, often in significant detail such as 'No pension may be lower than the existing monthly legal minimum wage. However, an Act may determine the cases in which periodical economic benefits which are lower than the minimum wage are paid to people with limited resources who do not fulfill the conditions required for the right to a pension.' (English version available at …). An interesting question I have no space to discuss here is whether the way in which pension rights receive stronger formulation in Latin American constitutions indicates bias towards the better-off. Pension expenditure in some countries, such as Brazil, represent a much larger share of GDP and are much less progressive than health, education, housing, and social assistance expenditure. Some work related rights are also amenable to precise and absolute formulation such as the right to a minimum wage, to maximum hours of work, to holidays, to work related injury compensation..

This type of formulation presents significantly greater complexity for the determination of the content of the obligation. There are several vague terms within it that require a great deal of specification before one can extract a minimally clear direction about what the state ought to provide to its citizens. 'Dignity', 'access', 'adequate', 'housing' are all highly indeterminate terms, open to a variety of possible interpretations.

To make things even more complex, the South African constitution expressly qualifies in subsection 2 the obligation through the equally vague notions of 'available resources' and 'progressive realization'. Although neither the Brazilian nor the Colombian constitutions do the same in express terms, this seems to follow logically from the way the provisions are worded and from the reality on the ground, as I will discuss further later on.

B. Complexity 1: Social Policy Intricacy and Variability

One might be tempted to wonder whether it would not have been more appropriate for the constitutional legislator to avoid such indeterminate provisions. Why not follow the model of absolute and clear obligations discussed above for all social rights? Would it not have been better for the South African Constitutional Assembly of 1994 to have passed a provision along the following lines:

> Housing will be provided for those who need it, *irrespective of contribution* to the social security system, and has as its aims:
>
> —the guarantee of accommodation of a minimum of one bedroom per person or couple, with a minimum of a working kitchen and bathroom with connection to the water supply, sanitation, waste collection, electricity and gas, to all individuals with disabilities and to the elderly who prove not to be able to subsist on their own or with the support of their family, in the terms specified by law.

A provision along those absolute lines for all social and economic rights would certainly simplify our task in this paper. But there are of course good reasons why such provisions are not to be found, not only in the South African constitution but in any other constitution that I am aware of in the areas of housing, health, and education.[24] Unlike social security, where we are talking about easily determinable benefits (i.e. monthly amounts of money) to be provided to easily identifiable groups of people (e.g. the elderly, the disabled, the retired, parents),[25] with social goods like health, education, and housing (and to a lesser extent also food and water) the precise content of the obligation is much more difficult to determine.

'Access to adequate housing', for instance, can have several different meanings. It can mean, in a very expansive interpretation, the free provision of equal accommodation to everyone, along the lines we think of public primary education in some countries.

[24] Some right to education provisions are formulated in absolute terms in US state constitutions. I am grateful to Jeff King for drawing my attention to this point.

[25] And some may be tempted to add with a hint of cynicism, where beneficiaries are mostly middle-class people with a lot of political leverage.

Or it can mean free (or subsidized) accommodation only to those who cannot afford housing in the private market with their own income (what we call 'social housing' in the United Kingdom). If the latter, which seems more in tune with the political morality and economy of most countries, there are several different possible means (i.e. different policies) the state can use to pursue that aim. It can simply give cash to the homeless for them to rent accommodation directly in the market. It can own accommodation and allocate it to the homeless. It can do both in combination. Whatever it chooses to do (and this very choice will involve intractable issues—more on which later), in any complex large market democracy it will demand a complex apparatus to administer the chosen policy (i.e. a Housing Department) that will need to carry out complex analyses and take difficult decisions to operate that policy in the real world. At a minimum, it will need to gather accurate information on homelessness, aim to match its available stock of accommodation to the demand, make sure the accommodation is safe and well maintained, etc. The areas of education and health are likely to present even greater complexity given that these social goods and the social needs they address are infinitely more complex than housing.

Here is the first good reason, thus, for why we don't find absolute and clearly specified constitutional obligations in the fields of housing, education, and health. These areas are simply *too complex* to be meticulously specified once and for all in the constitutional text. They require the formulation of highly complex policies, which demand collection and analysis of intricate information, design of multifaceted programmes and strategies, administration of human and material resources and, equally important, constant revision to adapt to changing circumstances and new technologies.

Once we reflect on this complexity for a while it starts to become clearer why constitutional provisions related to the rights to housing, education, and health are often phrased in vague and qualified terms. It is simply impossible to preemptively capture and freeze in absolute and precisely formulated obligations the exact content of the myriad of policies that states may employ when addressing the social needs of health, education, and housing.[26]

C. Complexity 2: Resource Scarcity

The complexity of social policy in the areas of housing, education, and health is further aggravated by a factor that makes the determination of the content of social rights obligations even more difficult, which I have deliberately left out of the discussion so far in order to highlight its importance: *resource scarcity*.

It would be great, from a social rights' supporter perspective, if the problems faced by the state in complying with its social rights obligations were only the technical ones highlighted above in the housing example. It is certainly challenging to manage a housing policy for the homeless in any large and modern market economy, but to do so in a context of *scarce resources* makes the task significantly more difficult. Yet this

[26] Frank Michelman evocatively refers to this issue as the '[r]aging indeterminacy' of social rights: Frank I. Michelman, 'The Constitution, Social Rights, and Liberal Political Justification' (2003) 1 International Journal of Constitutional Law 13.

is precisely the context in any country, including the richest ones, although of course the challenges tend to be greater the lower the level of economic development of the country.[27]

Let us keep focusing on the right to housing for a moment to see how significantly resource scarcity affects the determination of the obligations of the state. Recall, first, the formulation of the state obligation in Article 26 (1) of the South African constitution, which is the one that recognizes the issue in the most explicit manner: 'The state must take reasonable legislative and other measures, *within its available resources*, to achieve the progressive realisation of this right.'[28]

The first thing to note here is that the state's responsibility is not—neither in South Africa or in any other contemporary democratic regime—solely to provide access to adequate housing to the population. Any contemporary democratic regime has of course a myriad of other responsibilities not only in the area of housing and other social rights, but in other areas as well, such as the environment, national security, protection of property, civil and political rights, etc. These are often also recognized in the constitutional text, indicating their importance.[29]

The state requires considerable human and material resources to discharge these responsibilities.[30] As resources are limited (more or less severely according to context, but always limited), the point acquires tremendous importance. Due to resource scarcity, no state can, however rich, provide all public services and benefits to the population at their potentially highest available standard at the same time. The richer the country, the higher of course its capacity, *in principle*, to provide a higher standard of public services and benefits to its population. But to provide the highest available standard in all areas and at the same time is never possible, not even *in principle*.[31] Health alone would consume all the resources of even the richest country and that would still not suffice to provide the whole population with the highest available

[27] I say 'tend to be' here because another important variable is economic inequality. A poorer but more economically equal country may well have less scarcity challenges in the provision of social services than a richer but more unequal one. The classic comparison here is between the United States and other developed countries (less wealthy but more equal) such as the Scandinavian and other European ones.

[28] The issue of resource scarcity is also expressly recognized, of course, in Article 2 of the International Covenant on Economic, Social and Cultural Rights, from which the South African constitution has borrowed significantly:

> *Article 2* 1. Each State Party to the present Covenant undertakes to take steps, individually and through international assistance and co-operation, especially economic and technical, to the maximum of its available resources, with a view to achieving progressively the full realization of the rights recognized in the present Covenant by all appropriate means, including particularly the adoption of legislative measures.

[29] To use the South African constitution as an example, here are some of these responsibilities: (health care, food, water, and social security, Article 27; education, Article 29) but also civil and political ones (life, Article 11; freedom and security of the person, Article 12; freedom of religion, belief and opinion, Article 15; expression, Article 16; assembly, Article 17; association, Article 18; political rights, Article 19; access to courts, Article 34). The state also has constitutional responsibilities in the fields of labour relations (Article 23); the environment (Article 24); property and land rights (Article 25); protection of children (Article 28); language and culture (Article 30).

[30] Stephen Holmes and Cass R. Sunstein. *The Cost of Rights: Why Liberty Depends on Taxes* (New York: W.W. Norton, 1999).

[31] It is important to emphasize the expression 'in principle' because another important condition, which we will discuss further below, is the political ability and willingness of a state to invest in public services, something that varies significantly from country to country.

standard of health. To see this vividly all one needs to do is imagine the aggregate costs of providing all the expensive technology in treatment and equipment that continuously appears on the market to the whole of the population that may benefit even if slightly from it.[32] When one takes into consideration all the other areas mentioned above in which the modern state is expected to invest, the point seems even clearer.[33]

Another important reason for formulating social rights' obligations not only in a vague but also a qualified manner is therefore to allow for what we might call the *fact of resource scarcity*.[34] As the economic capacity of the state to provide housing (and education and health) depend on the same pot of limited resources available for all those other state responsibilities (security, environment, etc), the amount of resources available for any specific area is inextricably linked to the amount available to all others. The more a state spends on security, the less it has for health; the more it invests in the environment, the less is left for education; and so on and so forth. As it is simply impossible for any society to guarantee the satisfaction of everyone's numerous needs concomitantly, it is necessary for all societies to set priorities, that is, to decide which needs will receive attention and which will be postponed or even never satisfied.

III. What Role for the Courts?

Having tried to clarify these important differences in formulation and consequent interpretative latitude in constitutional social rights' obligations,we are now in a better position to address the main question of this chapter. This is because these differences have an important bearing on that question, which we could repeat now in summarized form for convenience. What we want to assess is *whether and how, as institutions of democratic regimes, courts are institutionally competent—that is, have legitimacy and capacity—to contribute to the enjoyment of social rights by the population*. As I will argue, the proper role of courts must necessarily vary according to the constitutional formulation of the social right in question. As a general rule, the more absolute and specifically formulated the right (or its corresponding obligation is),[35] the higher

[32] F. S. Vieira and I estimated the costs of doing this with only three new drugs for two diseases that affect a mere 1 per cent of the Brazilian population. It would cost around 4 per cent of Brazilian GDP: Octávio Luiz Motta Ferraz and Fabiola Sulpino Vieira, 'Direito à saúde, recursos escassos e equidade: os riscos da interpretação judicial dominante' (2009) 52(1) Dados 223–51. https://doi.org/10.1590/S0011-52582009000100007. These drugs featured constantly in right to health cases in Brazil. See also the debate on the costly hepatitis C drug: S. Iyengar et al., 'Prices, Costs, and Affordability of New Medicines for Hepatitis C in 30 Countries: An Economic Analysis' (2016) *Plos Medicine*, https://doi.org/10.1371/journal.pmed.1002032.

[33] This paragraph and the following draw on my chapter: 'What Course without Evils? Rare Diseases, Children's Right to Health and the Sustainable Development Goals', in Claire Fenton-Glynn (ed.), *Children's Rights and Sustainable Development. Interpreting the UNCRC for future generations* (Cambridge: Cambridge University Press, 2019).

[34] See King, *Judging Social Rights* (n. 3): 'My view is that the appropriate model for the text of a constitutional bill of social rights is to specify *explicit qualified obligations* in respect of *general or broadly stated interests or rights*. Doing this is an appropriate way to direct the courts that resource implications remain relevant to interpretation. However, if there is a class of interests where it can reasonably be assumed that the political support structure either is present or can be expected to be present, then it can be appropriate to state these as absolute obligations and for the courts to enforce them as such.'

[35] Some authors, such as David Bilchitz and Jeff King, argue that we should separate social rights into, on one hand, the interests they protect, and, on the other, the obligations they entail, that is, that these are not

the institutional competence (legitimacy and capacity) of courts will tend to be, and vice versa.

When their corresponding obligations are stated in absolute and precise form, such as is more common in rights to social security and assistance and some work related rights, they leave less room for disagreement and interpretation, that is, for the definition of their content. The task left is the more straightforward one of executing the clear commands of the constitutional norm. Conversely, when obligations are stated in vague and qualified fashion, such as in the rights to housing, health, and education in Colombia, Brazil, and South Africa for instance, the room left for interpretation—content definition—is not only rather ample, it also often involves the intractable questions of social policy design and administration in a context of inevitable scarcity of resources highlighted in the previous section.

As I will argue now in some detail, I believe courts' institutional competence tend to compare well to that of any other institution in the former scenario of absolute-precise obligations but leaves a lot to be desired in the latter one, of qualified-vague obligations.[36]

A concrete example will help us start the discussion. Let us begin with the easiest possible case. Imagine a Brazilian citizen who wants to claim the social assistance payment established in Article 205 of the constitution cited above. She goes to one of the offices of the National Institute of Social Security ('INSS'), and organ of the national executive government, with some form of identification that proves her age (identity card, birth certificate, passport) and declares that she is not able, on her own or with the support of her family, to subsist without the constitutional benefit. There is very little scope for the executive agency, the INSS, to determine if they ought to pay the

the same. My own view is that it is more appropriate to see rights and obligations as sides of the same coin and thus my references to social rights and obligations are made interchangeably in the text. I do not think much of practical consequence in the argument of this paper turns on this conceptual issue. For different views of the potential relevance of the different conceptualizations, see Bilchitz, (n. 20), and my review of his book: Octávio Luiz Motta Ferraz, 'Poverty and Human Rights' (2008) 28(3) Oxford Journal of Legal Studies 585–603.

[36] This is if course a simplification and thus my reference to these two scenarios as the main, not the only ones. In reality we are likely to encounter a multiplicity of scenarios involving a complex array of obligations, both absolute and qualified, with varying degrees of precision. Take, for instance, the case of the right to health in Brazil. Though the main obligation of the state is vague and qualified ('Article 196. Health is a right of all and a duty of the State and shall be guaranteed by means of social and economic policies aimed at reducing the risk of illness and other hazards and at the universal and equal access to actions and services for its promotion, protection and recovery.') other provisions of the constitution reduce somewhat this vagueness and, as a consequence, the latitude of interpretative discretion, such as the provision of Article 198 setting a duty on the state of minimum levels of investment in health. '2. The Union, the States, the Federal District, and the Municipalities shall apply each year, to health actions and public services, a minimum amount of funds derived from the application of percentages calculated upon the following: I—in the case of the Union, in the manner defined under the terms of the supplementary law provided for in paragraph 3; II—in the case of the States and of the Federal District, the proceeds from the collection of the taxes mentioned in article 155 and of the funds mentioned in articles 157 and 159, item I, subitem a, and item II, after deducting the portions remitted to the respective Municipalities; III—in the case of the Municipalities and of the Federal District, the proceeds from the collection of the taxes mentioned in article 156 and of the funds mentioned in articles 158 and 159, item I, subitem b, and paragraph 3. Paragraph 3. A supplementary law to be revised at least every five years shall establish: I—the percentages referred to in paragraph 2.'

constitutional benefit or not. All they need to do is establish, through the available evidence, if she qualifies both in terms of her age and her economic situation. No special institutional legitimacy or capacity is required for the task. For this very same reason, should the executive agency reject her claim, there would be little difficulty for the Judiciary to step in and adjudicate on the matter.[37]

Let us move now to a more complicated case. Imagine another Brazilian citizen who suffers from a certain medical condition, let us say HIV-AIDS. He goes to the local state health unit and demands treatment. Unlike in the social assistance example, the scope here is much wider for the state to determine if it has an obligation to provide the required treatment or not. This is because the constitutional obligation derived from the right to health is neither absolute nor specific. The constitution simply states, in Article 196, that 'health is a right of everyone and a duty of the state and shall be guaranteed by means of social and economic policies aimed at reducing the risk of illness and other hazards and at the universal and equal access to actions and services for its promotion, protection and recovery'. It does not specify that 'HIV treatment is a right of everyone', nor that 'the state has a duty to guarantee HIV treatment' to all those who need it. And this, as we saw in the previous section, is not an anomaly, but rather expected due to the fact of resource scarcity. The Brazilian state, like the Colombian, the South African and any contemporary democratic state, has a myriad of constitutional responsibilities to discharge with a limited pot of available resources. HIV treatment for our imagined citizen is only one of the potential competing things on which resources could be employed.

To avoid misunderstanding, note that I am not saying that HIV treatment is not part of the right to health or that the Brazilian state has no obligation to provide HIV treatment. All I am saying thus far is that such an obligation cannot be simply deduced from Article 196 of the Brazilian constitution, unlike in the social security example above. Whether our imagined citizen should be entitled to HIV treatment or not requires further consideration of the extremely complex issue of whether, within its available resources and in light of all its other constitutional responsibilities, the Brazilian state ought to provide such treatment not only to the claimant but to everyone else with the same condition. The same applies, of course, to any type of treatment or health intervention or, for that matter, any social right formulated in this qualified and indeterminate manner. I use HIV treatment only as an example.

We must bear in mind the extreme complexity of the task when assessing if the best institutional arrangement to address it ought to include any role for the courts and, if so, what role.

37 As a matter of fact, thousands of cases reach Brazilian courts from claimants who are denied this benefit. See D. W. L. Wang and N. P. Vasconcelos, 'Rights Adjudication and Policy Choices in Social Assistance: the Brazilian Supreme Federal Court and the Maximum Income Threshold for the Benefício de Prestação Continuada (BPC)' Novos estud. CEBRAP [online]. 2015, n.103, pp. 135–51. ISSN 1980-5403. https://doi.org/10.25091/s0101-3300201500030007.

A. The Consensus: Courts Should Play, at Most, a Complementary Role

We can start with what I believe is a reasonably widespread consensus. It is nicely expressed in the following passage by Jeff King:

> A just democracy depends on the guarantee of social human rights. In any such democracy that guarantee is delivered through a legislative programme of social rights, administered by a responsible executive, and buttressed by the existence of legal accountability. Constitutional judicial review of social rights can complement this process.[38]

It seems appropriate, from the perspective of both legitimacy and institutional capacity, that in a reasonably well-functioning democratic regime courts are attributed a *complementary* role, and not the leading one, in the determination of the specific content of the vague and qualified social rights' obligations included in the constitution. Under a reasonably well-functioning democratic regime, the elected bodies (the legislature and the executive) and the expert departments (the ministries of health, education, housing, etc) will be in a comparatively superior position (both from legitimacy and capacity perspectives) than courts to discharge this intractable task.

The reasons for this are as follows. The specification of the content of the vague clauses of the constitution require, as we saw, decisions on how much of a country's available resources are going to be allocated to each of these areas and how those resources will be invested, through different specific policies, to achieve the desired ends. These are not only extremely complex decisions, requiring a great deal of information and expertise in the areas involved (health, education, housing, etc) but also decisions characterized by a heightened level of uncertainty and disagreement among people.

To fully understand the complexity of the task, it is useful to distinguish these resource allocation decisions into different levels of generality: the *macro*, *meso*, and *micro* levels. *Macro level decisions* are those taken at the level of the whole government budget in the allocation of its total revenue[39] into the large areas of government such as social security, health, education, justice, environment, agriculture, security, sports, culture, etc. They form what is called the government's annual budget in public finances. *Meso decisions* are those taken at the level of each department in the allocation of the total budget among the several fixed expenses (capital and human resources), programmes and actions to be implemented. In health, for instance, that includes a complex array of decisions such as how much to spend in the recruiting and

[38] King, *Judging Social Rights* (n. 3), 187.

[39] By total revenue I mean the revenue the state collects through taxes, fees, profits from companies it controls, loans, international aid, etc. It is often called 'general government revenue' in the specialized literature and can be consulted in the so-called 'national accounts' in transparent countries. These are also decisions taken by the state, of course, and we could classify them as the super macro level. Another difficult question I cannot discuss here is whether to interpret 'maximum available resources' in an empirical and neutral manner, that is, as whatever a state collected as revenue in a given year, or a normative one, that is, as the level of total government revenue that a country ought to collect in order to fulfil its obligations. See R. E. Robertson, 'Measuring State Compliance with the Obligation to Devote the 'Maximum Available Resources' to Realizing Economic, Social, and Cultural Rights' (1994) 16(4) Human Rights Quarterly 693–714; Bilchitz (n. 20)

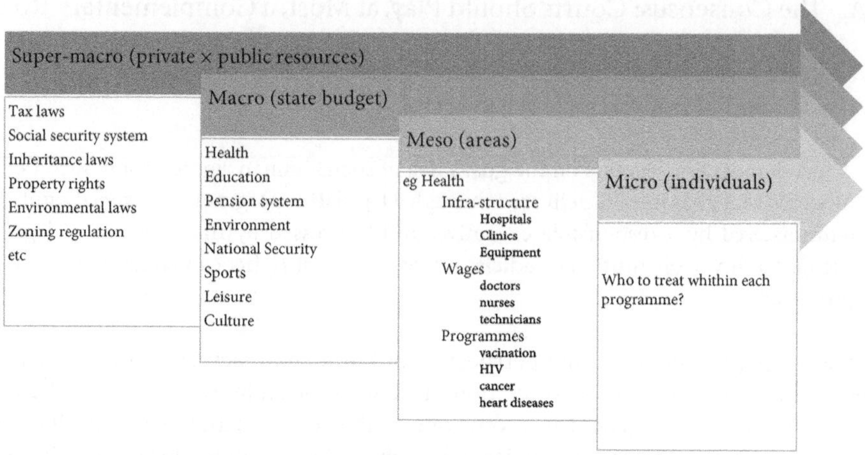

Fig. 10.1 Allocation Decisions at *micro*, *meso*, and *macro* levels

training of health personnel (doctors, nurses, technicians, etc); in the acquisition of health equipment; in the implementation of health prevention programmes; in each of the broad areas of medicine (cardio-vascular, oncology, infectious, neurology, etc); and many more. *Micro decisions* are taken within each programme and action and often involve the distribution of services among individuals. To use health again, think of the difficult decision faced by many health departments around the world about whom, among several individuals with similar needs, should have priority in the access of a certain scarce health resource, such as for instance renal dyalisis, hip replacement surgery, or an organ transplant.[40] Figure 10.1 shows the areas of decision making that fall under the *micro*, *miso*, and *macro* levels.

There is no precise single correct answer to any of these questions, that is, answers on which a reasonably extensive consensus can be formed. On the contrary, in any modern pluralistic society people will tend to disagree significantly about them depending on their political and moral views. Views will normally range from fierce opposition to any substantive government investment in any social service apart from law and order, that is, policing, national security, and courts to strong support of large-scale government investment in universal social policies such as health, education, housing, and social security, with many more others in between.[41]

It is these inevitable circumstances of complexity and uncertainty that explain the consensus that courts ought to normally exercise only a *complementary* role in the enforcement of social rights. The representative elected bodies, that is, legislatures and the executive, are better placed in terms of institutional legitimacy and capacity to

[40] The famous South African case of *Soobramoney* involved precisely such a decision: *Soobramoney v Minister of Health (Kwazulu-Natal)* (CCT32/97) [1997] ZACC 17; 1998 (1) SA 765 (CC); 1997 (12) BCLR 1696 (27 November 1997).

[41] John Rawls discusses this at length in his seminal book as the 'fact of reasonable pluralism': John Rawls, *Political Liberalism* (n. 17).

address these intractable and contested issues of resource allocation, design, and implementation of social policy. Their superior legitimacy stems from their representative nature, which furthers the fundamental democratic value of political equality. Their superior institutional capacity stems from the fact that modern governments, in reasonably well-functioning democracies, employ a wealth of public servants and advisers who are experts in a particular area of government responsibility and on public administration.

To go back to my HIV example, thus, we would expect a reasonably well-functioning democracy to have carried out reasonably comprehensive, open, and transparent debates in the legislature and executive branches before setting the macro health budget in light of the state's other myriad responsibilities, the meso health budget in light of the myriad health needs of the population, and the micro health budget in light of the more specific and ever changing circumstances of the local health area where our imagined claimant resides. We most of us would not want judges to be making any of these decisions in the place of legislators and administrators.

I expect most of what I have said so far to be reasonably uncontroversial but still worth clarifying and emphasizing.[42] Although few would argue that courts ought to completely take over from the legislature and executive the tasks of allocating the state's budget and designing social policy, the fact is that in some countries, notably in some Latin American ones, courts have actually operated in a way that has gone in precisely that direction, in some cases considerably so, as we will see in more detail below.[43] It was important therefore to re-emphasize why this would in principle be inappropriate from the institutional competence perspective adopted here.

We still need to address, however, a much more controversial issue: even if we agree that courts should not be the primary decision makers in determining the precise content of the specific social policies that vague social rights call for, what more precise

[42] The Colombian Constitutional Court emphasized this very point in its structural injunction in the displaced persons case, T-025: '[it]is not suggesting that the tutela may be used to order non-budgeted expenses or to modify budget planning as established by the legislature. It is not defining new priorities or modifying policies design by the legislature and developed by the executive.' inManuel José Cepeda Espinosa and David Landau, Colombian Constitutional Law. Leading Cases (New York: Oxford University Press, 2017), 181. Colombian constitutional law scholar Rodrigo Uprimny Yepes also expounds that view with approval: 'I think the difficulties of a judicial enforcement of social rights do not hinder the CCC from deciding these issues. That does not mean, however, that the consequences of those difficulties on the judicial function should be ignored. First of all, given the state's duty to fulfill social rights has a progressive character, which means that their satisfaction depends on the availability of resources, one must bear in mind that the interpretative task of the constitutional judge is certainly more difficult in this field. He or she must not only take into account the problem of limited resources, but also the progressiveness principle. Second, since social rights entail a public expense, the constitutional judge cannot ignore the crucial role that law has on the definition of social rights' content and mechanisms of protection, and must recognize the ample freedom of Congress to develop strategies for the satisfaction of those rights. In conclusion, the Constitution must be interpreted as an open but not neutral text; judges should orient their decisions towards the defense of its pluralist character and thus avoid adopting rigid formulas, in order to maintain the possibility of a vigorous democratic deliberation about social rights.' 'Should Courts enforce social rights? The Experience of the Colombian Constitutional Court', 18, https://www.dejusticia.org/wp-content/uploads/2017/04/fi_name_recurso_67.pdf, accessed 22 January 2019.

[43] For a rare dissonant view arguing that courts should engage in macro-allocation decisions, see Bilchitz (n. 20), 233.

complementary role are they legitimated to and capable of exercising, if any? This is the topic of the next section of this paper.[44]

B. The Court's Dilemma: To Interfere or not to Interfere

The intractability of the task of defining the specific content of some social rights leads to the following quandary about the proper role of courts in their enforcement. On one hand, as we saw in the previous section, we do not want courts to get embroiled in the allocation of budgets or the design and implementation of social policies. Given their comparatively superior institutional competence, we prefer legislatures and the executive to carry out these tasks. But on the other hand, as these are constitutional *rights*, we also think that the state should not be totally free to operate however it sees fit. Constitutional rights, at least in their traditional conception widely accepted in most democratic regimes, ought to imply some form of legal accountability on the representative branches of the state.[45]

Legal scholar Frank Michelman has captured the dilemma most eloquently as one between abdication and usurpation, even if in a deliberately exaggerated formulation:

> By constitutionalizing social rights, the argument often has run, you force the judiciary to a hapless choice between usurpation and abdication, from which there is no escape without embarrassment or discredit. One way, it is said, lies the judicial choice to issue positive enforcement orders in a pretentious, inexpert, probably vain but nevertheless resented attempt to reshuffle the most basic resource-management priorities of the public house-hold against prevailing political will. The other way lies the judicial choice to debase dangerously the entire currency of rights and the rule of law by openly ceding to executive and parliamentary bodies an unreviewable privilege of indefinite postponement of a declared constitutional right.[46]

As Michelman himself affirms, the problem is overstated, as these two extreme positions (abdication or usurpation) are not the only available ones. I agree (and will discuss other options available to courts later). We should not underestimate, however, the magnitude of the challenge of finding a role for courts that is at the same time within the boundaries of their institutional competences (i.e. legitimacy and expertise) *and* sufficiently meaningful to hold the political branches accountable.[47]

[44] This next section draws on my book, *Health as a Human Right. The Politics and Judicialisation of Health in Brazil* (Cambridge: Cambridge University Press, 2020).

[45] See Robert Alexy: 'This model is the expression of the idea ... that the fundamental rights of the German Constitution are positions that, from the point of view of constitutional law, are so important that the decision to guarantee them or not cannot be simply left to parliamentarian majority.' (my translation). Robert Alexy, *Teoria dos Direitos Fundamentais* (São Paulo: Malheiros Editores, 2008), 511–12.

[46] F. I. Michelman, 'The Constitution, Social Rights, and Liberal Political Justification,' (2003) 1(1) International Journal of Constitutional Law 13–34, 16. See also, on this topic, L. G. Sager, 'Fair Measure: The Legal Status of Underenforced Constitutional Norms' (1978) 91(6) Harvard Law Review 1212

[47] As he immediately adds after the passage quoted, 'The objection quite obviously is overstated': Michelman (n. 46). Yet his dismissal of the conundrum as not as important as often thought to be seems to me too quick. His reasons are that 'social rights can sometimes be 'negatively protected' by comfortably kosher forms of judicial intervention': Ibid., 17. As I discuss in the text, these 'kosher' forms are seen

Many academics and judges have been seriously grappling with this problem for some time now and have offered important contributions towards its better understanding and potential resolution. My aim in the remainder of this chapter is to add to this effort using the rich experience of two decades of health litigation in Brazil. As I mentioned in the introduction, the debate on the appropriate role of courts in adjudicating social and economic rights is far from academic. Health litigation in Brazil and elsewhere is perhaps one of the most prominent examples, though far from unique.[48] We have therefore a growing body of experience on which to draw to assess potential responses to the quandary highlighted above.[49]

I will start by discussing what, in my view, are unsatisfactory responses from which we can nonetheless still learn a great deal. I will then move on to more appropriate ones yet still somewhat problematic. I will then conclude with a suggestion about how we should deal with the seeming lack of a definitive solution to the conundrum.

1. Unsatisfactory responses: too much and too little judicial interference

Judges across the world have responded differently, often in radically opposite ways, to the challenge of social rights adjudication. In this subsection I discuss two rather extreme, radically opposite approaches adopted in different jurisdictions, focusing mostly on the adjudication of the right to health. They fall chiefly under the descriptions of abdication and usurpation in the passage quoted earlier from Frank Michelman. They are both overreactions to the conundrum. One simply evades it, the other simply ignores it.[50]

On the abdicative extreme, we have very deferential responses, in which it is argued that judges should *never* interfere with decisions made by the political branches regarding health policies and other social rights. Their limited institutional competences (legitimacy and expertise) are seen as an insuperable obstacle. Executive and parliamentary bodies are given an 'unreviewable privilege' to implement social rights

by many as not strong enough to protect social rights. His example of the South African case of *Minister of Public Works v Kyalami Ridge Association* is a good illustration. Minister of Public Works and Others v Kyalami Ridge Environmental Association and Others (Mukhwevho Intervening) (CCT 55/00) [2001] ZACC 19; 2001 (3) SA 1151 (CC); 2001 (7) BCLR 652 (CC) (29 May 2001).

[48] For discussions in the field of health in six different countries from Latin America, Africa, and Asia, see A. Yamin and S. Gloppen (eds.), *Litigating Health Rights: Can Courts Bring More Justice to Health?* (Cambridge, Mass.: Harvard University Press, 2011), 435; For education and health in four countries, see V. Gauri & D. M. Brinks (eds), *Courting Social Justice: Judicial Enforcement of Social and Economic Rights in the Developing World* (New York: Cambridge University Press, 2008). For a broader discussion of social rights in the courts of new democracies, see R. Gargarella, T. Roux, & P. Domingo, *Courts and Social Transformation in New Democracies: An Institutional Voice for the Poor?* (1st edn, London: Routledge, 2006).

[49] I have discussed some of this experience before in Octávio Luiz Motta Ferraz, 'Between Abdication and Usurpation: Social Rights in the Courts of Brazil, India and South Africa', in O. Vilhena, U. Baxi, & F. Viljoen (eds), *Transformative Constitutionalism: Comparing the Apex Courts of Brazil, India and South Africa*, (Pretoria: Pretoria University Law Press, 2013).

[50] See also Rosalind Dixon: 'In cooperative constitutional understandings, majoritarian political processes are often subject to serious blockages, such that very strong judicial deference to the legislature (super-weak judicial review)—or pure legislative supremacy—will tend to produce results that fall far short of a fully inclusive and responsive constitutional ideal.' Rosalind Dixon, 'Creating Dialogue about Socioeconomic Rights: Strong-Form versus Weak-Form Judicial Review Revisited' (2007) 5/3 International Journal of Constitutional Law 391–418, 402.

as they see fit. The only mechanisms of accountability under this view are political, that is, elections, demonstrations, the press, etc.

Not many commentators or courts seem to hold this more extreme view any longer, especially not when countries recognize social rights in the constitution and do not expressly qualify them as unjusticiable directives of state policy.[51] But it was once more popular, including among Brazilian judges, who for a decade or so held the view that the social rights of the Brazilian constitution were to be understood as so-called 'programmatic norms', that is, not to be directly enforced by courts but aimed exclusively at the legislature.[52] This 'super-deferential' stance is in my view unsatisfactory as it 'addresses' the conundrum by evading it. It eliminates from social rights, *a priori*, any measure of legal accountability.[53]

At the opposite, usurpative extreme, is the view that constitutionalization of social rights provides an automatic and sufficient mandate for judges to interfere strongly (i.e. provide strong remedies) with the decisions of the other branches whenever there is a violation of the right to health (as with any constitutional right). Little concern, if any, is expressed under this view about courts' lack of legitimacy or expertise. The conundrum is 'addressed', thus, by ignoring it, often under the problematic assumption that the constitution is clear about what needs to be done to implement the right to health and that courts are simply enforcing that right against recalcitrant legislative and executive bodies.

[51] Cass Sunstein is often wrongly cited as a proponent of this more extreme view against justiciability due to an article he wrote commenting on the debates about the then new constitutions of post-communist Eastern Europe. '*Many positive rights are unenforceable by courts.* Courts lack the tools of a bureaucracy. They cannot create government programs. They do not have a systematic overview of government policy. In these circumstances, it is unrealistic to expect courts to enforce many positive rights. Consider, for example, another provision in the Hungarian Constitution: "People living within the territory of the Republic of Hungary have the right to the highest possible level of physical health." How could courts enforce this right? The same problem appears for many (not all) of the positive rights, including the right to work, the right to a clean environment, and the right to training for the disabled.' See Cass Sunstein, 'Against Positive Rights. Why Social and Economic Rights *Don't* Belong in the New Constitutions of Post-Communist Europe' (1993) 2(1) East European Constitutional Review 35–8, 37. But he expressly clarified that his argument was aimed exclusively at Eastern European countries coming out of communist regimes and he later applauded the less deferential reasonableness approach of the South African Constitutional Court; see Cass R. Sunstein, 'Social and Economic Rights? Lessons from South Africa' (2001) 11(1) Constitutional Forum 123–32. Moreover, his main concern was perhaps not with judicial overreach, but rather that the judiciary would simply not be able to enforce these rights and, as a consequence, the constitution would be discredited as 'a mere piece of paper' and judges might even stop enforcing other rights as well. These concerns proved mistaken, at least in Hungary, Brazil, and elsewhere in Latin America. For Hungary, see A. Sajó, 'How the Rule of Law Killed Hungarian Welfare Reform' (1996) 5(1) East European Constitutional Review 31–41.

[52] Another example is perhaps the Irish judiciary. In *D v Minister for Education* [2001] 4 IR 259 (Irish Supreme Court), a case where the right to education, though included in the justiciable part of the Irish Constitution, was nonetheless deemed not to be subject to judicial enforcement beyond mere declaratory orders, as 'it is not the function of the court to make an assessment of the validity of the many competing claims on national resources'. As cited by M. Tushnet, *Taking the Constitution Away from the Courts* (Princeton: Princeton University Press, 1999), at 240. Note, however, that there is a difference between total non-justiciability and declaratory remedies.

[53] This 'super-deferential' approach might be appropriate if it becomes evident, empirically, that whenever courts try to interfere in certain areas, even when using very weak remedies, they end up making things much worse than they were before judicial interference, as I argued in section ... above.*Judging Social Rights* (n. 3).

This view is rather popular among some human rights activists and academics,[54] and has also spread in the past two decades across courts in some countries, most notably in Brazil and other countries in Latin America.[55] It is the prevalent view among judges in Brazil in the field of health.[56] The following passage from a leading decision of the Brazilian Supreme Federal Tribunal in a right to health case summarizes the approach:

> Between protecting the inviolability of the right to life and to health, an inalienable fundamental right guaranteed by the Constitution itself (art. 5º, caput and art. 196) or ensuring, against this fundamental prerogative, a financial and secondary interest of the state, I believe—once this dilemma is established—ethical and legal reasons impose on the judge one single and possible option: unswerving respect for life and human health ... The interpretation of a programmatic norm cannot transform it into a toothless constitutional promise ...[57]

This interpretation of the right to health as virtually an absolute right (I call it a 'right to everything') is in great part responsible for the significant growth of health litigation in Brazil and the extremely high success rates in such litigation, forcing the state to provide virtually any health benefit that litigants claim. It should be clear by now why this complete disregard for the health policies of the state is deeply problematic. First, it mistakes the nature of the constitutional obligations that flow from the right to health, taking for absolute and precise obligations what are in fact vague and qualified ones, that is, in need of specification involving complex decisions of resource allocation, policy design, and implementation. Moreover, when courts simply substitute the political branches' decisions for their own in this peremptory manner, they are not simply overstepping the boundaries of their legitimacy, they are also potentially distorting social policies and worsening inequalities, that is, producing a negative impact rather than contributing to the implementation of social rights.[58] As

[54] I believe this is the view of David Bilchitz, 'Giving Socio-Economic Rights Teeth: The Minimum Core and Its Importance' (2002) 119 South African Law Journal 484–501. See also Bilchitz (n. 20), 183–96, and my review of it: Ferraz (n. 35), 585–603.

[55] Courts in Colombia and Costa Rica seem to have also adopted this position at times; see A. Yamin & S. Gloppen (eds), *Litigating the Right to Health: Can Courts Bring More Justice to Health Systems?* (Cambridge: Harvard University Press, 2011). See also Octávio Luiz Motta Ferraz et al., 'Judging the Price of Life: Cost Considerations in Right-to-Health Litigation', in H. S. Aasen et al., *Juridification and Social Citizenship in the Welfare State* (Cheltenham: Edward Elgar, 2014), 121–45.

[56] It is important to note though that this assertive approach has not been applied consistently by Brazilian courts across all social rights. In housing cases and minimum wage cases, for instance, the courts have been notably less assertive than in health and education. See Octávio Luiz Motta Ferraz, 'Between Activism and Deference: Social rights adjudication in the Brazilian Supreme Federal Tribunal', in H. A. Garcia, K. Klare, & L. A. Williams (eds), *Social and Economic Rights in Theory and Practice: Critical Inquiries* (London: Routlegde, 2015).

[57] *Min. Celso de Mello* decision on the ARE 730.741/SP, cited by Min. Ricardo Lewandowski in ARE 724.293 (Rio Grande do Sul, 19.3.2013). My translation from the Portuguese. Full text, in Portuguese, available at the STF website: http://www.stf.jus.br/portal/processo/verProcessoPeca.asp?id=133345682&tipoApp=.pdf

[58] See also Octávio Luiz Motta Ferraz, 'The Right to Health in the Courts of Brazil: Worsening Health Inequities?' (2009) 11(2) Health and Human Rights, An International Journal; Octávio Luiz Motta Ferraz, 'Health Inequalities, Rights and Courts: The Social Impact of the "Judicialization of Health" in Brazil,' in Yamin & Gloppen (n. 57).

I demonstrate at length elsewhere, these negative effects are very real in the field of health litigation in Brazil.[59]

The tendency for social rights adjudication to gravitate towards one of these two problematic extremes is not negligible and explains, in great part, the heated debates that social rights' justiciability arouses between sceptics and supporters. [60] Those more concerned with the negative consequences of courts' overreach emphasize the perils of the usurpative tendencies of judges. Those more preoccupied with political neglect of rights stress the risks of abdication.

There is some exaggeration in both views, but we should not underestimate, I emphasize, the seriousness of either tendency. This is what makes the dilemma a real and important one. Let us look now into less extreme and more promising responses to the conundrum.

2. More promising (intermediate) responses

Responses that have actually tried to address the justiciability conundrum, that is, to strike a balance between the extreme super-deferential and super-assertive positions rather than evade or ignore the conundrum could perhaps be classified along a spectrum that goes from 'less interfering' to 'more interfering' forms of adjudication. I prefer to use these inelegant descriptors rather than say *weak* and *strong* forms of adjudication, or *procedural* and *substantive* forms of adjudication, because, as will become clear in the discussion below, I don't think that these qualifiers map perfectly onto what I call less and more interfering modes of adjudication.[61]

Less interfering forms of adjudication

Those more concerned with judicial overreach but still eager to find some meaningful role for courts tend to support forms of adjudication that fall under what I call the less interfering modes of adjudication (some might refer to them as *procedural*, or *weak* forms of adjudication). There are variants of these forms of adjudication, as we shall see, but they share the understanding that courts ought not to directly interfere with the *outcome* of decisions of the representative branches involving resource allocation and formulation of social policies simply because they think a better decision was available. But courts may still do quite a bit under these adjudication forms. At the less interfering end of the spectrum, they can review the *manner* in which legislative

[59] *Health as a Human Right* (n. 44). See also Ferraz, 'The Right to Health' (n. 58); Ferraz, 'Health Inequalities' (n. 58) .

[60] Landau seems to offer a plausible explanation for why some courts tend to adopt this problematic individualized assertive remedial approach in his excellent article, 'The Reality of Social Rights Enforcement': 'These tasks are difficult for courts to perform, and they may refuse to perform them because of a perceived lack of capacity or legitimacy. As I explain in more detail below, the fact that social rights have some aspects that are more easily assimilated to traditional rights enforcement, and other facets that would require courts to undertake radical tasks, is important. It means that in practice, courts are likely to enforce social rights either by issuing negative injunctions or by giving individualized remedies to individual plaintiffs. Such methods of enforcement will be least likely to get courts into serious trouble' Landau (n. 12), 196.

[61] For the most comprehensive treatment of the subject, see M. Tushnet, *Weak Courts, Strong Rights: Judicial Review and Social Welfare Rights in Comparative Constitutional Law* (Princeton: Princeton University Press, 2008). See also M. Tushnet, 'New Forms of Judicial Review and the Persistence of Rights—and Democracy-Based Worries' (2003) 38 Wake Forest Law Review 813; M. Tushnet, 'Social Welfare Rights and the Forms of Judicial Review' (2004) 82 Texas Law Review 1895.

and executive bodies have reached those decisions to guarantee that they have followed *due process*. Perhaps the most detailed formulation and defence of such a role for courts can be found in Jeff King's seminal *Judging Social Rights*. Here is how he describes the core of the approach:

> The special role of the court foreseen in contemporary constitutional adjudication and especially social rights adjudication is that it focuses on the process of decision-making in respect of the asserted human rights interest, rather than on the state's achievement of some particular state of affairs. It seeks to test the adequacy of the justification or reasoning underlying the public action or omission, the plausibility of its premises, and validity of its inferences, and at times the scope of participation afforded during that process, the availability of effective policy alternatives, and (where applicable) the compatibility of the resulting decision with the conceptual core of the asserted right. To prove that a right has been violated, it is not enough to show that someone has been incarcerated without a hearing, or evicted from a home despite substantial need, or was prevented from speaking at a political rally. We know only after assessing the state's justification, unless (in rare cases) the constitution states an absolute obligation that triggers an irresistible duty upon some conditions having been met.[62]

Due process is of course a broad term and, depending on how it is interpreted, will give courts more or less scope to interfere. The least interfering conception of due process involves the traditional grounds of rationality and non-discrimination present in the administrative law of many countries. A good example concerning the right to health is the famous UK case *Child B*. In this case, the claimant sought an order from the court to force the public health system (the National Health Service) to fund treatment which the health authority had decided not to fund within its budget, chiefly for priority-setting reasons. After stating that resources are not unlimited and must therefore be allocated in some way by the state, Lord Bingham, the leading judge in the case, concluded that courts should not interfere with such decisions unless there was a clear defect in the process, such as irrationality or discrimination:

> I have no doubt that in a perfect world any treatment which a patient, or a patient's family, sought would be provided if doctors were willing to give it, no matter how much it costs, particularly when a life was potentially at stake. It would however, in my view, be shutting one's eyes to the real world if the court were to proceed on the basis that we do live in such a world. It is common knowledge that health authorities of all kinds are constantly pressed to make ends meet. They cannot pay their nurses as much as they would like; they cannot provide all the treatments they would like; they cannot purchase all the extremely expensive medical equipment they would like; they cannot carry out all the research they would like; they cannot build all the hospitals and specialist units they would like. Difficult and agonising judgments have to

[62] King, *Judging Social Rights* (n. 3), 107.

> be made as to how a limited budget is best allocated to the maximum advantage of the maximum number of patients. That is not a judgment which the court can make.[63]

In a very similar South African case also involving the right to health the judges followed the same understanding when they refused to grant the claimant's request for renal dialysis treatment. The treatment had been refused on very similar grounds as in *Child B*, that is, for reasons of priority-setting in the context of scarce resources. Here is the Court's conclusion:

> The provincial administration which is responsible for health services in KwaZulu-Natal has to make decisions about the funding that should be made available for health care and how such funds should be spent. These choices involve difficult decisions to be taken at the political level in fixing the health budget, and at the functional level in deciding upon the priorities to be met. A court will be slow to interfere with rational decisions taken in good faith by the political organs and medical authorities whose responsibility it is to deal with such matters.[64]

More or less interfering modes of adjudication can be reached depending on how *rationality* is interpreted. As the development of British administrative law illustrates, rationality can be interpreted in a more restrictive manner, something close to madness ('so absurd or outrageous in their defiance of logic or morality that no reasonable person addressing the question would have come to the same conclusion', as in the classic *Wednesbury* case), but also in a more expansive manner, closer to proportionality.[65] The so-called reasonableness approach developed by the South African Constitutional Court after *Soobramoney*, in cases such as *Grootboom* and *TAC*, seems a good example of the latter.

The most thorough formulation of an expanded rationality approach to right to health adjudication, although not originally developed with courts in mind, is Norman Daniels' well received 'accountability for reasonableness' framework.[66] According to Daniels, a fair process of decision making in the allocation of scarce health resources displays four main characteristics: it is based on evidence (i.e. reasons), it is transparent, it is participatory, and it is subject to review.[67]

[63] *R v Cambridge Health Authority* [1995] 2 All ER 129. For a good discussion of the changes in British jurisprudence see, D. W. L. Wang, 'From Wednesbury Unreasonableness to Accountability for Reasonableness' (2017) 76(3) Cambridge Law Journal 642–70.

[64] *Soobramoney v Minister of Health (Kwazulu-Natal)* (CCT32/97) [1997] ZACC 17; 1998 (1) SA 765 (CC); 1997 (12) BCLR 1696 (27 November 1997).

[65] Wang (n. 58).

[66] Norman Daniels, *Just Health: Meeting Health Needs Fairly* (1st edn, New York: Cambridge University Press, 2008).

[67] Ibid., 300. It requires, at a minimum, 'the careful collection of evidence for interventions, the thorough review of arguments for establishing particular priorities, the involvement of all relevant stakeholders in the process, and transparency for all aspects of the process, including the rationales for the priorities adopted.' As he convincingly argues, given that reasonable disagreement about how to solve 'conflicts among claimants within and across rights' is inevitable and requires, thus, what he calls a procedural rather than a substantive solution, that is, a 'systematic rationale' to 'address the underlying moral disagreements among reasonable people.' Daniels' rather plausible point is that, since different reasonable principles of distributive justice will necessarily lead to different and reasonable conflicting answers, that is, people will reasonably disagree on what the correct one is, the solution can only be procedural. Ibid., at 328. I cannot engage here

Daniel Wang argues persuasively that British courts have adopted such an 'accountability for reasonableness' approach since *Child B*.[68] Keith Syrett provides a detailed defence of this approach as the most appropriate response to what I call the justiciability dilemma.[69]

Lawyers will immediately identify the proximity of many of these elements (transparency, rationality, participation, justification) with the procedural legal safeguards ('due process') present in the administrative law in most democratic legal systems.[70] Such a 'procedural' (or 'less interfering' as I prefer) accountability role is neither trivial nor easy to perform, unlike some critics often assume. Done well, it could potentially contribute to the improvement of the quality of legislative and administrative decision making on social policies in general and health policy in particular. As Wang shows in his excellent review of health litigation in the United Kingdom, 'by continuously requiring better reasons and procedural fairness .... [courts] have contributed to change the way in which the decisions about priority-setting in health care are made'.[71]

Yet this approach, focused on so-called procedural fairness rather than the correct outcome of the decision, does fall way short of what many people believe ought to be a strong protection of rights. For many, this model risks relegating social rights to a second-class position, rather different (i.e. weaker) from what is expected from genuine rights.[72] As much as the requirements of transparency, participation, and rationality go some way beyond the extreme super-deferential end of the spectrum of social rights' adjudication, they do not guarantee any particular substantive benefit to the right-holder, as rights are supposed to do according to many.

More interfering responses: the minimum core approach

It is a desire to afford stronger protection to social rights that motivates what I call 'more interfering' responses. Surely—one might claim—there is more courts could do to protect these rights than ensuring transparency, participation, and rationality in the decisions of the political branches?[73] Especially in less robust democracies, where the legislature and the executive are perceived to systematically fail to give due

in a deep analysis of Daniels' rich and complex proposal and the criticisms it has attracted. For a good discussion, see A. Rid, 'Justice and Procedure: How Does 'Accountability for Reasonableness' Result in Fair Limit-Setting Decisions?' (2009) 35(1) Journal of Medical Ethics 12.

68 Wang (n. 66). Daniels (n. 66), 328.

69 Keith Syrett, *Law, Legitimacy and the Rationing of Health Care: A Contextual and Comparative Perspective* (New York: Cambridge University Press, 2007), 266.. See also N. Daniels et al., 'Role of the Courts in the Progressive Realization of the Right to Health: Between the Threat and the Promise of Judicialization in Mexico' (2015) 1(3) *Health Systems & Reform* 229: 'the courts should, where they have the discretion, focus on promoting an equal right to health care for all, which requires a broad view of the entire health system and a focus on the fairness of allocation implications for different populations', 233.

70 Daniels himself highlights this: 'Accountability for reasonableness provides a systematic rationale for key elements of fair process in what is commonly thought to be part of a rights based approach.' (ibid., 328).

71 Wang (n. 66) 668–69. But Wang is not unambiguously positive about such changes. He aptly cautions against potential negative effects of the 'judge over your shoulder': 'fear of litigation may lead to what decision-makers would see as second-best policies.' Ibid., at 670.

72 See Bilchitz (n. 54), 119.

73 See also King entertaining a similar potential challenge to his approach: 'a judge's job is to define [a substantive core of the right] and require the state to implement it.' King, *Judging Social Rights* (n. 3), 97.

consideration to the social rights of the most vulnerable, courts ought to be able to force the state to respect, protect and fulfil the right to health (and other social rights) more strongly.

There is no doubt that, in an ideal scenario of legal accountability, it would be good if courts could legitimately and expertly provide stronger protection to the right to health and other social rights. It is beyond question that Brazil (and many other countries) could guarantee better health and other social goods recognized as social rights to its population than it currently does. If courts could make legislative and executive bodies improve their record this is surely what they ought to do as part of their duty to enforce rights recognized in the constitution.

When someone is found to have been arbitrarily imprisoned, we expect courts to order their immediate release; if someone is illegally prevented from registering to vote, we expect judges to issue a positive injunction ordering their prompt registration; if it is proven that a detainee has been tortured by the police, we expect the judiciary to condemn the official involved and make the state pay compensation to the victim.[74]

Less interfering modes of adjudication such as the reasonableness approach raise the justified apprehension of being perhaps too weak to protect fundamental rights. If these are *real* rights, the argument goes, some stronger measure of protection from courts is expected.[75]

The trouble is finding a role for courts that is at the same time stronger than the reasonableness approach and does not overstretch courts' institutional competences, especially when complex rights such as the right to health are at stake. The risk is not trivial and the consequences not negligible. Strong adjudication of the right to health in Brazil has meant, so far, two decades of reallocation of resources towards expensive health technologies of dubious priority in a chronically underfunded health system that struggles to universalize even the basics to the whole population. But perhaps the Brazilian model can be avoided. Perhaps there is a less deferential form of adjudication that conscientious judges may exercise without overstepping their legitimacy, overstretching their capacity, and generating the pernicious effects of the Brazilian model?

The most plausible such model seems to be the so-called *minimum core approach*. The basic idea of this approach is rather intuitive. It starts by recognizing that the social and economic rights to health, education, housing, etc of international human rights instruments and national constitutions provide little specific guidance on what states are under a duty to do. These legal instruments often say little about the amount of resources that states should invest in each social right let alone on how these resources should be allocated within each social right among the myriad of available options.[76] This is of course not a failure of legal draftsmanship, but rather a necessary

[74] As Mary Ann Glendon puts it: '... the language of rights is the language of no compromise. The winner takes all and the loser has to get out of town. The conversation is over.' Mary Ann Glendon, *Rights Talk: The Impoverishment of Political Discourse* (New York: The Free Press 1993), 9.

[75] As Rosalind Dixon notes: '... where a court order lacks any coercive dimension, it will have little direct impact on administrative inertia.' Dixon (n. 50), 412.

[76] Sometimes constitutions do ringfence resources for social rights, as was the case of the Brazilian Constitution'sAmendment 29 of 2000, which secured a minimum share of taxes for health..But this only reduces marginally the indeterminacy of social rights.

feature of these rights. It is precisely this indeterminacy, as we saw, that raises concerns about courts' institutional competence to hold legislative and executive bodies accountable to their social rights' constitutional duties and generates the justiciability dilemma. The minimum core provides an intuitive solution to the problem. If all courts had to work with were the vague statements that 'everyone has a right to the highest possible standard of health, education, housing etc affordable within available resources', it would be hard to see anything they could do beyond the reasonableness review discussed earlier. If, however, one can carve a more precise subset out of each of these generically formulated rights and claim that states are under a more urgent duty to respect, protect, and fulfil this 'core' than the 'rest' of the right, then courts (and international human rights adjudicative bodies) might exercise a stronger but still legitimate legal accountability role.

The *minimum core* is this subset of the right. If it 'exists', that is, if it can be plausibly justified and determined, it seems to strike a rather plausible golden mean between the extremes of deferential abdication and assertive usurpation. Given its purported *minimum* character, it seems to allow for just the right amount of tolerable interference by courts in the political process, leaving ample scope left for the political branches to go about their business of allocating scarce resources, and designing and implementing social policy. Yet, as they need to observe at least the minimum core, they are also subject to a reasonably strong measure of legal accountability, which is, as we saw, what many believe is lacking in the less interfering forms of adjudication such as the reasonableness approach. As Kate Young notes in her insightful article on the topic: 'With the minimum core concept as its guide, economic and social rights are supposed to enter the hard work of hard law.' [77]

This intuitive appeal of the minimum core idea emerges clearly from its most well-known official formulation, made by the UN Committee on Economic, Social and Cultural Rights in General Comment No. 3:

> 10.... the Committee is of the view that a minimum core obligation to ensure the satisfaction of, at the very least, minimum essential levels of each of the rights is incumbent upon every State party. Thus, for example, a State party in which any significant number of individuals is deprived of essential foodstuffs, of essential primary health care, of basic shelter and housing, or of the most basic forms of education is, prima facie, failing to discharge its obligations under the Covenant.[78]

Although the Committee did not expressly mention that the minimum core should be justiciable, nor all of its proponents advocate this position, my specific concern here is with the view that the minimum core may be an adequate response to what I am calling the justiciability dilemma.[79] For the idea of the minimum core to be operational

[77] K. Young, 'The Minimum Core of Economic and Social Rights: A Concept in Search of Content' (2008) 33 Yale International Law Journal 113–75, 114.

[78] CESCR General Comment No. 3: The Nature of States Parties' Obligations (Art. 2, Para. 1, of the Covenant) Adopted at the Fifth Session of the Committee on Economic, Social and Cultural Rights, on 14 December 1990 (Contained in Document E/1991/23)

[79] See J. Tasioulas, *Minimum Core Obligations. Human Rights in the Here and Now* (Washington, DC: World Bank, 2017), https://openknowledge.worldbank.org/handle/10986/29144; J. Tasioulas, *The Minimum Core of the Human Right to Health* (Washington, DC: World Bank, 2017), http://documents.

within this particular purpose of adjudication, the content of the minimum core of the particular right in question must be either clear (or subject to legitimate and competent determination by courts) and amenable to effective judicial enforcement.

Defining the minimum core

Many have argued that defining the content of the minimum core is ridden with the exact same kind of complexity and contestation involved in the definition of 'full' social rights, that is, that it involves the same intractable decisions on resource allocation and policy formulation that makes us question the legitimacy and capacity of courts. If this is so, we are back to the exact problem that the minimum core was supposed to solve in the first place.[80] Is it so?

I believe it is, but not for the reasons, nor to the extent often claimed by sceptics of the idea of the minimum core. Those who admit that defining the content of the minimum core presents important challenges often mention two main related difficulties: resource scarcity and the myriad of potential social policies available to advance essential levels of social rights and the likelihood of fierce disagreement about which ones should receive priority.[81] The argument goes along the following lines. Resources are so limited in many countries that not even a minimum core is affordable. The same intractable decisions about which social policies should be prioritized will therefore need to be made. How should a country prioritize its limited resources among several potential social policies, all equally essential? Should it universalize basic sanitation first or provide a minimum of clean water to everyone? Or should it put every child in primary school first? Or should it perhaps provide accommodation to the homeless as a top priority? The list of questions could go on and on. Focusing on essential levels might diminish the scale of the task compared to considering the 'full' right, but not by much when resources are severely limited.

worldbank.org/curated/en/194751515587192833/The-minimum-core-of-the-human-right-to-health both, accessed 23 June 2019.

[80] Young, among others, also raises doubt about the usefulness of the minimum core: 'Without this clarity, the concept cannot supply a predetermined content to economic and social rights, rank the value of particular claims, or set the level and criteria of state justification required for a permissible infringement. Indeed, I suggest that it is unlikely that the concept will ever offer the relative determinacy required for these three tests. Yet it can assist as an object of interpretive agreement—or disagreement—around claims for socioeconomic protection.' Young (n. 79), 116. See also *Government of the Republic of South Africa v Grootboom*, 2001 (1) SA 46 (CC), 32–3 rejecting a minimum core approach given the difficulties of establishing its content.

[81] Dixon, for instance, argues: 'It is quite possible, as an abstract theoretical matter, that there are answers to these questions that are both morally and constitutionally "right". However, as free and equal citizens, with extremely different life experiences and perspectives, it is also both likely and reasonable that South Africans should reach a variety of different answers to these questions. There is, thus, little chance of resolving these questions by reference either to collective South African understandings of the concrete content of sections 26 and 27, or agreed objective standards of constitutional or social morality in South Africa. Rather, rights-based controversies must be resolved in South Africa by more squarely democratic deliberative processes that attempt to give effect to constitutional understandings in the broader "constitutional culture".' Dixon (n. 50), 401. Jeremy Waldron has argued that, this, in turn, implies that there will be little basis for truly 'countermajoritarian' judicial enforcement of rights guarantees, since such enforcement would clearly fail to respect principles of equality among citizens in processes of democratic constitutional deliberation. Jeremy Waldron, *Law and Disagreement* (Oxford: Oxford University Press, 1999), 165–87.

These challenges are real, but it is important not to misapprehend their actual nature, as is easily and often done in the literature, somewhat muddling the search for a solution. Resource scarcity, in most countries today, should not be understood as *absolute insufficiency* of resources. Very few countries in the world today can genuinely claim that they are so poor that it would be simply impossible for them to guarantee universal access to 'essential foodstuffs, ... essential primary health care, ... basic shelter and housing, or ... the most basic forms of education' to the whole population. This was certainly the case for many countries in the 1960s, when the idea of recognizing social rights in international treaties was being fiercely debated.[82] It is certainly not the case now. To illustrate, even since the end of the Cold War, in the late 1980s, world GDP has almost quadrupled from US$ 22.6 trillion to US$ 75 trillion while the world population grew at a much lower pace (42 per cent).[83] That resulted in substantial gains in GDP per capita, which more than doubled from US$ 4.275 in 1990 to US$ 10.748 in 2017.[84] If we go further back to 1966, when the International Covenant on Economic, Social and Cultural Rights was adopted, world GDP was US$2.1 trillion, a *per capita* amount of a meagre US$628, that is, US$1.7 a day, or seventeen times lower than today.[85] As development economist Andy Sumner aptly puts it:

> ... economic growth since the Cold War has expanded national resources in developing countries, and consequentially the causes of much global poverty have become less about the lack of resources and more about questions of national inequality, and issues of social policy ... the poor now live in countries that are substantially better-off countries than a generation ago. The majority of global poverty is now in countries that many foreign aid donors see as sufficiently well off to reduce or end development aid ... In other words the context for poverty reduction efforts is now one of poverty amid growth and new wealth rather than, as it was towards the end of the Cold War, poverty reduction amid stagnation and insufficient domestic resources to address absolute poverty.[86]

Most countries today are therefore economically capable, in principle, to afford a pretty robust set of those essential social policies that human beings require to lead minimally decent lives (basic sanitation, essential immunization, clean water, sufficient food, basic primary education, basic shelter, etc). There will always be disagreement, of course, about the exact levels of provision a country could guarantee access to (e.g. how many litres per day of clean water, what quality of primary education, accommodation). But this is not the main challenge against the minimum core approach.[87]

[82] Back then, arguments that social rights were simply impossible to be implemented in most of the world (the infeasibility argument) were rather plausible. See M. Cranston, 'Are There Any Human Rights?' (1983) 112(4) Daedalus 1–17.

[83] https://data.worldbank.org/indicator/ny.gdp.mktp.cd?end=2015&start=1990, accessed 23 June 2019. World population in 1990 was 5.288 billion and is now 7.53 billion, that is, a 42 per cent growth. See https://data.worldbank.org/indicator/SP.POP.TOTL?view=chart, accessed 23 June 2019.

[84] Also in current dollars: https://data.worldbank.org/indicator/NY.GDP.PCAP.CD, accessed 23 June 2019.

[85] Ibid.

[86] See Andy Sumner, *Global Poverty* (Oxford: Oxford University Press, 2016), 1–3.

[87] For a definition of a minimum core in housing that no-one would disagree with, see the decision of Judge Davis on Section 28(1)(c) of the South African Constitution, holding that it did impose an obligation

We can all roughly agree on what an essential basket of health, housing, education, food, and water required for a minimally decent life is in the contexts of particular societies.[88] The problem is that the distribution of resources in most countries is such that a lot of people are still unable to enjoy these minimum social goods. Inequality, not insufficiency, is the main explanation for why so many people are still below the minimum core threshold.[89]

The right to health in Brazil provides a good illustration. Few people would reject that primary care for very young children and pregnant women should be part of the minimum core of the right to health everywhere, including in Brazil. If asked in a poll whether such care should be one of the top priorities of the health system, I doubt that many people would say no. Great strides have been made in Brazil towards reducing child, infant, and (less radically) maternal mortality in the past thirty years, in no small part because the Brazilian state (i.e. the successive governments in power since the 1988 constitution) has taken reasonably seriously the right to health included in Article 196 and has seen as part of its duties flowing from that right to implement policies, actions, and services aimed at the reduction of infant, child, and maternal mortality. It is also clear, however, that Brazil could do even better than it does in these areas given its level of economic development as an upper middle-income country. Costa Rica, a Latin American country with a similar GDP *per capita* to Brazil's, for instance, invests much more in public health and has much lower rates of infant, child, and maternal mortality than Brazil, showing that economic feasibility is not the cause of Brazil's underperformance.[90]

Once we understand that resource insufficiency is no longer an unsurmountable obstacle in most countries of the world for the enjoyment of a minimum core by everyone, we must approach the challenges to the definition of the minimum core in a different way. Our premises change dramatically and so must our conclusions. When it is simply unfeasible, due to absolute poverty, to guarantee a minimum core of each social right to everyone in a certain country, it is a highly complex and contested question

on the state where parents were unable to provide a child with basic shelter, defined as, at a bare minimum, 'tents, portable latrines and a regular supply of water (albeit transported)': Grootboom v Oostenberg Municipality and Others 2000 (3) BCLR 277 (C) paras 25–6 (S. Afr.). As cited in Dixon (n. 50), 400.

[88] Adam Smith's famous linen shirt passage in *The Wealth of Nations* provides a good illustration of the intuitive nature of the minimum core: 'By necessaries I understand, not only the commodities which are indispensably necessary for the support of life, but whatever the custom of the country renders it indecent for creditable people, even of the lowest order, to be without. A linen shirt, for example, is, strictly speaking, not a necessary of life … But in the present times, through the greater part of Europe, a creditable day-labourer would be ashamed to appear in public without a linen shirt … Custom, in the same manner, has rendered leather shoes a necessary of life in England. The poorest creditable person of either sex would be ashamed to appear in public without them … Under necessaries, therefore, I comprehend, not only those things which nature, but those things which the established rules of decency have rendered necessary to the lowest rank of people.' Adam Smith, *An Enquiry into the Nature and Causes of the Wealth of Nations* (London: W. Strahan and T. Cadell, 1776), Book 5, chapter 2.

[89] A longer version of this argument can be found in Octávio Luiz Motta Ferraz, 'Inequality, Not Insufficiency: Making Social Rights Real in a World of Plenty' (2014) 12(1) Equal Rights Review 77–94.

[90] Here arethe three rates in each country: infant mortality (Brazil: 7.8/1.000; Costa Rica: 5.7/1.000); child mortality (Brazil: 15.1/1.000; Costa Rica: 8.8/1.000); maternal mortality (Brazil: 44/100.000; Costa Rica: 25/100.000). World Health Statistics, World Health Organization, http://apps.who.int/gho/data/node.home, accessed 23 June 2019.

who should receive priority. Should we invest more on childcare, maternal care, or care for the elderly? Should we eliminate first hunger, homelessness, or illiteracy? We are in deep 'tragic choices' realm.[91]

Under the much more favourable circumstances of relative resource abundance currently prevailing in most countries in the world, we can say with confidence that the duties to respect, protect, and fulfil the minimum core of rights x, y, and z are being violated by many states that fail to guarantee such minimum levels to the whole of its population. To use the Brazilian example again, why not conclude that Brazil is in breach of its duty to guarantee the minimum core of the right to health to all infants, children, and pregnant mothers when, despite being an upper middle income country, its levels of infant, child, and maternal mortality are so high by international standards?

But this empirical clarification of the (in principle) affordability of the minimum core does not in itself establish its justiciability. It is one thing to show that (i) what the minimum core requires is reasonably clear and (ii) that there are enough resources in most countries in the world to guarantee it to the whole population and another to say that courts are therefore perfectly legitimized and capable to enforce the minimum core.

To take this additional step we would need to establish, further, that courts can effectively enforce the minimum core, that is, that when they interfere in governments social policies in the field of health and other social rights the outcome is indeed an improvement of the enjoyment of the minimum core in the relevant country. This is what the institutionalist approach I defended in Section I above recommends and the answer, as that approach also requires, is contextual, that is, can and do vary between different countries.[92]

The Brazilian example with the judicialization of the right to health is again useful in our inquiry. As I mentioned above, and have argued at much greater length elsewhere, health litigation in Brazil has not (with a few exceptions) focused on any of the main well-known minimum core deficiencies of the Brazilian health system. Whereas cases challenging the insufficiency and inequity of public health actions and primary care services in the poorest parts of Brazil are virtually non-existent, hundreds of thousands of cases come to the courts of the most developed cities every year (and mostly succeed) demanding more sophisticated and expensive secondary and tertiary care such as hospital treatments and medicines, which is hardly surprising given the significant inequalities in access to justice that prevail in Brazil. Moreover, a large proportion of that litigation is made up of claims for new and expensive medicines that the public system has decided not to fund within its limited resources for perfectly valid reasons, such as lack of evidence of safety, effectiveness, and-or cost-effectiveness. A small number of these drugs feature in thousands of claims and are responsible for a large part of the increasing costs of judicialization which, according to

[91] G. Calabresi & P. Bobbit, *Tragic Choices* (New York: W. W. Norton & Company, 1978), 18.

[92] My view seems to differ from Dixon's in that, unlike her, I believe that there is widespread consensus in most societies, and certainly in Brazil, about what the minimum core requires in terms of investment priority. The problem of justiciability, for me, is not therefore lack of societal consensus, but rather potential lack of judicial competence to enforce the minimum core. See Dixon (n. 52), 417.

estimates, could have reached about 3 per cent of the total health budget of the country and as much as 8 per cent of the budget of some states. The opportunity costs of such budgetary impact would be serious in any well-resourced health system. In a severely underfunded one like the Brazilian public health system (Sistema Único de Saúde - SUS) they are extremely concerning.

The type of health litigation currently prevalent in Brazil (the Brazilian Model) is clearly not capable, thus, *not even in principle*, to contribute to the improvement of the minimum core of the right to health of the Brazilian population. On the contrary, it exacerbates the system's equity problems by forcing the state at all administrative levels (federal, state, and municipal) to spend an increasingly larger part of its limited resources on health benefits (medicines and hospital treatment) and on individuals (those with access to justice) who are comparatively much better off than the large numbers who still lack some essential health actions and services. It does the very opposite to what the minimum core approach requires.

The failure of the judicialization of health in Brazil to advance the minimum core does not mean that it cannot succeed elsewhere. In my view, the famous *TAC* decision of the South African Constitutional Court may be a positive example of appropriate minimum core litigation.[93] If the institutional approach I adopt here is correct, in depth investigations of the sort I conducted in Brazil need to be carried out in each country so a conclusion as to the appropriateness of this more interfering model of adjudication can be reached.

IV. Conclusion

I have discussed in this chapter the thorny issue of social rights justiciability, that is, whether and how courts should enforce rights to health, education, housing, social security, social assistance, food, and water. I argued that the question should be addressed through what I described as an institutional approach, that is, through an investigation of the institutional competence—the legitimacy and capacity—of judges to contribute to the enjoyment of these rights by the population vis-à-vis the institutional competence of other institutional arrangements within a democratic regime—primarily but not exclusively legislative and executive mechanisms (section I).

I then argued that assessing the comparative institutional competence of these institutions requires, first, a better understanding of what exactly is involved in the implementation of these rights. That task involves, in turn, the determination of the actual content of these rights which varies, I claimed, according to the manner in which these rights are formulated in the specific constitution in question.

I then tried to show, through examples of actual constitutions from Colombia, Brazil, and South Africa, that social rights are formulated mostly in two different

[93] *Minister of Health v Treatment Action Campaign* (TAC) (2002) 5 SA 721 (CC). Whether the judicial order was effectively implemented is another question. My claim is simply that the decision itself seems to provide an example of how courts may competently determine the content of the minimum core in some cases.

ways: as *absolute* or *qualified* rights. The former, most often used for the rights to social security, social assistance, and some work related rights, *admit of no limitations*, not even resource scarcity based ones; the latter, most often used for the rights to health, education, and housing, not only *can be limited* by considerations such as resource scarcity, but are also usually couched in rather vague language, in great part due to their direct resource dependence, but also to the complexities involved in the design and implementation of the social policies required for their implementation.

These differences in formulation have a strong bearing on the issue of comparative institutional competence, or so I argued. Whereas *absolute rights* (which are also often clearly specified or capable of clear specification) present little difficulty of interpretation and implementation (and can in principle be enforced by courts without much problem), *qualified* (and often vaguely formulated) *ones* do. This is because the specification of the concrete obligations that they entail requires answering questions that are highly intricate and fiercely constestable; questions about the allocation of the scarce resources of a country's budget and the design and implementation of complex social policies. In these latter type of rights, which tend to be the case of the rights to health, education, and housing, the comparative institutional competence of courts to contribute to their implementation seems much more doubtful than in the former .

In a reasonably well-functioning democracy, it seems to me, representative (i.e. democratically accountable) institutions tend to be comparatively superior to courts—from an institutional competence perspective (in terms of legitimacy and capacity)—to resolve the intricate and contestable questions raised by those qualified rights. They ought thus to have the primary responsibility and prerogative to make those decisions without substantive interference from the courts. Courts could and should however exercise a measure of legal accountability through what I called *less interfering forms of judicial review*, that is, a review of the fairness of the decision-making process based on criteria such as transparency, non-discrimination, participation, and rationality.

It is true, as I conceded above, that less interfering forms of review cannot provide as assertive a protection to social rights as we have become used to expect when fundamental rights are at stake. But I believe that rejection of these forms as insufficiently strong and abdicative of courts' duties to protect fundamental rights may rely on the following intuitive assumptions that are not on reflection warranted. It might underestimate both the capacity of political and administrative bodies to interpret and implement in good faith their constitutional social rights' obligations and also the potential of less interfering forms of review to provide meaningful legal accountability.[94]

It might also overestimate the potential of more interfering forms of judicial review to protect fundamental rights and ignore their potential to generate negative effects. As I argued, the minimum core approach is in principle a legitimate model for courts to enforce social rights in a more interfering (strong) manner, yet in some

[94] This is of course an empirical and highly contextual issue, as different countries vary significantly in the quality and performance of their institutions, their levels of corruption, etc. All the same, many supporters of substantive judicial review of social rights seem to overlook this point. See Bilchitz (n. 56).

countries empirical evidence has shown that the results of such interference have been extremely negative, for example in health litigation in Brazil.

Less interfering forms of judicial review of the decision-making process of representative institutions, if performed well, can help improve both the quality and the fairness of that process, which is by no means an irrelevant contribution for courts to make in democratic regimes. In order to do it well and effectively, however, courts must be interested in understanding the intricacies of the work of legislatures and executives in the allocation of scarce resources, the design and implementation of social policies, and avoid pontificating about correct answers which are simply not provided by the constitutional text. As the American political scientist Robert Dahl insightfully stated, '[t]he democratic process is a gamble on the possibilities that a people, in acting autonomously, will learn how to act rightly'.[95] Judges ought to be an integral part in that enterprise, not the guardians that will purportedly save us from our mistakes.

[95] Dahl (n. 1), 192.

11
How can Rights be Individuated?

*David Bilchitz**

I. Introduction

It has become almost a mantra of international human rights law that all human rights are interdependent and interconnected. Yet, this statement is often accepted as a form of dogma without engaging with the questions it raises. If human rights are so intertwined, how do courts determine when one right should be applied instead of any other? How are rights individuated from one another? If they are distinct, in what way are fundamental rights interconnected?

In this paper, I consider these complex questions concerning the individuation and interconnection of fundamental rights specifically in relation to a particular right: the right to adequate housing. The catalyst for these explorations was the recent *Dladla* case[1] from South Africa where the Constitutional Court had to address whether the right to adequate housing applied. In doing so, the majority of the Court and the judgment of Justice Cameron outline starkly different approaches to the question of determining whether the case implicates the right to housing or other rights. In Section II, I will outline the key circumstances which led to the judgment and critically evaluate what might be termed the 'differentiation' approach adopted by the majority. Section III outlines the reasoning of Justice Cameron and critically evaluates what might be termed the 'integrated approach' outlined in his judgment. Section IV then turns to consider the approach adopted by the Constitutional Court of Colombia towards the individuation of the right to housing and its interconnection with other rights. The last section of this paper considers how these considerations play out practically in circumstances where there is a stark need to prioritize resources in circumstances of emergency and temporary accommodation.

This paper, ultimately, seeks to argue that in all judgments there is an understanding of a domain of distinctness which characterizes the right to housing. The differentiation approach, however, seeks to limit the right to housing to this domain whereas the integrated approach recognizes that this domain is partially constituted by the domain covered by other rights too. I argue that the integrated approach is preferable and that the right to housing should be conceived as a composite right that embraces other rights too. Far from losing its distinctiveness, this approach is able to capture fully why human beings have an interest in housing and the consequent obligations that should flow from such an understanding.

* I would like to thank Rafael Andres Gomez Campo for valuable research assistance on this chapter.

[1] *Dladla v City of Johannesburg*, 2018 (2) SA 327 (CC).

David Bilchitz, *How can Rights be Individuated?* In: *Constitutionalism.* Edited by: Alejandro Linares-Cantillo, Camilo Valdivieso-León, Santiago García-Jaramillo, Oxford University Press (2021).
DOI: 10.1093/oso/9780192896759.003.0012

II. *Dladla* and the Majority's Differentiation Approach

A. Background to the Case

This case emerged from a prior case—*Blue Moonlight Properties*[2]—in which the Court dealt with an application by a private company to evict a group of people from its property. The applicable right in *Blue Moonlight* was Section 26 of the South African constitution which reads as follows:

> 26. Housing
> (1) Everyone has the right to have access to adequate housing.
> (2) The state must take reasonable legislative and other measures, within its available resources, to achieve the progressive realization of this right.
> (3) No one may be evicted from their home, or have their home demolished, without an order of court made after considering all relevant circumstances. No legislation may permit arbitrary evictions.

The Court was concerned with an eviction and had, over time, outlined a number of principles in this regard. In *Blue Moonlight*, the Court made a number of far-reaching holdings: it held that private parties had a duty temporarily to allow unlawful occupiers to remain on their properties pending alternative accommodation being found for them; it also held that the local municipality had a duty—in the case of both private and public evictions—to provide alternative accommodation to individuals where they risked being rendered homeless. The Court ordered in this particular case that the city of Johannesburg had a duty to provide temporary accommodation for the occupiers after the date of eviction.[3]

The facts of the *Dladla* case relate to the manner in which the city gave effect to this order. It placed the people in a shelter run by a non-profit company–that went by the name MES–for destitute individuals. The management of the shelter told the people that it would allow them to remain there provided they complied with its rules, two of which were the subject of the court challenge. The *lockout rule* stated that residents could not remain at the shelter during the day (from 08h00 to 17h30) and they could not leave after 20h00. Those that returned after this time were not allowed in and had to sleep elsewhere (which often meant sleeping on the streets). This meant, for instance, that those on night shifts had nowhere to sleep during the day and were forced to wait outside the shelter and spend time in parks.

The second *family separation rule* involved separating out male and female residents. This meant that heterosexual couples could not remain in the same dormitory and male and female partners were separated. This situation meant that one of the parents—which often landed up being one of the women—had to take care of the children. In some cases, minor children were removed from their parents given the shelter was not a suitable place for them to live. A number of the applicants could not stand these oppressive rules and moved out of the shelter even if they lacked any alternative

[2] *City of Johannesburg Metropolitan Municipality v Blue Moonlight Properties*, 2012 (2) SA 104 (CC).
[3] *Dladla* (n. 1), para. 37.

accommodation. The *Dladla* case concerned an interdict to stop the city and MES from enforcing these rules.

B. The Reasoning of the Majority

The majority of the Court held that the prior order in *Blue Moonlight* was designed to ensure the provision of accommodation 'in accordance with the general legal standards applicable to the provision of temporary accommodation'.[4] It did not seek to limit other rights individuals have such as the rights to dignity, privacy, and freedom and security of the person.

Moreover, the majority recognized that the prior holding was made in terms of the right to housing. Section 26(2) requires that 'the state must take reasonable legislative and other measures, within its available resources', to achieve the progressive realization of the right to have access to adequate housing. Through providing temporary accommodation, the city was giving effect to its duty to 'take reasonable measures'. Yet, the Court held that the rules of the shelter did not themselves constitute measures in terms of Section 26(2). The Court held that the accommodation—absent the rules—would have been satisfactory. The accommodation essentially constituted the housing that was provided and was to be analysed in terms of Section 26(2). The rules imposed on the residents were separate to the accommodation and should be analysed independently to determine whether they implicate *other* rights in the constitution. This is the core holding which I will engage with below that articulates the 'the differentiation' approach.

The majority of the Court went on to hold that the applicants were entitled to the full guarantee of their fundamental rights in the temporary accommodation they were provided. The Court found the lockout rule violated a number of rights. In terms of the right to dignity, it held that the lockout rule forced the applicants onto the streets, providing no place for them to rest. It also seriously affected those who worked on nightshifts. It was paternalistic and did not respect people's ability to manage their own affairs. The rule also harmed the right to privacy of individuals who were forced onto the street during the day and denied their ability to have a place of their own or to retreat to. It also violated their right to freedom and security of the person as it endangered the applicants exposing them to crime on the street during the day and at night. One applicant was stabbed after being denied entry one night.

The majority of the Court also found that the family separation rule violated dignity that entitles people to engage in and maintain close personal relationships. It 'creates a vast chasm—between parents and children, between partners and siblings—where there should be only intimacy and love'.[5] This rule also fundamentally affected the movement of family members by denying children and partners of different sexes the right to visit one another when they wished—as such it violated their right to freedom and security of the person. These measures also violated their right to privacy.

[4] Ibid., para. 39.
[5] Ibid., para. 49.

Were these rules a justifiable limitation on these rights? The Court found that they were imposed on the basis of a contract between the city and MES. As such, they were not 'laws of general application' that are necessary to limit rights (in terms of section 36 of the Constitution). Consequently, there was no possibility to justify the rules and they were an unconstitutional infringement of the applicant's rights. The Court, consequently, directed the city and MES to stop enforcing these rules.

C. The Underpinnings of the Majority's Approach

The key dimension of the majority's judgment which I wish to focus on is its contention that the rules governing the residents' usage of the temporary accommodation were not 'measures' to be tested against the right to have access to adequate housing. As such, those rules were to be evaluated against their compatibility with three other rights in the bill of rights. The Court here, essentially, separates out what falls within the content of the right to housing and what falls within the domain of other rights. How does the Court individuate what falls within the domain of the rights in this instance?

Unfortunately, the reasoning of the Court is relatively sparse and so requires some reconstruction. The core consideration for the Court appears to have been the idea that, were the rules to have been removed, the accommodation would have been adequate. In other words, what is central to implicating the housing right, is the actual nature of the structure concerned. The right to housing essentially is about a particular space and structure which individuals require in order to conduct their lives. If that space and structure is adequate for meeting the human need for a place in which to live, the right to housing is not implicated. The rules that govern living within that structure are not intrinsic to the structure itself and so relate to other rights.

To distinguish what falls within the right to housing from the content of other rights, the Court has to adopt a particularly restrictive view of the right to housing. This view, I shall argue, is in tension with its own precedent, the approach of the UN Committee on Economic, Social and Cultural Rights, and is philosophically questionable.

First, in relation to its own precedent, the Constitutional Court in the *Grootboom* case stated expressly that the particular phrasing of the South African right—as being a right to have *access to* adequate housing:

> recognises that housing entails more than bricks and mortar. It requires available land, appropriate services such as the provision of water and the removal of sewage and the financing of all of these, including the building of the house itself. For a person to have access to adequate housing all of these conditions need to be met: there must be land, there must be services, there must be a dwelling.[6]

The Court's ruling in this earlier case interestingly extends the right to housing beyond simply land and a top-structure. The inclusion of services is not obvious: indeed,

[6] *Government of the Republic of South Africa v Grootboom*, 2001 (1) SA 46 (CC), para. 35

the South African constitution includes a right to have access to sufficient water which would be a clearer basis for a claim to water and sanitation services. The crucial point that the Court seems to be making is that one cannot consider housing in a way that is completely separate from the conditions under which people can inhabit such a home. Homes are meant to be lived in, and to provide circumstances conducive to human flourishing within them. As such, the interest in housing is not an interest in simply a bare structure but also the conditions surrounding the inhabiting of that structure. Consequently, if there are no opportunities to acquire water in or nearby the structure or to dispose of one's bodily waste, such a structure, according to the Court, does not meet the standards required by the right.

It could of course be argued that the Court in *Grootboom* focuses on very concrete infrastructure too: water pipes and sewerage lines. As such, it is possible to read it compatibly with the decision in *Dladla* which focuses on the actual concrete infrastructure surrounding a home. Yet, if we understand the reasoning behind the inclusion of services within the content of the right to have access to adequate housing, it seems necessary to recognize that *Grootboom* involves working with a more extensive conception of the right to housing. In other words, if the conditions for inhabiting a home matter—and this is the reason for the inclusion of services within the content of the right—then whether one can live in a home during all the hours of the day or whether one is able to live with one's partner or family surely also becomes a feature of understanding the nature of the human interest in a home.

This view is borne out by the General Comment of the United Nations Committee on Economic, Social and Cultural Rights on the right to adequate housing contained in Article 11 of the International Covenant on Economic, Social and Cultural Rights. The committee states there that the right to housing 'should not be interpreted in a narrow or restrictive sense which equates it with, for example, the shelter provided by merely having a roof over one's head or views shelter exclusively as a commodity. Rather, it should be seen as the right to live somewhere in security, peace and dignity'.[7] The committee provides a justification for this approach. First, it contends that the right to housing must be understood to be integrally linked to other human rights. The committee states that inherent dignity requires housing to be interpreted in relation to a range of considerations. These comments give expression to an integrated approach, yet raise squarely the question of what forms the unique content of housing in contradistinction to other rights. Secondly, the committee states that the focus should not simply be on housing but 'adequate housing'. It proceeds to identify seven aspects of the right which need to be taken into account in determining adequacy. They include: legal security of tenure; availability of services, materials, facilities, and infrastructure; affordability; habitability; accessibility; location; and cultural adequacy. The committee further emphasizes the interconnection between this right and other civil rights such as freedom of expression, freedom of association, and privacy.[8]

Philosophically, it also appears to be difficult to distinguish between the actual concrete infrastructure surrounding a home and the conditions under which individuals

[7] CESCR General Comment No. 4: The Right to Adequate Housing, http://www.refworld.org/pdfid/47a7079a1.pdf, accessed 8 November 2018, para. 7.

[8] Ibid., para. 9.

live in a home. Ultimately, the question comes down to why it is that individuals have an interest in a home. As human beings, there is a need for shelter from the elements, but the reasons human beings have an interest in a home are more expansive than this rationale. A home is a space of refuge from the rest of the world, a space in which one can eat and sleep, a space in which one can form a family and have friends over, a space of security and comfort, and a space conducive to growth. The Indian Supreme Court captured this when it wrote that 'for a human being it has to be a suitable accommodation which would allow him to grow in every aspect—physical, mental and intellectual'.[9] A home is a space and a structure but one that is there to enable us to realize our various interests involved in a flourishing life. The *Dladla* case is an important instantiation of this point: the city tried to reduce the interest of the individuals in housing simply to having a shelter in which to sleep at night. The case, however, illustrates the point that individuals need much more from a home than shelter alone, even a temporary one. Consequently, there are significant difficulties in interpreting the right to housing simply to cover structures without addressing the very point of those structures—which is to render the life of individuals who live therein as being of decent quality. There is, therefore, a problem with determining the content of particular rights and distinguishing them from others in ways that deprive them of their very purpose. This appears to be the key flaw of the majority judgment.

III. *Dladla* and Justice Cameron's Integrated Approach

A. Justice Cameron's Judgment

Justice Cameron reached the same conclusion about the unconstitutionality of the lockout and separation rules, yet his approach to deciding the matter was fundamentally different. He found that the rules in question were an integral part of the temporary accommodation provided. He reasoned:

> Temporary accommodation of necessity entails more than just providing a roof and four walls; it must include all that is reasonably appurtenant to making the temporary accommodation adequate. The provision of housing entails not only the delivery of a building or tent. The conditions the state attaches to the accommodation are part of its provision.[10]

Given this holding, Justice Cameron found that the rules governing the conduct of the inhabitants of necessity informed the adequacy of the housing it was providing. He stated: 'it cannot be that the provision of temporary accommodation implicates Section 26(2) while the rules designed to fulfil that provision do not'.[11] This is the more 'integrated approach' that I will engage with further below.

[9] *Shantistar Builders v Narayan Khimalal Totame* (1990) 1 SCC 520, para. 9.
[10] *Dladla* (n. 1), para 57.
[11] Ibid.

Justice Cameron also criticized the other minority judgment of Justice Jaftha. Justice Jaftha found that the shelter rules went beyond the court order the government was meant to implement and so were invalid. Justice Cameron stated that the order, however, simply required the provision of temporary accommodation without the specification of a number of issues such as the type of accommodation, the number of people per room, the ablution facilities, and much else. Ultimately, he held that the city was required to fill out the details and, in doing so, it had to act reasonably. That reasonableness standard was derived from Section 26: indeed, the fulfilment of a court order engaged the individuals' right to adequate housing.

Justice Cameron held that in the *Blue Moonlight* case, the Court situated the need to provide temporary accommodation within the housing right and the state's obligations in Section 26(2). In defending his view that this section applies (and its consequent reasonableness standard), he asked which right would apply if the temporary housing order was not governed by Section 26. He also asked what standards must govern the government implementation of an order for the provision of temporary housing: if there is no standard, then it needs to come back to the Court all the time. Instead, Justice Cameron argued the reasonableness standard in Section 26(2) governs the fulfilment of a court order. He proceeded to show how prior case law also supported placing temporary housing provision as falling within Section 26. He stated that: 'it would endanger a coherent understanding of government's duties in fulfilling its social and economic rights obligations—as well as vulnerable peoples' rights to delivery—if Section 26 were not implicated at all.'[12]

Consistent with his approach, Justice Cameron proceeded to determine whether the shelter rules were reasonable or not. Interestingly, he stated that his reasons were similar to those in the other judgments except that he rejects the focus of the majority on the requirement concerning a 'law of general application'. Seeing the rules were sourced in the court order in *Blue Moonlight*, he found that there was a law of general application. Nevertheless, the general rubric of his analysis lay in the reasonableness or otherwise of the measures taken by the city. The lockout rule he claimed was not strongly connected to any housing-related purpose and it seemed designed to force people to look for jobs. The rules were also demeaning and treated individuals as not properly worthy of consideration. Justice Cameron concluded that the shelter rules unlawfully limited the resident's right to dignity, freedom and security of the person, and privacy. Yet, he used this fact to reach a conclusion about the unreasonableness of the measures concerned. In other words, Justice Cameron saw the primary right that was applicable as being Section 26 of the constitution and its requirement that the measures taken to realize the right were reasonable. In determining reasonableness, however, in this context, the infringement of other rights could be considered and utilized to reach a conclusion about unreasonableness. Consequently, what Justice Cameron does involved placing the housing right as primary and then utilizing other *rights* to inform the content of the housing right.

[12] Ibid., para. 73.

B. The Underpinnings of Justice Cameron's approach

Whilst Justice Cameron's approach is more consistent with past case law, international instruments, and the political philosophy articulated above, it is not clear that he is correct that the reasonableness standard could only be derived from Section 26(2) in this instance. If other rights are used as a basis to determine compliance with the court order, then the question would still arise whether there was a reasonable justification for limiting those rights: given Justice Cameron's rejection of a narrow approach to determining the existence of a law of general application, a reasonableness standard could then be drawn from the enquiry concerning the limitation of rights (in terms of section 36 of the Constitution).

Moreover, the problems with the lack of content that is attributable to the reasonableness standard by the Constitutional Court in its socio-economic rights jurisprudence have been articulated by a number of academics. I have previously contended that the approach is itself empty and incapable of being rendered meaningful without some specification of the content of the rights in question.[13] Sandra Liebenberg too argues that the approach 'allows courts to elide an initial principled engagement with the purpose and underlying values of the relevant rights and the impact of the deprivations on the claimant groups'.[14] Justice Cameron's reasoning essentially bears out these points by having to reference the violations of other rights as the ground to find a failure of reasonableness relating to the right to housing. As the majority points out, these violations in and of themselves would be unacceptable. So the question is why is it desirable or necessary for Justice Cameron to utilize the reasonableness standard flowing from the right to housing in this instance? The point then is that there exists an alternative basis for sourcing a standard to evaluate the government's implementation of a court order: clearly the government must, as the majority holds, avoid violating other rights in the bill of rights. The question rather concerns whether the primary focus of analysis should be the right to housing or these other rights and what the distinctiveness is of these different approaches.

The *Dladla* case concerned the constitutionality of rules which affected the enjoyment of the accommodation in which people lived. Justice Cameron's approach is consistent with the philosophical point made above concerning the reasons why we value housing. Housing is not simply about a structure but about the kind of life we wish to live in that structure. Consequently, the conditions surrounding our ability to inhabit a house impact on our interests in housing. It is then artificial to divide housing from the other rights as was done by the majority.

This recognition translates into very different approaches to determining what forms part of the content of the right to housing. The majority's approach essentially tries to determine the particular content of the right to housing as a distinct right in a very narrow way that strictly seeks to define the boundaries between one right and another. In the process, as we saw, it does not fully capture many of our interests in the very right it is seeking to explicate. Justice Cameron's approach, however, differs in

[13] See David Bilchitz, *Poverty and Fundamental Rights* (Oxford: Oxford University Press, 2007), 161.

[14] Sandra Liebenberg, *Socio-economic Rights: Adjudication under a Transformative Constitution* (Cape Town: Juta, 2010), 175.

terms of the kind of right that housing in fact is. The housing right, for him, is a *composite* right which embraces multiple concerns and the interests protected by other rights as well. Thus, a house will not be adequate if it lacks privacy or fails to provide us with a sense of security: consequently, the very standard of 'adequacy' must embrace these other interests and the rights which protect them. On the view of housing as a composite right, questions of privacy and security of the person need to be utilized in defining the very nature of the entitlement itself.

This raises the question concerning the relationship between a *composite* right and more particular rights. In the case of *Soobramoney*,[15] the Court had to address the plight of an individual who was suffering from chronic kidney failure and had been refused treatment in a public hospital. The Court had to decide whether to utilize Section 11—the right to life—or the rights in Section 27 relating to access to health-care services and the right not to be denied emergency medical treatment. The Court stated that: '[i]n our Constitution, the right to medical treatment does not have to be inferred from the nature of the state established by the Constitution or from the right to life which it guarantees. It is dealt with directly in Section 27.'[16] The Court proceeded to conduct its analysis in terms of Section 27 and not Section 11. Consequently, the principle it articulates appears to be that 'when there is a specific entitlement that covers a matter, any claims or actions should be addressed towards that particular right rather than a more general right'.[17] I have in the past called this the *Principle of the Priority of the Particular over the General* (henceforth the PPG principle) and it can be seen to be part of and flow from a more general principle of subsidiarity utilized by the Court.[18] The question then arises as to how this principle applies in the context of the *Dladla* case.

If we take the housing right as a composite right, the PPG principle could arguably be utilized to support the approach of the majority. The argument would be that the violations of rights caused by the lockout and separation rules primarily relate to questions of privacy, freedom and security of the person, and dignity. Consequently, applying the above principle, those are the particular rights that should be utilized to conduct the analysis. However, in the context of the right to housing, it appears to me that there is something question-begging about this response.

The ultimate question concerning the application of this principle concerns when a claim or action is covered by a particular right and when it is not? The particular problem, in this instance, is the fact that the claim of the individuals relates to the quality of the conditions for inhabiting a dwelling. The conditions that have been imposed upon them implicate their privacy and security: yet, the people were concerned not about privacy and security in the abstract but inhabiting a space in which they could live and flourish. The violations that take place are not say physical attacks on

[15] *Soobramoney v Minister of Health (Kwazulu Natal)*, 1998 (1) SA 765 (CC).

[16] Ibid., para. 19. For a critique of this point, see M. Pieterse, 'A Different Shade of Red: Socio-Economic Dimensions of the Right to Life in South Africa' (1999) South African Journal on Human Rights 15, 372–85.

[17] David Bilchitz, 'Is the Right to Food Really Necessary?', in Vivienne Taylor and Sakiko Fukuda-Parr (eds), *Food Security in South Africa: Human Rights and Entitlement Perspectives* (Cape Town: UCT Press, 2015), 56.

[18] For a fuller discussion of the principle of subsidiarity in the South African context, see A. J. van der Walt, *Property and the Constitution* (Pretoria: Pretoria University Law Press, 2012), 35–7.

the person of the individuals: rather, the security violations emerge from an inability to have a place in which to rest securely. The primary concern here seems to be the nature of the housing available to the applicants. The other rights help to inform what constitutes acceptable housing.

Consequently, it does not seem to me that the PPG principle can apply in a simple way. Where there is a fundamental connection between the content of one right and that of other rights, what appears justifiable is to recognize the concerns relating to both as well as the interrelationship between them. In such instances, it will not be possible given the nature of a composite right such as housing simply to delineate its contours without considering its relationship with other rights that are engaged. Similarly, those other rights are closely connected to the right to housing and must be considered together with it in this context. Here, we see that there are indeed distinct concerns that may fall within the domain of particular rights, yet those concerns may well be interrelated in certain instances in ways that actually help determine the nature of the content of a more general right. Where this is so, decision making cannot proceed by simply considering the more particular right without losing the normative importance of the connection to the more general right. The particular and the general are interconnected and consequently the PPG does not apply.

Having considered the two approaches that have been outlined by the South African Constitutional Court, it is useful to consider another jurisdiction in which the relationship and interconnection between the right to housing and other rights has been explored. The Colombian Constitutional Court has a rich jurisprudence in relation to socio-economic rights and the right to housing in particular—the next section, consequently, analyses the background and context to its approach to the individuation of the right to housing.

IV. The Relationship between the Right to Housing and Other Rights in Colombia

A. Are Socio-Economic Rights Fundamental? The Background problem and Approaches to Dealing With it

In the 1991 constitution of Colombia it was not entirely clear to what extent socio-economic rights were justiciable given they were not placed in the chapter concerning 'fundamental rights'. The constitution maintained the traditional distinction between largely civil and political rights which were in the chapter entitled 'fundamental rights', and then had a separate chapter concerning socio-economic rights. The crucial implication of this division concerned whether or not socio-economic rights could be enforced through the special *tutela* process, which enables individuals to approach courts for a quick procedure to vindicate their rights. The Constitutional Court has increasingly brought socio-economic rights within the domain of fundamental rights that can be enforced through *tutela* actions. The initial approach of the Court was to establish what it termed a doctrine of 'connection'.

The reasoning in an early judgment on social security is illustrative of this approach. The right to social security, the Court held, 'acquires the character of fundamental when, according to the circumstances of the case, not acknowledging it raises the possibility of endangering other fundamental rights and principles such as life, human dignity, physical and moral integrity or the free development of personality of the elderly'.[19] The connection between a socio-economic right (like the right to social security) and more standard civil and political rights such as life and physical integrity becomes the basis for asserting that the former are as fundamental as the latter.[20]

The Court has adopted a similar approach to the right to housing. The right is itself enshrined in Article 51 of the Colombian constitution in the chapter on socio-economic rights. It reads:

> All Colombian citizens are entitled to live in dignity. The State will determine the conditions necessary to give effect to this right and will promote plans for public housing, appropriate systems of long-term financing, and community plans for the execution of these housing programs.

Whilst much of this language is rather programmatic and gradual in nature, the Colombian Court has held that, in a number of circumstances, the *tutela* action can be used to acquire speedy relief. For instance, in Decision T-495 of 2010, the Court was concerned about a serious situation where water was seeping into the house of the applicants due to a flaw in the sewerage system and causing damage to their home. The water was causing humidity, which was affecting the health of a 93year old as well as a minor child. The Constitutional Court defined decent housing there as involving a place, one's own or that of others, 'that allows the person to develop in minimum conditions of dignity and to satisfy their life projects'.[21] In defining decent housing, the Court proceeds to reference General Comment No. 4 as well as its own jurisprudence wherein it emphasizes that the content of the right to decent housing includes a structure that is able to offer 'adequate space for its occupants and to protect them from the cold, humidity, heat, rain, wind, or other threats to health, structural risks and disease vectors. It must also guarantee physical safety to the occupants'.[22] The Court concludes its analysis by emphasizing that the right to decent housing 'is intimately connected to the right to health, to life in decent conditions and to special considerations regarding the constitutional protection of children and older adults and can become a fundamental right depending on the specific case'.[23] After considering evidence of the health threats that the humidity was leading to, the Court found there was a violation of the right to housing given its deep interconnection with the right to health.

This case, interestingly, adopts the view that housing is itself a composite right that is connected to many other rights. These other rights are used to fill out its content

[19] Decision T-426 of 1992 (translated in M. J. Cepeda Espinosa & D. Landau, *Colombian Constitutional Law* (Oxford: Oxford University Press, 2017), 152).

[20] As Cepeda and Landau indicate (ibid. at 150), this notion became part of a 'connectivity' doctrine which led to the widespread enforcement of socio-economic rights. In recent years, the Court though has held that certain features of social rights are fundamental in their own right and do not depend on a connection with other rights.

[21] See Decision T-495 of 2010, para. 2.5.2.

[22] Quoting decision C-444/09 at para 2.5.7.3.

[23] Decision T-495 of 10, para. 2.5.3.

but also, particularly in the Colombian context, to determine its justiciability. Two interesting features emerge from the above case in this regard. First, clearly the right to health and housing overlap but do not merge: the domain of housing is considered to engage the space in which an individual may inhabit, yet in doing so the Court recognizes that it is necessary to consider the relevant ways in which the right to health can help condition the very content of what may be claimed. Secondly, the Court appears particularly concerned to adjudicate on violations of the right to housing where there is some degree of urgency or priority in the specific case. This feature of the jurisprudence relates to the problemcourts face in needing to justify their interventions in socio-economic rights cases. The case thus focuses on the right to health which clearly is of central importance to individuals and suggests that where there is likely to be a particularly damaging effect on this right flowing from housing conditions, the courts will intervene to protect the housing right. There is thus a focus on situations of priority—such as special groups that are at risk, harm to the basic minimum for survival, and serious harms to dignity.[24]

Interestingly, in another case, the Court finds that the right to 'decent housing implies, fundamentally, the satisfaction of the human need to have a space of privacy in which the person and the family can develop in conditions of dignity'.[25] Here we see the Court defines the right to housing in a complex way: on the one hand, its uniqueness relates to the fact that it concerns a 'space in which the person and the family can inhabit': that space, however, is specified with reference to other rights such as privacy and dignity. The right is also interpreted to include a space not just for an individual person but a family to inhabit—indeed, homes are the spaces in which humans, generally, are reared and experience their socialization into their families. The approach of the local government in the *Dladla* case (discussed above) to dividing families thus went against one of the core purposes of having a home at all. The Colombian Court thus clearly emphasizes that the nature of the space which individuals inhabit cannot be separated from other concerns.

More recently, the Court has held that many of the socio-economic rights have become fundamental in and of their own right given their connection to the fundamental values of the Colombian constitution and the state's obligations at an international level.[26] From the doctrine of connection, the Court's jurisprudence has thus evolved to regard the nature of the right to decent housing as fundamental in its own right —though, it still appears to justify this through its relationship with human dignity.[27] The Court places a particular emphasis throughout on the notion of dignity: indeed, in Decision T-227 of 2003 it states that one criterion for *fundamental rights* is that they are functionally aimed at achieving human dignity.[28] Any right can be determined to be fundamental where its violation leads to a threat to other fundamental values such as life, freedom, and equality.[29] In particular, the 'fundamental character'

[24] See also Decision T-125 of 2008.

[25] T-1017 of 2007, para 5.1.2.

[26] See, for instance, Decision T-585 of 2008. The Court has identified three ways in which socio-economic rights can acquire the character of fundamental: through transmutation; connection with a fundamental right, and by its ability to affect the vital minimum (Decision T-495 of 2010).

[27] Decision T-681 of 2016, Section IV., 3.

[28] Decision T-227 of 03, 11.

[29] Ibid.

of the right to housing can be achieved where it 'integrates contents inherent to respect for human dignity'.[30] In such circumstances, it can be given priority. Indeed, the Court also recognizes the fundamental character of the right to housing and the right to order immediate fulfillment of 'certain essential contents, like the protection of people in conditions of vulnerability'.[31] This has been of particular importance in relation to groups such as internally displaced persons and persons subject to extreme gender violence, which the Court has stated are subjects of special constitutional protection.[32]

Interestingly, the Constitutional Court of Colombia appears to determine the fundamental character of the right to housing by its reference to rights that are often of a higher level of abstraction—such as dignity. Indeed, arguably, dignity or worth is the foundation for all fundamental rights: tying the right to decent housing to dignity thus can be seen to provide a strong justification for its attaining the character of being of a fundamental nature.

In a sense, the Colombian Court was faced with a different problem to the South African Court. The latter was tasked with determining the content of an expressly recognized right of access to adequate housing and its interrelationship with other rights. The Colombian Court was faced firstly with justifying how the right to decent housing can be treated as a fundamental right—it thus goes up in layers of abstraction to a right to dignity. That justification then conditions the content it gives to the right: it does so through recognizing its composite nature and connection with other rights. Yet, its emphasis is very much on situations where there is a need to provide priority to specific individuals (or groups of individuals)—such as where there are especially vulnerable groups or where their needs are particularly serious. In the next section, I consider the implications of the debate surrounding the nature of the right to housing for situations of emergency or temporary accommodation.

V. The Nature of Housing Rights and Determining Standards of Provision for Emergency or Temporary Accommodation

A. Do Standards Diminish for Temporary Accommodation?

One of the complex aspects of the *Dladla* case relates to the fact that the claim under consideration was one concerning temporary accommodation: what were the standards applicable to such accommodation? In this case, the city claimed that, given that the court order related to temporary accommodation, it was contemplated that the rights of the applicants would be diminished. Indeed, it claimed that the temporary nature of the accommodation meant that what could be expected by the applicants was necessarily reduced. Its approach in providing limited accommodation based upon the two impugned rules, therefore, was reasonable in the circumstances.

As we saw, the majority of the Court refused to decide the case on the basis of reasonableness. Justice Mhlantla held that the order in *Blue Moonlight* meant that:

30 See Decision T-531 of 17, para. 5.2

31 Decision T-544 of 16, para. 4.4.

32 Decision T-531 of 17, para. 8.7.

> the city had to provide temporary accommodation in accordance with the general legal standards applicable to the provision of temporary accommodation. The order was made notwithstanding any other rights the occupiers had. The order certainly did not limit the rights in question in the present case, namely, the rights to dignity, freedom of security of the person and privacy.[33]

The majority, therefore, held that the nature of temporary accommodation essentially did not allow for the violation of other rights that were implicated.

Justice Cameron, on the other hand, based his ruling on the notion of reasonableness as we saw.One of the attractive facets of reasonableness for the Constitutional Court has been the fact that it allows for the tailoring of rulings to particular circumstances. Justice Cameron recognized in his judgment that it may, in fact, be reasonable to violate other rights in certain circumstances. He considers the fact that a measure could justifiably limit a right, for instance, in the provision of emergency housing, yet that limitation may not be justifiable when one considers the provision of non-emergency adequate housing. In situations of disaster such as fire and flood, ad hoc arrangements (which could include say a lockout or family separation rule) might be acceptable.[34] However, in the particular circumstances of this case, Justice Cameron found that the rules were unreasonable: they lacked any clear connection with a housing-related purpose (focusing on forcing people to seek work) and, ultimately, sent out a message which violated the individuals' dignity, suggesting they were less worthy of consideration.[35]

In the debate between the majority and the minority, once again, it seems to me that Justice Cameron has the better argument. There is a difference between temporary and permanent accommodation, and the circumstances in which temporary accommodation is needed may vary. As such, it is entirely conceivable say that in response to a flood or fire, a community hall may temporarily be needed to house individuals. That may not respect privacy, and there may be attempts to separate sexes to ensure safety for women (for instance). For a limited period, it would seem that the infringement of other rights in such circumstances is justifiable. The majority's holding is, therefore, too broad in suggesting that in providing temporary accommodation, the government can never infringe other rights.

There will, however, always be the need to evaluate the rationale behind any infringements in the particular circumstances.Of course, the same debate still arises as to whether that enquiry should be conducted in relation to the right to housing or another right which is implicated more closely. That debate takes a rather interesting turn in the context of temporary accommodation. For we are concerned in this case not with the ultimate standard of what is desirable; rather, we need to consider what must be provided temporarily.

It is necessary to distinguish different situations in which temporary accommodation may be needed. In some circumstances, such as in response to a fire or flood, there may be a need for emergency accommodation for a few days or weeks to help people

[33] *Dladla* (n. 1), para. 39.
[34] Ibid., para. 78.
[35] Ibid., para. 80.

avoid homelessness whilst enabling them to find new accommodation. On the other hand, there may be circumstances, such as in *Dladla* that resulted from poverty and a lack of a space to go to, where a temporary set-up could last for a year or even more. The latter circumstances involve more permanency than the former and it seems that, consequently, conditions will need to be better for medium-term temporary accommodation. The reason for this lies in the fact that a longer period affects the range of people's interests more significantly—for instance, one may be able to tolerate a very brief separation from a family member but a continuing dispensation such as that imposed in the *Dladla* case by the family separation rule can severely impact on one's familial relationships. There is clearly a spectrum here but there are circumstances where there is more urgency in some cases than in others. An interesting question that can be posed in relation to the whole issue of temporary accommodation relates to whether there is a hard minimum standard below which no accommodation may fall and, if so, how such a standard is to be determined.

B. Determining Minimum Standards for Temporary Accommodation

This question raises squarely the much-debated discussion around the possibility of defining a minimum core in relation to socio-economic rights. The United Nations Committee on Economic, Social and Cultural Rights recognizes an obligation on state parties to the covenant to 'ensure the satisfaction of, at the very least, minimum essential levels of each of the rights'.[36] The question that this approach raises is how to determine the essential levels of the rights in question. This is a large question which has attracted much academic attention.[37] For purposes of this chapter, I am concerned with the challenge posed by *Dladla* for a particular approach to the minimum core that I have advocated.

In *Poverty and Fundamental Rights*, I argue that the minimum core should be defined as the 'necessary preconditions for being free from threats to survival'.[38] Survival is clearly a necessary condition for being able to live any life at all, and achieve the sources of value in our lives. As such, it is essential for the enjoyment of any of the rights we are entitled to. It is also clear that there are goods and resources that we need in order to survive, and a survival threshold has the relative merit of being a hard boundary that has some degree of precision in terms of what is required.[39] There are some issues involved in defining the threshold, yet unlike any other it seems to provide us with a hard minimum below which no-one should fall. The *Dladla* case can, however, be seen to present a challenge to this notion of defining the minimum core. The

[36] General Comment No. 3, http://www.refworld.org/docid/4538838e10.html, accessed 16 December 2020, para. 10.

[37] See Bilchitz (n. 13), chapter 6; K. Young 'The Minimum Core of Economic Social and Cultural Rights: a Concept in Search of Content' (2008) 33 Yale International Law Journal 113–175.

[38] Bilchitz (n. 13), 39.

[39] It is not absolutely precise, but it is possible, for instance, to determine what the absolute limit is, for example, on survival without water: see, as just one instance, D. Spector, 'Here's How Many Days a Person Can Survive Without Water', https://www.businessinsider.co.za/how-many-days-can-you-survive-without-water-2014-5?r=US&IR=T, accessed 11 November 2018.

core it could be argued focuses on a very narrow conception of housing that concentrates simply on meeting material needs for shelter that individuals require to survive. Yet, the facts in *Dladla* show the insufficiency of focusing on such needs alone—people do not only require shelter that allows them to survive but also the conditions that enable them to be treated with a minimum level of decency, and respect for their privacy, security, and dignity. A simple approach to defining the minimum core in terms of survival is too minimal, and therefore defective.

In responding to this charge, it is necessary to understand the function of the minimum core concept. The idea is not meant to determine the full range of entitlements of individuals in relation to housing. It is rather meant to identify the very basic minimum that individuals need in relation to specific rights. That is helpful, for instance, in enabling a definition of what must be guaranteed in situations where it is not possible to realize a higher level of provision. Thus, in situations where refugees are suddenly displaced, in circumstances of flood or fire, or simply where a higher-level provision is beyond government capacity, it is necessary to determine a minimum below which people should not be allowed to fall. That minimum does not in any way mean that it is all that individuals can or should expect. This response raises the very debate that has been canvassed above between the majority and the minority in relation to the content of the right to housing.

The 'differentiation approach' of the majority sharply distinguishes between what falls under the housing right and what falls under other rights. In doing this, the majority in a sense seems partly to diffuse the challenge to the minimum core outlined above. The minimum core of the right to housing would be determined in relation to the actual concrete shelter that is provided from the elements. That could be defined in relation to what is required for survival. Any other considerations relating to privacy, security, or dignity are to be determined in relation to those specific rights. Arguably, some kinds of minimum standards could also be established in relation to those. By considering the minimum standards required in relation to each right, it would be possible to determine what individuals would be entitled to claim in any given circumstance. The benefit of this approach is that it does allow one some analytical clarity as to what housing entails in situations of emergency separately from these other rights. Yet, as was argued above, the problem is that it fails to recognize that the interest in housing is intimately connected with other human interests and so cannot purely be reduced to questions of bricks and mortar. Indeed, the approach appears to be incoherent on its own terms: if the standard of housing that is the absolute minimum is defined in terms of the necessary conditions to be free from threats to survival, then housing levels are determined in relation to what is necessary to protect life (or basic health). The level and nature of housing cannot be defined separately from the most foundational interests that individuals have. Housing and the basic conditions for human life can be seen to be fundamentally intertwined.

Justice Cameron, on the other hand, would probably reject this talk of minimums by focusing on the vague idea of reasonableness, and his approach would also lose the benefit of a very strict priority that needs to be given to this most urgent threshold. It, nevertheless, is interesting to consider what conceptually the 'integrated approach' would mean for developing a minimum core in relation to housing. For Justice Cameron, as we saw, housing is a composite right. This would render it more difficult to determine the minimum core separately from other interests. Instead, minimum standards would have to be set for housing which take account of the differing human interests involved in this area. Of course, survival and life could be of importance but the minimum required in relation to housing could probably not be set in terms of survival alone: it would have to take account of all the interests individuals have in this area. This approach would have the benefit of recognizing what appears true: namely, there are a range of reasons we require housing which are not simply reducible to shelter. The difficulty for this approach, analytically, lies in the fact that through taking cognizance of a range of human interests, it lacks the simplicity of definition of the narrower approach, creating a vaguer, less workable standard. It should be recognized, however, even on the integrated approach, the survival-based standard remains of importance: it is simply supplemented by the minimum standards from other rights that make up the composite right to housing. The problem for the integrated approach is that it could avoid the hard challenge—even recognized by Justice Cameron himself—which relates to the fact that there may be a need to prioritize certain dimensions of our interest in housing over others in real situations of emergency: privacy, for instance, may need to give way to ensuring basic shelter that protects life in such circumstances where no alternative exists.

This discussion highlights the conceptual impossibility, in a sense, of adopting a strict differentiation approach that fails to connect housing with other interests such as life. Where we do connect them though, it is necessary to recognize that the interests in question can have differing degrees of priority. In defining minimum standards, as a result, we must of necessity relate beyond the sphere of space and structure to the point of having housing: yet, in doing so, it is possible to recognize a spectrum whereby some of these interests such as life and health may, at times, take priority over others such as privacy and cultural adequacy. Of course, the higher level of decent or adequate housing should take account of all these interests: situations of emergency and temporariness require developing a ranking of importance of the specific interests implicated in the right to housing. A more complex integrated approach is thus preferable even in situations relating to minimum standards, but must itself recognize a differentiation amongst the interests implicated in the right to housing. A collapse of all these interests without recognizing the priority that some have over others cannot be what is required by recognizing the interconnection and interdependence of rights.

B. The Colombian Approach to Minimum Standards: A Need for Integrated Differentiation

As we saw above, the Colombian jurisprudence relating to the right to housing recognizes its integration with other interests. How does it fare when it engages with questions that concern defining the minimum level of such rights that is to be provided?

We see that the Colombian courts, in many ways, recognize that the level or standard of housing must be determined with reference to other interests. At times, though there is a conflation between minimum levels of provision and higher standards, without a clear differentiation between the two. This is one of the pitfalls that can occur when too many interests are combined.

We see the beginnings of this approach, in an early case, not in the area of housing but in relation to social security where the Court needs to formulate minimum standards. The Court stated that:

> [e]ven though the Constitution does not consecrate a right to subsistence, it can be deduced from the rights to life, to health, to work and to assistance, and to social security. People require a minimum of material elements to survive. The acknowledgment of fundamental rights in the Constitution aims to guarantee the economic and spiritual conditions necessary for the dignity of the person and the free development of his personality.[40]

The Court was concerned in this case with lack of payment of a pension to a senior citizen that he was entitled to on the death of his wife. It had to deal with the claim that there was a right to a minimum level of subsistence on the part of the pensioner. As we see in the above quote, the Court derives such a right from its connection with other rights. It does so by recognizing the need of individuals for resources to survive. Confusingly, though, in the next sentence it goes beyond this to recognize not simply the conditions for survival but a more extensive standard. The focus there is on dignity and free development of personality.

The Constitutional Court, as we saw above, initially determined its ability to decide *tutelas* on housing through emphasizing its connection to other fundamental rights. It did so specifically by recognizing a degree of urgency involved in meeting housing needs. Yet, for instance, in defining decent housing, the Court states that it involves having a place 'that allows the person to develop in a minimum of dignity and satisfy their life projects'.[41] This again seems to bring together two distinct levels of provision: a minimum of dignity appears to be a threshold that has a high degree of priority; yet, satisfying one's life projects involves a much higher standard of provision. The Court lumps the two together without enough thought being given to the differences between them.

We also see this trend in the case concerning internally displaced persons, yet the Court is a bit more careful in this instance and arrives at a more satisfactory threshold. The Court is also faced with the problem of defining a minimum level of entitlements that individuals may claim as a matter of priority pending the ability of the government to improve their conditions. The Court held that 'those welfare rights that are part of the minimum that should always be guaranteed to IDPs are those closely related to the preservation of life in dignified conditions proper for autonomous human beings'.[42] The function of defining such a standard was clear for the Court: namely, to determine a line between 'state obligations of a mandatory and urgent nature concerning the IDP population, and those that obviously should be satisfied, but do not have the same priority'.[43]

[40] Decision T-426 of 1992 translated and quoted in Cepeda & Landau (n. 19), 151.
[41] See Decision T-495 of 2010, para. 2.5.2.
[42] Decision T-025 of 2004 translated and quoted in Cepeda & Landau (n. 19), 185.
[43] Ibid.

The minimum standard defined by the Colombian Constitutional Court in the IDP case is a composite one. It focuses the minimum on the preservation of life and thus survival. Yet, it connects survival to dignity and the conditions that are proper for human beings to live autonomously. Thus, the Court articulates a concept of the minimum which is connected to survival but, also, gives expression to the reason we value survival: namely, that it conduces to a life in which individuals are treated with worth and can express, at least, some components of the good life for them (which the Court regards as involving autonomy). The standard outlined by the Court appears to go beyond a pure survival standard and so may not be the absolute minimum applicable in true emergency conditions. Yet, the threshold it identifies gives expression to a level of accommodation that individuals will, in all likelihood, be more satisfied with than the pure minimum core. As such, the Court is able to connect the various interests underlying a domain such as housing and do so in a way that is better suited to providing a threshold for temporary accommodation that extends into the medium term and in which people will spend a considerable period of time.

It is thus instructive to consider how the standard defined by the Colombian court may have played out in *Dladla*. *Dladla* was concerned with accommodation a little above the minimum core and the threshold identified by the Colombian Court could thus be a corrective both to the flaws of the majority and the minority judgment. In relation to the majority, the Colombian Court's definition would have obviated the need strictly to separate out the right to housing and the other rights under consideration. Instead, the Court could have asked whether the accommodation provided by the government was conducive to the preservation of life in dignified conditions proper for autonomous human living. Clearly, the lockout and separation rules violated dignity as well as a sense of agency on the part of the individuals concerned. In relation to Justice Cameron's judgment, there is a refuge into the vague notion of reasonableness to address the composite concerns involved in giving effect to the right to housing. Yet, the Colombian Court offers a way in which to provide a greater content to the threshold of housing provision that is required than Cameron does whilst also integrating the various dimensions of the composite right.

VI. Conclusion: The Porous Boundaries between Rights

This chapter considered a debate that emerged in the *Dladla* case between the majority and Justice Cameron concerning what fell within the ambit of the housing right. This raises an important question concerning how we delineate the borders between rights and the content of specific rights. The majority, as we saw, proposed an approach that sought rather strictly to separate the content of different rights by narrowing the scope of each. This might work in certain cases, yet in relation to the right to housing it seemed ultimately unable to account for the very reasons human beings are interested in housing, something recognized in prior case law of the Constitutional Court as well as the UN General Comment on the topic. Justice Cameron, on the other hand, recognized the interconnection of the various rights and sought to use the Constitutional Court's reasonableness standard as a basis for his decision making. When it comes to reasoning why the particular rules were unconstitutional, however, Justice Cameron's reasoning appears very similar to the majority. This underlines prior critiques about the emptiness of the reasonableness standard. What really matters, however, is the fact that he conceptualizes the housing right as essentially a composite right that requires reference to other rights for determining its content.

This debate is a more general one concerning the manner in which we delineate the content of rights. It seems that the way to do so must have reference, ultimately, to the interests that lie behind our having a particular right. In relation to housing, it is necessary to recognize with the minority and the Colombian Constitutional Court that these interests are composite in nature. That does not mean we cannot determine a specified content for the right to housing: it means, however, that that very content will overlap in some ways with the content of other rights in the specific domain of considering the nature of a structure for human habitation that will suffice.

The differences between the approaches were also raised in the context of a discussion of temporary accommodation. It is important to recognize that there are different degrees of 'temporariness', and in the *Dladla* case, there was a degree of permanence to the temporary accommodation. Nevertheless, the question arose concerning what could constitute minimum standards for temporary accommodation—that question in and of itself raised the issue of defining a minimum threshold in relation to specific rights. In the past, I have argued for the minimum core to be defined in relation to a survival-based standard. As was argued, however, this minimum is provided as a hard base-line below which no-one should fall. It is useful, for instance, in cases of emergency or where resources do not allow a higher standard to be provided. Even this minimum level, however, it was recognized is defined not in relation to housing alone but another core interest: preservation of life. Yet, the facts of *Dladla* address conditions not of a dire emergency but of relatively permanent temporary accommodation. In such circumstances, it is not possible to confine human interests involved in housing to bare survival; other dimensions of the right come into play. The Colombian Constitutional Court has, in its jurisprudence, often conflated thresholds relating to survival and higher levels of provision. Nevertheless, in the IDP case, it outlines a threshold that can provide guidance as to what standards temporary accommodation should meet that may last for a reasonable period of time. This involves ensuring any such housing provides shelter from the elements in conditions that ensure respect for the dignity and autonomy of persons.

This definition of a threshold for reasonably permanent temporary accommodation is really of vital importance given the scale of housing needs in many developing countries. Indeed, it is unlikely that in even ten to twenty years, everyone will be in housing that meets the full standards of adequacy. As such, there is a challenge to define what housing short of the fully adequate standard looks like. Such a lesser threshold must be conceptualized as lying between the minimum core and the higher sufficiency threshold.

This paper has argued that defining such a threshold cannot be done by attempting sharply to separate out housing interests from other interests as the majority in *Dladla* seeks to do. The housing right may relate particularly to spaces in which individuals inhabit, but what we require of those spaces is integrated into the rest of our lives. The debate about defining the content of a right such as housing goes to the core of why we value particular rights and how to capture the interrelationship between them. It also highlights the fact that certain types of rights such as housing may be of a different nature and require different treatment than perhaps a right such as the right to water. Rights identify distinct dimensions of the good for individuals, yet they are essentially connected by the fact that they are meant to enable individuals to live decent lives. The art of judging in this area thus requires a capacity to discern difference whilst having a sensitivity to relationships.

12
The Colombian Model of Structural Socio-economic Rights Remedies
Lessons from and for Comparative Experience

David Landau

The Colombian Constitutional Court has been one of the most active and creative in the world in responding to socio-economic rights violations. It has used a wide range of interpretive techniques and remedial approaches. Along with a few other courts around the world, such as the Indian and South African Supreme Courts, it has become one of the most 'canonical' courts on socioeconomic rights issues. This essay aims to take stock of one important part of the Court's legacy in comparative terms: its jurisprudence on structural remedies for socio-economic rights violations.

Without question, the Court's structural remedies have become a major part of its comparative legacy. This is especially true of two cases where the Court combined massive structural orders with a well-developed, and distinctive, monitoring mechanism: Decision T-025 of 2004, and Decision T-760 of 2008. These two cases dealt with massive failures in public policy towards internally displaced persons ('IDPs'), and the health-care system, respectively. These cases demonstrate what I will call the most distinctive flourishing of the 'Colombian model' of structural social rights enforcement. In many other cases, however, the Court has issued structural orders either without a monitoring mechanism or with a different, less-developed one in place.

Reflecting deeply on the Colombian model offers important lessons both comparatively and domestically. Section I briefly explains the Colombian model through an exploration of its two canonical cases. Section II argues that the jurisprudence that the Court developed to justify structural injunctions is an important guide for when courts should do so. It suggests that in certain cases, courts have a constitutional obligation to issue such a remedy, because they will respond more effectively to an underlying constitutional problem than with other approaches, such as individual orders. The Colombian jurisprudence helps to identify the conditions under which structural remedies should be issued.

Section III adds to this by arguing that, nonetheless, some omissions or weaknesses of the Colombian model of structural orders have become apparent over time. One is consideration of political context, which drives patterns of resistance and support for judicial efforts. The other is cost, both economic and opportunity cost, which has arguably been extremely high for the full-fledged Colombian monitoring process. These two points have important implications for the agenda-setting process, or the decision whether or not to issue structural remedies. They also have implications for the design

David Landau, *The Colombian Model of Structural Socio-economic Rights Remedies:* In: *Constitutionalism.* Edited by: Alejandro Linares-Cantillo, Camilo Valdivieso-León, Santiago García-Jaramillo, Oxford University Press (2021). © The various contributors.
DOI: 10.1093/oso/9780192896759.003.0013

of structural remedies. In particular, as I conclude in Section IV, they do not argue that the full-fledged Colombian model should be abandoned or cast aside, but rather that it should spark judicial and scholarly work on a guided form of experimentalism, in order to develop forms of the remedy that might be either less expensive or more responsive to particular political contexts.

I. The 'Colombian Model' of Structural Orders

The Colombian Constitutional Court has two major instruments, both unusually powerful in comparative terms. The first, called the public action, is an abstract review instrument that can be activated by any citizen, and which dates to the early twentieth century. The second was created in the 1991 constitution, and added to this abstract review an individual complaint mechanism called the *tutela*, which provides both informal and rapid relief for individuals aggrieved by constitutional violations perpetuated by state and (in some cases) non-state actors.[1]

The public action is most obviously useful for striking down laws, and thus this remedy is of somewhat limited use in protecting socio-economic rights in a developing context. The reason is because the biggest problem in these contexts is often the absence of positive state action, and it is difficult to use the public action to require such action. The Colombian Court has, nonetheless, at times been creative about the deployment of the public action. In a well-known series of cases, for example, the Court struck down a housing financing system called UPAC after that system threatened perhaps 100,000 homeowners with foreclosure during an economic crisis. The Court struck down aspects of the old system (such as the formula for setting interest rates and prepayment penalties)[2] and eventually the entire system,[3] but this threatened to create a legal vacuum. In order to induce Congress to pass a new law along lines suggested by the Court, it used a suspended declaration of unconstitutionality that gave the legislature time to construct a new system before the old one was invalidated.[4] Once the new law was passed, the Court upheld it but also made extensive use of conditional declarations of unconstitutionality, which upheld the law only if interpreted in accordance with the Court's own jurisprudence and views, in order to mold the law.[5] Thus, by modulating the effects of its decisions, the Court has sometimes been able to achieve a significant impact on socio-economic rights.

The *tutela* instrument can more easily impose positive obligations on the state. But there were real questions at the outset as to whether it could even be used to enforce socio-economic rights, since the instrument was only usable for 'fundamental rights'

[1] See Colombian Constitution, Article 86.

[2] See, e.g., Decision C-747 of 1999 (striking down capitalization of interest on housing loans); Decision C-252 of 1998 (same regarding prepayment penalties); Decision C-383 of 1999 (same regarding interest-rate formula).

[3] See Decision C-700 of 1999 (striking down the entire system on the grounds that it had been improperly promulgated by the president using decree powers).

[4] See ibid.

[5] See Decision C-955 of 2000.

and it was unclear whether socio-economic rights were fundamental.[6] The Court quickly resolved this ambiguity by holding that socio-economic rights could at least be enforced by *tutela* in cases where they were connected to rights that clearly were fundamental, such as life or human dignity.[7] Later, the Court would supersede this 'connectivity' doctrine by holding that in many cases, socio-economic rights such as the right to health were fundamental in their own right.[8]

The *tutela* instrument is quintessentially individualistic—its most obvious use in socio-economic rights cases is to provide a petitioner a health-care treatment, medicine, or pension that has been wholly or partially denied. But the Court developed a set of doctrinal tools allowing for structural remedies in socio-economic rights cases. In many cases, it began issuing both individual orders, designed to tackle the problems of the petitioner or group of petitioners, and structural orders designed to deal with the broader social problem identified by the case. The most extreme variant of this is the 'state of unconstitutional affairs' doctrine, which holds that when certain conditions have been met, there is a large, systemic gap between public policy and constitutional requirements, obligating the Court to issue a set of structural orders.

The first states of unconstitutional affairs were declared in the 1990s and dealt with issues such as massive prison overcrowding and problems in pension policy.[9] These early states of unconstitutional conditions included ambitious sets of structural orders, but no real monitoring system to ensure those orders were carried out. Critics have argued that the lack of a monitoring apparatus made the structural orders less effective than they would have been otherwise.[10] More subtly, it limited the ability of the Court to adjust the orders over time in response to evolutions in the scope of the problem. In the prisons case, for example, the orders eventually led to the construction of new facilities, but this response ignored other aspects of the problem, such as the social issues leading to criminalization and violence and over-reliance on criminal punishment.[11]

In 2004, the Colombian Constitutional Court issued a state of unconstitutional affairs dealing with the country's population of internally displaced persons.[12] This was an order on a truly massive scale, since roughly 10 per cent of Colombia's population, or 3–4 million people, had been displaced by the country's long-running internal armed conflict. Moreover, the problem was quintessentially polycentric in nature, since the IDP population needed access to a wide range of goods, beginning with registration into the system, and then reaching towards short-term needs like emergency aid, food, health care, job training, and housing, and longer-term, more complex

[6] See Colombian Constitution, Article 85 (defining certain rights as being of 'immediate application', and generally excluding socio-economic rights from the list).

[7] See, e.g., Decision T-426 of 1992 (protecting the right to a pension of an impoverished retiree by holding that the deprivation would impact his right to a 'vital minimum' needed for a dignified life).

[8] See, e.g., Decision T-760 of 2008.

[9] See, e.g., Decision T-153 of 1998 (prison overcrowding); Decision SU-068 of 1998 (social security system).

[10] See Cesar Rodriguez-Garavito, 'Beyond the Courtroom: The Impact of Judicial Activism on Socioeconomic Rights in Latin America' (2011) 89 Texas Law Review 1669, 1675 (arguing that the lack of a monitoring mechanism explains the case's 'overall low impact').

[11] See Libardo Jose Ariza Higuera & Mario Andres Torres Gomez, 'Constitución y Cárcel: La judicialización del mundo penitenciario en Colombia' (2019) 10 Revista Dereito y Praxis 630.

[12] See Decision T-025 of 2004.

rights such as reparations, restitution, and a right to return to one's home territory. The scope of the problem, of course, also potentially encompassed ameliorating the complex, multifaceted causes of displacement in Colombia. The Court held that while there was a well-drafted law governing the rights of IDPs, there was no effective public policy.[13] The issue essentially had little budget or bureaucratic capacity or coordination. The Court held that these failings were so severe as to warrant a declaration of a state of unconstitutional affairs. It thus consolidated a set of claims filed by different petitioners on the IDP issue, and issued an extensive set of structural orders in addition to individual orders designed to protect the rights of the petitioners.[14]

The innovation in the IDP case was to develop a sophisticated monitoring system. The initial *tutela* panel maintained jurisdiction over the case. It required a set of periodic reports from the government and from accountability institutions that it tasked with monitoring aspects of the problem, such as the national ombudsperson and the attorney general. It also recognized a civil society commission composed of a range of non-governmental organizations (NGOs) and experts on the issue, and asked this body to aid the monitoring process as well.[15] These various institutions reported back to the Court in various written reports, and also at periodic public audiences before the Court.[16] The audiences gave IDPs and civil society groups a chance to hold the state to account for its lack of progress on the issue.

Over time, the Court used this information to issue a huge number of follow-up orders.[17] It tended to proceed iteratively, giving its initial orders more definition and teeth over time. Moreover, it was able to put the focus on different sets of problems at different points in the case, and to shift its emphasis as the issue evolved. For example, the Court began by seeking to have the state construct a set of statistical indicators that would allow the government to assess the extent of the problem and its different dimensions.[18] It invited both the government and other groups, such as the civil society commission, to develop proposals, and through this process settled on a set of indicators. Over time, the Court moved on to other aspects of the problem, such as creating programmes that would protect especially vulnerable populations such as indigenous groups, Afro-Colombians, and women.[19]

The health-care decision in 2008 shared some similar aspects.[20] Here too, the order was very large in scope, since it dealt with systemic deficiencies in the country's health-care system. The Court again combined a series of individual *tutelas* and offered both individual and structural remedies. Its structural orders focused on various problems in the health-care system, requiring improvements to the 'subsidized' system to which

[13] See ibid.

[14] See ibid.

[15] See Rodriguez-Garavito (n. 10), 1685. The director of the monitoring commission was a political scientist affiliated with CODHES, an NGO focused on internal displacement.

[16] See ibid., 1694 (noting that there had been twenty-one public hearings on the case between 2004 and 2011).

[17] These orders can be found on the Court's webpage, http://www.corteconstitucional.gov.co/T-025-04/Autos.php accessed 5 December 2020.

[18] See, e.g., Auto 233 of 2007.

[19] See, e.g., Auto 092 of 2008 (focusing on the needs of female internally displaced persons ('IDPs')); Auto 004 of 2009 (focusing on indigenous IDPs).

[20] See Decision T-760 of 2008.

less affluent people belonged, expanding and improving the standard package of benefits, and improving the flow of resources.

The Court did not, in this case, issue a formal declaration of a state of unconstitutional affairs, but its overall model was nonetheless quite similar. It again maintained jurisdiction over the case, held periodic public hearings, and issued a series of follow-up orders.[21] It also acted to create or recognize similar civil society commissions, although with more mixed success than in the IDP case.[22] Rodriguez-Garavito argues that the Court exercised a relatively weak level of monitoring effort in this case, suggesting it should be placed between the IDP case where the Court had a forceful monitoring scheme and other cases like the prison case where it exercised very little.[23] But the level of effort waxed and waned over time (about which I will say more below), as the political context changed and created or foreclosed opportunities.[24]

The Colombian model of structural orders shares certain similarities with structural injunctions or orders found elsewhere, but at the same time it is distinctive in key respects. Compared to the well-known US experience with structural orders on issues such as school desegregation and prison reform, the Colombian model is actually more centralized: in US injunctions, cases were generally managed by trial court judges and localized to a particular state or city, whereas the Colombian cases were national in scope.[25] Because of the scale and centralization of the Colombian cases, the Court had to improvise especially effective monitoring devices, such as the civil society commissions, reporting practices, and public audiences. The Colombian cases may also be more 'dialogical' in nature—because of their broad scope, solutions have tended to emerge in an iterative fashion, through an interchange of ideas between the Court, civil society, and the state.

Structural orders are fairly rare in comparative terms in the enforcement of socio-economic rights, but a few other countries have experimented with them, such as India and Argentina.[26] Some of these cases are extremely creative and bear some similarities, such as the use of monitoring agents and drafting in of civil society, with the Colombian cases. But the Colombian Constitutional Court has developed a particularly clear model for issuing and enforcing structural orders, which consists of maintaining jurisdiction, delegating monitoring to civil society

[21] The follow-up orders in the health case can be found at http://seguimientot760.corteconstitucional.gov.co/.

[22] For a more detailed overview of the Court's interactions with civil society in this case, see David Landau, 'The Reality of Social Rights Enforcement' (2012) 53 Harvard International Law Journal 190, 228–9.

[23] See Rodriguez-Garavito (n. 10), 1694.

[24] See Section III below.

[25] For varying assessments of the US experience with structural injunctions, see Donald L. Horowitz, 'Decreeing Organizational Change: Judicial Supervision of Public Institutions' (1983) Duke Law Journal 1265; Malcolm M. Feeley & Edward L. Rubin, *Judicial Policy Making and the Modern State: How the Courts Reformed America's Prisons* (2000).

[26] See, e.g., Lauren Birchfield & Jessica Corsi, 'Between Starvation and Globalization: Realizing the Right to Food in India' (2010) 31 Michigan Journal of International Law 691 (discussing right to food litigation in India); Teresa Kramarz, Using the Courts to Protect the Environment in Argentina: Accountability Pitfalls When Judges Have the Last Word, Case Studies in the Environment, June 2018, http://cse.ucpress.edu/content/early/2018/06/25/cse.2017.000992 (discussing litigation to protect the Matanza-Riachuelo river basin).

and allied state institutions, holding public audiences, and issuing iterative follow-up orders.[27]

The degree of 'success' of these two cases is disputed in the scholarly literature. In this sense, the Colombian literature tracks broader debates about the effectiveness of structural orders. In the United States, for example, structural orders have been criticized on a number of different grounds such as lack of judicial capacity and legitimacy, although they have also been praised for their (relative) effectiveness in tackling difficult problems where there was no other effective institutional response.[28] Perhaps the Colombian experience can best be understood in similar terms: the cases have encountered many difficulties, and progress has been slow and uneven. But there has been real progress across a range of important issues, in contexts where the political system was broadly unresponsive to significant social problems over long periods of time.[29]

II. Justifying Structural Interventions

When should a court issue a structural remedy? The Colombian doctrines on this point, especially surrounding the state of unconstitutional affairs, offer a very useful starting point. They help to highlight the conditions under which structural orders make sense.

In the 2004 IDP case, the Court offered a fairly complete statement of the factors that should guide it in declaring a state of unconstitutional affairs. It held, based on prior case law, that it should make such a declaration when '(1) there is a repeated violation of the fundamental rights of many people, who therefore resort to tutelas claiming protection and overcrowding judicial courts—and (2) the origin of such an infringement is not exclusively ascribable to the authorities accused, but also to structural factors.'[30] The Court then expanded on these factors as follows:

> Among the factors evaluated by the Court in order to determine whether a state of unconstitutional affairs exists, it is worth mentioning the following: (i) the massive and generalized violation of various constitutional rights affecting a significant number of people; the prolonged omission of the authorities in compliance with their obligations to guarantee rights; (ii) the adoption of unconstitutional practices, like the adoption of the tutela as part of the procedure to guarantee the right at issue; (iii) the failure to issue legislative, administrative, or budgetary measures needed to avoid

[27] In 2015, the Brazilian Supreme Court imported the model of a state of unconstitutional affairs in a prisons case, although it remains unclear how much of the actual monitoring mechanism has been imported. See Thiago Luís Santos Sombra, 'The "Unconstitutional State of Affairs" in Brazil's Prison System: The Enchantment of Legal Transplantation', International Journal of Constitutional Law Blog (30 September 2015), http://www.iconnectblog.com/2015/09/the-unconstitutional-state-of-affairs-in-brazils-prison-system-the-enchantment-of-legal-transplantation/.

[28] See n. 25 above.

[29] The definitive account of the impact of the IDP case is Cesar Rodriguez-Garavito & Diana Rodriguez-Franco, *Radical Deprivation on Trial: The Impact of Judicial Activism on Socioeconomic Rights in the Global South* (2015). On the impact of the health case, see, for example, Alicia Ely Yamin, 'Colombia: Judicial Protection of the Right to Health: An Elusive Promise', in Alicia Ely Yamin & Siri Gloppen (eds), *Litigating Health Rights: Can Courts Bring More Justice to the Right to Health* (2011), 103.

[30] Decision T-025 of 2004.

> the infringement of rights; (iv) the existence of a social problem whose solution requires the intervention of various entities, requires the adoption of a complex and coordinated set of actions and demands a level of resources that demands an important additional budgetary effort; (v) if all the people affected by the same problem went to utilize the tutela to protect their rights, greater judicial congestion would be produced . . . [31]

The choice of remedy is sometimes treated in the literature as discretionary, at least compared to the interpretation of a right. But the Colombian jurisprudence, as noted above, suggests that under certain conditions, there is an obligation on a court to issue a structural order. The doctrine of a state of unconstitutional affairs is in part Colombia-specific, but it responds to considerations that should be relevant from a comparative perspective as well.

Most obviously, the choice to issue a structural remedy should respond to the scope of a problem. It makes the most sense to issue structural orders in cases where the scope of a problem is large. Moreover, structural responses are called for when the cause of a problem is itself structural—in other words, rather than being caused by isolated factors such as a single error or problematic office, it is a result of more widespread factors that are likely to sweep beyond the individual petitioners who have brought a lawsuit. This is particularly true where the scope of a problem is complex, and reaches beyond a single bureaucratic agency or set of actors. In such cases, it is less likely that the government will resolve a problem on its own.

Another factor is the relationship between individual and structural orders. As I have recently argued elsewhere, courts should carefully consider whether to issue the interaction between individual and structural remedies in deciding which type of order to issue for a given violation.[32] The Colombian jurisprudence clearly instructs the judge to consider the impact of individual remedies on the judicial docket: structural responses may be appropriate in cases where individual *tutelas* threaten to overwhelm the judiciary, again because of the sheer scope of a problem.

But the interaction between individual and structural remedies suggested by the test is also subtler. Courts should also consider the impact of individual remedies on the system of social provision itself. In some cases, as the Court has noted, an individual remedy such as the *tutela* may become a *de facto* requirement for receiving access to a socio-economic right. This suggests a significant bureaucratic failure, and moreover one that the judiciary may be contributing to. By offering individual relief to petitioners, a court may offer some relief from a broken social system, but this may also actually relieve pressure that would otherwise exist to reform the system.[33] In the meantime, those who lack the capacity or resources to bring a lawsuit are left without access to their socio-economic rights.

Compounding the problem, in many cases it appears that those bringing individual lawsuits on socio-economic rights issues in Latin America are relatively affluent, while

[31] Ibid.

[32] See David Landau, 'Choosing between Simple and Complex Remedies in Socioeconomic Rights Cases' (2020) 69 University of Toronto Law Journal, supplement 105–23. .

[33] See ibid.

the truly marginalized may be less likely to bring cases.[34] From a theoretical perspective, such an empirical result makes some sense because the poor are probably less likely to have access to information about their rights, and less likely to have the resources (such as a lawyer) needed to navigate the system. In such cases, one may worry that the transformative potential of social rights adjudication is reduced.

Right to health jurisprudence in Colombia has offered some evidence of these dynamics. The judiciary began issuing individualized *tutelas* on the right to health in the late 1990s; many of those seeking protection were middle-class plaintiffs reeling from an economic crisis.[35] This allowed thousands of Colombians to get access to health care that had been denied through normal channels.[36] But the Court's individual jurisprudence also introduced some new distortions into the system. For example, the Court held that treatments found outside the standard package of benefits, which were very expensive, needed to be provided in cases where those treatments impacted core rights such as life or human dignity.[37] In such cases, the state rather than the private insurer was supposed to pick up the tab.

This ruling helped to expand rights protection, but it also gave insurers strong incentives to deny coverage by arguing that a given treatment was outside rather than inside the standard package of benefits, since they would be reimbursed by the state if a court so held.[38] In turn, this fed more litigation.[39] The flow of resources within the system, for example regarding state reimbursements of these non-covered treatments, also became problematic. Moreover, empirical evidence suggests that despite the relative informality and simplicity of the *tutela*, most petitioners were relatively affluent formal-sector workers, rather than the most marginalized.[40] Thus, the Court in some ways was helping to provide relief from a flawed bureaucratic system for relatively privileged workers, but its jurisprudence was not improving the functioning of the system as a whole, and in some ways it actually introduced new distortions.

The 2008 structural case is best justified in this context. It was not simply the size of the problem—for example, the fact that health-care cases alone made up of a large portion of the *tutela* docket because of systemic failures of the health-care system. It was also that it had become clear that the Court's individualized jurisprudence was not resolving the underlying problem, and itself was causing problematic structural

[34] See Landau (n. 22) (discussing such effects in Colombian health litigation); Octavio Luiz Motta Ferraz, 'Harming the Poor through Social Rights Litigation: Lessons from Brazil' (2011) 89 Texas Law Review 1643 (finding distributive effects in health litigation in Brazil).

[35] See Pablo Rueda, 'Legal Language and Social Change During Colombia's Economic Crisis', in Javier A. Couso, Alexandra Huneeus, & Rachel Seider (eds), *Cultures of Legality: Judicialization and Political Activism in Latin America* (2010), 36 (documenting how middle-class petitioners used the 'vital minimum' concept during the country's deep economic crisis).

[36] See ibid.

[37] See Alicia Ely Yamin & Oscar Parra Vera, 'Judicial Protection of the Right to Health in Colombia: From Social Demands to Individual Claims to Public Debates' (2010) 33 Hastings International & Comparative Law Review 431, 448.

[38] See Katharine G. Young & Julieta Lemaitre, 'The Comparative Fortunes of the Right to Health: Two Tales of Justiciability in Colombia and South Africa' (2013) 26 Harvard Human Rights Journal 179, 190(noting that a major contributor to litigation was 'the result of attempts by EPS to get additional compensation for providing services and medicines that were already in the scheduled list by getting courts to order them').

[39] See ibid.

[40] See Landau (n. 22).

effects. There were equity concerns that the Court was not reaching those who did not file individual *tutelas*, especially many poorer citizens, as well as concerns that the Court's own individual jurisprudence had introduced new distortions into the health-care system. Some of the Court's most important orders thus focused on reaching the poor who were less likely to reach the Court: for example, it ordered the state to carry out a long-delayed legal mandate to equalize the package of benefits found in the 'subsidized' system usually used by poorer citizens and informal workers with the 'contributory' system for formal-sector workers.[41] The Court also responded to distortions exacerbated by its own jurisprudence: for example, it required that the standard package of benefits be completely revised so as to provide more clarity and updating in light of the Court's jurisprudence, and it demanded measures to improve the flow of resources within the system.[42]

The broad point shown by the Colombian test is that structural remedies can be justified, and indeed must be issued as a constitutional obligation, under certain conditions. These conditions depend not only on the scope of the problem, but also on the impact of other remedial approaches, such as individual remedies.

III. The Lessons of Experience: The Limits of the Colombian Model

At the same time, the (now extensive) experience with the Colombian model of structural remedies offers some important lessons about their effectiveness. These lessons do not go to the overall effectiveness of the remedy, for there is evidence that both the IDP and health cases achieved an important level of success. They go instead to other conditions needed to make the remedies effective, and which may limit their effectiveness in other situations.

One key point goes to cost. Both the IDP and health cases were quite costly, especially to a small institution like the Constitutional Court. Across both cases, the Court hired a large amount of additional personnel, as well as maintaining a busy follow-up chamber of justices to issue regular follow-up orders.[43] The cost to other institutions and actors, including civil society groups, accountability institutions such as the national ombudsperson and national attorney general, and the state bureaucracy, has also been extremely high. In effect, the Court created a new bureaucracy to manage these largescale problems, and that bureaucracy has persisted over a long period of time (over fifteen years in the case of the IDP decision). Evidence from the United States suggests that structural cases may take not only years, but decades.[44] Indeed, once created, for standard political and administrative reasons, such a bureaucracy may tend to persist even after its utility has decreased, or its core mission has been completed.

[41] See Decision T-760 of 2008.

[42] See ibid.

[43] See Rodriguez-Garavito (n. 10); Landau (n. 22).

[44] See, e.g., Joshua M. Dunn, *Complex Justice: The Story of Missouri v. Jenkins* (2008) (analysing a 1977 lawsuit, which lasted decades, aiming to desegregate Kansas City schools, and which the author argues was not ultimately successful).

The cost of the full Colombian model to the Court is thus very high, and unlike in the United States, where the work can be outsourced to district court judges, in Colombia most of it has been borne by the Constitutional Court itself. The upshot is that it would be impossible for the Court to use the full-fledged Colombian model on a large number of cases. Of course, the cost is not actually in issuing structural remedies, but rather in the monitoring mechanism. The Colombian Constitutional Court can and does issue structural orders fairly routinely, often without any monitoring mechanism. But as Rodriguez-Garavito has argued, the monitoring mechanism is what makes the Court's structural orders effective—without it, the prospects of achieving change on a major social issue seem to be remote.[45]

Experience suggests that the political context is also important to determining the success of this kind of structural case. The impact of the Constitutional Court's iterative orders over time depends on the reaction of state authorities and on the kind of pressure that can be placed on the Court by civil society groups and others. The Court has the ability to influence these factors through its own jurisprudence, but it is also in part dependent on it. The Court in both cases has depended on civil society and accountability institutions to make policy recommendations and to monitor compliance. Thus, in the IDP case, the relative success of the Court has depended in part on its reliance on a unified civil society commission that was skilled at pressuring the bureaucracy, as well as on the high level of general public support for IDP rights and the lack of overt political resistance.

The health care case tells a more complex story about changing windows of opportunity. The Court initially had more difficulty in assembling a cohesive civil society commission, given the wide range of different views on the health-care system. It also faced more active political resistance, which culminated in 2009 when the Uribe administration declared a state of economic, social, and ecological emergency to face a supposed crisis in the health-care system.[46] The administration's emergency decrees clashed with the Court's vision in treating health care more from a cost control perspective than as a constitutional right. For example, the decrees limited patients' ability to access treatments outside the standard package of benefits, and limited the ability of doctors to prescribe such treatment.[47] The massive protests and outcry against the emergency, which the Court eventually struck down,[48] played a role in changing the political context surrounding health care.[49] After the election in 2010, the new president Juan Manuel Santos signalled a more much conciliatory approach. The Court made a renewed push around 2011, bringing in new staff and holding new public audiences; eventually it made progress on compliance with many of its major orders. The Congress passed a new statutory law on health that included a ringing

[45] See Rodriguez-Garavito (n. 10).

[46] See Yamin & Parra-Vera (n. 37), 452.

[47] See ibid., 452–3.

[48] See Decision C-252 of 2010 (striking down the entire state of emergency because it was caused by factors that were 'known, structural, recurring, and foreseeable' in nature, although keeping some of the newly decreed taxes in place because of a financial crisis within the system).

[49] See Yamin & Parra-Vera (n. 37), 454 (noting that by February 2010, 'mass protests were taking place across Colombia' on the basis that health was a right).

affirmation of the Court's perspective, with its first article defining health as a 'fundamental right'.[50]

These two points, put together, place an emphasis on the agenda-setting role of the Court when deciding whether to issue structural orders with a monitoring mechanism. The Court plausibly lacks the resources to issue such a remedy for all significant social problems; in other words, structural remedies are a scarce resource. State failure is a problem everywhere;[51] in Global South contexts, however, problems of bureaucratic dysfunction and under-resourcing may be especially acute.[52] Welfare states may have huge gaps and may routinely fail, and thus may need to be constructed or reworked in fundamental ways. Certainly in Colombia, there remains a wide gap between the constitutional mandate of a 'social state of law' (*estado social de derecho*)[53] and reality on the ground. In such a context, there are potential scarcity problems—the existence of widespread social problems where a structural remedy could be justified may exceed the practical ability of the Court to actually provide such a remedy, given cost and other factors.

Thus, the Court should prioritize cases where it is likely to have sufficient political support to have an impact. Where the Court lacks civil society support, or political resistance is very high, it may be best for the Court to avoid issuing structural orders (at least for the moment) even in cases where it faces a significant social problem. These factors are unfamiliar ones for a court, at least to consider explicitly, but given the degree of the scarcity problem and importance of political context to the success of structural remedies, they must be faced when deciding whether such a remedy should be issued. Moreover, once the Court has issued a structural remedy, the same factors of political context should influence its decisions about how many resources to devote to compliance. As in the health care case, the Court should adjust to the political context, taking advantage of wider windows of opportunity to act.

IV. Beyond the Classic Colombian Model: A Call for Guided Experimentalism

The scarcity problem emphasized by the classic Colombian monitoring model, as exemplified by the IDP and health care cases, also acts as a call for renewed experimentation in the design of remedies. In particular, it suggests a need for other approaches that might lower the cost, to both the Court and other actors, of a structural remedy. The emphasis on political context suggests a very similar point. Just as the success of structural remedies depends heavily on patterns of civil society and political support and resistance, so too it may make sense for the design of those remedies to be responsive to that context.

[50] See Law 1751 of 2015, Art. 1 ('The present law has as its object to guarantee the fundamental right to health, to regulate it, and to establish its mechanisms of protection').

[51] See Michaela Hailbronner, 'Transformative Constitutionalism: Not Only in the Global South' (2017) 65 American Journal of Comparative Law 527 (arguing that discourses of state failure and constitutional transformation also resonate in Global North contexts such as Germany).

[52] See, e.g., David Landau & David Bilchitz, 'The Evolution of the Separation of Powers in the Global South and the Global North', in David Bilchitz & David Landau (eds), *The Evolution of the Separation of Powers: Between the Global North and the Global South* (2018) 1, 20.

[53] See Colombian Constitution, Article 1.

This is certainly not a call for abandoning the model pioneered in the IDP and health care cases, which has worked well in ameliorating massive social problems. It is instead a call for considering ways in which the approach might evolve over time and be made to vary in response to the scope of the problem and the nature of the political context.

In this sense, the proposal is somewhat similar to the ways in which the South African Constitutional Court has treated 'weak form' review in socio-economic rights cases. The paradigm case is *Grootboom*, where the Court issued a weak form order in a housing case that declared the state's policy unconstitutional because it failed to make adequate allowance for those in most immediate and dire need, but also refused to give any direct relief for the petitioners or to give the state detailed guidance on the form of the new policy.[54] But as Brian Ray has argued, most of the subsequent cases did not follow the same approach as *Grootboom*, although they were identifiably weak-form remedies.[55] The Court has instead focused in subsequent housing cases on various forms of 'engagement' remedies, where it has ordered the state to negotiate with affected parties to settle the case, with an evolving set of substantive or procedural constraints.[56] The South African judiciary has also experimented with other remedial approaches, such as denying eviction but requiring the state to pay damages to affected landowners for the construction of informal settlements.[57]

The Colombian approach has always been more assertive than the South African approach, and I would argue that it has more potential to realize constitutional rights. But the point is that the Colombian model, like the South African model, should not be treated as a rote formula, but rather as a basic approach to the problem and thus as an invitation to innovate in a way that is responsive to different kinds of problems and contexts.

Some of the subsequent Colombian cases suggest the potential for this kind of innovation. For the sake of space, I can only mention a few examples here. The first is a 2009 decision where the Court protected the rights of a group of informal trash recyclers in the city of Cali, who were threatened when the trash dump where they worked was closed for environmental reasons, and the city government offered no alternative possibilities.[58] The recyclers were backed by a fairly strong and well-organized civil society movement.[59] The discussion in the case is quite poignant, with the Court explaining in detail the extraordinary level of discrimination faced by this community and the way in which the city's actions affected the basic rights of dignified survival of a group that already faced extremely precarious living conditions. The Court issued a series of innovative remedies (although ones that built on an earlier series of cases involving informal recyclers in Bogotá). For example, the Court ordered the city to

[54] See *Government of the Republic of South Africa v Grootboom*, 2001 (1) SA 46 (CC).
[55] See Brian Ray, *Engaging with Social Rights: Procedure, Participation and Democracy in South Africa's Second Wave* (2016).
[56] See ibid.
[57] See *President of the Republic of South Africa and Another v. Modderklip Boerdery (Pty) Ltd*, 2005 (5) SA 3 (CC).
[58] See Decision T-291 of 2009.
[59] See Manuel Rosaldo, 'Revolution in the Garbage Dump: The Political and Economic Foundations of the Colombian Recycler Movement, 1986-2011' (2016) 63 Social Problems 351, 355–6.

suspend existing bidding processes that excluded recyclers, demanded the creation of a commission that would integrate them into future bidding processes, and required the creation of new programmes to provide job training and other benefits for the population.[60] It also required that the city set aside existing regulations, such as environmental rules, that excluded or hindered the work of the informal recyclers, until such time as the Court's other orders had been fully implemented.[61]

But the Court did not create a monitoring scheme. It relied instead on essentially 'fire alarm' mechanisms, which required civil society groups and the petitioners themselves to return to the Court in the event of non-compliance. The petitioners and their supporters did this in 2014, and the Constitutional Court found that there had been little progress on many of the major structural orders.[62] It issued new, more specific orders, but again without a clear monitoring mechanism.[63] One lesson of the informal recyclers case is that reliance on a fire alarm mechanism alone is not enough, even where the Court is operating in an area with strong, well-organized civil society groups. Just as the Court relies on civil society to help enforce its orders and to monitor compliance, civil society relies on the Court to put continuous pressure on the state, for example through the use of public audiences and updated orders.

Natalia Angel-Cabo and Domingo Lovera Parmo find, through an interview with the justice who authored the informal recycler decision, that the Court decided not to establish a new monitoring mechanism in part because of the scarcity problem noted above—it simply could not handle an additional monitoring process because of those already established.[64] But the context of the informal recyclers case suggests ways in which a monitoring mechanism might be created in ways that are potentially cheaper than the massive mechanisms set up in the IDP and health care cases. First, the informal recycling case was confined to one city, Cali—by focusing on geographically confined cases instead of problems with a nationwide scope like the IDP case, the Court might reduce the costs of monitoring. Moreover, fire alarm mechanisms can be combined with more robust forms of monitoring—for example, the Court could have scheduled public audiences once it heard complaints of significant non-compliance, rather than simply issuing follow-up orders. In short, there are a number of intermediate positions between establishing no monitoring mechanism at all and establishing the very expensive procedures set up the in IDP and health cases.[65]

Another interesting case is a series of orders between 2013 and 2015 dealing with Colpensiones, the Colombian agency charged with paying pensions. In a highly unusual case, Colpensiones approached the Court and asked it to declare a state of unconstitutional affairs involving the agency, because of a huge backlog and systemic

[60] See Decision T-291 of 2009.

[61] See ibid.

[62] See Auto 118 of 2014.

[63] See ibid.

[64] See Natalia Angel-Cabo & Domingo Lovera Parmo, 'Latin American Social Constitutionalism: Courts and Participation', in Helena Alviar-Garcia et al., (eds), *Social and Economic Rights in Theory and Practice: Critical Inquiries* (2015) 85, 95.

[65] See David Landau, 'Aggressive Weak Form Remedies' (2014) 5 Constitutional Court Review (South Africa) 244 (arguing that the distinction between strong form and weak form review is best thought of as a spectrum, and that there are many intermediate points depending on a court's procedures and level of assertiveness).

delays in paying benefits.[66] While asking for the declaration of a state of unconstitutional affairs effectively was an admission of massive structural problems in their own agency, Colpensiones nonetheless sought the decree because it was facing a large number of potential contempt sanctions from failing to pay orders obtained in individual *tutelas*.[67] The Court agreed to take over management of the case, suspending the contempt orders, and it issued orders requiring the agency to obtain sufficient resources to clear the backlog and to create a plan avoiding such problems in the future.[68] It monitored compliance through reporting and periodic public audiences, and in 2015 held that sufficient progress had been made so that it could deny the agency's request for relief from future contempt orders.[69]

From an agenda-setting perspective, the Colpensiones case is perhaps problematic because it demonstrates an agency effectively commandeering judicial resources to obtain relief from individual orders. Courts should of course be somewhat sceptical of state actors themselves seeking to set the judicial agenda. But at the same time, the case is significant in demonstrating the relationship between individual and structural orders. In the past, the Colombian Constitutional Court has usually kept the door open to individual claims even after issuing a structural remedy, but the Colpensiones case suggests at least one reason why this might not always be the optimal course. The threat of individual orders in *tutela* cases, and especially of contempt orders, can sometimes be a significant motive for bureaucratic action. Individual bureaucrats sometimes fear such orders. By strategically suspending individual claims, a court may in some cases help to leverage bureaucracies to comply with structural orders. And by hanging the threat of renewed individual orders over an agency as a penalty for poor compliance, the Court may be able to increase the leverage enjoyed by civil society groups and other monitors. Again, deploying such leverage may decrease the need for other, costlier mechanisms of compliance.

A third intriguing example of experimentation around the core model is provided by a set of decisions dealing with prison conditions. As noted above, in 1998 the Court issued a state of unconstitutional affairs orders because of prison overcrowding, and ordered the construction of new prisons.[70] The decision had no real monitoring mechanism—regardless, over time new prisons were built, although these did not fix the problem of prison overcrowding. In 2013, the Court re-examined the problem, found a state of unconstitutional affairs, and issued a new set of general orders that dealt with additional aspects of the problem, such as enjoyment of fundamental rights to health, work, and study within a prison context.[71] It also attempted to create a monitoring commission.[72]

In 2015, in a third major case, the Court went further in creating institutional mechanisms to follow its structural judgments on prisons.[73] In this case, it required

[66] See Auto 113 of 2013.
[67] See ibid.
[68] See ibid.
[69] See Auto 181 of 2015.
[70] See Decision T-153 of 1998.
[71] See Decision T-388 of 2013.
[72] See ibid.
[73] See Decision T-762 of 2015.

periodic reports from the government and created a monitoring group composed of a number of different state entities and checking institutions. It also required the creation of a sub-committee to work on certain technical issues, and required that the state work off a base of statistical indicators defined within the 2015 and 2013 decisions.[74] The Court reserved the right to take over monitoring and follow-up at any point, but did not create the same kind of internal structure (such as a standing judicial panel) that existed in the IDP and health cases.

The prisons context is interesting in showing how judicial responses to structural problems may evolve over time. As it became clear that initial processes were insufficient, the Court slowly evolved somewhat more robust monitoring mechanisms. The case also shows the Court grappling towards a potential intermediate ground where it creates robust monitoring mechanisms without unduly straining the Court's own resources. It is not clear to me whether the monitoring mechanism in the 2015 case will ultimately prove successful: scholars suggest that it has borne little immediate fruit.[75] Perhaps the Court has kept itself at too much of a distance; perhaps its monitoring processes have focused too heavily on the state, and not enough on civil society, which was arguably the key to success in the IDP and health cases.[76] But the prison context shows the Court grappling with newer ways to conceive of effective monitoring, rather than seeing the state of unconstitutional affairs as a fixed model.

Finally, comparative experience may also be useful in helping to guide remedial design in structural cases. In Colombia, the Constitutional Court used a standing panel of justices to issue follow-up orders, assisted by a number of staffers, including some working on the case at issue. But one point that comparative experience supports is that it is sometimes possible for high courts to delegate many of the monitoring costs to other institutions. In the United States, for example, structural orders effectively required by the Court's jurisprudence on school desegregation, prisons conditions, and other issues were actually managed by federal district court judges, rather than the Supreme Court itself.[77] This is a product of US civil procedure, where trials are managed at the district court level, and appellate courts are restricted to handling abstract issues of law. In other countries, such as India and Argentina, courts have relied on special masters or special commissions empowered to monitor compliance and issue follow-up orders.[78] Special masters have also been widely used in the United States as an aid to district courts.

To be sure, these kinds of institutions can have drawbacks, and may not work well under all conditions. Lower-court or ordinary judges, for example, are a far more difficult resource to tap in Colombia than in the United States. Historically, these judges had a far different vision of law, and at times expressed outright hostility towards the

[74] See ibid.

[75] See Ariza Higuera & Torres Gomez (n. 11), 650–1 (finding that the 'robust monitoring process' proposed by the Court, to date, 'has had little impact' on improving prison conditions on the ground).

[76] A key difference is that there is much less civil society support surrounding the prison issue, complicating the task of structural litigation. See ibid., 652.

[77] See (n. 25) above.

[78] See (n. 26) above.

Constitutional Court.[79] Over time, the dominant conception of law has evolved to become somewhat closer to that of the Constitutional Court, but the ordinary courts remain staffed by judges with a different conception of the judicial role. Special masters and similar mechanisms may also have drawbacks. In Argentina, for example, scholars have argued that the process was vulnerable to corruption and other problems in a major environmental case.[80] But these mechanisms show significant promise in lowering the costs of day-to-day monitoring, and so are worth consideration in Colombia and in other countries considering structural remedies.

Indeed, one recent case seems to show the Court moving towards this kind of decentralized model. In 2017, the Court declared a state of unconstitutional affairs regarding children of the Wayuu indigenous group, who were concentrated in a particular region of the country.[81] The Court held that there were systemic state failures leading to a failure to provide a battery of rights including health care, food, potable water, and political participation. It thus declared a state of unconstitutional conditions and created a complex and innovative monitoring system, but left the monitoring in the hands of a lower-level court, although reserving the right to intervene directly if necessary. The monitoring court in this case was the first instance *tutela* court, an administrative tribunal from the region where the violations occurred.

More direct forms of borrowing may also show some promise in particular contexts. For example, a couple of recent Colombian cases draw on the South African concept of 'engagement' to resolve constitutional problems.[82] In one recent case, for example, the Court ordered a process of meaningful engagement between the relevant governmental entities and the petitioners to resolve problems of access and quality of education in the North of Santander region of Colombia (including the necessity of children to cross an alligator-infested river to get to school).[83] This kind of order reflects a rather different approach than the dominant Colombian model, and has its own drawbacks (as an extensive South African literature demonstrates), but it may be the best approach in particular political and social contexts, and where there is adequate judicial and civil society supervision and guidance.

V. Conclusion

The Colombian Constitutional Court's experience with structural socio-economic rights issues is one of its greatest and most distinctive achievements, one justifiably celebrated both inside and outside the country. This paper has argued that the jurisprudence of the Court, and its experience applying structural remedies in cases like the IDP and health-care case, help to identify the conditions under which such remedies

[79] See Diego Eduardo Lopez Medina, *Teoria impura de derecho: La transformacion de la cultura juridica latinoamericana* (2004).

[80] See Kramarz (n. 26); Roberto Gargarella, 'Deliberative Democracy, Dialogic Justice, and the Promise of Social and Economic Rights', in Alviar-Garcia (n. 64) (noting that a corruption scandal greatly damaged the monitoring process).

[81] See Decision T-302 of 2017.

[82] See text accompanying nn 55–56 above.

[83] See Decision T-209 of 2019.

are likely to be the most effective approach and should be issued by courts as a matter of constitutional obligation. Such conditions include the size of a constitutional violation, of course, but also the sometimes perverse effect of other kinds of orders such as individual remedies, the changing political context in which a court is operating, and the cost of a remedy and its monitoring mechanism.

The influence of political context and cost also highlight a key point: the Colombian model should best be viewed as an invitation for further development and guided experimentation, rather than as a fixed formula for success. The Court should seek ways to develop different types of monitoring mechanisms that are less expensive and that respond to variations in political context. Existing case law gives some suggestions for how such mechanisms might be developed. For comparative scholars and courts, the Colombian experience is a fruitful source of evidence that structural remedies will often be the most effective way to realize socio-economic rights, especially in cases where problems are widespread and linked to bureaucratic failures.

Within Colombia itself, deployment of varied structural remedies in a form of guided experimentalism is the best alternative for future cases. Relying only on the traditional structural model found in the IDP and health cases may be too expensive, and there is an increasing sense that such an approach has reached the limits of its effectiveness. Relying only on individual remedies, however, will not always ameliorate the underlying causes of constitutional violations, and in some situations may actually worsen them. In many cases where constitutional violations are widespread, this chapter has argued, the Court should continue to issue structural remedies; likewise, it should continue to experiment with the form of those remedies in response to cost concerns and political context. Anything less would be an abdication of the Court's vital responsibilities as guardian of the constitution.

C)

Courts as Mediators or Courts Setting the Ultimate Standard of Fairness: Transitional Justice

13
The Resilient Constitution

*David Dyzenhaus & Alma Diamond**

I. Introduction

In the literature on transitional justice ('TJ'), the South African experience looms large just because it is an obvious example of a standard case of TJ. For example, in the leading work in TJ theory, Colleen Murphy identifies what she calls the four 'circumstances of transitional justice' which mark 'paradigm transitional societies'.[1] First, there is 'pervasive structural inequality' which can take the shape of economic, political, social, cultural, and legal institutional rules and norms that grant differential access to the goods that make for a valuable life and/or to the making of such rules and norms.[2] When inequality is pervasive, she says, the order is illegitimate and a right to rebel arises.[3] The second circumstance is 'normalized collective and political wrongdoing', that is, the 'actions or omissions of particular human beings that result in violations of human rights'.[4] The third circumstance is 'serious existential uncertainty'—the fact that the trajectory of the political community is in doubt.[5] Finally, there is 'fundamental uncertainty about authority'—an 'ambiguity about the standing of the political regime to rule and enforce rules'.[6] This flows from the fact that the state which has to manage the TJ process was deeply implicated in creating the first two circumstances.[7] As a result, authority in the transitional society must be able to accommodate a reckoning with the injustices of the past whilst also claiming legitimacy in building a just future.

For this reason, authority in transitional societies cannot be understood *de novo*. As Murphy explains, 'transitions are thought of as bridges, not complete breaks, between the past and the present'.[8] Her remark echoes the South African interim constitution of 1993 which mandated a TJ process and claimed that it provided 'a historic bridge between the past of a deeply divided society characterized by strife, conflict, untold

* We thank Whitney Taylor for comments on a draft, and Vicente F. Benítez-Rojas and Julián Huertas for memoranda on our argument which prompted important changes, though we should mention that we have not been able to do anything like full justice to their attempts to educate us better in the complexities of Colombian politics and constitutional jurisprudence.

[1] Colleen Murphy, *The Conceptual Foundations of Transitional Justice* (Cambridge: Cambridge University Press, 2017), 41, 43–66.
[2] Ibid., 43–9.
[3] Ibid., 47.
[4] Ibid., 52, 49–54.
[5] Ibid., 66–70.
[6] Ibid., 72.
[7] Ibid, 70–5.
[8] Ibid., 71–2.

David Dyzenhaus & Alma Diamond, *The Resilient Constitution* In: *Constitutionalism*. Edited by: Alejandro Linares-Cantillo, Camilo Valdivieso-León, Santiago García-Jaramillo, Oxford University Press (2021). © The various contributors.
DOI: 10.1093/oso/9780192896759.003.0014

suffering and injustice, and a future founded on the recognition of human rights, democracy and peaceful co-existence'.[9]

The metaphor of a bridge to describe the TJ process is profound. Even if the terrain on the other side of a bridge is very different from the terrain on which one starts one's crossing, it cannot be so different as to make bridging the gap impossible. There has to be secure ground on both sides if the bridge is to be anchored so that it does not collapse under its own weight, let alone the weight of the traffic across it. In other words, a TJ process poses a problem that is inextricably linked to, and that can only be solved in continuity with, the past. It also has to shape the future, a new political community out of a deeply divided society. The bridge of TJ therefore represents quintessentially existential, political problems.

If the problem and its solutions are political, it is not clear what the proper role of the courts and the law should be. The interdependence of the legal and the political, of 'transitional justice' and 'transitional society,' are apparent from the four circumstances of transition set out above: political and collective wrongdoing, and in response 'credible attempts to disrupt the status quo by overhauling pervasive structural inequality',[10] both sound like uses and abuses of collective political power. So does the establishment of pervasive structural inequality. However, the legal norms that maintain such inequality and the fundamental uncertainty about authority that arises as a result raise legal issues, substantive constitutional issues pertaining to authority. The circumstances of transition implicate not only power, but also authority. If the one side of the bridge had been mere power, law and authority could be understood *de novo* with the commencement of the transition process. The challenge of TJ arises precisely because this is not possible: law lives on both sides of the bridge.

The standard way of minimizing the implications of this fact is to enact a 'transitional constitution', one that mandates, as in South Africa, that a TJ process be undertaken. In contrast, a country such as Colombia which has a 'permanent constitution' suffers, as we will see, from the problem that its entrenched norms will seem to make any TJ process unconstitutional. However, the clarity and simplicity bought by a transitional constitution comes at a cost. It masks the continuity between past, present, and future when it allows courts to avoid directly gazing at the 'Gorgon head of power'.[11]

In this chapter, we examine this often-obscured continuity more closely and show that, upon inspection, there is no hard and fast distinction between a transitional constitution and a permanent one. Constitutions are better understood in terms of their resilience rather than as either transitional or permanent. Once we see this, it is clear that despite their differences, the TJ jurisprudence of the South African Constitutional Court is instructive more generally about the promise and the limits of both a TJ process and of constitutionalism. Whatever difficulties the Colombian TJ process faces,

[9] Constitution of the Republic of South Africa Act 200 of 1993, Schedule on National Unity and Reconciliation.

[10] Murphy (n. 1), 70.

[11] Hans Kelsen, in *Veröffentlichen der Vereinigung der Deutschen Staatsrechtslehrer*, vol. 3 (Walter de Gruyter, Berlin, 1927), 54–5: 'The question on which natural law focusses is the eternal question of what stands behind positive law. And whoever seeks the answer will find, I fear, neither an absolute metaphysical truth nor the absolute justice of natural law. Who lifts the veil and does not shut his eyes will find staring at him the Gorgon head of power.'

they do not mainly stem from the permanence of its constitution. Rather, they stem from the tensions inherent in any TJ process because it derogates from some of the very rights it is designed to promote.[12]

We venture to suggest that this claim is sound despite salient differences between the South African context at the time of the Truth and Reconciliation Commission ('TRC') and the Colombian context, which go beyond the permanence of its constitution. The current TJ process in Colombia is focused on the conflict between the Colombian armed forces and the guerilla group known as FARC. But while FARC and other guerilla groups began their activities at a time of political exclusion, and had their roots in popular concerns about pervasive social inequality, the 1991 constitution put an end to political exclusion. FARC, however, continued on the path of illegality, mainly because it had turned from politics to drug trafficking. Hence, the TJ process was not so much an attempt to turn away from an authoritarian past as one to bring into the political community a powerful but deeply unpopular group to which the state was too weak to respond. In addition, the human rights abuses with which the process is concerned are not those inflicted by the political elite on the oppressed population, but for the most part abuses inflicted by both FARC and the military on the civilian population in the course of the armed conflict. Finally, as we will sketch below, the legal situation in which the Colombian process was crafted was complicated and constrained by more legal considerations than the 1991 constitution.

As we show, South Africa's newly established Constitutional Court had to respond to an immediate challenge to the constitutionality of the TJ process because of its amnesty provisions, which permitted individuals on both sides of the conflict to escape punishment despite having perpetrated gross violations of human rights.[13] We argue that the TJ jurisprudence of the South African Constitutional Court is instructive more generally about the promise and the limits of both a TJ process and of constitutionalism even though there are always important political and legal differences in any particular context. We will also suggest that this tension between promise and limit is best managed by somewhat deflating expectations about what kind of justice a TJ process can produce. It is highly unlikely, perhaps impossible, for any such process to deliver the kind of justice that responds to pervasive structural inequality. At most it can produce a sense of belonging to what we term a 'jural community'. The bonds of such a community are forged by the rule of law, an idea better conveyed by the term

[12] We rely in this paper on earlier work on the South African TJ process, mainly, David Dyzenhaus, *Judging the Judges, Judging Ourselves: Truth, Reconciliation and the Apartheid Legal Order* (Oxford: Hart Publishing, 1998) and David Dyzenhaus, '*Leviathan* as a Theory of Transitional Justice' in Melissa S. Williams, Rosemary Nagy, & Jon Elster, (eds), *NOMOS LI: Transitional Justice*, (New York: New York University Press, 2012), 180.

[13] *Azanian Peoples' Organization (AZAPO) and Others v President of the Republic of South Africa and Others*, 1996 ZACC 16 (CC). After the TRC had concluded its work, the Court handed down two judgments on the implications of amnesty decisions made by the TRC's 'Committee on Amnesty'. We summarize these in a note below. The process was also challenged before lower courts: *Azanian People's Organization (AZAPO) and Others v Truth and Reconciliation Commission and Others*, 1995 4 562 (C); *Du Preez and Another v. Truth and Reconciliation Commission*, 1997 2 All SA 1 (A); *Niewoudt v Truth and Reconciliation Commission*, 1997 2 SA 70 (AD); *Truth and Reconciliation Commission v Du Preez and Another*, 1996 3 SALR 997 (C). The opinions of the lower courts generally displayed approaches and interpretations similar to those of the Constitutional Court.

that European languages other than English use in talking of an *estado de derecho* or the *Rechtsstaat*—the state governed by legal right.

Finally, we suggest that the task of building such a community is difficult enough in the circumstances of TJ without loading the process with the burden of responding to pervasive structural inequality. A TJ process brings into view something that philosophers from Hobbes to Kant have thought can't be dealt with as a matter internal to the juridical order, the fact that, as Hobbes put it, 'there is scarce a Common-wealth in the world, whose beginnings can in conscience be justified'.[14]

Kant elaborated the point as follows:

> A people should not *inquire* with any practical aim in view into the origin of the supreme authority to which it is subject ... For, since a people must be regarded as already united under a general legislative will in order to judge with rightful force about the supreme authority ... it cannot and may not judge otherwise than as the present head of state wills it to.... Whether a state began with an actual contract of submission ... as a fact, or whether power came first and law arrived only afterwards, or even whether they should have followed in this order: for a people already subject to civil law, these subtle reasonings are altogether pointless and, moreover, threaten a state with danger.[15]

A TJ process, however, requires a society to try to build a jural community while directly confronting the violence that lies at its actual foundation. Moreover, when courts are involved in managing the process, they do have to inquire into the 'origins of supreme authority' with the 'practical aim' of both maintaining and establishing the rule of law, precisely the kind of task that Kant deemed pointless and dangerous. Our discussion of the South African Constitutional Court's decision suggests why Kant was wrong.

II. Colombia's 'Permanent' Constitution

Colombia's Constitutional Court has already played a significant role in the current TJ process and doubtless will be called on again. A constitutional court or indeed any apex court that is charged with such a task is forced to confront complex problems about the legitimacy of its interventions. The claim that judges should be the 'guardians of the constitution' is controversial even when they do not have to decide existential questions about what makes the individuals subject to the law of the land part of one secure and stable political community. But questions like these are at the heart of any TJ process since it is an attempt to create one political community in a society that has been deeply divided.

The issue here is sharply posed by Juan E. Méndez, one of the towering figures in the field of human rights and TJ, at the beginning of his essay 'Constitutionalism and

[14] Thomas Hobbes, *Leviathan*, ed. Richard Tuck (Cambridge: Cambridge University Press, 1996), 486.

[15] Immanuel Kant, *The Metaphysics of Morals*, in Kant, *Practical Philosophy*, ed. and trans. Mary J. Gregor (Cambridge: Cambridge University Press, 1996), 461–2.

Transitional Justice'. Méndez asks: 'How do communities emerge from the rubble and make for themselves a new legal space?' His answer is TJ: the 'set of methods through which communities that have suffered gross and systematic violations of fundamental human rights seek to distance themselves from that past and move forward in a manner consistent with the need for justice for those who have suffered.' He also says that the 'objective … is to repair and rebuild within the confines of the rule of law'.[16] But, as he notes, this objective is difficult to achieve due to the tension between, on the one hand, constitutionalism and its commitment to the rule of law and, on the other, TJ.

This tension is manifested most dramatically in that TJ calls into question a fundamental norm of a political community that is ordered on constitutionalist lines: its commitment to the rule of law in that no person is considered to be above the law. As A. V. Dicey, the great English constitutional theorist put it, 'every man, whatever his rank or condition, is subject to the ordinary law of the realm and amenable to the jurisdiction of the ordinary tribunals'.[17] Dicey and other constitutional theorists emphasize that it is of special significance that state officials are subject to this norm. For if state officials are not subject to the law, the state will be lawless, even criminal, if state officials can act illegally with impunity. They will be able quite literally to get away with murder, as well as other heinous crimes.

Since a TJ process will standardly involve a grant of amnesty to people on both sides of the conflict who committed such crimes, it requires a serious derogation from this norm. Of course, the grant of amnesty will be conditional and there will standardly be a special tribunal set up to decide whether individuals meet the conditions, one of which might be a confession of guilt. But the establishment of such a tribunal that will not and cannot operate in accordance with the strict standards of a criminal trial appears to make things if anything worse from a rule of law, constitutionalist perspective.

One might suppose that the tension the Colombian Court has to manage is made easier by the fact that the process is taking place within the framework of a 'permanent constitution'—the constitution that was put in place in 1991.[18] In addition, the Colombian process avoids, to the greatest possible extent, the problem of granting immunity for human rights abuses, which reflects not only its design in the light of the constitution, but also the fact that Colombia accepts the authority of both the Inter-American Court of Human Rights and the International Criminal Court. Hence the

[16] Juan E. Méndez, 'Constitutionalism and Transitional Justice' in Michel Rosenfeld & Andràs Sajó (eds), *The Oxford Handbook of Comparative Constitutional Law* (Oxford: Oxford University Press, 2012) 1270, 1271.

[17] A. V. Dicey, *The Law of the Constitution*, ed. John Allison (Oxford: Oxford University Press, 2013), 100.

[18] We rely heavily in what follows on Manuel José Cepeda Espinosa & David Landau, *Colombian Constitutional Law: Leading Cases* (New York: Oxford University Press, 2017) and Carlos Bernal-Pulido, 'Transitional Justice Within the Framework of a Permanent Constitution: The Case Study of the Legal Framework for Peace in Colombia' (2014) 3 Cambridge Journal of International and Comparative Law 1136. We note that the 1991 Constitution was enacted in the framework of a demobilization and reconciliation process with some other guerrilla groups (most prominently the M-19). And one reason for guerrilla movements to re-enter civil life was precisely the idea of enacting a new constitution. Commanders of some of these groups were elected to the constituent assembly that enacted the constitution of 1991—the M-19 got one third of the seats of the Assembly. This participation led to several provisions of the original 1991 constitution that established amnesties in its 'transitory articles' in favour of former combatants and allowed them to run for office.

Colombian peace process was politically and legally more constrained than the South African one.[19] As a result, its TJ process stipulates 'effective restrictions on freedom' of from five to eight years for those who collaborate with the Prosecutor established in the 'Special Jurisdiction for Peace', and sanctions that range between fifteen and twenty years in prison for those who are found guilty after refusing to collaborate.[20]

In contrast, the standard TJ process aims to assist the creation of a new constitutional order that will replace the unjust past order, where one of the factors that made that order problematic was that it neither had a permanent constitution that contained a set of rights commitments, nor provided the institutional framework necessary to vindicate those commitments. With such a permanent constitution already in place, as well as the other legal constraints, it may seem that the process can be designed to bring the parties within the existing framework of the constitution, especially if it was designed, as Article 2 says, to 'ensure peaceful coexistence and the enforcement of a just order'. In short, with such a constitution in place, there is also in place a valuable asset for managing a process of TJ.

But in fact, the tension in Colombia seems to be made more acute by the existence of these constraints. While they resulted in a much smaller sacrifice of criminal justice than is usually the case in a TJ process, they also served to heighten the sense that an important sacrifice had been made. And sacrifice is intrinsic to any TJ process. That a justice process is 'transitional' indicates not only that there is a passage from one time to another—a passage from T_1 through T_2 to T_3. What makes T_1 a time that the society wishes to transition from is that it is a state of injustice such that groups in the society are excluded from the political community and their exclusion is marked by the human rights abuses that attend the exclusion. T_3 is the destination in which all will be part of the same political community, with their membership as such marked by the fact that their rights are secured by the constitutional order which the transition helps to bring about. But in order to reach T_3 in a context in which the perpetrators of human rights abuses on both sides of the conflict still hold power and are unwilling to participate in the process if the rights of the victims are fully vindicated as they would be in T_3, those rights have to be limited or even sacrificed to the extent necessary in T_2.

For this reason, those who frame a constitution to manage T_2 should ensure that it is a 'transitional constitution', one that makes express or implicit provision for the limitation and sacrifice of rights that can only be fully enjoyed in T_3 and so validates a TJ process. An 'explicit TJ provision' is one that states that during T_2 the demands of the transition will require the limitation or even sacrifice of rights. An 'implicit TJ provision' may be thought to exist when the constitution contains a standard proportionality clause—a provision that permits the limitation of rights guaranteed by the constitution—as long as it can be shown that the limitation is in the cause of a

[19] For example, the Inter American Court has developed a strict jurisprudence on the prohibition of amnesties applicable to Colombia. See Christina Binder, 'The Prohibition of Amnesties by the Inter-American Court of Human Rights' (2011) 12 German Law Journal 1203. For an account of the pressure put by the International Criminal Court on the Colombian government during the peace talks, see Rene Urueña, 'Prosecutorial Politics: The ICC's Influence in Colombian Peace Processes, 2003-2017' (2017) 111 American Journal of International Law 104.

[20] See Claudia Josi, 'Accountability in the Colombian Peace Agreement: Are the Proposed Sanctions Contrary to Colombia's International Obligations?' (2017) 46 Southwestern Law Review 401, 410.

legitimate objective and proportionate to achieving that objective. Ideally, the transitional constitution should have both, because the explicit TJ provision makes it clear that the objective is constitutionally legitimate while the implicit TJ provision provides a mechanism for evaluating the means devised to reach that objective.

That the Colombian Constitution is a permanent constitution is indicated by the absence of any explicit TJ provision. In addition, it makes no provision for the proportional limitation of the rights it guarantees. Thus, any TJ process would seem prima facie unconstitutional. Here we have the explanation of why having a permanent constitution in place may seem a liability rather than an asset if a society finds it necessary to go through a TJ process.

That liability was deepened by the past jurisprudence of Colombia's Constitutional Court. While permanent in the respect just described, the constitution was far from permanent in another since it provided three mechanisms for amendment. It can be amended by majority vote in the Congress in two consecutive sessions as long as the second vote commands an absolute majority. It can be amended by the people in a referendum once Congress has enacted a law providing for new articles. And it can be amended by a constituent assembly brought into being by a referendum proposed by Congress. In this respect, the constitution looks comparatively impermanent as all the processes, but especially the first of amendment by ordinary legislation, make it susceptible or even vulnerable to change.

It was against this backdrop that the Court came up with its 'substitution of the constitution' doctrine, its version of the 'unconstitutional constitutional amendment' argument that formally valid amendments may be unconstitutional if they offend the substance of the constitution. In the Court's version, a formally valid amendment would be unconstitutional if in substance it amounts to a 'replacement' of the constitution, one that 'denatures' a constitutionally protected right. This was a bold move, given that Articles 241 and 379 give the Court authority to review amendments on procedural grounds alone which could on standard maxims of statutory interpretation have been thought to indicate strongly that the constitution precluded the Court from developing this kind of substantive review jurisdiction. In addition, the doctrine of unconstitutional constitutional amendment is protected by the fact that the Court has devised a doctrine of precedent for its decisions about the constitution, although the Colombian legal system is civilian and so has no formal doctrine of precedent.

That the Court had taken this bold step, cemented by its doctrine of constitutional precedent, thus added to the obstacles presented by the existence of a permanent constitution which contains no provision for proportional rights limitation. For the last fact, at least as the Court's previous jurisprudence indicated, seemed to commit it to a process of syllogistic reasoning when it came to constitutional amendments that clearly violate constitutionally protected rights. It seemed, that is, fated to reason in the following way.

Major premise: in the Colombian permanent constitution, a constitutional amendment even if formally valid is invalid if it seeks a substantive replacement of the constitution.

Minor premise: any truly TJ process amounts to such a replacement.

Conclusion: the amendments that put in place the current TJ process are invalid.

But this bold Court was not deterred by the obstacles that its past interpretations and the constitution itself had created. Instead, it introduced two further innovations into its jurisprudence. First, it replaced its prior practice of syllogistic reasoning with the kind of balancing exercise that other courts had developed in jurisdictions where they are required to determine whether the limitation of a right is proportional and thus justified. The issue would no longer be whether a right would be 'denatured' by being significantly limited. Rather, the issue would be whether that limit is proportionate when balanced against principles that compete with the right, now conceived as a principle with weight rather than an all or nothing rule.[21] The Court thus introduced an implicit TJ provision of the kind I described into the constitution.

Secondly, the Court introduced an explicit TJ provision. The balancing of principles affected by the amendments would be against 'principles recognized to belong to the international and transnational legal framework for transitional justice, entrenching the goals of transitional justice: stable and lasting peace, reconciliation, and the end of political conflict'.[22] Article 93 of the constitution provides:

> International treaties and agreements ratified by Congress that recognize human rights and that prohibit their limitation in states of emergency have priority domestically.
>
> The rights and duties mentioned in this Charter shall be interpreted in accordance with international treaties on human rights ratified by Colombia.

The Court reasoned that Article 93 makes Colombia a monist jurisdiction, which means that the norms of the international human rights order in treaties ratified by Colombia are regarded as part of the 'constitutional block' or an integral part of the constitution.[23] In this way, the Court introduced a second implicit TJ provision into the constitution, this time an implicit explicit TJ provision, one that declares that the constitution is a transitional constitution, in terms of which for the sake of civil peace, measures may be adopted that limit constitutionally protected rights in ways that would in normal circumstances be prohibited.

But notice that the first sentence in Article 93 is a provision drafted with an eye on an authoritarian past and which aims to *preclude* rights limitation in states of exception or emergency. That would be in some tension with introducing TJ principles from international law to be balanced against constitutionally protected rights, now conceived as principles. For the introduction permits balancing in order that the state may respond to another kind of exception, that created by the amendments. It is then significant that when amendments were introduced that made up the 'Framework for Peace' in 2012, they were termed 'Transitory' Articles that created 'exceptional transitional justice mechanisms'. This terminology presupposes a dichotomy of norm and

[21] Bernal-Pulido (n. 18), 1151.
[22] Ibid., 1142–3.
[23] For an account of the Court's international law jurisprudence, see Carlos Arévalo & Julián Huertas, 'Not so Moderate: The Relationship between the Colombian Legal System and International Law', this volume.

exception where the permanent constitution represents the normal situation while TJ is the exceptional, time-limited situation.

One way of understanding the problem here is in terms of the constitutional theory of the fascist German thinker Carl Schmitt, who argued that the liberal idea of a constitution is intrinsically one of a permanent constitution the norms of which govern comprehensively the decisions of public institutions, including the legislature. Schmitt pointed out that exceptions will constantly arise that cannot be so governed. Nevertheless, a liberal constitution will attempt to normalize any exception by painting a veneer of legality over the exercise of political power that attempts to respond to the exception even when that exercise contravenes existing positive law. That legality is no more than a veneer will be exposed by the 'dilatory compromises' that liberal constitutionalists have to make in to keep the constitutional machine running. Tensions or even contradictions will inevitably result which may seem resolvable only by a quintessentially political decision about the identity of the political community, and thus not fit for judicial resolution. Liberal constitutionalists, including judges of this disposition, will try to postpone that kind of decision for as long as possible. But eventually the moment will come when the political sovereign—the true guardian of the constitution—will reveal himself by making the existential decision that establishes the identity of the political community.[24]

There is something to Schmitt's critique of liberal constitutionalism, which accounts for why even those who are not drawn to his apocalyptical understanding of the 'political'[25] still take on board the logic of his polemic against liberal constitutionalism. However, this logic cannot be simply assimilated into a liberal constitutionalist framework.

Schmitt is quite often misinterpreted as arguing only that liberal constitutionalism cannot be maintained if it contents itself with a formal theory of the constitution, one that says, for example, that if the constitution stipulates the formal requirements for amending it, any amendment is valid as long as it meets those requirements. That would be an absurd theory of constitutionalism, Schmitt points out. In England where there is parliamentary supremacy it would have the result that a formally valid statute that regulated the dentistry profession must be deemed as constitutionally valid as a formally valid statute that abolished democracy.[26] The lesson that liberal constitutionalists then take from Schmitt is that constitutionalism should be substantive, not formal.[27]

[24] Carl Schmitt, *Political Theology: Four Chapters on the Concept of Sovereignty* (Chicago: University of Chicago Press, 2005). Carl Schmitt, *Constitutional Theory*, ed. and trans. Jeffrey Seitzer (Durham: Duke University Press, 2008), 84–8. See also Schmitt's essays in Lars Vinx (ed.), *The Guardian of the Constitution: Hans Kelsen and Carl Schmitt on the Limits of Constitutional Law* (Cambridge: Cambridge University Press, 2015).

[25] Carl Schmitt, *The Concept of the Political*, trans. George Schwab (Chicago: University of Chicago Press, 1996).

[26] Schmitt, *Constitutional Theory* (n. 24), 71–2.

[27] See the leading treatment of this topic, Yaniv Roznai, *Unconstitutional Constitutional Amendments: The Limits of Amendment* Powers (Oxford: Oxford University Press, 2017), 75, in which the claim is made that after the war Gustav Radbruch revived Schmitt's idea of legality, as elaborated in Schmitt's 1932 *Legality and Legitimacy*, trans. Jeffrey Seitzer (Durham: Duke University Press, 2004). But as Schmitt's introduction makes clear, the entire book is a polemic against liberal constitutionalism and the rule of law written to clear the way for the authoritarian conservative politicians to whom he was close to seize power by legal means and then use that power to eliminate parliamentary democracy. That Hitler and the Nazis bested his

And it would seem that the lesson has been learned by the Colombian Court since it relied on Schmitt in formulating its doctrine of unconstitutional constitutional amendment.[28]

But the problem for the Court's TJ jurisprudence is that it aims to reach the conclusion that the seven amendments enacted between 2012 and 2017 are valid, while they are are substantively invalid by the terms of its past Schmittean replacement doctrine. For while the Court did declare parts of the amendments unconstitutional, it for the most part upheld their content, even resorting on occasion to a claim that replacement is a matter of degree, that is, that a little bit of substance abuse does not count. In effect, it thus permitted the installation of a new mini-constitution within the permanent constitution. In other words, the Court had to amend the constitution substantively in order to find the amendments valid, which meant that it could be accused of arrogating to itself the constituent power formally allocated by the constitution to a constituent assembly and to other processes.

The main point at stake here does not, however, depend on the claim that the amendments can be demonstrated to have been substantively invalid. Rather, it is that Schmitt would have thought that such questions are beside the point, which is not that liberal constitutionalism must learn to be substantive, but that constitutionalism cannot be both substantive and liberal. In his view, in the Colombian constitutional context the president would be the only candidate for guardian of the constitution since he is elected by the whole people and, as Article 189 says, 'symbolizes the national unity.' He thus stands above the partisan clashes of party-political conflicts and so was best placed to bring an end to the conflict with FARC. But that the person who held that office at the time was not in fact able to articulate an authentic vision of the identity of the Colombian people is revealed by the rejection in a plebiscite in 2016 of the 'Final Agreement' reached between FARC and the government and by the messy 'fast track' process that ensued in which the government resorted to Congress to get the amendment approved, a resort which the Court declared constitutional.[29]

On this view, a constitutional court is by definition faced with a burden of legitimacy that it cannot discharge because it is required to make political decisions. That fact can largely be ignored as long as the political conflicts the court resolves do not rise to a degree of intensity where it becomes clear that the identity of the political community is at stake. But as the conflicts do get closer to that level, so the impossibility

political friends in no way diminishes Schmitt's role in preparing the way for the destruction of the Weimar, rule of law state. In contrast, Radbruch's post-war writings were written as part of a revival of liberal jurisprudence against the kind of authoritarian legality that Schmitt championed. For illuminating discussion of Roznai, see Vicki C. Jackson, '"Constituent Power" or Degrees of Legitimacy?' (2018) 12 ICL Journal 319, https://www.degruyter.com/view/j/icl.2018.12.issue-3/issue-files/icl.2018.12.issue-3.xml.

[28] See Joel Colón-Rios, 'Carl Schmitt and Constituent Power in Latin American Courts: The Cases of Venezuela and Colombia', Victoria University of Wellington Legal Research Papers, Paper No. 24/2012, 23, note 79, http://ssrn.com/abstract=1621930.

[29] See Vincente Benítez-R, *Judicial Review of Constitutional Amendments in Times of Peace: The Colombian Case*, International Association of Constitutional Law Blog (26 April 2017), https://blog-iacl-aidc.org/test-3/2018/5/26/analysis-judicial-review-of-constitutional-amendments-in-times-of-peace-the-colombian-case (suggesting that the Constitutional Court altered its judicial review approach in cases that involved the Colombian peace process (shifting from a strict analysis to a soft scrutiny 'in times of peace').

of discharging that burden becomes more apparent, until the point where it becomes clear, as the *Daily Mail* claimed in the United Kingdom during the Brexit crisis, that the judges are the 'Enemies of the People'.[30]

It is thus also the case on this view that the Colombian Constitutional Court passed that level long ago. For it would be a mistake to date that event to the time it intervened to find the TJ process by and large constitutionally valid. Rather, the event took place as soon as it came up with its doctrine of unconstitutional constitutional amendment. Such a doctrine is a barely disguised judicial power grab and the power grabbed, in Schmitt's view, is the constituent power that can belong only to the people.

Here Schmitt could point to the deep irony of the process so far. Recall that the implicit, explicit TJ provision was built on principles of international law with their basis being an understanding of the constitution as monist in terms of Article 93. We noted that this provision is drafted with an eye on an authoritarian past and aims to preclude rights limitation in states of exception or emergency. Schmitt, of course, developed his argument based on the logic of norm and exception within an analysis of emergency powers both in history and in the Weimar Republic. So it would be highly interesting to him that an argument designed to show that it is the sovereign's task to make the friend/enemy distinction central to his own idea of how a political community is built, is deployed to bridge the gap between bitter enemies.[31]

It may seem that liberal Schmitteans, as we will refer to liberal constitutionalists who think that liberalism can absorb the logic of Schmitt's critique of liberal constitutionalism, can respond as follows. The Colombian situation shows precisely why the logic can be absorbed. Schmitt is in fact refuted by the trajectory of the Court's substantive jurisprudence. That the Court has progressively ratcheted up its substantive, political decision making, even deciding against its own prior substantive jurisprudence, and in the face of its own doctrine of precedent, shows that a constitutional court not only can successfully wield constituent power, but also can do so legitimately.

If that response were right, there would no reason for anxiety on the part of the Court when it comes to further interventions in the TJ process. But clearly there is such anxiety. Moreover, Schmitt would think his position vindicated by the facts of the Colombian situation. It is not only the Court that faces a legitimacy problem with the TJ process. The failed plebiscite also testifies to the widespread opposition to bringing a deeply unpopular group into the political community at the cost of amnesty for many of them as well as having to endure the spectacle of both having guerillas turned narco-criminals holding high political office and state officials who committed crimes keeping their jobs. The difficulties already encountered as well as those that

[30] James Slack, 'Enemies of the People: Fury Over 'Out of Touch' Judges who have 'Declared War on Democracy' by Defying 17.4m Brexit Voters and Who Could Trigger Constitutional Crisis', *Daily Mail* (3 November 2016,), https://www.dailymail.co.uk/news/article-3903436/Enemies-people-Fury-touch-judges-defied-17-4m-Brexit-voters-trigger-constitutional-crisis.html [https://perma.cc/MS66-Q28J.

[31] We understand that the Court relied in this regard on the work of Alfred Verdross, the Austrian international lawyer. But that only serves to compound the irony, as Verdross was a member of Kelsen's school of legal positivism. He did, we should note, try to take the Pure Theory of law in a natural law direction but that still leaves the irony intact. See Arévalo & Huertas (n. 23). On Verdross, see David Dyzenhaus, 'A Monistic Approach to the Internationalization of Constitutional Law' in Iulia Motoc, Paulo Pinto de Albuquerque & Krzysztof Wojtyczek (eds), *New Developments in Constitutional Law: Essays in Honour of Andràs Sajó* (The Hague: Eleven International Publishing, 2018), 97.

lie ahead are evidence of the fact that no decision has yet been taken that is capable of making the distinction between friend and enemy essential to establishing the identity of the Colombian political community. It is only under conditions of fractured political community that it may appear for a limited period that a constitutional court is the guardian of the constitution. To the extent it is successful, that will be at the cost of the very liberal constitutional principles of which the Court is supposed to be the guardian. One might say that such a court is doomed to fiddle with principle as the heavens fall.

Schmitt's line of thought cannot then be countered by constructing a liberal mirror image of Schmittean constitutionalism which curiously is the one he attributed to liberalism, with the addition of substance. For he himself presupposed an idea of the substantive constitution as a permanent constitution, the norms of which govern comprehensively the decisions of public institutions, including the legislature. But he thought that such a constitution can come into being only following a successful sovereign decision that establishes the political identity of a substantively homogeneous people. Such a decision is the sole secure basis for legitimacy and, on his account, legitimacy is an all or nothing property, one which does not admit of degrees. Moreover, it can only be enjoyed as long it is possible for the norm-enforcing and norm-applying institutions of the legal order to carry out their role without having to engage in controversial exercises of interpretation.

Hence, Schmitt's model of a well-functioning legal order is precisely the one associated with naïve versions of legal positivism that see law as having a predetermined factual content that judges and other legal officials can simply apply and enforce. It is not, however, so naïve if one supposes, as he did, that a society which has a thoroughly homogenous national culture, secured primarily by social institutions like the church, will relegate the legal order to the task of reinforcing a thoroughly pervasive, dominant political and social ideology, with the result that judges and other legal officials can always operate within the letter of the law. While Schmitt is notorious for his polemics against liberal formalism, exemplified in Kelsen's Pure Theory of law, he is a fan of what we can think of as substantive formalism, a formalism that ensures that the legal order faithfully reproduces the values of the dominant ideology.[32]

Schmitt's constitutional theory thus comes to the following conclusion about liberalism. Since liberalism is in principle opposed to his kind of politics of authenticity, it may strive for substance but never have it, with the tensions and contradictions in its attempt illustrated by the shifts and twists in the Colombian Constitutional Court's TJ jurisprudence. This problem is then illustrated by that jurisprudence.

But, to make things worse, it is the manifestation of an even deeper problem in the assumptions about justice in much of mainstream TJ theory.[33] First, many TJ theorists assume that transitions present problems of justice that are different in kind from those presented by stable societies. Secondly, they assume that transitions are radically discontinuous both with the bad past from which the transitional regime had to escape

[32] There is complete continuity in Schmitt's thoughts on this issue, from his very first work of 1912 which is organized around the theme of how to find a sociological solution to the problem of indeterminacy in law—*Gesetz und Urteil: Eine Untersuchung zum Problem der Rechtspraxis* (C. H. Beck: Munich. 1969).

[33] Here we rely on Dyzenhaus, '*Leviathan* as a Theory of Transitional Justice' (n. 12), 182–3.

and with the liberal democratic future into which it is hoped the society will emerge. These two assumptions require that we think of transitional regimes as exceptions to our ordinary theory of justice, the one appropriate for stable liberal democracies.

In other words, we take most TJ theories to be of the following type. They assume that the problem in a standard TJ process is to escape from the legacy of T_1 (the bad regime) by addressing it in T_2 (the transitional regime) in order to get to T_3 (stable, liberal democracy). Since in T_2 one is dealing with the legacy of illiberalism, the theory of justice appropriate for T_3 does not suffice. For example, even when officials according to the positive law of T_1 clearly were guilty of crimes but enjoyed impunity for political reasons, it might be that the circumstances of T_2 make it imprudent to punish them. For it is a characteristic of many transitional regimes that those who held power during T_1 decided that their growing weakness required entering T_2 but retain enough power to bring the transition to a crashing halt if they feel too threatened. Similarly, those who led the struggle against oppression and those who took up arms in that struggle will participate in a TJ process only on condition that they receive amnesty for the human rights abuses in which they were involved.[34]

Now, as already indicated, the Colombian TJ process is not standard in that T_1 and T_3 are assumed not to differ when it comes to the content of the standards of justice, but only in respect of the makeup of the political community in that T_3 will include members of FARC within the community. But that, as we have seen, makes life even more difficult because the TJ process is condemned by already existing constitutional commitments, the commitments of an existing permanent constitution. No one can deny this difficulty, given that the Constitutional Court had to craft a new set of constitutional doctrines to deal with it.

But it may seem that little morally speaking should turn on whether a TJ process is defective by the standards of the existing constitution at T_1 or by the standards of the constitution that will come into force at T_3. The main issue, that is, is that a TJ process is defective from the standpoint of liberal political morality. T_2 is a moment of moral exception—a kind of moral state of emergency—whether or not it is deemed such by the constitution that happens to be in place at T_1. It will then seem to follow that a permanent constitution that exists at T_1 and which incorporates such standards will make the dilemma of TJ jurisprudentially though not morally harder to deal with.

But that impression is misleading. We see at play here the same Schmittean logic of norm and exception that plays out in the Constitutional Court's jurisprudence. In fact, the problems of a moral theory that assumes that there are standards of morality that apply unless there is some state of exception that requires relaxing or sacrificing them are refracted in that jurisprudence. Put differently, the idea of a permanent constitution is problematic because it presupposes that there is such a thing as a permanent morality in the sense of a set of moral standards that provide the criteria for all or nothing judgments about legitimacy.

It is that presupposition that makes liberal constitutionalism vulnerable to the criticism that exceptional situations will raise challenges to its morality that can be answered only by an illiberal decision. Notice that the claim here need not be that the

[34] Murphy (n. 1) is an exception.

TJ process in Colombia is doomed to failure. It is only that if the process turns out to be successful, it will be because it was a process of injustice, one which constituted a community in which perpetrators of human rights abuses on both sides of the conflict are put beyond the reach of some of the most important norms of justice. Since in the nature of such conflicts the majority of such abuses would have been committed by agents of the state, whether by members of the armed forces or other state institutions, or by paramilitary groups acting as surrogates for the state, the result will be that state criminality will be declared to be constitutional. We now turn to the South African TJ process to see what lessons it might offer.

III. The South African 'Transitional' Constitution

South Africans generally look towards the 1994 transition as the dawn of a radically new normative order. Even though citizens awoke on 27 April 1994—the date on which the interim constitution came into force—in exactly the same material circumstances they had found themselves in the year before, the way they could understand themselves, and their society, had changed. This was equally the case for the courts and the legal system as a whole. The South African Constitution is perceived and revered in South African society as a sharp and decisive break with the past. This seems only natural: the arrival of constitutionalism was a remarkable feat for a society that was on the brink of violent civil war. As a former justice of the German Constitutional Court, Dieter Grimm, explained, constitutionalism is an achievement. It is an achievement because the constitution it envisages is both democratic and committed to the rule of law.[35]

The establishment of a democratic society was a new beginning in every sense of the word, of course. But the commitment to the rule of law did not originate in 1994, rather, it was *restored*. This is why Albie Sachs referred to the transition to constitutionalism as the '*realignment* of the law with justice'.[36] There had been a jural community during the apartheid era, albeit a deeply flawed one. The new constitution did not arise in a legal void. Rather, it revived a battered, bruised, and compromised principle of legality and established it firmly within a broader system of constitutional supremacy rooted in 'democratic values, social justice, and fundamental human rights'.[37]

The South African Constitutional Court has subsequently reaffirmed[38] that there 'always' have been common law principles of the rule of law and requirements of natural justice in the South African legal system. These principles had, as the Court said, been 'eroded and excluded' during apartheid, and as Arthur Chaskalson, the first President of the Court, was to acknowledge in a lecture in 2003, the apartheid legal system had threatened the very legitimacy of the Court and of law itself.[39] It is

[35] See David Dyzenhaus, 'Constitutionalism in an Old Key: Legality and Constituent Power,' (2012) 1 Global Constitutionalism 229, 234.

[36] Albie Sachs, *The Strange Alchemy of Life and Law* (Oxford: Oxford University Press, 2009).

[37] Constitution of the Republic of South Africa, 1996, Preamble.

[38] *The Pharmaceutical Manufacturers Association of South Africa and Another: In re Ex Parte President of the Republic of South Africa and Others*, 2000 (2) SA 674 (CC), paras 35–7.

[39] *AZAPO* (n. 13), para. 1. Arthur Chaskalson, 'From Wickedness to Equality: The Transformation of South African Law' (2003) 1 International Journal of Constitutional Law 590.

precisely for this reason that it is remarkable and important that the story of the 1994 transition be understood as a story of constitutional resilience.

This claim of constitutional continuity should not be overstated: the South African transition represented a 'stark and dramatic' break from the past.[40] The damage wreaked by the apartheid regime was immense: the past had been marred by wicked law.[41] Despite this, and in large part due to Arthur Chaskalson's careful steering of the Court's jurisprudence in its first decade, the new constitutional order is one that is rooted in an abiding respect for the rule of law.[42] We might recognize here faith in the role that law can play in a process of change and reconstruction. But this trust in and hope for law did not come out of nowhere. The history of resistance to apartheid is one in which the idea of law itself was often not the target of resistance, but its tool; and Chaskalson earned his place as President because of his prominence as a human rights lawyer in the legal struggle against apartheid, that is, as one of the lawyers who used the resources that law itself offered in the struggle against legalized oppression.[43] Law was sword and shield in apartheid South Africa: sword because the regime used legal institutions to construct and administer apartheid, shield because those very institutions offered tools for legal contestation and resistance.[44]

Thus, in another sense, the normative world in which South Africans found themselves in on 27 April 1994 was not altogether discontinuous with the world of the day before. So much was implied by the text of the interim constitution,[45] which in an epilogue entitled 'National Unity and Reconciliation' claimed the constitution as:

> a historic bridge between the past of a deeply divided society characterised by strife, conflict, untold suffering and injustice, and a future founded on the recognition of human rights, democracy and peaceful co-existence and development opportunities for all South Africans, irrespective of colour, race, class, belief or sex.
>
> The pursuit of national unity, the well-being of all South African citizens and peace require reconciliation between the people of South Africa and the reconstruction of society. The adoption of this Constitution lays the secure foundation for the people of South Africa to transcend the divisions and strife of the past, which generated gross violations of human rights, the transgression of humanitarian principles in violent conflicts and a legacy of hatred, fear, guilt and revenge.
>
> These can now be addressed on the basis that there is a need for understanding but not for vengeance, a need for reparation but not for retaliation, a need for ubuntu

[40] *Pharmaceutical Manufacturers* (n. 38), para. 40.

[41] Chaskalson, (n. 39).

[42] For a full account, see Stephan Ellman, *And Justice for All: Arthur Chaskalson and the Struggle for Equality in South Africa* (Montgomery: New South Books, 2020).

[43] See also former Deputy Chief Justice Dikgang Moseneke's reflection on Nelson Mandela's and Bram Fischer's Apartheid-era commitment to the rule of law, 'The Fourth Bram Fischer Memorial Lecture–Transformative Constitutionalism' (2002) 18 South African Journal on Human Rights 313. Moseneke was imprisoned from ages 15 to 25 on Robben Island because of his participation in the struggle against apartheid.

[44] Jens Meierhenrich, *The Legacies of Law: Long-Run Consequences of Legal Development in South Africa, 1652-2000* (New York: Cambridge University Press, 2008), 129–30.

[45] Constitution of the Republic of South Africa Act 200 of 1993.

> but not for victimisation. In order to advance such reconciliation and reconstruction, amnesty shall be granted in respect of acts, omissions and offences associated with political objectives and committed in the course of the conflicts of the past. To this end, Parliament under this Constitution shall adopt a law determining a firm cut-off date, which shall be a date after 8 October 1990 and before 6 December 1993, and providing for the mechanisms, criteria and procedures, including tribunals, if any, through which such amnesty shall be dealt with at any time after the law has been passed. With this Constitution and these commitments, we, the people of South Africa, open a new chapter in the history of our country.[46]

It continued:

> In order to advance such reconciliation and reconstruction, amnesty shall be granted in respect of acts, omissions and offences associated with political objectives and committed in the course of the conflicts of the past. To this end, Parliament under this Constitution shall adopt a law determining a firm cut-off date, which shall be a date after 8 October 1990 and before 6 December 1993, and providing for the mechanisms, criteria and procedures, including tribunals, if any, through which such amnesty shall be dealt with at any time after the law has been passed.

The interim constitution thus incorporated an explicit TJ provision of the sort thought necessary to make TJ measures constitutionally legitimate. In addition, the interim constitution contained an explicit, implicit TJ provision in Section 33 which provided that its entrenched rights 'may be limited by a law of general application, provided that such limitation shall be permissible only to the extent that it is ... reasonable; and ... justifiable in an open and democratic society based on freedom and equality; and shall not negate the essential content of the right in question ...'[47]

Pursuant to these constitutional provisions, the Promotion of National Unity and Reconciliation Act[48] which established the TRC was assented to on 19 July 1995. Negotiations about the exact form that the TRC would take had been fierce. It was clear that, amongst other things, the TRC had to function 'within a sound legal framework in a clear constitutional setting'; that the amnesty process proceeded on an 'individualized basis'; and that hearings be conducted 'in the open'.[49] The preamble of the Reconciliation Act located its purpose clearly within the paradigm of the constitutional bridge between the divided society of the past and a future that would be characterized by a recognition of human rights, peaceful co-existence, and democracy. It expressly noted that it was intended to provide for 'understanding but not vengeance,

[46] Schedule on National Unity and Reconciliation. Section 232 (4) of the constitution specifically provided that the status of the epilogue had to be considered on equal footing with the text and all other provisions of the constitution.

[47] The final Constitution of South Africa was adopted in 1996 and provided that: 'Notwithstanding the other provisions of the new Constitution and despite the repeal of the previous Constitution, all the provisions relating to amnesty contained in the previous Constitution under the heading "National Unity and Reconciliation" are deemed to be part of the new Constitution for the purposes of the Promotion of National Unity and Reconciliation Act.'

[48] Act 34 of 1995.

[49] Sachs (n. 36), 70–2.

reparation but not retaliation'. To this end, it identified a need to uncover the truth about past events, as well as the motivations for and circumstances of gross human rights violations.

The Act was to provide for:

> [T]he investigation and the establishment of as complete a picture as possible of the nature, causes and extent of gross violations of human rights committed during the period from 1 March 1960 to the cut-off date contemplated in the Constitution, within or outside the Republic, emanating from the conflicts of the past, and the fate or whereabouts of the victims of such violations; the granting of amnesty to persons who make full disclosure of the relevant facts relating to acts associated with a political objective committed in the course of the conflicts of the past during said period; affording victims an opportunity to relate the violations they suffered; the taking of measures aimed at the granting of reparation to, and the rehabilitation and restoration of the human and civil dignity of, victims of violations of human rights; reporting to the Nation about such violations and victims, the making of recommendations aimed at the prevention of the commission of gross violations of human rights.

The Act established the TRC, which consisted of three committees: the Committee on Human Rights Violations, the Committee on Amnesty, and the Committee on Reparation and Rehabilitation.[50]

The Committee on Amnesty was tasked with receiving, reviewing, and issuing decisions with regard to amnesty applications.[51] Commissioners were to be appointed by the President in consultation with his cabinet. Only 'impartial persons' who did not have high political office were eligible for appointment,[52] and on the five-person amnesty committees, one member had to be a judge.[53]

The Commission completed its work and handed its report over to President Nelson Mandela on 29 October 1998. The report has been described as a testament to the fact that TJ is a 'fragile good, dependent on an uneasy mixture of painful hindsight and patient hope'.[54] This was perhaps nowhere more true than in the context of amnesty.

The amnesty process was geared towards flexibility and fairness. The Committee could investigate matters at its discretion and could return applications with instructions to amend or to supply further information.[55] If it found that there was no need to afford a further opportunity for additional submissions, and it was satisfied that the application did not relate to an act that qualified for amnesty, the Committee could refuse the application.[56] The Committee could also grant amnesty without a hearing if it was satisfied: (1) that all the requirements had been met; (2) that there was no

[50] Section 3 (3).

[51] Section 19.

[52] Section 7.

[53] Section 17(3).

[54] Institute for Justice and Reconciliation, 'Truth Commissions and Transitional Justice: A Select Bibliography on the South African Truth and Reconciliation Commission Debate' (2001) 16 Journal of Law and Religion 69, 69.

[55] Section 19(1).

[56] Section 19(3)(a).

need for a hearing; and (3) that the act, omission, or offence in question was not a gross violation of human rights.[57] In all other cases, a hearing was required.[58] As a rule, all hearings had to be open to the public, although there was an application procedure to request that a hearing be held behind closed doors.[59] Section 11 of the Act required that victims had to treated with compassion and respect for their dignity, and this would form the main consideration of the Committee in deciding upon hearing formats and related procedural matters.

An application for amnesty would be granted if: (1) the application complied with the requirements set out in the Act; (2) the act, omission, or offence to which the application related was an act associated with a political objective and was committed in the course of the conflicts of the past; and (3) if the application had disclosed all relevant facts.[60] Section 20(2) and 20(3) of the Act clearly set the relevant criteria for deciding whether an act was associated with a political objective as well as the criteria on which such a decision had to be based. For reasons that will become apparent later, we want to highlight the last of the seven conditions that attached to Section 20(3) which related to 'political objective': (f) 'the relationship between the act, omission or offence and the political objective pursued, and in particular the directness and proximity of the relationship and the proportionality of the act, omission or offence to the objective pursued'.[61] The effects of amnesty were set out in Section 20(7):

> (a) No person who has been granted amnesty in respect of an act, omission or offence shall be criminally or civilly liable in respect of such an act, omission or offence

[57] Section 19(3)(b).
[58] Section 19(4).
[59] Section 33.
[60] Section 20(1).
[61] Section 20(3): 'Whether a particular act, omission or offence contemplated in subsection (2) is an act associated with a political objective, shall be decided with reference to the following criteria:

(a) The motive of the person who committed the act, omission or offence;
(b) the context in which the act, omission or offence took place, and in particular whether the act, omission or offence was committed in the course of or as part of a political uprising, disturbance or event, or in reaction thereto;
(c) the legal and factual nature of the act, omission or offence, including the gravity of the act, omission or offence;
(d) the object or objective of the act, omission or offence, and in particular whether the act, omission or offence was primarily directed at a political opponent or State property or personnel or against private property or individuals;
(e) whether the act, omission or offence was committed in the execution of an order of, or on behalf of, or with the approval of, the organisation, institution, liberation movement or body of which the person who committed the act was a member, an agent or a supporter; and
(f) the relationship between the act, omission or offence and the political objective pursued, and in particular the directness and proximity of the relationship and the proportionality of the act, omission or offence to the objective pursued, but does not include any act, omission or offence committed by any person referred to in subsection (2) who acted-
    (i) for personal gain: Provided that an act, omission or offence by any person who acted and received money or anything of value as an informer of the State or a former state, political organisation or liberation movement, shall not be excluded only on the grounds of that person having received money or anything of value for his or her information; or
    (ii) out of personal malice, ill-will or spite, directed against the victim of the acts committed.'

and no body or organization of the State shall be liable, and no person shall be vicariously liable, for any such act, omission or offence.

The Constitutional Court has decided three matters arising out of the Reconciliation Act, the first a challenge to the Act itself, the other two questions about its scope. We focus here on the first, the *AZAPO* decision.

The applicants were the relatives of political activists and opponents of apartheid (amongst others, Steve Biko who died of assaults while in police custody), and the political organization AZAPO. They instituted the action on their own behalf, but also on behalf of the broader public interest.[62] Their application challenged the constitutionality of the Reconciliation Act as a whole. In the alternative, they challenged the constitutionality of the parts of the Act dealing with amnesty.

Before the Constitutional Court, the applicants focused on the constitutional right of access to courts, arguing that the consequence of amnesty was unconstitutional because it deprived citizens of the right to insist that wrongdoers be properly prosecuted and punished.[63] According to the applicants, such a right was protected in Section 22 of the constitution,[64] which provided that: '[e]very person shall have the right to have justiciable disputes settled by a court of law or, where appropriate, another independent and impartial forum'. In the alternative, the applicants argued that if the consequences of Section 20(7) of the Reconciliation Act were constitutional, such constitutionality would only extend to criminal liability. Wrongdoers, even if granted amnesty from state prosecution under the Act, should still remain civilly (delictually) liable.[65] Finally, it was also argued that even if wrongdoers could not be held criminally or civilly liable, the state should still be held vicariously liable for damages and losses caused by agents acting on its behalf.[66]

The Court found against the applicants on all three arguments. It acknowledged that the Reconciliation Act infringed on the right of access to courts but noted that the constitution does allow for the limitation of rights in certain circumstances. Moreover, in this case, the limitation of the right in question flowed out of another constitutional provision.[67] Therefore, the limitation of the right of access to courts was constitutionally valid as a means of achieving the legitimate purpose of 'a constructive transition towards a democratic order'.[68] In its reasoning, the Court attached much significance to the instrumental value of amnesty as a way of bringing the truth about the past to light. This also convinced the Court to reject the applicant's second argument: if civil

[62] Section 7(1)(a) and (b)(iv) of the interim constitution (Constitution of the Republic of South Africa Act 200 of 1993) and Section 38(d) of the final constitution of the Republic of South Africa allows anyone acting in the public interest to approach a competent court with an allegation that a right in the Bill of Rights has been infringed or threatened, and the court to then grant appropriate relief.

[63] *AZAPO* (n. 13), para. 8.

[64] The applicants were relying on Section 22 of the interim constitution (Constitution of the Republic of South Africa Act 200 of 1996). The equivalent provision in the final constitution is in Section 34, providing that: 'everyone has the right to have any dispute that can be resolved by the application of law decided in a fair public hearing before a court or, where appropriate, another independent and impartial tribunal or forum'.

[65] *AZAPO* (n. 13), para. 33.

[66] Ibid., para. 39.

[67] Ibid., para. 14.

[68] Ibid., para. 32.

liability was to be allowed, the objective of truth-telling would still not be served.[69] The Court therefore concluded that amnesty had to cover civil liability as well.

The final issue was the civil liability of the state for the actions of its agents. In this case, the objective of truth-telling did not justify amnesty: perpetrators would still be incentivized to come forward with the truth even if the state were to be held vicariously liable for harm caused. However, the majority of the Court found that the state did not have the resources to compensate for all the harms of the past, and that the legislature had legitimately used its discretion in prioritizing rebuilding and reconstruction over compensation for the past.[70] In a concurring opinion, Justice Didcott disagreed with this reasoning, but concluded with the majority that amnesty should cover state liability, because '[o]nce the truth about the iniquities of the past has been established and made known, the book should be closed on them so that the catharsis thus engendered may divert the energies of the nation from a preoccupation with anguish and rancour to a future directed towards the goal which . . . the Constitution . . . [has] set.'[71]

The main judgment, written by Ismail Mahomed, Deputy President of the Court, contains several passages which are worth quoting in full in support of our argument. First, there is his elaboration of the metaphor of the constitution as a bridge in the context of his justification of the amnesty process:

> The alternative to the grant of immunity from criminal prosecution of offenders is to keep intact the abstract right to such a prosecution for particular persons without the evidence to sustain the prosecution successfully, to continue to keep the dependents of such victims in many cases substantially ignorant about what precisely happened to their loved ones, to leave their yearning for the truth effectively unassuaged, to perpetuate their legitimate sense of resentment and grief and correspondingly to allow the culprits of such deeds to remain perhaps physically free but inhibited in their capacity to become active, full and creative members of the new order by a menacing combination of confused fear, guilt, uncertainty and sometimes even trepidation. Both the victims and the culprits who walk on the 'historic bridge' described by the epilogue will hobble more than walk to the future with heavy and dragged steps delaying and impeding a rapid and enthusiastic transition to the new society at the end of the bridge, which is the vision which informs the epilogue.[72]
>
> Even more crucially, but for a mechanism providing for amnesty, the 'historic bridge' itself might never have been erected. For a successfully negotiated transition, the terms of the transition required not only the agreement of those victimized by abuse but also those threatened by the transition to a 'democratic society based on freedom and equality.' If the Constitution kept alive the prospect of continuous retaliation and revenge, the agreement of those threatened by its implementation might never have been forthcoming, and if it had, the bridge itself would have remained wobbly and insecure, threatened by fear from some and anger from others. It was for this reason that those who negotiated the Constitution made a deliberate choice,

[69] Ibid., paras. 34–6.
[70] Ibid., paras. 43–5.
[71] Ibid., para. 59.
[72] Ibid., para. 18.

preferring understanding over vengeance, reparation over retaliation, ubuntu over victimisation.[73]

Secondly, there is his description of the 'result':

> at all levels, ... a difficult, sensitive, perhaps even agonizing, balancing act between the need for justice to victims of past abuse and the need for reconciliation and rapid transition to a new future, between encouragement to wrongdoers to help in discovery of truth and the need for reparations for the victims of that truth, between a correction of the old and a creation of the new. It is an exercise of immense difficulty interacting a vast network of political, emotional, ethical and logistical considerations. It is an act calling for judgment falling substantially within the domain of those entrusted with lawmaking in the era preceding and during the transition period. The results may well often be imperfect and the pursuit of the Act might inherently support the message of Kant that out of the crooked timber of humanity no straight thing was ever made. There can be a legitimate debate about the methods and mechanisms chosen by the lawmaker to give effect to the difficult duty entrusted upon it in terms of the epilogue. We are not concerned with that debate or the wisdom of its choice of mechanisms but only with its constitutionality, That, for us, is the only relevant standard.[74]

Finally, there is his response to the question of the bearing South Africa's international law obligations had on the amnesty provisions. First, Mahomed found that, under the interim constitution Section 231(3), an act of legislation contrary to South Africa's international obligations would override those obligations. But, second, he found that in any case the amnesty provisions were not inconsistent with the obligation adduced in argument—the Geneva Conventions of 1949 and its associated Protocols—which required that there be 'effective penal sanctions' for the kinds of crimes covered by the provisions. For he found that in the international literature and in the Conventions themselves there was a distinction between, on the one hand, a conflict between states, and, on the other, a conflict within a state between the state and dissident forces and that in respect of the latter the need for amnesty was recognized.[75] He said of the latter:

> The erstwhile adversaries of such a conflict inhabit the same sovereign territory. They have to live with each other and work with each other and the state concerned is best equipped to determine what measures may be most conducive for the facilitation of such reconciliation and reconstruction. That is a difficult exercise which the nation within such a state has to perform by having regard to its own peculiar history, its complexities, even its contradictions and its emotional and institutional traditions. What role punishment should play in respect of erstwhile acts of criminality in such a situation is part of the complexity.[76]

[73] Ibid., para. 19,
[74] Ibid., para. 21.
[75] Ibid., para. 30.
[76] Ibid.

He thus concluded that the provisions could not be said to be a breach of South Africa's international law obligations:

> The amnesty contemplated is not a blanket amnesty against criminal prosecution for all and sundry, granted automatically as a uniform act of compulsory statutory amnesia. It is specifically authorised for the purposes of effecting a constructive transition towards a democratic order. It is available only where there is a full disclosure of all facts to the Amnesty Committee and where it is clear that the particular transgression was perpetrated during the prescribed period and with a political objective committed in the course of the conflicts of the past. That objective has to be evaluated having regard to the careful criteria listed in section 20(3) of the Act, including the very important relationship which the act perpetrated bears in proportion to the object pursued.[77]

In making these observations, Mahomed was drawing attention to the rule of law like features of the operation of the Amnesty Committee, and earlier he stressed the independence of the committee that made these determinations.[78] Justice Didcott, in his judgment on the issue of civil liability, also emphasized this feature when he said that both the Committee on Amnesty and the Committee on Reparation and Rehabilitation appear to be rateable ... as 'independent and impartial tribunals' in respect of the guarantee in Section 22 of the interim constitution of the right '... to have justiciable disputes settled by a court of law or, where appropriate, another independent and impartial forum' ; although, as he immediately pointed out, the matters that would be decided by these committees could not be characterized as the decision of 'justiciable disputes'.[79] He elaborated the point later in his judgment as follows:

> The statute does not, it is true, grant any legally enforceable rights in lieu of those lost by claimants whom the amnesties hit. It nevertheless offers some *quid pro quo* for the loss and establishes the machinery for determining such alternative redress. I cannot see what else it might have achieved immediately once, in the light of the painful choices described by Mahomed DP... and in the exercise of the legislative judgment brought to bear on them, the basic decision had been taken to substitute the indeterminate prospect of reparations for the concrete reality of legal claims wherever those were enjoyed. For nothing more definite, detailed and efficacious could feasibly have been promised at that stage, and with no prior investigations, recommendations and decisions of the very sort for which provision is now made.[80]

In making these observations, both judges were pointing out that while the provisions of the Act derogated from the rule of law requirement in Section 22 of the constitution, the derogation was only a partial one, which could be justified as reasonable in the context for which the explicit TJ provision of the constitution had been crafted.

[77] Ibid, para. 32.
[78] Ibid, para. 20.
[79] Ibid, para. 53.
[80] Ibid., para. 65.

Notice that Section 22—'[e]very person shall have the right to have justiciable disputes settled by a court of law or, where appropriate, another independent and impartial forum'—does little more than restate Dicey's formulation of the rule of law principle that 'every man, whatever his rank or condition, is subject to the ordinary law of the realm and amenable to the jurisdiction of the ordinary tribunals'. In addition, the common law principle of rule of law that had been part of South African law since 'colonial times' remained alive (perhaps more accurately: was revived). Now, common law constitutional principles had been 'subsumed' in the new constitution, where, in so far as they might continue to be relevant to judicial review, they gain force from the constitution[81] where they are enshrined in Section 39.[82] The Constitutional Court has affirmed that 'there can be no difference' between principles of legality under common law and after 1994. What had changed, in the words of Chaskalson, was that the 'legal watershed' of 1994 shifted constitutionalism from the realm of common law to prescripts of a written supreme constitution:[83]

> the principles of common law have [not] ceased to be material in the developments of public law. These well-established principles will continue to inform the content of administrative law and other aspects of private law, and will contribute to their future development. But there has been a fundamental change. Courts no longer have to claim space and push boundaries to find means of controlling public power. That control is vested in them under the Constitution ... Whereas previously constitutional law formed part of and was developed consistently with the common law, the roles have been reversed. The written Constitution articulates and gives effect to the governing principles of constitutional law.[84]

Thus, while the new constitution made it possible for courts to decide on the issues implicated by the Reconciliation Act without having to claim space and push boundaries, it did not fundamentally change the principles upon which such issues were to be decided. We now turn to investigate the implications of this phenomenon.

IV. Bridges and the Rule Of Law

As we pointed out, the metaphor of a 'bridge' to describe a TJ process is profound. There has to be secure ground on both sides if the bridge is to be anchored so that it does not collapse under its own weight, let alone the weight of the traffic across it. In the TJ context, the point we wish to bring out is nicely made by the editors of a collection on TJ that one has to take into account 'the paradox of the probable and the unnecessary':

81 *Pharmaceutical Manufacturers* (n. 38), para. 33.

82 Constitution of the Republic of South Africa, 1996, Section 39(c) ('The Bill of Rights does not deny the existence of any rights or freedoms that are recognized or conferred by common law, customary law or legislation, to the extent that they are consistent with the Bill').

83 *Pharmaceutical Manufacturers* (n. 38), 45.

84 Ibid., para 45.

'The impact of truth and justice policies on a new democracy depends on starting conditions or the initial balance of power; in other words, the more likely the implementation of such policies is because of a favorable balance of forces, the less necessary they are to ensure a process of democratization.' In other words, one might want to qualify somewhat Méndez's claim that the question of TJ is 'How do communities emerge from the rubble and make for themselves a new legal space?' For there has to be something much better than rubble on one side of the bridge. But, as the editors also point out, whatever the effect of such policies on democratization, they form 'crucially important moral and political demands which are, even if imperceptibly, part of a changing climate that places respect for human rights at the forefront within and between national communities.'[85]

The starting condition here is the resource the apartheid legal order offered at T_1– the common law legal order in which there was Westminster-style parliamentary supremacy. One should not infer from the fact that the apartheid legal order was a common law legal order in which Parliament was supreme that it therefore lacked a constitution.

This legal order, and its common law constitutional principles, was the abutment that made it possible for the arch of the interim constitution to stretch to the abutment of the order put in place by the final constitution of 1996. While as suggested above, the architects of apartheid used law as an instrument for building the 'pervasive structural inequality', which Murphy identifies as the first circumstance of TJ, it was the case, as also suggested, that law offered a resource to challenge that inequality.

It was precisely because the legal order had a constitution that law could be used as a resource in the struggle against apartheid, including the struggle against the racist and politically oppressive laws enacted by the supreme parliament. This was the 'unwritten' constitution amounting to the values maintained by judges independent of the executive who ensured that when public officials act in the name of the law, their actions are congruent not only with the letter of the law, but also with principles of reasonableness, equality, and liberty.[86]

Now it was the case that only a minority of judges could be counted upon always to interpret the law so as to maximize its consistency with these principles, and since these judges were mostly in the lower courts, they were often, even usually, overruled by judges higher up the hierarchy. Even more significantly, it was also the case that statutes could be and were used as a blunt tool to override such interpretations and could be and were drafted so as preemptively to preclude such interpretation.

To the extent this happened, official action was put beyond the reach of the law, even its letter, since judges could no longer ensure that officials had a legal warrant for their action. In short, to that extent the state became explicitly lawless. However, to the extent it did not happen, judges were able to maintain what the American legal theorist Lon L. Fuller called 'fidelity to law'.[87] Only as long as that was possible was it

[85] Alexandra Barahona De Brito, Carmen Gonzalez-Enriquez, & Paloma Aguilar (eds), *The Politics of Memory: Transitional Justice in Democratizing Societies* (Oxford: Oxford University Press, 2001), 314.

[86] See David Dyzenhaus, *Hard Cases in Wicked Legal Systems: Pathologies of Legality* (2nd edn, Oxford: Oxford University Press, 2010).

[87] Lon L. Fuller, 'Positivism and Fidelity to Law: A Reply to Professor Hart' (1958) 71 Harvard Law Review 630.

the case that the formal characteristics of the legal order were preserved, that is, a legislature charged with enacting law, officials charged with implementing the law, and an independent judiciary charged with ensuring that the law is what the officials implemented. And that preservation made meaningful, even during the darkest times, the practice of human rights lawyering which Chaskalson championed.

Two tentative conclusions follow. First, there is a necessary connection between the substantive values of the rule of law and the formal characteristics of legal order that impart a degree of intrinsic legitimacy to legal order. Secondly, and following, while the ideology of apartheid was of course thoroughly unjust the legal order in which it was maintained was to some degree legitimate. These two conclusions indicate why the apartheid legal order had a constitution that could not be reduced to apartheid ideology, but which was in fact in some tension, even contradiction, with that ideology. There are, one could say, certain kinds of political substance—Schmittean substance—that the unwritten constitution of a common law legal order resists. One could also say that the apartheid legal order had a permanent constitution, one that could be amended only at the cost of 'denaturing' the legal order. But we prefer to term its constitution 'resilient,' one that was capable of springing back even after being subject to extreme pressure as long as the rulers maintained their commitment to governing within the limits of the law.

Whichever term one uses, it is important to see that the standard TJ context of South Africa has more in common with the non-standard Colombian context than the distinction between transitional and permanent constitutions would lead us to suppose. The human rights violations for which both state officials and those on the other side of the conflict may receive amnesty in T_2 were criminal during T_1, which is one of the factors that creates the uncertainty about authority. But it is precisely at this point that the paradox of the probable and the unnecessary has bite, and here it is useful to understand the legal order at T_1 when the circumstances of transition obtain in an 'apartheid state'.[88]

This term is inspired by the actual apartheid state. But we use it for the moment in a more generic sense to describe a particular kind of legal order, one in which a significant group of legal subjects are relegated to second class status by either legal norms or social norms, or both; they are, that is, subject to pervasive structural inequality. Members of this group who resist their oppression whether by legal or illegal means are subjected to human rights abuses that amount to normalized collective and political wrongdoing, and they retaliate in kind.

It is crucial to the characterization of this state as an apartheid state that these abuses are illegal by the law of the land at T_1. This point can be appreciated by placing the apartheid state on what we can think of as a continuum of legality. This continuum stretches from the rule of law state at one end, as described by Dicey, to, at the other end, the 'dual state', the term coined by the German political scientist and lawyer Ernst Fraenkel to describe the Nazi state.[89] Fraenkel argued that the Nazi state consisted of

[88] We rely here on David Dyzenhaus, 'Dugardian Legal Theory' in Tiyanjana Maluwa, Max du Plessis, & Dire Tladi (eds), *The Pursuit of a Brave New World in International Law: Essays in Honour of John Dugard* (Leiden: Brill Nijhoff, 2017), 3.

[89] See Ernest Fraenkel, *The Dual State: A Contribution to the Theory of Dictatorship* [1941], Jens Meierhenrich, Intro. (Oxford: Oxford University Press, 2017).

two states that existed side by side: the 'normative state', which contained for the most part what remained of the law and institutions of the Weimar legal order, and the prerogative state, which consisted of the apparatus of the Nazi Party wherein the leader's will (his actual will or his will as interpreted by subordinate officials) was the ultimate source of authority. Fraenkel pointed out that the rule of law did not obtain in Nazi Germany because the law of the normative state governed relationships between individuals and between individuals and state institutions only as long as officials in the prerogative state did not find such government inconvenient. Put positively, a Nazi official could override the law or the institutions of the normative state whenever this was thought to be in the interests of the Party, which were considered to be synonymous with the interests of the German nation.

Fraenkel thus contrasted the dual state with the rule of law state, the 'classical definition' of which he found in this sentence of Dicey's: 'the Rule of Law may be used as a formula for expressing the fact that with us the law of the constitution, the rules which in foreign countries naturally form part of a constitutional code, are not the source but the consequences of the rights of individuals, as defined and enforced by the Courts.'[90] Fraenkel concluded that the rule of law did not obtain in Nazi Germany because the protections of the normative state were subject to the discretion of Nazi officials.

But what may give the dual state at least a toehold at one end of the continuum of legality is that when matters were decided within the normative state, they were decided according to law.[91] Of course, the closer things get to dominance by the prerogative state, the closer a dual state comes to falling off the continuum. In contrast, an apartheid state is firmly on the continuum. Indeed, in two respects it is a perverse example of a rule of law state, as is illustrated by the actual South African apartheid state.

First, all inhabitants of apartheid South Africa were subject to the same general law. However, the racial laws of apartheid carved out vast exceptions to the rule of general law—the legal regimes that dominated the lives of black South Africans, subjecting them to severe discrimination. These regimes were for the most part run by specialized agencies and officials, and they relegated black South Africans to a second-class status in almost all aspects of life—social, economic, and political. Secondly, while the security laws of the state gave its officials vast resources to deal with political opposition more or less as they pleased, officials in the police, the military, and the security services engaged in widespread, illegal acts—ranging from torture to murder—in their bid to stamp out opposition. But just because this activity was illegal, it did not make the apartheid state into a dual state. That the officials who engaged in these acts enjoyed impunity was because the law was not enforced, not because it could be put aside at will.

[90] Ibid., 156, quoting from Dicey (n. 17), 119.

[91] In his preface to the 1974 German edition of the book, Fraenkel, who practiced law in Germany from 1933 to 1938, says:

> In the final phase of my legal practice, I frequently described my work to friends as that of a switchman ... That is, I regarded it an essential part of my efforts to ensure that a given case was dealt with under the auspices of the 'normative state', and not end up in the 'prerogative state'. Colleagues with whom I was on friendly terms confirmed that they, too, had repeatedly worked towards making sure that their clients were punished in a court of law ... (Fraenkel (n. 89), xix.

The very idea of impunity implies that a punishable act took place which should have been punished but was not, whereas in the dual state an official can render an act not punishable by fiat. Those same acts remained punishable after the formal end of apartheid. But they were not going to be punished for two main reasons. First, the state lacked the resources necessary to effectively investigate and prosecute the crimes. Secondly, in the nature of these crimes it is very difficult to get evidence other than from the testimony of those directly involved.

Had South Africa retained parliamentary supremacy, which was a serious option during the transition, there would then have been no way for the applicants in *AZAPO* to mount a formal constitutional challenge to the amnesty provisions of the Reconciliation Act. The courts would have had no option but to defer to the legislative choice. But the Act would still have been problematic from the perspective of the common law constitution and its implementation and interpretation would have been vulnerable to challenges on the basis of the principles of that constitution, just as the laws that established apartheid were vulnerable.[92]

This much is clear from the decision by the Supreme Court of Appeal in the *Du Preez* case,[93] where the Court did in fact rely on 'principles of natural justice,' common law constitutional principles. In this case, it was argued that persons implicated in TRC hearings have a right to be informed about testimony that implicates them, as well as a right to be given access to the relevant statements and documentary evidence.[94] Even though the Reconciliation Act itself did not provide expressly for such rights, the Court found that it could decide the matter by relying on principles of natural justice found in the common law and ultimately read such rights into the Reconciliation Act.[95]

Particularly, the Court relied upon the *audi alteram partem* principle, which it characterized as a 'rule of natural justice which comes into play whenever a statute empowers an official to do an act or give a decision'.[96] The Court found that such natural justice principles are impliedly incorporated into the National Unity and Reconciliation Act.[97] The *audi* principle was considered by the Court as one facet of 'the general requirement of natural justice that ... public official or body concerned must act fairly'.[98] In deciding what a principle of fairness might require, the Court referred to English case law[99] to find that there is a duty in accordance with common law principles of natural justice upon the Commission and Committee to 'act fairly

[92] The Constitutional Court decided two further cases on the amnesty provisions well after the process had come to a close: *Du Toit v Minister of Safety and Security*, 2009 ZACC 22 (CC) and *The Citizen 1978 (Pty) Ltd and Others v McBride and Others*, 2011 ZACC 11 (CC). Since neither involved a constitutional challenge, both could have been disposed of using the resources offered by the common law. It would have made no difference, that is, to the outcome had South Africans opted to have a common law constitution in the 1990s.

[93] *Du Preez and Another v Truth and Reconciliation Commission*, 1997 (3) SA 204 (A).

[94] Ibid., 230F–G.

[95] Ibid., 230I.

[96] Ibid., 231C.

[97] Ibid., 231D.

[98] Ibid., 231F.

[99] *Doody v Secretary of State for the Home Department and Other Appeals* [1993] 3 All ER 92 (HL), 106d–h; *R v Secretary of State for the Home Department, ex parte Hickey and Others (No. 2) and Other Appeals* [1995] 12 All ER 490 (QB) 497a–h; *Re Pergamon Press Ltd* [1970] 3 All ER 535 (CA), 593a–f.

towards persons implicated to their detriment by evidence or information coming before the Committee in the course of its investigations and/or hearings'.[100]

Accordingly, the Commission was found to have a duty to disclose and give timely notice to persons implicated in testimony in terms of common law principles of natural justice.[101] Justice Corbett concluded: 'It seems to me that in a case such as this procedural fairness demands not only that a person implicated be given reasonable and timeous notice of the hearing, but also that he or she is at the same time informed of the substance of the allegations against him or her, with sufficient detail to know what the case is all about.'[102]

In the interests of justice and to protect the victims, however, the Court refused to also read into the statute a duty on the committee to disclose the identity of the victims in question. That would be 'going too far' in terms of infringing upon victims' safety and privacy. We see here how common law constitutional principles—principles that were in existence in T_1—had to be balanced against the interests of the TJ process in T_2.

Similarly, one could consider in this regard one feature of the amnesty process emphasized earlier and which was also highlighted by Mahomed in his judgment—that the political objective with which an act was carried out 'had to be evaluated having regard to the careful criteria listed in Section 20(3) of the Act, *including the very important relationship which the act perpetrated bears in proportion to the object pursued*'. This proportionality requirement was not in fact enforced by the Amnesty Committee, and was perhaps unenforceable given that the brutality of the killings and torture could never be considered proportionate to a political objective which was after all ruthlessly to eradicate political opposition to an unjust regime. It is plausible to claim that the success of the process upheld as constitutionally valid in *AZAPO* depended on this requirement not being enforced. But that it was not enforced rendered each amnesty decision vulnerable to a challenge that the committee had not properly exercised its discretion as required by the letter of the law. And had such a challenge been mounted, the court that heard it would have had to engage in much the same kind of reasoning as the Court did in the *AZAPO* case, because in issue would have been whether a provision of the Act should not be enforced because of the importance to the transition of the TJ process. If, as we suspect would have been the case, the decisions would have been upheld as valid because in the context the proportionality requirement was unenforceable, the court would have then placed even greater emphasis on the other rule of law like aspects of the amnesty process.

In other words, the amnesty provisions were problematic in terms of the permanent constitution in force at T_1. While these problems would not have permitted a court to consider striking down the statute, and hence deference to legislative choice was total in one respect, in another it was not, as a court could have 'read out' of the statute the proportionality requirement, just as it 'read into' the statute in the *Du Preez* case the requirements of natural justice. Similarly to the *Du Preez* case, when it came to the hearing requirements, a court could have 'read into' the statute more stringent rule of law requirements than the letter of the law stipulated, though it would have had to

[100] *Du Preez* (n. 93), 233B–C.
[101] Ibid., at 234H.
[102] Ibid.

take into account the context of transition and the bridging aspect of T_2, even though it may not have come up with that particular metaphor to describe the situation. It, just like the Constitutional Court, would have had to help shore up that bridge at the same time as keeping an anxious eye on the rule of law. Moreover, on the flipside it is not the case that deference played no role in the Constitutional Court's jurisprudence, even though it was armed with all the tools of contemporary constitutionalism. As Mahomed emphasized at the end of his judgment in *AZAPO*, when it came to the design of the amnesty process, as long as amnesty itself was constitutionally permissible, the 'choice of alternatives legitimately fell within the judgment of the lawmakers. The exercise of that choice does not . . . impact on its constitutionality.'[103]

We turn now to an evaluation of the achievement of the Court in this matter and its relevance to the Colombian context.

V. TJ as an Education in Legality

Jonathan Allen has argued that the kind of justice achieved by the South African TRC should be understood in terms of what he calls 'justice as recognition' and 'justice as ethos'.[104] In regard to the first, the work of the Committee which heard from victims—the Committee on Human Rights Violations—supports the restoration of the rule of law by drawing attention to the 'evil consequences resulting from apartheid and the officially sanctioned transgressions of the rule of law'. The hearings 'demonstrate the consequences of a lack of public commitment to justice and the rule of law and thus show the importance of such a commitment. In this sense the TRC supports legal recognition in a context where law's equal recognition of all responsible agents has been grossly distorted.'[105]

In regard to the second, justice as ethos involves the demonstration of how, under apartheid, people's sense of justice was corrupted. Justice became equated with the ideology of the group one happened to belong to, rather than serving as a standpoint from which any particular ideology might be criticized. This equation in turn led to an impoverished view of public discourse—politics is either a dirty business or a noble calling in which the end justifies the means. But neither of these views permits any operation for a sense of injustice; and that sense is required if the transitional government is to preserve legitimacy and a commitment to the constraints of the rule of law, constraints which will make it possible for citizens to call government to account for injustice.[106]

Allen's ideas of justice as recognition and justice as ethos are not meant to be discoveries of new kinds of justice.[107] Rather, they are labels for processes that serve the transformation of an unjust society into a just one. But the justice they serve is little more than the justice of the rule of law, the kind of justice which has to be in place before order becomes something worth having and which also makes it possible for a

[103] *AZAPO* (n. 13), para. 50.

[104] Jonathan Allen, 'Balancing Justice and Social Unity: Political Theory and the Idea of a Truth and Reconciliation Commission,' (1999) 49 *University of Toronto Law Journal* 315, 328–32, 335–8.

[105] Ibid., 330–1.

[106] Ibid., 336–8.

[107] Here we rely on Dyzenhaus, '*Leviathan* as a Theory of Transitional Justice' (n. 12), 201–7.

society to decide other kinds of political issues in a civil fashion. If that is right, then most of the debate about TJ should be boiled down to one about how to achieve the rule of law.

This boiling down, even deflation, might cause disappointment not only to those who see in TJ and the work of truth commissions something altogether new and exciting, but also to the political activists who risked much to bring about the transition. As one such activist—Bärbel Bohley—from the former German Democratic Republic—famously complained of the transition that followed German reunification: 'We expected justice, but we got the *Rechtsstaat* instead.'[108] But justice as ethos is an education in the claim that there is a kind of justice that transcends the ideology of the particular group that happens to be in power, and is thus able to use law legitimately to achieve its ends. And if an education in legality cannot be other than an education in how justice transcends particular ideologies, it must be the case that an education in the first kind of justice entails an education in the second.

The tragedy of any TJ process is that it aims at doing more than bringing people fully into the jural community. In addition, it aims at bringing about a more general transformation of the society, in particular of the pervasive structural inequality that largely lies behind the human rights abuses incurred in both maintaining and resisting the structure. Indeed, it was common to describe South Africa's post-apartheid constitutional dispensation using a term that went way beyond 'transitional'. It was and is still sometimes seen as an experiment in 'transformative constitutionalism', a term coined by Karl Klare, who defined it as a:

> ... long-term project of constitutional enactment, interpretation, and enforcement committed (not in isolation, of course, but in a historical context of conducive political developments) to transforming a country's political and social institutions and power relationships in a democratic, participatory, and egalitarian direction. Transformative constitutionalism connotes an enterprise of inducing large-scale social change through nonviolent political processes grounded in law.[109]

Klare insisted that, in the new legal order, methods of interpretation had to change. The constitution, according to him, invited a new self-reflection and imagination when it came to legal reasoning. Legal reasoning had to become conducive of the transformative goals of the constitution.[110]

Not all scholars agreed with Klare about the extent to which legal interpretation had to change. Some argued that common law methods of interpretation were to be adapted, but not abandoned.[111] But perhaps the most sobering assessment came from Chaskalson, who said in 2012:

[108] A. James McAdams, *Judging the Past in Unified Germany* (Cambridge: Cambridge University Press, 2001), 7.

[109] Karl E. Klare, 'Legal Culture and Transformative Constitutionalism' (1998) 14 South African Journal on Human Rights 146, 149.

[110] Ibid., 156.

[111] Lourens M. Du Plessis, 'The Jurisprudence of Interpretation and the Exigencies of a New Constitutional Order in South Africa' (1998) 20 Acta Juridica 8.

> Transformation contemplates an improvement in the lives of people, households and communities, achieved over time by institutionalising policies, programmes and projects to that end. The arms of government primarily responsible for this are the legislature and the executive. Judges hold office under the Constitution ... The role of judges in relation to transformation is therefore governed by the provisions of the Constitution and the law.[112]

As he pointed out, his former Court the previous year 'again drew attention to the centrality of the constitutional commitment to social justice, to the fact that millions of people were still compelled to live without adequate housing, and to the concern that 'seventeen years into our democracy, a dignified existence for all in South Africa has not yet been achieved'.'[113]

It is in light of this realization that some have suggested a flaw in the metaphor of constitution as a bridge. Perhaps it was naïve to conceive of the law as a way to get society from T_1 to T_3. This thought allowed South Africans to view the abyss that the bridge spans as unavoidable but temporary and the bridge as linear progression.[114] One could say that that the two sides of the bridge don't look that different,[115] and the abyss is not that temporary. If that is the case, the limits of law become apparent, and the hopes of South Africans should shift towards political process.

But there was a successful transition in that the flaws of the apartheid state, understood in the more technical sense suggested in the last section, were corrected and in that the other three of Murphy's four circumstances of transition were removed. The racial laws of apartheid which relegated black South Africans to a second-class status in almost all aspects of life are gone as are the security laws which gave officials vast resources to deal with political opposition more or less as they pleased. And while South Africa remains an extremely violent and crime-ridden society, the nature of the violence has changed. It is no longer the violence of 'normalized collective and political wrongdoing' deployed in order to maintain pervasive structural inequality. Moreover, there is neither 'serious existential uncertainty' nor 'fundamental uncertainty about authority'. The majority of South Africans are committed to parliamentary democracy within the framework of the final constitution. That is the achievement of T_3.

We want to suggest that both the TRC and the *AZAPO* decision played an important role in getting South Africans across the bridge to T_3 because they offered what we can think of as a spectacle of legality. While the term might seem to convey the sense of an appearance of something without its substance, the Oxford English Dictionary offers as its primary meaning: 'A specially prepared display of a more or less public nature (esp. one on large scale) forming an impressive or interesting show for those watching it'. The spectacle was one in which individuals on both sides of the conflict renounced

[112] Arthur Chaskalson, 'Without Fear, Favour or Prejudice: the Courts, the Constitution and Transformation' (2012) (August) Advocate 34.

[113] Ibid., 36, quoting from *City of Johannesburg Metropolitan Municipality v Blue Moonlight Properties 39 (Pty) Ltd and Another* (CCT 37/11) [2011] ZACC 33.

[114] A. J. van der Walt, 'Dancing with Codes—Protecting, Developing and Deconstructing Property Rights in a Constitutional State' (2001) 118 South African Law Journal 258, 258–60.

[115] Ibid.

violence and submitted themselves to the judgment of an independent tribunal, by which we mean both the Committee on Amnesty and the Constitutional Court.

Because a successful application for amnesty resulted in no punishment for the applicant, and because the tribunal was not a court of law, the amnesty process fell far short of the ordinary standards set by the rule of law. As we pointed out, these standards were constitutionalized in the interim constitution in Section 22. But that did not make the shortfall more constitutionally problematic than it would have been in terms of the unwritten constitution of T_1. It only made it more spectacular—the subject of a full-out constitutional challenge.

That permitted the Court to emphasize the following features of the amnesty process: first, that the shortfall was constitutionally mandated; second, that while it was a shortfall, it was not a total derogation; third, that there was a justification for having such a process to get from T_1 to T_3 because it made it possible for erstwhile enemies to agree to submit to the judgment of the institutions of legal order. In displaying that justification, the Court made it clear that the ultimate constitutional value is civil peace—the peace of a jural community. In this way, the Court confronted the violence at the foundation of the new political order with the kind of practical aim that Kant thought both pointless and dangerous. The point was to educate South Africans in legality in order to respond directly to the dangers of continued conflict.

This is the advantage of having in place a written constitution with entrenched rights. It serves to highlight the rule of law stakes in a way that an unwritten constitution cannot. Moreover, it highlights them within a spectacle of legality, in which the actors adopt the role of legal subjects thus showing their willingness to submit to the judgment of an impartial arbitrator. Within that spectacle the spectacle that is still to unfold—the TJ process with its own tribunals—can be shown to the extent possible to be itself a spectacle of legality, thus creating the bridge to T_3. But that the shortfall would have been equally problematic under the unwritten constitution helps us to understand the importance of the quality of constitutional resilience.

This quality is obscured by a Schmittean doctrine of unconstitutional constitutional amendment, one which relies on an idea, however muted, of a constituent power wielded by judges. Judges who exhibit fidelity to law do not work in the register of power, no matter how formally powerful their position is in the constitutional order. They work in the register of authority and, moreover, in the register of constitutional or legal authority, which is by definition a constituted authority. As long as they stick to that task, they can do more than maintain the jural community. They can facilitate its expansion by helping to bring within it not only individuals and groups who had been relegated to second class status, but also individuals and groups who had taken up the cause of armed resistance to that relegation.

If the jurisprudence of the Colombian Constitutional Court can be understood as having moved from an understanding of the constitution as permanent to one of resilience that, we suggest, does not represent a new power grab by the Court. Rather it signals an understanding of the role of a court in maintaining a constitutional order even in the face of existential threats to that order. The task of judges who manage a transition is then to educate their audience through the measures they take in the related matters of justice as recognition and justice as ethos. But that is no different from their task in times of normality. The only difference is that during a TJ process judges should be primarily guided by the aim of achieving a condition of legality which will make it possible for the state to get on with a different task—remedying the circumstance of pervasive structural inequality.

14
Judging the Justice of the Colombian Final Agreement

*Colleen Murphy**

I. Introduction

After fifty-two years of conflict, the Final Agreement to End the Armed Conflict and Build a Stable and Lasting Peace (hereafter Final Agreement) between the Colombian government and the Revolutionary Armed Forces of Colombia (hereafter FARC) is now being implemented.[1] However, divisions within Colombian society are real, and opposition to the Final Agreement on the part of some remains deep. Thus, the pursuit of peace is a fragile enterprise.

One cause of the fragility of the Colombian peace process is moral in nature. An important source of opposition to the Final Agreement concerns whether justice is achieved in the treatment of past wrongs. In this paper I take up this concern and focus on the question: by what standards should we evaluate the justice of transitional justice (TJ) processes for dealing with past wrongs outlined in the Final Agreement? That is, what are the criteria that must be satisfied for such wrongs to be said to have been dealt with *justly*? It is worth noting the difference between the question I take up and the kinds of questions typically examined in the literature on TJ. Studies of TJ are characteristically social scientific in orientation and concerned with understanding the choices transitional societies do make, either in terms of the factors that influenced such choices or in terms of the societal impact of processes adopted. My question, by contrast, is a question about how we should think about the morality of the choices a given society makes. Should we view the Final Agreement as a success from the perspective of justice, both as envisioned in its text and as currently being implemented?

In the first section, I provide some background to the Colombian case. I focus specifically on the mechanisms of TJ outlined in the Final Agreement, and the objections to those processes as articulated in responses to the October 2016 failed plebiscite on the September 2016 version of the Final Agreement. The revisions subsequently made following the failed plebiscite did not substantively alter the form such mechanisms

* Earlier versions of this paper were presented at McMaster University as part of conference, 'Global Perspectives on Peace: The Colombian Peace Process with FARC' organized by Jorge Fabra, Nancy Doubleday, and Andres Molina Ochoa; the Melbourne University Law School Legal Theory Workshop; and the 2019 academic conference of the Colombian Constitutional Court on the 'Colombian Constitutional Court in a global perspective'. I am grateful for the feedback provided in both venues. I also thank Sebastian Machado, Lulu Weis, and Carlos Bernal-Pulido for their feedback on previous drafts.

[1] For the English translation of the Final Agreement, see http://especiales.presidencia.gov.co/Documents/20170620-dejacion-armas/acuerdos/acuerdo-final-ingles.pdf accessed on 7 December 2020.

Colleen Murphy, *Judging the Justice of the Colombian Final Agreement* In: *Constitutionalism*. Edited by: Alejandro Linares-Cantillo, Camilo Valdivieso-León, Santiago García-Jaramillo, Oxford University Press (2021). © The various contributors.
DOI: 10.1093/oso/9780192896759.003.0015

would take and thus the source of moral concern with them. After outlining the processes for dealing with past wrongs and the sources of moral debate about them, I go on in the second section to outline the substantive view of TJ developed in my book *The Conceptual Foundations of Transitional Justice.*[2] The third section then applies that framework to the Colombian case, arguing that the processes for dealing with past wrongs outlined in the Final Agreement satisfy criteria of TJ, though whether that justice will be realized depends on the process through which the Final Agreement is implemented. The fourth section then turns to the constitutional dimensions of implementation. Multiple constitutional amendments have been and will continue to be necessary in order to implement the Final Agreement. Drawing on examples from Northern Ireland and South Africa, I discuss the temporal dimension of constitutional change and then distinguish three different forms of constitutional change, each of which addresses a different form of prior injustice.

II. Background to the Final Agreement

The process leading to the formal adoption of the Final Agreement was long and very complex, encompassing negotiations between the FARC and Colombian government begun in 2012.[3] The negotiations focused on six central issues: rural reform; political participation; illicit crops; victims; the termination of conflict; and how to implement and endorse any agreement. These negotiations culminated in an intricate and comprehensive agreement comprising over 300 pages, which was formally signed by Colombian President Juan Manuel Santos and FARC leader Rodrigo Londoño, known as Timochenko, on 26 September 2016 in Cartagena, Colombia. Following that signing, there was a public plebiscite on the Final Agreement on 2 October 2016. Part of the impetus for holding the plebiscite was to bolster the legitimacy of the Final Agreement within Colombian society. In an unanticipated outcome that shocked the nation and the international community, the plebiscite failed by 0.5 per cent. 50.2 per cent voted no and 49.7 per cent voted yes, with 60 per cent of the Colombian population abstaining from participating.[4] The failed plebiscite led to a consultation with a large group of stakeholders within Colombian society to seek suggestions for modifications to the agreement. Forty-one days later a joint communique was issued stating a revised agreement was in place that addressed fifty-six of the fifty-seven themes for revision that emerged from the process of consultation. On 1 December 2016 the Colombian Congress ratified the Final Agreement.

The necessity of including measures to respond to victims is clear once we consider the numbers of such victims. Colombia's current population is forty-eight million

[2] Colleen Murphy, *The Conceptual Foundations of Transitional Justice* (New York: Cambridge University Press, 2017).

[3] Another related subject for moral evaluation is the process by which the Final Agreement was designed. I restrict my focus here to the evaluation of the terms outlined in the Final Agreement itself.

[4] Numerous analyses following the failed plebiscite tried to explain the unanticipated outcome, pointing to factors like the weather that may have influenced turnout as well as lack of information that could have shaped the manner in which individuals voted. However, such explanations are not relevant for my purposes in this paper.

people. According to the Victim's Unit, more than eight million have registered as victims since 1985.[5] This includes seven million individuals forcibly displaced; 260,000 individuals killed; 46,000 enforced disappearances; 30,000 hostage takings; 17,500 rapes and other forms of sexual violence; 10,000 cases of torture. Those directly harmed by the conflict are many; indirectly all Colombians have been affected.

I want to focus in the remainder of this section on the claims of justice that were implicit and explicit in the explanations of why individuals voted as they did in the October plebiscite. But before turning to these views I want first to summarize the processes for dealing with past wrongs outlined in the Final Agreement. Some details about the structure and functioning of these processes changed between the version of the Final Agreement that was put to the vote in the plebiscite in October and the version that was ratified by the Colombian Congress. However, the changes did not alter substantively the basic structure of the TJ processes and, importantly, did not alter the features of those processes that were the source of moral concern.

One component of the Final Agreement is the Special Jurisdiction for Peace ('JEP'). This consists of a set of judicial bodies that investigate, establish facts, and, where applicable, levy penalties for the crimes that fall under its jurisdiction. The JEP is comprised of Colombian judges with ten foreign expert observers. It will operate over a ten-year period with the possibility of an extension of an additional five years. Rulings from the JEP can be appealed to the Constitutional Court. Wrongs that fall under its jurisdiction fall into two main groups. In the first group are wrongs committed for political reasons but that do not rise to the level of war crimes or crimes against humanity; an example would be the crime of rebellion. Perpetrators of this category of wrongdoing are eligible for amnesty if they offer a full confession and wrongs committed were not for personal enrichment. Into the second category of crimes are gross human rights violations that are not eligible for amnesty or pardon and that were not committed for personal enrichment. For this set of crimes there will be three different categories of penalties. For those who fully and immediately confess to wrongs committed, they will be eligible to serve between five and eight years in zones of restricted liberty, during which time acts of reparation and restoration will be performed. Such acts could include, for example, clearing land mines, repairing damaged infrastructure or participating in rural development projects. Individuals who recognize responsibility for wrongdoing later will be eligible for prison sentences of between five and eight years. Individuals who do not confess or recognize responsibility for wrongs but are found guilty by the JEP will serve prison sentences of between fifteen and twenty years.

In addition to the JEP, the Final Agreement makes provisions for a truth commission. This commission was established on 5 April 2017 and its mandate is to 'find out what happened in Colombia that led to the victimization of 8 million'.[6] It has three years to function and has eleven members. The actors of interest in the truth commission are both FARC and state agents. A wide range of wrongs are the subject of its

[5] Amnesty International 2016/2017, Annual Report for Colombia, https://www.amnesty.org/en/countries/americas/colombia/report-colombia/ accessed 7 December 2020.

[6] Ariaan Alsema, 'Colombia Creates Historic Truth Commission' Colombia Reports, 5 April 2017, https://colombiareports.com/colombia-creates-historic-truth-commission/.

focus, including mass transfers of land. Finally, the Final Agreement makes provisions for a Missing Persons Search Unit and for reparations for victims of the conflict.

There are other features of the Final Agreement worth highlighting for the way they shape moral evaluations of the TJ processes. First, the Agreement includes a commitment to political representation for the post-FARC political party, the Common Alternative Revolutionary Force. That party will have ten automatic congressional seats between 2018 and 2026. There are provisions for rural development programmes. There is a scheme for the decommissioning of weapons, a process which has already been completed. There is also a programme for the reintegration of FARC members following periods spent in 'Temporary Zones for Normalization'.[7] Such zones are to be monitored by the United Nations.

In an article published by the British newspaper *The Guardian* shortly after the October 2016 plebiscite, a range of views about the justice of the Final Agreement were expressed.[8] One set of views rested on the claim that justice requires giving perpetrators what they deserve, and what perpetrators deserve is punishment. Therefore, because the JEP does not guarantee punishment, but grants amnesty to non-war criminals; permits time spent in zones of restricted liberty for war criminals; and allows war criminals to serve in political office; the terms for dealing with wrongdoing laid out in the Final Agreement are unjust. Sample quotes reflecting this position include the following: 'The agreement gave the wrong message to society as criminals were rewarded with injustice, money and political representation.' Echoing a similar perspective another interviewee stated: 'Santos was giving more than deserved to the narco-guerrillas. Political liberties shouldn't be granted to terrorists guilty of atrocities.' Putting the same point even more directly, another interviewee stated: '[I want] a fairer deal that meets the following conditions: That Farc members responsible for war crimes go to jail instead of having a secure place on the senate.'

By contrast, another set of views conceptualized TJ as a compromise between peace and justice, with differing judgments taken as to whether the balance struck in the Final Agreement was just. For one yes vote: 'The peace accord is an imperfect document but I thought the balance between peace for the country and justice for victims was fair.' Whereas another individual who voted no claimed a 'little more compromise by the rebels, regarding material reparation for victims and justice' was needed.

A third and final set of views appealed to a notion of justice different to that of retribution. Justice requires unity or the overcoming of divisions within Colombian society. Or justice requires participation, where the importance of having a say on policies that will impact one is emphasized. Consider the following yes vote explanations: '[T]he results show a sharp divide ... The departments in the center ... voted against the accords while the departments in the rural periphery, including many areas which have been most impacted by the economic and social costs of the conflict, overwhelmingly

[7] Isabella Flisi, "The Reintegration of Former Combatants in Colombia' (Feb 2017) *Oxford Research Group*, https://www.oxfordresearchgroup.org.uk/Blog/the-reintegration-of-former-combatants-in-colombia accessed on 7 December 2020/

[8] 'Colombians Divided on Failed Referendum: "We Need to Move Forward"', *The Guardian*, 4 October 2016, https://www.theguardian.com/world/2016/oct/04/colombia-farc-peace-deal-referendum-readers-reactionaccessed on 7 December 2020. Quotes in the following three paragraphs are all taken from this article.

supported the accords.' Similarly emphasizing the importance of unity, another yes vote stated: 'The peace agreements are ... about unity. We need to unite as a country. The plebiscite showed just how divided we are. Even worse, how indifferent we are.'

The various viewpoints expressed above raise questions about what exactly the criteria we should be using to evaluate the justice of TJ processes are. Are the salient criteria those articulated by theories of retributive justice? Or is justice rather best conceptualized as a compromise between retributive justice and other moral considerations? Or is justice instead not about retribution, but rather about other kinds of concerns such as societal unity? Each of these views is intuitively plausible as accounts of the justice of TJ, and it is not immediately obvious on what basis we should judge a particular view as better or worse than another.

In the next section, I articulate my framework for conceptualizing TJ. In brief, TJ at its core is about the just pursuit of societal transformation. I explain why this is the core concern of TJ and what the just pursuit of societal transformation entails. In the third section I apply my view to Colombia, contrasting my view with the three views on justice outlined in this section and evaluate the Final Agreement from within my framework. The fourth then considers the implications of TJ so conceived for constitutional change.

III. Transitional Justice

In *The Conceptual Foundations of Transitional Justice*, I approach the question of TJ by drawing on the methodology for theorizing about justice articulated by the eighteenth-century Scottish philosopher David Hume.[9] Hume famously claimed that a set of circumstances of justice generate a particular problem of justice it becomes necessary for a community to address and possible to resolve. Principles of justice then provide guidance on how a community should resolve a given problem. For Hume, the central problem of justice concerned the stabilization of property. This becomes a problem, he claimed, when specific circumstances exist including, for example, limited scarcity of goods. He illustrated why limited scarcity of goods is salient by considering the contrasting set of circumstances of extreme abundance and extreme scarcity. When goods are abundant, Hume argues, the stabilization of property is not necessary. There is no important purpose served by specifying and articulating who owns which good when the same good can be easily replaced. At the opposite end, in a circumstance of extreme scarcity stabilization of property is a futile exercise. When faced with the question of survival, property rules will not constrain individuals from taking what they need to survive.

The central insight of Hume is that principles of justice are context-dependent. They become operative or salient in a specific set of circumstances of justice. This is because principles of justice are problem or question-responsive, providing guidance

[9] Murphy (n. 2). For discussions of Hume on the circumstances of transitional justice see David Hume, *A Treatise of Human Nature*, ed. L. A. Selby-Bigge, (2nd edn, Oxford: Oxford University Press, 1739/1978); David Hume, *An Enquiry Concerning the Principles of Morals*, ed. Tom L. Beauchamp (Oxford: Oxford University Press, 1751/1998)

for a concrete question of justice facing a community. Following Hume, then, suggests that before it is possible to adjudicate among competing understandings of the principles that ought to be used to evaluate processes for dealing with past wrongdoing, it is necessary first to articulate the circumstances of justice characterizing transitions. Only then is it possible to identify the central question of justice that is at issue and articulate principles that will provide guidance for dealing with that question.

There are, I argue, four circumstances of justice that characterize paradigmatic transitional societies. I briefly summarize each in turn. I then argue that the salient question of justice is how to justly pursue societal transformation. Finally, I articulate principles for societal transformation and its just pursuit.

A. Circumstances of Transitions

The first circumstance is what I call *pervasive structural inequality.*[10] The subject matter of this circumstance is the basic terms for interaction among citizens and between citizens and officials. 'Structural' signals the dominant role of institutions in defining these basic terms. The institutions that shape interaction are many, including legal, political, social, cultural, and economic institutions. They shape interaction by virtue of how their rules and norms govern who is eligible to engage in certain pursuits or actions and who is eligible to shape the rules themselves. Political rules and norms shape the conditions that must be satisfied for someone to be eligible to hold public office, and political and legal rules shape the powers that may be legitimately exercised if one holds such an office. Part of the rules and norms include penalties for their infraction. Such rules and norms can be unequal in two senses. They can be unequal in the sense that different groups enjoy differential freedom to do and become various things of value. For example, the educational opportunities, the prospects for entering politics, the possibilities for employment vary. Rules can be unequal in a second sense, by virtue of the different ability various individuals or groups of individuals enjoy to shape the institutional rules and norms themselves. When inequality is pervasive, the institutional order is illegitimate in the sense that there exists a right to rebel on the part of citizens. Revolution, and not simply reform, is permissible. A paradigm case of pervasive structural inequality is apartheid South Africa. Inequality can be targeted on the basis of other identities or on the basis of regional location; it can also be pervasive in a less intentionally targeted manner.

The second circumstance of transitions is what I call *normalized collective and political wrongdoing*. By wrongdoing I mean violations of human rights. Wrongdoing is normalized in an empirical sense; it becomes a basic fact of life around which individuals must orient their conduct. The anticipation of being arrested if speaking out against the government, and the anticipation of being tortured if arrested, irrespective of whether such arrest and torture would be permissible according to declared legal rules, becomes part of what one must take into deliberation when considering whether to speak out. Wrongdoing is collective in the sense that it is characteristically

[10] These four circumstances are discussed at length in Murphy (n. 2), chapter 1.

carried out by groups and targets groups. It is political in two ways. First, wrongdoing is done for the sake of furthering political objectives; acquiring control of territory, maintaining a regime, or contesting a regime in power are the reasons for the commission of wrongdoing. Second, wrongdoing is committed by agents of the state or agents acting with the permission of the state or by agents contesting the state. Sexual violence and rape, disappearing of citizens, killing, and torture are some of the many forms such wrongdoing may take. It is common in transitions for categories of perpetrator and victim to overlap in many instances. Such complex victims may be victims of wrongdoing, and then go on to commit wrongdoing themselves.[11]

The third circumstance of TJ is what I call *serious existential uncertainty*. The subject matter of this circumstance is the basic trajectory of a political community. When that trajectory is seriously uncertain, it is profoundly unclear in what direction a community is heading. There may have been a truce signed, but it is uncertain whether the terms of the truce will be upheld and, if upheld, whether the truce will be followed by a return to violence or an extended period of calm. It is uncertain whether elections will be held as scheduled and, if held, whether results will be respected. Many attempted transitions to democracy fail; conflict or repression resumes. In the circumstance of serious existential uncertainty it is thus objectively uncertain whether a transition attempted will ultimately be successful. The aspiration to end conflict or repression does not entail that this will in fact take place. This means subjectively it is very difficult for both members of transitional societies and international observers to know what the most accurate narrative is to tell about unfolding events.

The fourth circumstance of transitions is *fundamental uncertainty about authority*. The state is characteristically implicated in the wrongs which are now the subject of responses such as truth commissions and reparations. The basis of the authority of the state to deal with wrongs in which it is characteristically implicated must be established.

We can contrast the four circumstances of transitions articulated above with what I call the circumstances of stable democracies. These are the circumstances implicitly or explicitly assumed to be present when theorists develop accounts of retributive, corrective, or distributive justice. *Limited structural inequality* is such that while the freedom enjoyed by all individuals to do and become things of value and to shape the institutionally defined terms of interaction are unequal, the inequality does not threaten the legitimacy of the institutional order. Reform, not revolution, is needed. *Deviant individual and personal wrongdoing* is ordinary criminality. Violations of rules forbidding violations of human rights are the exception, not the rule. They are committed by individuals targeting other individuals for reasons that are personal; greed, jealousy, ambition, fear, or recklessness explain why someone committed this wrong. *Minor existential uncertainty* obtains such that the trajectory of a political community is not seriously in doubt. Where there is *narrow uncertainty about authority*, the authority of a particular individual to hold a specific office may be questioned or there

[11] I take the label of complex victims from Luke Moffett. See Luke Moffett, 'Reparations for "Complex" Victims: Navigating Complex Identities of Victim–Perpetrators in Reparation Mechanisms' (2015) 10 International Journal of Transitional Justice 146. doi:10.1093/ijtj/ijv030.

may be narrow debates about which branch should deal with a given question. But the authority of the institutional order itself is not in question.

B. The Question or Problem of Justice in the Circumstances of Transitions

Against the background of the four circumstances of transitions (pervasive structural inequality, normalized collective and political wrongdoing, serious existential uncertainty, and uncertainty about authority) I now turn to identifying the salient question or problem of justice in this context. After briefly discussing why retributive justice is not the salient notion of justice, I turn to outlining my understanding of the notion of justice that is.[12]

Using the standards of retribution as the standards by which to assess processes of TJ is intuitively plausible. Theories of retributive justice take up the question: what counts as a just response to perpetrators of wrongdoing? Responding to perpetrators of wrongdoing is certainly a prominent issue in contexts of transition. Despite this initial plausibility, however, there are reasons for concern with using retributive theories as guides to what justice requires in transitional contexts. According to the retributivist, perpetrators of wrongdoing deserve to suffer proportional to the culpability and suffering caused. In explaining why the retributive answer to the question of the just treatment of perpetrators is the correct answer, accounts of retributive justice aim to respond to two sources of scepticism. The first is scepticism about the moral difference between the suffering wrongdoing inflicts and the suffering constitutive of punishment; here the worry is that instead of meting out justice punishment is instead inflicting an additional wrong. The second is scepticism about the state as an appropriate agent of punishment. Here the worry is that the intentional infliction of suffering by the state is incompatible with its recognition of the moral equality of all citizens; punishment is, in other words, outside the boundaries of the legitimate exercise of authority by the state. In defending the retributive answer to the question of the just treatment of perpetrators, retributivists argue that punishment is different because it has a different moral function: it aims to restore a status quo ante of equality that wrongdoing disrupted.[13] In Herbert Morris' view, punishment restores the distribution of benefits and burdens that punishment upset.[14] In Jean Hampton's view, punishment restores the moral equality between victim and perpetrator which wrongdoing upset by countering the false moral claim about the value of the victim wrongdoing expressed.[15] Implicit in both accounts is the assumption that there is a prior background situation of equality that wrongdoing as an isolated act disrupted.

[12] The argument against retributive justice, corrective and distributive justice as the salient notion of justice, and the argument for my own positive account of the question of transitional justice is in Murphy (n. 2), chapter 2.

[13] There are some retributivists, such as Michael Moore, who take the core retributive principle to be a bedrock moral intuition not requiring further argumentation. However, this response will not suffice in the circumstances of transitional justice. As the quotations from Section I highlight there are conflicting intuitions about what justice requires.

[14] Herbert Morris, 'Guilt and Suffering' (1971) 21(4) Philosophy East and West 419–34

[15] Jean Hampton, 'Correcting Harms Versus Righting Wrongs: The Goal of Retribution' (1992) 39 UCLA Law Review, 1659–702.

The state, on these views, is the appropriate agent to mete out punishment because it is an impartial agent with respect to the wrongdoing and the central representative of a community and its values.

When we shift to the circumstances of transitions, however, the retributive explanation of the justice of punishment is not compelling. The state's authority to punish cannot be assumed but needs to be established. Insofar as a state in transition is representative of a community's values, it represents values at least some of which need repudiation. Moreover, punishment cannot be taken to restore a prior situation of equality between perpetrator and victim which wrongdoing disrupted; there was no prior situation of equality that existed given pervasive structural inequality. Insofar as a situation of equality between victim and perpetrator is to be achieved, punishment of an individual perpetrator cannot by itself fulfil this aim, for the threat to that equality is not the function of the isolated act of one individual. Finally, and most fundamentally, responding to perpetrators of wrongdoing is, at most, part of the problem of justice in the circumstances of transition. Focusing exclusively on perpetrators of wrongdoing misses the broader context which enabled wrongdoing to occur in a characteristically systematic and widespread manner.

A better way of framing the question or problem of justice in the circumstances of transition, I argue, is: what constitutes the just pursuit of societal transformation?[16] The first two circumstances of TJ (pervasive structural inequality as well as normalized collective and political wrongdoing) make transformation necessary. The third circumstance (serious existential uncertainty) makes transformation possible. Absent such serious uncertainty, there is no real prospect for changing the status quo. Serious existential uncertainty creates a situation in which a society may go in a direction different from where it was before. As I explain in greater detail below, the circumstance of normalized collective and political wrongdoing also makes it necessary to evaluate the justness of the pursuit of transformation.

What is the substantive content of the just pursuit of societal transformation? The most salient form of transformation needed is relational transformation. It is the overhauling of the terms for interaction among perpetrators, and between perpetrators and victims, among citizens and between citizens and officials, that is needed. For it is only in so doing and thereby altering how members of a transitional society interact will the aim of preventing a recurrence of conflict and repression and, with it, wrongdoing be achieved.

In my first book, *A Moral Theory of Political Reconciliation*, I develop and defend a substantive account of political reconciliation, which forms the basis of my view of societal transformation in my account of TJ.[17] Relational transformation, I argue, has three core components. The first is the establishment and/or strengthening of the rule of law, where I follow Lon Fuller in understanding the rule of law to require ongoing cooperative action by and interaction among citizens and officials to ensure there is

[16] The language of transformation is increasingly prominent in the literature on transitional justice.

[17] Colleen Murphy, *A Moral Theory of Political Reconciliation* (New York: Cambridge University Press, 2010). Reconciliation is generally understood to be the process of repairing damaged relationships. I discuss transformation specifically in Murphy (n. 2), chapter 3.

in fact governance of conduct on the basis of legal rules.[18] Characteristically, conflict and repression weaken the rule of law, by for example eroding congruence between declared legal rules and their enforcement. The second component of transformation is establishing threshold conditions such that default trust of citizens and officials becomes reasonable. I conceptualize trust as an attitude of optimism about the competence and lack of ill-will of the trusted; competence is defined in a role-specific manner, relative to the duties and responsibilities associated with the role of citizen or of official. The third component is establishing threshold levels of genuine opportunities to be respected; recognized as a member of one's political community; participate in institutions; and avoid poverty.[19] These three components, I argue, articulate the institutional, attitudinal, and interpersonal conditions that must be in place for citizens and officials to interact on the basis of mutual respect for agency and reciprocity.

The question of TJ is not limited to societal transformation but also includes its just pursuit.[20] This is because processes of TJ pursue transformation via dealing with past wrongs. Those wrongs had particular victims and perpetrators. To simply pursue societal transformation in the most efficient or effective manner risks treating perpetrators and victims of wrongdoing as mere means, thereby failing to recognize the particular moral claims to which being a victim or perpetrator give rise. The 'just pursuit' of transformation signals the necessity of treating victims and perpetrators in a fitting and appropriate manner. There are, I argue, a number of factors that inform judgements about whether a response is fitting and appropriate. One factor is whether it contributes to the moral aims associated with responses to victims and perpetrators, aims which are widely recognized in the literature on moral philosophy and on TJ. These aims in the cases of perpetrators include repudiating wrongdoing, holding perpetrators accountable by judging them to have been responsible for the wrong, and contributing to non-recurrence. In the case of victims these aims include condemning wrongdoing, acknowledging the status of victims as rights bearers and as members of their political community, and providing reparation. Another factor is the relationship between the responder and respondent. Examining reactive attitudes illustrates why. Resentment is taken to be a reactive attitude it is appropriate for victims to have towards perpetrators, but not for third parties or bystanders to wrongdoing; indignation is an appropriate attitude for such parties. Also informing judgements of appropriateness is the nature of the wrong done. The protests by prisoners in Northern Ireland during the Troubles offers an example of the importance of this condition. In the blanket protest, followed by the dirty protest and hunger strike, prisoners were contesting the change of status that rendered them ordinary criminals. The protest was designed to force the government to re-recognize prisoners as political prisoners of an armed conflict who had committed political, not ordinary criminal, wrongs. Finally, the cultural context in which a response to wrongdoing is adopted is salient. Many of the central moral aims listed above are expressive in nature; acknowledgement,

[18] See Lon Fuller, *The Morality of Law* (rev. edn, New Haven, CT: Yale University Press, 1969).

[19] I understand 'genuine opportunities' in the sense of capability. The presence or absence of such opportunities is a function of what individuals have (e.g., resources, knowledge, skills) and what they can do with what they have (e.g., given the institutional structure).

[20] I discuss the just pursuit of transformation in Murphy (n. 2), chapter 4.

condemnation, and recognition fall into this category. This means it is necessary to consider what kind(s) of processes could plausibly count as expressing, for example, acknowledgement, in a given context. This last factor highlights the fact that it is a mistake to think that any single form of response is required for victims and/or perpetrators to be treated in a fitting and appropriate manner. There may be contextual variability in what responses will be fitting and appropriate, where the limits to this variability will be set by the factors listed above.

For the expressive aims of responses to wrongdoing to be achieved, and indeed for societal transformation itself to be facilitated by TJ processes, it is necessary that the design, implementation, and then subsequent evaluation of such processes be holistic.[21] By holistic I mean that processes should be designed and implemented jointly or as a package, rather than approaching the process of dealing with past wrongs in a piecemeal fashion. In transitions the expressive meaning of a particular response is impacted by what else does or does not occur in a particular transitional context. This is because processes for dealing with past wrongs face risks in transitional contexts that are not present in the same way in the circumstances of stable democracies.[22] Specifically, any process for dealing with past wrongs risks failing to be seen as and thereby serving as an instrument of justice. Trials risk being seen as 'victor's justice', reparations as 'blood money', and truth commissions as mere words. When seen in these ways processes not only fail to treat victims and perpetrators appropriately, they also fail to contribute in any meaningful sense to relational transformation, and can serve instead to further entrench extant relational patterns. Countering these risks and establishing that processes are processes of *justice*, requires enacting not a single but a set of processes jointly undertaken to deal with past wrongs. Together, these processes can underscore that the truth is not mere words but words that will be used in ways that will facilitate transformation and will provide the basis for offering reparations to those harmed.[23]

One final comment about my account of TJ is worth highlighting before turning to the specific case of Colombia. I conceptualize the relationship between the requirements of societal transformation and the requirements to treat perpetrators and victims of wrongdoing appropriately as structurally analogous to the relationship between the two parts of just war theory. Just war theory is standardly taken to comprise two sets of moral requirements. The first set of requirements, *jus ad bellum*, specifies the conditions that must be satisfied for war to be permissibly undertaken. These conditions include acting for a legitimate reason (e.g., self-defence) and with legitimate authority. The second set of requirements, *jus in bello*, specify the constraints that must be respected during the conduct of war itself. Importantly, non-combatants may

[21] I discuss this point in detail in Murphy (n. 2), chapter 4.

[22] On this point, see Pablo de Greiff, 'Theorizing Transitional Justice', in Melissa S. Williams, Rosemary Nagy, & Jon Elster (eds), *NOMOS LI: Transitional Justice* (New York: New York University Press, 2012), 31–77.

[23] The important work being done by social scientists in understanding the societal impact of different combinations of processes can prove invaluable in understanding what set of mechanisms is likely to contribute to transitional justice. See, e.g., Hugo Van der Merwe, Victoria Baxter, & Audrey Chapman, *Assessing the Impact of Transitional Justice: Challenges for Empirical Research* (Washington DC: United States Institute of Peace Press, 2009); Tricia D. Olsen, Leigh A. Payne, & Andrew G. Reiter, *Transitional Justice in Balance: Comparing Processes, Weighing Efficacy* (Washington DC: United States Institute of Peace, 2010).

not be intentionally targeted in conflict. War can fail to be just in two ways, by being undertaken illegitimately and/or by being conducted in ways that violate the *jus in bello* constraints. Analogously, I see the requirements of societal transformation are the overarching reason for the sake of which TJ processes are undertaken. But the demands of fitting and appropriate treatment of perpetrators and victims constrain how that transformation may be permissibly pursued. Thus, just like with war, processes of TJ may fail to be just in one of two ways: by failing to contribute to societal transformation or by failing to treat victims and perpetrators in a fitting and appropriate manner.

IV. Application to Colombia

My account of TJ aims to provide an articulation of the considerations that are salient from the perspective of justice when evaluating choices about TJ processes in a specific context. It also provides the considerations to appeal to when defending or critiquing the justice of choices made. To apply my framework to Colombia it is first necessary to establish that the circumstances of TJ are satisfied in that context. For it is only with the presence of the four circumstances of TJ that the problem of TJ as I articulate it is salient and the principles of TJ provide a normative guide.

The four circumstances of TJ are I believe satisfied in the current context of Colombia. There is first pervasive structural inequality. Indeed, one of the sources of the ongoing conflict over the past five decades is the differential life prospects and ability to shape terms of interaction among those who live in rural areas and those who live in the urban centres. This divide can also be seen as tracking racial divisions among more indigenous populations and non-indigenous groups.[24]

Second, Colombia has had normalized collective and political wrongdoing as a constitutive feature of the conflict between the Colombian government and the FARC. This is evidenced by the statistics listed in the first part of this paper on the numbers of individuals displaced, killed, taken as hostage, disappeared, subject to rape or other forms of sexual violence, and/or tortured. The structure of the JEP is predicated on the political nature of at least a substantial portion of these cases, and eligibility for participation in the JEP tracks membership as a state actor or as a member of the group contesting the state's authority. A significant portion of the Colombian population were direct victims of the conflict, but all Colombians were indirectly affected by knowing someone who was such a victim. Thus, anticipation of the kinds of wrongs now subject to the TJ process became a basic fact of life around which conduct needed to be oriented. Many cases are cases of complex victims.

There is currently significant uncertainty as to the long-term prospects of success for the peace process itself. There is hope and optimism that the Final Agreement is in fact final. There has been some progress on the implementation of legislation needed to realize the processes and commitments articulated in the Agreement itself. At the same time, there remains opposition to all or parts of the terms of the Final Agreement both among politicians, including the current President of Colombia Ivan Duque, and

[24] Joel Gillin, 'Understanding the causes of Colombia's conflict: Inequality', Colombia Reports, 7 January 2015, https://colombiareports.com/understanding-colombias-conflict-inequality/.

among the general public. And acts of violence threaten to undermine the progress made.[25]

Finally, authority comes into question in different ways. One way is in terms of legitimacy of the Colombian government adjudicating wrongs in which agents of the state are implicated in certain cases. Another way is in terms of the legitimacy of members of the post-FARC party who are implicated in wrongdoing and are now serving in official roles; some of the quotations in the first part of this paper indicate opposition to this inclusion.

Because the four circumstances of transition are satisfied in the Colombian case, the standards by which we ought to assess the TJ processes established are the standards set by the just pursuit of societal transformation. It is thus a mistake to claim, as the first set of claims considered in Section I did, that justice necessarily requires punishment of perpetrators of wrongdoing. It is also a mistake, as some quotes in the second set of views claimed, to conceptualize the Final Agreement as a compromise between peace and justice. Insofar as compromises may be necessary, they will not be compromises between peace and justice. For the societal transformation being sought is itself a form of peace, and by facilitating its processes also facilitate justice. Compromises may be necessary, but such compromises will be between satisfaction of the requirements of societal transformation and the requirements of the fitting and appropriate treatment of perpetrators and victims. Or there may be compromises between TJ as an important goal or aim of such processes and other aims that are salient for Colombian society.

How does the Final Agreement fare when evaluated from the perspective of the demands of societal transformation and the demands of fitting and appropriate treatment of both perpetrators and victims? The terms as laid out in the text of the Final Agreement outline conditions that, if implemented, will meaningfully contribute to the just pursuit of societal transformation. First, the commitment to rural development, to the reintegration of former FARC combatants, and to political participation on the part of the post-FARC party indicate recognition of the necessity of countering the structural inequality that underpinned and was a source of the conflict itself.

Second, these commitments are combined with a comprehensive set of processes for dealing with past wrongdoing. The comprehensiveness of the set (including a truth commission, reparations, criminal trials, and a unit focused on those disappeared) jointly bolster the expressive function each process individually may have. That is, they jointly counter at least in their structure the risk of failing to be and to be seen as instruments of justice. Reparations can less plausibly be claimed as 'blood money' to silence victims given that the JEP and the truth commission will be operating as well. In other words, the propensity of such processes to express meaningful acknowledgement of victims, robust condemnation of wrongdoing committed on all sides, and recognition of victims as rights bearers is strengthened by the holistic manner in which wrongdoing is treated. In terms of perpetrators, processes satisfy the constraints of the just pursuit of transformation if they can be said to hold perpetrators accountable, by

[25] Cristobal Vasquez, 'The Hardest Part is yet to Come for Colombia's Peace Agreement', World Policy Blog (7 March 2017), http://worldpolicy.org/2017/03/07/the-hardest-part-is-yet-to-come-for-colombias-peace-agreement/accessed 7 December 2020 .

judging them responsible for wrongdoing and ideally encouraging perpetrators to accept responsibility and make reparations. The JEP is predicated on judging the actions under its mandate as wrongful and, through the structure of its operation, aims to incentivize perpetrators to explicitly acknowledge and accept responsibility for their actions and, in the case of the restricted zones of liberty, engage in acts of reparation. It also includes accountability in the form of criminal punishment for those convicted who confess late in the process or not at all.

Insofar as processes for dealing with past wrongs can express the moral objectives associated with the fitting and appropriate treatment of perpetrators and victims, they are more likely to facilitate broader transformation by underscoring the commitment to non-repetition and by reducing serious existential uncertainty. In contexts of serious uncertainty processes that may not otherwise have broader significance for the trajectory of a community can come to assume such significance as citizens and observers seek tangible signs of where a community is heading.[26] By underscoring a commitment to deal with past wrongdoing and the underlying sources of the conflict, the components of the Final Agreement, if implemented as envisioned, could meaningfully contribute to broader relational change.

The full implementation of the Final Agreement requires ongoing political will. At the time of writing, there are reasons to worry as to whether the requisite political will is going to be maintained in the long term. Duque, whose campaign platform included opposition to the terms of the Final Agreement especially concerning the JEP, recently defunded the truth commission and is currently seeking other changes to the structure of the JEP.[27] How significant the impact on the implementation of the Final Agreement Duque's efforts will be remains to be seen.

V. Constitutional Dimensions

The Final Agreement is a document with a moral vision for transformative change for Colombia. The Constitutional Court unanimously ruled on 11 October 2017 that the Final Agreement has normative force and, together with international law, will inform interpretations of laws passed to implement the Final Agreement.[28] The process of implementing the Colombian Final Agreement and passing the multiple constitutional amendments needed for this purpose are ongoing. In this section I discuss the temporal dimension of TJ and three types of constitutional changes that occur in the

[26] This point is discussed in detail in Murphy (n. 2), chapter 4.

[27] Adriaan Alsema, 'Duque Defunds Colombia's Truth Commission', Colombia Reports, 20 February 2019, https://colombiareports.com/duque-defunds-colombias-truth-commission/accessed on 7 December 2020; Julia Symmes Cobb & Luis Jaime Acosta, 'Colombia Court Says Cannot Yet Rule on Possible Changes to Peace Law,' Reuters, 20 March 2019, https://www.reuters.com/article/us-colombia-peace/colombia-court-says-cannot-yet-rule-on-possible-changes-to-peace-law-idUSKCN1R12TFaccessed on 7 December 2020.

[28] Gonzalo Ramirez-Cleves, 'The Colombian Constitutional Court Rules that the Peace Agreement is Mandatory for Three Presidential Terms', I.CONnect: International Journal of Constitutional Law Blog (27 October 2017), http://www.iconnectblog.com/2017/10/the-colombian-constitutional-court-rules-that-the-peace-agreement-is-mandatory-for-three-presidential-terms/ accessed on 7 December 2020.

pursuit of TJ. I highlight the source of prior injustice each is designed to address.[29] My discussion draws on the cases of Northern Ireland and South Africa.

That there are constitutional implications of TJ is not surprising. As the Greek philosopher Aristotle noted more than two thousand years ago, constitutions reflect the basic conception of justice ordering a political community.[30] Insofar as the ordering of a political community reflects—in part or as a whole—a conception of justice that is indefensible, constitutional change will be necessary. More specifically and drawing on the account in Section II, TJ requires transformation in the terms structuring interaction among citizens and between citizens and officials. Constitutions articulate the structure of government, the scope of the legitimate exercise of power by government officials, and the basic rights and claims of citizens. Constitutionally recognized rights set basic parameters for the rights and duties of citizens and officials, the process through which a citizen can become a public official in some capacity, and the limits on a government's authority. Thus, TJ will have constitutional implications, because constitutions provide a primary architecture of the relationships in need of transformation.

The language of transformation might suggest that following a transition there will be a comprehensive rejection of an old constitution and immediate establishment of a new constitution that creates a fundamentally different framework for governance and for relational possibilities within a political community. However, in fact not every transition leads to a new constitution. Moreover, constitutional changes are often gradual and occur over an extended period of time. [31] What is true in the case of constitutions is true for other dimensions of transformation as well. Transformation of political relationships requires, for example, cultivating the conditions under which trust among citizens who have historically been divided and among citizens and officials when such trust is absent. Such conditions and their influence on the attitudes taken towards fellow members of a political community cannot arise immediately, but attitudes will only change, if they do change, over time. As I wrote in the conclusion of my book on political reconciliation:

> Rebuilding political relationships in the aftermath of civil conflict and repressive rule is enormously complicated and difficult, given the comprehensive and often extraordinary changes demanded of political relationships in transitional contexts. Few transitional societies will be able to achieve the required changes in political relationships immediately, or even in a short-term period, following a transition to democratic governance; very likely the process of reconciliation will occur over an extended period of time. In some contexts the achievement of more than minimal reconciliation may not be possible. Thus, as a corrective to current discussions, my analysis suggests that discourse about political reconciliation be framed more explicitly in terms of degrees of achievement and the promotion of specific kinds of repair,

[29] For an excellent analysis of time in politics, see Elizabeth Cohen, *The Political Value of Time: Citizenship, Duration, and Democratic Justice* (New York: Cambridge University Press, 2018).

[30] Aristotle, *Nicomachean Ethics*, trans. Terence Irwin, (2nd edn, Indianapolis: Hackett Publishing, 1999), V.1.1129b11–19; Aristotle, *The Politics*, trans. T. A. Sinclair, (rev. edn, New York: Penguin Classics, 1981), III.12.1282b16–17.

[31] Ruti Teitel, *Transitional Justice*, New York: Oxford University Press (2002), 201.

remaining ever mindful of the damage that remains to be addressed and of the long road to rebuilding political relationships that characteristically remains ahead.[32]

The temporal dimension of relational transformation and the implications of that temporal dimension for constitutional change are vividly illustrated in ongoing discussions in South Africa about land expropriation without compensation. Drafted in 1993 by representatives of twenty-six political parties and then endorsed by the outgoing apartheid government in Act 200 of 1993, the 1993 interim constitution paved the way for fully democratic elections and a transition away from apartheid.[33] It contained constitutional principles entrenching basic rights of citizenship for all South Africans, including political rights, language and cultural rights, and educational rights. Following the first fully democratic elections in 1994 in which all South Africans enjoyed the right to vote, the newly elected government set about drafting a permanent constitution, the constitution of the Republic of South Africa of 1996.[34] The interim and final constitution codified basic principles of equal citizenship and non-racism as well as non-sexism and entrenched equal rights for all South Africans regardless of race, in contrast to rights denied to many under the apartheid order.

The interim constitution contained a commitment to amnesty as a way of fostering reconciliation and solidifying a peaceful bridge between the apartheid past and democratic future of South Africa. The South African Truth and Reconciliation Commission ('TRC') was a key process established for dealing with wrongdoing committed during the course of apartheid in a manner that was consistent with that amnesty commitment; individuals implicated in wrongs that fell under the mandate of the TRC were eligible for amnesty if they fully disclosed such wrongs and could demonstrate they were committed for political reasons.[35] The TRC focused on the extraordinary violence (specifically killing, abduction, torture, and severe ill-treatment) committed in contestation of or defence of the apartheid order.[36] While critical to address these wrongs, the TRC did not address the wrong of apartheid itself, the institutionalized discrimination on the basis of race and ethnicity in which it consisted. Citing the TRC's own Final Report, Mahmood Mamdani notes that apartheid was characterized as 'institutionalized discrimination on racial, ethnic or religious grounds involving the violation of fundamental human rights and freedoms and resulting in seriously

[32] Murphy (n. 17), 192.

[33] Interim Constitution of South Africa, https://www.gov.za/documents/constitution/constitution-republic-south-africa-act-200-1993 accessed on 7 December 2020.

[34] The Constitution of the Republic of South Africa, Act 108 of 1996, https://www.gov.za/documents/constitution/constitution-republic-south-africa-1996-1 accessed on 7 December 2020.

[35] 'In order to advance such reconciliation and reconstruction, amnesty shall be granted in respect of acts, omissions and offences associated with political objectives and committed in the course of the conflicts of the past. To this end, Parliament under this Constitution shall adopt a law determining a firm cut-off date, which shall be a date after 8 October 1990 and before 6 December 1993, and providing for the mechanisms, criteria and procedures, including tribunals, if any, through which such amnesty shall be dealt with at any time after the law has been passed.' https://www.gov.za/documents/constitution/constitution-republic-south-africa-act-200-1993accessed on 7 December 2020.

[36] South African Truth and Reconciliation Commission, https://www.justice.gov.za/trc/ accessed on 7 December 2020.

disadvantaging of a population'.[37] The harms of this institutionalized system suffered by entire communities on the basis of racial classification included 'forced relocation, forced disruption of community and family life, coerced labor through administrative and statutory regulation of movement, and so forth'.[38] The failure to deal with the harms associated with apartheid itself and these specific harms was one of the main criticisms raised by scholars such as Mamdani against the TRC.

The current President of South Africa, Cyril Ramaphosa, has indicated that the African National Congress will seek a constitutional amendment to permit land expropriation without compensation, an amendment he supports. Allowing land expropriation without compensation would require a constitutional amendment to change Section 25 of the South African Constitution, which deals with property, and as currently written allows for expropriation of property for a public purpose only if compensation is given.[39] The sought amendment aims to address what the TRC did not, by providing redress for the economic inequality and patterns of ownership of land that continue to align strongly with race.[40] Many questions remain concerning whether the amendment will be passed and, if so, how it will be implemented. What is most salient for my purposes is an aim of the change, which is to contribute to relational transformation by establishing conditions in which all citizens can avoid poverty and participate in political and economic institutions.[41]

The experience of South Africa is not unique, and suggests that the constitutional implications of the pursuit of the transformation of political relationships in Colombia will exist for some time; this is true even if the pace of amendments at the present time is increased through the fast track option. In recognition of the constitutional implications of the Final Agreement and out of a concern to avoid undue delay in or potentially negatively impact on the political will needed for the implementation of the Final Agreement, Congress passed a constitutional amendment, which the Constitutional Court upheld, that establishes a 'fast track' process for the passage of constitutional amendments bound up with the implementation of the Final Agreement. This process reduced the procedural requirements and constrained the parameters of permitted Congressional alteration of proposed amendments, enabling a more rapid implementation of the Final Agreement.[42]

[37] Mahmood Mamdani, 'Amnesty or Impunity? A Preliminary Critique of the Report of the Truth and Reconciliation Commission of South Africa (TRC)' (2002) 32(3–4) Diacritics 33–59, quoting the TRC's Final Report at 54.

[38] Ibid., Mamdani characterizing apartheid in his own words.

[39] Constitution of the Republic of South Africa.

[40] Luke Daniel, 'Land expropriation report adopted by Parliament', The South African, 10 December 2018, https://www.thesouthafrican.com/news/land-expropriation-adopted-by-parliament/accessed on 7 December 2020/; Anita Powell, 'South Africa's Controversial Land Expropriation Stirs Emotions, Uncertainty', VOA News, 11 September 2018, https://www.voanews.com/a/uncertainty-emotions-high-amid-south-africa-talks-of-no-compensation-land-expropriation-/4567355.htmlaccessed on 7 December 2020).

[41] Luke Daniel, 'Land Expropriation without Compensation: What's Next for South Africa', The South African, 14 January 2019, https://www.thesouthafrican.com/land-expropriation-update-south-africa-2019/ accessed on 7 December 2020. On these conditions of relational transformation, see Murphy (n. 2), chapter 3.

[42] Ramirez-Cleves (n. 28); http://es.presidencia.gov.co/normativa/normativa/ACTO%20LEGISLATIVO%2001%20DEL%207%20DE%20JULIO%20DE%202016.pdf.

In addition to noting the temporal dimension of the pursuit of relational transformation in general and through constitutional amendments specifically, we can identify different forms of constitutional changes that will be apt as a response to past wrongdoing and distinctive historical sources of structural inequality in political relationships. While not intended to provide a complete taxonomy, I discuss below three kinds of such change, drawing on South Africa and Northern Ireland and indicating in a preliminary manner where similar changes may be or have been seen in Colombia.

First, against a history of *de facto* discrimination and marginalization of one or more groups within a political community, anti-discrimination protections and procedural reforms in governance may be necessary. The problem to which such protections and reforms are a solution is not fundamentally a problem with constitutionally rights recognized and/or the framework of governance itself, but rather with how in practice rights were respected and governance occurred.

Northern Ireland provides an instructive case for this first point. At the root of the conflict in Northern Ireland are conflicting national identities. The national identify conflict is one between nationalists, who are overwhelmingly Catholic and identify as Irish, and unionists, who are overwhelmingly Protestant and identify as British. Nationalist political parties historically have sought reunification of Ireland, while unionists wish to retain the place of Northern Ireland within the United Kingdom. Ethno-nationalist divisions were exacerbated by residential and educational segregation coupled with historical discrimination against and political marginalization of the nationalist/Catholic minority community in Northern Ireland. This was especially true during the period between 1922 and 1972, when the Parliament of Northern Ireland (Stormont) operated, per the requirements of the Government of Northern Ireland Act of 1920.[43] During these decades, gerrymandering of districts effectively guaranteed the complete control of government by unionist political parties. The 1960s civil rights movement began as an effort to protest discrimination as well as police misconduct and brutality against Catholics. The failure of any effective response to the demands at the core of the civil rights movement initiated a period of violent conflict known as The Troubles, which lasted until the Good Friday Agreement/Belfast Agreement ('GFA') of 1998.[44] Paramilitary violence was a core feature of the violence, pitting nationalist paramilitary groups, such as the Irish Republican Army ('IRA'), against unionist paramilitaries, such as the Ulster Volunteer Force ('UVF'). From 1972 until the GFA, the British government ruled Northern Ireland directly.

The terms of the GFA required constitutional changes in both the United Kingdom and the Republic of Ireland. The GFA outlined provisions for the creation of a democratic assembly, to replace direct rule by the British government in Northern Ireland, as well as for the creation of Councils across the entire island of Ireland (and so between Northern Ireland and the Republic of Ireland) and between the British and Irish governments.[45] To create the Northern Ireland Assembly, the British government repealed the Government of Northern Ireland Act of 1920 and then passed the

[43] John McGarry & Brendan O'Leary, *Explaining Northern Ireland: Broken Images* (Oxford: Wiley-Blackwell, 1995).

[44] The Belfast (Good Friday) Agreement, https://www.gov.uk/government/publications/the-belfast-agreement.

[45] Ibid.

Northern Ireland Act of 1998.[46] The Northern Ireland Act established the Northern Ireland Assembly and the positions of the First Minister and Deputy First Minster in Northern Ireland, the Northern Ireland Human Rights Commission, and the Equality Commission for Northern Ireland. These latter two commissions specifically aimed to ensure that human rights for all people of Northern Ireland were respected and to guard against discrimination. To guard against a repetition of the political marginalization of one community, the First Minister and Deputy First Minister stand for election jointly, and represent both communities. Another safeguard against discrimination and marginalization articulated in the GFA and included in the Northern Ireland Act of 1998 is a requirement that all votes within the Northern Ireland Assembly on especially contentious matters get a majority of votes from designated nationalists and unionists. The commitment in the Colombian Final Agreement to reserve a set of Congressional seats for the Common Alternative Revolutionary Force, the post-FARC political party, can be seen as one way of providing an institutional space for political participation of those previously excluded.

The inclusion of anti-discrimination measures and procedural safeguards were necessary but not sufficient to address the sources and consequences of conflict in Northern Ireland. Importantly, such measures did not address the root cause of conflict, namely, the conflict of national identity and affiliation. More broadly, anti-discrimination measures and procedural safeguards will be insufficient for dealing with injustice surrounding the basic definition of citizenship itself: who counts as a (full) citizen and what rights citizens are taken to enjoy. What is necessary in these cases is a fundamental alteration of the definition of citizenship itself. This is the second kind of constitutional change in transitional contexts.

In South Africa this alteration was made explicit in the post-apartheid interim and final constitutions when citizenship and equal citizenship rights were extended to all South Africans regardless of race, ethnicity, religion, and/or gender. The form the changes to citizenship took in Northern Ireland, however, were different. Against the background of an implicit denial of the national identity of one community and in the context of conflicting national identities between communities, the alterations made aimed to recognize the identity that had been denied and provide conditions for navigating in a just manner the conflicting affiliations. For this purpose, principles of self-determination and consent by the people of Northern Ireland with respect to the future of Northern Ireland guided the GFA and the subsequent text of the Northern Ireland Act of 1988 and the Nineteenth Amendment to the constitution of the Republic of Ireland. The Northern Ireland Act of 1988 and the Nineteenth Amendment of the Irish Constitution recognized the choice of staying within the United Kingdom or joining the Republic of Ireland as a choice to be made by the people of Northern Ireland. If a majority decided to bring about a united Ireland than they could do so.[47]

[46] Northern Ireland Act of 1998, https://www.legislation.gov.uk/ukpga/1998/47/content accessed on 7 December 2020.

[47] Part 1 of Section 1 of the Northern Ireland Act of 1988 states: '(1) It is hereby declared that Northern Ireland in its entirety remains part of the United Kingdom and shall not cease to be so without the consent of a majority of the people of Northern Ireland voting in a poll held for the purposes of this section in accordance with Schedule 1. (2) But if the wish expressed by a majority in such a poll is that

Moreover, the birthright of people of Northern Ireland to identify as British or Irish or both was recognized; this right would not be affected by any future change in the status of Northern Ireland itself. The Nineteenth Amendment of the Irish constitution revised Article 29 to include a commitment to recognize the birthright of every person born on the island of Ireland to membership in the Irish nation and to Irish citizenship.[48] The creation of an all-Ireland, North/South Ministerial Council, British-Irish Intergovernmental Council, British-Irish Council aimed to further strengthen connections between the people of Northern Ireland and both the British and Irish governments.[49]

A third kind of constitutional change in transitional contexts is bound up with the establishment of processes for dealing with past human rights violations. As mentioned earlier, in South Africa this took the form of an explicit commitment in the interim constitution to enacting an amnesty provision for those responsible for human rights abuses during the course of the conflict.[50] In Northern Ireland, by contrast, no specific requirement for dealing with past wrongdoing was laid out. Instead, the GFA recognizes the importance of acknowledgement of, and support for, victims of the conflict and the importance of police reform moving forward. These commitments were realized through the Northern Ireland Victims Commission and the Commission on Policing for Northern Ireland (or Patten Commission).[51] In Colombia, the changes to the judiciary made in order to allow for the functioning of the JEP reflect constitutional changes of this third type.

VI. Conclusion

This paper has evaluated the justice of the Colombian Final Agreement, arguing that its provisions as laid out satisfy the requirements of TJ though for that justice to be realized the terms of the Final Agreement must be implemented. I then noted the significant constitutional implications in general of the pursuit of relational

Northern Ireland should cease to be part of the United Kingdom and form part of a united Ireland, the Secretary of State shall lay before Parliament such proposals to give effect to that wish as may be agreed between Her Majesty's Government in the United Kingdom and the Government of Ireland.' https://www.legislation.gov.uk/ukpga/1998/47/section/1; 'It is the firm will of the Irish nation, in harmony and friendship, to unite all the people who share the territory of the island of Ireland, in all the diversity of their identities and traditions, recognising that a united Ireland shall be brought about only by peaceful means with the consent of a majority of the people, democratically expressed, in both jurisdictions in the island. Until then, the laws enacted by the Parliament established by this Constitution shall have the like area and extent of application as the laws enacted by the Parliament that existed immediately before the coming into operation of this Constitution.' http://www.irishstatutebook.ie/eli/1998/ca/19/enacted/en/print.

48 http://www.irishstatutebook.ie/eli/1998/ca/19/enacted/en/print.

49 John Morison, 'Constitutionalism and Change: Representation, Governance, and Participation in the New Northern Ireland' (1998) 22(4) Fordham International Law Journal 1608–27.

50 1993 Interim Constitution of South Africa, http://www.justice.gov.za/trc/legal/sacon93.htm.

51 Independent Commission on Policing for Northern Ireland, 'A New Beginning: Policing in Northern Ireland', http://cain.ulst.ac.uk/issues/police/patten/patten99.pdf.

transformation. I also discussed the temporal dimension of constitutional changes in transitional contexts. Finally, I outlined three different forms of constitutional change that are common in transitional contexts, each of which addresses a different source of prior injustice, highlighting where such changes are or might be necessary in the context of Colombia.

15

The Transitional Justice Model in Colombia vis-à-vis the Inter-American Human Rights System

Amidst the Conventionality Control and the National Margin of Appreciation

Juana I. Acosta-López & Cindy Vanessa Espitia-Murcia[*]

I. Introduction

On 24 November 2016, the Colombian Government and FARC-EP signed the 'Final Agreement to End the Armed Conflict and Build a Stable and Lasting Peace' (Final Agreement). The Final Agreement enshrines the principles and commitments agreed upon by the parties in respect to: (i) rural reform; (ii) political participation; (iii) bilateral and definitive ceasefire and cessation of hostilities; (iv) solution to the problem of illicit drugs trafficking; and (v) the 'Holistic System for Truth, Justice, Reparation and Non-Recurrence (SIVJR by its acronym in Spanish).[1]

Regardless of the legal and political debates concerning the legal value of the Final Agreement at the domestic level,[2] today the transitional justice model (TJM), particularly the SIVJR, is an integral part of the Colombian political constitution of 1991.[3] Furthermore, the Colombian Constitutional Court validated the conformity of the Final Agreement and its implementation legal frame with essential constitutional principles.[4] Nevertheless, the relationship of the SIVJR with the Inter-American Human Rights System ('IAHRS') is yet to be assessed by the Inter-American Court of

* This paper is a result of the research project '*Justicia transicional: alcance, límites y desafíos del componente de justicia en el modelo colombiano*' of the Research Group on International Law of Universidad de La Sabana (Bogotá, Colombia). We would like to express our special gratitude to Giovanny Vega-Barbosa (LLM) for his input in the translation and review of this paper.

[1] High Commissioner for Peace, 'Final Agreement to End the Armed Conflict and Build a Stable and Lasting Peace' (24 November 2016) https://peacemaker.un.org/sites/peacemaker.un.org/files/Colombia%20Nuevo%20Acuerdo%20Final%2024%20Nov%202016_0.pdf, accessed on 12 December 2020.

[2] Álvaro Amaya & Valeria Guzmán, 'La naturaleza jurídico-internacional de los Acuerdos de Paz y sus consecuencias en la implementación' (2017) 30 International Law 42–60.

[3] Legislative Act No. 1 of 2017, 'por medio del cual se establecen instrumentos jurídicos para facilitar y asegurar la implementación y el desarrollo normativo del acuerdo final'; Juana Acosta-López & Carlos Arévalo Narváez 'Constitucionalización del sistema integral de verdad, justicia y reparación en Colombia: algunos comentarios sobre la participación política y la responsabilidad del mando', in Instituto Español de Estudios Estratégicos *Cuadernos de estrategia* (Ministerio de Defensa de España, 2017).

[4] Constitutional Court of Colombia, Judgment C-674 of 2017.

Juana I. Acosta-López & Cindy Vanessa Espitia-Murcia. *The Transitional Justice Model in Colombia vis-à-vis the Inter-American Human Rights System* In: *Constitutionalism*. Edited by: Alejandro Linares-Cantillo, Camilo Valdivieso-León, Santiago García-Jaramillo, Oxford University Press (2021). © The various contributors. DOI: 10.1093/oso/9780192896759.003.0016

Human Rights (IACtHR). In its analysis, the IACtHR will have to decide if the particular Colombian TJM meets the human rights obligations of the state provided for the American Convention on Human Rights (ACHR), and further, if the Constitutional Court properly carried out the so-called conventionality control.[5]

In short, this paper seeks to demonstrate that, in light of the relevant international normativity and case law, the Colombian TJM, especially the justice tools of the SIVJR, are likely to successfully withstand the conventionality control. Given the early stage of implementation, we will focus on the formal design of the TJM rather than on its operation.

First, this article contains a description of the design and structure of the SIVJR in the Final Agreement. The principle of 'integrality' is governing and transversal to the whole TJM. This principle entails that it is not possible to understand the available judicial and extra-judicial mechanisms in isolation. Accordingly, every analysis about the adequacy and effectiveness of the SIVJR must be made bearing in mind that those mechanisms are complementary to each other, the fundamental rationale being that only through symbiotic interaction can those mechanisms achieve the intended final objectives of the TJM.

Second, the justice tools of the TJM will be analysed against the mandates deriving from victims' rights to justice, truth and reparation, and non-recurrence. This study will take into account that Colombia's due diligence obligations not only include investigating, prosecuting, and punishing human rights violations, but also preventing those violations, guaranteeing non-recurrence, and uncovering the truth. These obligations are intermingled and cannot be interpreted in a vacuum. In fact, the inter-dependence of the obligations is reinforced in a transitional context.

Finally, we will propose a model for the just and proper balance between the notions of conventionality control and national margin of appreciation. In particular, the position is advanced that a context of transition from a non-international armed conflict ('NIAC') to peace requires the interaction between these two doctrines to be re-assessed. The view is that states parties to the ACHR are better placed to design and implement the necessary mechanisms and platforms to move to a stable and lasting peace.

II. Design and Structure of the SIVJR in the Final Agreement

In the Final Agreement, the SIVJR is strictly required to follow four objectives. First, to promote the integral protection of victims' human rights. Second, to guarantee accountability by establishing the responsibility of the participants in the NIAC. Third, to work towards the uncovering and clarification of the truth. Fourth, to consolidate the termination of the NIAC and to impede the emergence of new forms of violence.[6] The SIVJR, which includes and combines judicial and extra-judicial mechanisms, has the following organs:[7]

[5] *Almonacid Arellano v Chile*, IACtHR App. 12.057, 26 September 2006.
[6] Final Agreement (n. 1).
[7] Legislative Act No. 1 of 2017 (n. 3).

1. *The Truth, Coexistence and Non-Recurrence Commission* (Truth Commission).[8] This is a temporary extra-judicial organ tasked with four main functions,[9] namely: (i) to clarify the human rights and international humanitarian law ('IHL') violations and breaches committed in the course of the NIAC; (ii) to provide the society with ample explanation on the complexity of the Colombian conflict; (iii) to promote the recognition of the victims and the acknowledgement of the individual and collective responsibilities of those who participated in the conflict; (iv) to promote reconciliation and coexistence in the territories as a guarantee of non-recurrence.[10]

   In particular, the Truth Commission has a three-year mandate to clarify and promote the recognition and/or acknowledgement of: (i) practices and facts that constitute grave violations of human rights and IHL; (ii) the collective state responsibility by FARC-EP, or any other group or organization with participation in the conflict; (iii) the impact of the NIAC in society, in the exercise of political rights, on the victims, and in those who directly participated in it; (iv) the historical context—the original and multiple causes of the conflict; and (v) the factors and conditions that allowed or contributed to the continuation of the NIAC, among other affairs.[11] The Truth Commission started its mandate on 28 November 2018.
2. *Special Unit for the Search of Persons deemed as Missing in the Context and due to the Conflict (Special Unit).*[12] This is a high-level special unit of a humanitarian and extra-judicial nature, whose goal is to direct, coordinate, and contribute to the implementation of humanitarian actions for the searching and identification of all the people deemed as missing due to the NIAC who are still alive. In the cases of those deceased, whenever possible, the Special Unit should work for the location and dignified delivery of their remains.[13]
3. *Special Jurisdiction for Peace* ('JEP').[14] This organ is composed of a number of judicial panels for justice. In its twenty-year term it is tasked with judging those who bear most responsibility for crimes that constitute serious violations of international human rights law and grave breaches of IHL that were committed during the sixty-year NIAC.[15] Its jurisdiction is prevalent in respect of conducts committed before 1 December 2016, relating directly or indirectly to the NIAC.[16] According to the Statutory Act No. 1957 of 2019 on the Administration of Justice of the JEP (Statutory Act), the main function of this organ is to secure, by reasonable means within its reach, truth, justice, reparation, and guarantees of non-recurrence for the victims.[17] In accordance

[8] Final Agreement (n. 1), 9. See also 79, 84, 89, 131.
[9] Ibid., 138.
[10] Legislative Act No. 1 of 2017 (n. 3), Articles 2, 11; Decree 588 (2017); Final Agreement (n. 1).
[11] D. 588 (n. 10), Article 11.
[12] Final Agreement (n. 1), 9, 134.
[13] Final Agreement (n. 1), 138; Legislative Act No. 1 of 2017 (n. 3), Article 3.
[14] Final Agreement (n. 1), 138.
[15] Legislative Act No. 1 of 2017 (n. 3); Statutory Law (2019); Judgment C-674 of 2017 (n. 4).
[16] Legislative Act No. 1 of 2017 (n. 3), Article 6.
[17] Ibid., Article 28.

with the Final Agreement and Legislative Act No. 1 of 2017,[18] the various mechanism and measures for truth, justice, reparation, and non-recurrence 'cannot be interpreted in isolation', since they are part of an integral system.[19] Moreover, the SIVJR was envisaged to be governed by the transversal principles of: (i) restorative justice; (ii) centrality of victims' rights; (iii) effective participation of victims; (iv) conditionality; and (v) investigation of patterns.[20]

III. The SIVJR and the Rights to Justice, Truth, and Reparation in the Inter-American Human Rights System

The political debate in Colombia has focused almost exclusively on one of the subcomponents of the SIVJR: the JEP. One of the reasons is that the JEP has authority to select both the most responsible perpetrators and the most serious crimes. In other words, not all crimes or actors will be prosecuted by the JEP. Further, even those convicted for the most serious crimes would be eligible for alternative punishments, including the deprivation of liberty without imprisonment.[21] This has triggered criticism to the effect that the JEP may revert to impunity.

Under the ACHR, Colombia not only has the obligation to investigate, prosecute, and punish, but also to prevent human rights violations,[22] to guarantee the non-repetition and recurrence of such violations,[23] to uncover and clarify the truth,[24] to guarantee security, and to maintain the public order.[25] These obligations cannot be interpreted individually; they are interdependent,[26] with interdependence being accentuated in contexts of transition.[27] This implies, for example, that in the transitional justice scenario it is not possible to analyse the obligation to investigate, prosecute, and punish human rights violations without taking into account that judicial truth has considerable limits.[28] The accused has little incentive to contribute to the truth

[18] Ibid., Article 1.

[19] Final Agreement (n. 1), 139.

[20] Ibid., 153

[21] Ibid.

[22] *Velásquez Rodriguez v Honduras*, IACtHR App. 2.521, 29 July 1988; *Gelman v Uruguay*, IACtHR App. 13.431, 24 February 2011; *Lopez Soto v. Venezuela*, IACtHR App. 12.797, 26 September 2018.

[23] *Rio Negro Massacres v Guatemala*, IACtHR App. 844-05, 4 September 2012; *Las dos erres massacre v Guatemala*, IACtHR App. 652-04, 24 November 2009; María Londoño, *Las garantías de no repetición en la jurisprudencia interamericana* (1st edn, Universidad de La Sabana, Bogotá, Colombia, 2014).

[24] *Bámaca Velásquez v Guatemala*, IACtHR App. 11.129, 25 November 2000; *El Mozote and nearby places v El Salvador*, IACtHR App. 10.720, 25 October 2012; *Coc Max v Guatemala*, IACtHR App. 11.550, 22 August 2018.

[25] *Montero-Aranguren et al (Detention Center of Catia) v Venezuela*, IACtHR App. 11.699, 5 July 2006; *Neira Alegria et al. v Perú*, IACtHR App. 10.078, 19 January 1995; *Alvarado Espinoza v Mexico*, IACtHR App. 12.916, 28 November 2018.

[26] *Cepeda Vargas v Colombia*, IACtHR App. 12.531, 26 May 2010.

[27] *Verdad, justicia y reparación: Cuarto informe sobre la situación de derechos humanos en Colombia*, IACHR OEA/Ser.L/V/II. Doc. 49/13 (2013).

[28] Annette Pearson, 'Is Restorative Justice a Piece of the Colombian Transitional Justice Puzzle?' (2017) 5 Restorative Justice 293; Johanna Sköld, 'The Truth about Abuse? A Comparative Approach to Inquiry Narratives on Historical Institutional Child Abuse' (2016) 45 History of Education 492; James Meernik & Jose Raul Guerrero, 'Can International Criminal Justice Advance Ethnic Reconciliation? The ICTY and Ethnic Relations in Bosnia-Herzegovina' (2014) 14 Southeast European and Black Sea Studies 383.

in an ordinary trial.[29] Therefore, it is not wise to subject the uncovering of the truth exclusively to the results of ordinary criminal procedure.[30] Given these limitations, transitions require complementary extra-judicial mechanisms, such as truth commissions.[31] Under exceptional circumstances, especially when the balancing of principles is required, states must direct their efforts to guarantee at the highest possible level every single one of their international obligations. Nonetheless, as can be anticipated, compliance with these obligations in contexts of transition from NIAC to peace is especially complex.[32]

It is also crucial to bear in mind that, according to the IACtHR, where complex cases are concerned, the obligation to investigate implies the duty to direct the efforts of the state apparatus to uncover criminal structures.[33] In transitional settings, where massive violations have occurred, this is not possible without concentrating efforts on the investigation of those who bear the greatest responsibility, and without encouraging the structural components of the criminal organization to participate in non-judicial mechanisms to provide information that contributes to unveiling the causes of violence and to preventing their recurrence.[34]

The system designed in the peace agreement aspires to comply with all of the aforementioned interdependent obligations, based on an all-inclusive strategy for transitional justice involving different judicial and extra-judicial tools,[35] in tandem with a policy of holistic reparation and guarantees of non-recurrence. The Final Agreement and its implementation legal frame also includes FARC-EP's commitments, among which we can find the commitment to lay down arms, to acknowledge responsibility, to contribute to the clarification of truth, the full reparation of victims, and to release hostages and illegally recruited minors.[36]

[29] *Sin la verdad no puede haber justicia y reparación, ni paz y reconciliación*, OHCHR, 13 June 2005; Brian Grodsky, 'Weighing the Costs of Accountability: The Role of Institutional Incentives in Pursuing Transitional Justice' (2008) 7 Journal of Human Rights 353.

[30] Juana Acosta-López & Cindy Espitia, 'Pasado, presente y futuro de la justicia transicional en el Sistema Interamericano de Derechos Humanos' (2017) 30 International Law: Revisto Colombiana 9–40.

[31] Louise Mallinder, 'Can Amnesties and International Justice be Reconciled?' (2007) 1 International Journal of Transitional Justice 208.

[32] Darryl Robinson, 'Serving the Interests of Justice: Amnesties, Truth Commissions and the International Criminal Court' (2004) 14 European Journal of International Law 481; Diane Orentlicher, 'Settling Accounts: The Duty to Prosecute Human Rights Violations of a Prior Regime' (1991) 100 Yale Law Journal 2537.

[33] *Cepeda Vargas v Colombia* (n. 26); *Pacheco León et al. v Honduras*, IACtHR App. 484-04, 15 November 2017; *Isaza Uribe et al. v Colombia*, IACtHR App. 10.737, 20 November 2018.

[34] A review of comparative practice shows the importance of adopting such mechanisms in instances where multiplicity of victims and victimizers are identified. For example, in Bosnia & Herzegovina, the prosecutor's office adopted the document 'Orientation Criteria for Sensitive Rules of the Road Cases' (2004) in which: (i) characteristics were identified to allow the classification of cases as 'highly sensitive cases' and 'sensitives', these being the only ones that were subject to criminal prosecution; (ii) the procedure was fixed to distribute the cases between the competent organs. See Bogdan Ivanisevic, 'A Chance for Justice? War Crime Prosecutions in Bosnia's Serb Republic' (2006) 18(3) Human Rights Watch 6–7. In Argentina, in 1984, the state prosecutor adopted criteria for the selection of cases and the most responsible in order to proceed to the prosecution of the Military Junta who ruled the country in the 1970s. Similarly, in Indonesia, the National Commission on Human Rights has, in practice, focused its work on the analysis of the most serious cases. Cf. Morten Bergsmo, *Criteria for Prioritizing and Selecting Core International Crimes Cases* (2nd edn, Torkel Opsahl Academic Epublisher, 2010).

[35] Citizen Security and Human Rights, ICHR OEA/Ser.L/V/II (2009)

[36] Statutory Law (2019) (n. 15), Articles 4, 13, 18, 39.

In light of the above, in this section the analysis is made with respect to the transversal principles of the SIVJR using the international obligations of the state concerning victims' rights to truth, justice, and reparation as the relevant benchmark. In parallel, we will present their specific views about the notion of 'selection'. Our purpose will be to show that both the principles and the structure of the TJM withstand the conventionality control, under not only the obligations arising out of the IAHRS, but under a wider and growing *corpus juris* governing transitional justice.

A. The Principle of Restorative Justice

According to Transitory Article 1 of Legislative Act 1 of 2017,[37] and Article 1 of the Statutory Act,[38] restorative justice constitutes a guiding paradigm by virtue of which all actions carried out by the JEP will endeavour to repair the damage caused to the victims, particularly, with the aim 'to put an end to the situation of social exclusion that the victimisation has caused'. This means that the conditions of those beneficiaries of the rationalization of the criminal action[39] and the sanctions imposed on those actually condemned,[40] shall effectively adopt a restorative logic as opposed to a retributive one.

The conception of justice in Colombia's TJM finds support in the decisions of international tribunals recognizing its importance especially with regards to creating reconciliation scenarios and for the protection of victims.[41] This notion of justice also acknowledges that a violation of human rights is relevant not only because it is a breach of the law but also because it harms and causes damage to the victims and the community. This explains that the focus is on the affected party and on the re-establishment of the social contract that the violation broke.[42]

As noted by Colleen Murphy, the concept of restorative justice has not yet been sufficiently developed or delimited.[43] Moreover, Colleen Murphy, Pablo de Greiff, and David Dyzenhaus are of the opinion that in a TJM the expectations over results should always be modest. Nonetheless, it can still be sustained with a great deal of support in the very basic purpose underlying a transitional model, which is to repair the affected social relations and to re-establish confidence among citizens,[44] including with respect

[37] Legislative Act No. 1 of 2017 (n. 3), Article 1.

[38] Statutory Law (2019) (n. 15), Article 13

[39] Ibid., Article 39.

[40] Ibid., Articles 97, 127, 128, 140.

[41] Pablo de Greiff, 'Report to the Human Rights Council on the Foundation of the Mandate and the Importance of a Comprehensive Approach' (A/HRC/21/46, 9 August 2012) https://www.ohchr.org/Documents/HRBodies/HRCouncil/RegularSession/Session21/A-HRC-21-46_en.pdf, accessed 7 February 2019.

[42] United Nations Office on Drugs and Crime, 'Manual sobre programas de justicia restaurativa' (2006) 1(1) https://www.unodc.org/documents/justice-and-prison-reform/Manual_sobre_programas_de_justicia_restaurativa.pdf, accessed 7 February 2019.

[43] Colleen Murphy, 'Transitional Justice: A Conceptual Map', in Krushil Watene & Jay Drydyk (eds), *Theorizing Justice: Novel Insights and Future Directions* (Rowman & Littlefield, 2016), 33.

[44] Colleen Murphy, 'Judging the Justice of the Colombian Final Agreement', this volume; David Dyzenhaus & Alma Diamond, 'The Resilient Constitution', this volume ;Pablo de Greiff, 'Algunas reflexiones acerca del desarrollo de la Justicia Transicional' (2011) Anuario de Derechos Humanos 7.

to the relevant institutions and the consolidation a reconciliation scenario.[45] If this is in fact the goal of a process of transition, then restorative justice plays a vital role.

B. The Centrality of Victims' Rights

The Inter-American Commission of Human Rights (IACmHR), the IACtHR, and the former UN Special Rapporteur on the promotion of truth, justice, reparation, and guarantees of non-recurrence, among others, have stressed the view that in transitional justice scenarios states shall direct all their efforts to secure and guarantee victims' rights. In particular, states should aim to: (i) uncover the truth of the facts and establish the corresponding responsibilities;[46] (ii) direct all the efforts to investigate, prosecute, and punish those responsible for international crimes;[47] and (iii) promote the reparation of the victims as well as the non-recurrence of the human rights violations.[48]

The Colombian TJM has been conceived under this type of logic. Transitory Article 12 of Legislative Act 1 of 2017[49] and Article 13 of the Statutory Law[50] expressly recognize the 'centrality of the victims' rights' as a guiding principle for the operation of the JEP. By virtue of this, every action carried out within the JEP shall consider as a transversal axis: (i) the rights of the victim to truth, justice, reparation, and non-recurrence; and (ii) the gravity of the suffering inflicted because of the gross human rights violations and grave breaches to IHL during the NIAC.[51]

In this framework, the rights of the victims shall be guaranteed by the state through: (i) a regime of conditions pursuant to which the beneficiaries of the mechanisms for the rationalization of the criminal action must contribute to the searching of persons deemed as missing, the uncovering of the truth, and the reparation of victims, and must acknowledge their responsibilities and commit themselves to non-recurrence;[52] (ii) the investigation, prosecution and sanction of the grave violations of human rights;[53] (iii) the uncovering of the truth through a dialectic process and with the active participation of the victims;[54] (iv) the consolidation of an accountability system for all the various participants in the NIAC;[55] and (v) the materialization of a regime of sanctions with a restorative approach,[56] among other mechanisms.

[45] Paul Seils, 'The Place of Reconciliation in Transitional Justice' (2017) 1(1) International Center for Transitional Justice, https://www.ictj.org/sites/default/files/ICTJ-Briefing-Paper-Reconciliation-TJ-2017.pdf, accessed 7 February 2019.

[46] *Terrones Silva et al. v Perú*, IACtHR App. 422-03, 26 September 2018; *La Cantuta v Perú*, IACtHR App. 11.045, 29 November 2006; *Verdad, justicia y reparación: Cuarto informe sobre la situación de derechos humanos en Colombia*, IACHR OEA/Ser.L/V/II. Doc. 49/13 (2013).

[47] *El Mozote* (n. 24)

[48] *Terrones Silva et al.* (n. 46); *La Cantuta* (n. 46); *Verdad, justicia y reparación* (n. 46).

[49] Legislative Act No. 1 of 2017 (n. 3), Article 12.

[50] Statutory Law (2018) (n. 15), Article 13.

[51] Ibid.

[52] Ibid., Article 20.

[53] Legislative Act No. 1 of 2017 (n. 3), Articles 1, 5, 16; Statutory Law 1957 of 2019, (n. 15) , Articles 2, 8, 13, 19, 28, 29, 42 45.

[54] Statutory Law 1957 of 2019, (n. 15), Article 20.

[55] Legislative Act No. 1 of 2017 (n. 3), Article 1.

[56] Statutory Law (2010) (n. 15), Article 127.

C. The Effective Participation of Victims

There is consensus among human rights bodies on the importance of the participation of victims in judicial processes where the uncovering of the victimizing facts takes place.[57] The essential role played by victims, and the corresponding state duty to secure such participation, is even stronger in transitional justice processes aimed at lasting national reconciliation[58]

Pursuant to Legislative Act No. 1 of 2017[59] and the Statutory Law,[60] the Colombian TJM, and especially the process carried out by the JEP, is premised on the principle of victims' participation. This principle materializes in three specific scenarios of empowerment. First, victims have the possibility to participate throughout the judicial activity, including all the relevant hearings and sessions.[61] Second, victims are entitled to file reports and deliver information to the JEP about the victimizing facts and the corresponding responsibilities.[62] Finally, victims can participate in the definition, following-up, and monitoring of compliance with the conditions and the sanctions granted and imposed by the JEP.[63]

D. The Principle of Conditionality

The regime of conditionality in transitional justice scenarios has not yet been amply developed or approached in light of the relevant international human rights obligations. Moreover, there are few experiences of peace-building processes implementing such a regime.[64] Nevertheless, several human rights bodies, including the IACmHR;[65] the former UN Special Rapporteur on the promotion of truth, justice, reparation, and guarantees of non-recurrence;[66] the Colombian Constitutional Court;[67] and a sector

[57] *González Medina and family v Dominican Republic*, IACtHR App. 11.324, 27 February 2012; *Radilla Pacheco v Mexico*, IACtHR App. 11.324, 27 February 2012; *Bulacio v Argentina*, IACtHR, 18 September 2003; Pablo de Greiff, 'Report of the Special Rapporteur on the Promotion of Truth, Justice, Reparation and Guarantees of Non-Recurrence' (A/HRC/36/50, 21 August 2017) https://documents-dds-ny.un.org/doc/UNDOC/GEN/G12/158/58/PDF/G1215858.pdf?OpenElement, accessed 7 February 2019.

[58] Ibid.

[59] Legislative Act No. 1 of 2017 (n. 3), Article 5.

[60] Statutory Law (2019) (n. 14), Article 14.

[61] Final Agreement (n. 1); Legislative Act No. 1 of 2017 (n. 3), Articles 1, 5, 12, 14, 15, 75, 92; see Judgment C-674 of 2017 (n. 4).

[62] Final Agreement (n. 1); Statutory Law (2019) (n. 15) Articles 79B, 79C, 79H, 80.

[63] Final Agreement (n. 1); Legislative Act No. 1 of 2017 (n. 3), Articles 1, 5, 11, 13, 18, 20, 25; Statutory Law (2019) (n. 14), Articles 13, 31, 38, 39, 79, 92, 97, 114.

[64] For example, South Africa, with the recent creation of the Truth and Reconciliation Commission. The South African Final Agreement provides for as follows: 'anyone seeking amnesty for crimes defending or opposing apartheid would have to tell the Truth Commission details of what they did and have their names and the events they were involved in published. Once granted amnesty, they could never be prosecuted or sued for their activities.' Cf. Janine Clark 'Reconciliation via Truth? A Study of South Africa's TRC' (2013) 11(2) Journal of Human Rights 189.

[65] *Verdad, justicia y reparación* (n. 34).

[66] de Greiff (n. 57).

[67] Constitutional Court of Colombia, Decision C-579 of 2013.

of academic scholarship[68] have highlighted the importance of subjecting criminal law benefits in transitional justice contexts to strict compliance with the conditions that were envisaged to result in the realization of victims' rights to truth, justice, reparation, and non-recurrence.

These bodies and commentators share the view that the minimum conditions that must be demanded in order to access and keep enjoying the mechanisms for the rationalization of the criminal action are: (i) the surrendering of the weapons; (ii) the acknowledgement of responsibility; (iii) the commitment to non-recurrence of the victimizing facts; (iv) the contribution to the reparation of the victims; and (v) the contribution to the uncovering of the truth in respect of the victimizing facts.[69]

Pursuant to Legislative Act No. 1 of 2017 and Law 1820 of 2016, the conditionality regime is recognized as a principle of the TJM. It has also been considered by the Colombian Constitutional Court as a structural component of the SVJR,[70] since it allows for the harmonization, on one hand, of the state's faculty—according to IHL—to grant criminal law benefits as part of the process of peace-building, and on the other hand, of its duty to protect victims' rights to truth, justice, reparation, and non-recurrence under international human rights law.[71]

In conformity with the set of legal and constitutional provisions referred to above, the general conditions governing the granting of benefits in the Colombian TJM are as follows:[72]

- to contribute to the uncovering of truth;
- to commit to non-recurrence;
- to contribute to the reparation of the victims; and
- to provide information to aid with the work of the Special Unit for the Search of Persons Deemed as Missing;

In the case of former FARC-EP members, the granting of criminal law benefits will be additionally subjected to compliance with the following conditions:[73]

- to surrender weapons;
- to actively contribute to the success of the civil life re-integration process; and
- to surrender minors.

The Constitutional Court, in its analysis of the Final Agreement's legal framework and seeking to delimit the scope of the conditionality principle, has underlined, first,

[68] *Verdad, justicia y reparación* (n. 34); de Greiff (n. 41); Decision C-579 of 13 (n. 67); Instituto de Justicia Transicional, *Las pautas de Belfast sobre Amnistía y Responsabilidad* (Belfast, 2012) 25 (hereinafter Instituto de Justicia Transicional, *Las pautas de Belfast)*

[69] *Las pautas de Belfast* (n. 68).

[70] Judgment C-674 of 2017 (n. 4).

[71] *El Mozote* (n. 24); *Gelman* (n. 22); *Almonacid Arellano* (n. 5); *Gomes Lund v Brasil*, IACtHR App. 12.113, 24 November 2010; *Barrios Altos v Perú*, IACtHR App. 11.811, 14 March 2001; de Greiff (n. 57).

[72] Statutory Law (2019) (n. 15), Article 20.

[73] Ibid.

that verification of compliance with the above-mentioned requirements shall be made both at the time of granting the benefit and subsequently in order to determine the continuous granting of the benefit,[74] and second, that the organs of the JEP shall carry out the relevant analysis in accordance with the principles of proportionality, reasonability, and graduality.[75]

Although there are not enough legal sources allowing affirmation that the principle of conditionality is in and of itself an international obligation binding upon states in instances of transitional justice, there is no doubt that it materializes the necessary articulation that must exist among the various mechanisms for the attainment of truth, justice, reparation, and non-recurrence, all in favour of the victims.[76]

E. Investigation by Patterns

The IACtHR,[77] and the Special Rapporteur on the promotion of truth, justice, reparation, and guarantees of non-recurrence,[78] have declared that the state, in contexts of massive human rights violations, have the duty, as part of the obligation to investigate, to uncover and discern the patterns of macro-criminality that allowed and sustained those scenarios.

In the legal and constitutional framework that sets out the foundations for the JEP, in compliance with the standards referred to above, a guiding parameter is the analysis of the cases, not in isolation, but in conjunction, in order to identify the common characteristics. The purpose is that, from a global perspective, the complex structure of the criminality responsible for the human rights violations within the jurisdiction of the JEP can be established.[79] In this respect, it is worth taking into account the JEP's methodological guide for the prioritization of cases and situations. According to this guide, the Judicial Panel for Acknowledgement of Truth, Responsibility and Determination of Facts and Conduct shall proceed in three main stages: (i) 'to group together', defined as the construction and delimitation of provisional universes; (ii) 'concentration', defined as the series of actions preliminary to prioritization, that permit the Chamber for Recognition of Truth, Responsibility and Determination of Facts and Behavior (SRVR by its acronym in Spanish) to focus its work on specific groups of persons or cases; (iii) prioritization, defined as the application of strategic criteria allowing the SRVR to determine the order and allocation of resources for case analysis.[80]

[74] Final Agreement (n. 1); Legislative Act No. 1 of 2017 (n. 3), Articles 5, 14, 33, 35, 50; Statutory Law (2019) (n. 15), Article 20.

[75] Decision C-007 of 2018 and Judgment C-674 of 2017 (n. 4).

[76] de Greiff (n. 41).

[77] *El Mozote* (n. 24); *Rochac Hernández et al. v El Salvador*, IACtHR App. 731-03, 14 October 2014; *Contreras et al. v El Salvador*, IACtHR App. 12.494, 31 August 2011.

[78] de Greiff (n. 41).

[79] Statutory Law (2019) (n. 15), Articles 19, 79, 114.

[80] JEP, 'Criterios y metodología de priorización de casos y situaciones en la Sala de Reconocimiento de verdad, de responsabilidad y de determinación de los hechos y conductas', 28 June 2018, 4.

F. The Selection Tool in Light of the Obligation to Investigate, Prosecute, and Punish

The concern may be validly raised that the Inter-American jurisprudence prohibits the selection of cases. Particularly, because the Tribunal, even in transitional cases, has stated that prosecution for every responsible perpetrator of a gross human rights violation or an international crime is required.[81] However, the Inter-American Court has developed some considerations that might allow us to conclude that a selection mechanism isn't by itself against the ACHR or the international obligations of the states in transitional contexts.

First, in its 2012 judgment, *Masacres de El Mozote v El Salvador*, the Court analysed the transition from armed conflict to a *negotiated* peace. Here the Court took an important step in departing from its post-dictatorship case law. On one hand, it took into account international humanitarian law, especially Article 6.5 of Protocol II Additional to the Geneva Conventions and the customary rule 159 that promotes granting 'the broadest possible amnesty' at the end of hostilities, with the exception of 'persons suspected of, accused of, or sentenced for war crimes'. And on the other hand, it acknowledged the way in which peace was agreed upon in El Salvador and the limits that the country imposed on itself for the prosecution and punishment of human rights and IHL violations.[82]

In *Herzog v Brazil*, the Court also stated that the nature of the transition has an impact on the scope of the state's obligation to punish. In particular, the Tribunal highlighted that a different international regime arises in a transition from armed conflict to peace. Both cases demonstrate that: (i) transitions from armed conflict have different rules; and (ii) the obligation to punish doesn't imply the punishment of every case or violation of human rights.[83]

Second, in their concurring opinion in *El Mozote*, five out of seven judges (including the president of the Court) affirmed that the degree of justice that can be achieved in a transition from conflict to peace 'is not an isolated component . . . but part of an ambitious process of transition towards mutual tolerance and peace'. Furthermore, they emphasized that: (i) there is no universally applicable solution since each context is different; (ii) where victims can be counted in the hundreds of thousands it is necessary to create exceptional mechanisms which include both judicial and non-judicial components; and (iii) the isolated application of criminal penalties would only produce an 'apparent relief' in the situation of victims, but not a transformation of the conditions that gave rise to the violations.[84] The prioritization or selection of cases—as part of a holistic transitional justice strategy that is different from any the IACtHR has ever had the opportunity to review—seemingly fits within these parameters.

[81] *Members of the Village of Chichupac and Neighboring Communities of the Municipality of Rabinal v Guatemala*, IACtHR App. 12.788, 12 March 2019; *Coc Max* (n. 24); *Terrones Silva et al.* (n. 46).

[82] *El Mozote* (n. 24), Concurrent Opinion, Diego García-Sayán.

[83] *Herzog et al. v. Brazil*, IACtHR App. 12.879, 15 March 2018.

[84] *El Mozote* (n. 24) Concurrent Opinion, Diego García-Sayán

Third, the Court also established in *Santo Domingo* that there is no obligation to clarify all the facts or classification of the facts to fulfil the duty to punish:

> 171. All things considered, in the circumstances of this case, what is relevant for the Court is that the domestic organs for the administration of justice have already made an extensive determination of several implications of the State's responsibility for the facts, irrespective of the levels of individual, criminal or disciplinary responsibility of State agents or private individuals, definition of which corresponds to the domestic jurisdiction, even if not all the facts or classifications of the facts have been sufficiently or fully investigated or clarified.[85]

In addition, in *Yarce v Colombia*, the Tribunal: (i) urged the state to continue with the implementation of the investigation mechanisms adopted, as prioritization and selection strategies; and (ii) did not declare the international responsibility of Colombia, although it had not judged all the perpetrators.[86]

Finally, in the compliance supervision of the *Mozote* case, the president of the Tribunal concluded that the selection mechanism adopted in El Salvador may violate the right of the victims and ignore the scope of the reparations ordered by the Court, regarding to access to justice. However, in this decision the president also suggested that a selection mechanism is not itself against the ACHR. For the president, those mechanisms could be necessary in transitional contexts.[87] Such considerations were not overruled by the Court.[88]

Despite an absence of a unified position before the Inter-American Court, the preliminary judgments reveal that the obligation to punish, in transitional contexts, doesn't imply to judge every case and every perpetrator and, thus, a selection mechanism is not by itself prohibited.

That conclusion is particularly important because Colombia, in its transitional justice model, has conceived a prohibition of amnesties for international crimes or grave violations of human rights, but has established a selection mechanism for cases and most responsible.[89]

In addition, in its decisions regarding the implementation of the Final Agreement, particularly Decisions C-080/18,[90] C-007/17,[91] and C-674/17,[92] the Colombian Constitutional Court noted that the criminal law benefits as part of the peace talks' compromise are compatible with the relevant international obligations, specifically the obligations to investigate, prosecute, and punish gross human rights violations and grave violations of IHL.

[85] *Santo Domingo massacre v Colombia*, IACtHR App. 12.416, 30 November 2012.
[86] *Yarce et al. v. Colombia*, IACtHR App. 231-05, 25 November 2016.
[87] *Case of the Massacres of El Mozote and surrounding areas v El Salvador*. Urgent Measures and Monitoring Compliance with Judgment. Order of President of the Inter-American Court of Human Rights, IACtHR, 8 May 2019.
[88] *Case of the Massacres of El Mozote and surrounding areas v El Salvador*. Urgent Measures and Monitoring Compliance with Judgment. Order of President of the Inter-American Court of Human Rights, IACtHR, 3 September 2019.
[89] Statutory Law (2019) (n. 15), Article 19.
[90] Constitutional Court of Colombia, Decision C-080 of 2018.
[91] Ibid.
[92] Judgment C-674 of 2017 (n. 4).

IV. Amidst the Conventionality Control and the National Margin of Appreciation

The Inter-American Court of Human Rights has developed the conventionality control doctrine since its decision in *Almonacid Arellano v Chile* in the following terms:

> The Court is aware that domestic judges and courts are bound to respect the rule of law, and therefore, they are bound to apply the provisions in force within the legal system. But when a State has ratified an international treaty such as the American Convention, its judges, as part of the State, are also bound by such Convention. This forces them to see that all the effects of the provisions embodied in the Convention are not adversely affected by the enforcement of laws which are contrary to its purpose and that have not had any legal effects since their inception. In other words, the Judiciary must exercise a sort of 'conventionality control' between the domestic legal provisions which are applied to specific cases and the American Convention on Human Rights. To perform this task, the Judiciary has to take into account not only the treaty, but also the interpretation thereof made by the Inter-American Court, which is the ultimate interpreter of the American Convention.[93]

This doctrine has since been further developed in the IACtHR's jurisprudence, and the requirements determining an adequate application of the ACHR by American states are more demanding each day.[94] Indeed, beyond the scope and content of the decision in *Almonacid Arellano*, the IACtHR has posited that the conventionality control shall be carried out by all public authorities,[95] not only the judiciary, and that the analysis has to be carried out in light of the Inter-American jurisprudence binding each state, but also in accordance with the parameters established in its advisory opinions[96] and compliance resolutions.[97] All in all, at the core of the conventionality control doctrine lies a conception that there are standards common to all states, which are relevant in the purpose of building what some scholars and theorists have referred to as a *ius constitutionale commune*.[98]

Without prejudice to some criticism and troublesome issues regarding the conventionality control, this tool is by all account one of the more significant developments for the judicial dialogue between national and international courts.[99] The question

[93] *Almonacid Arellano* (n. 5).

[94] *Dismissed Employees of Petroperú et al. v Perú*, IACtHR App. 11.830, 24 November 2006; *Caso Boyce et al. v Barbados*, IACtHR App. 12.480, 20 November 2007; *Heliodoro Portugal v Panamá*, IACtHR App. 12.408, 12 August 2008; *Radilla Pacheco* (n. 57); *Andrade Salmón v Bolivia*, IACtHR App. 12.872, 1 December 2016.

[95] *Gelman* (n. 22).

[96] *OC-21/14*, IACtHR, 19 August 2014; *OC-22/16*, IACtHR, 26 February 2016.

[97] Pablo González, 'La doctrina del control de convencionalidad a la luz del principio de subsidiariedad' (2017) Estudios Constitucionales 55.

[98] Armin Von Bogdandy, 'Ius Constitutionale Commune in Latin America: A Look at a Transformative Constitutionalism' (2015) 34 Revista Derecho del Estado; Armin Von Bogdandy, Héctor Fix Fierro, & Mariela Morales Antoniazzi (eds), *Ius constitutionale commune en América Latina: Rasgos, potencialidades y desafíos* (1st edn, Ciudad de Mexico, Mexico, Universidad Nacional Autónoma de México 2014).

[99] Eduardo Ferrer Mac-Gregor, 'Interpretación conforme y control difuso de convencionalidad: El nuevo paradigma para el juez mexicano' (2011) Estudios Constitucionales 531; Manuel Morales, 'El

is, however, whether the conventional control should be applied with the same intensity and under the very same parameters previously defined by the IACtHR in its general case law, to contexts of transition, and to the particularly complex Colombian transition from a protracted NIAC to peace. Answering this question becomes even more urgent when one realizes that the most highly qualified domestic and international publicist agree to affirm that each context of transition is different and that, accordingly, seeking to find unique common standards or borrowing from foreign models is a big mistake, although a sadly common one in countries facing transition scenarios.[100]

But should uniformity be the final aim, and is it precisely the conventionality control's main purpose to promote the identification and establishment of common standards, which should then be the scope of the conventionality control in contexts of political transition? Moreover, what is the degree of latitude or deference that international courts and particularly the IACtHR should give states in the design of transitional justice models? Even more importantly, which would be the cases, decisions, or referents of comparative assessment that should guide or set the point of departure for national authorities in carrying out the conventional test in contexts of transition? In the IACtHR's docket, the *El Salvador* case is certainly the most proximate to the Colombian situation. However, we must be cautious not to rely excessively on the decision and standards structured in the *Mozote* judgment. Indeed, not only are the contexts different, but also the contents and focus of each peace agreement differ in important aspects. For instance, the Final Agreement is premised upon the idea that, in the Colombian context, the state's obligations can only be fulfilled to their maximum potential when efforts are focused on complying with all obligations in the ACHR, and not only with the obligation to investigate and punish. For this reason, the view defended here is that the Colombia's TJM would withstand the conventionality control test before the IAHRS. Even though such mechanisms can imply a restriction of some rights contained in the ACHR, they do not necessarily constitute a violation of the treaty.[101]

The most complex challenge in this part of the analysis is to determine the level of deference that organs of the IAHRS ought to show states when reviewing individual petitions directly or indirectly concerning the TJM. Faced with an event of great historical significance, the organs of the Inter-American System would be loath to deviate from the international community's decision to support the end of the conflict in

control de convencionalidad y los sistemas de protección de los derechos humanos americano y europeo. Su recepción en el caso argentino y español' (2017) 21 Anuario Iberoamericano de Justicia Constitucional.

[100] 'Report to the Human Rights Council on the Foundation of the Mandate and the Importance of a Comprehensive Approach' (A/HRC/21/46, 9 August 2012); Colleen Murphy, 'Transitional Justice: A Conceptual Map', in Krushil Watene & Jay Drydyk (eds), *Theorizing Justice: Novel Insights and Future Directions* (Rowman & Littlefield, 2016), 33; Rodrigo Uprimny, 'Las enseñanzas del análisis comparado: procesos transicionales, formas de justicia transicional y el caso colombiano', in Rodrigo Uprimny (ed.), *Justicia transicional sin transición* (DeJusticia, 2006), 25.

[101] For an analysis of the reasons that justify that *self-restraint* and how these reasons have been used by the ECtHR, see Dean Spielmann, 'Allowing the Right Margin: The European Court of Human Rights and the National Margin of Appreciation Doctrine: Waiver or Subsidiarity of European Review?' (2015) 14 Cambridge Yearbook of European Legal Studies 381.

Colombia, and the implementation of a carefully negotiated deal. However, there is a difference between supporting the TJM in the abstract, and evaluating its implementation in concrete cases—particularly with regards to victims who argue that their specific violations were not investigated or repaired. Indeed, while the Final Agreement and the selection policy should be analysed under the conventionality control test when considered in the abstract, the analysis will certainly be different and more difficult in individual cases.

In our view, the only possible and coherent response that the organs of the IAHRS can provide when dealing with individual cases is one through the lens of the margin of appreciation doctrine. This would imply a recognition that international organs should show deference to the discretional capacities of national authorities regarding human rights issues falling under their jurisdiction.[102] Remarkably, however, the margin of appreciation has never been adopted by the IACtHR. On the contrary, the doctrine is seen with suspicion and caution by many of the Court's judges and by human rights defenders in the Americas. The scepticism stands in contrast to an enthusiastic and prospective application of the same doctrine by the European Court of Human Rights ('ECtHR'), especially after the Brighton Declaration.[103] In this respect, our view is that the IACtHR should re-examine the relevance of this doctrine. Ultimately, a margin of appreciation gives effect to the principle of subsidiarity, recognized since the preamble of the ACHR as a pillar of the IAHRS, and one that is especially apt in contexts of transitional justice where the very different historical, political, and social circumstances demand unique solutions.[104]

One must also bear in mind that the Colombian context is not only unique but a very complex one. Among the intrinsically complicated circumstances it combines, one can mention: (i) the existence and maintenance of strong democratic institutions firmly adhered to the rule of law notwithstanding a protracted NIAC of more than sixty years; (ii) the operation of several organized armed groups in its territory (guerrillas, heavily armed drug-trafficking groups, illegal paramilitary units, criminal bands, etc.); (iii) the background and backlash of a failed plebiscite for peace and several peacebuilding attempts that have failed during the implementation stage; (iv) a constitutional jurisprudence recognizing and mandating obligations beyond those existing and binding Colombia in the international realm; (v) a spectrum of complex and complementary international human rights obligations that did not exist nor governed transitional process in the late 1980s and 1990s; (vi) a transitional process without constitutional modification; and (vii) more than eight million victims, that is, an unprecedented scenario of massive human rights violations.

[102] Howard Yourow, *The Margin of Appreciation Doctrine in the Dynamics of European Human Rights Jurisprudence* (1st edn, Martinus Nijhoff Publishers, 1996).

[103] Mikael Madsen, 'Rebalancing European Human Rights: Has the Brighton Declaration Engendered a New Deal on Human Rights in Europe?' (2017) 9 Journal of International Dispute Settlement199; Janneke Gerards, 'Margin of Appreciation and Incrementalism in the Case Law of the European Court of Human Rights' (2018) 18 Human Rights Law Review 495; Robert Spano 'The Future of the European Court of Human Rights—Subsidiarity, Process-Based Review and the Rule of Law' (2018) 18 Human Rights Law Review 473.

[104] Juana Acosta & Maria Londoño, 'Juicio de sustitución: la participación política de excombatientes como desarrollo del marco democrático participativo', in Kai Ambos (ed.), *Justicia de transición y Constitución II: Análisis de la sentencia C-577 de 2014* (Konrad Adenauer Stiftung, 2015).

In our opinion, the analysis of the IACtHR in respect of individual petitions directly or indirectly concerning the TJM should include one additional element: that in the Colombian case there is an imminent risk of return to war. In the previous cases where the IACtHR assessed the conventional conformity of transitional justice models the analysis was made at least fifteen years after the initiation of the transitional process. That was the case of El Salvador, where twenty years had passed since the signing of the peace agreement.[105] In those years, the state was allowed to move towards a crucial point of 'no-return'. Previous experiences abroad show that the first four years after the implementation of peace agreements are in fact when the transitional move is more vulnerable. Comparative practice shows that in those years the uncertainty is especially acute for the demobilized, and this may influence a potential failure in the peacebuilding process. In this vein, since some petitions related to the Colombian TJM have already been filed before the IACtHR,[106] the conventionally control test will be made at a critical and decisive stage of the implementation of the Final Agreement, one which is however still very far from the so-called 'point of no return'.[107]

The ideas expressed above are certainly not an invitation for the IACtHR to give its blessing to any norm or provision in the TJM even if overtly contrary to Colombia's international obligations. Our proposal is rather for the analysis of the American tribunal to be made with especial prudence and full conscience of the effects that any decision is likely to cause in the still fragile peacebuilding process in Colombia. For this reason, an adequate balance between the notions of 'conventionality control' and 'national margin of appreciation'—whatever its particular designation by the Inter-American organs—is deemed essential in the context of transitional justice and especially in the dialogue between domestic and international court.

The approach proposed here seems all the more relevant when one notices that, in the jurisprudence of the Colombian Constitutional Court, a national margin of appreciation in the definition of transitional justice mechanisms has already been recognized.[108] Although a national court, the Colombian Constitutional Court enjoys great respect among its peers in the American Region and beyond, as well as within the organs of the IAHRS, precisely because of its firm and explicit adherence to international human rights standards.[109] Although the words 'conventionality control' are scarce in the case law of the Colombian Constitutional Court,[110] its material application is easily discernible and has been recognized by the IACtHR.[111] Importantly,

[105] *El Mozote* (n. 24).

[106] IACmHR, 'CIDH presenta caso sobre Colombia ante la Corte IDH' (Press Release, 25 July 2018) http://www.oas.org/es/cidh/prensa/comunicados/2018/162.asp, accessed 7 February 2019.

[107] Juan Pablo Acosta et al. 'Perspectiva holística de la reintegración en el Acuerdo de Paz en Colombia' (2019) Draft.

[108] Juana Acosta-López & Cindy Espitia 'La justicia transicional a la luz del derecho internacional: la perspectiva de la Corte Constitucional de Colombia', in Juana Acosta-López, Paola Acosta, & Daniel Rivas, *De Anacronismos y Vaticinios: Diagnóstico sobre las relaciones entre el derecho internacional y el derecho interno en Latinoamérica* (Bogotá Universidad Externado de Colombia, 2017); Constitutional Court of Colombia, Decision C-577 of 2014; Decision C-579 of 2013 (n. 67); Decision C-795 of 2015; Decision C-052 of 2012; Decision C-694/15; Decision C-286 of 2014; Decision C-180 of 2014; Decision C-684 of 2015.

[109] *Gelman* (n. 22); González (n. 97).

[110] Acosta-López et al., 'Diagnóstico sobre las relaciones entre el derecho internacional y el derecho interno en Latinoamérica', in Acosta-López, Acosta, & Rivas (n. 108).

[111] *Duque v Colombia*, IACtHR App. 12.841, 26 February 2016.

beyond a mere formal quotation or reference to international obligations, the more than seventy decisions dealing with transitional justice-related matters show that the Constitutional Court has carried a good faith conventional control while at the same time recognizing for itself a certain margin of configuration or appreciation, particularly in the design of transitional justice mechanisms. The tendency in the decisions of the Constitutional Court has been to identify a wider margin of appreciation for some matters or issues, and a narrower one for some others. In some other cases, it has considered that certain questions, for example the political participation of former members of FARC-EP, is not governed by international law and accordingly remains a domestic affair.[112]

What is then the degree of deference of latitude that the IACtHR should grant to the Constitutional Court in its analysis of the SIVJR? The answer not only comes with legal relevance for the decisions already pronounced by the domestic constitutional tribunal, which are likely to be examined by the IACtHR. As noted before, the answer is by all accounts more pervasive since the position of the IACtHR will affect the long-term sustainability of the SIVJR as a whole. In this respect, a bottom-up dialogue will be of utmost importance. One must recall in this regard that the IACtHR has already acknowledged, in the cases of *Rochela v Colombia*[113] and *Vereda la Esperanza v Colombia*[114] concerning the 'Ley de Justicia y Paz',[115] that domestic judicial analysis was consistent not only with the Colombian Constitution but also with the ACHR.

In respect of the selection tool or methodology, the Constitutional Court, in its most recent analysis of the Statutory Law of the JEP, adopted two views about the nature of this strategy in light of victims' right to justice in transitional justice contexts.[116] The Constitutional Court considered that the selection tool is an exception to the obligation to investigate, prosecute, and punish. However, it also expressed the view that it is the best means to secure and guarantee the rights of the victims to truth, justice, and reparation. This is because the selection of cases: (i) allows for a more effective and efficient use of the limited resources of the state; (ii) directs the state's efforts to guarantee the access to justice of the victims in a reasonable time; (iii) allows the investigation to be directed towards a general identification and understanding of the macro-context; (iv) promotes accountability under objective, public, and transparent criteria; and (v) contributes to overcome the tensions between the demands for justice and peace.[117]

The dichotomy described above—the rationalization mechanism is an exception to the state's obligation to investigate but the most adequate mechanism to guarantee the rights of the victims—was the result of the Constitutional Court's attempt to achieve a

[112] Acosta-López and Espitia (n. 108) and Acosta and Londoño (n. 104).

[113] *Rochela massacre v Colombia*, IACtHR App. 4202, 11 May 2007.

[114] *Vereda La Esperanza v Colombia*, IACtHR App. 12.251, 31 August 2017.

[115] See Law No. 795 of 2005. This instrument was created as part of the demobilization process for the members of 'Autodefensas Unidas de Colombia'.

[116] Decision C-080 of 2018 (n. 90).

[117] This is because the experiences in other countries show that *de facto* selection of cases constitute a common phenomenon in transitional justice scenarios. In Argentina, although there are pre-defined criteria for selection in the relevant legal framework, in practice the cases addressed since 2003 have been subject to prioritization, not in light of the gravity of representativeness of the crimes but on the basis of: (i) the diligence of the judicial authority; and (ii) the initiative of the victims of their lawyers. Cf. Bergsmo (n. 34).

necessary compromise between two positions that were probably dividing the justices within the court. Regardless of the compatibility of these two views, the IAHRS should take into account the reasoning exposed by the Constitutional Court to sustain the constitutionality and conventionality of the selection mechanism.

To the multiple and varied considerations already assessed before one may add the fact that international human rights obligations should be interpreted in connection with obligations under international criminal law. With special relevance in this respect, the communications of the prosecutor of the ICC have underlined the factual impossibility of dealing with the total number of cases deriving from a scenario of massive human rights violations. Accordingly, and in support of Colombia's strategy, the prosecutor has encouraged domestic authorities to define 'clear, justified and proportionate' criteria for the prioritization and selection of cases.[118] Surely the IACmHR will not ignore these statements when it comes to analysing the agreement's design and its implementation. It is noteworthy that the Inter-American *ratio decidendi* concerning previously negotiated peace agreements refers, among others, to international criminal law as *lex specialis* when dealing with international crimes.[119] Hence, the ICC prosecutor's views should be welcomed by the IAHRS organs as a significant input.

As already voiced by the prosecutor, the Agreement in Colombia is a historical achievement. Although she warned that Colombia could not avoid or negate the obligation to effectively prosecute those most responsible for the commission of international crimes, she also expressed satisfaction that the Final Agreement does not allow amnesties for those crimes.[120] The communication also emphasized the important role of the JEP in guaranteeing the fulfilment of the obligations to investigate, prosecute, and punish the most responsible for crimes committed during the NIAC. Moreover, it recognized that victims, and their right to justice, have been at the centre of the peace process, and cautioned that peace is intrinsically related to the satisfaction of victims' right to justice. This communication is of fundamental value, since it evinces the prosecutor's political will to respect and support Colombia's TJM and the ongoing process. Although her opinions are not legally binding and the prosecutor of the ICC maintains competence over the situation in Colombia, it can be expected, by virtue of the principle of good faith, that the ICC will treat any agreement that falls within the same parameters previously raised similarly.

Turning now to the issue of suspended, reduced, and alternative sentences, neither the ACHR nor the IAHRS jurisprudence exclude their application. Moreover, neither the ACHR nor the developing case law support the contention that prison penalties are necessarily required. Accordingly, in this respect the doctrine of the national margin of appreciation is the most appropriate tool. Indeed, one must recall that back

[118] Juana Acosta-López & Ana Idárraga, 'Alcance del deber de investigar, juzgar y sancionar en transiciones de conflicto armado a una paz negociada: convergencias entre el Sistema Interamericano de Derechos Humanos y la Corte Penal Internacional' (2019) Revista Estado de Derecho, Bogotá,, 55–99.

[119] James Stewart, 'The Role of the ICC in the Transitional Justice Process in Colombia' (2018) 1(1) International Criminal Court, https://www.refworld.org.es/pdfid/5b4e15b74.pdf, accessed 8 February 2019; Acosta-López & Idárraga (n. 118).

[120] Fatou Bensouda, 'Statement of ICC Prosecutor, Fatou Bensouda, on the conclusion of the peace negotiations between the Government of Colombia and the Revolutionary Armed Forces of Colombia—People's Army' (2016) 1(1) International Criminal Court, https://www.refworld.org.es/pdfid/5b4e15b74.pdf, accessed 8 February 2019.

in 2015, the ICC's deputy prosecutor affirmed, in reference to the Colombian case: (i) that the Rome Statute does not prescribe specific type or length of sentences; (ii) that in sentencing, states have wide discretion; and (iii) that effective penal sanctions may take many different forms.[121] In a similar vein, as recent as 2018, the deputy prosecutor noted that the mechanisms for the rationalization of the criminal action envisaged by Colombia were 'compatible with the States' obligation to investigation and prosecute the most serious crimes, among them war crimes, as an established principle in international law'.[122] At the same time, he stated: 'effective penal sanctions may take different forms, as long as they serve appropriate sentencing objectives of retribution, rehabilitation, restoration and deterrence.'[123]

These pronouncements by the office of the prosecutor of the ICC support the argument that states enjoy considerable latitude in the design of transitional justice models. Albeit with a clear limit preventing states denying minimum requirements governing the investigation, prosecution, and sanctioning of international crimes, Colombia is entitled to design and implement the mechanisms that it deems most suitable to its particular reality, needs, and context. This also supports our argument that notwithstanding a necessary and unavoidable human rights international protective mantle, Colombia can legitimately claim a margin of appreciation in conducting the conventionality control when assessing the design and implementation of its TJM.

IV. Conclusion: Some Challenges and Difficulties in the Phase of Implementation

Although the signing of the Final Agreement was a historic moment, putting an end to a sixty-year NIAC with FARC-EP, Colombia is facing an even greater challenge at the implementation stage. The current political context is agitated and polarized rendering implementation highly uncertain. A source of even greater concern is the realization that there is a huge risk that armed violence will return, partly because of the strengthening of FARC-EP's dissident branches, and partly because of the current failure in the peace talks with ELN, one of the still operational guerrillas.

In Colombia, the impact of the Inter-American jurisprudence has historically had an important impact on the protection of human rights. However, given the still vulnerable stage of the peace-making process, the decisions adopted by the organs of the IAHRS concerning the TJM will be decisive for its implementation. One should not forget that a decision by the IACtHR can order the amendment of national legislative, including at the constitutional level, and accordingly, can substantively affect both the content and implementation of the Final Agreement, and thereby the previous assumptions and expectations of the parties involved. The Inter-American organs are thus in front an equally challenging responsibility. The question is moreover far from

121 James Stewart, 'Transitional Justice in Colombia and the Role of the International Criminal Court', Bogotá, 13 May 2015, 1–20..
122 Ibid., 131.
123 Ibid., 142.

hypothetical since cases concerning the Colombian TJM have already reached the tribunal.

In our opinion, the IACtHR can choose between various possible paths, all of them with profound consequences for Colombia. One option is to decide to explicitly pronounce detailed standards and criteria that should guide Colombia and other countries in their transitional policies. In this type of approach, one already publicly requested by one NGO in a public hearing before the IACtHR,[124] the tribunal can decide to order the JEP to adopt the Inter-American criteria for the selection of cases and those most responsible for the commission of international crimes. Another option is to decide to order, as already requested by the IACmHR in an emblematic case of massive human rights violations in times of armed conflict, that all facts and all those responsible for the crimes be investigated, prosecuted, and punished, with a special emphasis placed on individual reparation by the judiciary.[125]

A different type of approach would be for the IACtHR to adopt a model, similar to the one proposed in this work, to adequately balance the conventionality test and the margin of appreciation—or its equivalent. In the particular case of Colombia, the IACtHR could, on one hand, verify that the design of the TJM, as contained in the Final Agreement, and the complementary norms and constitutional jurisprudence, do not contravene basic prohibitions in contexts of transition. Of importance in this analysis is the fact that the conformity of the system with the applicable human rights international law was already made by a Constitutional Court previously commended for its enthusiastic adherence to international standards; in addition, that consistency with the relevant norms of international criminal law, as the *lex specialis* when dealing with international crimes and those most responsible for their commission, was also supported by the office of the prosecutor of the ICC. On the other hand, after verifying compliance with the aforementioned minimum requirements, the IACtHR could grant Colombia a wide margin of appreciation in order to complete the design and implementation of the judicial and extra-judicial mechanisms.

Whatever the approach of the IACtHR and its position on the scope of deference and latitude recognized to the state, it should always be kept in mind that it has never dealt with a TJM similar or even closely proximate to the Colombian one. It is indeed an ambitious model that integrates important lessons from peace-building processes in other countries, where each component and mechanism should be interpreted as complementary to one another. In consequence, the organs of the IAHRS are strongly invited to avoid decisions deriving from fragmented analysis of the human rights involved. Such type of reasoning, albeit in all likelihood inspired by a *pro personae* principle of interpretation, would be nugatory of the principle of integrality, the very fundamental bedrock of the SIVJR.

124 *Public hearing. Villamizar Durán v Colombia* (IACtHR, 30 October 2017) https://vimeo.com/239111338, accessed 8 February 2019.

125 IACmHR, 'CIDH presenta caso sobre Colombia ante la Corte IDH' (Press Release, 25 July 2018) http://www.oas.org/es/cidh/prensa/comunicados/2018/162.asp, accessed 7 February 2019

16

Righting Wrongs or Wronging Rights?

An Ethical Perspective on the Colombian Integrated System for Transitional Justice

Diana Acosta-Navas

Colombia is currently undergoing the implementation phase of a holistic and ambitious system of transitional justice, aimed to facilitate the end of a protracted internal conflict: the 'Integrated System for Truth, Justice, Reparation and Non-Repetition' (hereinafter 'Integrated System'). Even though the peace agreement with FARC-EP is characterized for its focus on victims' rights, the Integrated System is constituted by institutions that circumvent the ordinary means of recognition and enforcement of these rights. For this reason, there is little agreement over what constitutes enforcing victims' rights within this institutional framework, and the moral justification of some of the accord's key components remains the matter of intense debate in the country. This chapter situates the debate that has taken place in Colombia in a wider ethical debate regarding the conditions of satisfaction of victims' right to justice and attempts to draw a conceptual bridge between the two opposing views.

I focus on the ethical justification of transitional justice measures, as opposed to its legal dimension. First, I employ conceptual analysis to dissect the different conceptions of justice that inform proponents' and detractors' arguments. Secondly, I argue that addressing this dispute requires carefully threading between the two argumentative camps, as arguments on both sides suffer from a common problem: they fail to fully tailor their normative framework to the non-ideal empirical conditions in which such institutions are implemented. From this discussion I draw out a proposal that synthesizes the ethical concerns behind both positions and attempts to overcome the diagnosed flaws. I argue that an appropriate acknowledgment of the circumstances in which transitional justice institutions are implemented should inform a standard of justice that neither fully brackets the respect for individuals' entitlements nor disregards the need to correct existing structural injustice.

I.

Over the course of five decades, more than 8.5 million Colombians have been the victims of targeted murders, massacres, kidnapping, terrorism, sexual violence, extortion, and forced displacement.[1] The peace accord with FARC, which was later recorded

[1] 'Basta Ya! Colombia: Memorias de Guerra y Dignidad', Grupo de Memoria Histórica 42 (2013) http://www.centrodememoriahistorica.gov.co/descargas/informes2013/bastaYa/basta-ya-colombia-memorias-de-guerra-y-dignidad-2016.pdf. See also Gobierno Nacional de Colombia, *Registro único de Víctimas*

Diana Acosta-Navas, *Righting Wrongs or Wronging Rights?* In: *Constitutionalism*. Edited by: Alejandro Linares-Cantillo, Camilo Valdivieso-León, Santiago García-Jaramillo, Oxford University Press (2021). © The various contributors.
DOI: 10.1093/oso/9780192896759.003.0017

into Legislative Act No. 1 of 2017, marks the beginning of a peace-building process that seeks to correct the injustices caused by the conflict and address some of the factors that enabled its persistence over the course of five decades. One of its distinctive features, according to its architects, is the centrality of victims both during the negotiation stage and in the accord itself. The various measures introduced by the accord seek to jointly address victims' rights to truth, justice, reparation, and non-repetition.

The Integrated System constitutes a holistic approach to the difficult issue of justice for those responsible of international crimes committed as part of the civil conflict. It is the first framework of transitional justice that has been agreed upon since the signing of the Rome Statute and the creation of the International Criminal Court ('ICC'). The Integrated System encompasses various components: the Special Jurisdiction for Peace ('SJP'); the Search Unity for Disappeared Persons; the Commission for the Clarification of Truth, Coexistence and Non-Repetition; and the Program for Holistic Reparation, which builds on the 'Victims' Act' (Law No. 1448 of 2011) and introduces new measures for individual and collective reparation. This system is also part of a broader institutional structure aimed at terminating the conflict between FARC and the Colombian state. Its initiatives range from innovative approaches to the problem of illicit drug trafficking and rural reform, to measures that promote the political participation of the main stakeholders of the conflict, and programmes for disarmament, demobilization, and reincorporation of ex-combatants (DDR).

Although the SJP is designed to uphold victims' dignity, it has been strongly criticized. The debate has specifically revolved around the extent to which the system upholds the rights of victims; whether it permits the Colombian state to meet its international obligations; and whether it promotes impunity. While both supporters and detractors of the Integrated System agree that victims' rights to truth, justice, reparation, and non-repetition ought to be upheld, there remains disagreement over the implications of the right to justice, and its relation to the other rights. Some see the state's recognition of this right as directly entailing its duty to prosecute all perpetrators of international crimes and punish them in accordance with the legal standards of the country. Others suggest that it can be satisfied through a holistic approach that trades off the number of prosecutions and the severity of punishments for the adoption of other complementary measures that promote a broader sense of justice.

The phrasing of the Rome Statue itself leaves some room for disagreement. Article 53(1)(c) states that the prosecutor of the ICC may decide against undertaking prosecutions that would be otherwise admissible on the grounds that pursuing them would not be in the *interests of justice*. The Office of the Prosecutor ('OTP') policy takes a narrow view of what constitutes the interests of justice and states that in any case there should be a strong presumption that undertaking prosecution will serve the interests of justice. It thus excludes the consideration of political circumstances and the safeguarding of peace negotiations as sufficient conditions to rule out prosecutions. However, while it distinguishes the interests of justice from the interests of peace

Agosto 1, 2017 https://rni.unidadvictimas.gov.co/RUV accessed on 31 August 2017; Kathryn Sikkink et al., 'Evaluation of Integral Reparations Measures in Colombia' (2015) https://pdf.usaid.gov/pdf_docs/PA00KSXQ.pdf accessed on 4 March 2019.

and security, it explicitly states that the concept is broader than one of pure criminal justice, leaving some minimal room for interpretation[2]

Likewise, the OTP encourages complementary measures like truth seeking, reparations programmes, institutional reform, and traditional justice. The Office thus endorses adopting comprehensive approaches that incorporate complementary efforts to address impunity. And though it does not endorse ponderation or tradeoffs between prosecutions and other measures, it does appear to recognize a role for the latter in serving the interests of justice.

Different parties take different views on this policy.[3] While defenders of peace negotiations argue that the OTP's definition of the interests of justice is overly narrow, detractors seem to believe that it is not sufficiently so. At the heart of this debate lies a disagreement regarding the breadth and content of our conception of justice and the specific entailments of the right to justice. On the one hand, the narrow view takes the right to entail the states' duty of prosecution and punishment for all perpetrators of international crimes (a duty which befalls on the ICC when states are unable or unwilling to undertake such prosecutions). On the other hand, the broad view maintains that the interests of justice can be better served by a holistic response that takes other transitional measures into account and trades off severity of punishment for the sake of a more comprehensive approach.

Below I analyse each of these positions as they are voiced by various actors at the domestic and international spheres. I argue that each position is informed by a specific conception of justice and dissect the philosophical underpinnings of each. I also argue that neither of these operative concepts are appropriate to characterize the entailments of victims' right to justice, or to assess a set of transitional justice measures as the Colombian Integrated System.

II.

From early on, the transitional justice measures in the peace accord have been criticized for promoting impunity. In a 2015 analysis of the peace agreement, Human Rights Watch objected that the sanctions for international crimes contemplated in the accord 'do not reflect accepted standards of appropriate punishment for grave violations and make it virtually impossible that Colombia will meet its binding obligations under international law to ensure accountability for crimes against humanity and war crimes'.[4]

[2] International Criminal Court, Office of the Prosecutor, Policy Paper on the Interests of Justice (2007), https://www.icc-cpi.int/nr/rdonlyres/772c95c9-f54d-4321-bf09-73422bb23528/143640/iccotpinterestsofjustice.pdf, accessed on 4 March 2019, 8.

[3] See International Criminal Court, Informal Expert Paper, 'The Principle of Complementarity in Practice' (2005), https://www.icc-cpi.int/RelatedRecords/CR2009_02250.PDF, accessed on 4 March 2019; Amnesty International, 'Open letter to the Chief Prosecutor of the International Criminal Court: Comments on the concept of the interests of justice' (2015), https://www.amnesty.org/en/documents/IOR40/023/2005/en/, accessed on 4 February 2019; Human Rights Watch, 'The Meaning of "the Interests of Justice" in Article 53 of the Rome Statute' (2005), https://www.hrw.org/news/2005/06/01/meaning-interests-justice-article-53-rome-statute, accessed on 4 March 2019.

[4] Human Rights Watch, 'Analysis of Colombia-FARC Agreement' (2015), https://www.hrw.org/news/2015/12/21/human-rights-watch-analysis-colombia-farc-agreement, accessed on 4 March 2019.

Domestically, one of the most systematic objections to the Integrated System can be found in a report submitted by the Attorney General's Office in 2015.[5] The document advocates for the use of more stringent punitive measures, stressing that individuals responsible for serious crimes should be effectively deprived of liberty and excluded from participation in public office. It argues that, as a signatory of the Rome Statute, the Colombian state is committed to prosecuting and punishing all international crimes. It claims that, though the Rome Statute allows sentence reductions, it does so only insofar as the initial sentencing is proportional to the crime and the rights of victims are satisfied. Hence, in failing to abide by standards of proportionality, the Colombian state enables impunity, violating its international obligations, and victims' rights.

Defenders of this view argue that punishment in accordance with recognized standards is needed to serve three fundamental social functions. First, it serves an instrumental role as a deterrent for crime: in the absence of sufficiently stringent punitive measures there is no guarantee of non-repetition. Secondly, they claim, punishment *dignifies the victim*, by expressing disapproval of the crimes committed against him.[6] Thirdly, punishment *dignifies the perpetrator*, because it constitutes an act of submission to, and reconciliation with, society. Thus, they defend strict punitive measures for their instrumental value as a deterrents, while also emphasizing their non-instrumental, expressive, and retributive value.

More recently, controversy has ensued over some key aspects of the statutory law for the special jurisdiction for peace.[7] After its approval by the Constitutional Court, the Statutory Law has been objected by the nation's Office of the Prosecutor and the current administration. Critics insist that the Integrated System promotes impunity by limiting punitive responses to the intellectual authors of international crimes; due to its provisions on reparations, which, they claim, are insufficient to guarantee that victims are holistically repaired; due to the limits imposed on state bodies to carry out investigations independently of the SJP; and due to its treatment of individuals who continue to engage in criminality after the signing of the peace accord. There is a common denominator in these objections: namely, the underlying view that the punitive responses to international crimes outlined in the Act enable impunity and thus fail to satisfy victims' right to justice.

Given their particular view of punishment, these objections sit most comfortably in the theoretical frame of retributivism. Generally speaking, retributive views hold that punishment is the morally required response to wrongdoing because it is what wrongdoers *deserve*. In this framework, punishment must be of an offender, and for an offence. The seriousness of the offence, along with community's standards, should determine the severity of the punishment.[8] Furthermore, punishment ought to be imposed by the state or an authoritative body representing the moral community.

[5] *Mínimos Penales Para Máximos Responsables* (2015), https://www.procuraduria.gov.co/portal/media/file/200815DOCUMENTO.pdf, 68, accessed on 2 January 2021.

[6] Ibid., 56.

[7] Néstor Humberto Martinez, 'Ley Estatutaria de la JEP, Carta para el Presidente Ivan Duque' (2019), https://docs.google.com/viewerng/viewer?url=http://caracol.com.co/descargables/2019/02/18/b5835ff3b9e2b06ba7aead5e2c98efb9.pdf, accessed on 4 January 2019.

[8] Antony Duff, 'Retributive Punishment—Ideals and Actualities' (1991) 25 Israel Law Review 422.

Importantly, though retributivists recognize the deterring effect of punishment, they don't regard this as the central justification for it.

The notion that punishment is what the perpetrator deserves helps make sense of the thought that it can be dignifying for perpetrators: punishing individuals who commit wrongful actions recognizes their status as rational members of a moral community with shared standards of acceptable behavior. By failing to punish them, however, we fail to hold them answerable for their actions, and hence, we diminish their responsibility for their own actions and their status as members of the community.

Retributivist views also conceive of punishment as what is owed to the victims of wrongdoing. As stated above, defenders of these ideas think of punitive responses as vindicating and dignifying victims. Some versions of retributivism conceive of wrongdoing as offsetting a base-line of equality between individuals. A wrongful action denies the victim's dignity through the denial of her entitlements. It expresses a negative message about the victim's status and tries to establish the degradation of the victim and the superiority of the perpetrator.[9]

Punishment is required to correct this imbalance. By 'lowering' or 'defeating' the perpetrator, punishment 'elevates' the victim and nullifies the wrongdoer's message of superiority, thus re-establishing equality. In this view, the state's authority as the representative of the moral community confers great importance to the act of punishment. When exercised by the state, it expresses the community's recognition of the victim's status. Conversely, the state's failure to punish an offender may further diminish the value of the victim: 'a decision not to punish wrongdoers ... is also expressive: it communicates to the victim and to the wider society the idea that such treatment, and the status it attributes to the victim, are appropriate.'[10]

Other versions of retributivism hold that the function of punishment is not to defeat the perpetrator but rather to hold her accountable for her actions and to recognize the victim's entitlements.[11] If interpersonal accountability is damaged when one person violates another's rights, restoring it can re-situate perpetrators as members of the moral community. Likewise, punishment dignifies the victim insofar as enforcing

[9] Jean Hampton, 'Correcting Harms versus Righting Wrongs: The Goal of Retribution' (1992) 39(6) UCLA Law Review 1659–702.

[10] Ibid., 1684.

[11] This form of retributivism goes hand in hand with a widespread conception of 'claim rights', according to which p has a set of rights against q, if and only if q has a correlative set of directed duties towards p. This bipolar relation presupposes that p has normative authority to demand certain treatment of q, and q is accountable to p for failing to comply with those demands. In creating causes of action, civil law creates a normative arc between persons, via relations of liability, which crystallizes a set of rights with correlative duties. This *legal* standing embodies the state's recognition of citizens' *moral* standing to hold others accountable and renders their claims enforceable. Criminal law operates somewhat differently, as retributive responses are not an exercise of authority by the victim, but rather by the moral community as a whole. In this view, crimes constitute failures to respect the authority of the law and punishment holds offenders responsible for such failures. By accepting punishment, perpetrators recognize the authority of the state. Hence, they are not 'defeated' but 'held accountable' or 'answerable' to the moral community they belong to (Ariel Zylberman, 'Why Human Rights? Because of You' (2016) 24(3) Journal of Political Philosophy 321–43; W. Hohfeld & Walter Wheeler Cook, *Fundamental Legal Conceptions: As Applied in Judicial Reasoning: and Other Legal Essays* (Legal classics library) (New Haven: Yale University Press, 1920); Stephen L. Darwall, 'Justice and Retaliation' (2010) 39(3) Philosophical Papers 315–41; Stephen L. Darwall, *Morality, Authority, and Law: Essays in Second-Personal Ethics* I (Oxford: Oxford University Press, 2013)).

the perpetrator's accountability *is* enforcing the victim's authority to demand certain forms of treatment that are deemed appropriate for members of the community.

According to this view, a right to justice entails that the state *owes* it to the victims to prosecute those who violated their rights, and grants victims the authority to demand that the state honour that commitment. This is because the state's recognition of our moral entitlements is embodied in its legal recognition of rights. However, in the absence of an enforcement mechanism, rights are nothing more than a mere formality. Recognizing a right thus entails using the state's coercive power to back individual's entitlements and carries along a commitment to enforce the victim's authority when he is not able to do so himself.

A key to understanding these rationales is that they are profoundly informed by notions of individual desert and procedural justice. In these views, the justification for punitive responses is grounded on what each of the actors deserve. The perpetrator *deserves* to be punished for having violated someone else's rights. The victim *deserves* to be vindicated because his claims and entitlements were not respected. Further, it relies on the notion that individual dessert is honored by following the procedures agreed upon by the moral community.

In this sense, the kind of retributivism at play in critics' objections seems to be *individual* and *historical*: how an individual acts (or is acted upon) calls upon a specific response, the nature and severity of which is determined by the standard procedures that the community has agreed upon. Neither the broader context in which these actions occur nor the outcome that punitive responses may bring about are relevant factors to their justification.

It follows from this view that justice is only served when each individual gets what she deserves as established by standard procedures that the community has agreed upon as appropriate responses for the kind of conduct that she undertook or underwent. Such standard procedures constitute the ordinary mechanisms for the enforcement of citizens' rights and claims, as they are recognized by constitutions or international treaties. For this reason, transitional institutions that bypass or circumvent these mechanisms are regarded as promoting impunity and failing to honour victims' right to justice.

There is a deep flaw in this rationale, however. Both the notion of individual desert and the notion of community-sanctioned procedures presuppose certain conditions of validity, which often fail to hold in the contexts in which transitional justice institutions are implemented. The two variants of retributivism I describe above regard punishment as a corrective response that reinstates the prior balance that was disturbed by wrongful actions. They thus assume a prior state of equality and mutual accountability that ought to be reinstated. They also assume the prior recognition of both individuals as members of the moral community, and of their entitlements, which the state ought to honour. Finally, they assume the existence of shared standards of conduct and shared procedural norms for addressing deviations.

Absent any of these conditions, retributive responses fail to fulfil the social functions described above. Hence, though retributivist accounts of punishment are not exactly ideal theories, their view is based on a series of idealizing assumptions. They are conceived, that is, to operate in an imperfect world, but not in what Pablo de Greiff refers to as the 'very imperfect world' of political transitions and peace-building processes.[12] Following Murphy's argument, I outline five reasons to think that the validity conditions of retributivism are unlikely to hold in the context at hand.

First, retributivists embrace a proportionality constraint. For punishment to be justified, in their view, it ought to be proportional to the wrong that was committed. Putting aside the technical hurdles involved in figuring out what constitutes 'proportional punishment', we can assume there are decision procedures that match the severity of punishment to the seriousness of the offence. These procedures are informed by attributions of responsibility for specific actions to specific individuals. Their validity is grounded on the assumption that, for any given crime, we can determine the extent of individuals' responsibility in its commission. However, in the context of civil conflict where the responsibility for each wrongful action is distributed among large groups of people, respecting proportionality constraints is close to impossible.[13]

Secondly, retributive views must assume that wrongdoing is individual and exceptional. Only thus can they claim that it violates shared norms and standards of conduct. However, when wrongdoing is sufficiently widespread, one could argue that it becomes normalized, which may shift the standard of what is considered acceptable behaviour in a given community.[14] Societies that undergo peace-building efforts after periods of protracted violence may often face such an absence of uniform norms of respect for others.[15] When this is the case, it is harder to see wrongful acts as challenging community standards. Likewise, it is hard to see how punishment is meant to restore the pre-existing situation, or why that would be a morally worthy function.

Thirdly, the view assumes a state of rough equality before the law and claims that punishment is necessary to reinstate it. Thus, it assumes that victims' rights were previously enforced, as were the perpetrators'. However, normalized wrongdoing is barely compatible with an institutional arrangement that provides equal protection of citizens' rights. The situation of victims in these circumstances seems to be one of "pervasive structural inequality": a kind of inequality that is embodied in flaws of the institutions that dictate and enforce the terms of interpersonal interactions.[16]

Fourthly, retributivism assumes the state to be the legitimate representative of the community, with the authority to enforce the community's moral standards. An illegitimate state, by this account, would not have the moral standing to punish, because it does not represent the moral community. Insufficient recognition of individual rights and involvement in wrongful actions could challenge the legitimacy of a state, and thus disable it from the moral role of enforcing the community's standards.

Lastly, adding to Murphy's argument, the retributive framework presupposes a clear division between the categories of victims and perpetrators. Individuals in each category *deserve* a distinctive kind of treatment to restore their status as equal members of the community. However, circumstances of horizontal violence,[17] where there

[12] Pablo de Greiff, 'Theorizing Transitional Justice' (2012) 51 Nomos 31–77.

[13] Colleen Murphy, The Conceptual Foundations of Transitional Justice (Cambridge: Cambridge University Press, 2017).

[14] Colleen Murphy, *The Conceptual Foundations of Transitional Justice* (Cambridge: Cambridge University Press, 2017).

[15] de Greiff (n. 12).

[16] Murphy (n. 13).

[17] Iván Abad Orozco, *Sobre los límites de la conciencia humanitaria: Dilemas de la paz y la justicia en América Latina* (Bogotá, Editorial Temis: Universidad de los Andes, 2005).

is a large overlap between these two categories may be harder to accommodate for retributivists. It may be the case that some victims of human rights violations have themselves committed serious crimes, in which case there is a possible argument to the effect that they waived their moral rights. Likewise, perpetrators who commit crimes *because* they have been victimized, such as child soldiers or the victims of forced recruitment, may not be deemed fully culpable. Even the strictest retributivists may hesitate to claim that these individuals *deserve* the same punitive response as someone who undertook wrongdoing willingly.[18]

In summary, although retributivists see punishment as being the required response to individual actions regardless of their context, certain conditions are required to validate their rationale. Failing to recognize the absence of such validity conditions in the context of a peace-building society vitiates their moral arguments.

However, retributivism does capture an important moral insight: unless it is purely formal, the state's recognition of individuals as equal right bearers requires the establishment and employment of enforcement mechanisms. Relatedly, procedural standards not only give us a robust sense of what it means to respect individual entitlements, but they also give us evidential grounds to determine that the state's obligations have been met. Such a procedure-based conception of the right to justice wears its conditions of success on its sleeve, so to speak. When each individual is given their due in compliance with established procedures, the claim that the right to justice has been satisfied is rather uncontroversial. I return to these points at the end of the following section.

III.

Section II outlined some of the objections that have been raised against the transitional justice measures adopted by the Integrated System. In response to these arguments, various actors have expressed their support, including victims' representatives. When asked during an interview what kind of justice he and other victims wanted for the perpetrators of the terrible crimes that afflicted his community, Léyner Palacios, a victims' leader and representative replied:

> The one we have always practiced. The kind of justice we demanded was the same one we practiced. Indigenous people in the Department of Chocó, when someone makes a mistake, we do not exclude them from the community but rather we give them a job in the community. We, in our experience and in our practice, have felt that it is more effective to put people to work and to have them relate to the community, because that actually allows them to change their behavior. We do not believe that justice is solely punitive, putting people in prison. I think that means revictimizing victims, for

[18] From a retributivist perspective, having been victimized may act as a *mitigating factor*, informing proportionality calculations. In this way, a perpetrator who is also a victim may deserve punishment nonetheless, though a less strict form thereof. However, this response overlooks the perspective of the victim. From his standpoint, the perpetrator's history should be irrelevant to the gravity of the crime and to the victims' entitlements.

> a very simple reason: the person who is imprisoned has to be sustained by the victims. It is with our taxes that they pay for their sustenance, because they can't work! So, we thought: how is this possible? For us, the kind of justice that we have been practicing in the community is one that contributes to mending the errors we have made and correcting them with concrete actions that repair and restore that error. You aren't just put away for the people to sustain you and for people who are offended by our behavior to feel revictimized. No, it is rather, let's get him out put him to work and let him restitute ... This is why today we are suggesting to the actors who victimized us to return to the territories and with their work we can start rebuilding everything that was damaged in the conflict.[19]

Palacios's response synthesizes some of the key ideas of restorative justice, as they were famously voiced by Archbishop Desmond Tutu. In his account of the South African Truth and Reconciliation Commission, Tutu describes the paradigm of restorative justice as one concerned with 'the healing of breaches, the redressing of imbalances, the restoration of broken relationships, a seeking to rehabilitate both the victim and the perpetrator, who should be given the opportunity to be reintegrated into the community he has injured by his offense'.[20]

Both Palacios and Tutu articulate a conception of justice as the mending of what was broken by acts of wrongdoing: interpersonal relationships between victims and perpetrators; community relations and bonds; property and territory. Especially prominent in Palacios's words is the rejection of an intrinsic moral value in retribution. Rather, he focuses on the further damages, both material and psychological, that the punishment of perpetrators inflicts on victims. From his point of view, a restorative response is far superior, as it is it more effective in attaining certain valuable outcomes: rehabilitating perpetrators, rebuilding their relationships with the community, and recuperating affected territories.

The Integrated System incorporates these elements from restorative justice. Nevertheless, its architects insist that its response to human rights violations goes beyond a purely restorative or pragmatic one. As articulated by Humberto de la Calle, the chief government negotiator during the peace talks with FARC,

> The equation should not be how much to sacrifice justice for the sake of peace. This is not a new version of restorative justice. There are components of retributive and restorative justice. The concept of impunity goes beyond the imposition of punishments, it is the response to victims ... transitional justice is much broader than criminal symmetry. It is the search to instill new values in justice: the reestablishment of trust that these events shall not be repeated and that nobody is above the law.[21]

[19] Léyner Palacios, cited in Patricia García-Ríos, 'Peace and Justice In Colombia: Finding a Balance after 50 Years of War', Harvard Kennedy School Case Program, https://www.hksslate.info/wp/Colombia/.

[20] Desmond Tutu, *No Future without Forgiveness* (1st edn, New York: Doubleday, 1999), 55.

[21] Cited in Alfredo Molano, 'De la justicia transicional' (2013), https://www.elespectador.com/noticias/politica/de-justicia-transicional-articulo-458204, accessed on 4 March 2019.

Other advocates of the Integrated System have also argued in favour of an enriched conception of justice, which recognizes the state's duty to prosecute perpetrators but allows weighing this duty against other, potentially conflicting, ones. This conception justifies certain trade-offs between criminal justice and the forward-looking prevention of human rights violations.[22] Its advocates claim that it is in line with international law, as it can be accommodated under the Rome Statute as furthering the interests of justice and consider this to be a more robust notion of justice than strict retributivism:

> For real justice, reform of the national judiciary may be necessary, building a criminal justice system for all. Justice should include reparations for victims—most especially when the perpetrator was the state. Those implicated in serious crimes should be removed from the security forces. And for many victims, the first demand is to learn the truth, and to have that truth officially recognized. If these components are included in peace talks—and if, importantly, the plans are credible and likely to be implemented—then the 'interests of justice' would be served by a successful conclusion of the peace agreement and robust implementation.[23]

A broad understanding of the interests of justice includes the promotion of structural reforms, truth seeking initiatives, and reparations programmes.[24] These are seen as part and parcel of a comprehensive effort that promotes justice more broadly. This enriched conception of justice operates at a wider structural level, and not only at the level of individuals' (or collectives') concrete actions. Unlike its retributive counterpart, it is not centred on individual desert. Rather, it broadens its focus to collective responsibility for the institutional arrangements and material conditions that served as enabling factors for widespread acts of wrongdoing.[25]

By this account, justice is not served solely by prosecuting and punishing individual perpetrators. It requires corrective measures to counteract the institutional flaws that enabled the conflict to initiate and endure. Truth-seeking initiatives, reparation programmes, and institutional reforms are not just additives to a right that is satisfied by criminal prosecutions. Rather they are the mechanisms that set in place the necessary conditions for justice in the broader sense and guarantee that victims' rights are fully recognized and enforced.

The philosophical foundations of this view are twofold. On the one hand, it is founded on the recognition that the validity conditions for retributive responses are often absent in the contexts where transitional justice measures are designed and implemented. Hence, the view stems from the denial of a moral imperative for strict retributive responses to individual wrongdoing in these circumstances. Rather, the

[22] Rodrigo Uprimny & Nelson Camilo Sánchez, 'The ICC and Negotiated Peace: Reflections from Colombia (2015), https://www.opendemocracy.net/en/openglobalrights-openpage/icc-and-negotiated-peace-reflections-from-col/, accessed 4 March 2019.

[23] Priscilla Hayner, 'Does the ICC Advance the Interests of Justice?' (2014), https://www.opendemocracy.net/en/openglobalrights-openpage/does-icc-advance-interests-of-justice/, accessed on 4 March 2019.

[24] Priscilla Hayner, *The Peacemaker's Paradox: Pursuing Justice in the Shadow of Conflict* (New York, NY: Routledge, 2018).

[25] Catherine Lu, *Justice and Reconciliation in World Politics* (Cambridge: Cambridge University Press, 2017), 36

conditions of a large-scale political transition are seen as calling for a different application of justice: one that addresses past wrongs but is also forward-looking.[26]

On the other hand, these views are informed by the perception of a need for deeper and broader transformations. Their advocates recognize that the prosecution and punishment of all perpetrators would be insufficient to secure the enforcement of victims' rights unless the background conditions are also addressed through a comprehensive approach.[27] Thus, they argue, holistic approaches to transitional justice are justified because they contribute to bringing about various features of what we consider to be a just society:[28] reconciliation,[29] social transformation,[30] economic and social justice,[31] rule of law,[32] democratic deliberation and participation,[33] etc.

In this respect, defenders of the holistic view may consider the punishment of perpetrators to be an appropriate response, insofar as it furthers justice in the broad sense. Other responses to wrongdoing are also regarded instrumentally. Truth-seeking initiatives, for example, are seen as laying the grounds for necessary transformations and promoting various forms of accountability.[34] Truth commissions are often described as having a therapeutic and reconciling value for victims;[35] as serving to condemn wrongdoing and uphold the rule of law;[36] promoting democratic values;[37] and as

[26] André du Toit, 'The Moral Foundations of the South-African TRC: Truth as Acknowledgment and Justice as Recognition', in Robert I. Rothberg & Dennis Thompson (eds), *Truth v. Justice: The Morality of Truth Commissions* (Princeton University Press, 2000), 122; Ruti Teitel, *Transitional Justice* (Oxford; New York: Oxford University Press, 2000); Ruti Teitel, *Globalizing Transitional Justice : Contemporary Essays* (New York: Oxford University Press, 2014).

[27] Diana Acosta-Navas, 'The Search for Truth and the Dignity of Victims: Analysis of the Colombian Peace Accord, Harvard Human Rights Journal, Online Symposium on Transitional Justice (2017), https://harvardhrj.com/2017/10/online-symposium-on-transitional-justice.

[28] Lu (n. 25).

[29] Tutu (n. 20); Lu (n. 25).

[30] Colleen Murphy, 'Transitional Justice, Retributive Justice and Accountability for Wrongdoing', in C. Corradetti, N. Eisikovits, & J. Rotondi (eds), *Theorizing Transitional Justice* (Farnham; Burlington, VT: Ashgate, 2015); Colleen Murphy, *The Conceptual Foundations of Transitional Justice* (Cambridge: Cambridge University Press, 2017). Colleen Murphy, 'Judging the Justice of the Colombian Agreement', this volume.

[31] Louise Arbour, 'Economic and Social Justice for Societies in Transition' (2007) 40(1) New York University Journal of International Law and Politics 1–28.

[32] de Greiff (n. 12); David Dyzenhaus & Alma Diamond, 'The Resilient Constitution', this volume.

[33] Amy Gutmann & Dennis Thompson, 'The Moral Foundations of Truth Commissions', in Rothberg & Thompson (n. 26); de Greiff (n. 12); Krista Thomason, 'Transitional Justice as Structural Justice', in Corradetti, Eisikovits, & Rotondi (n. 30).

[34] Diana Acosta-Navas & Carlos Reyes, 'From Combatants' Boots', in F. Diaz Pabon, *Truth, Justice and Reconciliation in Colombia : Transitioning from Violence* (Milton: Routledge, 2018).

[35] Martha Minow, *Between Vengeance and Forgiveness: Facing History After Genocide and Mass Violence* (Boston: Beacon Press, 1998); Elizabeth Kiss, 'Moral Ambition Within and Beyond Political Constraints: Reflections on Restorative Justice, in Rothberg & Thompson (n. 26); Margaret L. Popkin & Naomi Roth-Arriaza, 'Truth as Justice', in Neil J. Kritz,.*Transitional Justice: How Emerging Democracies Reckon with Former Regimes* (Washington, D.C.: United States Institute of Peace Press, 1995); Du Toit (n. 26).

[36] Lucy Allais, 'Restorative Justice, Retributive Justice, and the South African Truth and Reconciliation Commission' (2011) 39(4) Philosophy & Public Affairs 331–63.

[37] Leigh Payne, *Unsettling Accounts: Neither Truth nor Reconciliation in Confessions of State Violence* (Durham: Duke University Press, 2008); Amy Gutmann and Dennis Thompson (n. 33); de Greiff (n. 12); Thomason (n. 33).

laying the ground for structural reforms, as they may reveal the flaws that enabled widespread wrongdoing in the first place.[38]

To summarize, defenders of the broad conception of justice advocate for circumventing ordinary routes for criminal redress and favouring a comprehensive approach. This approach trades off the number of prosecutions and the severity of punishments for the possibility of pursuing complementary measures like truth-seeking initiatives and reparations programmes. Unlike retributive conceptions of justice, the views in this family don't ground their normative force on individual desert or standard procedures. Rather, they derive their normative force from the promise that the institutional arrangements they advance will contribute to bring about morally valuable outcomes, which will affirm victims' status as equal citizens and right-bearers.

In the Colombian Integrated System, neither truth-seeking, nor reparative, nor punitive measures are regarded as self-standing responses. They constitute an integrated set of responses, which should promote victims' rights and dignity as a whole. Thus, for instance, the SJP integrates truth-telling and the provision of reparations as *sine qua non* conditions for perpetrators to receive judicial benefits. In this way, when amnesties or sentence reductions are granted to perpetrators of serious crimes, they are given in exchange for truth and reparation. Victims' right to justice in this framework is not violated, but rather addressed holistically, by measures that contribute to truth, reparation, and non-repetition. Furthermore, these measures are designed to produce inputs to inform broader institutional reforms, aimed at guaranteeing the future enforceability of their rights. From this perspective, we could define a broad criterion for the satisfaction of justice in transitional contexts along the following lines: an institutional arrangement satisfies victims' right to justice if any limitation of their rights, as they are ordinarily conceived, contributes to bring about a social and structural transformation that promotes the future recognition and enforceability of their rights.

However, this conception of justice is not free from problematic assumptions. Though it is informed by the recognition that transitional justice measures are implemented in a very imperfect world, it fails to fully grasp the normative significance of that fact. Whereas retributivist positions fail to acknowledge that non-ideal circumstances vitiate the validity conditions for retributive responses, the holistic approach fails to appreciate that those very conditions can also undermine their goal-oriented rationales. Let me explain.

Unlike procedure-based justifications, the outcome-based justifications for transitional justice measures have no clear conditions of success. Lacking a procedural guide, the success of such institutions can only be assessed by their results. However, beyond the attainment of the promised outcomes, there is no moral framework for their assessment. This is problematic for at least three reasons.

Firstly, the outcomes that these institutions are meant to bring about are often described in terms with vague satisfaction conditions, such as 'reconciliation' or 'the rule of law'. These terms denote normative ideals that social arrangements can aspire to, but are only likely to approximate. It is worth pointing out that the formulation of outcomes in terms of these normative ideals is neither accidental nor a function

[38] Rama Mani, *Beyond Retribution: Seeking Justice in the Shadows of War* (Cambridge, UK : Malden, MA: Polity Press ; Blackwell, 2002), 100; Acosta-Navas (n. 27).

of stylized academic language. There are good reasons why advocates of these institutional arrangements should use this kind of language. On the one hand, there are political reasons. The implementation of these measures is usually a matter of controversy, so their advocates need to present them in ways that appeal to the public interest. On the other, as De Greiff has argued,[39] to be seen as applications of justice, transitional justice measures ought to reaffirm values and norms that are lacking in a certain community. Hence, their goals and ends must be presented in terms of normative ideals that convey the importance of those norms and values.

It thus seems fundamental to the project of transitional justice that it sets normative ideals as its overarching goals. But this means that the only kind of assessment we have available is to contrast outcomes against the normative ideals they promise. This strategy is highly problematic. In her recent book on the advancement of human rights, Kathryn Sikkink[40] warns us against measuring progress by comparing realities and ideals. Because ideals cannot be attained, and sometimes not even approximated, any comparison that uses them as measures will downplay the actual progress and achievements that have been made. However, in the absence of an alternative mode of assessment, we are left in the dark as to the extent to which they contribute to satisfy victims' rights in general, and their right to justice in particular.

Secondly, holistic approaches create the challenge of assessing their aggregate results, given that none of their individual components is capable of bringing about justice in the broad sense of the term. On their own, truth-seeking initiatives may be seen as pure facades for impunity; reparations can be seen as grossly inadequate compensations; etc.[41] It is through their joint action that they can be regarded as promoting justice. However, we lack specific criteria to understand how they should interact and what outcomes can be reasonably expected from their co-operation.

Thirdly, and most importantly, in the very imperfect world of transitional societies, normative ideals are even harder to approximate. The same non-ideal conditions that justify circumventing retributive responses are likely to hamper institutions' capacity to produce results that meet or even approximate normative goals. If their advocates are correct, transitional justice institutions will be implemented in a context of institutional weakness, serious structural flaws, and in some cases strong political opposition. If this is the case, the background conditions for implementation will hamper any effort at producing the large-scale reforms that they adopt as their goals.

This insight is elegantly stated as the *paradox of the probable and the unnecessary.*[42] The paradox suggests that any degree of success by a system of transitional justice requires the operation of political, social, and economic forces that lie outside the reach of these institutions. When these forces are favourable for the transition, the institutions are superfluous. When they aren't, institutions are unlikely to succeed. Some

[39] de Greiff (n. 12).

[40] Kathryn Sikkink, *Evidence for Hope: Making Human Rights Work in the 21st Century (Human Rights and Crimes against Humanity)* (Princeton: Princeton University Press, 2017).

[41] de Greiff (n. 12), 37.

[42] Alexandra Barahona De Brito, Carmen González Enríquez, & Paloma Aguilar, *The Politics of Memory and Democratization: Transitional Justice in Democratizing Societies* (Oxford: Oxford University Press, 2001).

defenders of a holistic view of transitional justice seem to lose sight of this fact.[43] And yet, when we narrow our focus to specific measures, there seems to be deep frustration with the attained outcomes of reparations programmes[44] and the alleged reconciliatory powers of truth commissions,[45] let alone the more ambitious goals of structural justice and social transformation.[46]

Proponents of holistic transitional justice measures, thus capture the insight that retributive responses are unlikely to guarantee the satisfaction of victims' rights, unless a comprehensive response is employed to promote a deeper change. However, they suffer an analogous problem to that of retributivists. While the latter fail to recognize that transitional contexts vitiate the moral argument for retributive responses, the former fail to acknowledge that the large-scale outcomes that would allegedly justify these measures are unlikely to be attained in such contexts. When the entire normative force of the proposal is derived from the promise to obtain certain results and the likelihood of obtaining those results is very low, the moral justification for the proposal is tenuous at best. This seems to lead to the unfortunate conclusion that transitional justice arrangements, however well-designed they are, are bound to fail by their own standards.

IV.

The last two sections argued that the debate concerning the Integrated System of transitional justice can be framed as part of a deeper disagreement regarding the content and implications of a key concept, namely that of victims' right to justice. They analyse the conceptual underpinnings of each view, to reconstruct their justificatory structures and identify the crucial insights they capture. Lastly, they argue that, even though both approaches attempt to formulate a set of morally appropriate responses to wrongdoing, neither one fully incorporates the fact that these responses are implemented in

[43] Pdraig McAuliffe, 'Structural Causes of Conflict and the Superficiality of Transition', in Corradetti, Eisikovits, & Rotondi (n. 30).

[44] Cristián Correa, 'From Principles to Practice Challenges of Implementing Reparations for Massive Violations in Colombia' (2015), https://doi.org/10.1163/2210-7975_HRD-9808-2015002; James Robinson, 'La miseria en Colombia' (2016) 76 Desarrollo Y Sociedad 9–90; Frances Thomson, 'Land Restitution in Colombia: Why so Few Applications? (2017) 56 Forced Migration Review 35–36; Julia Zulver 'Feasible Justice: Has Colombia Over-Promised and Under-Delivered Reparations for its 8.6 Million Victims?' (2018), https://www.justiceinfo.net/en/reparations/37686-feasible-justice-has-colombia-over-promised-and-under-delivered-reparations-for-its-8-6-million-vic.html, accessed on 4 March 2019).

[45] Kimberly Theidon, 'Reconstructing Masculinities: The Disarmament, Demobilization, and Reintegration of Former Combatants in Colombia' (2009) 31(1) Human Rights Quarterly 1–34; Hugo Van Der Merwe and Audrey R. Chapman, *Truth and Reconciliation in South Africa: Did the TRC Deliver?* (Philadelphia: University of Pennsylvania Press, 2008); Payne (n. 37).

[46] It is for this reason that Pablo de Greiff warns transitional justice scholars against a *conceptual indiscipline in the field*, which consists of the attribution of ends and goals to transitional justice mechanisms without the support of a judicious functional analysis that can lead us to believe that such mechanisms have the capability to attain the ends attributed to them: Jaramillo L. García, Vicente R. Benítez,. 'Somos magníficos en el diseño legal, pero no en su implementación' (2019) https://www.elespectador.com/noticias/judicial/somos-magnificos-en-el-diseno-legal-pero-no-en-su-implementacion-de-greiff/accessed on 4 March 2019 .

a context of large-scale wrongdoing and institutional weakness, nor do they fully appreciate the extent to which this fact undermines their justificatory strategies.

Defenders of retributive views understand that, unless individuals' entitlements are honoured in ways that abide by clear standards, there is no clear measure for what constitutes upholding their rights. However, they fail to grasp the fact that the circumstances of transition are such that neither the notion of individual entitlements nor that of community standards can be taken for granted. Holistic views of justice are based on the insight that, absent a broader and deeper reform, the recognition and enforcement of victims' rights will remain a formality. However, they fail to acknowledge that the very structural flaws that undermine retributive responses also compromise the institutions' ability to bring about such reforms. Since comprehensive approaches to transitional justice derive their normative force from such a promise, they cannot succeed by their own standards.

The crucial insights in these views can be articulated as follows. Retributivist views, on the one hand, insist that respect for individual rights requires responses that abide by conventional procedures to honour individuals' entitlements. On the other, holistic views insist that such responses will fall short of upholding victims' rights, as they will not suffice to produce the structural conditions in which these responses are both possible and legitimate exercises of justice. Synthesizing the two, we could suggest that the aim of these measures should be to set such conditions in place. That is, in the circumstances of transition, responses to wrongdoing should be oriented towards creating appropriate conditions that enable and legitimize the future exercise of standard procedures for redress.

Per Section II, the validity conditions for retributive responses are the following: (1) the prior recognition of victims and perpetrators as full members of the moral community; (2) mutual accountability among members and between members and the state; and (3) shared norms and standards of conduct. With these conditions in place, the validity of retributive responses could be restored alongside a robust affirmation of individual entitlements and the legitimacy of standard procedures.

As suggested above, the imperfect conditions in which transitional measures are implemented are likely to hamper their ability to bring about a transformation of sufficient depth and breadth to attain these conditions. However, falling short of an ideal is not equivalent with failure, and progress can be measured by comparing the results of these institutions with either prior states or a relevant comparison class of similar efforts.[47] In fact, work in the social sciences has progressed in developing and applying comparative assessments for institutions' ambitions and achievements.[48] By these measures, the efforts in Colombia are far broader and more ambitious than any other such programmes 'both in absolute terms and relative to population size'.[49]

Importantly, however, in the realm of moral justifications, not just any measure of progress counts as success, and we still require guidelines to judge whether progress

[47] Sikkink (n. 40).

[48] Sikkink et al. (n. 1); Pham, Phoung, Vinck, Patrick, Marchesi, Bridgett, Johnson, Douglas, Dixon, Peter J., & Sikkink, Kathryn (2016) 'Evaluating Transitional Justice: The Role of Multi-Level Mixed Methods Datasets and the Colombia Reparation Program for War Victims' Transitional Justice Review 1–37. doi: http://dx.doi.org/10.5206/tjr.2016.1.4.3

[49] Sikkink et al. (n. 1), 3.

amounts to upholding victims' rights. So we need to formulate a threshold condition, which is more concrete than normative ideals, does justice to the notion of individual entitlements, is capable of capturing partial progress, and is yet sufficiently broad that it can be adapted to non-ideal contexts of application.

I end this section with a suggestion for future work, in what appears to be a promising direction. I suggest that the relevant threshold should be defined in terms of the creation of fertile capabilities[50] that enable victims to bring about social and structural transformations to guarantee the robust enforcement of their rights in the future. The notion of a capability is useful, insofar as it is intimately connected with that of individual entitlements, though it is richer than a mere formal or procedural conception thereof. It should be understood as a substantial individual liberty, which encompasses factors internal to the individual and environmental enabling conditions.[51] In this sense, a capability is not simply created through the formal recognition of rights, it requires an institutional arrangement where individuals are enabled to exercise their rights, and thus encompasses a broader social and political dimension. Securing capabilities for victims to bring about social and structural transformations entails clearing institutional obstacles for their exercise of civil and political rights.[52] This includes: securing conditions that enable their political participation; engaging in truth-seeking efforts that enable victims' testimonies to reveal the structural flaws that allowed their victimization; and promoting reparation programmes and institutional reforms that respond to the findings of truth commissions.

By centering on capability creation, the ethical assessment of transitional justice measures need not focus on institutions' ability to bring about large-scale outcomes. Rather it asks whether their design lays reasonable grounds for victims to be able to bring about these transformations through their agency. By this rationale, victims' rights and entitlements are upheld when the limitations of their ordinary rights are embedded in an institutional design that aims to remove structural obstacles that prevent them from exercising their civil and political liberties in ways that drive the necessary social transformation. Institutions that meet this standard will be such that, even though they block ordinary enforcement channels for victims' rights, they also lay the grounds for them to right the wrongs of structural injustice and widespread wrongdoing.

By focusing on capabilities, this approach could address the concern that transitional justice institutions simply put aside individual victims' entitlements in order to pursue long-term and large-scale goals. A capability-oriented ethical framework is focused on the creation of conditions for victims' individual entitlements to gain substantial traction. The framework could thus reinforce the recognition of victims as agents and full members of a community of mutually accountable moral equals. At the same time, the approach is prospective and forward-looking, as it recognizes the

[50] De-Shalit, Avner, & Wolff, Jonathan. (Oxford: Oxford University Press, 2007). Disadvantage (Oxford Political Theory)..

[51] Martha Nussbaum, *Creating Capabilities: The Human Development Approach* (Cambridge, MA: Belknap Press of Harvard University Press, 2011).

[52] Ibid.; Amartya Sen, *Development as Freedom* (New York: Knopf, 1999).

moral need to bring about social transformations that lead to shared norms and standards of respect for others.

This suggestion opens several avenues for future inquiry. In particular, the question of what concrete conditions ought to be met by a transitional justice system to secure the transformational capabilities it puts forth as its key ethical standard. Future work in this area should delineate at least: (1) the category of transformational capabilities; (2) assessment methods for capability creation; (3) specific criteria for the felicitous co-operation and integration of various transitional justice measures; and (4) a threshold condition for success that allows would-be designers, critics, and implementers to measure moral progress.

Ultimately, this framework's value will rely on its ability to establish clearer normative goalposts. To serve this purpose, these would need to be clearly grounded on the empirical conditions in which transitional justice is implemented. Simultaneously, they must honour the notion that these measures are not simply a pragmatic compromise, but constitute an exercise of justice that addresses the rights of those whose rights have been denied.

IV

THE ROLE OF INTERNATIONAL, COMPARATIVE AND FOREIGN LAW IN DOMESTIC CONSTITUTIONAL LAW: DIALOGUE AMONG THE GLOBAL SOUTH

A)

The Use of Foreign Precedents, A 'Global South' Monologue or a Conversation among Equals?

17

International and Foreign Law in Domestic Constitutional Law

A Comparative Examination of the Practice in United States and Post-Conflict Countries

Muna Ndulo

I. Introduction

Traditionally, when speaking of international law and domestic law, the theories of dualism/monism/modified dualism come to mind. In spite of the debate, it is generally recognized that international law and domestic law have their own sphere of application. At the international level states cannot invoke provisions of domestic law as justification for any internationally wrongful act that implicates state responsibility.[1] At the domestic level, international law applies either as part of the domestic law directly according to the constitution, or via transformation subject to the constitution.[2] Countries like South Africa constitutionally mandate their courts to consider international law when interpreting the bill of rights.[3] Similarly, the Colombia constitution

[1] *Elettronica Sicula SpA (ElSI) (US v Italy)* [1989] ICJ Rep. 15, 175; Article 27 Vienna Convention on the Law of Treaties (VCLT); Article 3 Draft Articles on State Responsibility; *Avena* and other *Mexican Nationals (Mexico) v United States of America* case [2004] ICJ Rep., para. 12,65; *LaGrand (Germany) v United States* case [2001] ICJ Rep., paras 466, 497–8; *Lockerbie* case Questions of Interpretation and Application of the 1971 Montreal Convention arising from Aerial Incident at Lockerbie (*Libyan ArabJamahiriya v United States of America*) [1992] ICJ Rep., paras 3, 32; *Applicability of the Obligation to Arbitrate Case*, [1988] Advisory Opinion Concerning the Applicability of the Obligation to Arbitrate under Section 21 of the United Nations Headquarters of 26 June 1947. ICJ Rep, paras 12, 34; *Polish National in Dazing Case* Treatment of Polish Nationals and other Persons of Polish Origin or Speech in Danzing Territory, Advisory Opinion, 1932 PCIJ Rep, Series A/B, No. 44, 24, para. 21.

[2] For instance, *Paquete Habana v US*, 175 US 677,700 (1900): International law is part of our law and must be ascertained and administered by the courts of justice of appropriate jurisdiction as often as questions of right depending upon it are duly presented for their determination. The constitution of Russia, 1993, Part 4, Article 15 states: 'generally recognized principles and norms of international law and the international treaties of the Russian Federation shall constitute an integral part of its legal system. If an international treaty of the Russian Federation establishes rules other than those provided for by the law, the rules of the international treaty shall apply. The constitution of Kenya, 2010, Article 2 (5) provides: The general rules of international law shall form part of the law of Kenya; 2 (6) provides: 'Any treaty or convention ratified by Kenya shall form part of the law of Kenya under this constitution.'

[3] 1996 South African constitution, Article 39 states: 'When interpreting the Bill of Rights: (a) must promote the values that underlie an open and democratic society based on human dignity, equality and freedom; (b) must consider international law and foreign law.'

Muna Ndulo, *International and Foreign Law in Domestic Constitutional Law:* In: *Constitutionalism.* Edited by: Alejandro Linares-Cantillo, Camilo Valdivieso-León, Santiago García-Jaramillo, Oxford University Press (2021). © The various contributors.
DOI: 10.1093/oso/9780192896759.003.0018

incorporated international law in its domestic legal system.[4] Domestic courts use the jurisprudence from foreign case law and international law to: strengthen a decision based on domestic law; for direct resolution of a dispute on the basis of international law; as a guide for interpreting domestic law; and for establishing a jurisprudential principle based on international law.

The impact of international law in constitutional texts can be observed in the way it has influenced constitutional texts adopted in the post democratization period in the new constitutions of states like South Africa, Kenya, and Colombia. This has happened more markedly in post-conflict/transitional states. Decolonized countries, post-conflict countries, and transitional countries, due to political and historical reasons, are to a large extent, founded upon norms guaranteed and promoted by modern international law: the right to self-determination, civil and political rights, socio-economic rights, and humanitarian law. These norms are not the exclusive property of international law, but are recognized as belonging to all human beings everywhere, and are universally recognized as vital ground rules for the ordering of human societies entering into any social contract to form a sovereign or international community consisting of states, individuals, and international organizations. International law has helped advance socio-economic rights and civil-political rights throughout the world. International norms also help to promote and strengthen the rule of law, and the judiciary, and the efficacy of the checks and balances between the different branches of the government. International law and foreign law help in the interpretation of the constitutional provisions in domestic jurisdictions. International law and foreign decisions sometimes act as gap-fillers in interpreting the bill of rights as well as standard setting. The role of international law in one country is not limited to a discussion about whether international decisions are binding or not but includes a discussion as to whether international law can act as a significant facilitator and promoter of constitutionalism and the rule of law in the country. Indeed international law can be weaponized to secure the rule of law and inspire law reform in a country. For example, in the remarkable case of *Attorney General v Unity Dow*,[5] where international human rights norms were used to declare unconstitutional citizenship laws that discriminated against women and provided that a child took her father's citizenship, but could not take that of her mother. The Court declared that it was guided by the Convention for the Elimination of all Forms of Discrimination against Women ('CEDAW') to which Botswana was party. It reasoned that Botswana's ratification of CEDAW had to mean something. It concluded that Botswana, as a member of CEDAW and the International Covenant on Civil and Political Rights ('ICCPR'), was under an obligation to observe the doctrines of anti-discrimination contained in the conventions. This chapter will seek to develop the themes identified above and interrogate the role of international and foreign law in domestic constitutional law. The issue is looked at

[4] 1991 constitution of Colombia, Article 9 reads: 'The foreign relations of the state are based on national sovereignty, on respect for the self-determination of the people, and on the recognition of the principles of international law approved by Colombia ... '. Article 93 states that: 'International treaties and agreements ratified by Congress that recognize human rights and prohibit their limitation in states of emergency have domestic priority. The rights and duties mentioned in this chapter will be interpreted in accordance with international treaties on human rights ratified by Colombia.'

[5] 1992AHRLR 99. (Bots.)

with specific reference to South Africa and the United States. South Africa is chosen because of its post-conflict status and the United States because it is often seen as a country that is not too friendly towards international law and foreign decisions. We demonstrate, in the end, that both countries use international and foreign law to aid them in the interpretation of aspects of their constitutions.

II. Human Rights Treaties, International Tribunals, and Domestic Courts

As between treaties and foreign court decisions, domestic courts have tended to rely more on treaties than foreign court decisions to resolve the cases brought before them. Although readily apparent, it is important to point out why treaties are the preferred way of establishing international law. First, the substantive rules of treaties are relatively easy to determine as they are contained in easily accessible texts. Secondly, the problem of state consent (obligation of state to follow) is largely mitigated in treaties because they are usually entered into through a recognizable affirmative act by the nation entering into them (this being an executive signature, a parliamentary statute, or a combination thereof). Third, treaties resemble in form and sometimes in substance, the controlling documents that pertain to domestic governance. Finally, treaties are more accessible to a domestic constituency and therefore might be more favoured and accepted by such constituency.

The emergence of international human rights tribunals has altered the types of available enforcement mechanisms for international law. Although often cited , there are some issues with these tribunals that limit the application of their jurisprudence to domestic constitutional matters. After the end of the Cold War, tribunals like the International Criminal Tribunal for the former Yugoslavia ('ICTY') and the International Criminal Court for Rwanda ('ICCR') were set up in response to massive human rights violations in those regions. This followed international consensus to end impunity for grave human rights violations. However, these courts' jurisdiction was confined to crimes from these specific regions and to international crimes. As a result, the reach of these tribunals only extended to punishment in specific contexts informed by regional law. The International Criminal Court ('ICC') was established following the need for a permanent court and for a tribunal that would have broader geographical reach.

One noticeable US case in which international tribunals cases were referenced to by a domestic court was *Hamdan v Rumsfeld*.[6] The matter in that case had stemmed from understanding the legality of the United States' own military tribunals at the domestic and international level, so the issue does not completely square up with constitutional matters relating to fundamental rights, etc. It is instructive, however, to see how a US court relied on international norms to interpret a US statute in a sensitive security matter. However, conspiracy as a crime was not recognized as a violation of the law of war, and the only 'conspiracy' crimes that have been recognized by international

[6] 548 US 557 (2006).

war crimes tribunals (whose jurisdiction often extends beyond war crimes proper to crimes against humanity and crimes against the peace) are conspiracy to commit genocide and a common plan to wage aggressive war, which is a crime against the peace and requires for its commission actual participation in a 'concrete plan to wage war'. The Court looked to the International Military Tribunal at Nuremburg for guidance. Even though the Court recognizes the Nuremburg Tribunal, it qualifies this reference with the line '[t]he Anglo–American concept of conspiracy was not part of European legal systems and arguably not an element of the internationally recognized laws of war'.[7]

Thus, international law decisions resulting from comparative analysis by domestic courts, as a means for the promotion of international human rights and creation of law, have the potential to acquire a certain domestic legitimacy that rulings from international tribunals—that are far-removed from the general populace—do not. Therefore, even though the European Court of Human Rights ('ECtHR'), whose decisions can formulate the interpretation of other human rights conventions and treaties, has a powerful voice as a promoter of international human rights law, its decisions on their own, have relatively little impact on the rest of the world not covered by its jurisdiction.[8] It is important to note that the total sample of cases where the US Supreme Court has referenced international law as persuasive is small. Of those cases, the majority of instances where the Court has decided constitutional matters using outside sources were referencing foreign domestic law, rather than international law. Taken even further, the substantive issues that reference outside international law are siphoned off from other issues and are limited.

The Court often mixes international law with foreign domestic law, thus creating confusion and unclear application as to purpose and weight. The Court has taken an ad hoc approach, rather than methodological one. However, one of the prime areas of case law that finds arguably with the most international law underpinnings is within Eighth Amendment Jurisprudence following *Roper v Simmons*.[9] Cases from other contexts are included later, but this analysis of the Eighth Amendment by scholars serves as a foundation for understanding the extent that international law is used.

III. Eighth Amendment, Capital Punishment, Foreign Cases, and International Law

This foray into the realm of non-US sources of law stems from the framing of the analysis of Eighth Amendment claims which are evaluated with an eye to 'evolving standards of decency' that are the hallmarks of 'a maturing society'. As such, the Court has continuously opined that such standards take into account international opinion and therefore, by 'society', it is intended to include 'all humanity' rather than a more insular

[7] Telford Taylor, *Anatomy of the Nuremberg Trials: A Personal Memoir* (New York: Skyhorse Publishing, 1993), 36

[8] See J. G. Merrills, *The Development of International Law by the European Court of Human Rights* (2nd edn, Manchester: Manchester University Press, 1995), 18 r

[9] 543 US 551, 575 (2005).

American outlook.[10] In its 1988 *Thompson v Oklahoma* decision,[11] the Court ruled that the death penalty was an unconstitutional violation of the Eighth Amendment where applied to persons who were under the age of 16 when they perpetrated their crime. The Court, in a footnote, noted that 'three major human rights treaties explicitly prohibit juvenile death penalties'. The three treaties that the Court then referred to were the ICCPR, the American Convention on Human Rights, and the Geneva Convention Relative to the Protection of Civil Persons in Time of War. However, the extent to which the Court provided guidance in weighing the value of these treaties was limited only by characterizing them as 'major'.

In *Stanford v Kentucky*,[12] the Court held that the death penalty could be applied to minors under the age of 18. In this case, it was primarily the dissent that referred to the international law sources. The dissent made reference to the same three human rights treaties ratified by the United States stating that: 'In addition to national laws, three leading human rights treaties ratified or signed by the United States explicitly prohibit juvenile death penalties.'[13] Additionally, the dissent also added a resolution to the same effect that had been passed by the UN Economic and Social Council, endorsed by the General Assembly of the UN, and adopted by the 7th United Nations Congress on the Prevention of Crime and the Treatment of Offenders. Interestingly enough, the resolution doesn't qualify as a human rights treaty, but is soft law. It does not have the same significance in the hierarchy of sources reflected in Article 38 of the ICJ statute. However, the Court does not distinguish the weight of each source of law

One of the key cases in this context is *Roper v Simmons*,[14] which overruled *Stanford* and declared the execution of minors under 18 as unconstitutional. Within the Court's decision, a paragraph is spent discussing why, based on international norms, the death penalty should not apply to juveniles.[15] The decision referenced numerous international human rights treaties. They included the UN Convention on the Rights of the Child, the African Charter on the Rights and Welfare of the Child, International Covenant on Civil and Political Rights, ICCPR, and the American Convention on Human Rights. The Court then rebuts respondents' use of countries like Iran, Pakistan, Saudi Arabia, Yemen, Nigeria, the Democratic Republic of Congo, and China as countries who used to execute juveniles in 1990, but have since abolished the practice. Why the Court chose to refer to respondents' use of this statistic and these specific countries, which are often at odds with the United States on domestic and international issues, is unclear. In a separate dissent, Justice O'Connor disagreed with the outcome, but reiterated that foreign and international law have a role in Eighth Amendment analysis, because the inquiry required in this context 'reflects the special character of the Eighth Amendment, which, as the Court has long held, draws its meaning directly from the maturing values of civilized society'.[16]

[10] 487 US 830 (1988) (citing *Trop v Dulles*, 356 US 86, 102 (1958)).
[11] Ibid.
[12] 492 US 361.
[13] Ibid., 389–90 (Brennan, J., dissenting).
[14] (2005) 543 US 551.
[15] Ibid., 575.
[16] Ibid., 604–5.

An interesting characteristic of that decision that Glensy[17] mentions is that Justice Scalia's own dissent in *Roper* emphasized that referencing the UN Convention on the Rights of the Child as persuasive means that signing on to one part of it denotes that other sections must be adopted as well since it is a document that finds its strength as a whole. At the time, Justice Scalia meant that the US may also have to adopt the portion of the Convention prohibiting life without parole for juveniles, which was adopted by the Court in *Graham v Florida.*[18] In that decision, the majority cited exactly the same article of the same treaty that Justice Scalia had identified five years earlier, stating that this treaty prohibited the imposition of 'life imprisonment without possibility of release ... for offences committed by persons below eighteen years of age'. In *Roper*, the Court made a bold stance on the role of foreign law in US constitutional interpretation and stated: 'Yet, at least from the time of the Court's decision in Trop, the Court has referred to the laws of other countries and to international authorities as instructive for its interpretation of the Eighth Amendment's prohibition of "cruel and unusual punishments"'.

In this context, the 'climate of international opinion' around determining appropriate punishment has been a relevant part of the actual analysis. The Court looked to 'historical development of the punishment at issue, legislative judgements, international opinion, and sentencing decisions ... made before'.[19] Another example of the use of foreign jurisprudence for guidance in the context of the Eighth Amendment is the *Hamdan v Rumsfeld* decision . The Court's opinion in *Hamdan*, dealt with the constitutionality and legality of military commissions as they relate to domestic law and international law. This section focuses on the international law. Salim Ahmed Hamdan, a Yemeni citizen, was Osama bin Laden's driver. Captured in Afghanistan in 2001 by members of the United States Armed Forces, he was transferred to the United States detention centre at Guantánamo Bay in 2002. By an order of the President of the United States, Hamdan was designated to stand trial before a United States military commission for charges of conspiracy to commit multiple offences, including attacking civilians and civilian objects, murder by an unprivileged belligerent, destruction of property by an unprivileged belligerent, and terrorism.

In the Court's opinion: '[t]he military commission convened to try Hamdan lacked power to proceed because its structure and its procedures violated both the UCMJ and the Geneva Conventions. Four of us also conclude ... that the offense with which Hamdan has been charged is not an "offens[e] that by ... the law of war may be tried by military commissions.'[20] Although quite extensive, the Court opinion focused on how Common Article 3 of the Geneva Conventions undermined the use of the military commissions through the Authorization to Use Military Force. Neither Hamdan's alleged agreement with bin Laden and others to commit war crimes, nor a single act occurred in a theatre of war or during a war (34–6). Furthermore, conspiracy is not a war crime: it has rarely, if ever, been tried as such in the United States by any military

[17] Rex D. Glensy, 'Constitutional Interpretation Through Global Lens' (2010) 75 Missouri Law Review 1171.

[18] 130 S. Ct. 2011 (2010).

[19] *Enmund v Florida*, 458 US 782 (1982).

[20] *Hamdan* (n. 6), 557, 567.

commission and does not appear in either the Geneva or Hague Conventions, the major treaties on the law of war (40, 46).

Trial by the military commission in question also fails because its procedures violate the Uniform Code of Military Justice and the rules and precepts of the law of nations (49–60). Furthermore, the military commission violates the Geneva Conventions (62). Irrespective of whether or not the Geneva Conventions are judicially enforceable, the rights guaranteed under the Convention form part of the laws of war, and military commissions are obliged to comply with the laws of war (65). The Court added that at the very least Common Article 3 to the Geneva Conventions applies to *Hamdan*, which requires that he be tried by a regularly constituted court—military commissions are not such courts (69–72). Specifically, the international instruments used included the Geneva Convention for the Amelioration of the Condition of the Wounded and Sick in Armed Forces in the Field ('GC I'), Geneva Convention for the Amelioration of the Condition of Wounded, Sick and Shipwrecked Members of Armed Forces at Sea ('GC II'), Geneva Convention relative to the Treatment of Prisoners of War ('GC III'), and Geneva Convention relative to the Protection of Civilian Persons in Time of War ('GC IV'). However, international human rights law was a source of considerable disagreement between the Justices: on the enforceability of the Geneva Conventions, a five-to-two split; on the applicability of Common Article 3 to the war with al Qaeda, a five-to-two split; and on the meaning of Common Article 3, a five-to-three split.

IV. Equal Protection: Education and International Law

Outside of Eighth Amendment cases, the Court has used international law to interpret other constitutional provisions, with a particular focus on the Equal Protection and Substantive Due Process clauses. This is the case because, like the standards announced for the Eighth Amendment, the Equal Protection and Substantive Due Process clauses embody norms such as fairness and liberty 'that transcend[] borders', and therefore lend themselves to a certain universality of approach. Within the Substantive Due process analysis, the Court seeks to protect practices that are 'implicit in the concept of ordered liberty'.

In *Grutter v Bollinger*,[21] the Court referenced international law in upholding the University of Michigan Law School's affirmative action programme. In her concurrence, Justice Ginsburg cites the International Convention on the Elimination of All Forms of Racial Discrimination and CEDAW. Both support the proposition that affirmative action programmes are remedial in nature and must be reviewed periodically so they can be phased out once the goals of equality are achieved. Here, the Court, again, left out the significance of mentioning the two international treaties or how much weight should be given to them. What is interesting is that the decision referenced the fact that the first treaty had been ratified by the United States. This was clearly done to give it more significance in the analysis. In contrast, it's important to note again that CEDAW is an international treaty that the United States has signed,

[21] 539 US 306 (2003).

but has not ratified. However, many localities within the United States have adopted some of the CEDAW ordinances and resolutions. *Grutter* is another example of the issues that arise with citing international treaties that the United States has not completely supported.

V. Substantive Due Process: *Lawrence*, Sexual Orientation, and International Law

In *Lawrence v Texas*,[22] the US Supreme Court struck down the Texas anti-sodomy statute as an unconstitutional violation of due process. The decision referred to international law in critiquing the earlier Supreme Court decision in *Bowers v Hardwick*.[23] In that decision, Justice Burger made a note that sodomy was universally condemned and criminalized in all Judeo-Christian Western civilizations.[24] One of the significant takeaways was when Justice Kennedy drew on international law to debunk Burger's claim, specifically noting that a case decided by ECtHR five years before *Bowers* had reached the exact opposite result, to universal approval.[25] This was used to show that western society had evolved.

While Justice Ginsburg in *Grutter* only cites two international treaties, Justice Kennedy provides substantial insight into the motivation and reasoning behind his citations to a case from the ECtHR and not just a treaty. In *Lawrence*, international law (of the regional law variety) provided a communing function of linking the US Constitution to the European Convention on Human Rights (ECHR) as well as a counter to the obviously erroneous arguments uttered by Chief Justice Burger in *Bowers*. For the *Lawrence* majority, it was not enough to merely rule in favour of the petitioners, they also had to clarify that Bowers was being unceremoniously dumped as a colossal error from its inception. This could not be clearer in the words of Justice Kennedy: 'Bowers was not correct when it was decided, and it is not correct today.' In one of the few times noted, international law was used squarely as a means of changing precedent and showing error of an earlier decision . Here the international treaties and tribunals that were cited were UN resolutions or covenants like the ICCPR, Inter-American Convention on Human Rights, Geneva conventions, UN Convention on the Rights of the Child, and the African Charter on Peoples and Human Rights. The ultimate irony is that while the Court gave weight to these treaties, the United States is not a party to most of the conventions cited.

In *Knight v Florida*,[26] Justice Breyer assumed the mantle of Justice Frankfurter by making continuous references to international and foreign law.[27] The case involved the constitutionality of extensive delays prior to executions being considered cruel and unusual punishment. In his dissent, Justice Breyer made clear reference to the Supreme Court of Zimbabwe's decision and holding that 'delays of five and six

[22] 539 US 558 (2003).
[23] 478 US 186 (1986).
[24] *Lawrence v Texas*, 539 US 558 (2003).
[25] *Dudgeon v United Kingdom* (1982) 4 EHRR, 149; IHRL 31 (ECHR 1981) 45 ECtHR 52.
[26] 528 US 990 (1999).
[27] Ibid.

years' were 'torture or inhuman or degrading punishment or other such treatment'.[28] Ironically enough, Justice Breyer debated with Justice Scalia and considered the reference to be a 'tactical error' since they considered Zimbabwe 'not the human rights capital of the world'. This comment , is important as it points to how forum selection is made as to which countries to look to in citing foreign cases on constitutional matters. The US Supreme Court clearly looks to countries that follow similar democratic practices to those of the United States , even where a decision exists on the point in a country not fitting that description.

VI. Determining Which Countries Courts Choose to Cite

It is clear that the Court engages international and foreign law for certain cases dealing with fundamental human rights, such as the death penalty, in addition to equal protection and due process issues.However, in decisions like *Roper*, where the Court engaged in extensive international and foreign law references, there was a clear delineation that European democracies bear a more appropriate source for comparative analysis from non-European democracies. An examination of the *Lawrence decision reveals that the Supreme Court cited* sources from traditional democratic allies, such as the United Kingdom and Canada. They did not engage the jurisprudence of any other countries.

Roper is again informative on this issue, although still not completely clear. First, it is important to note the countries that were used to draw a contrast on how bad the United States was doing by still executing juveniles. Other statistics could have been used, but the year 1999 and the countries (Iran, Pakistan, Saudi Arabia, Yemen, Nigeria, the Democratic Republic of Congo, and China) were used to show that if they were considering juvenile executions unconstitutional, then the United States is completely behind. Although seemingly harmless, this statistic stands out more because the Court then turns to support its point by picking the model nation and looking at the United Kingdom. The Court could have looked to any of the seven countries listed to see how they rationalized changing their own foreign domestic law stances; however, they did not.

As noted above, the Court used the United Kingdom because the 'United Kingdom's experience bears particular relevance here in light of the historic ties between our countries and in light of the Eighth Amendment's own origins'.[29] Predictably, Justice Scalia caught on to this selective endorsement and blasted the majority by engaging in his own negative comparative analysis by pointing out that, while the United States is looking to the United Kingdom for guidance on this issue, other nations in Europe (Netherlands, Britain, Germany, Australia, and France) refused to adopt policies and constitutional viewpoints similar to the United States These countries rejected the exclusionary rule, the separation of church and state doctrine, and the fundamental right to have an abortion. Justice Scalia faced a blowback from Justice O'Connor, but

[28] 'Catholic Commission for Justice & Peace in Zimbabwe v. Attorney-General' [1993] 1 Zimbabwe Law Reports 242, 251, 282 (S).

[29] *Roper v Simmons*, 543 US 551, 577 (2005).

the important point was made that the United States has engaged international law, not just on issues where domestic law is silent, but on key constitutional matters where Court precedent exists. Further, Justice Scalia shows that the United States also engaged these sources just because they came from '"like-minded" foreigners'. He challenged the Court to cite sources origination from nations outside traditional allies.

VII. South African Constitutional Court and International Law and Foreign Law

During the past three decades new constitutions have appeared in many parts of the world, often in the aftermath of civil wars, but also in response to demands for more democratic political systems or for resolution of institutional crises. Some remain pieces of paper that have made little impact while others have been successful and have become the source of norms that shape societies and governance. Many of these new documents embrace international law. In this section of the chapter we look at the experience of South Africa. The South African constitution adopted in 1996 after the end of apartheid enjoins judges to have regard to international law applicable to the rights entrenched in the constitution. Article 39(1) provides that when interpreting the Bill of Rights, a court, tribunal, or forum—(a) must promote the values that underlie an open and democratic society based on human dignity, equality and freedom; (b) must consider international law; and (c) may consider foreign law. This brings international human rights law into the centre of human rights adjudication in South Africa. This means that the judges can learn and draw on human rights decisions based on international human rights conventions. Similarly important is the learning to be found in comparable foreign law. While judges are not obliged to have regard to such comparable foreign case law, they are able to do so in terms of Section 39(1)(c). This section allows them to look at the law of human rights as it is developing in other jurisdictions.

VIII. The Bill of Rights, International Law, and the South African Constitution

In *The Republic of South Africa v Makwanyane and Another*,[30] the Court considered the constitutionality of the death penalty. Chaskalson P, in the context of Section 35(1) of the interim constitution,[31] stated that:

> [P]ublic international law would include non-binding as well as binding law. They may both be used under the section as tools of interpretation. International

[30] Constitutional Court of South Africa (1995) CCT/3/94.

[31] Section 35(1) of the interim constitution reads as follows: 'In interpreting the provisions of this Chapter a court of law shall promote the values which underlie an open and democratic society based on freedom and equality and shall, where applicable, *have regard to public international law applicable to the protection of the rights entrenched in this Chapter, and may have regard to comparable foreign case law*.' [Emphasis added]

> agreements and customary international law accordingly provide a framework within which [the Bill of Rights] can be evaluated and understood, and for that purpose, decisions of tribunals dealing with comparable instruments, such as the United Nations Committee on Human Rights, the Inter-American Commission on Human Rights, the Inter-American Court of Human Rights, the European Commission on Human Rights, and the International Labor Organization, may provide guidance as to the correct interpretation of particular provisions of [the Bill of Rights].[32]

The Court pointed out that comparative 'bill of rights' jurisprudence would no doubt be of importance particularly in the early stages of the transition when there is no developed indigenous jurisprudence to draw on. In its decision to abolish the death penalty as unconstitutional the Court surveyed jurisprudence from the United States; the ICCPR; the ECHR; and case law from India, Tanzania, Canada, and Germany.

In *Hoffman v South African Airways*,[33] Mr Hoffman applied for job as a flight attendant with South African Airways. At the end of the selection process he was found to be the most suitable candidate for the position. Engagement was subject to a pre-employment medical examination. The medical examination found him to be clinically fit and thus suitable for employment. However, a blood test showed that he was HIV positive. The company informed him that he could not be employed in view of his HIV positive status. The labour court found that the airline's company practice was not unfairly discriminatory. Mr Hoffman took the matter to the Constitutional Court alleging that the refusal to employ him amounted to unfair discrimination. The Court concluded that the refusal by the airline to employ Mr Hoffman violated his right to equality guaranteed by Section 9 of the South African constitution. In order to strengthen its argument the Court referred to South Africa's international obligations on discrimination. It stated:

> The need to eliminate unfair discrimination does not arise only from Chapter 2 of our Constitution. It also arises out of international obligations. South Africa has ratified a range of antidiscrimination Conventions, including the African Charter on Human and Peoples Rights. In the preamble to the African Charter, member states undertake, amongst other things, to dismantle all forms of discrimination. Article 2 prohibits discrimination of any kind. In terms of Article 1, member states have an obligation to give effect to the rights and freedoms enshrined in the Charter. In the context of employment, the ILO Convention 111, Discrimination (Employment and Occupation, Convention, 1958 proscribes discrimination that has the effect of nullifying or impairing equality of opportunity or treatment in employment or occupation. In terms of Article 2, member states have an obligation to pursue national policies that are designed to promote equality of opportunity and treatment in the field of employment, with a view to eliminating any discrimination.[34]

[32] *S v Makwanyane and Another* [1995] ZACC 3; 1995 (3) SA 391 (CC), 1995 (6) BCLR 665 (CC), para. 35.
[33] Constitutional Court of South Africa (2000) CCT17/00.
[34] Ibid.

Relying on the provisions of the South African constitution and international law, the Constitutional Court concluded that Mr Hoffman was denied equal treatment.

In a case dealing with the right to housing, one of the fundamental socio-economic rights, as an example, Article 26 of the Constitution of South Africa provides that:

> Everyone has the right to have access to adequate housing. (a) The state must take reasonable legislative and other measures, within its available resources, to achieve the progressive realization of this right (b) No one may be evicted from their home, or have their home demolished, without an order of court made after considering all the relevant circumstances. No legislation may permit arbitrary evictions.

It is not explicitly clarified in the constitution what constitutes 'adequate' or 'reasonable' legislative and other measures of government, and what satisfies 'progressive' realization of the right to housing. When it came to the positive obligation of the government on guaranteeing the right to housing, the Constitutional Court relied on international law to fill the gaps and thereby facilitated the achievement of the Bill of Rights. In *Grootboom*,[35] Mrs Irene Grootboom and the other respondents were rendered homeless as a result of their eviction from their informal homes situated on private land earmarked for formal low-cost housing. They applied to the Cape of Good Hope High Court for an order requiring the government to provide them with adequate basic shelter or housing until they obtained permanent accommodation and were granted certain relief. The appellants were ordered to provide the respondents who were comprised of children and their parents with shelter. The judgment provisionally concluded that 'tents, portable latrines and a regular supply of water (albeit transported) would constitute the bare minimum'. The appellants, who represented all spheres of government responsible for housing, challenged the correctness of that order before the Constitutional Court.[36] The Constitutional Court, in paragraphs 26–33 of its judgment, examined the relevant international law, in particular the International Covenant on Economic, Social and Cultural Rights ('ICESCR'), recognizing that 'every state party is bound to fulfil a minimum core obligation by ensuring the satisfaction of a minimum essential level of the socio-economic rights, including the right to adequate housing'.[37] However, read together with the Constitution and South Africa's situation, the Court observed:

> As will appear from the discussion below, the real question in terms of our Constitution is whether the measures taken by the state to realize the right afforded by section 26 are reasonable. There may be cases where it may be possible and appropriate to have regard to the content of a minimum core obligation to determine whether the measures taken by the state are reasonable. However, even if it were appropriate to do so, it could not be done unless sufficient information is placed before a court to enable it to determine the minimum core in any given context. In this case,

[35] *Government of the Republic of South Africa v Grootboom* (2000) ZACC 19; 2001 (1) SA 46; 2000 (11) BCLR 1169.

[36] Ibid., para. 4.

[37] Ibid., para. 30.

we do not have sufficient information to determine what would comprise the minimum core obligation in the context of our Constitution. It is not in any event necessary to decide whether it is appropriate for a court to determine in the first instance the minimum core content of a right.[38]

In interpreting 'progressive' realization of the right to housing, the Court referred to Article 2.1 of the ICESCR[39] and concluded: 'Although the committee's analysis is intended to explain the scope of states parties' obligations under the Covenant, it is also helpful in plumbing the meaning of "progressive realization" in the context of our Constitution. The meaning ascribed to the phrase is in harmony with the context in which the phrase is used in our Constitution and there is no reason not to accept that it bears the same meaning in the Constitution as in the document from which it was so clearly derived.'[40] The General Comment of ICESCR quoted by the Constitutional Court reads:

> Nevertheless, the fact that realization over time, or in other words progressively, is foreseen under the Covenant should not be misinterpreted as depriving the obligation of all meaningful content. It is on the one hand a necessary flexibility device, reflecting the realities of the real world and the difficulties involved for any country in ensuring full realization of economic, social and cultural rights. On the other hand, the phrase must be read in the light of the overall objective, indeed the raison d'être, of the Covenant which is to establish clear obligations for States parties in respect of the full realization of the rights in question. It thus imposes an obligation to move as expeditiously and effectively as possible towards that goal. Moreover, any deliberately retrogressive measures in that regard would require the most careful consideration and would need to be fully justified by reference to the totality of the rights provided for in the Covenant and in the context of the full use of the maximum available resources.[41]

In conclusion, the Court decided that:

> Neither section 26 nor section 28 entitles the respondents to claim shelter or housing immediately upon demand. The High Court order ought therefore not to have been made. However, section 26 does oblige the state to devise and implement a coherent, coordinated Programme designed to meet its section 26 obligations. The Programme that has been adopted and was in force in the Cape Metro at the time that this application was brought, fell short of the obligations imposed upon the state by section 26(2) in that it failed to provide for any form of relief to those desperately in need of access to housing.[42]

[38] Ibid., para. 33.
[39] Please note that South Africa signed the ICESCR but had *not* yet ratified it at the time of this judgment. The ratification was made in 2015. Even before the ratification, the Constitutional Court referred to ICESCR frequently.
[40] *Grootboom* (n. 35), para. 45.
[41] General Comment 3 of 1990, para. 9.
[42] *Grootboom* (n 35), para. 95.

Grootboom is an early decision of the South African Constitutional Court. It was given in 2000, only three years after the entering into force of the constitution, and seven years after the end of apartheid, and at the time when the ICESCR was not even ratified by South Africa. Following the *Grootboom* case, Chapter 12 of the National Housing Code was introduced, entitled 'Housing assistance in emergency housing circumstances', and provides for assistance to people who find themselves in a housing emergency for reasons beyond their control. Eleven years after *Grootboom*, the Constitutional Court in *City of Johannesburg Metropolitan Municipality v Blue Moonlight Properties* read Chapter 12 together with Article 26 of the Constitution, with elaborative interpretation of the reasoning and conclusion in *Grootboom*, and finally held:

> The City's interpretation of Chapter 12 as neither permitting nor obliging them to take measures to provide emergency accommodation, after having been refused financial assistance by the province, is incorrect. The City is obliged to provide temporary accommodation.[43]

IX. Separation of Powers, Securing Checks and Balances, and International Law

In *United Democratic Movement v Speaker of the National Assembly and Others*, the Constitutional Court was asked to answer the essential question of whether the Speaker of the National Assembly was correct in saying that neither the constitution nor the Rules of the National Assembly allow her to authorize a vote by secret ballot for the motion of no confidence in the then-President Zuma. It was argued that the constitution is silent on the concrete way of voting on the motion of no confidence. What was really before the Court was the Court's judicial power to interpret the other branches' power and/or obligation under the constitution and the corresponding boundary of the separation of powers. Given that the domestic constitutional law, and even the whole domestic context provided limited guidance on this highly sensitive issue, the Constitutional Court looked at European Union law and foreign laws in Africa to make convincing arguments on the meaning and effectiveness of a secret ballot. Referring to those laws was extremely helpful, not only because they showed the common concern of guaranteeing the check and balance between the legislative and the executive, and the reasonable solution to that concern—the effective voting method; but also because it strengthened the legal reasoning of the Constitutional Court's judicial interpretation of such a significant check and balance issue, and ensured that the Court was not easily criticized for dangerous judicial-overreach, which is always a risk when the Court is providing a check on the executive.

[43] *City of Johannesburg Metropolitan Municipality v Blue Moonlight Properties 39 (Pty) Ltd and Another* [2011] ZACC 33; 2012 (2) BCLR 150 (CC); 2012 (2) SA 104 (CC), para. 96 (emphasis added).

The relevant part of the judgment reads:

> The proper exercise of the power to prescribe a voting procedure in a motion of no confidence proceedings would partly depend on why the Constitution prescribes a secret ballot for the general elections and a contested election of the President and the Speaker. Beginning with European electoral instruments, article 5 of its Convention on the Standards of Democratic Elections, Electoral Rights and Freedoms in the Member States of the Commonwealth of Independent States provides: 'The Parties hereto proceed from the assumption that observance of the principle of secret balloting means exclusion of any control over voters' expression of will, provision for equal conditions for free choice'.

The Court also looked at case law from Botswana and Zimbabwe. In *Botswana Democratic Party v The Speaker*, the Court of Appeal of the Republic of Botswana noted that the secret ballot voting system in Parliament— 'is rather an arrangement put in place by the National Assembly for the effective exercise of the Members' right to vote without outside influence or coercion which could render the right an empty one'. And this was also explained by the Supreme Court of Zimbabwe in the following terms:

> The legislature chose the secret ballot for its optimum benefits ... The prescription of a secret ballot as the method for the election of the Speaker [by members of the legislature] is based on the acceptance of the principle that it promotes and protects freedom of expression of choice of a preferred candidate without undue influence, intimidation and fear of disapproval by others.[44]

Finally, the Constitutional Court concluded that:

> Our interpretation of the relevant provisions of the Constitution and the rules makes it clear that the Speaker does have the power to authorize a vote by a secret ballot in a motion of no confidence proceedings against the President, in appropriate circumstances. The exercise of that power must be duly guided by the need to enable effective accountability, what is in the best interests of the people and obedience to the Constitution.[45]

X. International Law, Rule of Law, and Constitutionalism

The role of international law in one country is not only about binding or not binding, applying or not applying, obligations of the government towards the international community or its own citizens, but can also act as a tester, and in return, a significant facilitator of constitutionalism in a country. Indeed, International law can be weaponized to secure the rule of law. South Africa's withdrawal from the ICC and later withdrawal of that withdrawal as a result of the judiciary holding the executive's conduct

[44] *United Democratic Movement v Speaker of the National Assembly and Others* [2017] ZACC 21; 2017 (8) BCLR 1061 (CC); 2017 (5) SA 300 (CC), paras 70–2.

[45] Ibid., para. 90.

as unconstitutional, read together with the judiciary checking the executive's not arresting Mr Al-Bashir as requested by the ICC before that withdrawal, provides a perfect example of international law promoting the rule of law.

In 2005 the Security Council referred the situation in Darfur, Sudan to the ICC (Resolution 1593 of 6 June 2005). On 4 March 2009 the Pre-Trial Chamber issued an arrest warrant for Al-Bashir, and on 12 July 2010 a new arrest warrant with additional charges was issued. In 2015, when Al-Bashir attended the African Union summit in Johannesburg, a non-governmental organization ('NGO'), the Southern African Litigation Center ('SALG'), filed a request in the Pretoria High Court, for the arrest of Al-Bashir so that he could be handed over to the ICC. The request was granted. South Africa did not arrest and surrender him to the ICC despite the arrest warrant issued by the Court and despite the fact that South Africa is a state party to the ICC and was obligated to cooperate under the ICC Statute. It resulted in a formal non-cooperation proceeding at the ICC, and a public hearing taking place on 7 April 2017.

This situation was submitted to South Africa's High Court and Supreme Court of Appeal, both of which ruled that the government's failure to arrest Al-Bashir was unconstitutional. Although, unfortunately, at the time of the judgment Al-Bashir had left South Africa already.

The High Court held that:

> The Respondents are quite aware of the provisions of ss. 1 and 2 of the Constitution which declares that the State is founded on the supremacy of the Constitution and the rule of law. They are also aware of the constitutional enjoinder that international agreements bind the Republic, especially those that have been ratified (s. 231). They are obviously bound to comply with domestic legislation and obviously the Implementation Act. They must also be aware of s. 165 of the Constitution [on judicial authority].

At this stage, on a common sense approach, there are clear indications that the order of Sunday 14 June 2015 was not complied with. It is for this reason that we are moved to state that:

> A democratic State based on the rule of law cannot exist or function, if the government ignores its constitutional obligations and fails to abide by court orders. A court is the guardian of justice, the corner-stone of a democratic system based on the rule of law. If the State, an organ of State or State official does not abide by court orders, the democratic edifice will crumble stone-by stone until it collapses and chaos ensues.[46]

The Supreme Court of Appeal decided that:

> The conduct of the Respondents in failing to take steps to arrest and detain, for surrender to the International Criminal Court, the President of Sudan, Omar Hassan

[46] *Southern Africa Litigation Centre v Minister of Justice and Constitutional Development and Others* [2015] ZAGPPHC 402; 2016 (1) SACR 161 (GP); 2015 (5) SA 1 (GP); [2015] 3 All SA 505 (GP); 2015 (9) BCLR 1108 (GP), paras 37.1, 37.2.

Ahmad Al Bashir, after his arrival in South Africa on 13 June 2015 to attend the 25th Assembly of the African Union, was inconsistent with South Africa's obligations in terms of the Rome Statute and section 10 of the Implementation of the Rome Statute of the International Criminal Court Act 27 of 2002, and unlawful.[47]

After the events surrounding of Al-Bashir, and based on the argument that the 'ICC is targeting Africa', South Africa (the executive branch) decided to withdraw from the Rome Statute and submitted the application of withdrawal to the UN Secretary General on 19 October 2016. According to the Rome Statute such withdrawal would take effect one year after the application. The withdrawal notice was challenged as unconstitutional. On 22 February 2017, South Africa's High Court decided that the declaration of withdrawal was unconstitutional and invalid. Essentially, the case concerned 'the separation of powers between the national executive and parliament in international relations and treaty-making'.[48] The High Court stated that:

> The primary question is whether the national executive's power to conclude international treaties, also includes the power to give notice of withdrawal from international treaties without parliamentary approval. Related to that is an ancillary question whether it is constitutionally permissible for the national executive to deliver a notice of withdrawal from an international treaty without first repealing the domestic law giving effect to such treaty. At the heart of the dispute is the withdrawal of South Africa from the Rome Statute of the International Criminal Court (the ICC).[49]

South Africa ratified the Rome Statute on 27 November 2000 and on 16 August 2002 passed the Implementation Act, which created a legal framework for cooperation with the ICC, the effective implementation of the Rome Statute, and a structure for the national prosecution of international crimes to bring perpetrators to justice in domestic courts or in the ICC. The provision at issue was Article 231 of the constitution which provides that:

(1) The negotiating and signing of all international agreements is the responsibility of the national executive.
(2) An international agreement binds the Republic only after it has been approved by resolution in both the National Assembly and the National Council of Provinces, unless it is an agreement referred to in subsection (3).
(3) An international agreement of a technical, administrative or executive nature, or an agreement which does not require either ratification or accession, entered into by the national executive, binds the Republic without approval by the

[47] *Minister of Justice and Constitutional Development and Others v Southern African Litigation Centre and Others* [2016] ZASCA 17; 2016 (4) BCLR 487 (SCA); [2016] 2 All SA 365 (SCA); 2016 (3) SA 317 (SCA), Order para. 4.1.
[48] *Democratic Alliance v Minister of International Relations and Cooperation and Others* [2017] ZAGPPHC 53; 2017 (3) SA 212 (GP), para. 1.
[49] Ibid.

National Assembly and the National Council of Provinces, but must be tabled in the Assembly and the Council within a reasonable time.

(4) Any international agreement becomes law in the Republic when it is enacted into law by national legislation; but a self-executing provision of an agreement that has been approved by Parliament is law in the Republic unless it is inconsistent with the Constitution or an Act of Parliament.

The Republic is bound by international agreements which were binding on the Republic when this constitution took effect. The Court reasoned:

> A notice of withdrawal, on a proper construction of s 231, is the equivalent of ratification, which requires prior parliamentary approval in terms of s 231(2). As correctly argued on behalf of the DA, the act of signing a treaty and the act of delivering a notice of withdrawal are different in their effect. The former has no direct legal consequences, while by contrast, the delivery of a notice of withdrawal has concrete legal effects in international law, as it terminates treaty obligations, albeit on a deferred basis in the present case. Also, this argument overlooks the explicit provisions of article 127(1) of the Rome Statute, which provide that a state may withdraw 'by written notification addressed to the Secretary-General of the United Nations'. The notice of withdrawal deposited by the Minister of International Relations is the written notification envisaged in the article. Although the withdrawal does not take effect until a year later, that notice constitutes, at international level, a binding, unconditional and final decision of withdrawal from the Rome Statute.

As the Constitutional Court explained in paragraph 96 of *Glenister v Republic of South Africa*[50] , a resolution by parliament in terms of s 231(2) to approve an international agreement is 'a positive statement ... to the signatories of that agreement that parliament, subject to the provisions of the Constitution, will act in accordance with the ratified agreement'. Therefore, the approval of an international agreement in terms of Section 231(2) creates a social contract between the people of South Africa through their elected representatives in the legislature and the national executive. That social contract gives rise to the rights and obligations expressed in such an international agreement. The anomaly that the national executive can, without first seeking the approval of the people of South Africa, terminate those rights and obligations, is self-evident and manifest.

What is more, it is trite law that where a constitutional or statutory provision confers a power to do something, that provision necessarily confers the power to undo it as well. In the context of this case, the power to bind the country to the Rome Statute is expressly conferred on parliament. It must therefore, perforce, be parliament which has the power to decide whether an international agreement ceases to bind the country. The conclusion is therefore that, on a textual construction of Section 231(2), South Africa can withdraw from the Rome Statute only on approval of parliament and after the repeal of the Implementation Act. This interpretation of the section is the most

[50] CCT 41/08

constitutionally compliant, giving effect to the doctrine of separation of powers so clearly delineated in Section 231. The fact that Section 231 does not expressly say that only parliament has the power to decide on withdrawal from the Rome Statute, is no bar to this interpretation.[51] Consequently the High Court held that: 'The notice of withdrawal from the Rome Statute of the International Criminal Court, signed by the first respondent, the Minister of International Relations and Cooperation on 19 October 2016, without prior parliamentary approval, is unconstitutional and invalid.'[52] As a result, South Africa withdrew that withdrawal and stayed a state party to the ICC.

XI. Conclusion

The preceding discussion has demonstrated the extent to which domestic courts in the United States and South African jurisdictions resort to international law and foreign law in the resolution of disputes before them. It shows that the courts do take into account foreign law and international law whenever they deem it appropriate. They do so under the following conditions: when they feel that a domestic norm can be clarified in the light of international norms; in view of the deficiencies or inadequacy of the domestic norm the judge relies on an international standard to develop a judicial rule with which the dispute can be settled; where a dispute could be settled on the basis of domestic law but with an alternative reference to international law the judge can either underline the fundamental nature of the principle or right that is already recognized in domestic or corroborate the interpretation of national law. For example in the Zimbabwe case of *Makoni v Commissioner of Prisons CCZ 8/16 (13 July 2016) Zimbabwe Constitutional Court*, the Court struck down the provisions of the Prisoners Act that excluded all life-term prisoners from the formal process of consideration by the Parole Board. The Court relied on foreign and international legal authorities to discern an emerging global consensus that life imprisonment without the possibility of parole constitutes cruel and degrading punishment. The Court referred to decisions of the European Court of Human Rights addressing irreducible life imprisonment.[53] This should be encouraged as at one level the practice in a not too insignificant manner promotes uniform interpretation of international law and promotes the progressive advancement important norms worldwide. This is especially important in the field of human rights. It is also especially empowering to courts in developing countries and post-conflict societies, and a source of knowledge for both judges and lawyers. It allows them to tap into the jurisprudence that has been developed by other courts when they faced similar issues. In terms of which foreign jurisprudence the courts should be looking at, Glensy's[54] observations are useful. The

[51] Ibid., paras 47, 52, and 53.
[52] Ibid., order para. 1.
[53] Andrew J. Novak, 'Towards a Global Consensus on Life Imprisonment Without Parole: Transnational Legal Advocates and the Zimbabwe Constitutional Court's Decision in Makoni v Commissioner of Prisons' (2018) 62 Journal of African Law 2; *Kafkaris v Cyprus* (2009) 49 EHRR 35; *Vinter & Others v United Kingdom* (App nos 66069/09,130/10 & 3896/10), 9 July 2013.
[54] Rex D. Glensy, 'Which Countries Count? Lawrence v. Texas and the Selection of Foreign Persuasive Authority' (2005) 45 Virginia Journal of International Law 357.

author identified three criteria that courts seem take into consideration when seeking to consult foreign law in the context of domestic constitutional adjudication: (1) the democratic credentials of the nation from which the law is being sought with a marked preference for those nations whose law is processed from a system of checks and balances that owes its ultimate source of legitimacy to the people; (2) the societal character and culture of the nation from where the proposed law is coming with an eye towards spotting those embedded socio-cultural features that create a commonality between that nation and the other state; and (3) the specific context of the case where the inquiry is into the nature of the doctrine being examined by the Court and whether it shares characteristics that transcend national borders.

18

The Inter-Institutional Dimension of the Fundamental Rights Revolution

The Colombian–American Implications of the Franco-European Experience

Mitchel Lasser

I. Introduction

This chapter offers an inter-institutional analysis of the explosive rise of fundamental rights in the French legal system over the last couple of decades.This rise has occurred not only with breathtaking speed, but also with remarkable thoroughness: it has lead very quickly to the spread of fundamental rights claims, debates, and jurisprudence within all corners of the French judicial system, from the Constitutional Council to the Conseil d'Etat to the Cour de cassation.

The French experience offers a potential treasure trove of comparative insights for scholars interested in examining the possibility that Latin American countries might follow a similar course.After all, many Latin American countries share two key characteristics with their French counterpart that are—as this article explains—essential ingredients of the French and European fundamental rights transformation: (1) they are jurisdictionally complex civil law systems; and (2) they are part of a regional treaty organization (in the Latin American case, the Inter-American system) with which they regularly interact through their judiciaries.

Of course, the explosive rise of fundamental rights in the French context is undoubtedly due, at least in part, to important social and intellectual developments. At the domestic level, France has been increasingly fragmenting along pluralistic lines. This fragmentation has posed ever greater challenges to French republicanism, which has traditionally stressed the unitary nature of both 'the general will' and the 'general interest'. The result has been a marked rise in individual and group oriented pluralism increasingly expressed in fundamental rights terms.

This trajectory functions at the supra—or transnational level as well. As political communities have become increasingly complicated cross-nationally as well as intra-nationally, fundamental rights have risen dramatically in importance. Fundamental rights have served in effect as a *lingua franca* across jurisdictions: they operate as a common legal denominator and as a pool of common legal terms transferable within and across the European polities. By focusing on individuals (including firms) and their fundamental rights, courts have found a cross-culturally operative technique

Mitchel Lasser, *The Inter-Institutional Dimension of the Fundamental Rights Revolution* In: *Constitutionalism*. Edited by: Alejandro Linares-Cantillo, Camilo Valdivieso-León, Santiago García-Jaramillo, Oxford University Press (2021). © The various contributors.
DOI: 10.1093/oso/9780192896759.003.0019

for resolving disputes that ostensibly steers clear of bigger aggregation/polis-building enterprises.

This common social and intellectual momentum has likely been reinforced by the fall of the Berlin Wall and by the incorporation of ex-Soviet bloc and/or ex-totalitarian states into the Western European legal order. This liberalizing and anti-communist reaction has taken legal form not only via the constitutional process within these states, but also by their adherence to such symbolically charged rights-based institutions as the Council of Europe and the European Court of Human Rights.[1] In short, both the internal fragmentation and the external aggregation of political communities have contributed to the stunningly rapid rise of the fundamental rights idiom throughout Europe.

But this is not the entire story. As Part II of this chapter explains, the fundamental rights revolution is also a matter of the complex—and often competitive—inter-institutional dynamics that increasingly define the judicial arena in our ever more globalized legal space. These judicial dynamics are particularly visible and pressing in contemporary Europe for two reasons. First, the European judicial arena possesses two layers of powerfully operational courts: the domestic and the European judiciaries. Second, almost all national judiciaries in Europe belong to the civil law tradition; as a result, they typically possess multiple and often quite distinct judicial hierarchies, each headed by its own 'supreme court'. In fact, even the European judiciary is led by two different courts, the European Court of Justice ('the ECJ') and the European Court of Human Rights ('the ECtHR').

The European domestic and supranational judicial orders therefore possess a distinctive structural feature: they deploy a plethora of high courts that operate in an overlapping and richly interactive judicial environment. As a result, all of these high courts are now scrambling to master and direct the emergent fundamental rights regime; and some are better positioned to do so than others.

This multiplicity of high courts leads to a group dynamic that reinforces the recourse to the fundamental rights idiom and contributes to its increasing dominance. Almost every European judicial player now faces powerful pressures to jump on the fundamental rights bandwagon or be left intellectually and institutionally behind. Each judicial institution must accordingly deploy and seek to control this rising idiom, even if doing so threatens to refashion or even replace that institution's traditional role definition. This has prompted a frantic race to the 'top' of an increasingly unitary doctrinal, procedural, jurisdictional, and intellectual scheme: the evermore powerful and ubiquitous fundamental rights framework.

Part II of this chapter offers a succinct case study of the dramatic circulation of fundamental rights pressures between the numerous high courts in play at the intersection of the domestic and supranational European judiciaries. It briefly examines the

[1] Of course, some of the motives for such adherence are deeply practical: candidate countries for the EU must effectively sign onto the European Convention on Human Rights ('ECHR') fundamental rights regime. Seethe 'Copenhagen Criteria' for accession to the EU, Bulletin of the European Community 6/1993, I.13.

ongoing 'fair trial' litigation (conducted under Article 6-1 of the European Convention on Human Rights) challenging the decision-making procedures used by the numerous high courts designed on the French judicial model.

This analysis, which I explain in detail elsewhere,[2] focuses on the French and European high courts. It explains that what appears at first blush to be a simple case of external European (and, in particular, ECtHR) pressures on the French judiciary to modify its traditional decision-making procedures actually represents a far more complex and highly charged set of interactions between multiple French and multiple European courts. This examination could easily and fruitfully be expanded to include other national high courts, ranging from those directly involved in the 'fair trial' litigation (such as the Belgian, Dutch, and Portuguese supreme courts) to others particularly prominent in the rise of fundamental rights (such as the Bundesverfassungsgericht, the German Federal Constitutional Court). But as will soon become apparent, the multifaceted interaction between the French and European courts is more than sufficient to suggest the key structural dynamics currently driving the European fundamental rights revolution.

For heuristic purposes (and for heuristic purposes only), I adopt a four-part analysis that examines the four basic types of judicial pressures that operate between and within the European and the French courts: (1) European pressures on the French courts; (2) French pressures on the French courts; (3) French pressures on the European courts; and (4) European pressures on the European courts. This highly structured approach offers two advantages. First, it organizes an otherwise confusing morass of interactions between a wide range of domestic and international courts. Secondly, working systematically through this simplified analytic structure eventually demonstrates that the French and European judicial orders are increasingly difficult to disentangle, both theoretically and practically: interventions at every level constitute interventions at all others.

This analysis comes to several conclusions. I state them straightforwardly right now in order to help the reader work through the institutional complexities that follow. First, the current inter-institutional dynamics are prompting a group convergence of all domestic and European high courts on the fundamental rights idiom, however disruptive this may be to the particular courts in question. As the French and European example demonstrates quite clearly, there appears to be no effective opt-out of the fundamental rights framework for any of these courts.

Second, this all-but obligatory convergence has forced these courts to translate their prior procedural, doctrinal, and conceptual schemes into fundamental rights terms. This translation process has proven to be not only deeply competitive, but often quite creative as well: numerous individual, group, and institutional interests are in play; the stakes are patently major; and the results are not preordained. This has led to widely

[2] See Mitchel Lasser, *Judicial Transformations: The Rights Revolution in the Courts of France and Europe*(Oxford: Oxford University Press,2009). See also the précis of that monograph: Mitchel Lasser, 'The Judicial Dynamics of the French and European Fundamental Rights Revolution', in Gordon Silverstein, DonaldKagan,&Diana Kapiszewski(eds),*Consequential Courts: Judicial Roles in Global Perspective* (Cambridge: Cambridge University Press, 2013), 289.

divergent interpretations of how to construct and implement the emerging fundamental rights framework.

Third, the struggle to master and direct these legal developments has further reinforced the rising fundamental rights regime. The domestic and supranational European judiciaries function in an inter-institutional context whose group dynamics have created a strong incentive regarding fundamental rights. The most empowering strategy for any given court is not to attempt to evade the often disruptive fundamental rights regime; not only does such a refusal appear retrograde, it leaves the institution at the interpretive, doctrinal, and institutional mercy of those who have taken the opposite tack. The more effective strategy is to embrace and even seek to lead the emerging regime by aggressively developing expansive fundamental rights positions. This 'maximalist' approach is the most effective means to disable and trump troublesome interpretations by legal competitors, to maintain control over one's own institution, and to exercise institutional and intellectual leadership of the emerging judicial order. The net result has been a one-way ratchet: all courts are motivated not only to expand their recourse to fundamental rights constructs, but also to generate expansive readings of those constructs.

Part III of this chapter briefly discusses the potential relevance (and irrelevance) of this Franco-European analysis for Colombia and other Latin American countries. In keeping with the analytic orientation of this article, it focuses almost entirely on key institutional features that might affect such relevance.First, it discusses the multiplicity of high courts in play at the domestic level in Colombia and elsewhere in the Americas.After all, Colombia follows the same basic institutional model as the French legal system; it too possesses multiple and quite distinct 'judicial hierarchies', each headed by its own 'supreme court': the 'ordinary courts', headed by the Corte Suprema de Justicia; the 'administrative tribunals', headed by the Consejo de Estado; and the Corte Constitucional, which resolves constitutional challenges to legislation.But unlike Colombia, several Latin American countries possess relatively unitary judiciaries. This necessarily reduces the number and diversity of high courts, which may accordingly affect the competitive judicial dynamics at work.

Secondly, Part III recognizes that this diminished judicial diversity is even more pronounced at the supranational level.Unlike Europe, which offers both the ECJ and the ECtHR, the Americas really only possesses one major judicial player at the supranational level: the Inter-American Court of Human Rights ('IACtHR').This too may significantly affect the circulation and intensification of fundamental rights pressures in the Latin American context.

Thirdly, Part III addresses judicial institutional diversity of another sort: the lower courts within the national systems.One of the ECJ's most effective institutional gambits was to adopt an open-door policy towards these lower national courts.Not only would litigants not have to exhaust domestic remedies before having recourse to the Luxembourg Court, but the ECJ staunchly refused to permit the national high courts to act as a filter—never mind as a barrier—for references made by those lower courts. This institutional policy empowered the lower courts to bypass, and thereby to exert significant pressures on, their hierarchical superiors within the national judiciaries.

The requirement to exhaust domestic remedies prior to bringing cases before the Inter-American Commission and the IACtHR puts the Latin American national high courts in a very different position than their European counterparts.The exhaustion requirement significantly decreases the number and diversity of courts in play. Although this does not completely insulate the high national courts from the pressures that inferior courts might wield, it likely reduces them a great deal.Indeed, the same holds true for the IACtHR, which is spared both the number and the diversity of challenges it might otherwise face.

In a similar vein, Part III addresses the IACtHR's decision to respect how national legal systems choose to distribute the competence to interpret and apply constitutional and international norms among their national courts.It questions the effects of this doctrine on the inter-institutional dynamics within the countries of Latin America: by allowing these countries to maintain their internal jurisdictional and institutional boundaries, this doctrine may make it less likely that all national judicial institutions will converge on the same doctrinal structures—namely, human rights—, which may reduce their incentives to internalize, promote, and eventually compete over them.It suggests that the IACtHR's doctrine may effectively permit a single national high court to function as the primary (if not quite exclusive) filter for national cases to move to the supranational level, once again limiting the institutional competition regarding human rights developments.

Finally, the article examines whether the IACtHR's doctrines of 'conventionality control' and of the 'block of constitutionality', which appear to promote the internalization and spread of Inter-American human rights norms, may paradoxically contribute to confining them.By forcing the member state courts to treat Inter-American human rights norms as national constitutional law, the doctrine may actually allow national jurisdictional boundaries to limit their enforcement to specialized constitutional courts. Although this concentration may increase the leverage of those particular courts over other domestic actors, it may also allow them to resist the interpretive and institutional pressures that might otherwise have been exerted not only by other national high courts, but also by the IACtHR itself.

The chapter concludes with a few words of caution about the limits of its methodological approach.By focusing its analysis almost exclusively on the structural features and the inter-institutional dynamics of the domestic and supranational courts in Europe and Latin America, this chapter steers studiously clear of the numerous political, social, ideological, and other contextual issues that would have to be taken seriously into account to produce a meaningful comparative analysis of the Inter-American and European judicial systems.This chapter avoids these issues not because they are unimportant, but, to the contrary, because they are *so* important that they deserve far more extensive treatment than can be offered at this stage of my research.The goal of this chapter is much more modest: it merely seeks to highlight the existence of inter-institutional dynamics that might contribute significantly to the spread of the fundamental rights idiom within judicial institutions operating at the intersection of the national and supranational domains.

II. The Franco-European Analysis

A. The Traditional French Judicial Model: The Pre-Existing Equilibrium

The French legal system has traditionally been defined—procedurally, doctrinally, institutionally, structurally, and intellectually—by its distinctive brand of republicanism. The classic French package has consisted of four fundamental and interlocking features: (1) a unitary conception of the general will and of the general interest;(2) the supremacy of the legislature as the voice of the general will;(3) a strict separation of the judiciary from the political branches of government; and (4) a commitment to elite and expert institutional decision-making. These features have traditionally been understood to entail several more, including:(5) the refusal of judicial review;(6) the establishment of separate administrative and constitutional tribunals;(7) a doctrine of the 'sources of the law' that refuses to grant the ordinary judiciary law-making powers;(8) the theory of '*la loiécran*', which shields legislation from administrative review regarding its compatibility with the constitution or with international obligations;(9) legality-based—as opposed to fundamental rights-based—administrative review; and (10) institutionally-oriented—as opposed to individually-oriented—judicial decision-making procedures.

Article 6 of the 1789 Declaration of the Rights of Man and of the Citizen declares: '*La loiestl'expression de la volontégénérale*' ('Legislation is the expression of the general will'). This statement of principle establishes the core of the traditional French understanding of law. Political will is, in good Rousseau-ianfashion, general; it is not divisible into subgroups, never mind into the conflicting rights and interests of individuals.[3]

The supremacy of general legislation requires a strict separation of the judiciary from the political branches of government. The Revolutionaries established this strict separation as early as August 1790, when they passed the Law on Judicial Organization: judges were explicitly forbidden to interfere with legislative and administrative decisions.[4] Far from adopting a system of checks and balances, this approach unambiguously rejects judicial review.

That said, the French system has long been far more flexible and nuanced than has traditionally been portrayed. Although judicial review of the acts of the political branches has been anathema, the French established a series of specialized administrative tribunals within the executive branch to perform quasi-judicial review of the executive.

Furthermore, although the ordinary judiciary was explicitly denied law-making powers,[5] the courts have neither been, nor were they intended to be, passive actors in

[3] Ezra Suleiman, *Politics, Power and Bureaucracy in France: The Administrative Elite* (Princeton: Princeton University Press, 1974),24–9, 297–323; Sudhir Hazareesingh, *Political Traditions in Modern France* (New York, Oxford: Oxford University Press, 1994), 155–71; Jean-Jacques Rousseau (Dunne. Trans.), *The Social Contract and the First and Second Discourses* (New Haven and London: Yale University Press, 2002),164–82, 193–96, 214, 227–30. In fact, Article 3 of the 1958 constitution goes to the bother of spelling out that:'No portion of the people may arrogate to itself, nor may any individual arrogate to himself, the exercise [of national sovereignty]'.

[4] French *Code de l'organisationjudiciaire* tit. II, arts 10, 13, 16–24 August 1790.

[5] French Civil Code,Articles 5 and 1351.

the French legal order. Portalis, the Civil Code's primary author, made the point expressly: codified legislation could only establish the general outlines of the law; judges (and academics) would necessarily have to work out the specifics and adapt the law to the demands of a society in constant change.[6]

Institutional and professional structures were designed to ensure the accountability and representativeness of French judges. These judges spend their entire careers within a unified and hierarchical judicial institution.[7] Because they have tested into the system by formal state examinations, have been trained for their office by state educational institutions, and been promoted by state-defined and state-managed meritocratic means, the judiciary as a whole bears the imprimatur of elite republican representation.[8]

Having gone to such effort to select, train, and organize its judges, the French system then gives them the necessary procedural and institutional means to manage the application and development of *la loi*'s broad provisions. The judicial decision-making process of the French high courts is accordingly dominated by the courts themselves: in some important sense, it is the court, not the litigants, who are understood to be appropriately representative of the state and of the citizenry at large.

Once the parties have submitted their written pleadings, it is therefore the judicial panel that effectively takes responsibility for the case. Partisan oral argument by the parties all but withers away, as elaborate and multi-stage internal discussions between key judicial magistrates—such as the Advocate General and the judicial *rapporteur*—take centre stage.[9] Shielded from public view, judicial debates unfold in absolute candour and without fear of political retribution.

This sequestering approach also produces an important secondary effect: it greatly diminishes the argumentative and doctrinal control that these judges can exert through their cryptic, collegial, single-sentence, and syllogistic judgments. The syllogism also stands as a powerful reminder: only legislation constitutes the true expression of the general will.

This supremacy ofthe general will has traditionally meant that the ordinary judiciary—or, for that matter, the quasi-judicial administrative tribunals—cannot call *la loi* into question, whether on domestic (constitutional) or international (treaty/convention) grounds. Even when the administrative tribunals review executive branch actions at the behest of disgruntled citizens, they traditionally do so not so much in order to vindicate the rights of the individual, but rather to ensure that the state has acted according to the state's own standards of appropriate behaviour. This review has therefore traditionally been focused not on the *individual*'s fundamental constitutional *rights*, but on the *legality* of the *state*'s actions.

[6] Jean-Etienne-Marie *Portalis,Discourspréliminaire, prononcé le 24 thermidor an VIII, translated and reprinted in Otto Kan-Freund, Claudine Levy and Bernard Rudden, A Source Book on French Law –* (Oxford: Clarendon Press, 1991), 233–35.

[7] Mitchel Lasser, *Judicial Deliberations: A Comparative Analysis of Judicial Transparency and Legitimacy* (Oxford: Oxford University Press, 2005), 182–5.

[8] Ibid., 331–4.

[9] Antoine Garapon & IoannisPapadopoulos, *JugerenAmérique et en France: Culture juridiquefrançaise et common law* (Paris: Odile Jacob, 2004), 110–12.

Finally, the Fifth Republic's treatment of constitutional review reflected almost all of these traditional assumptions. It therefore adjusted, rather than subverted, the traditional equilibrium between the ordinary courts, the administrative tribunals, and the political branches. First, constitutional review was established to police the division between the legislature and the executive branches, not to protect fundamental rights from legislative or governmental encroachment. Second, individuals could not trigger such review; only a small set of major State actors could file constitutional complaints. Third, the newly created Constitutional Council was established *outside* of the judiciary. Finally, the Council could only perform review *a priori*, that is, while the challenged legislative act was still a pending bill. Once the bill had been passed into law, and had thus become the formal expression of the general will, it was no longer subject to challenge.[10]

B. European Pressures on the French Judicial System: The Domestic Order Thrown into Flux

1. General External Pressures

The traditional model just described has certainly not been the product of a static legal or judicial history. Slowly developed and deeply entrenched over the course of the last two centuries, the model had nonetheless reached a recognizable—if undoubtedly complex and somewhat malleable—state of equilibrium. But in the last few decades, it has been undergoing a stunningly rapid and sweeping transformation.

The first important pressures for the current transformation emerged from the European legal plane. In 1964, the ECJ began insisting on the supremacy or 'precedence' of European law over conflicting national law.[11] This doctrine called on national courts to refuse to apply national laws inconsistent with European law; in effect, it required judicial review, albeit in the name of European law.

Given the traditional model described above, it should come as no surprise that the French legal system did not exactly rush to adopt this jarring new doctrine. Indeed, it was not until 1975 that the Cour de cassation took the step demanded by the ECJ in 1964. It is a testament to the lasting power of the classic French approach, however, that the Conseil d'Etat and the Constitutional Council refused to follow suit for almost fifteen more years: it was not until 1989 that the Conseil d'Etat finally buckled under by overturning its own jurisprudence.[12] This shift represented an important moment in the acceptance of European law; but it was a truly monumental event in the internal history of French law. The theory of the *loiécran* had finally fallen, and with it the primacy of legislation and of the general will, if only in the context of European law.

This development threw the French legal order into a state of disequilibrium. The new role adopted by the French courts meant that individuals could now seize the ordinary and administrative courts to block the operation of French legislation in the name of *European* rights (including fundamental rights) of EU or ECHR origin. But

[10] As we shall see, the design features of the Fifth Republic's mode of constitutional review have since been significantly modified. See text accompanying n.26 below.

[11] Case 6.64 *Costa v E.N.E.L.*[1964] CMLR 425.

[12] SeeJudgment of the Conseil d'Etat of 20 October 1989 (*Nicolo*), (1989) Rec. Lebon 190.

these same individuals could *not* do so in the name of domestic *French* rights, even of constitutional status.

This discrepancy had a dual effect. First, the sudden availability of justiciable European rights constituted a bonanza for individuals and firms searching for a basis to challenge unfavorable legal outcomes at the national level. Secondly, this new turn to superior European norms not only empowered the national judiciary vis-à-vis the political branches, but also disrupted the traditional French mode for reviewing the acts of the executive branch. Quasi-judicial review of the executive had been an integral part of the French legal order since at least 1799, when Napoleon established the Conseil d'Etat.[13] Over the ensuing two hundred years, the Conseil developed a sophisticated jurisprudence for challenging executive rules and acts, which has been applied throughout the country by a large administrative court hierarchy.

European rights jurisprudence accordingly challenges French administrative jurisprudence rather directly. Elaborated by the ECtHR and the ECJ, this jurisprudence undermines the institutional leadership of the Conseil d'Etat, which traditionally elaborated the bases for reviewing state acts. This institutional shift also challenges the conceptual structure and very ethos of French administrative jurisprudence. Review had been steeped in French republican notions. It was grounded in a series of 'legality' doctrines traditionally oriented towards the state: the key issue was whether the state had behaved according to proper administrative morality.[14] But the increasingly dominant European approach offers a more liberal perspective: its key question is whether the rights of the individual—including theirfundamental rights—have been violated.[15]

2. Targeted External Pressures

Plaintiffs have now successfully wielded these newly justiciable European rights to overturn a whole series of specific French legal rules, ranging from the non-recognition of sex changes to the calculation of VAT taxes.[16]Amazingly, plaintiffs have even leveraged their European rights to target the decision-making procedures traditionally deployed by all the French high courts. This 'procedural' litigation has proven to be immensely disruptive: it subjects the ethos and practices of these proud 'supreme courts' to the critical appraisal of foreign courts on the basis of an unfamiliar fundamental rights logic.

In a major and ongoing line of decisions handed down over the last ten years, the ECtHR has struck repeatedly at the decision-making procedures of the high courts designed on the French model.[17]In doing so, it has condemned precisely those practices

[13] Neville L. Brown & John Bell, *French Administrative Law* (Oxford: Clarendon Press, 1998), 46–48.

[14] I owe the elegant term 'administrative morality'to Brown and Bell. See ibid. 216.

[15] These two approaches could of course be fused: the violation of an individual's rights could, for example, be treated as a violation of state morality.

[16] See,e.g., Court of cassation judgments of 11 December 1992, JCP, *jurisprudence* no. 21991, p. 41 (conclusions Jéol); Joined cases C–177/99 and C–181/99 *Ampafrance v Directeur des services fiscaux de Maine-et-Loire* (2000) ECR I–7013.

[17] The ECtHR cases specifically condemning the French supreme courts only date back to 1998; but the first ECtHR decision to condemn the French model of judicial decision-making dates to 1991 when the ECtHR censured the similar procedures utilized by the Belgian Cour de cassation. See*Borgers v Belgium*, 214 ECtHR (Ser. A) 22 (1991); *Reinhardt and Slimane-Kaïd v France*, 1998-II ECtHR 640; *Kress v France*, 2001-VI ECtHR 1; *Martinie v France*,App.58675/00 (12 April 2006), [2006] ECHR 392.

and institutional structures that reflect the classic French republican understanding of the judicial role: stressing the importance of permitting the individual litigant to take an active role in litigation, it has criticized the French high courts' characteristically closed and institutionally-oriented decision-making procedures.

These French procedures were traditionally designed to permit two key judicial figures—the *rapporteur* and an advising magistrate (known as the 'Advocate General' at the Cour de cassation or the '*Commissaire de gouvernement*' at the Conseil d'Etat)—to lead the judicial panel in intensive and candid debates about how to decide cases in such a manner as to promote the general interest and the public good. As a result, the litigants would almost always wave their nominal right to engage in oral arguments: once they had submitted their written pleadings, their role in the decision-making process was effectively over.

Elaborating a fundamental rights perspective that stresses the right of individuals to take an active role in litigation, the ECtHR has found much to fault in the traditional French procedures. In particular, it has insisted that individual litigants be granted access and response rights with respect to the key internal documents generated within the French preparatory judicial debates. First, because the judicial advisor might put forward damaging arguments, the litigant must be allowed to receive the advisor's conclusions in advance in order to respond to them as necessary at oral arguments. Second, the judicial advisor must not be put in a privileged position by gaining access to the otherwise unavailable report and draft judgments of the *rapporteur*. Finally, the advisor must also be removed from the judicial panel's final deliberations, lest he be perceived (accurately or not) to gain an argumentative advantage.

The ECtHR's Article 6-1 'fair trial' jurisprudence could hardly have done a more thorough job of pitting its individual fundamental rights perspective against the French judicial system's republican self-understanding. Reducing the prototypically republican figure of the judicial advisor to little more than a potential opponent of the individual litigant, it undermines the governing logic of the French system, namely, that it is the judicial institution—rather than the individual and self-interested litigant—that best represents the general interest and the public good. The ECtHR instead placed the individual litigant in a privileged position: by dint of theirfundamental procedural and substantive rights, theyhad to be empowered to play an analytically and procedurally central role, even at the expense of the French courts' traditional structure, ethos, and practices.

C. French Pressures on the French Judicial System: Internal Motivations

The French legal order has thus been subjected to tremendous pressures from the European rights-based approach in general and the ECtHR's 'fair trial' jurisprudence in particular. But it has also been exerting major pressures on itself at the same time. These internal motivations and dynamics are caused in large measure by the broad and enduring structural design of the French courts.

As is the case in most civil law systems, the French 'judiciary' is organized into several distinct hierarchies. The 'ordinary''judicial' courts, headed by the Cour de cassation, handle civil and criminal litigation. The 'administrative' tribunals, headed by the Conseil d'Etat, are instead housed within the executive branch. This distinction is not merely formal. Ordinary French judges receive their educational and vocational training at the Ecole Nationale de la Magistrature, the national judge school. Administrative judges, however, receive theirs at the particularly prestigious Ecole Nationale de l'Administration, which trains all high-ranking executive branch civil servants. They are therefore prepared above all not to be judges, but to manage state affairs. For its part, the Constitutional Council is a free-standing (and largely political) institution, distinct from both the ordinary and the administrative tribunals.

This division of 'judicial' turf into subparts has prompted somewhat competitive inter-institutional motivations and dynamics. On the sociological front, the high executive judges look upon their civil/criminal counterparts with a certain disdain. The former are the cream of the elite management team that composes the 'state nobility' (to use the term coined by Bourdieu[18]); the latter are mere judges. On the institutional front, the Constitutional Council has come to play an increasingly prominent role in defining the proper structure and operation of the state, a field previously dominated by the Conseil d'Etat. And on the doctrinal front, the partitioning of the 'judiciary' has fostered interpretive complexities: even if the jurisdictional field is divided between the three hierarchies, the three institutions periodically elaborate doctrines in related and even overlapping fields.[19]

The addition of a strong European presence on the French legal scene has greatly multiplied the number and the stakes of such competitive judicial interactions; this has added another layer of internal motivation for the assorted French courts' institutional responses. First, European law represents a whole new field of action on which French judicial institutions can compete. Secondly, to conquer the European legal terrain is to occupy the high ground for French domestic law purposes: European law is, both by its own definition and by French constitutional standards, superior to French law. Thirdly, European law cuts across the key jurisdictional and doctrinal divisions that we have been describing: corporate, environmental, or other European regulation can generate litigation in any of the domestic judicial hierarchies. These factors have in essence thrown the French courts into an ongoing negotiation regarding their respective roles, domains, and powers.

The fundamental rights doctrines of the ECtHR offer the clearest example of the collapsing of domestic divisions and distinctions. ECHR law is superior law; it must be applied by all state actors (including the courts); and it therefore operates across the board in disputes litigated in any and all of the judicial hierarchies. This alters the nature and intensity of the competition between the three major 'judicial' institutions. Now that European law bridges the substantive and jurisdictional divisions between the three major institutions, the classic partitioning of the French 'judicial' field blurs: all three must increasingly interpret and apply the same (superior) fundamental rights principles.

[18] Pierre Bourdieu (Clough, trans.), *The State Nobility: Elite Schools in the Field of Power* (Stanford: Stanford University Press, 1996).

[19] For example, 'tort' doctrines are elaborated in both the ordinary courts (for private injuries) and the administrative tribunals (for public ones). Similarly, procedural rights of 'defendants' have been elaborated in the ordinary, administrative, and constitutional courts, albeit in somewhat different contexts.

The internal motivations and dynamics of the French judiciary were already apparent decades ago when the ECJ insisted that the 'precedence' (i.e. superiority) of European law required domestic courts to refuse to apply conflicting national norms. Deeply attached (professionally, institutionally, and intellectually) to the French republican tradition, the Conseil d'Etat was dead set against recognizing the precedence of European law and violating the doctrine of '*la loiécran*' by exercising review over French legislation. Composed primarily of major French political figures similarly attached to existing national traditions and power structures, the Constitutional Council was not much more enthusiastic. Indeed, having recently granted itself the power to review legislation for substantive violations of fundamental rights incorporated into the 1958 French constitution, the Council was in no rush either to adopt another deeply controversial position or to subjugate the authority of its constitutional mission to routine European legal norms. The Cour de cassation, however, had excellent motivations for staking out a different (and pro-European) position: not only could it drastically empower itself relative to the legislative branch,[20] but it could also greatly increase its standing relative to the Conseil d'Etat and the Constitutional Council. By dutifully following the ECJ's demands, not only would it adopt the mantle of the open-minded, progressive, and commercially sensitive institution, it could suddenly wield legal materials superior to those handled by its sister institutions. The results followed suit: in 1975, the Cour was the first French 'supreme court' to set aside a *loi* that conflicted with a European norm; the Constitutional Council began to waver noticeably in the mid-1980s; and the Conseil d'Etat finally caved in 1989.[21]

Similar French inter-institutional motivations and dynamics have been unleashed repeatedly in the face of European legal pressures. The ongoing Article 6-1 'fair trial' litigation offers a particularly clear and telling example. The Conseil d'Etat has steadfastly resisted the ECtHR's 'fair trial' jurisprudence. Advancing arguments so tenuous as to border on the disingenuous, it has done all in its power to maintain its traditional understanding of republican procedures. It has refused to remove its judicial advisor (the '*Commissaire de gouvernement*') from its internal deliberations; and it has offered litigants as little as possible in the way of information and response rights.[22]

The Cour de cassation, however, has jumped on the opportunity presented by the ECtHR's jurisprudence to institute a major overhaul of its decision-making procedure. These reforms significantly increase the capacity of individuals, firms, and interested parties to intervene aggressively in the decision-making process. In all important cases, the *rapporteur* must now disclose her report's legal analysis not only to the parties well in advance of oral argument, but also to the public at large: it is to be published alongside the final judgment in the Cour's official reports. As a result, the judicial advisor (the advocate general) no longer obtains privileged access to internal judicial

[20] This is the so-called 'empowerment thesis.'See Joseph Weiler, 'The Community System: The Dual Character of Supranationalism' (1981) 1 Yearbook of European Law 268 Joseph Weiler, 'A Quiet Revol;ution: The European Court and Its Interlocutors' (1994) 26 Comparative Political Studies 510.

[21] SeeCass. mixte, judgment of24 May 1975, D. 1975, 497 ('*Jacques Vabre*'); Judgment of the Constitutional Council 86-116 of 3 September 1986, (1986) Recueil des decisions du Conseil Constitutionnel 135; Judgment of the Conseil d'Etat of 20 October 1989 ('*Nicolo*'), Rec. Lebon 190.

[22] Lasser (n. 2, 2009), 93–4. Even the Conseil d'Etat's recent reforms changing the title of the judicial advisor from 'the Commissaire de gouvernement' to the 'Rapporteur public' are designed to resist the ECtHR's jurisprudence. See Article R 733 of the Code de justice administrative.

information: not only can theyonly receive the same 'objective report' as the litigants, but they have been banished altogether from the Cour's pre- and post-oral argument deliberations. Finally, the litigants can respond either orally or in writing to the advisor's conclusions to the court. In short, the Cour has chosen to shift the balance of procedural power noticeably in the direction of private parties at the expense of the advocates general. The Article 6-1 'fair trial' litigation has thus triggered a schism between the Conseil d'Etat and the Cour de cassation, which again reveals the latent structural and intellectual tensions between these two domestic high courts.

This window into the internal diversity of the French judiciary holds great analytic importance for the examination of the French judicial system, of the European judicial system, and of the interaction between the two. On the French side of the equation, the tensions between the Cour and the Conseil demonstrate that the institutional and intellectual threat (or promise) posed by the rise of the European courts and of the fundamental rights idiom affects different institutional players quite differently. Put simply, their motivations differ.

Furthermore, the institutional schism between these two high courts hardly exhausts the wide range of domestic responses. Even within the Cour de cassation, which has taken a pro-European law and fundamental rights-friendly approach, there is endless disagreement about what such stances actually require. All of the fundamental rights norms need to be interpreted; and the range of possible interpretations is obviously quite large. Some factions wish to interpret these fundamental rights in a dignitarian fashion that empowers disadvantaged groups relative to the state and to powerful private interests. Others seek, to the contrary, to interpret them in such a fashion as to protect vested economic and property rights from the disruptions threatened by such a dignitarian approach. The key is to recognize that, despite their disagreements, all of these French institutions and factions have converged on fundamental rights as the appropriate mode of legal analysis, as each jockeys to control the development of supremely powerful fundamental rights within the domestic legal order.

Moreover, the institutional competition on the fundamental rights front has developed simultaneously with regard to French constitutional norms. The reasons for this are both structural and doctrinal. First and foremost, the Constitutional Council has traditionally been limited to abstract *a priori* review of legislation. As a result, it only got one crack at reviewing a given piece of legislation.[23] Once it had given the law its blessing, the ordinary and administrative courts took over that law's interpretative development. Although these courts could not formally review the law and declare it unconstitutional, they could—and necessarily often did—apply it in light of their own interpretations of constitutional norms.

The Constitutional Council has had only very weak means to control such ongoing constitutional interpretation of both legislative and constitutional norms.[24]

[23] The constitutional revision of 2008 and subsequent interpretive developments have modified this somewhat. See,e.g., Dominique Rousseau and Pasquale Pasquino (eds.), *La question prioritaire de constitutionnalité: une mutation réelle de la démocratieconstitutionnellefrançaise?* (Paris: Mare & Martin, 2019).

[24] Perhaps the most important of these powers is the capacity to condition its approval of legislation on interpretive reservations (JohnBell, *French Constitutional Law* (Oxford: Clarendon Press, 1992), 53–55; John Bell, *French Legal Cultures* (London: Butterworths, 2001), 217–19. This approach seeks to control the potential meaning and application of the challenged legislation over time. But there exists no formal policing mechanisms for enforcing such reservations.

Individuals could neither petition the Council directly nor refer concrete judicial interpretations to the Council for further constitutional review. The Council therefore had only the first say in constitutional interpretation;[25] but the ordinary and administrative courts would then elaborate their own interpretations in a relatively decentralized fashion.[26]

The absence of an important 'state action doctrine' compounds this interpretive decentralization. Almost any litigant in any private controversy can put forward arguments couched in fundamental rights terms, thereby triggering further constitutional interpretations. In this manner, contract clauses have been challenged on the grounds that they violate the right to exercise a profession, malpractice liability has been imposed in the name of the dignitarian right to bodily integrity, and the like.[27]

The combination of external pressures, internal motivations, and institutional structures has thus led fundamental rights (of both European and French origin) increasingly to dominate the French legal terrain in almost all domains. The advent of fundamental rights thus challenges the structural, institutional, and doctrinal divisions that have traditionally partitioned the French judicial order into relatively distinct subparts. As we shall soon see, it challenges the division between the French and European judicial orders as well.

D. French Pressures on the European Judicial System: External Pressures in Reverse

The pressures exerted between the European and French judicial orders are not a one-way street. The institutional roots of the returning pressures can be inferred from the internal tensions and motivations just described: the multiplicity of domestic high courts. The European courts are negotiating their relationship with a multifaceted and fractured set of French judicial institutions whose own inter-institutional motivations function as strongly on the domestic level as on the European one. The judicial chess match is therefore being played on at least two levels at once, with moves on either level affecting the relationships on the other.

This reality presents strong opportunities for the European judiciary. Because European law qualifies as superior (if only by ECJ doctrine), it is relatively easy for European legal institutions to enlist the support of tactically insightful domestic counterparts, who now function as agents for European legal progress in the national legal order. Internal French judicial motivations thus offer welcoming points of entry for European fundamental rights pressures.

[25] Even this power is debatable: the Conseil d'Etat actually has the first say, as it gives advice to the government about the constitutionality of proposed legislation (Bell (n. 24, 1992), 45).

[26] The recent amendment of the French constitution has changed this state of affairs, though it is not yet clear how significantly. The addition of Article 61-1 now allows references to be made to the Council in concrete cases. Although this opens the door for *a posteriori* review of legislation (undoubtedly a major development), it establishes the Cour de cassation and the Conseil d'Etat as the gatekeepers to the Conseil. This effectively maintains the partial autonomy of these high courts' interpretive powers in the constitutional realm (Lasser (n. 2, 2009), 300–1).

[27] See, e.g., Cass. Soc., 10 July 2002, D. 2002, 2491, note Serra; Cass. 1re civ., 9 October 2001, D. 2001, 3470, rapport P. Sargos, note D. Thouvenin.

But this state of affairs also imposes significant costs. The multiplicity of domestic high courts, when combined with the interpretive leeway of fundamental rights norms, leaves the development of European law vulnerable to the interpretive decisions taken by self-interested domestic legal institutions. The Article 6-1 fair trial litigation provides an excellent example of this dynamic.

When the ECtHR started condemning French high court decision-making procedure some ten years ago, the French courts had some tough decisions to make about how to respond. The range of possibilities was quite large. For example, the 1998 *Reinhardt* decision condemned the unequal ('imbalanced') access given to the reporting judge's work product in Cour de cassation cases (the judicial advisor received all of this preparatory material prior to oral arguments, while the litigants received none).[28] Furthermore, the 2001 *Kress* judgment held that the judicial advisor at the Conseil d'Etat (the 'CDG') could not legitimately retire with the sitting judicial panel to participate in post-oral argument judicial deliberations, lest the appearance be given that he might press his arguments in a prejudicial fashion.[29]

The French supreme courts could legitimately adopt a wide range of potential responses, each premised on more or less expansive or restrictive interpretations of the ECtHR's jurisprudence.[30] For example, the requirement that the litigants receive the same access as the advisor to the judicial materials prepared in advance of oral arguments does not settle how much access should be given to what kind of information.

As we have seen, the Conseil d'Etat and the Cour de cassation adopted fundamentally different tacks in the face of the ECtHR's decisions. The Conseil stonewalled as best it could by refusing to remove the judicial advisor from its final deliberations (it merely required him to remain silent). But the Cour de cassation removed him not only from the final deliberations (as apparently required by the ECtHR's *Kress* judgment), but also from the preparatory ones that take place before oral argument. Indeed, the Cour used the ECtHR's jurisprudence as a springboard to rework its decision-making procedures in a manner that significantly increased the procedural rights of litigants, interested parties, and the public at large.

We can learn a great deal from this type of interchange. First, even in instances in which a European court has settled an issue in a seemingly straightforward fashion, there nonetheless remains more than enough room for ongoing interpretive effort at the domestic level.

Second, expansive domestic interpretations of European law in effect become European law, if only for domestic purposes. That is, the Cour's expansive interpretation of what was required by the ECtHR's jurisprudence functions as the meaning of European law in France. The Cour's procedural modifications were made in the name of European law; and the ECtHR has few viable means of policing, never mind overriding, this interpretation. On the practical level, the ECtHR can only effectively oversee a tiny percentage of the cases that raise fundamental rights issues arising

[28] SeeReinhardt (n. 17) 666.

[29] *Kress* (n. 17),70–2.

[30] Nick Huls underlines this interpretive agency in his insightful analysis of the Dutch Hoge Raad's expansive interpretations of EU law and jurisprudence. SeeNick Huls, 'The Dutch Hoge Raad: Judicial Roles Played, Lost, and Not Played', in Silverstein, Kagan, & Kapiszewski(n.2), 181.

from the Convention: there are limits to how many cases an institution composed of only one judge per country can possibly handle. As a prudential matter, things are not much better. Faced with the recalcitrance of the Conseil d'Etat, could the ECtHR really object to the exuberance of the Cour de cassation, thereby jeopardizing the Cour's ongoing support of the ECHR project? As a legal matter, furthermore, on what basis could the ECtHR criticize the Cour? The Convention and its ECtHR interpretation set minimum fundamental rights standards, not maximum ones. Beyond this minimum level, domestic legal actors are free to read the Convention as liberally as they like.

These factors demonstrate that expansive domestic interpretations of European law exert strong pressures not only within a given domestic level order, but also on the European one, to the point that they effectively become European law. Within the national legal order, they specify what European law requires. At the European level, the ECtHR has excellent prudential reasons to adopt such interpretations as its own. In fact, these expansive domestic interpretations even operate *between* different domestic orders: expansive positions taken by the *Belgian* courts, supported (almost by necessity) by the European ones, exert pressures on their *French* counterparts.[31]

This cycle of pressures reveals an essential attribute of the ongoing fundamental rights explosion. Domestic legal actors have powerful incentives to frame their interpretations in expansive fundamental rights terms. To adopt a contrary tack is to invite sanction. But to take an expansive approach is deeply empowering. When artfully done, it helps to insulate the domestic court from effective European intervention,[32]while permitting that court to exercise intellectual, institutional, jurisdictional, and doctrinal leadership on both the national and the supranational levels.

This dynamic has helped to fuel the fundamental rights revolution. Every major domestic judicial institution has good reason to engage in the increasingly frantic 'race to the top' of the fundamental rights regime, in which the courts seek to recast their preexisting doctrinal and intellectual frames in fundamental rights terms. This dynamic exerts tremendous pressures back on the European judicial order, as it fosters a decentralized fundamental rights one-upmanship that the European courts cannot effectively control. The internal motivations of the French courts thus manifest as external pressures imposed on the European courts.

E. European Pressures on the European Judicial System

The European courts are by no means immune to these fundamental rights pressures. As the last section suggested, the domestic courts can back the European ones into something of a corner: by casting their domestic judgments as expansive interpretations of European fundamental rights norms, they can pressure the European courts to ratify and even adopt these interpretations. But that is not all. The European judiciary is no more unified than its domestic counterparts: it is headed by two preeminent

31 Lasser (n. 2, 2009), 201.

32 Daniela Caruso, 'Private Law and Public Stakes in European Integration: The Case of Property' (2004) 6 European Law Journal 751.

courts, the ECJ and the ECtHR, which have strong internal motivations of their own to pressure each other quite strongly on the fundamental rights front.[33] It should not be surprising, therefore, to see that the European courts reproduce many of the same inter-institutional dynamics that characterize the domestic judicial terrain.

As in the domestic arena, the European courts are situated differently with regard to fundamental rights. The ECtHR is on its home turf when elaborating fundamental rights doctrines. Such work represents its jurisdictional, institutional, and doctrinal raison d'être. The ECJ, however, is in a very different situation. It has long exercised review over actions taken by the EU institutions. But such review was based not on fundamental rights, but on the four 'legality' grounds listed in Article 263 (ex 230) of the EC Treaty: 'lack of competence, infringement of an essential procedural requirement, infringement of [the] Treaty or of any rule relating to its application, or misuse of powers.' As knowledgeable readers will recognize, this legality framework faithfully reproduces the state-oriented good governance approach deployed domestically by the Conseil d'Etat: the four traditional grounds for reviewing the legality of French administrative actions are none other than *incompétence*, *vice de forme*, *violation de la loi*, and *détournement de pouvoir*.[34]

The explosion of fundamental rights doctrines accordingly challenges the conceptual and doctrinal framework of the ECJ, which was derived directly from the Conseil d'Etat. As might be expected, the ECJ has met this challenge with some resistance: it only accepted to develop a fundamental rights jurisprudence when faced with mounting institutional threats. These pressures came from at least two directions. Classic EU analyses stress the first: pressure exerted by domestic constitutional courts, especially the German Federal Constitutional Court. The Federal Constitutional Court threatened to protect the fundamental rights of German citizens against encroachment by the acts of the Community institutions unless the Community (and the ECJ in particular) took on this task in a manner substantially similar to German constitutional protections.[35] But our analysis highlights a second, European, motivation that complements this domestic pressure: the ECJ was also increasingly threatened by the ECtHR, whose evermore bold and influential fundamental rights analyses of governmental action challenged its own legality-based approach.[36]

Pushed from both directions, the ECJ had little tactical choice but to hop onto the fundamental rights bandwagon, regardless of how unsettling this may have been to its

[33] The struggle for institutional, intellectual, and doctrinal leadership of the European high courts was on the verge of entering a new and potentially explosive phase: if the EU had acceded to the European Convention system, the ECJ would suddenly have become directly subject to the ECHR's jurisdiction. See n.47 and accompanying text.

[34] Brown and Bell (n. 13), 239.

[35] When the ECJ did so, the Federal Constitutional Court suspended its own review. *Re WünscheHandelsgesellschaft* ('*Solange II*') (1987) 3 CMLR 225, 265. See also *Brunner v European Union Treaty* (1994) 1 CMLR 57, 89 BverfGE 155.

[36] The centrality of the ECtHR and of its rights-based analyses has since been formalized in the EU legal order. The Charter of Fundamental Rights of the European Union, which took effect in 2000, established that the EU's institutions (including the ECJ) would respect fundamental rights 'as they result,' *inter alia*, from the ECHR and 'the case-law of the [ECtHR]'. It even specified that insofar as it 'contains rights which correspond to rights guaranteed by the [European Convention], the meaning and scope of those rights shall be the same as those laid down by the said Convention': Charter of Fundamental Rights of the European Union, Article 52(3).

traditional prism. Tellingly, however, it did so in a manner that faithfully reproduced the Conseil d'Etat's approach: it started to develop its own fundamental rights jurisprudence under the rubric of 'general principles of [European] Community law'.[37] This solution—since enshrined in Article 6-2 of the Treaty of Amsterdam—parrots the Conseil d'Etat's creative elaboration of such 'general principles of law' under the rubric of the cardinal French administrative notion of 'legality';[38]and it offers the same basic tactical advantage: it allows the ECJ to partake of, be responsive to, and influence the existing fundamental rights regimes (both domestic and European), while also establishing the legal independence of the ECJ and its fundamental rights doctrines.

These startlingly vivid institutional, conceptual, and doctrinal parallels between the ECJ and the Conseil d'Etat support several conclusions. At the most general, systemic level, the European courts are gradually organizing themselves as a complexly integrated judicial order; and they are doing so along recognizable domestic lines. Not only do they replicate the basic institutional division between fundamental rights-oriented 'constitutional' courts (the ECtHR playing the role of the Constitutional Council) and legality-oriented 'administrative' courts (the ECJ playing the role of the Conseil d'Etat), but they are reproducing both the tensions, motivations, and solutions that characterize these domestic judicial orders. This confirms our analysis of the fundamental rights dynamics that have been operating at the national level; justifies its transposition to the supranational level; and illustrates its relevance to the increasingly porous and interactive environment at the intersection of these two domains.

The Article 6-1 fair trial litigation reveals quite clearly the operation of these dynamics. In theory, this litigation should not have been a bone of contention between the ECJ and the ECtHR: the former is not subject to the latter's jurisdiction.[39] The litigation has nonetheless spilled over into the Euro-European realm, because the decision-making process of the ECJ is so clearly patterned on the French model.[40] In fact, this procedural link between the ECJ and the French high courts has been stressed by almost all parties involved as a means to exert leverage on one another.

These Euro-European Article 6-1 debates have played out in multiple venues. First, the ECtHR has explicitly and repeatedly addressed the ECJ's judicial decision-making processes in litigation concerning similar practices employed by the French and Belgian supreme courts. ECtHR majority decisions have worked hard to distinguish ECJ from national supreme court decision-making practices: it would be highly impolitic for the ECtHR to condemn the practices deployed by its august European

[37] These general principles were to be inspired by the 'constitutional traditions common to the Member States' and by the ECHR. See,e.g., Case 44/79 *Hauer v Land Rheinland-Pfalz*(1979) ECR 3727.

[38] Developed most aggressively and expansively in the post-war years, these general principles have permitted the Conseil to crystallize a set of overarching principles of legality that ground the French state and its actions.Seeconclusions of CDG Fournier in *Syndicat général des ingénieurs-conseils*, 26 June 1959, Rec. Lebon 364; 5 May1944 *Dame Trompier-Gravier* and Conseil d'État 26October1945, *Aramu*, Leb. 213.

[39] The EU has still not acceded to the ECHR. The ECJ ruled in 1996 that accession was outside the scope of EU's competences. SeeAccession by the Communities to the European Convention for the Protection of Human Rights and Fundamental Freedoms, Opinion 2/94, 1996 ECR I-1759, para. 35. The Lisbon Reform Treaty then called for such accession. SeeArticle 6(2) Treaty on European Union. But in its notorious 2014 Opinion 2/13, the ECJ blocked the negotiated accession from taking place. SeeCase C-2/13, Opinion 2/13 of the Court, EUR-Lex document, 62013CV0002 (18 December 2014).

[40] For more on these procedural parallels and their limits, seeLasser (n. 2, 2009),chapters 4 and 7.

colleague.[41] Dissenting ECtHR judges have, to the contrary, stressed Franco-ECJ parallels as a means to critique the majority's developing jurisprudence in a (largely unsuccessful) attempt to shield French-style supreme courts from ECtHR condemnation.[42] Indeed, the national high courts under review have done the same, both in domestic litigation and when defending themselves before the ECtHR.[43]

Second, the Article 6-1 litigation has also surfaced before the ECJ itself. In effect, the ECtHR's 6-1 jurisprudence has all but forced the ECJ to defend its traditional judicial decision-making procedures against the claim that they violate the fundamental right to a fair trial in a manner comparable to those of the French, Dutch, Belgian, and Portuguese supreme courts. In *Emesa Sugar vAruba*, the ECJ took matters in hand by issuing an order that held explicitly that its procedures do not run afoul of fair trial guarantees.[44]

This exchange demonstrates a number of key points. First, the ECtHR has been exerting significant pressure on the ECJ through the development of its fundamental rights doctrines, even though it does not formally exercise jurisdiction over its sister court. Secondly, the ECJ has understood that it has no choice but to meet this challenge directly on its own fundamental rights terms: it must make an effort to seize control of the fundamental rights analysis insofar as possible, lest it be at the mercy of less favorable interpretations. Thirdly, the ECJ is nonetheless in a disadvantageous position in these exchanges. Fundamental rights analysis is not the traditional source of its jurisdictional or doctrinal power. Worse, the ECJ finds itself in a defensive posture, as it must fend off the suggestion that its own decision-making procedures violate the fundamental right to a fair trial. This puts the ECJ in the awkward and seemingly retrograde position of fighting a rearguard action against fundamental rights protections.

The ECJ has nonetheless held firm, claiming the authority to make its own fundamental rights determinations. Relying on its self-availed—and Treaty and Charter ratified—power to interpret fundamental rights norms as 'general principles of law',it has even taken the dramatic tack of challenging the ECtHR overtly: by explicitly refusing to follow the Strasbourg court's Article 6-1 fair trial jurisprudence, the ECJ is in effect challenging the ECtHR's leadership in the fundamental rights arena.

Tellingly, the ECJ could hardly have picked less congenial ground on which to make its stand. It was the very institution charged with having violated the fundamental rights norms in question; its analysis was therefore inescapably self-interested, if not self-serving. Worse, the ECJ was effectively forced to frame its self-defence as a restrictive, rather than an expansive, fundamental rights interpretation: the ECJ had to conclude that the litigants' fair trial rights did not extend to the decision-making procedures at issue. The ECJ's very willingness to stand its ground under such unfavourable circumstances demonstrates the severity of the threat posed by the ECtHR's

[41] See, e.g., *SeeDelcourt v Belgium*, 11 ECtHR. (Ser. A) 1 (1970), para. 30; *Kress*(n. 17), paras 52, 86.

[42] Seedissenting opinion of Judge Van Compernolle and of Judges Gölcüklü, Matscher, and Pettiti in *Vermeulen v Belgium*, 1996-I ECtHR 224 (1996); *Reinhardt*(n. 17), Dissenting Opinion of Judge De Meyer, n. 13; Partly dissenting opinion of Judges Wildhaber, Costa, Pastor Ridruejo, Kūris, Bîrsan, Botoucharova, and Ugrekhelidze in *Kress*(n. 17), para. 11.

[43] See,e.g., *Kress* (n. 17),para. 62.

[44] SeeOrder of the Court in Case 17/98*Emesa Sugar (Free Zone) NV v Aruba*, 2000 ERC I-665.

Article 6-1 jurisprudence: backed against the wall, the ECJ had to claim fundamental rights authority more forcefully, lest the ECtHR dominate the field completely.

Equally telling, the ECJ defended its decision-making procedures in terms that reproduced unabashedly those put forward two years earlier by the French Conseil d'Etat.[45] By closing ranks in this manner, the ECJ presented the ECtHR with a threateningly unified front against its developing jurisprudence. In so doing, the ECJ effectively recognized that it and the Conseil d'Etat are structurally, intellectually, doctrinally, and procedurally kindred institutions; the rise of the fundamental rights idiom and of fundamental rights courts subjects both courts to deeply analogous pressures. These structural parallels confirm that the European courts are indeed organizing themselves into an integrated judicial order along recognizable domestic lines.

On a micro level, the ECJ's pugnacious approach, and to a lesser extent, the Conseil d'Etat's foot-dragging method, appear to have succeeded: the ECJ eventually backed off its increasingly frontal attack by accepting the minor window-dressing reforms that the Conseil d'Etat had grudgingly and strategically instituted as a stalling and face-saving tactic.[46]But on the macro level, all the judicial institutions involved—from the Conseil d'Etat, to the Cour de cassation, to the ECJ, to the ECtHR—were actively negotiating these conflicts through the unitary intellectual and juridical prism of fundamental rights.

In conclusion, the Franco-European analysis presented above demonstrates the full extent to which the French and European judiciaries have both been undergoing major reconstructions. On its side, the French judicial system has rapidly turned itself evermore completely and explicitly into a fundamental rights-based regime. This has triggered a major realignment of French judicial doctrines, procedures, jurisdictions, and ideologies. All French 'courts' now interpret constitutional rights when handling litigation, even if formal constitutional review has traditionally been vested solely in the Constitutional Council. When combined with the establishment of fundamental rights review of European derivation, the French judicial order has shifted ever further from its traditional package of republican-inspired attributes.

The French constitutional amendments of July 2008 offer the latest and clearest indication of this transformation. The addition of Article 61-1 opens the door for *a posteriori*concrete review of legislation on behalf of individuals: it allows references to be made by the Cour de cassation and the Conseil d'Etat to the Constitutional Council in ongoing litigation. This means, by definition, that all judicial (and/or quasi-judicial) branches of the French legal order are suddenly and explicitly important players in triggering judicial review of legislative norms on constitutional fundamental rights grounds. One can only assume that this represents the death knell of the general will as classically defined.

[45] Seeibid., drawing heavily from *Esclatine*, Conseil d'Etat,29July, 1998, D. 1999, at Jur. 85, concl. Chauvaux, at 89.

[46] SeeDécretNo 2009-14 du 7 janvier 2009 relatif au rapporteur public des juridictionsadministratives et au déroulement de l'audiencedevantcesjuridictions, https://www.legifrance.gouv.fr/affichTexte.do?cidTexte=JORFTEXT000020046644&categorieLien=id accessed on 4 January 2021.

Meanwhile, the European judicial orders have been reconstructing themselves at the same time. As the 'fair trial' case study demonstrates so clearly, not only have they been carefully negotiating their relationship with the multiple national high courts within the European Member States, but these interactions have also profoundly affected the interactions between the ECJ and the ECtHR.

Of course, the teleology of these inter-European judicial interactions once appeared to be clear: the eventual accession by the European Union to the European Convention on Human Rights. This accession, called for by the Lisbon Treaty that went into force in 2009,[47] would in practice have placed all EU institutions—including of course the ECJ—under the ultimate fundamental rights supervision of the ECtHR. But this seemingly straightforward solution, which would in theory have created a single ultimate European judicial authority in fundamental rights matters, never came to pass. In 2014, the ECJ published its Opinion 2/13, which declared that the EU could not legally accede to the ECHR under the terms of the Draft Agreement in Accession. The ECJ would therefore continue to be able to maintain its independence from the ECtHR, which guaranteed that the competitive inter-institutional dynamics would continue to operate in full force at the intersection of the European domestic and supranational judicial orders.

III. The Colombian/Latin American Parallel

The final substantive part of this article raises questions, but offers few answers. Its basic purpose is to ask what the Franco-European analysis provided above may suggest regarding the elaboration of human rights jurisprudence in Colombia and other Latin American countries that operate under the ambit of the Inter-American system of human rights.

In accordance with the analytic orientation of this article, this part focuses almost exclusively on the institutional and jurisdictional features that might inform such an inquiry. Specifically, it raises five such features and offers initial thoughts about their potential impact on the sorts of inter-institutional dynamics that we observed in the Franco-European context: (A) the centralized or decentralized structure of national 'judicial' hierarchies; (B) the centralized or decentralized structure of supranational/regional judicial courts; (C) the capacity of lower courts to access supranational/regional courts directly; (D) supranational judicial respect for a country's internal jurisdictional boundaries; and (E) the adoption of doctrines that require national courts to treat supranational human rights norms as national constitutional law. This list is by no means intended to be exhaustive. Nor is the analysis provided meant to be conclusive: I mean only to suggest avenues of study. And finally, as I will explain clearly in the conclusion, I understand this kind of inter-institutional examination to be only one component of a much broader and more detailed study of the political, institutional,

[47] See Treaty of Lisbon amending the Treaty on European Union and the Treaty establishing the European Community, OJ C306, 17 December 2007, Article 6(2).

legal, ideological, economic, and other factors that might impact upon the development of human rights norms, institutions, and mentalities within a given juridical and social order.

A. The (De-)Centralized Structure of National 'Judicial' Hierarchies

The first important structural variable involves the centralized or decentralized configuration of national 'judicial' hierarchies. I once again place the term 'judicial' in quotes in order to stress the seriousness with which such decentralization can be treated. As per the French model, legal systems can categorically refuse to concede that the institutional entities that decide constitutional or public law disputes qualify as judicial courts in the first place. As a result, these institutional entities can be housed outside of the judiciary altogether.

Such 'judicial' decentralization can then help to generate the kind of competitive inter-institutional dynamics of the sort described in Part II. If a legal system possesses distinct 'judicial' hierarchies, each led by its own high 'court', then the table is set for these institutions to compete for jurisdictional, doctrinal, political, and intellectual leadership. But such competition can be of lesser or greater importance. On the one hand, these inter-institutional rivalries can be rather benign. After all, an institutional division can simply reflect a jurisdictional division: cassation can govern civil and criminal matters, the Council of State can govern public law matters, and the constitutional 'court' can resolve constitutional challenges. True, such jurisdictional divisions will never be perfectly clean, as there is always going to be some degree of overlap; and this is bound to cause some friction over jurisdictional borders and their associated doctrinal specificities. Such competition can therefore remain of relatively low intensity as long as existing jurisdictional divisions lead each institution to remain more or less in its own lane.

The superimposition of a supranational dimension can, however, transform such rivalries into something far more pressing and profound. As we have seen in the French context, the addition of the supranational dimension gives the national courts a new and different field on which to engage and compete with each other. This alone is disruptive, offering new and interesting possibilities for some domestic institutions, while offering more threatening possibilities for others. But the arrival of supranational law does something else: it links these domestic courts together in a truly novel manner. Before the arrival of supranational law, these courts—each housed at the top of its own jurisdictional hierarchy—could have relatively little interface. They handled their respective kinds of cases, applying their own type of law. Except in relatively exceptional cases, these institutions could have relatively little to do with each other. But the arrival of supranational law changes all this: suddenly, these disparate institutions are all applying the same law. Now joined together via common substantive law, these previously siloed institutions all converge on the same legal turf. The decentralized institutional framework, when interacting with this newly integrated normative structure, can thus yield particularly competitive dynamics.

How might this play out in the Colombian and Latin American context?It depends. The first thing to recognize is that the institutional features that we examined in the Franco-European example do exist to some extent in the current Latin American environment.But they exist very unevenly from country to country.[48]In some respects, for example, Colombia follows a similar institutional model to France: it possesses multiple and distinct 'judicial hierarchies', each headed by its own 'supreme court': the Corte Suprema de Justicia leads the 'ordinary courts'; Consejo de Estado leads the 'administrative tribunals'; and the Corte Constitucional resolves constitutional challenges to legislation.Colombia thus possesses the same three independent supreme 'judicial' institutions as France, except that in the Colombian case, there is no need to use quotation marks: Article VIII of the 1991 Colombian constitution clearly designates all three as part of the judicial branch ('la Rama Judicial').Whether the fact that all three institutions fall under the formal category of the 'judiciary' affects the potential inter-institutional competition between them, or whether their relatively short terms of office (eight years non-renewable[49]) does so, however, is less than clear.

If we broaden our field of view to look at other Latin American states, it becomes immediately obvious that most possess far more integrated judiciaries.Argentina, Mexico, Costa Rica, Nicaragua, El Salvador, Panama, Honduras, Uraguay, Paraguay, and Venezuela, for example, all have unitary judiciaries headed by a single supreme court and possess no distinct constitutional court.[50]Chile, Brazil, Guatemala, and Bolivia, however, offer mixed models by establishing dual high jurisdictions: a supreme court and a separate institution whose predominant function is to resolve constitutional questions.[51]

Viewed from this perspective, it becomes clear that Colombia (along with Ecuador) is something of an outlier among Latin American countries for deploying the disaggregated three-headed judicial model that can routinely be found in Europe, such as in France, Italy, Poland, Portugal, Belgium, the Netherlands, the Czech Republic, and so on.[52]If then, the multiplicity of high courts within national legal systems contributes to the development of inter-institutional competition, which helps to drive the development of supranational fundamental rights norms, one might expect that this reduced level of national high court diversity within the countries of Latin America might decrease the institutional motivation to turn to, foreground, and promote fundamental

[48] As is the case, for that matter, in Europe.

[49] Articles 233 and 239 of the Colombian constitution of 1991.

[50] Constitution of Argentina of 1853 (reinstated in 1983, amended through 1994), Part 2, Title I, Section III; constitution of Mexico (1917, amended through 2015), Title III, Chapter IV; constitution of Costa Rica of 1949 (amended through 2011) Title XI; constitution of Nicaragua of 1987 (amended through 2005), Title VIII, Chapter V; constitution of El Salvador of 1983 (amended through 2014), Title VI, Chapter III; constitution of Panama of 1972 (amended through 2004), Title VII, Chapter 1; constitution of Honduras of 1982 (amended through 2013), Title V, Chapter XII; constitution of Uruguay of 1966 (reinstated in 1985, amended through 2004), Section XV; constitution of Paraguay of 1992 (amended through 2011), Part II, Title II, Chapter III; constitution of Venezuela of 1999 (amended through 2009), Title V, Chapter III.

[51] Seeconstitution of Chile of 1980 (amended through 2012), Chapter 8; constitution of Brazil of 1988 (amended through 2014), Chapter III (2) and (3); constitution of Guatemala of 1985 (amended through 1993), Chapter IV; constitution of Bolivia of 2009, Part II, Title III.

[52] Germany actually deploys an even more multi-headed model, with five constitutionally established Federal Supreme Courts, in addition to the Federal Constitutional Court. SeeBasic Law of Germany of 1949 (amended through 2012), Articles 92–95.

and human rights norms.Whether this holds true in practice requires further, detailed research.

B. The (De-)Centralized Structure of Supranational/Regional Courts

The diminished judicial diversity that we have just examined at the national level is even more pronounced at the supranational level.Europe, after all, possesses two powerful supranational/regional courts: the ECJ and the ECtHR; and as we examined in Part II(E) above, this judicial multiplicity has generated fiercely contested jurisdictional, doctrinal, intellectual, and institutional tensions.Neither the Luxembourg nor the Strasbourg Court can afford to cede leadership over fundamental rights issues to the other.Indeed, the ECJ went to great lengths to construct its fundamental rights jurisdiction and jurisprudence out of whole cloth long before the EU had enacted its Charter of Fundamental Rights in 2000, never mind before this Charter was finally formally enshrined in the EU Treaty system in 2009.And having done so, it can hardly be surprising that the ECJ would have protected its hard-won jurisdiction by any means necessary, including by blocking the EU from signing onto the ECHR, which would have subjected the ECJ to supervision by the ECtHR.[53]

By all indications, the Americas possess no equivalent judicial diversity at the supranational level.The IACtHR is the only major judicial institution in play, as the Andean Court of Justice has—to this point—played too limited a role in too limited a jurisdictional pool: the Andean Community consists, after all, of only four Member States: Bolivia, Colombia, Ecuador, and Peru.The IACtHR need not, therefore, compete aggressively to maintain its regional leadership in the supranational human rights arena, which again reduces the level of inter-institutional pressure.

C. Vertical Judicial Diversity

Limiting the number of independent *national* and *supranational* high courts may very well decrease the type of competitive dynamics that have helped to drive the fundamental rights revolution in the European judiciary.But there exists a third axis of judicial diversity that has proven extremely productive in the European context: the *lower* national courts.True, the ECHR calls for the exhaustion of domestic remedies for a complaint to be filed in Strasbourg,[54] which effectively turns national supreme courts into gatekeepers to the ECtHR.But the ECJ made sure to demolish the power of national supreme courts to exercise this type of control over their own lower courts.In a series of tactically brilliant judgments, the ECJ systematically tore down any national

[53] SeeCase C-2/13 (n. 39).

[54] Article 35 of the ECHR states: 'The Court may only deal with the matter after all domestic remedies have been exhausted . . .'

impediment that might limit the capacity of lower domestic courts to refer cases directly to the ECJ without supreme court interference.Most importantly, no national rules could prevent any domestic court or tribunal from independently and directly referring a question of European law to the ECJ.[55]

This seemingly technical procedural policy was paradigm shifting in multiple respects.Suddenly, every court and tribunal in every small town in every Member State could raise questions of European law directly with the ECJ in Luxembourg.This effectively turned all national courts into European courts.By the same token, national supreme courts were denied the capacity to demand that European legal questions be systematically forwarded to them for their ultimate consideration, which would have empowered those high courts not only to play a far more dominant role in determining the meaning of European law within the domestic legal system, but also to find creative ways *not* to refer European legal questions to the ECJ.This would have greatly empowered the national high courts in their interactions with the ECJ, which would have become dependent on those high courts for the purposes of gaining relevance within the national judicial and legal systems.

Instead, the lower domestic courts were effectively empowered to bypass their hierarchical superiors within the national judiciaries.Not only had the supreme courts lost control over their own judicial hierarchies, but the lower national courts could actually exercise greater power when acting within the ambit of European law than they could when applying national law.Far from being able to stem the turn to European law, the national supreme courts had been placed in such a compromised position that they had to join in this Europeanization lest they be bypassed altogether.In effect, the ECJ had licensed and secured the emergence of intensely competitive inter-institutional pressures *within* the national legal systems by undercutting the supreme courts' traditional powers over their inferior courts.This left the high courts with no good alternative to jumping on the European fundamental rights bandwagon; to do otherwise would put them at risk of being outflanked by their lower courts, the ECJ, and any other high courts willing to take a more European-friendly approach.

The Inter-American system does not appear to put comparable dynamics into play within the national judicial hierarchies.Article 46 of the American Convention on Human Rights ('ACHR') specifically demands that 'the remedies under domestic law have been pursued and exhausted' in order for a claim to be admitted by the Inter-American Commission.[56]This requirement firmly entrenches the authority of the domestic high courts, which cannot easily be bypassed by their hierarchical inferiors.

True, litigants can press their claims and this will push supreme courts to consider fundamental rights claims under the threat of eventual IACtHR sanction.But the threat is distant in time, remote in likelihood, and elsewhere in effect.After all, it takes a long time to exhaust national remedies, for a case to be brought before the

[55] SeeJoined Cases 146 &166/73*Rheinmuhlen-Dusseldorf v Einfuhr-und Vorratsstelle Get-reide*,European Court Reports 1974-00033.

[56] ACHR, Article 46(1)(a).

Inter-American Commission in Washington, for negotiations to conclude, and for a case to eventually be brought before the IACtHR in Costa Rica.Indeed, given the miniscule number of cases actually decided by the Court—it functions, after all, but parttime—, the threat of judicial sanction remains quite remote in all but the most egregious and high-profile conflicts.Furthermore, such sanction, if ever it does come to pass, will be directed first and foremost at the state *qua* state, and especially at its political—not judicial—institutions.

By all indications, this long and tortuous American path cannot compare to the European-style threat of an immediate lower court reference to the supranational court, which bypasses the high national court altogether and directly calls the regional court into play (and the national high court into question).That European model, elaborated by the ECJ (*not* the ECtHR) primarily in the context of its preliminary reference procedure to resolve questions of EU law interpretation, inserts the supranational court directly into national judicial proceedings, effectively empowering the lower courts to challenge their national hierarchical superiors.But this dynamic is all but foreclosed by the obligation to exhaust national remedies before bringing a claim under the Inter-American Convention.Neither the domestic high courts, nor the IACtHR itself, are likely to face comparable pressures to resolve a large number of pressing claims forwarded by the lower national courts.

D. The Respect for Internal Jurisdictional Boundaries

The three variable features discussed so far consist of structural features inherent in the institutional framework in which the Inter-American system functions.In particular, the IACtHR has no say in the number of national and supranational courts; nor is it responsible for demanding the exhaustion of remedies, which is a requirement written into the Convention.The Court and national high courts have, however, chosen to adopt two other doctrinal policies that may impact significantly on the kinds of inter-institutional dynamics that have helped to fuel the European fundamental rights revolution.For its part, the IACtHR has chosen to respect jurisdictional boundaries within the national legal orders; and it has adopted and elaborated the doctrine of 'conventionality control' in a manner that reinforces national institutional and jurisdictional structures even as it has demanded respect for Inter-American human rights norms.As we shall see in the next section, this respect for internal jurisdictional boundaries has been further strengthened by the national judicial elaboration of the doctrines of the 'block of constitutionality', which domesticates human rights norms.These doctrinal policies may accordingly temper, rather than stimulate, the reordering that human rights jurisprudence might provoke within the legal orders of Latin America.

The first of these doctrinal policies—'conventionality control'—addresses a deeply practical question: if the national legal systems are required to abide by Inter-American human rights norms, what are national judges to do when asked to apply domestic law that appears to run afoul of those norms?The simple answer is the categorical one: refuse to apply it.But this simple answer has the weakness of simplicity: it fails to recognize the diversity of approaches that national legal systems may take regarding the power of judges to exercise different kinds of judicial review.In many Latin American countries, judicial review is decentralized, which allows ordinary judges to examine the constitutionality of legislative acts.[57] But in others, and most notably in Colombia, constitutional review is concentrated in a single constitutional court.To ask ordinary courts in the latter type of jurisdiction to set aside national law that runs afoul of supranational law is therefore to ask them to violate the most basic dictates of their constitutional orders.

And yet, this is precisely what the IACtHR appeared to do in its famous judgment in*Almonacid-Arellano v Chile*:

> 123. ... However, when the Legislative Power fails to set aside and / or adopts laws which are contrary to the American Convention, the Judiciary is bound to honor the obligation to respect rights as stated in Article 1(1) of the said Convention, and consequently, it must refrain from enforcing any laws contrary to such Convention.
>
> The observance by State agents or officials of a law which violates the Convention gives rise to the international liability of such State, as contemplated in International Human Rights Law, in the sense that every State is internationally responsible for the acts or omissions of any of itspowers or bodies for the violation of internationally protected rights, pursuant to Article 1(1) of the American Convention.149
>
> 124.The Court is aware that domestic judges and courts are bound to respect the rule of law, and therefore, they are bound to apply the provisions in force within the legal system. But when a State has ratified an international treaty such as the American Convention, its judges, as part of the State, are also bound by such Convention. This forces them to see that all the effects of the provisions embodied in the Convention are not adversely affected by the enforcement of laws which are contrary to its purpose and that have not had any legal effects since their inception. In other words, the Judiciary must exercise a sort of 'conventionality control' between the domestic legal provisions which are applied to specific cases and the American Convention on Human Rights. To perform this task, the Judiciary has to take into account not only the treaty, but also the interpretation thereof made by the Inter-American Court, which is the ultimate interpreter of the American Convention.[58]

Had this doctrinal policy held, it would have put all national courts throughout Latin America in play as vectors for the transmission of human rights, and would accordingly have created the type of judicial free-for-all that has propelled the spread and development of EU law.

But the IACtHR did not maintain this blanket policy for long.Less than two months later, it backtracked on its sweeping *Almonacid-Arellano* ruling: although the Court confirmed that national judges 'should exercise not only a control of constitutionality, but also of "conventionality"*ex officio* between domestic norms and the American

[57] This still leaves open the question of the direct effect of the Inter-American Convention in such jurisdictions. SeeAlexandra Huneeus, Constitutional Lawyers and the Inter-American Court's Varies Authority' (2016) 79 Law & Contemporary Problems179, 203. But this issue lies beyond the scope of our analysis.

[58] *Almonacid-Arellano et al. v Chile*, 2006 IACtHR (Ser. C) 154 (26September 2006) (citations omitted).

Convention', it now qualified this rule by stating that such control (i.e., review) should 'evidently [be exercised] in the context of their respective spheres of competence and the corresponding procedural regulations'.[59]This important new qualifier effectively meant that the Inter-American system of human rights protection would henceforth defer to the basic jurisdictional and institutional structure of the Member States: if a given country concentrated its consideration of human rights violations in a single judicial institution (such as a constitutional court), so be it.The IACtHR would not insist—as in the ECJ model—that every judicial entity independently exercise such control/review.[60]

The IACtHR's respectful stance towards the institutional and jurisdictional structures of the Member States' courts may further temper the inter-institutional dynamics that might otherwise propel a rapid and competitive convergence on human rights norms and discourse.In particular, those judicial systems that *do* possess complex judicial systems that deploy separate constitutional courts (including those possessing an even more complex institutional architecture *à la française*)—that is,the very ones that might be *most* conducive to fractious inter-institutional competition for human rights leadership—, would not have to set such dynamics in motion: the IACtHR would not require that Inter-American human rights norms be applied across the board, which would require the ordinary courts to step on the toes of the constitutional courts, thereby overriding and likely undermining national jurisdictional divisions.

E. Constitutionalization: The Doctrines of 'Conventionality Control' and of the 'Block of Constitutionality'

Finally, it may be worth questioning whether the adoption of the doctrines of 'conventionality control' and of the 'block of constitutionality,' which appear to promote the internalization and spread of Inter-American human rights norms, may simultaneously limit their rapid spread throughout the legal orders of the Americas.

On the one hand, it is self-evident that these doctrines promote the internalization and spread of Inter-American human rights.If, as the Court made clear in its famous *Almonacid Arellano* judgment, 'the [national] Judiciary is bound to honor the obligation to respect rights as stated in Article 1(1) of the [Inter-American] Convention, and consequently, it must refrain from enforcing any [national] laws contrary to such

[59] *Dismissed Congressional Employees (Aguado-Alfaro et al.) v Peru*, 2006 IACt.HR (Ser. C) 158 (24 November 2006), para. 128.

[60] The IACtHR has confirmed this 'evident' qualifier. See*Radilla-Pacheco vMexico*, 2009 ICtHR (Ser. C) 209 (23 November 2009), para. 339. See alsoEduardo FerrerMac-Gregor, 'Conventionality Control: The NewDoctrine of the Inter-American Court of Human Rights'(2015-2016)109 American Journal of International Law Unbound93, 97. Judge Mac-Gregor has worked hard to promote a creative reading of the qualifier: he argues that just because the IACtHR has accepted that some national judges do not have the power to set aside legislation within their own legal systems does not mean that those judges cannot exercise conventionality control by creatively interpreting domestic norms in such a manner as to bring them into line with Inter-American human rights norms (including the interpretation that the IACtHR has given to such norms). SeeConcurring opinion ofEduardo Ferrer Mac-Gregor in *Cabrera García and Montiel Flores v Mexico*, 2010 IACt.HR (Ser. C) 220 (26 November 2010),para. 37.

Convention' and domestic judges must therefore 'exercise a sort of 'conventionality control' between the domestic legal provisions which are applied to specific cases and the American Convention on Human Rights',[61] then there is no question that Inter-American rights accordingly become relevant within all judicial systems in the Americas.

On the other hand, the domestic high courts have gradually tended to choose a distinctive doctrinal mechanism for making such human rights norms effective within their respective national judicial systems: the doctrine of the 'block of constitutionality'.According to this doctrine, which comes in a wide array of national variants, Inter-American human rights tend not to be treated as straightforwardly effective within the national orders.Instead, these rights are incorporated into the national constitutional orders themselves: they become part of the national constitutional regime.[62]

This approach, which has spread through much of the Americas since its early emergence in Panama, Costa Rica, Colombia, and Peru almost thirty years ago,[63] turns international human rights norms—and Inter-American human rights norms in particular—into national constitutional law.This internalization obviously makes such norms effective within the national legal order.But the manner in which it does so may also lead to a fairly clear chain of command within the domestic legal realm: after all, the human rights norms become domesticated as national constitutional law.This constitutionalization process places national constitutional judges in the privileged position of dominating the debates concerning the meaning and eventual import of these norms within the national legal, political, and constitutional order: if the human rights debates are officially recognized as constitutional in nature, then it is above all the constitutional judiciary that is empowered to resolve them.

In some respects, this prioritization of constitutional law returns us to the analysis suggested in Sections A and D above.Because Latin American countries offer varying degrees of judicial specialization (and thus varying degrees of jurisdictional and institutional differentiation), they are likely to respond differently to the internalization of Inter-American human rights as domestic constitutional law.For those countries with decentralized constitutional adjudication, all courts will be able to access and deploy these human rights norms.But for those countries with centralized constitutional adjudication (such as Colombia), it is the constitutional court that will likely be empowered to dominate human rights litigation.That said, the very existence of centralized constitutional adjudication, especially in countries(such as Colombia) with French-style diversification of judicial institutions, results in the establishment of multiple high courts that can compete for control of human rights claims. But such competition hinges on maintaining thesupranational as well as domestic character of the apex norms to be applied.It is precisely the European provenance of EU and ECHR

[61] *Almonacid-Arellano*(n. 58), paras 123–4.

[62] For a particularly useful account and analysis of the emergence and development of the doctrine throughout the Americas, seeManuel EduardoGóngora-Mera, 'The Block of Constitutionality as the Doctrinal Pivot of a *Ius Commune*', in Armin vonBogdandy et al. (eds), *Transformative Constitutionalism in Latin America: The Emergence of a New Ius Commune* (Oxford: Oxford Univ. Press, 2017), 235.

[63] SeeManuel Eduardo GóngoraMera, *Inter-American Judicial Constitutionalism*(San Jose, Costa Rica: Inter-American Institute of Human Rights, 2011, 169.

fundamental rights norms that removes the capacity of any given high court in any given country to claim authoritative capacity to interpret those norms to the exclusion of other national courts.In other words, it is the maintenance of the European character of European fundamental rights norms that permits and even promotes the inter-institutional competition over fundamental rights interpretation.

This suggests that the elaboration of the doctrine of the 'bloc of constitutionality' may indeed be a clever form of institutional and jurisdictional, as well as interpretive, domestication of Inter-American human rights norms.The doctrine places the Colombian Constitutional Court, to pick the obvious example, in the tactically enviable position not only of handling Inter-American human rights norms as if they were national constitutional norms, but also of preempting interference from potential institutional competitors (such as the Corte Suprema de Justicia or the Consejo de Estado).Compared to supreme courts operating in integrated judicial orders in which all courts have access and recourse to constitutional norms, specialized constitutional courts can therefore monopolize constitutional discourse especially effectively, although this is likely to be counterbalanced by the ability of the supreme courts to exercise more direct hierarchical control.

Whether such outcomes should be lauded or decried lies beyond the scope of this article.The point of our analysis is merely to suggest that the elaboration of the 'bloc of constitutionality' doctrine may well reduce the level of inter-institutional competition that—as the European exampledemonstrates so well—can actively contribute to the rapid expansion of fundamental rights discourse.If a given Latin American country offers an integrated judiciary (with 'decentralized' constitutional decisionmaking), then primary interpretive authority will ultimately fall on the national supreme court. And if it offers a decentralized structure of national 'judicial' hierarchies (with 'centralized' constitutional decisionmaking), then primary interpretive authority will ultimately fall on the national constitutional court.Under either permutation, the 'bloc of constitutionality' doctrine, precisely by turning supranational law into national law, appears to concentrate human rights control in a single national high court, rather than foster inter-institutional rivalry to exercise such control.

IV. Conclusion

This article has described the judicial dynamics underlying the explosive rise of fundamental rights in the Franco-European context in order to suggest further lines of inquiry in the Inter-American context.The Franco-European experience strongly suggests that the interaction between multiple supranational courts, when coupled with the interaction between multiple national high courts, can help to foster a highly competitive judicial environment in which a plethora of institutional players clamour to master and control the development of fundamental rights, leading to a self-reinforcing rise in the prevalence and dominance of fundamental rights jurisprudence.

This dynamic is suggestive for the development of the Inter-American system. As this article has suggested, the judicial orders in the Americas hold a good deal in common with their European counterparts, including multiple levels and types of courts, justiciable human rights, and so on.As we have seen, however, they also possess features that may tend to reduce the intensity of the competitive inter-institutional dynamics that have helped to fuel the European fundamental rights revolution.In particular, their national judiciaries are somewhat more centralized.They possess only one major supranational court: the IACtHR.Their lower national courts cannot directly access the IACtHR.The IACtHR shows greater respect for internal domestic jurisdictional boundaries.Finally, the 'bloc of constitutionality' doctrine makes it somewhat easier for a single national high court (whether it be the constitutional court or the supreme court) to take primary control over human rights issues.The net result is an institutional structure that appears somewhat less conducive to the explosive rise of human rights throughout the judicial orders of the Americas.

This article's tentative drawing of Euro-American parallels and distinctions also suggests avenues for further research on the European plane.To what extent, for example, should the success of the ECHR system be attributed not the ECHR system itself, but to the fortuitous existence of the EU system?After all, without the EU, the ECJ, and the preliminary reference procedure (including in particular the ECJ's open-door policy towards the lower courts of the EU's Member States), would the competitive judicial dynamics of the fundamental rights revolution ever have been unleashed?Similarly, would those dynamics have been so chaotic and fruitful had national constitutional courts been able to put the 'constitutional bloc' doctrine into effect, thereby empowering them to centralize, and thus exert significant control over, fundamental rights challenges brought under European law?

And this is to say nothing of institutional and professional issues of a more practical kind.Would the competitive inter-institutional dynamics behind the European fundamental rights revolution have developed had the ECJ been a part-time judicial college deciding a handful of cases a year?After all, the ECJ disposes of many hundreds of cases each year.[64]The IACtHR, by contrast, functioning in a part-time capacity a few times a year, delivers less than two dozen contentious judgments annually.[65]This tiny caseload, directed at the most large-scale governmental abuses, seems unlikely to generate the type of broad and pervasive rights-based litigation and jurisprudence that now characterize the European legal domain.

To perform a more thorough examination of the factors that might impact upon the development of human rights norms, institutions, and mentalities in the Americas and beyond, one would then have to take account not only of the types of inter-institutional issues addressed in this chapter, but also of much broader and much more specific professional, political, ideological, economic, and other factors.On the more specific professional front, for example, one would need to understand the relationship

[64] Indeed, we may soon be able to say that it disposes of *thousands* of cases per year. In 2017, the ECJ and the General Court completed 1,594 cases:https://curia.europa.eu/jcms/upload/docs/application/pdf/2018-04/ra_pan_2018.0421_en.pdf accessed on 4 January 2021.

[65] As states the Court's 2017 Annual Report: 'During 2017, the Court issued a total of fourteen judgments, divided into ten judgments on preliminary objections, merits, reparations and costs, and four interpretation judgments.'Inter-American Court of Human Rights, 2017 Annual Report, https://www.corteidh.or.cr/sitios/informes/docs/ENG/eng_2017.pdf, 52 accessed on 4 January 2021). The 2016 Annual Report states: 'In the course of 2016, the Court delivered twenty-one judgments, divided into fourteen judgments on preliminary objections, merits and reparations and costs, and seven interpretation judgments.'Inter-American Court of Human Rights, 2016 Annual Report, https://www.corteidh.or.cr/sitios/informes/docs/ENG/eng_2016.pdf, 54 accessed on 4 January 2021.

between the judges and their own 'judicial' institutions, as well as the relationship between those institutions.As soon as one pays closer attention, it becomes obvious that the apparent similarities between, for example, the French and Colombian judicial models can be vastly overstated.The judges of the French Cour de cassation and Conseil d'Etat, for example, spend their entire working lives within the ambit of their respective institutions.Once having gained entrance to the Conseil d'Etat upon graduation from the *Ecole nationale de l'administration*, a conseiller d'Etat will likely spend the totality of their forty-year career under the organizational umbrella of the Conseil. The members of the Colombian Consejo de Estado or Corte Suprema de Justicia, however, only serve a single non-renewable eight-year term.[66]Given these short terms, is there any reason to expect that the high courts of the Colombian judiciary would feel either the institutional loyalty of their French counterparts or the impulse to engage in the type of competition for inter-institutional leadership that characterizes the French juridical field?

What, furthermore, are the much broader background political—never mind social and economic—conditions in which these courts operate and how might this affect the spread of fundamental rights discourse and jurisprudence?What might be the effect of the much-discussed authoritarian and military legacies in the Americas?Or of the well-documented limitations on the reach of judicial authority—and of legality in general—in the region?In short, is there any reason to assume that rights, procedures, courts, discourses, and so on mean the same thing, occupy the same positions, or serve comparable functions in the different jurisdictions throughout the Americas, never mind when comparing the Americas and Europe?

These are of course extremely difficult—if not intractable—conceptual and methodological questions.This chapter was primarily meant to offer up the European example to American eyes.Having done so, its conclusions are intentionally modest and provisional.It merely means to suggest (1) that the fundamental rights revolution in Europe has been fuelled in part by powerful interinstitutional dynamics, (2) that similar inter-institutional features do appear to exist in the Inter-American context as well, but (3) that for a series of distinctive structural, constitutional, procedural, and doctrinal reasons, these inter-institutional features appear somewhat less prone to trigger and sustain the type of competitive inter-institutional dynamics that have helped to turn fundamental rights jurisprudence into such an important force throughout the European domestic and supranational legal domains.To say more will require further research.

[66] Article 233 of the Colombian constitution of 1991.

19

The Changing Role and Reception of International Law in Domestic Constitutional Law

Some Thoughts about Latin America and Europe

Marie-Christine Fuchs

I. Introduction

On 10 December 2018, we celebrated the seventieth anniversary of the Universal Declaration of Human Rights,[1] which was adopted on that date in 1948 by the United Nations General Assembly. That same day, Colombia, as one of the fifty-eight Member States of the United Nations, voted in favour of its adoption. Worldwide awareness of the need for the protection of rights at a global level, based on the fact that all human beings are born free and equal in dignity and rights, arose after the atrocities and devastation caused by the Second World War. With the adoption of the Universal Declaration, a new framework for the protection of rights, in particular human rights, was born and continues to be developed gradually in Colombia, as in other countries. It finds its expression in a growing number of agreements and conventions guaranteeing these rights, which have a multilevel dimension in a globalized world.

At the global level, seventy years ago the Universal Declaration was constituted as the first substantial norm putting into practice the global content of human rights and fundamental freedoms.[2] This Universal Human Rights System ('UHRS') was conceived to complement its Member States human rights' protection mechanisms and to supervise their actions.[3] However, as there is no court which has jurisdiction to control compliance and execution of, *inter alia*, the nine principal human rights treaties which were adopted under the aegis of the United Nations as well as the application of

[1] See the Universal Declaration of Human Rights at https://www.ohchr.org/EN/UDHR/Documents/UDHR_Translations/spn.pdf accessed on 7 December 2020.

[2] After its adoption, the basic principles which it enshrines found precision and further elaboration in numerous procedural and substantive rules contained in more than 200 international treaties, conventions, and protocols as well as extra-conventional mechanisms and general principles of international law.

[3] T. F. Mégre, 'Nature of Obligations' in D. Moeckli (ed.), *International Human Rights Law* (Oxford University Press, 2010), 124–49.

Marie-Christine Fuchs, *The Changing Role and Reception of International Law in Domestic Constitutional Law:* In: *Constitutionalism.* Edited by: Alejandro Linares-Cantillo, Camilo Valdivieso-León, Santiago García-Jaramillo, Oxford University Press (2021). © The various contributors. DOI: 10.1093/oso/9780192896759.003.0020

the resolutions of the Human Rights Committee, some have called the UHRS a 'toothless tiger'.[4]

In addition to the UHRS, regional human rights protection regimes have been developed; these include the Inter-American Human Rights Protection System ('IAHRS') in the Americas[5] and the European Human Rights System ('EHRS') in Europe. From the perspective of constitutional judges, this level might be more visible and impactful because, other than the UHRS, there exist regional courts in Latin America (the Inter-American Court of Human Rights ('IACtHR')) as well as in Europe (the European Court of Human Rights (ECtHR)) competent to interpret the respective regional human rights catalogues and to ensure compliance with regional treaties by condemning those Member States which have formerly accepted their jurisdiction[6] and are now infringing on those norms to repair the damage caused.[7] Thus, in accordance with the jurisprudence of the IACtHR, in Latin America, not only constitutional judges, but all public servants in the countries that have signed the American Convention on Human Rights ('ACHR'), ought to design, interpret, and apply all national norms in the light of and in compliance with the Convention (so called 'conventionality control'[8]) and thus become, *ex officio*, inter-American judges.[9]

[4] Kristen D. A. Carpenter, 'The International Covenant on Civil and Political Rights: A Toothless Tiger' (2000) 26 North Carolina Journal of International Law and Commercial Regulation 1–55, https://scholarship.law.unc.edu/cgi/viewcontent.cgi?article=1684&context=ncilj accessed on 7 December 2020.

[5] For more details, see César Rodríguez Garavito & Celeste Kauffman, 'From Orders to Practice: Analysis and Strategies for Implementing Decisions of the Inter-American Human Rights System, in The Inter-American Human Rights System – Changing Times, ongoing challenges, Due Process of Law Foundation' (2016), chapter 7, 249–84.

[6] In Europe, all members of the Council of Europe have signed the ECHR and have thus accepted the jurisprudence of the ECtHR. In the Americas, out of the thirty-five Organization of American States ('OAS') Member States twenty are subject to the IACtHR's jurisdiction so far: 'Argentina, Barbados, Bolivia, Brazil, Chile, Columbia, Costa Rica, the Dominican Republic, Ecuador, El Salvador, Guatemala, Haiti, Honduras, Mexico, Nicaragua, Panama, Peru, Suriname, and Uruguay'. Annual Report, Inter-American Court of Human Rights (2019), Protecting Rights, 12, https://www.corteidh.or.cr/docs/informe2019/ingles.pdf accessed on 7 December 2020.

[7] See ECHR, Articles 32, 46 and ACHR, Articles 62, 68.

[8] This so-called 'conventionality control' was first introduced by the IACtHR in *Case of Almonacid Arellano et al. v Chile*, Judgment of 16 September 2006, Series C 154. If an interpretation in compliance with the ACHR was impossible, the courts would have to disapply the respective national rule (Eduardo Ferrer Mac-Gregor, 'Conventionality Control. The New Doctrine of the Inter-American Court of Human Rights' (2015) 109 American Journal of International Law Unbound 93). Thereby, not only the ACHR itself, but also its interpretation by the IACtHR were binding for all Member States, including such cases in which a Member State was not involved as a party (ibid., 98). The conventionality control is derived from ACHR, Articles 1.1, 2 and 29 as well as from the principle of '*pacta sunt servanda*' (ibid.). See also Ariel Dulitzky, 'An Inter-American Constitutional Court? The Invention of the Conventionality Control by the Inter-American Court of Human Rights' (2015) 50 (1) Texas International Law Journal 49 et seq., https://law.utexas.edu/faculty/publications/2015-An-Inter-American-Constitutional-Court-The-Invention-of-the-Conventionality-Control-by-the/download accessed on 7 December 2020 and Jorge Contesse, 'Judicial Backlash in Inter-American Human Rights Law?' (2 March 2017) International Journal of Constitutional Law Blog, http://www.iconnectblog.com/2017/03/judicial-backlash-interamerican/ accessed on 7 December 2020. On the obligation of officials such as judges and judicial operators to exercise conventionality control, see Florentin Meléndez, 'Instrumentos internacionales sobre derechos humanos aplicables a la administración de la justicia – Estudio constitucional comparado, Konrad Adenauer Stiftung' (10th edn, 2019), 40

[9] See IACtHR, *Case of Trabajadores Cesados del Congreso v Peru*, Judgment of 24 November 2006, Series C 158, para. 128; *Case of Cabrera García and Montiel Flores v Mexico*, Judgment of 26 November 2010, Series C 220, para. 225; for more details, see Eduardo Ferrer Mac-Gregor & Carlos Pelayo Moller, 'Article 2', in Christian Steiner & Marie-Christine Fuchs (eds), *Comentario a la Convención Americana de Derechos*

In Europe, we even rely on two regional human rights protection systems so that—counting in the respective national systems—human rights protection in Europe is of tripolar nature:[10] Although the Convention for the Protection of Human Rights and Fundamental Freedoms ('ECHR')[11] adopted within the Council of Europe and the jurisprudence of the ECtHR remains the principal reference for regional human rights protection in Europe,[12] with the ratification of the Treaty of Lisbon, as of 2009 the Charter of Fundamental Rights of the European Union[13] is legally binding for all Member States of the European Union (with the exception of Poland and the United Kingdom), having the rank of primary EU-legislation.[14] Therefore, the Charter became subject to the binding jurisprudence of the Court of Justice of the European Union ('CJEU') and has been gaining importance in European human rights protection of late.

In this context, particularly in EU Member States, the relationships, interferences, and (potential) hierarchies between the human rights catalogues provided by their respective constitutions, the EU-Charter and the ECHR, as interpreted by their respective courts, the ECtHR, the CJEU, and the national constitutional courts, have become increasingly more complex.[15] Although Article 6 of the Treaty of the European Union ('TEU') explicitly stipulates that the EU will accede to the ECHR in order to clarify their relations, especially due to a broadly discussed ruling of the CJEU in 2014,[16] which rejected a concrete accession proposal, and although recently accession negotiations have been resumed,[17] this has not yet occurred. However, given that the texts of

Humanos, Rights (2nd edn, 2019), 76, https://dialogoderechoshumanos.com/component/edocman/articulos-cadh-ii-edicion/parte-1-capitulo-1/articulo-2-convencion-americana-sobre-derechos-humanos accessed on 11 December 2020; Gonzalo Aguilar Cavallo, 'Obligatoriedad del control de convencionalidad a la luz del derecho de los tratados, Anuario Mexixano de Derecho Internacional (Vol. 19, 2019), 357–98.

[10] See Aida Torres Perez, 'Conflicts of Rights in the European Union: A Theory of Supranational Adjudication' (2009), 27: 'three spheres of human rights protection'.

[11] https://www.echr.coe.int/Documents/Convention_SPA.pdf accessed on 7 December 2020.

[12] See Héctor Fix-Zamudio, 'La Corte Europea de Derechos Humanos y el derecho de amparo internacional', in Héctor Fix-Zamudio & Eduardo Ferrer Mac-Gregor (eds), *El Derecho de Amparo en el Mundo* (2006), 1105; Joaquín Brage Camazano, 'Stratisburgum locutus, causa finita'. El 'amparo intereuropeo' ante el Tribunal de Estrasburgo, última intancia de tutela de los derechos fundamentales en Europa', in Héctor Fix-Zamudio & Eduardo Ferrer Mac-Gregor (eds.) *El Derecho de Amparo en el Mundo* (2006), 1035 et seq.

[13] Official Journal of the European Communities (2000/C 364/01). The Charter of Fundamental Rights of the European Union was adopted in 2000.

[14] TEU, Article 6, para. 1.

[15] With respect to the European Union's possible accession to the ECHR, see Ricardo Alonso García, 'Análisis crítico del veto judicial de la UE al CEDH en el Dictamen 2/13, de 18 de diciembre de 2014' (2017) 32 Working Papers on European Law and Regional Integration (WP IDEIR no. 26, 2017), 1–29, https://www.ucm.es/data/cont/docs/595-2015-11-25-Binder1.pdf accessed on 7 December 2020.

[16] European Court of Justice ('ECJ'), Opinion No. 2/13. In this opinion the CJEU rejected the compatibility of the proposed Agreement for EU Accession to the ECHR, based on a very broad, perhaps exaggerated defence of the principle of autonomy of the EU. The Court based the rejection on several points, including the lack of coordination between Article 53 of the Charter and Article 53 of the ECHR in order to ensure that the level of protection in the Charter would not be affected.

[17] On 1 July 2020 Germany took over the Presidency of the Council of the EU. The programme for the six-month Presidency includes the objective of continuing negotiations on the EU's accession to the ECHR, see 'Together for Europe's recovery, Programme for Germany's Presidency of the Council of the European Union, 1 July to 31 December 2020', 18, https://www.eu2020.de/blob/2360248/e0312c50f910931819ab67f630d15b2f/06-30-pdf-programm-en-data.pdf accessed on 7 December 2020.

the EU Charter and the ECHR are for the most part consonant, in daily practice conflicts rarely arise.[18] Nevertheless, they may occur. In the latter case there is no binding norm or authority competent to resolve the conflict.[19]

In spite of the growing importance of global and regional human rights protection throughout the last decades, in the practical reality of national constitutional judges in both Europe and Latin America, no matter if states are conformed as federations[20] or as centralized states, the most relevant level of protection of rights still seems to be the national level, the most important norm being the constitution, the 'norm of the norms' which creates and empowers national constitutional courts. However, the existence of national (and sub-national), regional, and, finally, international protection mecanisms provide states with a large range of instruments and opportunities for improving the effective materialisation of human rights. At the same time it implies challenges and in some cases provokes conflicts and even fundamental resistance. For national constitutional courts, such as Colombia's, the question arises as to whether, and in what sense, this multilevel architecture affects, and should affect, their jurisprudence.

II. Reception of International Law in Domestic Constitutional Law: A Methodological Dilemma?

From a methodological point of view, those who have to apply human rights norms at various levels face not only the difficulty of knowing about them all and how they are interpreted by constitutional and regional courts, but also of facing and resolving—prima facie—complex problems of their normative hierarchy as well as exercising conventionality control (countries which have acceded to the ACHR) and constitutional review in a coherent manner. This multilevel establishment of fundamental rights in the form of principles, of general and abstract rules, represents a challenge for legal operators in their daily work in applying and interpreting ordinary laws, and for

[18] The EU Charter refers to the ECHR, and states that the rights contained therein have the same importance and scope as the corresponding rights under the Charter, with the exception that, as provided in Article 53 of the Charter, the EU reserves the right to provide greater protection than the ECHR. Even before the adoption of the EU Charter, in accordance with the EU Treaties, the rights established by the ECHR have been recognized as general principles of EU law (TEU, Art. 6 III), although without binding effect.

[19] Such a conflict has not yet occurred because the ECJ has repeatedly declared that it accepts a precursor role in the ECtHR. This is highlighted by C-145/04 *Spain v United Kingdom* [2006] ECR I-7917, in which the ECJ followed the ECtHR's ruling in *Matthews v United Kingdom* (1999) 28 EHRR 361. See also Johan Callewaert, 'The European Convention on Human Rights and European Union Law: A Long Way to Harmony' (2009) 6 European Human Rights Law Review 770, citing a number of cases in which the ECJ followed the rulings of the ECtHR.

[20] Federations, such as Mexico or Germany, usually count on a fourth level of human rights protection as the level of the constitution of the respective confederated state. As could recently been observed in the case of the new constitution of the State of Mexico City which came into force in 2017, counting Mexico City in as the 32nd department of Mexico, the addition of another level of protection of fundamental rights may give rise to complex questions about jurisdictional relationships and authority with regard to the protection of rights, especially in states which have a diffuse system of constitutional review and if the level of the federated state has a higher human rights protection standard than the national level or vice versa. See further, Centro de Estudios Sociales y de Opinión Pública, 'Las implicaciones de la Constiución Política de la Ciudad de México' (2018), Working document No. 287, 34

law schools, which must provide tools of interpretation, argumentation, and application of domestic law in accordance with convention principles.

Irrespective of whether a state follows a monistic or dualistic legal tradition or a concept in between those two extremes,[21] these concepts only impact the way that international law finds reception in internal law. It is for each state to decide what rank to assign to international law in its domestic legal system.[22] From a constitutional judge's perspective the legal value and rank of international treaties and conventions in the domestic law of its respective country mainly depends on how it is defined in the constitution as almost all modern Magna Cartas give a constitutional status to international human rights treaties.[23] These treaties, or at least certain categories of treaties, sometimes occupy a supra-constitutional rank. Alternatively, they may occupy the same rank as the national constitution, or even an infra-constitutional rank, above or at the same level as ordinary laws.[24]

In Colombia, for example, at first blush international human rights conventions ratified by Congress seem to have a supra-constitutional rank because the constitution stipulates that they 'prevail' over domestic law (Article 93 of its constitution).[25] However, the Colombian Constitutional Court constantly speaks of a 'constitutional bloc' composed of the constitution and those treaties with constitutional status.[26] Judicial review checks the compatibility of any state action or omission with the 'constitutional bloc' placing the constitution and those treaties with constitutional status at the same level.[27] In Germany, on the contrary, in accordance with its constitution and

[21] Although there are multiple variations of both monism and dualism, the two systems can be characterized as follows. According to monist theories, international law and national law form part of a single legal system; in case of conflict, either international law or national law would prevail over the other, depending on the individual legal system. In the dualist legal tradition, on the other hand, international law and national law are considered two separate legal systems independent from each other; thus, international law has to be incorporated into national law, which can be achieved either by declaring it directly applicable in the national legal system or by transforming it into national legislation. See Madelaine Chiam, *Monism and Dualism in International Law*, Oxford Bibliographies, 2018, doi: 10.1093/obo/9780199796953-0168, https://www.oxfordbibliographies.com/view/document/obo-9780199796953/obo-9780199796953-0168.xml accessed on 7 January 2020; Paolo G. Carozza, 'Subsidiarity as a Structural Principle of International Human Rights Law' (2003) 97 (1) American Journal of International Law 38–79, 63–4.

[22] Dulitzky (n. 8), 53.

[23] Dulitzky (n. 8), fn 64 for Latin America.

[24] Meléndez (n. 8), p. 24.

[25] See Jaime Orlando Santofimio Gamboa, *El concepto de Convencionalidad* (2nd edn, Colombia: Universidad Externado, 2018), 183; Meléndez (n. 8), 25. Article 93 of the Political Constitution of Colombia establishes that 'international treaties and conventions ratified by the Congress which recognize human rights and prohibit their limitation in states of emergency prevail in the domestic legal system' and that '(t)he rights and duties enshrined in (the) Constitution shall be interpreted in accordance with the international human rights treaties ratified by Colombia.'.

[26] Santofimio (n. 25), 187ff; Alejandro Ramelli, 'Sistema de fuentes del Derecho Internacional Público y "bloque de constitucionalidad" en Colombia' (2004), 11 Cuestiones Constitucionales -Universidad Autónoma de México, July–December 2004, 157–8.

[27] See, e.g., Rodrigo Uprimny discussing how Columbia's judicial system interprets and uses 'bloque de constitucionalidad' in, 'El Bloque de Constitutionalidad en Colombia: Un Análisis Jurisprudencial y un Ensayo de Sistematización Doctrinal 10' (2005), https://www.dejusticia.org/wp-content/uploads/2017/04/fi_name_recurso_46.pdf accessed on7 December 2020)
To give an example, in Decision C-291 of 2007, the Constitutional Court of Colombia held that the prohibition of taking hostages constitutes a binding rule of *ius cogens* in Colombia, even though the International Convention Against the Taking of Hostages had not been formally incorporated into domestic Colombian law. Furthermore, the Court clarified in this decision that not only the human rights treaties, but also customary norms of international law may form part of the so-called 'constitutional bloc', which means they

the jurisprudence of its Federal Constitutional Court ('FCC'), ordinary international treaties have the rank of ordinary federal law[28] and therefore they have an infra-constitutional status in the legal system.[29] This only differs with regard to the primary law of the European Union which, given the supra-national character of the EU, as a matter of principle prevails over the German Constitution.

However, it is worth noting that, in general, constitutions in Latin America tend to give international human rights treaties a higher rank in their national legal systems than their counterparts in Europe, although in general this does not mean that there is better compliance with international law and jurisprudence on this side of the ocean.[30] Therefore, one could dare to say that, at the end of the day, the rank of international law in the domestic legal system does not resolve the substance of the issue: almost all constitutional judges interpret ordinary laws not only in light of their own constitution, but also in accordance with ratified international law. Many also accept the interpretation of the constitution itself in accordance with international treaty law adopted by their respective country.[31] However, what would happen if there was an incompatibility or conflict between the solutions of the same case under national constitutional law and international law, which could not even be resolved by applying established principles of legal interpretation?

The German Constitution, for example, assigns special protection to the 'core' of international human rights. Although the ECHR in Germany has the rank of ordinary law, the FCC has 'self-imposed' a duty to interpret human rights in the constitution 'in light of' the ECHR and the jurisprudence of the ECtHR[32] as part of its general doctrine of constitutional interpretation in accordance with public international law. However, in cases involving conflicts between the constitution and the Convention that cannot be resolved applying all possible and licit hermeneutical methods, it still gives greater weight to the constitution.[33] Thus, the interpretation of the German constitution 'in light of' the Convention has its limits.[34]

have *ius cogens* status for the Colombian State. Decision C-291 of 2007 (per Justice Manuel José Cepeda Espinosa); see also 47; Santofimio (n. 25), 194.

[28] Decisions of the Federal Constitutional Court (BVerfGE, for its initials in German) 74, 358, 370; 82, 106, 120; 111, 307, 317; 128, 326, and 367. See in this regard, Thomas Giegerich, 'Wirkung und Rang der EMRK in den Rechtsordnungen der Mitgliedstaaten', in Oliver Dörr, Rainer Grote, & Thilo Marauhn (eds), EMRK/GG Konkordanzkommentar (2nd edn, 2013) vol. I, chapter 2, 82, points 46 et seq.; Jörg Polakiewicz & Adriana Kessler, 'Das Streikverbot für deutsche BeamtInnen', (2012), NVwZ, 841–5, 843.

[29] Rudolf Streinz, 'Article 59', in Michael Sachs (ed.), *Grundgesetz Kommentar* (7th edn, 2014), 1363–87, margin number 65a. Within the German normative hierarchy, and from the perspective of the FCC, the Convention shares the same legal status and has the same level as its approval law, which is an ordinary law.

[30] See, e.g., Ellen L. Lutz & Kathryn Sikkink, 'International Human Rights Law and Practice in Latin America' (2000) 54 (3) Legalization and World Politics 633–59, https:www.jstor.org/stable/2601347 (accessed 7 December 2020). The authors explore the level of legalization of, and compliance with, three different international human rights treaties and find that, in the past, the actual practice in Latin American countries often fell short of their international commitments (see 639).

[31] For Colombia see Article 93, para. 2 of the Colombian constitution.

[32] BVerfGE 74, 358, 370; 82, 106, 120; 111, 307, 317; 128, 326, 367.

[33] BVerfG, NJW 2004, 3407 (3408); T. Thomas Haug, 'Die Bedeutung der EMRK in Deutschland und ihre Auslegung durch den EGMR' (2016), AfP, 223, 225; Felix Ekardt & Verena Lessmann, ‚EuGH, EGMR und BVerfG - Die dritte Gewalt im transnationalen Mehrebenensystem' (2006) Kritische Justiz, 381, 387.

[34] BVerfGE 111, 307, 50; Angelika Nussberger, 'Auswirkungen der Rechtsprechung des Europäischen Gerichtshofs für Menschenrechte auf das deutsche Arbeitsrecht, European Symposium of the Federal Labor

Even with respect to EU law, which has a supra-constitutional rank in Germany (see Article 23 of the German constitution), the German FCC, maintains 'reserve authority' to review the application of EU law in exceptional cases or to exercise *ultra vires* review in—its opinion—obvious and manifest cases of abuse of authority by EU bodies. This contravenes the jurisprudence of the CJEU, which does not accept limits on the supremacy of EU law.[35] With respect to EU human rights protection, in its famous '*Solange II*' formula, the FCC says that it will not exercise constitutional review of German laws derived from EU law only as long as the EU guarantees the protection of fundamental rights at a level that is substantially comparable to the level of protection guaranteed by the constitution and respects its 'essential content'. Although the FCC has created the principle of 'openness' towards EU law, it reserves its faculty to declare EU law unconstitutional if the EU significantly exceeded its competence[36] as it has recently demonstrated by declaring parts of the EU's Public Sector Purchase Programme (PSPP) non-binding 'ultra vires' acts.[37]

In Colombia, the constitution itself stipulates that in case of incompatibility between the constitution and the law or any other judicial norm, the constitution (Article 4) always prevails. Corresponding to this, the Colombian Constitutional Court has constantly preferred constitutionality control over conventionality control, letting the constitution prevail in most of the cases even over those treaties that form part of the 'constitutional bloc' in case of conflict.[38]

It seems consistent that as a policy matter the German FCC and the Colombian Constitutional Court—like other constitutional courts or tribunals around the world—had to come to this result because both organs were created and empowered by their national constitution.[39] From their perspective, as long as a state continues to exist as such, the national constitution is the prevailing reference in cases of indissoluble conflicts of laws, regardless of the formal rank of international treaties in the domestic legal system, because the constitution is the 'law of laws' from which the legal

Court of Germany' Erfurt (26 and 27 April 2012), 18, https://www.bundesarbeitsgericht.de/symposion/rev_nussberger.pdf accessed on 7 December 2020.

[35] The CJEU has consistently insisted that European law prevails over national legislation. The principle of supremacy of European law was introduced by the CJEU in *Costa v ENEL* in 1964, where the CJEU understood that the European Community created its own legal system, which 'became an integral part of the legal systems of the Member States and which their courts are bound to apply'. See Case 6/64, *Costa v ENEL*, [1964] ECR 587, 593.

[36] BVerfG NJW 2009, 2267 (2272)—*Lissabon*.

[37] On 5 May 2020 the FCC issued its judgment in the proceedings on the European Central Bank's (ECB) PSPP, in which, for the first time, the FCC found that EU institutions—the Court of Justice of the European Union (CJEU) and the ECB—had exceeded their powers and that the resulting ultra vires acts do not bind Germany; see, Isabel Feichtner, 'The German Constitutional Court's PSPP Judgment: Impediment and Impetus for the Democratization of Europe' (July 2020) 5 (21) German Law Journal 1090–103, https://www.cambridge.org/core/journals/german-law-journal/article/german-constitutional-courts-pspp-judgment-impediment-and-impetus-for-the-democratization-of-europe/A70F08BCA58E1C821EBBC84A4DCE3D2E accessed on 7 December 2020.

[38] The Columbian Constitutional Court has constantly held that it is not a 'conventional judge'; see Judgments C-028 of 2006, C-750 of 2008, C-446 of 2009, C-1189 of 2000, C-025 of 2004, and C-442 of 2011; for more detailed explanations, especially on the exceptional cases in which the Colombian Constitutional Court most recently gave preference to international treaties over the Colombian constitution, see Santofimio (n. 24), 193 et seq.

[39] See also Dulitzky (n. 8), 54.

value of other laws, including international and regional human rights, is derived.[40] Thus, states are, as a matter or principle, free to choose how and at what level they incorporate international treaties into their national legal system.[41] In order to underline their position they invoke the traditional 'principle of subsidiarity', which governs the allocation of public authority in systems of multilevel governance and shows a preference for functions at the lowest level thus establishing the premise that national authorities still are the primary guardians of human rights.[42]

On the contrary, regional courts argue that Member States have voluntarily signed international treaties. However, in the moment they accepted them as binding, as well as the jurisprudence of their respective courts, it is their obligation to adapt their internal law including the constitution. If domestic judges are therefore obliged to check the compatibility of all state action, whether constitutional or legislative, with the regional human rights treaties, as it demands the conventionality control principle in Latin America created by the IACtHR with respect to the ACHR, this means that these treaties must always be at a higher legal level then the constitution.[43] We seem to be confronted with a methodological dilemma. But who has the last word to resolve it?

III. Emerging Political Challenges to the Multilevel Protection of Human rights

Besides the methodological problems mentioned above, international and regional human rights courts are currently facing an increasing number of different forms of socio-political or judicial resistance from their Member States, especially if their cases deal with topics which are politically sensitive or which touch upon the core prerogatives of state sovereignty.[44] Indeed, in many cases, Member States of regional or international human rights protection systems do not want to, or even believe that they *cannot*, comply with international law or the jurisprudence of regional organs of, for

[40] See in Germany, BVerfGE 37, 271—*Solange I*; BVerfGE 126, 286—*Honeywell*; Peter J. Spiro, 'Treaties, International Law, and Constitutional Rights' (2003) 55(5) Stanford Law Review 1999–2028; Jorge Alejandro Amaya, 'El diálogo interjurisdiccional entre tribunales extranjeros e internos como nueva construcción de las decisiones judiciales', in Luiz Arcaro Conci & Luca Mezzetti (eds), *Diálogo entre Cortes* (2014), 55–72. In Colombia, see Article 4 of the constitution, which explicitly stipulates that the constitution is 'the norm of the norms' and that in cases of incompatibility between the constitution and other laws the constitution always prevails.

[41] Carozza (n. 21), 62; Dulitzky (n. 8), 57.

[42] Isabel Feichtner, 'Subsidiarity', in Wolfrum (ed.), *Max Planck Encyclopedia of Public International Law* (2007), para. 1 ff.; Jorge Contesse, 'Contestation and Deference in the Inter-American Human Rights System' (2016), 79 (2) Law and Contemporary Problems 123–145, 145. Also, the IAHRS was conceived as complementary to national rights protection (see therefore Dulitzky (n. 8), 52).

[43] Nestor Pedro Sagüés, 'El "control de convencionalidad", en particular sobre las constituciones nacionales' (2009), 1 LXXIII LA LEY, 2, http://www.joseperezcorti.com.ar/Archivos/DC/Articulos/Sagues_Control_de_Convencionalidad_LL_2009.pdf accessed on 7 December 2020.

[44] See Ximena Soley & Silvia Steininger, 'Parting Ways or Lashing Back? Withdrawals, Backlash and the Inter-American Court of Human Rights' (2018) 14 (2) International Journal of Law in Context 237–57, who speak of a 'backlash' in the IAHRS. Likewise, see Jorge Contesse, 'Judicial Backlash in Inter-American Human Rights Law?', International Journal of Constitutional Law Blog (2 March 2017), http://www.iconnectblog.com/2017/03/judicial-backlash-interamerican/ accessed on7 December 2020; Alexandra Huneeus, 'Courts Resisting Courts: Lessons from the Inter-American Court's Struggle to Enforce Human Rights' (2011) 44 Cornell International Law Journal 493.

example, the IAHRS and the EHRS.[45] This is due to various aspects: a combination of a lack of political will and opportunity, budgetary and technical restrictions, and traditional moral and social concepts that still prevail, especially in the Latin American region, and which are subject to constant change. In this respect, in every society fundamental rights constitute an objective order of values, a kind of mirror of our societies and their functioning. The aforementioned socio-political aspects have an influence on the interpretation of our constitutions. Thus, conflicts that appear between international law and the domestic legal order often reflect the expression of socio-political divergences, rather than legal or methodological problems.

Growing resistance is reinforced especially in such Latin American and European countries with emerging nationalistic tendencies whose societies are being seduced by populism, which tends to replace human rights political programmes and messages with hate speech. They put into question the entire 'raison d'etre' of multilateral human rights treaty systems. In extreme cases such as Venezuela, the jurisprudence of the Inter-American Court has been uprooted.[46] In the European case, no less worrisome, states such as Russia and Turkey are weaving new arguments for ignoring the jurisprudence of the ECtHR, resorting to a number of arguments, including to the concept of constitutional identity.[47] Some authors have even spoken of a 'crisis of compliance' in global and regional human rights systems, given the growing number of decisions of the IACtHR[48] and the ECtHR[49] still pending implementation.[50]

In less extreme cases, tendencies to limit regional human rights protection, some of which subscribe to a more reductionist concept of democracy, find their expression in growing controversies about the scope of the margin of appreciation of national judges applying the jurisprudence of regional human rights courts.[51] In Europe, for

[45] See Laurence Burgorgue-Larsen, 'The Powers of the Court to Monitor Compliance with its Judgments', in *The Inter-American Court of Human Rights—Case Law and Commentary* (2011), 190.

[46] For more information, see the OEA's press release, http://www.oas.org/es/cidh/prensa/comunicados/2017/058.asp accessed on7 December 2020).

[47] European Commission: Turkey 2018 Report, 30; Anastasia Berger, 'Aktuelle Entwicklungen zur Bindung an die Entscheidungen des EGMR in Russland (2016), Ost/Letter-2-2016, 4.

[48] See the IACtHR's respective publications at https://www.corteidh.or.cr/casos_en_supervision_por_pais.cfm accessed on7 December 2020) .

[49] See the respective annual report of the Council of Europe at https://rm.coe.int/annual-report-2017/16807af92b accessed on7 December 2020).

[50] In Europe, by the end of 2019, 5,231 ECtHR judgments (out of more than 21,600 judgments delivered until then) were pending implementation supervised by the Committee of Ministers of the Council of Europe (See 13th Annual Report of the Committee of Ministers 2019, 58, https://rm.coe.int/annual-report-2019/16809ec315–accessed 11 December 2020); ECHR Overview 1959-2018, 3, https://www.echr.coe.int/Documents/Overview_19592018_ENG.pdf accessed on7 December 2020). In Latin America, on the other hand, 223 cases (out of approx. 400 judgments delivered) were at the stage of monitoring compliance by the end of 2019 (see IACtHR, Annual Report 2019, 66, https://www.corteidh.or.cr/docs/informe2019/ingles.pdf – accessed 11 December 2020).

[51] In certain cases, the ECtHR grants its Member States a margin of appreciation with regard to the interpretation and application of the ECHR, which is further substantiated by its case law. The doctrine of margin of appreciation has already been developed in the first judgments of the ECtHR (see, e.g., *De Wilde, Ooms and Versyp v Belgium*, ECtHR App. 2832/66, Judgment of 18 June 1971) and affects the level of control by the Court in the respective case. The latter is of importance when determining whether an infringement of the Convention rights was necessary and hence justified or not (Franz Mayer, 'Einleitung', in Ulrich Karpenstein & Franz Mayer (eds), *EMRK—Kommentar, 2. Ed.*, (Munich: C. H. Beck, 2015), 14). The doctrine reflects the principle of subsidiarity, and is based on the assumption that national authorities–being closer to the problems they are facing on the national level–will be in a better position to protect human rights adequately with regard to the individual national circumstances (Laurens Lavrysen, 'System

example, although the Council of Europe's recent Copenhagen Declaration published in April 2018[52] was ultimately much more favourable than expected, the regressive draft of this Declaration presented on 5 February 2018 and sponsored by the former Danish Presidency of the Council of Europe[53] has provoked alarm amongst human rights activists and academics.[54] Some have even spoken about a crisis of the system or an attempt to dismantle the independence of the ECtHR as the draft tried, at least formally, in an ambiguous and confusing way 'to reinforce the subsidiary nature of the European guarantee system but also to bolster the legal status of the state's margin of appreciation'.[55]

In Latin America a similar debate came to light exactly one year later in April of 2019 due to a letter sent to the Inter-American Commission on Human Rights by the (former) right-wing or extreme right-wing governments of Argentina, Brazil, Colombia, Chile, and Paraguay.[56] Also these states claimed greater respect for the principal of subsidiarity as a cornerstone of the distribution of powers within the IAHRS and the introduction of a considerable degree of state autonomy or a margin of appreciation in the application of the IACtHR's decisions, although the margin of appreciation doctrine so far has been alien to this system.[57] Ironically, in the letter the five states mentioned above invoke archaic arguments of sovereignty similar to the ones brought forth by the former socialist governments of Hugo Chávez in Venezuela

of Restrictions', in Pieter Van Dijk, Arjen Van Hoof, & Leo Zwaak (eds), *Theory and Practice of the European Convention on Human Rights* (Cambridge: Intersentia, 2018), 327). This applies in particular to sensitive socio-political areas concerning religion, moral values, or sexuality, where there is no common European standard. (Maria Angélica Benavides Casals, 'Die Auslegungsmethoden bei Menschenrechtsverträgen: Die Rechtsprechung des Europäischen Gerichtshofs für Menschenrechte und des Interamerikanischen Gerichtshofs für Menschenrechte', Nomos (2010), 135). In this way, the ECtHR implicitly indicates that there might be more than just one appropriate solution when it comes to balancing out the rights under the Convention.

52 Available at https://www.echr.coe.int/Documents/Copenhagen_Declaration_ENG.pdf accessed on7 December 2020.

53 Janneke Gerards, 'The Draft Copenhagen Declaration and the Court's Dual Role—the Need for a Different Definition of Subsidiarity and the Margin of Appreciation', 2018, para. 4, https://strasbourgobservers.com/2018/02/28/the-draft-copenhagen-declaration-and-the-courts-dual-role-the-need-for-a-different-definition-of-subsidiarity-and-the-margin-of-appreciation/ accessed on7 December 2020).

54 Helga Moelbeak-Steensig, 'Something Rotten in the State of Denmark?', VerfBlog (26 April 2018), https://verfassungsblog.de/something-rotten-in-the-state-of-denmark/ accessed on7 December 2020).

55 Argelia Queralt Jiménez, 'The Copenhagen Declaration: Are the Member States about to Pull the Teeth of the ECHR?', VerfBlog (9 April 2018), https://verfassungsblog.de/the-copenhagen-declaration-are-the-member-states-about-to-pull-the-teeth-of-the-echr/ https://www.corteidh.or.cr/docs/informe2019/ingles.pdf, accessed 11 December 2020..

56 See https://minrel.gob.cl/comunicado-de-prensa-ministerio-de-relaciones-exteriores-ministerio-de/minrel/2019-04-23/105105.html accessed on7 December 2020); http://www.rfi.fr/es/americas/20190627-quien-quiere-limitar-el-sistema-interamericano-de-derechos-humanos accessed on7 December 2020).

57 Andreas Follesdal, 'Exporting the Margin of Appreciation: Lessons for the Inter-American Court of Human Rights' (2017) 15 (2) International Journal of Constitutional Law 359–37; ; Dominic McGoldrick, 'Affording States a Margin of Appreciation: Comparing the European Court of Human rights and the Inter-American Court of Human Rights' in Carla Buckley, Alice Donald, & Philip Leach (eds.), *Towards Convergence in International Human Rights Law* (Brill 2016), 323–65; Yuval Shany, 'Toward a General Margin of Appreciation Doctrine in International Law?' (2006) 16 (5) European Journal of International Law 907–40, 929.

or Evo Morales in Bolivia with respect to the IAHRS some years ago.[58] If the petitions mentioned in the letter were implemented or became a trend in the region, the regional system of human rights protection in Latin America would suffer a serious backlash.

IV. Why Should we Overcome the Difficulties?—Opportunities and Advantages in the Multilevel Protection of Rights

Taking into consideration the above, it is thus worth reflecting on the question: What added value is provided, for example, by the human rights jurisprudence of regional courts if the states already have a broad catalogue of these rights in their respective national constitutions and a constitutional court that guarantees their materialisation? In the first place it has to be mentioned that functions of jurisprudence of regional human rights courts are at least threefold: their sentences have a function of correction, confirmation, and harmonization of national constitutional jurisprudence. They can correct national decisions which are not in line with regional human rights treaties, which have therefore been critizized and thus need readjustment by regional court. Perhaps more importantly, regional jurisprudence has a confirmation function if constitutional court rulings that provoked great controversy at a national level receive the 'seal' of Strasbourg or San Jose for being in compliance with conventions and thus are 'reapproved'.[59]

And thirdly, regional human rights courts in their sentences automatically exercise a harmonization function in reconciling different national constitutional standards and in seeking their coherence by interpretation of law and by identifying the most protective scenario as a guiding approach.[60] Due to the nature of the ECtHR and the IACtHR as regional courts, their decisions necessarily constitute compromises that mediate between the heterogeneities and peculiarities of the states under their jurisdiction. This is a consequence of the multinational composition of their organs, as a result of which it is inevitable that these decisions occasionally come into conflict with the normative, historical, cultural, and ethical characteristics of their Contracting States. Despite this, however, it is not too bold to point out that, although we are facing a great diversity of culture, including law culture, that enriches our continents and which should not be inhibited and suppressed, the jurisprudence of regional human rights courts helps to construct a kind of shared common Inter-American or European human rights judicature, that in the end will support the promotion of regional integration through

[58] Statement of José Manual Vivanco, Director of Human Rights Watch with respect to the letter; see https://www.eltiempo.com/mundo/eeuu-y-canada/denuncian-ataque-de-colombia-y-otros-paises-contra-la-cidh-353034 accessed on7 December 2020); https://www.elespectador.com/noticias/elmundo/bolivia-podria-retirarse-de-cidh-articulo-411002 accessed on7 December 2020).

[59] See Nussberger (n. 34), 20.

[60] Eduardo Ferrer Mac-Gregor & Argelia Queralt Jiménez, 'El control de convencionalidad americano y el efecto de cosa interpretada europeo¿ dos caras de una misma moneda?', in Javier Roca García & Encarna Cuenca Carmona (eds), ¿ Hacia una globalización de los derechos? (2017), 133 ff.

law.[61] Several decades of regional human rights jurisprudence in Latin America and in Europe has facilitated an every day higher convergence of national human rights catalogues and supranational human rights conventions so that true conflict of norms nowadays barely occur.[62]

Apart from this, from the perspective of the justiciable, we have learned from our violent near history in Europe as well as in Latin America that the guarantee of a high level of protection of human rights is, and must be, a regional and international task, which complements national jurisprudence and can even replace it in disgraceful cases in which national courts and the executive powers do not comply with their obligations towards their citizens to efficiently protect their rights. By assuming a kind of 'external watchdog' function regional human rights systems are an indispensable mechanism to strengthen stability and peace in the region. As regards the IACtHR, although compliance with the sentences of the IACtHR is sometimes characterized as low,[63] the impact of the Court's sentences, which goes far beyond linear compliance, is enormous with multipolar forms of incidence.[64] It has forever changed the continent's face as we think, for example, in the annulment of amnesty laws[65] or creation of truth

[61] Similarly, the theory of the 'Ius Constitutionale Commune en América Latina' calls for a regionally rooted constitutionalism secured by supranational human rights guarantees in Latin America; to this end, its representatives advocate close ties between constitutional, international, and comparative law in order to achieve a mutual reinforcement between national constitutional law and international law (Armin von Bogdandy, 'The constitutionalization of international law in Latin America - Ius Constitutionale Commune en America Latina: Observations on Transformativ Constitutionalism' (2015), AJIL, Volume 2015, 109–114, https://www.cambridge.org/core/services/aop-cambridge-core/content/view/365FC299C450C7F8CFC7FCF5A7938204/S2398772300001264a.pdf/ius_constitutionale_commune_en_america_latina_observations_on_transformative_constitutionalism.pdf, accessed 11 December 2020; Armin von Bogdandy et al. 'Ius Constitutionale Commune en América Latina: A Regional Approach to Transformative Constitutionalism', Max Planck Institute for Comparative Public Law & International Law (MPIL) Research Paper No. 2016-21, in Armin von Bogdandy et al. (eds), *Transformative Constitutionalism in Latin America* (New York: Oxford University Press, 2017), 17–51, https://ssrn.com/abstract=2859583 accessed on7 December 2020). Dulitzky speaks of an 'inter-American' constitution in Dulitzky (n. 8), 64.

[62] Rainer Arnold, 'The Convergence of the Fundamental Rights Protection in Europe' (2016), 52 Ius Gentium: Comparative Perspectives on Law and Justice, Springer, 2 ff., doi 10.1007/978-94-017-7465-9; Amaya (n. 40), 64, refers to the 'fertilization' within the national jurisprudence caused by the jurisprudence of the international courts. See also Tom Ginsburg, Zachary Elkins, & Beth Simmons, 'Getting to Rights: Treaty Ratification, Constitutional Convergence, and Human Rights Practice' (2013) 54 Harvard International Law Journal 61–95 on the template role of the Universal Declaration of Human Rights and the ICCPR.

[63] Fernando Basch et al.,'The Effectiveness of the Inter-American System of Human Rights Protection: A Quantitative Approach to Its Functioning and Compliance with Its Decisions' (2010) 12 SUR-International Journal on Human Rights, 9; Eduardo Bertoni, 'El Sistema Interamericano de Derechos Humanos-SIDH-y La (Real?) Falta de Apoyo Regional' (2017) 20 Iuris Dictio, Revista de Derecho, 87–104; Darren Hawkins & Wade Jacoby, 'Partial Compliance:A Comparison of the European and Inter-American Courts of Human Rights' (2010) 6 Journal of International Law and International Relations, 35; Alexandra Huneeus, 'Courts Resisting Courts: Lessons from the Inter-American Court's Struggle to Enforce Human Rights' (2011) 44 Cornell International Law Journal, 493.

[64] Par Engstrom (ed.), *The Inter-American Human Rights System. Impact Beyond Compliance* (Palgrave Macmillan, 2019); René Urueña, Beatriz Eugenia Sanchez, & Sergio Anzola, 'Después Del Fallo: El Cumplimiento de Las Decisiones Del Sistema Interamericano de Derechos Humanos. Una Propuesta de Metodología' Bogotá: Uniandes/Documentos Justicia Global (2015); .

[65] *Barrios Altos v Peru*, IACtHR Judgment of 14 March, 2001, Series C 75; *Gelman v. Uruguay*, Judgment of 24 February 2011, Series C 221; *Gomez Lund et al. ('Guerrilha do Araguaia') v Brazil*, Judgment of 24 November 2010, Series C 219.

commissions as a consequence of IACtHR rulings which gave way to the persecution of crimes against humanity resulting from dictatorship and civil war.

V. Concepts and Ideas to Mitigate Methodological Challenges

How then to resolve the methodological challenges described above? How to answer the old question of who has the last word? What to do in case of apparently 'indisoluble conflicts' in between different human rights norms if the traditional concept of the hierarchy of norms does not always provide satisfactory solutions? First of all it has to be mentioned, that usually catalogues of human rights are formulated in such a general and abstract manner, that in almost all cases conflicts should be 'resolvable' with traditional hermeneutical measures without the necesity to 'invent' new ones. Therefore, if ultimately a constitutional judge claims to have identified an 'indissoluble conflict,' in most of the cases, having a closer look to the divergence, it is less a legal problem in the sense of a real and indissoluble conflict of norms.

If there really is a need for new law conflict resolving techniques, the *pro personae* principle created by the IACtHR two decades ago[66] has to be mentioned. The essence of the benefit of multilevel protection of human rights finds its intrinsic expression in this principle according to which 'human rights norms should be interpreted as extensively as possible when recognising individuals' rights and, by contrast, as restrictively as possible when the norm imposes limits on the enjoyment of human rights'.[67] Thus, apart from being a hermeneutic mecanism, as a normative conflict resolving technique[68] among different existing human rights norms applicable to the same case, it requests the application of the one that most benefits the justiciable concerned.[69] Thus, apparent tensions between human rights prescriptions should not be resolved by hierarchical frameworks or rules of speciality but ought to be determined by the subjective purpose of human rights norms as being the one which guarantees individuals' rights in the widest sense.[70] Undeniably, it is still necessary to generate more

[66] IACtHR, *Certain Attributes of the Inter-American Commission on Human Rights*, Advisory Opinion, 16 July 1993, para. 50; IACtHR, *Compulsory Membership in an Association Prescribed by Law for the Practice of Journalism*, Advisory Opinion, 13 November 1985, para. 52.

[67] Mónica Pinto, 'El principio pro homine: Criterios de hermenéutica y pautas para la regulación de los derechos humanos', in Martîn Abregú & Christian Courtis (eds), *La aplicación de los tratados sobre derechos humanos por los tribunales locales* (Editores del Puerto,1997), 163. On the *pro personae* principle, see also Gonzalo Aguilar Cavallo & Humberto Nogueira Alcalá, 'El principio favor persona en el derecho internacional y en el derecho interno como regla de interpretación y de preferencia normativa', (2016) 84 Revista de Derecho Público 13–43. doi:10.5354/0719-5249.2016.43057; Alejandra Rodiles, 'The Law and Politics of the Pro Persona Principle in Latin America', in Helmut Philipp Aust & Georg Nolte, *The Interpretation of International Law by Domestic Courts* (2015), 157 ; Yota Negishi, 'The Pro Homine Principle's Role in Regulating the Relationship Between Conventionality Control and Constitutionality Control' (2017) 28 (2) European Journal of International Law 457, 473.

[68] Hayde Rodarte Berbera, 'The Pro Personae Principle and its Application by Mexican Courts' (2017) 4 Human Rights Review 1–27.

[69] Karlos Castilla, 'El principio pro persona en la administración de justicia' (2009) 1 (20) Cuestiones Constitucionales Revista Mexicana de Derecho Constitucional, 71–8, http://dx.doi.org/10.22201/iij.24484881e.2009.20.5861 accessed on7 December 2020).

[70] See, for first 'traces' of the application of the *pro personae* (or *pro homine*) principle in the jurisprudence of the Colombian Constitutional Court, Santofimio (n. 24), 196, citing, *inter alia*, Judgment T-352 of 2016.

processes of interrelation between the different levels of protection of rights in order for it to become a real 'plus' for citizens. Moreover, the *pro personae* principle meets its limits in cases of conflicting rights of two or more individuals, as it is not able to provide an answer to the delicate question of which of these individuals' rights is to prevail over the other. In striking a balance between the different conflicting rights, they cannot always be interpreted as extensively as possible as the *pro personae* principle would require. Nevertheless, the efficient realization and implementation of the *pro personae* principle is one of the most urgent tasks for combating the gap that still exists between laws and theories and realities, especially those in Latin America, so that human rights are effectively materialized.[71]

Beyond the *pro personae* principle doctrine, there have to be mentioned more recent manifold efforts and intents to replace the traditional 'hierarchy and subsidiary-orientated', exclusive concepts to explain the relationship between human rights norms at different levels with more convergent, inclusive concepts. The latter seak to interprete national, regional, and global human rights architecture as a whole 'universe of norms' instead of considering them as separate normative systems .[72] In this context, some authors have brought forward that the principle of subsidiarity has to be rethought and evolved in the sense that it provides a tool for the effective protection of human rights rather than impairing it.[73] It has been argued that focus should be placed on the positive aspect of the principle of subsidiarity:[74] priority should still be given to the protection of human rights at the local level. However, in cases where the local authorities are unable to ensure the effective protection and promotion of these fundamental guarantees, the 'higher level', that is, the regional entity has the inherent right and even the duty to intervene.[75] As *Carroza* puts it, the principle of subsidiarity serves as a tool to 'balance both the idea of noninterference and that of intervention or assistance'.[76] *Dulitzky* uses the term 'integration principle'; according to him the sense of embedding international

[71] On the progress of the *pro personae* principle in Latin America, see Flavia Piovesan, 'Latin American *Ius Constitutionale Commune* in Human Rights and Impact of the Inter-American System: Features, Potential and Challenges', in Armin von Bogdandy, Mariela Morales Antoniazzi, & Eduardo Ferrer MacGregor (n. 8), 564 et seq..

[72] Ibid., 564–570; Óscar Parra Vera, 'La justiciabilidad de los derechos económicos, sociales y culturales en el Sistema Interamericano a la luz del artículo 26 de la Convención Americana . El sentido y la promesa del caso Lagos del Campo, in: Eduardo Ferrer Mac- Gregor, Mariela Morales Antoniazzi, & Rogelio Flores Pantoja (eds), *Inclusión, Ius Commune y Justiciabilidad de los DESCA en la Jurisprudencia Interamericana – El Caso Lagos del Campo y los Nuevos Desafios,* Instituto de Estudios Constitucionales del Estado de Queretaro, México (2018), 181–234; Gabriela Kletzel & Camila Barretto Maia, 'The Challenge of Complementarity in Latin America's New Institutional Architecture for Human Rights', in *The Inter-American Human Rights System* Washington: Due Process of Law Foundation (2016), 17–52 (Chapter 1).

[73] Juana Acosta López, 'El resurgir de la subsidiariedad en el Sistema Interamericano de Derechos Humanos: El caso de las transiciones políticas', Working Paper (2019); Carozza (n. 21), 38–79.

[74] Yota Negishi, 'The Subsidiarity Principle's Role in Allocating Competences between Human Rights Courts and States Parties: The Hybrid Model of Centralized and Diffused Conventionality Control of Domestic Law'. In Ius Constitutionale Commune na América Latina; (2016) 3, Diálogos Jurisdicionais e Controle de Convencionalidade: Coleção Direitos Humanos e Constitucionalismo Regional Transformador, Brasil: Juruá Editora, 125–160; Carozza (n. 21), 38–79.

[75] Ibid.

[76] Carozza (n. 21), 79.

or regional human rights treaties into the national legal systems is to provide viable and effective solutions where justifications for subsidiarity fail.[77]

Thus, a more holistic, flexible vision of the multitude of human rights norms can help to see it as a complementary, comprehensive eco-system which gives a *de facto* legitimization to the most effective norm for each particular situation. This vision helps us to overcome the schematic and categoric principle of subsidiarity and the interpretation of progressive rulings of regional courts as threats to the core prerogatives of state sovereignty and to fight back the backlash against regional human rights systems.[78]

VI. Fighting Back the Backlash through Dialogue

Apart from new methodological concepts and the creation of new interpretation methods, which serve to resolve conflicts of norms arising between different human rights protection systems, as we have seen above, the apparent 'conflict' almost always lies buried in differences at the political, social, cultural, or economic level of the respective state, which carry weight on the constitutional judges' willingness to interpret the respective norm in a convergent way or not. Even the most elaborate theory and conflict resolving technique will not be able to resolve these kinds of 'indissoluble conflict'. Their solution will only depend on the willingness of each state to cooperate and to overcome these socio-economic differences. Therefore, in the end, adopting a more pragmatic perspective, the only really promising method to overcome differences is the intent to achieve a mutual understanding and a real jurisprudential dialogue among the courts, a frank, convincing, and sustainable discourse; a multi-dimensional debate of different modalities.[79]

First, this dialogue should consist of constant and, if possible, institutionalized vertical exchanges by Member States' constitutional tribunals, courts, and chambers with international and regional human rights protection bodies, not only through mutual jurisprudential references and the interpretation of national law pursuant to regional treaties or the jurisprudence of the respective regional court. A real 'cross-fertilization'[80] between conventional and constitutional rights is desirable. This does not necessarily mean that a constitutional court should literally adopt or even copy the reasoning of the regional court. Rather, it should entail a good faith effort to adapt the domestic legal system and the factual and legal situations of each individual case to the jurisprudence of the regional court and, therefore, to the respective convention or treaty even in case of socio-cultural differences. Constitutional

[77] Dulitzky (n. 8), 54; see, with respect to the integration principle in the context of the ECHR, e.g., Lawrence R. Helfer, 'Redesigning the European Court of Human Rights: Embeddedness as a Deep Structural Principle of the European Human Rights Regime' (2008) 19 European Journal of International Law 125, 136–37.

[78] Huneeus (n. 44), 493; Soley & Steininger (n. 44), 237–57.

[79] See in this regard Gonzalo Aguilar Cavallo, 'El diálogo multinivel / The Multilevel Judicial Dialogue', in Luiz Guilherme Arcaro Conci & Luca Mezzetti, *Diálogo entre Cortes* (2015), Conselho Federal, Brasilia, 149, 182–3.

[80] Amaya (n. 40), 64.

and regional courts must find their individual '*modus vivendi*.' In other words, they should ideally involve in a reciprocal situation of giving and receiving.[81] To give an example, although in theory the relationship between the German FCC and the ECtHR in cases of conflict between their respective jurisprudence remains uncertain, in practice throughout recent years they have constructed a stable and prosperous relationship of cooperation between the courts through mutual review and consideration, which has permitted them to resolve almost all possible confrontations by dialogue. This has not always been like this: Especially in the last decade of the twentieth century Germany had some difficulties in complying with the judgments rendered by the ECtHR. The compliance problems almost all originated from differing historical and cultural conceptions in Germany and in the ECHR. These differences were revealed, *inter alia*, by the 'historical dispute' or the 'ping pong game' between the FCC and the ECtHR in the cases of Princess Caroline of Monaco, where the FCC and the ECtHR took differing views on how to balance the freedom of the press on the one hand and the right to private and family life on the other;[82] or with regard to the application of unlimited subsequent preventive detention, which was possible in Germany for many years as it was not considered as a 'penalty' in the sense of Article 7 of the ECHR.[83] However, in its famous case '*M*',[84] the ECtHR found a violation of Articles 5 and 7 of the ECHR, amongst others, due to an infringement of the concept of *nulla peona sine lege* (no penalty without a law) as well as the retrospective imposition of punishment.

This divergence, especially regarding these two cases, can be explained by the fact that the relationship between the ECtHR and the German FCC was characterized by tension, rivalry, or confrontation, sometimes even by outright conflict for many years. In this more or less strained situation, the mutual rapprochement of the German courts and the ECtHR in the Caroline case,[85] and the complete overhaul of

[81] Paola Andrea Acosta Alvarado, 'El diálogo judicial interamericano, un camino de doble vía hacia la protección efectiva', Luiz Arcaro Conci & Luca Mezzetti (Ed.) *Dialogo entre Cortes* (2016), Universidad Externado de Colombia, 237 – 239.

[82] *Von Hannover v. Germany*, ECtHR App. 59320/00, Judgment of 24 June 2004; *Von Hannover v. Germany (No. 2)*, ECtHR (GC) App. 40660/08 & 60641/08, Judgment of 7 February 2012; *Von Hannover v. Germany (No. 3)*, ECtHR App. 8772/10, Judgment of 19 September 2013.

[83] German criminal law provides the possibility of a person's lifelong detention, even after they have served the longest possible penalty of imprisonment which can be imposed in Germany (fifteen years). If the offender continues to pose a threat to society after serving the custodial sentence of fifteen years, the state may order his preventive detention in the greater interest of the general public. This form of confinement or detention—which, according to the German understanding, does not constitute a punishment in a strict sense, but rather a corrective and preventive measure—could even be imposed retroactively.

[84] *M v. Germany*, ECtHR App. 19359/04, Judgment of 17 December 2009.

[85] In reaction to the ECtHR judgment, the highest civil court in Germany (the *Bundesgerichtshof*, BGH) had to lower the standard of protection of the freedom of the press, hence achieving a better balance between the conflicting rights and introducing a model of gradual protection: The concept of 'absolute personalities of contemporary history' does not justify a general prevalence of the freedom of the press. On the contrary, each case requires individual consideration, taking into account the specific circumstances of the case as well as the contribution made by the respective article to the public debate (BGH, Judgment of 6 March 2007, VI ZR 51/06). This judgment of the BGH was subsequently declared compatible with the German Constitution by the FCC (BVerfG, 1 BvR 1602/07). The ECtHR, for its part, shifted its position towards the German one and approved the outcome of the German judicature on this issue following its first decision in the case of Caroline of Monaco (*Von Hannover v. Germany (No. 2)*, ECtHR (GC), App. 40660/08 & 60641/08, Judgment of 7 February 2012.

the legislation on preventive detention by the German parliament in 2015, aligning it with the judgment in '*M*', were welcomed with considerable relief. The cited cases corroborate that, even in situations of differing historical and cultural conceptions, a relationship based on cooperation and dialogue regarding the implementation of the decisions can lead to satisfactory results for both sides.

Secondly, it is necessary to strengthen the horizontal relationships at an inter-state and at a regional level intra- and inter-continent in order to establish an institutional exchange amongst constitutional courts[86] and amongst regional courts.[87] This horizontal exchange helps analysing challenges that all states and regional courts have in common, and recognizing the different strategies for confronting these challenges even those of socio-cultural nature. In terms of the interstate dialogue, it is interesting to investigate how, for example, the analysis of the states' compliance with certain regional court measures has the potential to help other states with similar problems make progress in complying with adverse decisions. Although the domestic law of other states and the decisions of their courts have no binding legal value for other countries, their constitutions and constitutional court decisions can serve as an important source of inspiration in the resolution of legal problems in a given state. One example of this is the influence in Latin America of the jurisprudence of the German FCC with respect to its famous concept of '*Drittwirkung*',[88] the radiation effect of fundamental rights between private parties, which the FCC established in 1958 with the famous '*Lueth*' decision.[89]

Furthermore, human rights should not only be a matter of interest for jurists, they should be everyone's cause. Consequently, we must expand our concepts and our means in order to promote and defend them. We must investigate in an inter- and multi-disciplinary dialogue with, for example, sociology, economics, and the political sciences, and with civil society in general, as well as by means of art, journalism, and cinema, which transmit messages that are much clearer and more readable for citizens, in contrast to court decisions, which are sometimes too long and loaded with complex legal language. Finally, this multilevel human rights system needs dialogue facilitators.[90] Dialogue is a construction that does not come out of nowhere. On the contrary, it is the result of an arduous process of consensus building and the exchange of ideas between relevant actors at all levels.

86 On jurisdictional dialogue, see Roberto Dias & Michael Freitas Mohallem, 'El diálogo jurisdiccional sobre derechos humanos y el surgimiento de la red internacional de cortes constitucionales', in: Luiz Arcaro Conci & Luca Mezzetti (Ed.) *Dialogo entre Cortes* (n. 38) (2016), Universidad Externado de Colombia, 273 - 313.

87 As regards the mutual influence and the impact of the jurisprudence of the IACtHR on the ECtHR, see María Díaz Crego, 'The Impact of the Jurisprudence of the Inter-American Court on the European Court of Human Rights' (2015), DERECHO PUCP – Revista de la Facultad de Derecho, No. 75, 31–56.

88 While regional courts are very reluctant to implement this concept, the IACtHR has addressed it on a larger scale, mainly in Advisory Opinion 18/03 on the legal status of immigrants. This report, which continues to receive attention, assumes the possibility of a direct effect of fundamental rights between private persons. Javier Mijangos y Gonzales, 'The Doctrine of *Drittwirkung der Grundrechte* in the Jurisprudence of the Inter-American Court of Human Rights' (2008), InDret 1, Barcelona, 1 – 31.

89 BVerfGE 7, 198ff., 15.01.1958–1 BvR 400/51.

90 See Soley & Steininger (n. 44) on the role of civil society and compliance partners in diffusing criticism of the IAHRS.

VII. Conclusion

To conclude, the parallelisms in the threats to the rule of law and democracy that our societies are currently facing have shown us the need for analysing legal problems in a more comprehensive and joint manner. We are on the way to internationalization, a globalization of our rights and our constitutions which even an apparent 're-birth' of nationalistic tendendies will not be able to stop. In times of 'shrinking spaces' we should remember the indespensable advantages of multilevel rights protection instead of combatting them on a theorical and *de facto* level. All actors involved should make an effort to achieve viable pragmatic compromise solutions in cases of conflicts of norms instead of insisting on their socio-political and cultural differences. From their birth, from their conception, human rights have been universal, indivisible, and interdependent forming part of an effective but yet fragile eco-system that we have to protect. It is time to act accordingly.

20

Not so Moderate

The Relationship between the Colombian Legal System and International Law

Carlos Arévalo & Julián Huertas

I. Introduction

The Colombian legal system is massively intertwined with international law, ranging from human rights law and international humanitarian law ('IHL') to investment, environmental, labour, and trade law. Furthermore, Colombia is usually portrayed internationally as a law-abiding country with a constant tradition of respecting international norms.[1] In recent times, for instance, these features have proven instrumental concerning the Colombian peace agreement with FARC and the enforcement of decisions issued by international tribunals.[2] In this regard, the Colombian Constitutional Court has been a relevant actor in shaping the relationship between municipal and international rules.

The Court has issued landmark rulings on the enforcement of social rights, limits to the powers of the executive branch, as well as Congress; budget-related questions, and contentious social issues, among a myriad of critical examples in which treaties have been instrumental.[3] The Colombian Constitutional Court has decisively defined the role of international law in Colombia. Since 1998, the Court has stated that classical *moderate monism* is the model that best explains how the Colombian order relates to international law. However, this chapter shows that the actual practice of the Court does not fit that theory. Drawing upon the practical aspects of the traditional theories that have struggled to explain the interaction between international and domestic law (monism and dualism), the analysis of the Colombian state's position concerning international law, especially treaties, is carried out from the Colombian Constitutional Court's case law.

[1] For example, former French Prime Minister Dominique de Villepin on an address given in Paris in an event organized by Procolombia, 24 October 2019, declared: 'Colombia is a democratic, law-abiding country and, as a result, foreign investors know they can rely on legal and political guarantees ... it's very important to have a functional Government.' https://www.investincolombia.com.co/news/650-french-ex-prime-minister-singled-out-colombia-as-an-investment-destination-and-exporting-platform.html, accessed 9 December 2020.

[2] Courtney Hillebrecht & Alexandra Huneeus, with Sandra Borda, 'The Judicialization of Peace' (2018) 59 Harvard International Law Journal 279.

[3] See generally Manuel José Cepeda-Espinosa, 'Judicial Activism in a Violent Context: The Origin, Role, and Impact of the Colombian Constitutional Court' (2004) 3 Washington University Global Studies Law Review 529.

Carlos Arévalo & Julián Huertas, *Not so Moderate:* In: *Constitutionalism*. Edited by: Alejandro Linares-Cantillo, Camilo Valdivieso-León, Santiago García-Jaramillo, Oxford University Press (2021).
DOI: 10.1093/oso/9780192896759.003.0021

To grasp the Court's position in this regard, Section II of the chapter illustrates how the theory proposed by the Court in 1998 is not compatible with Alfred Verdross's moderate monism, and the way some scholars have interpreted it. Section III analyses the mechanism for the reception of international law in the Colombian legal system. Section IV deals with the question of the status of international law at the local level, as well as the implications of this interaction for the international responsibility of the state when it breaches international obligations. Lastly, the conclusion discusses whether it is plausible to describe the interaction of the Colombian system with international norms under the relevant categories proposed under the monist-dualist framework and identifies the essential elements that explain this interaction.

II. Moderate Monism in the Court and the Legal Scholarship

In the landmark Decision C-400 of 1998, the Court introduced what it called *moderate monism* as the model that best explains how the Colombian legal order relates to international law.[4] The Court examined the tension between constitutional Article 4, which enshrines the supremacy of the Colombian constitution in the domestic order,[5] and Article 9, which provides that foreign relations must be guided by the principles of international law.[6] Specifically, the Court examined the conflict between the supremacy clause and the *pacta sunt servanda* principle and held that the constitution takes precedence over any other norm and source of law, both domestic and international. In addition, the Court ruled that domestic authorities should grant precedence to domestic rules—especially the constitution—in case of conflicts that cannot be harmoniously solved.[7]

Based on the constitution and the contributions of monist and dualist authors like Hans Kelsen, Alfred Verdross, and Carl Heinrich Triepel, the Court dismissed *constitutional monism* because the state cannot justify the breach of international obligations based on national rules, not even its constitution. It also rejected *international monism* (because of the supremacy clause) and *dualism* since the coexistence of two heterogeneous legal orders cannot be accepted. Rather, the Constitutional Court declared that Colombia embraces moderate monism and supported its finding on Verdross's writings.[8] Nevertheless, differing from the Court's conclusion, Verdross proposed an international monism by which international law prevails in cases of conflict with domestic law.[9] In fact, the Colombian Court misrepresented some of the

[4] This description of the Court's moderate monism is based on Julian Huertas-Cárdenas, 'Monismo moderado colombiano: examen a la teoría oficial de la Corte Constitucional desde la obra de Alfred Verdross' (2016) 132 Vniversitas 197–234.

[5] Constitution of Colombia, Article 4.

[6] Ibid., Article 9.

[7] Decision C-400 of 1998.

[8] The Court cited the 6th edition of the Spanish translation of *Völkerrecht*: Alfred Verdross, *Derecho Internacional Público* (Madrid: Biblioteca Jurídica Aguilar, 6th edn, translation by Antonio Truyol y Serra, 1982).

[9] See Bardo Fassbender, 'The United Nations Charter as Constitution of the International Community' (1998) 36 Columbia Journal of Transnational Law 541–4; Thomas Kleinlein, 'Alfred Verdross as a Founding Father of International Constitutionalism?' (2012) 4 Goettingen Journal of International Law 408.

foundations of Verdross's proposal in order to make the *pacta sunt servanda* principle compatible with the constitutional primacy, but has never adopted an international moderate monism.[10]

After advancing its theory, the Court has barely addressed this type of theoretical issue again. But in more recent and critical rulings, it has declared that Decision C-400 of 1998 is the binding precedent on conflicts between international and domestic laws.[11] Therefore, it remains to be established which analytical approach, if any, guides the Colombian state in its relationship with international rules. Although it is clear that moderate monism is not an adequate theory to describe it, it is still necessary to understand Colombia's position.

Before presenting the constitutional norms that address the interaction between the domestic order and international law, it is useful to examine how some scholars have inaccurately accepted that the doctrine introduced by Judgment C-400 of 1998 satisfactorily explains the position of the Colombian state. First, some authors think that the moderate monism invented by the Court defends an indirect primacy of international law.[12] Nevertheless, this opinion ignores that, as will be seen later, the supremacy of the human rights norms that are part of the 'constitutional block'[13] is the exception to the rule according to which the constitutional norms are above any other norms, including international ones.[14] Additionally, while some authors assume that moderate monism and dualism share some important elements,[15] other constitutional law scholars praise the Court for adopting the moderate monist approach that harmonizes domestic and international law.[16] Even international law scholars believe that the Verdrossian theory actually guides the Constitutional Court's view.[17] Of course, there have also been critical comments towards the theory of moderate monism presented by the Court, but even this criticism takes for granted that moderate monism is in effect the model adopted by the Colombian Court.[18]

[10] See Huertas-Cárdenas (n. 4), 217–24.

[11] See Decision C-269 of 2014, Section 4.2.3.

[12] María Angélica Prada, 'La Integración del Derecho Internacional en el Sistema Colombiano', in George Bandeira, Aida Torres, & René Urueña (eds), *Protección Multinivel de Derechos Humanos* (Barcelona: Universitat Pompeu Fabra, 2013), 368.

[13] The constitutional block (or 'block of constitutionality') is composed of those norms and principles that, without formally appearing in the articles of the constitutional text, are used as parameters of the constitutionality control of the laws (constitutional judicial review), since they have been normatively integrated into the constitution, by various means and by mandate of the constitution itself. They are therefore true principles and rules of constitutional value, that is, they are norms located at the constitutional level, even though they may sometimes contain reform mechanisms different from the norms of the constitutional article *stricto sensu*. See Decision C-225 of 1995.

[14] Constitution of Colombia, Article 93: 'International treaties and agreements ratified by Congress that recognize human rights and prohibit their limitation in states of emergency have domestic priority. || The rights and duties mentioned in this Charter will be interpreted in accordance with international treaties on human rights ratified by Colombia.'

[15] Edgar Hernán Fuentes Contreras, 'Papel jurisdiccional en la aplicación de las normas internacionales laborales en el derecho interno colombiano' (2010) 1 Revista Análisis Internacional 221.

[16] Manuel Fernando Quinche, *El control de constitucionalidad* (Bogotá: Pontificia Universidad Javeriana & Grupo Editorial Ibañez, 2nd edn, 2014), 287.

[17] Juan José Quintana, *Derecho Internacional Público Contemporáneo* (Medellín: Ediciones Jurídicas Gustavo Ibañez, 2001), 48.

[18] See Laura Victoria García-Matamoros, 'Control de constitucionalidad de los tratados públicos a la luz del Derecho Internacional' (1999) 1 Revista Estudios Socio-Jurídicos 130–2.

The interpretations cited above reflect how unfamiliar Verdross's theories are in Colombia and the extent to which the Court's theory has generated considerable confusion among scholars. With these examples, the need for a better understanding of the position of the Colombian system, in light of the constitution and the case law of the Court, becomes apparent.

III. Reception of International Law in the Colombian Legal System: Automatic Incorporation or Transformation?

The conception of the unity of the legal system is one of the differentiating elements between the monist and dualist schools. Therefore, it is essential to establish what international law's reception mechanisms are in the Colombian legal system in order to determine the relationship, whether unified or not, of international and domestic law. To correctly analyse the reception mechanisms, it is necessary to distinguish between treaties on the one hand, and custom and other sources of international law on the other.

The monist reception mechanism is the automatic incorporation of international norms, which entails that international norms have direct application or effect within the state without the need for national legislation that converts them into national law. In contrast, transformation is the dualist reception mechanism, which demands that international law be converted into domestic law—usually through a Congressional act— so that they may acquire application or effect within the state.[19]

Both mechanisms reflect a particular view of the sovereignty of the state and the binding force of international law for states.[20] Since the Colombian constitution does not explicitly indicate whether it adopts automatic incorporation or transformation techniques, it is crucial to find out whether Colombian law requires the transformation of international rules into domestic legislation. For this purpose, distinguishing the type of source of law becomes necessary.

A. Treaties

The reception of treaties in Colombia involves the executive, legislative, and judicial branches, and is done through a Treaty Passing Act (TPA).[21] First, through a TPA, Congress passes a bill that authorizes the government only to ratify the treaty.[22] The same can be said of the review undertaken by the Constitutional Court.[23] The objective

[19] Gideon Boas, *Public International Law: Contemporary Principles and Perspectives* (Cheltenham: Edward Elgar, 2012) 136.

[20] André Nollkaemper, 'The Effects of Treaties in Domestic Law', in Christian Tams et al. (eds), *Research Handbook on the Law of Treaties* (Cheltenham: Edward Elgar, 2014), 124–30.

[21] Constitutional Court, Decision C-864 of 2006; Constitutional Court, Decision C-252 of 2019.

[22] Alejandro Ramelli, 'Relaciones entre el derecho internacional y el derecho interno', in René Urueña (ed.), *Derecho Internacional: Poder y Límites del Derecho en la Sociedad Global* (Bogotá: Ediciones Uniandes, 2015), 523.

[23] Constitution of Colombia, Article 241, para. 10.

of TPAs is not to assimilate a treaty to national legislation, but to limit the power of the executive to bind the state internationally. The constitutional articles do not seek to incorporate a treaty domestically and through legislation, but to ensure that the international obligation arising from a treaty conforms to domestic law.

Legislation approving treaties has particular characteristics that differentiate it from ordinary legislation. For example, TPAs can only be proposed to Congress by the executive (usually the president, the minister of foreign affairs, or the minister of the relevant sector for the treaty).[24] In the same way, Congress only has the power to either simply approve TPAs—with reservations and interpretative declarations—or reject them. Unlike the regime applicable to ordinary legislation, TPAs only authorize the executive to bind the Colombian state, but this will only happen once the exchange of notes has been perfected, or the ratification has been deposited.[25] Therefore, the Congressional approval and the presidential sanction for a treaty are not enough to bind the state.

It is important to make clear that, while the process for the adoption of treaties in Colombia includes a TPA, that does not mean that treaties need a law approving them to be invoked if they have already been ratified.

The Court has clarified that, unlike the system of reception of the constitution of 1886, the 1991 constitution does not require the transformation of international norms into national legislation.[26] In the same 2009 ruling, the Court emphasized that the 1991 constitution replaced the then-prevailing dualism with automatic incorporation so that treaties could be invoked before local authorities without it being necessary to reproduce its text in an ordinary law (i.e. a statute).[27] An exception provided for in the constitutional text is found in International Labour Organization treaties, since the international labour agreements ratified by Colombia are part of domestic legislation.[28] This exception confirms that treaties other than labour treaties are not part of domestic legislation. In other words, the explicit mention of Article 53 requires that this type of treaty be assimilated with the national legislation precisely because the other treaties are not transformed into domestic legislation.[29]

Hence, the constitution does not require that treaties have to be transformed into national legislation so that they have legal effects in the domestic order. In other words, automatic incorporation is the treaties' reception mechanism in the Colombian legal system. Colombian authorities, therefore, apply international law sources and not domestic legislation when they enforce international law. However, the study of the position of the Colombian state would be incomplete if it ignored the rulings of the Constitutional Court.

In this sense, the constitutional block created by the Court in 1995 raises questions regarding the reception of human rights treaties in the domestic order. The

[24] Olga Ríos, Nicolás Carrillo, & Carlos Arévalo, 'The Protection of Immunity in Colombian Law' (2018) 3 The Yearbook of Diplomatic & Consular Law 5–10.

[25] Germán Cavelier, *Régimen Jurídico de los tratados internacionales en Colombia* (Bogotá: Legis, 3rd edn, 2000), 134–41.

[26] Decision C-615 of 2009, para. 5.1.

[27] Ibid.

[28] Constitution of Colombia, Article 53.

[29] Decision C-401 of 2005.

constitutional block has been broadly studied by constitutional law scholars and has been used to understand the constitutional status of human rights treaties.[30] But despite its importance, the theory of the constitutional block poses a conceptual paradox for international law. In effect, as previously explained, the basic notion of the constitutional block refers to the existence of constitutional norms that do not appear directly in the constitutional text.[31] According to the theory of the block, constitutional Article 93 provides for the special status of human rights treaties in the national legal order. Because of this reception clause, some international standards are *incorporated* into the constitution. Put differently, Article 93 allows the Constitutional Court to integrate norms and principles that are not formally found in the articles of its text.[32]

Since the founding idea of the block is the *integration* to the constitution of norms included in treaties, those norms are converted into constitutional parameters of judicial review or, at least, into hermeneutical criteria to establish the meaning and scope of constitutional norms.[33] The doctrine of the block raises the question of the direct application of international law in the internal order. In other words, the doctrine elaborated in numerous judgments of the Court can lead to the conclusion that, to the detriment of the very existence of international law, what is applied is not human rights treaties, but the same constitution that has incorporated treaties and 'transformed' them into the constitution.

Nevertheless, this theoretical paradox does not reflect the judicial practice by which domestic authorities do apply international instruments and not domestic norms that incorporate international law. The discrepancy between the theory of the block of constitutionality and its practical application is explained by the purpose of the doctrine of the block. With this jurisprudential creation, the Court can use the treaties mentioned in Article 93.1 to examine national standards under constitutional review.[34] As in other Latin American nations,[35] the Court sought a mechanism through which it could achieve this goal, adapted a notion of French origin,[36] introduced it to Colombian law, and asserted that human rights treaties are part of the constitution. It is relevant, therefore, to question whether Article 93 actually required the creation of a theory such as the constitutional block to ensure the prevalence of human rights treaties in the domestic legal system.

A possible alternative interpretation of the notion of the block would be to understand the constitution broadly and not just as normative text. In this regard, constitutional pluralism proposes understanding the constitution not as a single document,

[30] See Alejandro Ramelli, 'Sistema de fuentes del derecho internacional público y bloque de constitucionalidad en Colombia' (2004) 11 Cuestiones Constitucionales 157–75; Rodrigo Uprimny, 'El bloque de Constitucionalidad en Colombia. Un análisis jurisprudencial y un ensayo de sistematización doctrinal' (Dejusticia, 2005), https://www.dejusticia.org/wp-content/uploads/2017/04/fi_name_recurso_46.pdf accessed 9 December 2020 .

[31] Uprimny (n. 30), 3.

[32] Prada (n. 12), 371–2.

[33] Decision C-225 of 1995.

[34] Manuel Fernando Quinche Ramírez, 'El Control de Convencionalidad y el Sistema Colombiano' (2009) 12 Revista Iberoamericana de Derecho Procesal Constitucional 169.

[35] See René Urueña, 'Domestic Application of International Law in Latin America', in Curtis A. Bradley (ed.), *The Oxford Handbook of Comparative Foreign Relations Law* 567–70 (Oxford University Press, 2019).

[36] See Conseil Constitutionnel, Decision 71–44 DC of 16 July 1971.

with normative superiority, reinforced and comprehensive stability,[37] but in a substantive way, as an articulated order that seeks to guarantee human dignity through organization and limitation of power.[38] However, to date, the Constitutional Court has not given any indication of accepting this approach. That is why, although the doctrine of the constitutional block has not received academic analysis from the perspective of the direct application of international law, it is necessary to raise this problem for future developments.

As a conclusion regarding the mechanism of reception of treaties, both the constitution and the constitutional judicial practice reject the transformation of international norms into local legislation as a requirement for having effects at the domestic level. Rather, the Constitutional Court adopts a monist model, as the technique of automatic incorporation operates in the Colombian legal order.

B. Customary Law and Other Sources of International Law

In the absence of rules governing the reception of international customary law, the Court has pointed out that international obligations have their source 'both in the public treaties that it has ratified, as in international custom and the general principles of law'.[39] Although there is no specific clause that defines the reception of custom into domestic law, the Court has given special treatment to customary IHL through Article 214 of the constitution.[40] Furthermore, before the introduction of the doctrine of the constitutional block, the Constitutional Court defended the automatic incorporation of customary IHL.[41]

Subsequently, the Court has interpreted the doctrine of the constitutional block extensively so as to apply it to the custom relating to human rights and IHL too.[42] The same logic applies to human rights and IHL provisions that are *ius cogens* norms.[43] The Court has also applied this reasoning of automatic incorporation of custom not only to IHL, but also to customary norms in general as a source of international law.[44] On the other hand, principles of international law are automatically incorporated into the Colombian legal system with the same binding force that treaties hold.[45]

[37] See Paola Andrea Acosta, 'Más allá de la utopía: Del diálogo interjudicial a la constitucionalización del derecho internacional. La red judicial latinoamericana como prueba y motor del constitucionalismo multinivel', doctoral dissertation (2015) https://eprints.ucm.es/28119/, 190–1, accessed 9 December 2020.

[38] See Paola Andrea Acosta Alvarado & Julián Eduardo Huertas Cárdenas, 'Teorías sobre la relación entre el derecho interno y el derecho internacional en la jurisprudencia constitucional colombiana', in Juana Inés Acosta López, Paola Andrea Acosta Alvarado, & Daniel Rivas Ramírez (eds), *De Anacronismos y Vaticinios: Diagnóstico Sobre las Relaciones entre el Derecho Internacional y el Derecho Interno en Latinoamérica* (Bogotá: Universidad Externado de Colombia, 2017), 695–704.

[39] Decision C-1189 of 2000, para. 2.3.

[40] See generally Alejandro Ramelli Arteaga, *La Constitución Colombiana y el Derecho Internacional Humanitario* (Bogotá: Universidad Externado de Colombia, 2000) .

[41] Decision C-574 of 1992.

[42] Decision C-291 of 2007.

[43] Decision C-027 of 1993.

[44] Decision C-291 of 2007.

[45] Decision C-1189 of 2000, para. 2.3.

Finally, other types of decisions, such as the precautionary measures of the Inter-American Commission on Human Rights, are also automatically incorporated into domestic law without an act of transformation.[46] Similarly, the rulings of the Inter-American Court of Human Rights ('IACtHR') are binding in the Colombian legal system and do not need to be transformed into local legislation.[47]

Thus, on the question of whether Colombian law requires the transformation of international norms into domestic legislation, it is clear that both the constitution and the constitutional jurisprudence have followed the monist model. Even the reception of the treaties, which are incorporated through legislation approved by Congress and reviewed by the Constitutional Court, moves away from the dualist conception that demands the transformation of international norms.

In this regard, judges and other Colombian authorities can—and, in fact, they do—apply international law directly. Now it is necessary to analyse the status of such norms once they have been incorporated into the domestic order.

IV. The Status of International Law in Colombia: Its Rank and Consequences for the International Responsibility of the State

This section presents (A.) the Court's attempts to establish a general system of relations between domestic and international norms, and (B.) the implications of those relationships on the international responsibility of the state.

A. General Relations between International Law and Domestic Norms from Constitutional Jurisprudence

The C-400 of 1998 ruling marked a milestone because it laid the foundations for the relationship between the Colombian system and international law. Although the Court tried to establish the relationship between local and international law, it actually only focused on the constitution and omitted national legislation. This first attempt of systematization was complemented by Decision C-1189 of 2000, which also referred generically to 'the moderate primacy of international norms in the domestic order'.[48] However, the Court has been aware of the insufficiency of addressing in an undifferentiated manner the question of the hierarchical rank of international law in Colombia.[49] For this reason, numerous judgments have distinguished the type of international source and the regime that source belongs to, which gives rise to the possibility of five types of relationships: (i) international norms of a supra-constitutional nature; (ii) international norms of constitutional rank, and, therefore, supra legal-;

[46] Decision T-558 of 2003.

[47] Decision C-715 of 2012, para. 2.3.

[48] Decision C-1189 of 2000, para. 2.2.

[49] So far, the most comprehensive ruling in this regard is Decision C-269 of 2014. For a critical account of the Court's explanation, see Paola Andrea Acosta Alvarado et al. 'Diagnóstico sobre las relaciones entre el derecho internacional y el derecho interno. El caso colombiano' (2018) 16 Estudios Constitucionales 369.

(iii) infra-constitutional but supra-legal international standards; (iv) international standards of legal status; and (v) infra-legal international standards.

One of the Court's most important findings refers to *ius cogens* norms, irrespective of the sources that originate such rules. In Decision C-269 of 2014, the Court acknowledged the supra-constitutional status of *ius cogens* norms. This is the only category of norms the Constitutional Court has deemed superior to the constitution. Likewise, it can be said that it is the most authentic sample of international monism, notwithstanding the Court's rejection of this possibility in 1998 because it was portrayed as a radical doctrine. The rules of *ius cogens* turn out to be the only real exception to the principle of constitutional primacy enshrined in constitutional Article 4.

On the other hand, and speaking only of international legal sources, the treaties on human rights and IHL have constitutional status. Customary norms relating to the same subject hold the same status too.[50] Since Decision C-225 of 1995, the Court introduced the doctrine of the constitutional block. Through this creation, the Court held that human rights and IHL treaties are *integrated* into the constitution. In subsequent jurisprudence, the Court differentiated two types of the constitutional block in accordance with the two paragraphs of Article 93: the block 'in a strict sense' (*stricto sensu*), and 'in a broad sense' (*lato sensu*).[51] In the former case, the block consists of those principles and norms expressly enshrined in the constitution—those that are found in the constitutional text—as well as human rights treaties whose limitation is prohibited during states of exception.[52]

Based on the second paragraph of Article 93, the *lato sensu* block would include treaties that establish human rights that may be limited during states of exception and are a parameter to perform constitutional judicial review of domestic legislation.[53] The particular feature of the block in the broad sense is its interpretive function, unlike the *integrative* function of the *stricto sensu* block. The treaties of the *lato sensu* block have an inferior status than those referred to in the *stricto sensu* block.[54] However, beyond this conceptual distinction, it should be noted that treaties on human rights and IHL prevail over other national sources, except the constitution. This means that without formally appearing in the constitutional text, they are used as parameters for the judicial review of legislation. In short, the treaties on human rights and IHL prevail in the domestic order but not over the constitution. On the other hand, the Court clarified in Decision C-269 of 2014 that treaties that establish territorial borders are, in fact, part of the block in the strict sense.[55]

However, it is still essential to answer the question about the status of international law in the domestic order, as it constitutes one of the defining issues on the interaction between local and international law.[56] The constitutional block is an exception to the

[50] Decision C-291 of 2007.

[51] David Landau, 'Vulnerable Insiders: Constitutional Design, International Law and the Victims of Armed Conflict in Colombia' (2017) 57 Virginia Journal of International Law 686–7.

[52] Decision C-225 of 1995.

[53] Decision C-191 of 1998.

[54] Decision C-067 of 2003.

[55] Decision C-269 of 2014, para. 4.4.

[56] Janne E. Nijman & André Nollkaemper, 'Introduction', in Janne E. Nijman & André Nollkaemper (eds), *New Perspectives on the Divide between National and International Law* (Oxford University Press, 2007), 1–14.

general regime. In Decision C-191 of 1998, the Court held that treaties, in general, are not part of the constitutional block and, therefore, they do not have a higher status than ordinary laws.[57]

In turn, since the assessment of the non-prevalence of treaties vis-à-vis domestic legislation is built on the distinction between 'constitutional block/ordinary treaties', the same reasoning applies to international customary law. The Court has stated that treaties and customary law have the same legal status.[58] Consequently, there being no reason to differentiate it, nor jurisprudence that refutes it, it is logical to conclude that international custom also has legal status in Colombian law. The exception to this idea is customary human rights and humanitarian law that is integrated into the constitutional block. This means that, in the domestic domain, national authorities could supersede or modify a treaty or an international custom by enacting legislation that overrides an international rule. Accordingly, the overriding of international sources of law by national authorities could entail the breach of the obligations contained in them. This would entail an internationally wrongful act resulting in the (international) responsibility of the state.

Needless to say, the ratification of a treaty could modify previous national legislation too, but this is not surprising nor problematic from the vantage point of international law. Now, it is worth questioning whether, for practical purposes, the equal status of treaties and national legislation would not eventually lead to the prevalence of the latter over the former.[59] That is to say, the legal status of treaties could lead to granting, in practice, even infra-legal status to treaties. If a conflict arises between the two domestic and treaty-based norms, the last-in-time national rule would prevail, which would mean that the treaty could have, in practical terms, lower rank than the domestic legislation.

To illustrate the consequences of assigning legal status to treaties, it is worth examining conflicts between national legislation and treaties that are not part of the constitutional block. The Court's Decision C-358 of 1997 examined the constitutionality of Article 577 of Decree 2550 of 1988 (the Military Penal Code then in force), for opposing international diplomatic law. According to Article 277 of the Military Penal Code, the registration of the office or residence of the consuls could be made provided that the consul or the person in charge of the property was previously notified. However, at least three treaties ratified by Colombia establish that it is not enough to 'give notice' for a national authority to enter the residence or the premises of the mission, but rather that the consent or authorization of the consul or the person in charge is required. This is provided for in the Vienna Convention on Diplomatic Relations of 1961; the Vienna Convention on Consular Relations of 1963; and the Convention on Consular Agents of 1928. The conflict between the two norms is apparent, and the Court acknowledges it.[60] Faced with the controversy, the Court declared itself

[57] Decision C-191 of 1998, para. 6.

[58] Decision C-291 of 2007.

[59] This debate echoes the controversy around the *last-in-time* rule applied by the US Supreme Court to solve conflicts between treaties and federal statutes. See Louis Henkin, 'The Constitution and United States Sovereignty: A Century of 'Chinese Exclusion' and its Progeny' (1987) 100 Harvard Law Review 853; Julian G. Ku, 'Treaties as Laws: A Defense of the Last-in-Time Rule for Treaties and Federal Statutes' (2005) 80 Indiana Law Journal 319.

[60] Decision C-358 of 1997, para. 4.

inhibited, because international treaties do not constitute—by the mere fact of being treaties—part of the constitutional block and, therefore, they are not a parameter to review domestic legislation.[61] Only the norms integrated into the block can be used as review parameters, and since the treaties confronted in this case are not part of the block, it was inappropriate to examine the claim of whether the domestic law (the Military Penal Code) was unconstitutional. For the Constitutional Court, it is the responsibility of ordinary judges to decide in individual cases as to whether a violation of national law or international diplomatic law has taken place, but not through judicial review undertaken by the Court.

On that account, it is reasonable to conclude that, according to the Constitutional Court, treaties have legal status in Colombia. This general rule finds three significant exceptions, which are explained by virtue of its substantial content, namely: treaties or other sources that incorporate *ius cogens* norms (of supra-constitutional rank), border delimitation treaties (of constitutional rank), and treaties on norms of human rights and IHL integrated into the constitutional block. Thus, clarifying the standing of international law in the Colombian legal system (knowing the legal value of international obligations), makes it possible to evaluate the responsibility of the state, derived from the breach of its international duties, both in the domestic and international order, as follows.

B. The Implications of the Relationship between International Law and Domestic Norms in the International Responsibility of the State

The relationship between international law and domestic norms is closely associated with the particular understanding of the responsibility of states at the international level. It also constitutes a relevant element to identify the position of every national legal system in this matter. In effect, the breach of an international obligation that is attributable to the state (an internationally wrongful act) generates state responsibility. Hence, the solution of normative conflicts is not only a local issue. Each state must confront the international consequences of its acts before other states and other actors, like international organizations and private investors. Now, a vision of dual responsibility of the state is incompatible with the monist school. According to monism, in the face of the violation of an international norm by a state act or some domestic legislation, the state will have the same responsibility domestically and internationally. Since the system is one, the existence of two or more conflicting norms is not valid simultaneously, just as it is not valid for an act of the state to be lawful in one order and illegal in the other.[62]

[61] Ibid., para. 8.

[62] A practical example of this monist view of state responsibility can be found in the decisions of international tribunals. In particular, the IACtHR has developed the monist-inspired idea of 'conventionality control'. See Eduardo Ferrer MacGregor, 'Conventionality Control: The New Doctrine of the Inter-American Court of Human Rights' (2015) 109 American Journal of International Law Unbound 93.

On the contrary, for dualism, it is viable to 'split' the responsibility of the state into two dimensions: based on the same conduct, an act of the State could be declared legal in the national legal order but illegal in the international one. Thus, the possible responsibility of the state may be dual: giving rise to international responsibility while remaining valid within the domestic legal order.

In Colombia, the unity or duality regarding international responsibility has been a central aspect of the Colombian moderate monism. In Decision C-400 of 1998, the Constitutional Court declared that the constitution prevails over the rest of the norms (except for *ius cogens* norms, as clarified in Decision C-269 of 2014). This position supports the primacy of the constitution at the domestic level if a conflict with an international norm arises. In those cases, the Court held, '... for the national judge and other authorities, the principle that constitutional law precedes international order prevails, for which treaties have the status that the constitution assigns them. Therefore, a Colombian judge is obliged to ignore a treaty that violates the constitution.'[63] The inevitable consequence of this guideline for local authorities is that, in cases of conflict of sources of law, they must breach an international obligation when no other harmonizing solution is available.

Logically, such an act will give rise to international responsibility. This situation, observes the Court, should require the competent authorities to adapt either the domestic or international rules to resolve the contradiction. In particular, the Constitutional Court holds that in cases of conflicts between constitutional norms and international provisions, the President of the Republic and Congress should reform the constitution to avoid engaging the international responsibility of the state; or, depending on each case, to modify the international obligation in order to avoid state responsibility.

An interesting application of this reasoning is seen in Decision C-252 of 2019, in which the Court reviewed the constitutionality of the bilateral investment treaty ('BIT') between Colombia and France.[64] The Constitutional Court could have avoided a future conflict between the BIT and the constitution when it conditioned the treaty's ratification to some shared interpretations on significant provisions of the BIT.[65] Colombia now has to convince France to agree on the joint interpretative declaration following the understanding set by the Court. Though it is an unprecedented ruling that creates an additional burden for the executive branch, it may prove effective in avoiding the international responsibility of the Colombian state. It may also give some leverage to the government in renegotiating an agreement with a stronger developed economy, and it may lead to a better deal.[66]

Still, the duty of preventing acts that may give rise to the international responsibility of Colombia does not alter the rule for the resolution of actual legal conflicts. The local

[63] Decision C-400 of 1998, para. 45.

[64] Under the Colombian constitution, the domestic approval of treaties starts after the executive has signed the treaty and presents it to Congress for approval. The bill of the TPA follows the same procedure of ordinary bills. Once Congress approves the bill, the president must submit it to the Constitutional Court, which will examine the constitutionality of both the treaty and its TPA. Only then, can the president ratify the treaty, meaning that it enters into force at the international level.

[65] Decision C-252 of 2019, para. 460.

[66] See Eyal Benvenisti, 'Reclaiming Democracy: The Strategic Uses of Foreign and International Law by National Courts' (2008) 102 American Journal of International Law 241–4, 241.

judge and other operators remain subject to the obligation to enforce domestic law—particularly the constitution—in cases of conflict with international standards. Article 4 is rigorously imposed and shapes the legal system, though the Court acknowledges that this guideline is only applicable to national authorities. It does not claim that international tribunals accept the primacy of the constitution over international norms, which suggests the possibility of a dual system of state responsibility.[67]

The clarification made in Decision C-400 of 1998 is relevant because it shows that the Constitutional Court's starting point is the existence of two systems in which two types of opposing responsibilities can emerge. The claim on the plurality of the system seems not to be consistent on this point with international monism, nor with the moderate monism proposed by Verdross. The original moderate monism was indeed characterized not only by defending the superiority of international law, but by foreseeing the possibility of conflicts relating to the primacy of one or another type of norm.

Nevertheless, this moderate monism of the Vienna school states that such an anomalous situation in which a local norm can still be valid despite opposing an international norm '... is only for *internal and provisional purposes*'.[68] Verdross stresses that while there may be a valid domestic norm despite opposing international law, such validity will only be real within the state, and will also be provisional. This 'provisionalness' is explained by the fact that a state adversely affected by the rule of another state, contrary to international law, has the possibility of demanding the repeal or non-application of the said national norm. And the breaching state—the one that has enacted the norm—is obliged to do so.[69] Thus, conflicts between domestic and international norms will be resolved in favour of the international order.

Regardless of the virtues or weaknesses of Verdross's analysis, it is unavoidable to conclude that the Constitutional Court's approach to the dual responsibility of the state contrasts with the monist approach. It is not acceptable to assert that the Colombian Court embraces the tenets of moderate monism. While the original moderate monism requires the subjection of domestic law to international rules, the jurisprudence discussed here evidences that the Court's misinterpretation of Verdross's work paves the way for the international responsibility of the state. Consequently, the Constitutional Court is inclined towards a quasi-dualist position concerning the international responsibility of the state.

V. Conclusion: From Moderate Monism to Moderate Sovereigntism?

The problem of the status of the international norms in the local order does not admit a general and straightforward answer from the so-called classical theories: monism and dualism. Although the Colombian constitution and the Court do not require the transformation of treaties into national legislation—and in this sense, it is not a dualist reception system—its jurisprudence does embrace the basic idea of dualism as

[67] Decision C-400 of 1998, para. 49.
[68] Verdross (n. 8), 96.
[69] Ibid., 96.

to the status of international sources. In this regard, the Constitutional Court favours the dualistic thesis of the legal status of treaties and other international law sources. Of course, this must be complemented by the fact that, together with the *ius cogens* norms, the treaties on human rights, IHL, and border delimitation hold a unique position in Colombian law. In this regard, the regime applied to these types of norms manifests a stark international monism, but it is an exceptional situation. As important as they are, these types of treaties constitute only a part of international law. It is not accurate to state that the supremacy of those norms in the national order is predicable of the entire order because, as the Court itself has acknowledged, its constitutional status is exceptional.

It seems that the answer to the question about the status of general international norms is at some point between constitutional monism and dualism. It combines elements of both doctrines. It is not acceptable to suggest a purely constitutional monist model. Although the constitution prevails, and treaties are equated with national legislation—the central concept of monism of domestic law—the Court recognizes that there are two legal systems and that the Colombian state cannot invoke its domestic law at the international level to justify the breach of an obligation. Because of the acceptance of *pacta sunt servanda* at the international level, one can identify a moderate version of constitutional monism.

However, it is also at this point that dualism acquires significant validity. Triepel's footprints loom large not only in terms of the status of treaties in domestic law, (with the consequence that a last-in-time statute may practically supersede a treaty) but also in the solution of the conflict between local and international law. According to the Court, in cases of non-reconcilable normative conflicts, local authorities should apply domestic law even if that entails committing an internationally wrongful act. But at the same time, the hypothetical international responsibility of the state will not affect the domestic order, which shows a dualist approach, as analysed in the previous section.

This leads to the conclusion that, with the crucial exception of norms on human rights, IHL, and border delimitation, the Colombian Constitutional Court follows a position that can be described as sovereigntist or statist. Beyond the possible nuances in the constitutional monism law and dualism, the common element in the Court's case law is the supremacy of domestic legislation over treaties in general. In this sense, we can speak of a strong conception of state sovereignty, which is expressed in the status of international norms and in the way of understanding the international responsibility of the state. Despite its numerous statements in support of international law in general, the Court has tended to favour a vision that, domestically, strengthens the power of the state vis-à-vis international norms. As has been discussed throughout this chapter, the so-called classical theories of monism and dualism fail to define Colombia's position in this matter.

However, it is also true that, on some occasions, the Court's decisions have not been systematic nor rigorous. Even so, it is possible to identify in its case law a statist inclination in relation to international law. Of course, theoretical coherence is not an absolute, not even the most important goal for a constitutional tribunal. Following a pragmatic attitude, the Court has found in international law a useful tool to advance significant social, political, and economic changes. Above all, and in spite of the more academic rulings handed down in its first ten years, the Constitutional Court is not concerned about drawing systematic precedents. Through its strategic and flexible use of international rules, the Court has left the door open to meet social and political demands.[70] This has led the Court to achieve remarkable results. Nonetheless, it has come at the cost (perhaps modest) of systematic thought.

In sum, more than a theory or a school of thought, the characterization of constitutional case law as mostly sovereigntist may help understand the central features of such judicial decisions and, in turn, avoid unsuccessful classifications. The idea of a sovereigntist or statist disposition of the Court over international law may seem novel in the Colombian academic literature, especially because several scholars only focus on the constitutional block. However, the gaps in the local doctrine exposed in this research demonstrate the need to address the theory and practice of the Constitutional Court without a narrow preconception. There are sufficient elements to understand the position of the Court in this regard.

[70] See, e.g., the role of international law in constitutional amendments within the framework of the most recent peace process. Carlos Bernal Pulido, 'Transitional Justice within the Framework of a Permanent Constitution: The Case Study for the Legal Framework for Peace in Colombia' (2014) 3 Cambridge Journal of International & Comparative Law 1136.

Index

For the benefit of digital users, indexed terms that span two pages (e.g., 52–53) may, on occasion, appear on only one of those pages.